WRITING, RESEARCHING, COMMUNICATING

Communication Skills for the Information Age

WRITING, RESEARCHING, COMMUNICATING

Communication Skills for the Information Age

Second Edition

KEITH WINDSCHUTTLE

ELIZABETH ELLIOTT

McGraw-Hill Book Company Sydney

New York St Louis San Francisco Auckland Bogatá
Caracas Hamburg Lisbon London Madrid Mexico Milan
Montreal New Delhi Oklahoma City Paris San Juan
São Paulo Singapore Tokyo Toronto

National Library of Australia Cataloguing-in-Publication date:

Windshuttle, Keith, 1942–
Writing, researching, communicating.

Rev. ed.
Bibliography.
Includes Index.
ISBN 0 07 470052 9.

1. Communication in management. 2. Commercial correspondence.
3. Business report writing. 4. English language—Business English.
I. Elliott, Elizabeth II. Title

658.45

Produced in Australia by Oldstyle Publishing Services Pty Ltd for
McGraw-Hill Book Company Australia Pty Limited
4 Barcoo Street, Roseville NSW 2069, Australia
Typeset in Australia by Asset Typesetting Pty Ltd, Sydney
Printed in Australia by McPherson's Printing Group

CONTENTS

INTRODUCTION
HOW TO USE THIS BOOK

This is a revised edition of a book which in the last five years has established itself as a leading text in tertiary education courses in Australia. It has been written by two authors who have each had a number of years of experience, both in teaching these skills to students in universities and colleges of advanced education and in practising our own skills in the publishing and broadcasting industries. Between us, we have written eight books, several hundred articles for journals and magazines, more than twenty reports for governments, and a television series. In other words, our experience derives not only from teaching in this field but from making a living as writers in the outside world.

This book is not simply a localised version of an overseas text. It has been written specifically for Australian readers and uses Australian examples throughout. We want to emphasise, however, that we recognise and endorse the best international standards and approaches. This is particularly important today, because the theory and practice of communications is now dramatically different to that of twenty years ago. The decade of the 1990s is the scene of major changes in terms of the employment available and the way that people relate to one another in organisational life. We discuss these changes in detail in the chapters that follow but, briefly, they are as follows.

- The information sector is now the largest in the economy and most people today work on information-related tasks.
- Older hierarchical organisations, with their top-down management methods, are being replaced by structures in which there is a much freer flow of information and responsibility.
- The twin ethos which pervades the thinking of successful organisations today is the provision of quality in output and service to clients.
- The ability to communicate with people of other cultures is now an economic imperative, both for doing business internationally and for relating to our own multicultural workforce and clientele.
- There is a renewed emphasis today on the question of ethics in organisational life, and especially on the ethical implications of communications.

We have revised our book to locate it squarely within these new directions in social, vocational and organisational life. As a result, all the practices and skills that we teach and advise are both immediately relevant to the 1990s and consistently derived from a coherent, up-to-date theory of communications and its role in society.

This new edition has a re-organised and much expanded chapter structure. The number of chapters has been increased from thirty-nine to fifty. The book also contains a range of new aids within each chapter to assist teachers and students develop the kinds of communication skills that are now in demand. These pedagogical aids include:

- at the start of each of the twelve major parts of the book: a discussion with a prominent Australian communicator about his or her theory and practice
- within each of the major parts: a new, up-to-date reading list of key texts useful for student reference
- within each of the major parts: a revision list of key points made in the text
- at the start of each of the fifty chapters: a list of objectives to be pursued and skills to be developed
- at the end of each chapter: key points, questions for discussion and relevant exercises
- as a running commentary through each chapter: major points and summaries of techniques
- throughout the entire book: new, up-to-date illustrations, specimens and examples of documents cited in the text

More than ever, we are aware of the need to clear away many of the myths surrounding communication practice. We are especially concerned to scotch the notion that it takes some sort of special inbred talent for a person to be a good writer, speaker or communicator. This is a view derived from an earlier era when only a small number of people had these roles and is completely out of place today when almost everyone needs to develop these abilities. Writing, speaking and relating to others are no more nor less difficult than any other human skills. What they require is good teaching, a capacity to learn from experience and plenty of practice.

We want to strongly emphasise the word practice. You cannot learn to write, speak or communicate well by reading alone. For this reason we have included exercises at every point we thought appropriate and have made as many suggestions for further practice and group discussion as we could. People need to work their way, rather than simply read their way, through the book. We have re-ordered the chapters in the way that we believe most people develop communication skills. However, we have not wanted to be dogmatic about this. Each chapter is written so that it is self-contained and can be read without any dependence on other parts of the book. We realise that few people will go through the whole book from beginning to end. Most will want to focus on particular chapters or parts.

We also believe that a book of this kind should develop a full complement of communication skills. We have not confined ourselves solely to the basic needs of communicating in the workforce—such as letter and report writing, interviews and speaking at meetings—but have extended our scope much wider to include such areas as research essays, journalism, technical writing, survey research, the use of statistics, illustration, submission writing, editing, lobbying, public speaking and handling the media. We have described present patterns of professional practice in all these areas so that readers who work at it can hope to reach acceptable standards of professionalism themselves.

As often as we could, we have related this discussion to both the traditional and the new technologies available. In the last decade, the scope of communication practice has expanded considerably, thanks to changing employment practices and the development of new technology. For example, the use of personal computers in low-cost desktop publishing systems has led a great many organisations—companies, clubs, community groups, schools and colleges, associations and societies—to produce their own magazines and journals. In-house publishing today is being conducted at a professional level and many people need the skills of the journalist to make their prose style and articles equally professional. There is also the growing need for many organisations to influence the wider society through lobbying techniques and use of the media.

As well as this, we believe that professional communicators in the media have a great deal to teach the rest of us about communication styles and the ways to approach an audience. People new to the information industries and those who are increasingly using information skills in their employment need to learn as much as they can from those who have traditionally made a living in these areas.

In preparing this new edition, we were greatly assisted by research assistants Margaret Kerr and Rachel Chalmers. Margaret Kerr conducted and wrote all the interviews with the twelve prominent communications practitioners who are discussed at the start of each of the major parts of the book. We are grateful to all those who were interviewed, both for giving us their valuable time and for sharing with our readers their ideas, their practices and their ideals.

We also benefited greatly from the thoughtful reviews and advice offered by a number of lecturers in communications and related fields, in particular Dianne Bromley, Joe Gaha, Jenny Davies, Warwick Goodenough, Beth Shade, Rod Chinery, Lorelle Champion and Elspeth Browne. We have incorporated a number of their suggestions into this revised edition and we are confident it is the better for them.

Keith Windschuttle
Elizabeth Elliott

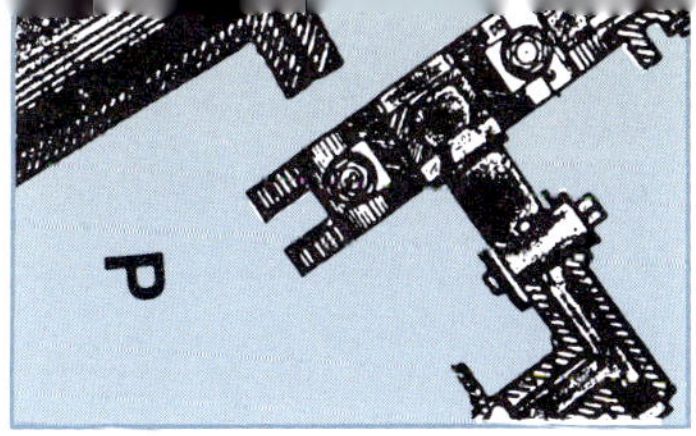

PART

I

FOUNDATIONS OF COMMUNICATION

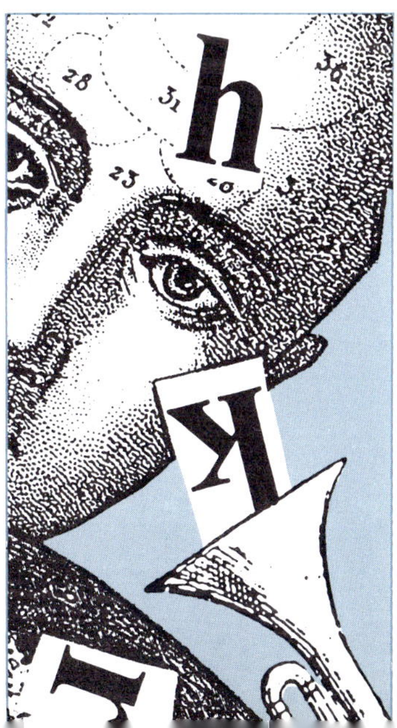

PROPHET OF THE INFORMATION SOCIETY

Barry Jones is now widely recognised as one of the few who correctly predicted the emergence of the Information Age. His vision of the future, however, offers us a choice of optimistic or pessimistic directions.

Barry Jones is best known in Australia as a politician in the House of Representatives but he is better known internationally as the author of one of the most prescient works of the last decade. His book, *Sleepers, Wake! Technology and the Future of Work,* originally published in 1982 and since reprinted fifteen times, was reissued in 1990 in a revised edition by Oxford University Press. It is widely recognised as having defined most clearly the nature of the information society we now inhabit and of the opportunities and problems this society presents. The book has been translated into Chinese, Japanese, Korean and Braille and has enjoyed best-seller status for ten years.

According to Jones, the information society is one where the productive activity that generates most wealth and employs most people has shifted from primary, secondary and tertiary sectors into what he calls the quarternary sector. The primary sector is agriculture and mining which employed most people in the nineteenth century; the secondary sector is manufacturing and construction which was a major employer until the end of the 1960s; the tertiary sector is transport and retailing which today is the second largest employer; and the quarternary sector is information processing which today employs more than any other.

The accompanying graph shows trends in each of the four sectors in Australia over the last hundred years. The accompanying table indicates the type of work that is done in the quarternary or information sector. It includes publishers, accountants, scientists, writers, bankers, real estate agents, actors and musicians. The trends in Australia, Jones emphasises, are not unique but are typical of the types of changes that have also occurred in most European and North American countries. The information sector not only employs more people but is where most new wealth is being generated. For instance, by 1990 the combined revenue of the Australian

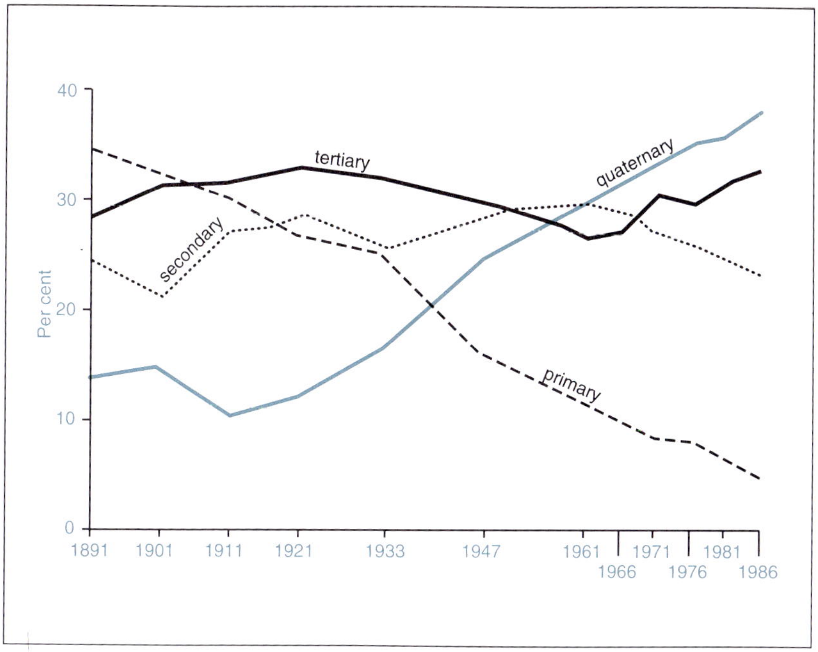

Australian labour force in paid employment: four-sector analysis 1891–1986 (per cent)

media industries (print, radio and television) plus telecommunications and other information technology was about $12 billion compared with the Australian automotive industry's revenues of about $10 billion and the textile industry's revenue of about $1 billion.

The force that is driving the growth of the information sector, Jones says, is technological change. 'The central argument of my book—that technologically based transitions create revolutionary economic and social changes—is controversial,' he acknowledges. 'The thesis is disputed by many and arouses hostility, if not contempt, from most professional economists,' he adds. Nonetheless, most of the social and economic changes he predicted ten years ago have actually been confirmed, a record which few economists can claim.

Among the predictions he made which have since been borne out are the following.

- The number of people working in large-scale, routine and repetitive employment (especially office work and processing of routine financial transactions) will decline, to be replaced by computerised operations which are cheaper, faster and more accurate.

- There will also be fewer jobs in service industries which rely on centralised computer-controlled technology such as telecommunications, printing and some public utilities.

- Manufacturing will use fewer workers, especially in older industries which either go out of business or become computerised. However,

Table A

Categories of information workers

Collecting, interpreting and transferring information		*Collating, mediating, negotiating with information*	
Public servants	Translators	Lawyers	
Statisticians	Diplomats	Union officials	
Librarians	Scientists	Members of Parliament	
Mathematicians	Accountants		
Bankers	Economists		
Meteorologists	Academics		
Clergy			
Transmitting, disseminating information, ideas, techniques and aesthetic experience		*Conceptualising*	
Writers	Teachers	Architects	Town planners
Musicians	Actors	Philosophers	
Dancers	Painters/Sculptors		
Recording and publishing		*Facilitating information flow*	
Photographers	Printers	Secretaries	Couriers
Publishers	Designers	Office workers	
Sound recordists		Communications workers	
Lighting technicians		Postal workers	
		Computer engineers	
Information base agencies		*Analysing probabilities*	
Real estate workers		Insurance workers	
Travel agents		Bookmakers	
Mixed functions (part information)		*Providing professional information*	
Customs officers	Police	Psychologists/psychiatrists	
Theatrical workers		Physicians	Pharmacists

Source: House of Representatives Standing Committee on Long-Term Strategies (1991), *Australia as an Information Society: Grasping New Paradigms.*

Australia will also develop a small but growing, export-oriented, high technology manufacturing industry.

- Society and industry will become increasingly conscious of environmental issues, pollution and the depletion of resources. The recycling of materials and the miniaturisation of technology will become major techniques used to save energy.

- Politics will lose much of its ideology. Political parties will agree on the major issues and disagree only on less important questions. Complex problems will be seen as technical in nature and left to technicians to resolve.

- The social structure will be more divided between the information rich, that is, those who are highly educated, employed and affluent, and the information poor, that is, early school leavers and the unskilled who suffer increased unemployment, boredom and frustration.

Despite predicting what would happen, Jones also emphasised that we should not be fatalistic about the future. Rather than regarding change as unstoppable, we should see ourselves as facing options to be taken from within a given framework. To a certain extent, this is also what has happened. For example, when Jones wrote the first edition of his book, Australia had one of the lowest rates of participation at senior school level and at university in the Western world. Within a decade, however, this had been turned around as large numbers of young people saw increased education as one of the keys to the new types of jobs that were emerging.

Nonetheless, Jones still warns us against complacency. The new economy is clearly growing at both ends of its scale—the numbers of haves and have nots are both increasing while those of the middle ground are shrinking. He argues that we need to develop new types of employment, aimed more at satisfying individual needs. Some of the fields he originally identified as growth areas, notably research, tourism and leisure, have fulfilled his predictions but others have declined faster than he anticipated.

Temperamentally, Jones says, he is still an optimist. He thinks that by lateral thinking, human beings can find new approaches to the obvious social and economic problems they are facing.

The information society of the future has the potential, he believes, to be 'a creative era in which Mozartian man and woman can evolve'. But if we fail to respond creatively, we will be left with the dark side of the options. 'If we remain imprisoned in the linear thinking so congenial to bureaucrats, capitalists and commissars, the future will be a period of unemployment, alienation and unprecedented social crises.'

CHAPTER

1

THE NATURE OF COMMUNICATIONS IN THE INFORMATION AGE

After studying this chapter, you will:

- understand some of the implications of the enormous growth of information over the past decade
- recognise where this has and where this has not affected the nature of communicating
- understand why communication practices within organisations are changing
- know the strengths and weaknesses of the various models of communication theory
- be aware of the ethical implications of communication practice

THE INFORMATION EXPLOSION

We now live in an era when large numbers of people employ communication skills in their everyday work. The fastest growing part of the economy is the information and communications sector. In Australia, Canada and the United States, 40 per cent of the working population is in information occupations. The average for all the developed countries is now more than one-third and the figure is growing every year. In all these countries, more than twice as many workers are employed in the information sector as in manufacturing. Not only has there been a rapid growth in the number of specialist information workers such as market researchers, finance personnel, data processing professionals, media workers and monitors, evaluators and reporters of various kinds, but many more people have to use information skills as part of their jobs in more traditional occupations.

The fastest growing part of the economy is the information and communications sector. In Australia, Canada and the USA, 40 per cent of the working population is in information occupations.

The days when most people worked primarily with their hands on farms, factories and building sites are fast disappearing. Today, the successful farmers are those who spend more time on their computer terminals studying information about market trends, prices, new technology, scientific developments and weather conditions than they do on the land itself. In advanced manufacturing plants, computer-controlled processes and robots actually make the products while the human employees spend their time studying, designing and refining the production process so that it is more efficient and can be adapted quickly to changes in market demand. Most building components today are prefabricated in factories and only a minimum of work is completed on site. The growth area in building employment is for designers, organisers and managers—the information and communications personnel. In other words, we are moving to the stage when everyone will have information tasks as part of their employment.

In a great deal of the discussion about the Information Age there is an assumption that, unless people understand computer programming languages and are familiar with the architecture of the silicon chip, they will be left out. This is misleading. Computers today have reached the stage where anyone can be taught to use them without great difficulty. Computers are increasingly becoming specialised devices that are built into the products we use. A fair comparison is driving a motor car. To drive it, you need to know how to use the controls but you don't need to understand the workings of the internal combustion engine. Similarly, you don't need to know anything about the computer software used by a bank when you use a computer-controlled automatic teller; nor about the telecommunications principles involved in the stationary-orbiting satellite to make an international telephone call. In some computer devices there is more involved. For instance, it still takes some time to become proficient in the computer software that governs word processing, accounting spreadsheets or filing and retrieving from databases. But there is no need for anyone operating these systems to have been trained in computer systems analysis or programming. Computers, telecommunications systems and other kinds of new technology have reached the stage where they are serving rather than dominating people in their working relations with each other.

Employment in the Information Age is much more about the way people relate to one another rather than to technology.

Technology is allowing much greater quantities of information to be made available to people but it is not really altering the *quality* of the information we need to use to communicate with each other.

This all has important implications for communicating. Technology is allowing much greater quantities of information to be made available to people but it is not really altering the *quality* of the information we need to use to communicate with each other. When using a word processor or sending a written message by fax, you still need to compose your message in clear, informative and attractive prose. You can have a telephone conversation via a satellite with someone on the other side of the world, or conduct a video conference which allows several people in different parts of the country to see and talk to each other through telecommunications links; but the virtues of good speech and conversation, such as being interesting, informative, well prepared and attentive, are just as necessary in this setting as in a more normal meeting. The Information Age, then, is something of a paradox. On the one hand, more people are being employed to spend more of their time using sophisticated technology to communicate with each other. On the other hand, the traditional values embodied in good communication practice have not been lost but are, in fact, in greater demand than ever. We should regard the Information Age as an era in which we have much greater opportunity than ever before to share our knowledge and experiences and to get to know other people's needs, demands and tastes.

The Information Age demands that most people become not just receivers but the active producers of messages. They need to be able to write and speak well and to relate to their fellows in positive ways.

The real difficulty for most people will be to learn how to communicate with each other. Over the last five or six generations, people in the developed countries have devoted most of their energies to mastering nature and our use of the physical world. A small number of people have been the organisers, managers and designers. The majority of people were educated basically to read or listen to instructions, not to initiate messages of their own. Today, however, the Information Age demands that most people become not just receivers but the active producers of messages. They need to be able to write and speak well and to relate to their fellows in positive ways. Unfortunately, too few people have gained these skills and education systems have not developed sufficient strengths in fostering them.

HUMAN RELATIONS IN THE INFORMATION AGE

A great many books have been written in the last thirty years about communication within organisations. They have identified many of the problems that arise within companies, government departments, community groups, educational and other institutions as failures of communication. The problems include employees resisting the introduction of new procedures and technologies, duplicated efforts within large bureaucracies, certain groups feeling nobody consults them or considers their needs and, often, a general aimlessness or lack of direction.

Many of these books were written for people in management positions. They offer managers various charts and models of how an effective communication system should operate within an organisation. They often draw up possible alternatives. Top management can communicate directly with departmental heads (such as the financial manager, production manager, advertising manager, etc.) or there could be a buffer zone of senior managers between the top person and the departments. The heads of the departments might communicate directly with each other or they might have to send all their messages up to top management before they can go down again to other departmental heads. Relations between managers and workers on the factory or office floor can also be drawn up as direct links or via supervisors or through some other channel. Most of these books have one thing in common. They assume that communication always goes downwards, from top to bottom. Their main aim is to tell managers how to get those below them to do what managers want. The effectiveness of communication is measured by how well those on the receiving end understand and respond to what they are told to do. Issues usually defined by these books as problems of communication are the distortions that can occur when messages are passed down across several managerial levels. Like rumours that are passed on by several people, they point out, the final version of a top manager's instructions can vary greatly from the original. Some of these books do admit that communication should flow upward as well as downward but they see the opportunity for this in very limited terms. Workers can have suggestion boxes to send their ideas to managers; small shareholders can ask questions at annual general meetings to express their views to the board. Needless to say, neither of these channels has ever proven adequate to the task of effectively communicating the attitudes of either employees or shareholders to those at the top.

The most successful firms and the most successful nations are those that employ communication networks that transmit information not only downward but upward as well as from one side to the other.

Communication of this kind might have sufficed in the days when many organisations were run as if management had all the knowledge and expertise and those on the bottom had few ideas to contribute to the running of the organisation. In the assembly line techniques pioneered by Henry Ford, each worker had one limited task to perform over and again and, in such a setting, there was no room for the employee to contribute anything but labour.

Today, however, these practices are no longer effective. The most successful firms and the most successful nations are those that employ communication networks that transmit information not only downward but upward, as well as from one side to the other. The fact that the majority of workers are now either fully or partially employed on information tasks shows we are in a process of radical change in which information is increasingly *shared* throughout organisations. Managers are no longer the sole source of knowledge and instruction. They have grown increasingly dependent upon the communication they receive from all regions of their organisations. Increasingly, well-run organisations of any kind—whether they are private firms, government bodies, public utilities or community associations—are those in which clear and effective communication systems flow freely and efficiently.

Everyone in an organisation today needs to think more about their relationships with other people. We all need to develop the ability to put ourselves in the other person's position and to see things from their point of view.

Developing a shared communication system does not mean adopting some trendy psychological analysis or therapy, nor plunging into the latest version of communication theory. It does, however, mean that everyone in an organisation needs to think more about their relationships with other people. We all need to develop the ability to put ourselves in the other person's position and to see things from their point of view.

Consulting, negotiating, listening and interpreting are communication skills that are every bit as important as writing and speaking. We are in a new era but, in many ways, we don't measure up to its potential. The legacy of the past has left too many of us with too few communication skills. As we said before, we have a small number of people who know how to compose and send messages; and we have a large number who are familiar only with the receiving end. The demands of the Information Age will force this situation to change.

To respond to the opportunities of the new era, we need to recognise two cardinal points: first, everyone should be trained to become a communicator in both the sending and receiving sense; and second, the old models of top-down communication are now out of date and are, in fact, a hindrance to the development of the potential before us. We need to develop new models of communication networks and skills or, what is the same thing, new ways for people within organisations to relate to one another. Communication deserves to move to centre court in the development of our administrative and organisational techniques.

THEORIES OF COMMUNICATION

Just as the practice of communication within organisations has shifted over recent decades, so too has communication theory. If we look at the broad contours of communication theory since the Second World War, we can see there has been a long-term change of emphasis from the original theories which focused on those who initiate communications to the most recent theories which focus on their audiences.

THE 1940S: ENGINEERING MODELS

Early theories of communication were developed for the telecommunications industry by engineers, especially those working for Bell Telephone Laboratories in the United States during the Second World War.[1] The model defined by Shannon and Weaver conceived of communication as a matter of transmitting a whole message intact from sender to receiver. This model saw problems of communication in essentially engineering terms. The two major problems it identified were, first, interference along the line and, second, fade-out or dissipation of the message as it was transmitted. Translated into business terms, this model held that an organisation should try to provide as little scope for interference and fade-out as possible. As it travelled from management down to employees, a message should go through as few terminals or repeater stations (that is, other people such as middle managers and supervisors) as possible. The more direct the route, the more effective the communication.

THE 1950S AND 1960S: PSYCHOLOGICAL THEORIES

In the 1950s and 1960s, a human dimension was added to the model. Psychologists argued that people were not mere terminals or receiving

1. For a more detailed history of communication theory, see John Fiske, *Introduction to Communication Studies*, Routledge, London, 1990

stations. An individual received messages through his or her own perceptual apparatus, in particular the eyes and ears. The message sender had to be aware that this apparatus would provide its own shape and distortion to any message. The psychologists also pointed out that the kinds of messages received by human beings involved far more than simply the words that were sent. People are emotional creatures and pick up many emotion-related signals in any message. Signals such as gestures with the hands, face and body, emphases on particular words and phrases, irony and sarcasm, pauses and even silences all added their own content to any piece of communication. Communication theory, the psychologists argued, needed to address the far more complex array of meanings that the sender of a message was likely to transmit.

Signals such as gestures with the hands, face and body, emphases on particular words and phrases, irony and sarcasm, pauses and even silences all added their own content to any piece of communication.

THE 1970S: CULTURAL ENCODING AND DECODING

In the 1970s, sociologists and social theorists came into the field. Against the psychologists' focus on individuals in the communication process, this new group emphasised that any communication theory had to take into account the social phenomena of language and culture. Language was influenced by culture, these theorists argued, and communication was a process in which a signal was 'encoded' by the sender with meanings drawn from a culture, and then 'decoded' by the receiver. Signals or signs were always heavily laden with cultural and political meanings, whether we intended it or not. Movements, objects, symbols and even colours conveyed meanings in very complicated ways that required detailed analysis. Language was a shared cultural medium and its social function needed to be understood by any theory of communication.

Signals or signs are always heavily laden with cultural and political meanings, whether we intend it or not. Movements, objects, symbols and even colours convey meanings in very complicated ways.

The 'encoding/decoding' thesis was developed at the University of Birmingham by a group of Marxists, headed by Professor Stuart Hall, who were working in social theory and media studies.[2] They used the thesis to try to explain how the media, especially newspapers, television programs and advertisements, indoctrinated its audiences with political messages that supported conservative attitudes about social change. The 'encoding/decoding' thesis is now widely recognised by academics in the field as being flawed and out of date, but there are still some recent business communication textbooks which are unaware of this.[3] It is ironic that when they give a brief overview of communication theory to their business studies readers, these textbooks use a thesis that was developed by Marxists to explain how business oppresses the workers!

The encoding/decoding thesis shifted the focus of communication studies from the sender of the message, who had been the main concern of earlier theories, to the message itself. The text of the message was thought to exert a great deal of influence over what audiences could do with it.

2. See Stuart Hall, Dorothy Hobson, Andrew Lowe and Paul Willis (eds.) *Culture, Media, Language*, Centre for Contemporary Cultural Studies, University of Birmingham, Hutchinson, London, 1980.

3. For example, Michael Galvin, David Prescott, Richard Huseman, *Business Communication: Strategies and Skills*, Holt, Rinehart and Winston, Sydney, 1992, pp. 16-17.

However, in recent years, critics of this thesis have argued that it greatly underestimates the role of the audience in making its own interpretations of the messages on offer.[4] Theory has finally reached the stage where it now focuses on the most important part of the communication chain, the receiver.

THE 1990S: AUDIENCE-FOCUSED COMMUNICATIONS

Communication theorists are now beginning to recognise something that professional communicators have known all along, that audiences bring their own expectations and prejudices to their reading, listening and viewing and that they never accept precisely what they are told.

Communication theorists are now beginning to recognise something that professional communicators have known all along, that audiences bring their own expectations and prejudices to their reading, listening and viewing and that they never accept precisely what they are told.[5] They are always involved in reading between the lines, that is, in not only determining *what* is being said but in asking *why* it is being said, and what might have been left out. Anyone who writes or speaks to the public is virtually forced to use this as their guiding principle. You can never get inside the mind of someone else to know precisely what they are thinking but, when writing or public speaking, your main concern should always be how the audience is likely to respond: will they understand what you are saying, will they do what you want, or will they have an agenda of their own?

Throughout this book we have adopted this attitude to the audience as our own guiding principle. You have to respect your audience, to treat your readers and listeners as equals, and to communicate with them in ways you would want them to communicate with you. You need to recognise that any failure to communicate, either through lack of clarity or by not being sufficiently engaging or interesting, is not the fault of the audience but is always the responsibility of the sender of the message who has not taken the audience's needs sufficiently into consideration. An audience-focused approach to communication is not merely something that is justified by the communication theory of the 1990s. It is now, and always has been, the basis of the *practice* of all successful communicators.

THE ETHICS OF COMMUNICATION

The Information Age spans both the 1980s and the 1990s. There is, however, a noticeable difference between these two decades which has important implications for communication practice. The 1980s was a period that was characterised by selfishness, greed and sharp practices. These qualities were found right throughout our political, business and social organisations. They were not, of course, confined to Australia. We took our models from the United States and the United Kingdom where the 'greed is

4. A summary of critiques of the encoding/decoding thesis is in Stuart Cunningham and Graeme Turner (eds.), *The Media in Australia: Industries, Texts, Audiences*, Allen & Unwin, Sydney, 1993.

5. Keith Windschuttle argued this point in his 1984 book, *The Media*, Penguin. For an overview of recent research into audiences *see* Cunningham and Turner, *The Media in Australia*, pp. 267–305.

good' philosophies originated. The collapse of the fortunes of many of those who lived by these codes, and their subsequent public disgrace, has led to a different ethical environment in the 1990s. No one expects the former qualities to disappear, for they are embedded in the human nature of all of us. Nonetheless, it is clear that they will be treated with far less tolerance and sympathy in the decade ahead than they were in the one now past. This is becoming apparent in the growing number of organisations which are producing written codes of ethics for the guidance of all their personnel.

Whether or not a formal code exists, communication practice should always be couched within an ethical framework. The central ethos might be summed up as: communicate with others in the way you want them to communicate with you. In terms of the various groups and individuals with whom we all interact, an ethical attitude towards communication could be summarised as follows.

Whether or not a formal code exists, communication practice should always be couched within an ethical framework. The central ethos might be summed up as: communicate with others in the way you want them to communicate with you.

- People outside your organisation such as clients, suppliers, public officers, and the community at large. Your objective should be to communicate in a way that produces mutual understanding. In some cases, there can be serious legal consequences if your written communications are found to be untrue and you can be held personally responsible. In other cases, you are under no obligation other than your personal standards to avoid disinformation and misleading others. Today, most people are occupationally mobile and never work for the same organisation all their working lives. Perpetuating lies on behalf of an organisation with which you have only a temporary relationship is a poor basis for building a career. Being known as a person of character is a much sounder strategy.

- Your superiors. Everyone has the temptation to cover up their mistakes when they occur, and to exaggerate their own achievements, especially to those who will decide our prospects for promotion. However, no organisation can function properly when those in authority are given misleading or inaccurate information. In the long run, if information is really important, any lies that are told will be uncovered anyway. Being honest and accurate about your activities is an obligation you owe to those who employ you.

- Your subordinates. You have a similar obligation to those whose activities you supervise. They have a right to know information about matters which affect both their work and their well-being. They are also entitled to know that personal information about them will be handled with discretion.

- Your colleagues. You should act in an ethical manner when communicating with your fellow workers. Taking credit for someone else's work, spreading malicious gossip, or trying to make a co-worker look bad, are dishonourable practices that, in the long run, are more likely to rebound onto your own reputation. However, even if they don't backfire and you actually gain by cheating, the victory is unlikely to give you any satisfaction because you will always know you won it, not on your own merit, but by unethical methods.

KEY POINTS: Chapter 1 The nature of Communications in the Information Age

- Information and communications are now the fastest growing part of the economy. In Australia, Canada and the United States, 40 per cent of the working population is employed in information occupations.
- Technology allows much greater *quantities* of information to be made available to people, but it is not really altering the *quality* of the information we need. Good speech and conversation and clear, informative and attractive prose remain essential.
- Writing, speaking and relating do not require any inborn talent. They are no more or less difficult than any other human skill and, like any other human skill, they can be learned.
- Everyone should now be trained to become a communicator.
- The old models of top-down communication are out of date. We need to develop new communication networks and skills.
- Communication theory began in the 1940s with a focus on the sender of a message. By the 1970s it had shifted to the message itself or the text. In the 1990s, theorists are now paying most attention to the receiver, that is, the audience. In other words, theory has now reached the point where the practice of professional communicators has always been.
- In the aftermath to the 'greed is good' decade of the 1980s, ethical practices have become as important in communication practice as they have in other professional areas. The central ethos should be: communicate with others in the way you would want them to communicate with you.

QUESTIONS FOR DISCUSSION

1. Has technology changed the underlying nature of human communication?
2. How has organisational change affected the practices of communicating?
3. What is the area to which communication theory in the 1990s is paying most attention? Why is this?
4. Within an organisation, is it always ethical to tell the whole truth and nothing but the truth? Describe some exceptions and discuss their ethical implications.

EXERCISES

1. Read the first chapter of Barry Jones' book *Sleepers, Wake!* Write a summary or draw a diagram to outline the stages he identifies from 'pre-industrial' to 'post-service' society.
2. Look at the occupations listed in Table A: Categories of Information Workers, page 4. Write a list of the types of writing, speaking and other forms of communicating that each job entails. You will need to look at vocational guidance literature for a description of each occupation.
3. Look at some recently published textbooks on business management, especially those which discuss such concepts as Total Quality Management and Service Quality Assurance (see the reading list at the end of Chapter Thirty-One). Discuss how much emphasis each book places on communication within the organisation.
4. Draw up a set of recommendations to govern the ethics of communication at an organisation with which you are familiar.

CHAPTER 2

DEVELOPING GOOD COMMUNICATION PRACTICE

After studying this chapter, you will:

- understand the foundations of good communication practice
- understand the range of purposes people have when they try to communicate
- recognise the need to spell out to yourself your own communication purposes
- recognise the importance of planning what you are to say before you say it
- develop a sense of the presence of the reader whenever you write

There are two things to do before you engage in sending any form of communication—written, spoken, illustrated or any other kind. First, decide what you want to say and, second, work out a plan of how to say it. This may seem very obvious when seen here in cold print but it is advice that very few people put into practice. When most people want to say something to others they simply plunge in, composing their message as they go along. The result is a speech or talk that rambles around the issue, digressing and making points that are not quite relevant to the issue. At times the speaker is lost for words and the conclusion is often limp and unconvincing.

When writing essays and reports, most people make the same mistake. They start by writing the first few points that come into their head and then simply add on points as they come to mind. This approach guarantees that writing will be a tortuous process in which the author is often lost for direction and has to agonise over how to fit his or her successive ideas into the mess that already lies there on the page. This experience of writing is slow and painful. It always involves several drafts and re-drafts and persuades many people that they have not got 'the talent' for writing. In reality, though, they lack not talent but technique. With a different approach, writing would come much easier to them and would also be a far more pleasant experience for their readers.

People who have good communication skills take a quite different approach. Before they put their fingers to the keyboard or step up to the microphone, they decide exactly what they want to get across to their audience and they work out a plan for the message that will do the job. The message and the plan can vary enormously: it might be an elaborate and complicated scene-by-scene plot for a novel set out in note form on a huge wall chart; or it might be three main points that someone at a meeting decides inside his or her head while waiting to get the nod from the chair. But whatever the size or difficulty of the communication, the basic principle remains the same: know what you are going to say and plan how you will say it *before* you do anything else.

Before they put their fingers to the keyboard or step up to the microphone, people who are good communicators decide exactly what they want to get across to their audience and they work out a plan for the message that will do the job.

DETERMINING YOUR PURPOSE

People always communicate for some reason but for many their reasons are not always clear, even to themselves. Communications have a very wide range of purposes. Some of them are:

- to get across some information or knowledge
- to persuade someone to take an action
- to express sympathy or support
- to persuade people to reject one set of ideas for another
- to entertain or amuse an audience
- to make someone feel confident about themselves

- to gain a victory over an opponent
- to rouse people to excitement
- to lull them into a sense of security

Most messages contain not one of these purposes but several, and some will be more important than others. Despite this complexity, the simple act of asking 'What is this message intended to do?' will in most cases produce a fairly clear answer. The real problem is not that the answer is difficult but that too few people bother to ask the question. The result is that their message lacks direction from the outset. This makes it much harder to write or to say what you want. It also makes it much more likely that the person on the receiving end will misunderstand what you mean and what you intend.

If you fail to identify your purposes, your message lacks direction from the outset. This makes it much harder to write or to say what you want. It also makes it much more likely that the person on the receiving end will misunderstand what you mean and what you intend.

Let's take an example of a familiar kind. You work with someone who has a way of doing one small job, say filing new order forms, that is mildly irritating to everyone else in your department because it involves them all in some unnecessary extra work. Apart from this, the person is a valued employee and a pleasant workmate. You have to tell this person to do the filing a different way. If you think about this message for any time at all, you should realise that it needs to do two jobs at once. It must persuade the person to act differently but it must also reassure him or her that you are only being critical about this one point, and not giving a broad hint that the person is no longer wanted at all. This dual purpose means you would approach this person with quite a different communication to the one you might have used if you had not stopped to think.

Or take a different example. You have to write to the head office of your organisation to ask for funds to expand one of your activities. If you did not stop to question your purposes, you might think your letter adequate if it does two things: (1) justifies the expansion, and (2) requests the money. However, in a case like this a third purpose may well be necessary: that of explaining the activity itself. Once you have started to clarify to yourself what your purposes are, it might become apparent that some people in head office do not have a very clear idea of what you are doing. You will realise you cannot assume that everyone who reads your request and is party to the decision will have this knowledge. Trying to justify the expansion of an activity that remains unexplained to those you are approaching is not the best way to get what you want.

It cannot be emphasised too strongly that you should always start the communication process by asking the basic question, 'What am I trying to do?'

It cannot be emphasised too strongly that you should always start the communication process by asking the basic question, 'What am I trying to do?' Once you have clarified your purpose or purposes, you have eliminated the most likely sources of wasted effort and confusion, for both yourself and your audience.

DEVELOPING A PLAN OR STRUCTURE

By far the most important part of any form of communication is its structure. This is the order in which ideas are presented. The structure is the process which moves the audience from ignorance to understanding of what you want to communicate. To do this effectively it is essential to develop your structure before you start. The central principle is: *know what you are going to say before you say it.* You should keep to this principle at every level of writing or speaking. You should have a plan for the piece as a whole, a plan for its main divisions, its sections, paragraphs and even sentences.

Let's start with the example of an author writing a book. This might appear to be a daunting kind of example because the great majority of people reading this will obviously have less ambitious goals, at least in the short term. However, the principles for a long book or a short essay are basically the same and, anyway, book writing is not really all that daunting. It is not confined to people with a special kind of intellectual capacity. What you need far more is a good technique and, of course, plenty of time. We can't give you the time but the technique is certainly available.

The central principle is: *know what you are going to say before you say it.*

For anyone planning to write a book, the first thing to do is to draw up a list of chapter headings. In other words, the first thing to write is the Table of Contents. Like any plan, you should be prepared to make changes to this list—two or three chapters on the list may eventually be collapsed into one; another might be expanded into two chapters; some new chapters might be added as you proceed and some from the plan might be dropped altogether. But, no matter how flexible your plan might be, you still need it to give you an overview of the whole book so that you can comprehend its whole direction from start to finish as you go along. You can look at the list of chapters—in effect, put the whole of the book inside your head at one time—and think whether they really represent the overall scope that you wanted and which your readers need. You can question whether the overall direction really goes somewhere, that is, builds upon itself so that by the time readers get to the end they have actually been on a journey that has led them to some new understanding of the subject.

You cannot create this direction as you go along. Once you have started writing, you become heavily involved with the material immediately in front of you and it is very difficult to think about both this and the wider outcome of the whole book. To be sure your book really says what you want, you have to plan it all in advance. Most good authors find that, part of the way through, they realise their original plan was inadequate or in need of some modification. So they develop a new or altered structure and fit what they have already written into this. They then continue with the new structure or plan as their basic guideline. In other words, they are always working from a plan of the whole piece.

Once you have started writing, you become heavily involved with the material immediately in front of you and it is very difficult to think about both this and the overall outcome.

Writing an article for a magazine or a chapter for a book involves precisely the same technique. The article needs its own plan which means dividing it into sections according to the main points you want to make. Give these sections headings that are fairly descriptive of the actual content. It is probably best to keep these headings within the text of the final version you write (in the same way that the five headings around which we planned the chapter you are reading now have been left in the text). Some people dislike internal headings within articles and essays because they think they interrupt the flow of the text and are unaesthetic. We disagree. Headings are very useful in a text, especially non-fiction like this, because they allow the reader to 'see' as well as read the structure of the article. This provides a reminder of where the reader has been and gives easy reference points if anyone wants to go back over a major point that has been made. It is true that headings can be overdone and become irritating but, on balance, they are better included than left out.

Once the major sections have been determined and given their headings, the next thing to do is develop a plan to govern the order of the paragraphs within those sections. Each paragraph should contain a significant point that contributes to the one being made in the section as a whole. This means that the plan for paragraphs is the development of a case. It plays the same role as the development of the list of chapters for a whole book. It allows you to see whether you have included all the points the case needs and whether the order or direction is right and convincing. You should write out a series of small or abbreviated headings that stand for each paragraph, think about them and perhaps rearrange them. When you are satisfied your paragraph plan is right, you can start to think about writing the first paragraph.

Headings are very useful in a text, especially non-fiction like this, because they allow the reader to 'see' as well as read the structure of the article.

Planning does not, however, stop at this point. Many authors actually draw up a small plan for each paragraph, or at least for a group of paragraphs. Most paragraphs have from two to ten sentences (except in news journalism which is a special case we discuss in Chapter Eighteen). Each paragraph should make one clear point, usually in the last sentence, though sometimes in the first. The supporting sentences normally provide evidence or reasoning to back up the main point. In other words, a paragraph is a mini-argument which has to persuade the reader just as the article as a whole does. So a plan of the internal structure of sentences within each paragraph is needed to perform the same role as the much broader plans already discussed. The plan for a paragraph can be fairly sparse—a series of words or abbreviations will usually do—but no less important for that.

Some readers may now baulk when we say that they need a plan for each sentence. You might now think we are overdoing this. We still want to insist, however, that this is the best way to proceed. Obviously, it would be silly to tell you to write down the plan for a sentence in point form, for that would mean almost writing the sentence itself. What is important, however, is to plan the sentence *in your head* before writing it down. If you start to write a sentence without thinking how it will end, you will, as we said earlier, always find writing difficult and unpleasant. You will be stuck with a beginning onto which you have to fit a middle and an end. You will end up with convoluted prose that is as difficult to write as it is to read. Writing will not only be hard work, it will be slow work. People who are fast writers are usually those who have developed the habit of tossing around within their heads several versions of the sentence they want *before* they write down one word of the sentence. Once they work out what they want to say, they then write it out without hesitating, without correcting themselves or having to stop to think how they are going to finish.

People who are fast writers are usually those who have developed the habit of tossing around within their heads several versions of the sentence they want *before* they write down one word of it.

The relationship between a writer and sentences is like that of a computer to its printer. The central processor of a computer can make millions of decisions a second but it is a very slow business to get material out of the computer onto paper because even fast printers can produce at speeds measured in only hundreds of characters per second. The writer's brain, like a central processor, can test out several versions of a sentence at great speed (much faster, in fact, than any computer). It is far more efficient to search for the right sentence at this stage than to start the comparatively slow print-out phase of writing and trying to get the sentence right as you go along.

When using your brain to test different versions of what you intend to say, it is much easier to use short sentences than long ones. By the time you have finished mentally composing a long sentence you will probably have forgotten how it started. A short sentence of twenty words or less is relatively simple to compose in your head.

Short sentences are one of the keys to successful writing. They are an essential part of the process of knowing what you will write before you actually write it.

Short sentences are one of the keys to successful writing (and are the basic practice of journalists, as we discuss in Chapter Eighteen). They are an essential part of the process of knowing what you will write before you actually write it. And this, we cannot emphasise too strongly, is the basic strategy behind all good writing.

DRAFTING AND EFFICIENCY

One of the basic principles of communication ought to be efficiency. Unfortunately, this principle is not as well recognised as it ought to be. Part of the blame for this lies with a small number of literary writers who, in describing their technique, have admitted to writing anything between five and ten drafts of a work before they are satisfied with it. There is also the well-known comment by Oscar Wilde who, when asked what he had done all day, said he had spent the morning taking a comma out of one of his plays and the afternoon putting it back again. Now, the great volume of work that Wilde turned out indicates that we should not take his comment seriously and that it was probably a sarcastic rejoinder to someone who thought writers never really worked hard. And, probably, only a few of those who do large numbers of drafts need to make a living from writing. People who are professional writers cannot afford to take this much time over any one piece and, anyway, real professionals never need to go over their work this many times. The modest rates of payment made to journalists and authors in most countries usually mean that they have to be as economical as they can with their time. A long drafting process is a luxury they cannot afford.

A long drafting process is a luxury professional writers cannot afford.

The objective in any form of communication should be to get it right the first time. In a public talk, of course, this is usually all that is possible. There is little opportunity to go back and make corrections to what you have said. If you try to correct your words or expression, you simply communicate a lack of confidence in what you are saying. It would have been better, in most cases, to have let the original stand.

The more writing practice you get, the fewer should be your drafts.

When writing, your long-term goal should be to get to the stage where your first draft is your final draft. Some people will take a long time, perhaps years, to reach this goal. However, it is one that is within the reach of every person who has to use writing as part of his or her work. The key to reaching the goal is practice. The more writing practice you get, the fewer should be your drafts. If you develop the habit of planning your work the way we have recommended in this chapter, your early efforts may have some unclear or awkward expressions but your basic structure will be right. This means re-drafting will be a matter of changing words and phrases and rewriting some sentences, not re-ordering the whole piece.

The best way to tackle a re-draft is to put away your first draft (preferably overnight) and do something else to get the words out of your head so that when you return you are reading from a fresh viewpoint. Make your corrections, then put the piece away again. Come back again and repeat the process until you are satisfied. The more practice you get as a writer, the fewer drafts you should aim for. Your ultimate goal of one draft as final draft means, in reality, that you write a piece once, then put it away. When you come back, your second look should be to correct your first version, not to rewrite it. The original should be able to stand basically as it is but with a few touch-ups here and there. Most professional writers operate this way and it is the most efficient method there is for writing and checking your work.

SELECTING THE MEDIUM

How can you tell whether a message will be relayed best in writing, in speech, or by an illustration? There are no hard and fast rules to follow. You have to consider each case on its merits in terms of the advantages and disadvantages of each communication medium.

Writing has at least four advantages.

First, it is a permanent record. It may be read and stored, retrieved and read again many times and it does not change. There are many kinds of message where permanence is desirable—where the information is important, where it brings together difficult or complicated ideas, or where the expression is particularly apt, or moving, or amusing and is worth keeping for its own sake.

The advantages of writing:
- it is a permanent record
- it reaches a large audience
- it can be reproduced in many forms
- the writer has time to consider words carefully

Second, writing allows you to reach a much larger audience than could be present in one place to hear someone talk. Writing can be reproduced in multiple print runs and can be sent to many people in locations at great distances from each other.

Third, writing can be reproduced in a variety of forms such as books, articles, pamphlets, letters, brochures, newspapers and computer printouts. Despite the variety of the print medium, the actual words, or even the original typeset letters, can be reproduced precisely from one to the other.

Fourth, the writer has the time to consider written words carefully, to polish and re-draft them before sending them off to readers. This allows the writer to say precisely what he or she wants to, and avoids the poor expression and misunderstandings that often characterise speech.

The main disadvantage of writing is that it takes time and is more difficult than speech. People can speak instantaneously but writing is a much slower process. Children, for instance, learn to speak at a very young age but they need another six to ten years before they gain any proficiency as writers. Another disadvantage is that it takes a long time to question, challenge or disagree with a writer in print and for the writer to reply. It can take several issues of a newspaper or magazine for a debate in print to be argued out, but a debate in speech can be accomplished on the spot.

When should you use illustrations with your writing? The old cliché that a picture tells a thousand words is certainly true but, funnily enough, pictures can rarely stand on their own without words. Photographs in newspapers or books usually need captions to explain them. Drawings or graphs are often meaningless unless they relate to a point made in an accompanying text. Illustrations, whether photographs, drawings or graphs, should be primarily regarded as material that supports, confirms or provides background to the words of the text.

When should you use illustrations? The simple but correct answer is as often as possible. If you are writing an article, try to find or take photographs that show the things you are writing about. Overall, the principles behind the use of illustrations should be to employ them as often as possible but to keep them subordinate to the words in the text.

THE READER OVER YOUR SHOULDER

Most of us learn to write at school but, in one sense, this is not a very satisfactory place to acquire the skill. The relationships that exist between students and teachers foster a certain kind of writing which is the opposite of the type needed by most people when they enter the workforce. At school, college or university, a group of students write their essays for an audience of one, the teacher, and the students assume that the teacher knows more than they do about the subject. This assumption of knowledge by the reader of their essays means that there are a great many points that do not have to be spelled out by students, especially basic points that all 'insiders' to the topic would know. The aim of students is to impress teachers with their broad knowledge of the subject and their mastery of the more complex debates in the area.

At work, on the other hand, one person writes a report or an article that is meant to be read by several or many other people. The task of the report is usually to tell these other people things they do not know. The style demanded in the workplace is not a display of erudition or argumentation but the use of simple, concise English to convey information directly, without wasting time. The part that most people find most difficult about writing for an audience, rather than an individual, is knowing how much knowledge to take for granted. This is not something that students have to think about at all—they assume when they are writing that the teacher will know more than they do, no matter how well they have researched the topic. But the writer for an audience has to be constantly aware of this issue.

The style demanded in the workplace is not a display of erudition or argumentation but the use of simple, concise English to convey information directly, without wasting time.

When you are writing for people who know less than you do about a subject, you cannot drop names and assume that readers will know who you mean or the significance of the person, place or object concerned. You have to continually put yourself in the readers' position and ask whether what you have written is clear to all of them. When you are writing a report for a small group of colleagues, you can take a fair amount of knowledge of the subject for granted but it is better to err on the side of

When writing for the public at large, you have to assume far less knowledge and to fill in enough of the background of everything you say to make the whole piece clear to someone who comes to your writing fairly ignorant of the subject matter.

caution and spell out in detail any point that you think your colleagues might not be fully informed about. When writing for a wider audience, or for the public at large, you have to assume far less knowledge and to fill in enough of the background of everything you say to make the whole piece clear to someone who is fairly ignorant of the subject matter. Newspaper journalists who write for mass audiences have refined this practice over many years. When talking about even very famous people, for instance, they still spell out enough background detail for the reader to 'place' the person concerned. They would not write: 'Bob Hawke entered hospital today with a suspected broken vertebrae.' Rather, they would write: 'Former Australian prime minister, Bob Hawke, entered hospital today with a suspected broken vertebrae.' The same is true of politicians whose names are never regarded as sufficient identification. Their public office has to be noted in each news story in which they appear. In later chapters we discuss the techniques of journalism in more detail but it is worth remembering the basic point made here when engaged in any kind of writing.

Another fundamental difference in the relationship between writer and reader in school compared to the outside world is the issue of being impressive. When writing is offered to be assessed and given a mark out of ten or out of 100, the student author usually adopts a prose style calculated to be noticed and writes a long rather than a short essay. Writing at work or for publication demands the opposite approach. The best writing here gets its ideas across with a minimum of fuss; in fact, it is not noticed as 'writing' at all. It is simple, direct and concise, designed to be both written and read quickly. It works best when it is least intrusive, when the relationship between writer and reader is one in which the ideas and information seem to be transmitted directly from mind to mind, with as little interference as possible from the written words. The words are simply the medium of that transmission process.

Writing works best when it is least intrusive, when the relationship between writer and reader is one in which the ideas and information seem to be transmitted directly from mind to mind, with as little interference as possible from the words on the page.

In 1943, the English poet and novelist, Robert Graves, with co-author Alan Hodge, wrote a book on prose writing called *The Reader over Your Shoulder*. The book has been hard to get for some years but its title is worth preserving. It provides a vivid image that urges writers to constantly remember the reader's presence. Whatever is written on the page in front of you has to be perfectly clear not to you but to that other person. As a critic of your own work, you have to move yourself out of the author's seat and read your work from the perspective of that reader standing over your shoulder. Is every word, phrase and passage clear to that reader? Does he or she read your work the way you intended? Retain a sense of the imminent presence of the reader in everything you write.

KEY POINTS: Chapter 2 Developing good communication practice

- Before engaging in any form of communication, first, decide what you want to say, and second, work out a plan how to say it.
- Once you have clarified your purpose or purposes, you have eliminated the most likely cause of wasted effort and confusion, for both yourself and your audience.
- It is essential to develop your structure before you start. Know what you are going to say before you say it.
- You can improve your writing by planning chapters, paragraphs and even sentences in advance.
- Efficiency is a basic principle. The better your first draft, the less rewriting you will have to do.
- Use illustrations as often as possible, but keep them subordinate to words.
- When writing, take the perspective of the 'reader over your shoulder'.

QUESTIONS FOR DISCUSSION

1. What are the dangers of not determining your purpose before you start speaking or writing?
2. Why is it important to work out a plan or structure before you try to communicate a message?
3. What are the advantages and disadvantages of writing as a communication medium?
4. Why is it important to retain a sense of the presence of the reader whenever you write?

EXERCISES

1. Draw up a plan of at least ten chapters for your autobiography. Then select one of these chapters, and prepare a plan for it.
2. Draw up a plan for a five-minute speech about your family background, life history and personal interests to be given to a group of people who do not know you.
3. Watch a current affairs program on television in which a politician is interviewed at some length. Make a note of the issues discussed in the interview which are not explained clearly enough for the average viewer to follow. Write what questions you think should have been asked to make these issues more understandable.

CHAPTER

3

THE ELECTRONIC REVOLUTION

After studying this chapter, you will:

- understand the significance of the electronic revolution in the area of communications
- know why professional writers prefer to work on computers
- recognise the wide range of tasks that small computers can handle
- understand why everyone in the future should have keyboard skills

In the past decade, electronic technology has transformed communications in ways that few people could have once imagined. The technology has eliminated a great many of the repetitive tasks and drudgery that was once involved in paper-based communication systems and allowed people to become both more proficient and more creative. We are fortunate to be living in an age that is going through a technological revolution that is every bit as revolutionary as the invention of the printing press and moveable type. Caxton and his printers freed books from being the preserve of scholars in the monasteries and made them widely available, a move which eventually allowed everyone in society to become readers. Today's electronic technology has the potential to free writing and publishing from being the preserve of a minority and to allow everyone to become their own writer and publisher.

Today's electronic technology has the potential to free writing and publishing from being the preserve of a minority and to allow everyone to become their own writer and publisher.

COMPUTERS AND WORD PROCESSORS

By far the best piece of technology yet invented for writers is the word processor. There were originally 'dedicated' word processors that handled this type of work and nothing else. More recently, small personal computers have become available which come with software packages that will handle word processing, filing and accounting.

The great virtue of word processing is its flexibility and adaptability. You can correct simple typing mistakes, insert and delete words and passages, and move paragraphs and much longer parts of a text from one position to another. Successive drafts are all done on the one text—there is no need to retype the whole piece after you have made corrections or changes. The text is typed onto the computer's screen where all the corrections and changes are also made. Once you are satisfied with the final version, you can print it out onto paper using a computer printer.

The word processor is by far the most useful piece of technology yet invented for writers.

Laser printers for personal computers are now available which can give you close to the professional quality of typesetting. But even the cheaper type of printers—ink jet, bubble jet and more recent versions of dot matrix printers—allow high quality printing which is perfectly suitable for most communication tasks.

A good idea of the practical difference that computer systems can make to writing may be gained from the experience of the Australian novelist Thomas Keneally. For much of his writing career he adopted an approach that combined handwriting and dictation. 'I used to write the first draft in longhand,' he explained to the *Australian* newspaper, 'and then go through it cutting and pasting in new sections and correcting sentences. Then I would use that to dictate a second draft, which I would have typed. After that I would edit the typed draft, cutting and pasting again and adding new sentences in balloons all over the pages. When that was typed it was ready to go to the publisher.' Keneally added that his first drafts by hand 'tended to be a little florid, while I was too clipped when I dictated'. In 1984, he bought a computer with a word processing package. 'The first draft on the computer is very different. When I've finished with my cutting and pasting [on the computer] the first draft is much closer to the finished result: it's practically in the form you could send to the publisher. The novel is in the stage which would have taken four drafts to reach before.'

'When I've finished on the computer, the first draft is much closer to the finished result: it's practically in the form you could send to the publisher. The novel is in the stage which would have taken four drafts to reach before.'

There are many computers and word processing systems on the market and it is not easy to choose between them. Built into almost all word processing software today are dictionaries to check your spelling, an electronic thesaurus, a program to check your grammar, and a routine to count how many words in a document. The top-of-the-market word processing software packages handle just about every conceivable need in professional writing, such as:

footnotes
references
bibliographies
indexes
chapter and section headings
page and paragraph numbering
table of contents
tables of figures
justified pages
graphs
drawings and clip art

You can have a wide choice of typefaces reproduced in any size and in bold, italic or underline. Some have a very useful 'outlining' feature that allows you to plan the structure of an article or report in terms of headings and subheadings, and then to fill in the body text under the appropriate headings.

Word processing is one technology that can make you a better writer. No one who makes a substantial part of their living out of writing can afford not to use one today.

DESKTOP PUBLISHING

Desktop publishing is very suitable for companies, clubs, community groups and organisations in the production of their reports, presentations, proposals, newsletters, employee and customer bulletins, direct mail campaign material and for correspondence

Linked to a laser printer plus some typesetting and page layout software, a good word processor becomes a desktop publishing system. Desktop publishing is the production of print quality pages comprising headings, subheadings, text and artwork in a similar form to that found in magazines. The pages from the laser printer can be then sent to an offset printer for a large print run or to a copier for a smaller number of copies.

Desktop publishing is very suitable for companies, clubs, community groups and organisations in the production of their reports, presentations, proposals, newsletters, employee and customer bulletins, direct mail campaign material and even ordinary correspondence.

An organisation can set up a desktop publishing system for a relatively modest outlay—about twice the cost of a personal computer plus printer. The savings compared to commercial typesetting are substantial—the in-house cost per page is about one quarter the cost of the commercial product. There is also the question of time saved. Instead of the several days turnaround that is the norm with outside typesetting and layout, a desktop publishing system can produce material on the spot.

DATABASE AND SPREADSHEET SOFTWARE

Two other useful computer tools for writers are the database and the spreadsheet. An ordinary, non-computer database is simply a collection of information like a card index, a library index or a phone book. We use these systems all the time but generally they become bulky, they are slow at retrieving data, they are slow to be updated and you cannot manipulate the data easily, that is, make comparisons and draw relationships between the records in the database. Spreadsheets are useful for any task that involves calculating numbers, especially if you want to produce an instant graphic summary of a range of figures.

In a computer database, you fill out records on the computer screen in much the same way as you would fill out cards for an index. For example, on each record in a mailing list of the staff of a school you might enter Name, Organisation, Address, Telephone, Subject, Date of Recruitment. Like an ordinary card index you could use these records to produce a mailing list to use to send a memo to all teachers on the staff. Computer databases can also read each record in a selective way. This allows you to produce selective mailing lists based on, say, Subject. You could use it to send a memo to only the maths and science teachers on the list; or to only those members of staff who have had less than two years service.

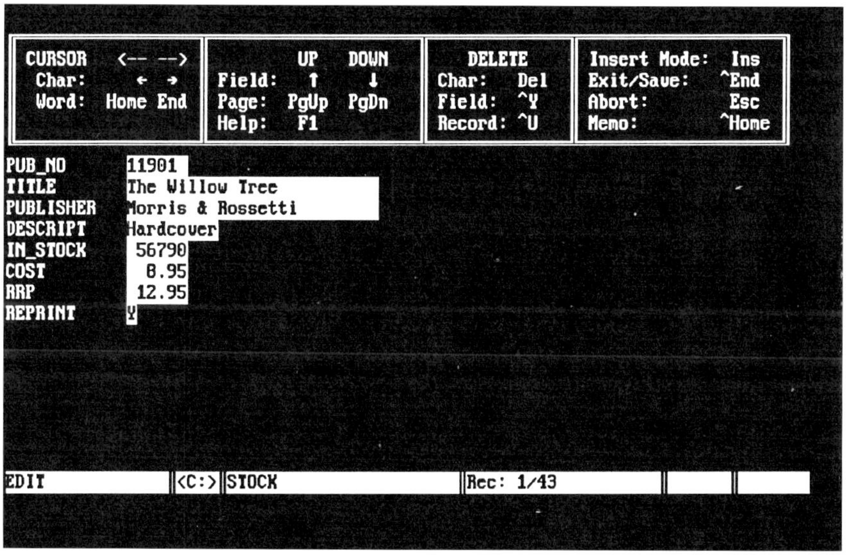

Database software allows you to record and alter information in a number of fields

Unlike a card index which can become large, unwieldy and slow to use, even a small database on a personal computer can hold between 50 000 and 100 000 records and still give very fast access. Database software for personal computers can handle a wide range of tasks including:

scheduling appointments
keeping track of projects

maintaining research files
analysing questionnaires
planning meetings and conferences
creating mailing systems
managing contract and employment applications
tracking business expenses
handling purchase orders
analysing accounts
managing inventories
analysing production costs

COMMUNICATIONS TECHNOLOGY

As well as communicating with the outside world from a desktop computer, communications modems are also increasingly being used in portable computers in order to communicate from the field back to the office. People whose jobs take them on the road—journalists, sales people, engineers, architects, geologists and the like—can prepare data and reports on their portable computer at a remote site.

Another very useful computer product for the writer is a communications modem. This gives you access to the information held in major public databases. The most readily accessible and useful in Australia is Discovery which is conducted by Telecom. For very modest charges, you can tap into a great range of specialist news and information (such as the value of the Australian dollar, share prices, sporting results) and—especially valuable—the major figures from the Australian Bureau of Statistics.

There is also the Ausinet system which is accessible through personal computers or through most libraries that have computers. Ausinet can give you full text reproductions of major daily newspapers. It can also produce bibliographies and reading lists on a great range of subjects or combinations of subjects. For instance, if you are a student writing an essay on the Great Depression in Australia and you want to know more about health conditions, you can request Ausinet to produce all titles that have the indexed descriptions 'Great Depression', 'Australia' and 'Health' in common. Within minutes, the computer will print out the list for you. Some of the bigger libraries can also access via satellite some of the very large international databases which provide similar services to Ausinet but which provide information produced in a large number of countries and in many languages. These tend to be expensive but for a thesis or major project, the cost is usually worthwhile.

As well communicating with the outside world from a desktop computer, communications modems are also increasingly being used in portable computers in order to communicate from the field back to the office. People whose jobs take them on the road—journalists, sales people, engineers, architects, geologists and the like—can prepare data and reports on their portable computer at a remote site. Then, through the modem built into the machine, they can use telephone lines to transmit their data back to their head offices. The modem sends the data at high speed and with complete accuracy.

CD-ROM

One of the major innovations of the past five years has been the linking of the CD systems which play music to computers. This allows the storage of vast quantities of information on one CD. (CD-ROM stands for Compact

Disk—Read Only Memory, which means the information on the CD cannot be altered by the person using it, the way a floppy disk in a computer can be changed.)

Today, you can get on one CD any one of the following:

- the whole 26 volumes of Compton's *Encyclopedia*
- 21 volumes of Grolier's *Encyclopedia*
- full dictionaries of 12 foreign languages
- the complete *Oxford English Dictionary*
- the complete works of Shakespeare plus 2000 other classic texts
- every telephone book in Australia (all capital city directories and all regional directories in all states)

CD-ROM is an amazingly useful technology that has made a huge quantity of information available for the writer right at his or her desk.

One of the common criticisms of the Information Age is that human beings cannot cope with it all. There is now an 'information explosion' of such dimensions that no one can keep up with the knowledge in any subject any more, it is often said. If we were using traditional tools such as card files and manual typewriters and making our requests by mail this might be true. But the development of database software, public databases, CD-ROM and communication systems—all of which are available to anyone with a personal computer costing $1000 upwards—provides us with the means to be both more selective in gaining information most suited to our needs, and more extensive in discovering and accessing information from anywhere in the world. The Information Age is developing the technology for its own management. The big challenge is for users to recognise the potential and respond to it in creative ways.

KEYBOARD SKILLS

Business executives have traditionally thought that using a keyboard was beneath their dignity. More recently, women who wanted to pursue careers in management were advised not to learn to use the keyboard. Once their superiors found they could type, it was often argued, they would be relegated to traditional female office roles and miss the promotions they deserved.

However, we believe that technology has now reached the stage where everyone—men, women, managers, non-managers—should be able to use the keyboard. The Information Age is demanding that an increasing number of people develop writing skills. Proficiency on the keyboard should be regarded as an integral part of this development. Whatever form of technology you use to compose—handwriting, dictation, typing or word processing—your personal output will be enhanced if you can use a keyboard at some stage in the process. Of all the writing skills, the use of the keyboard is one of the easiest to acquire. The best way to learn is through a software package that teaches typing (such as the Australian-developed *Typequick* which is distributed worldwide by IBM) and to practise on an office or home computer.

All children at school today should be taught the keyboard and any adult thinking seriously about his or her career prospects should make the acquisition of keyboard skills a high priority.

All children at school today should be taught the keyboard and any adult thinking seriously about his or her career prospects should make the acquisition of keyboard skills a high priority.

Of course, no amount of high technology can disguise the fact that something is badly written. As we noted in Chapter One, technology cannot affect the quality of the messages we use to communicate with each other. For the potential of the Information Age to be borne out, we need a complementary change in the ability of most people to be able to write well. We are confident, however, that this change will come. After the advent of printing, the availability of cheap books created a widespread demand for literacy which eventually led to the mass education system. Similarly, the ready access that many people now have to relatively inexpensive computerised word processing, typesetting, desktop publishing and copying systems, means that there should be a parallel growth in demand for skills in writing and publishing. One of the aims of this book is to help foster this growth by assisting our readers to gain a professional level of ability in these areas.

KEY POINTS: Chapter 3 The electronic revolution

- The development of electronic technology for communications promises to be as revolutionary as the invention of the printing press and moveable type.
- Just as the availability of books created mass literacy, small computers, word processing and desktop publishing software have the potential to turn many people into writers and publishers.
- One thing retarding this development is a prejudice among executives against using the keyboard.
- However, technology has reached the stage where everyone should learn the keyboard as a matter of course—starting with school age children.
- The potential of the technology can only be realised if large numbers of people learn to write well.

QUESTIONS FOR DISCUSSION

1. Why does electronic technology have the potential to be as revolutionary as the invention of printing?
2. Technology has created an information explosion. Can we handle it?
3. Does everyone need to learn to use the keyboard?
4. What is more important than technology in communication practice? Why?

EXERCISES

1. If you have never used a word processor, visit a library or computer retail store and ask to be given a demonstration of a word processing system. Type in a headline and some sentences of your own. Format the headline in large, bold type. Obtain a printout of your work.

2. Go to a major library near you. Obtain from the librarian a full list of all the electronic services provided by the library.

3. At the same library, ask if you can have access to a computer Bulletin Board Service. Dial up a bulletin board and report on its contents.

REVISION LIST FOR PART I

FOUNDATIONS OF COMMUNICATION

- The information sector has emerged as the biggest single employer in Australia and most Western countries. It also generates the most wealth.
- Computers and communications technology are generating a revolution in economic values and social change.
- The implications for employment and education are that both need a greater focus on the development of communication skills.
- We do not, however, need to change the quality of our communications—rather to use our existing methods better and to spread them to a wider cross-section of the population.
- Writing and publishing, which were once the preserve of a minority, will become common to many.
- The old models of top-down communication are out of date. We need to develop new communication networks.
- The basis of good communication practice lies in deciding what you will say before you say it, that is, on determining your purpose and planning your message.
- It also involves treating your audience as equals and being able to put yourself in their shoes to determine what they need to know about what you want to tell them.
- The evolution of computer technology has now reached the stage where it can actually make you a better writer.
- Keyboard skills need to become as widespread as literacy. Everyone in the information sector, and many related areas, needs to learn to use the keyboard. The skill should be taught to children in schools.

PART I
KEY TEXTS AND FURTHER READING

Castle, Robert, Lewis, Don and Mangan, John (eds), *Work, Leisure and Technology*, Longman Cheshire, Melbourne, 1986.

Cunningham, Stuart and Turner, Graeme (eds), *The Media in Australia: Industries, Texts, Audiences*, Allen & Unwin, Sydney, 1993.

Drucker, Peter, *Post-Capitalist Society*, Butterworth-Heinemann, Oxford, 1993.

Fiske, John, *Introduction to Communication Studies*, Routledge, London, 1990.

Forester, Tom (ed), *Computers in the Human Context*, Blackwell, Oxford, 1989.

Francis, Dave, *Organisational Communication*, Gower, London, 1987.

Graves, Robert and Hodge, Alan, *The Reader Over Your Shoulder*, Random House, New York, 1979.

Jones, Barry, *Sleepers, Wake! Technology and the Future of Work*, Oxford University Press, Melbourne, 1990.

Kreps, G., *Organisational Communication*, Longman, New York, 1990.

More, E. and Laird, R., *Organisations in the Communications Age*, Pergamon Press, Sydney, 1985.

Popcorn, Faith, *The Popcorn Report*, Random House Australia, Sydney, 1992.

Windschuttle, Keith, *The Media*, Penguin Books, Ringwood, 1988.

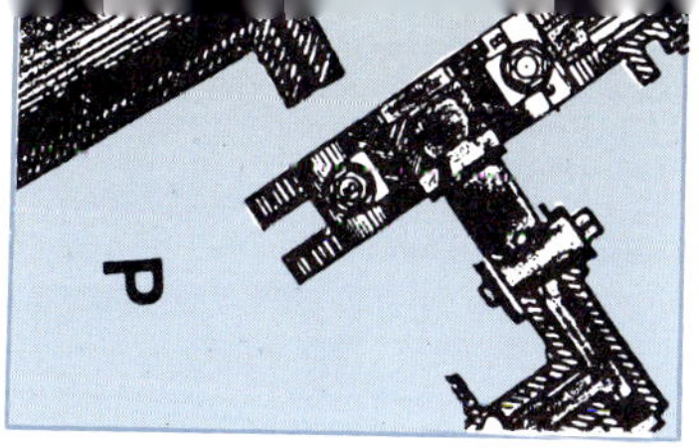

PART

II

WRITING FOR THE ORGANISATION

DEVELOPING BUSINESS WRITING SKILLS

How Peter Aspinall fosters writing competency among staff of the AMP Society.

The importance of training its staff in written communication is something that Australia's largest life insurance group, the AMP Society, has recognised for many years. Today, when computers are used to generate a great deal of business correspondence, the content and focus of business writing courses have had to be adapted to the new environment.

Peter Aspinall is manager of competency development at AMP. His staff, based in Sydney and Melbourne, co-ordinate a variety of training programs on a national basis.

'Most of the people who attend our written communication courses (part of our competency development program) are those who tend to construct their own letters, such as staff in our direct customer-service positions. They specifically respond to requests and complaints for which a formatted letter would not be appropriate. People in our investment division, who write to clients or organisations with which we regularly deal, also find the courses helpful,' he says.

He explains that the people in the investment areas of the company may be relatively junior in grade, but senior in terms of authority and accountability. Many are graduates. However, he says he is concerned by the low standard of written skills exhibited by many of these university-trained specialists.

'This deficiency has something to do with the nature of the content-based programs they go through at different educational institutions. There is little in the way of skills development, in a written or oral sense,' says Aspinall.

He stresses that the written communication classes presently run by the AMP are not corrective English classes, although up until about two years ago, remedial English classes were run for those interested. A surprising number of people from English-speaking backgrounds attended.

'Our course concentrates on the different forms of written material a person is likely to come across in the organisation and would be expected to produce. It deals with such subjects as report writing, simple business letters and memo and precis writing. We mainly address elements such as purpose, style and content. We emphasise the importance of brevity, simplicity and clarity,' he says.

Until about five years ago, the AMP published its own house style guide but the use of it has now lapsed. Aspinall explains that the majority of employees no longer compose their own writing and that the notion of a business organisation having its own written code is a dying practice.

'The appropriate business language comes through the computer-formatted letters, almost by osmosis. So I guess you could say we're indoctrinating our younger employees in a style we would prefer them to use,' he states.

Those people who go to the written communication classes, held over a four and a half day-block, are assumed to have an HSC level of ability in reasoning, comprehension and problem-solving. The program doesn't attempt to develop their ability to express themselves any further than that, but it does deal with relevant forms of writing in the employees' respective roles.

The classes are also significant because they are used as assessment tools. If it is discovered that somebody doesn't have an appropriate grasp of written English, then action can be taken to help. Depending upon the co-operation of their line-manager, an in-house trainer may help these employees during working hours, or else the AMP may organise outside assistance.

Aspinall adds that the company is now starting to introduce entry-level tests in literacy and numeracy, especially among those applicants seeking work in the customer-service division.

'The literacy test involves general comprehension and the matching and selection of written material. The numeracy test places emphasis on practical mathematical skills which, naturally, are valued in our kind of organisation,' he says.

The tests have been introduced to set and maintain a certain standard of ability or competency.

'We've identified the main flaws in written communication to be in the areas of sentence and paragraph construction, logic, sequence, context and the inability to clearly distinguish between concrete and abstract levels of ideas,' he states.

The AMP's competency development program also aims to present training sessions relevant to the three groups of managers in the company: senior officers (section heads and department heads), managers (junior executive positions) and chief managers/general managers (heads of particular divisions or business units). These sessions focus on staff management, conflict resolution and personal empowerment. However, they may also deal with instruction in report writing or written material associated with project work.

The AMP arranges for the New South Wales Education Department to conduct two other courses, English as a Second Language and English in the Workplace, which are run on a periodic basis in working hours. These are primarily attended by people in the organisation from non-English-speaking backgrounds who work with computer data in the information systems area.

'All of our training courses are "sold" to employees on the basis that we would expect most people to have some degree of ambition. If you have difficulties in a specific area, but want to progress, then there are some ways in which problems can be identified and rectified. But the employee is expected to work hard to improve,' says Aspinall.

Staff training has been a feature of the AMP Society since the 1930s, with written communication skills, time-management and numeracy skills being taught since the 1950s. Aspinall has been with the organisation since 1985 and it was his decision to place the training functions under the umbrella of 'competency development'. He felt that the concept of 'training' produced notions of everybody dutifully trooping off to classrooms in procession, and it may therefore have been an intimidating term.

Aspinall says there are two major philosophies behind the AMP's competency program which other organisations may find worth considering. First, he says that no organisation owes anybody a career and companies don't exist to provide every element of development and training for an individual. He adds, though, that if people have the self-interest, incentive and ambition, then an organisation should be active in helping them develop competencies. Second, there are certain skills and abilities which the AMP regards as being crucial, so it enables employees to acquire expertise by providing the facilities for them to do so.

'Until five years ago, the emphasis in the AMP was for acquisition of knowledge and very little attention was paid to how well a person could do something with that knowledge. The situation has now been reversed and we are looking at how skills can be used to increase productivity and produce better results in the workplace.'

CHAPTER

4

WRITING STYLE

After studying this chapter, you will be able to:

- write clearly and intelligibly for a wide range of readers
- recognise the use of jargon and avoid it at all cost
- understand the importance of using special terminology sparingly, if the same idea can't be expressed in lay terms
- express ideas in a concrete style, rather than using florid, abstract language
- increase your fluency by keeping your sentences short and dramatic

WRITING AND READERS

When you are reading good writing, you are almost unaware that it is there.

Good writing is simple, direct and clear. It conveys precisely what the writer intended and it is easily understood by readers. This remains true whether you are writing an academic essay, a business letter, a legal document, a scientific treatise or a letter to a friend. No special styles need to be adopted for different types of documents or different audiences.

Many people reading this now will probably have doubts about what we are saying. If you pick up an academic journal you will find most articles have a dense prose style and contain a large number of words and concepts that are impossible to understand. Most business letters use a set of traditional phrases and expressions that you need to know to understand the whole meaning. Yet we still want to insist that good writing is not like this. The best academic, business, scientific or any other kind of writing is that which calls least attention to itself, which is not designed to be impressive or formidable in any way. When you are reading good writing, you are almost unaware that it is there.

Books on how to write have made this point for a long time. It is almost fifty years since one of the best of these, Sir Ernest Gowers' *Plain Words*, castigated public servants everywhere for the awful officialese that they wrote to each other and to the public. Much of the archaic, unintelligible language produced by the bureaucracies of government and big business left both readers and writers equally confused. A great deal of it took six sentences to say something that could have been said in one. It was complicated and inefficient.

Why, then, is bad writing still so prevalent? One of the main reasons is the set of relationships that develop within occupational groups. People who work with a subject every day get tired of pronouncing their most frequently used words and phrases in full every time they use them. They quickly produce shorthand to describe the main tools and procedures of their trade. They often develop forms of slang and jargon all of their own. Anyone who has read an article about computers will know what we mean. Unless you have a reasonably good understanding of the field, these articles make no sense at all. Occupational shorthand is, to a certain extent, acceptable and even unavoidable when some new product or technique is being discussed. However, it is usually overdone and usually based on the false assumption that everyone is as familiar with the subject as the author. While writers have to assume readers have some degree of understanding of the subject matter, they should err on the side of caution and, if in doubt, explain what they mean when they use special terminology.

People use jargon not just for convenience but mainly to exclude others from understanding what they are talking about.

In other cases, occupational groups develop their own forms of language for very elitist reasons. They use jargon not just for convenience but to exclude others from understanding what they are talking about. The most notorious group here are lawyers. The laws that govern the relations between people ought to be understood clearly by all citizens in any society that calls itself democratic. However, the law has become shrouded in mystery because it is expressed in inaccessible language. Lawyers often say this is necessary to be precise. Their critics have long argued, however, that it has really occurred to make ordinary people dependent on lawyers to translate legal language into understandable English.

University academics, especially in the arts and humanities, are often in the same boat. In many academic disciplines, fairly ordinary ideas are dressed up in an inaccessible language that makes the people who can converse in these terms appear far wiser than they really are. One of the worst offenders is the field of communications itself. There are a number of competing theories of communications taught in universities and colleges. Some of these theories are expressed in forms of jargon and are unintelligible to anyone outside these departments.

> The overall intention of effective communication must, certainly, be to 'win the consent' of the audience to the preferred reading, and hence to get him to decode within the hegemonic framework. Even when decodings are not made, through a 'perfect transmission', within the hegemonic framework, the great range of decodings will tend to be 'negotiations' within the dominant codes—giving them a more situational inflexion—rather than systematically decoding them in a counter-hegemonic way. 'Negotiated' decodings, which allow wide exceptions to be made in terms of the way the audience situates itself within the hegemonic field, but which also legitimate the wider reach, the inclusive reference, the greater overall coherence ...

Obfuscation like this (written by Stuart Hall, a Professor of Sociology at Britain's Open University) is unintelligible to most people who earn their living as professional communicators, such as journalists, television producers and radio broadcasters, let alone the people who compose the audiences who are being discussed here. The aim of using jargon is the same wherever it occurs—to assert a false authority and superiority for the insiders who speak the language and to thus create a market for their services which would not otherwise exist.

Writers should treat their audiences with the same respect and attention that they would want themselves.

Good communication practice should reject such tactics. Writing, above all, should be open and accessible. It should be widely understood among its intended audience. In an age when more people than ever before are writing as part of their job, the writer cannot assume any superiority over his or her audience. Writers should treat their readers as equals; as people who will probably be writing for them in turn at another time. In the Information Age, when good communications are necessary for most jobs, the people who will be most successful are those who don't waste the time of their audiences with digressions or attempts to be impressive. The best writers will be those who present their readers with information in a clear and economical form. In other words, they treat their audiences with the same respect and attention that they would want themselves.

NOUNS AND ADJECTIVES

Nouns are words that stand for the objects or things in a sentence. The more concrete and vivid your nouns, the stronger your writing. Try to choose nouns carefully so they will stand alone and not need any support from adjectives. The fewer adjectives used to describe nouns the better. Many people think that to create an accurate picture of an object in the reader's mind you need to pile on adjectives until you have created the effect you want. The opposite, however, is true. The more adjectives you use to qualify a noun, the more you divide the reader's attention and the more you diminish the impact a well-chosen noun can make. Compare:

They towed away the crumpled, twisted, misshapen car.
They towed the wreck away.

One well-chosen word is more powerful than a convoluted description.

Good writers dole out their adjectives sparsely so that when they do use one, it breaks the rhythm established and so stands out sharply. Compare the impression made by a tree on a plain to one in the middle of a forest.

When you feel adjectives are really necessary to create an emotion or to portray a scene it is often better to keep them separate from the noun concerned and to attach them to the verb.

The strong, deep river flowed.
The river flowed strong and deep.

VERBS AND ADVERBS

Verbs convey motion and the more concrete and active they are, the better. Verbs should be doing or making things rather than passively indicating relationships. Compare:

The bridge is between the north and south sides of the city.
The bridge connects the city, north to south.

Adverbs divert attention from verbs in the way adjectives do to nouns. The well-chosen verb is almost always to be preferred to the verb heavily qualified by adverbs. Compare:

He ran neatly, quickly and evenly up the hill.
He trotted up the hill.

Active voice creates a momentum that carries the reader along with it.

ACTIVE AND PASSIVE VOICE

Verbs can be used actively or passively. This is usually described as using active voice or passive voice. In most cases it is better to choose active voice. This will make your writing more direct in individual sentences. Passive voice usually slows writing down and clogs it up. Over longer passages, the continued use of active verbs creates a momentum that carries the reader along with it. Compare:

Her father took the car and drove to the hills. *(Active)*
The car was taken by her father and was driven to the hills. *(Passive)*

The verb *to be*—'am', 'is', 'are', 'was', 'were'—turns an active verb into a passive one. Where possible, avoid using this verb. It conveys no motion or action. It only acts to connect or relate two ideas to each other and in many cases its use signals a writer's laziness more than anything else. One of the reasons academic writing is often boring and difficult to follow is its continued use of passive voice. For example: 'The equipment was examined and was found to contain no evidence of anything which would have caused it to collapse.' This writer should have said: 'When I examined the equipment, I found nothing to cause it to collapse.'

Don't take this advice too literally. There are times where the verb *to be* is perfectly appropriate and where the passive form of a verb communicates your meaning better than the active form. In general, when correcting your writing, go through and change all passive forms of verbs into active forms, except where the passive is essential to your meaning.

SIMILES AND METAPHORS

A simile is a phrase that compares one thing to another: 'The plane was like a silver bird.' It usually uses 'like' or 'as'. A metaphor is also a comparison but it says that something actually is another thing: 'The Samurai were tigers on the battlefield.' Both are sometimes called 'figures of speech'. Like adjectives and adverbs, they can be easily overused. Because Shakespeare used figures of speech frequently, many people still think writing is more impressive when it contains more, rather than less, of them. In Shakespeare's time, however, language of this kind was common to everyday speech and thus natural to the period.

Figures of speech lose their effectiveness if used over and over again.

Today, similes and metaphors are easily overdone and hard to use in an impressive way. If used without restraint, they can turn a passage into a joke. It is best to avoid using them except for special occasions. Used frequently, they appear pretentious; used rarely, they can be just right for those occasions when a striking phrase is really warranted.

CONCRETE AND ABSTRACT WORDS

Writing that is vivid and alive most often employs concrete words rather than abstract ones. Concrete words are those which stand for real things or actions in the world and which may be seen, felt or otherwise picked up by the senses. All concrete words are, in a sense, abstract in that they represent the real world instead of actually being real themselves. Nonetheless, there are some words that are more abstract than others. Words that are more abstract are those which refer more to ideas and concepts and less directly to reality.

Never cloud your meaning with vague and rambling observations.

When you use concrete nouns and verbs, your writing assumes more of the quality of a motion picture within the mind of the reader. The names of concrete objects, people, colours and movements stimulate the reader's imagination and memory and help re-create the reader's own experiences of life. Writing is most effective and most pleasurable to read when it is maintained at the concrete level. Following this rule does not mean you have to abandon abstract ideas or give up intellectual concepts and debates—humanity's greatest intellectuals have all preferred the concrete side of the equation. Rather, by grounding your writing as closely as you can to the real world of experience, you avoid the tendency to drift into the obscurity, confusion and waffle that characterises a great deal of abstract writing.

RHYTHM

All good writers have rhythm. Their prose has a flow or movement that feels right. Rhythm in writing need not be even nor smooth nor predictable like the rhythm in a popular song. It can be more like the rhythm in a symphony which varies considerably but nonetheless has a unity which it conveys to the whole piece. When rhythm is present in prose it carries the reader along with a momentum that makes reading pleasurable. All stories that are hard to put down have this momentum, and all good literary writers are masters of rhythm. Writers of non-fiction works as mundane as reports and submissions might imagine that such literary heights are beyond them. However, if these types of writing are to do the best job of persuading their readers to take the actions they recommend then the writers should use all the techniques at their disposal. They should also remember that when a piece of writing lacks rhythm, it breaks the flow of the reader's thought, it makes reading hard work and thus lessens its chances of being convincing.

How do you get rhythm? First, you follow the advice already given in this chapter. Keep adjectives and adverbs to a minimum. In particular, use the active rather than the passive voice wherever possible. Prefer short, concrete words to long abstract ones. Further, keep sentences short. Long sentences are harder to write and harder to read. Most newspaper journalism has rhythm and it is usually fast paced because its sentences are short. Some newspapers advise journalists to keep within a limit of twenty-five words per sentence. You should regard this as a useful rule of thumb. It is not a hard and fast principle that can never be transgressed but try to keep to it more often than not.

In terms of maintaining rhythm, the most important word or phrase in a sentence is the last. Because a full stop makes people pause, the weight of a sentence naturally falls onto the end. The last word or phrase should therefore be significant and, if possible, memorable. Compare:

He decided he had gone there for the last time.
He decided that was the last time he would go there.

In the first sentence the weight falls on 'last time' and the weight of the sentence falls more on his decision in relation to its timing than it does with the place. In the second, the place takes the significance of the decision. The last word or phrase is not important in every sentence, however. The best way to determine those sentences where this does matter is by reading your words aloud.

Most of us are better speakers than we are writers because we have more practice. As a result, we have a better sense of rhythm in our speech. This prompts two sorts of advice. First, try to write as you speak. Don't think that you have to change your tone of voice when putting words on paper. Keep your writing flowing in the same way as your speech. Second, when you re-check what you have written, read the words aloud and listen to how they sound. You will soon detect any discordant expressions. While you are developing your writing skills, reading your work aloud to yourself is always a very useful critical exercise. Do it when you can.

KEY POINTS: Chapter 3 The electronic revolution

- Good writing is simple, direct and clear.
- Jargon is used as a short-cut or to preserve the privilege of an elite. Good communication practice should reject unintelligible writing and deliberate obfuscation.
- Instead of qualifying with adjectives and adverbs, choose the right noun or verb in the first place.
- Used frequently, similes and metaphors can appear pretentious. Used rarely, they can have just the right effect.
- Writing should tend towards the concrete, not the abstract.
- To maintain rhythm through your prose, try to write as you speak, and read aloud what you have written.

QUESTIONS FOR DISCUSSION

1. Is it always better to write business documents in simple, direct language? Are there any times when it would be better to use official-sounding and important-looking terms and phrases?
2. Take one of the defining documents of your own institution, such as its prospectus, calendar, handbook, or policies and procedures document. Examine the statements which describe the aims and objectives, the mission statement or something of similar importance. Are they well expressed? Could you write them better?
3. Which groups of people in society often use their own jargon? Why? Are there any occasions when the use of technical terms would be justified?
4. Find a passage in a book, magazine or newspaper which you think contains rhythm. How has it been achieved?

EXERCISES

Rewrite the following sentences keeping adjectives and adverbs to a minimum, using active rather than passive voice and employing concrete rather than abstract words.

1. A negative reply has been received from them.
2. Prospective first homebuyers, whether firmly committed or tentative inquirers, are advised that generous, readily available subsidies are obtainable as from today from the state government of Victoria, to the extent of a maximum of $8000.
3. Our organisation wishes to advise you that unsolicited inquiries of this kind from potential suppliers are not normally or frequently given high priority.
4. Persistent, chronic and inexcusable unpunctuality will be firmly and swiftly rewarded by non-negotiable dismissal.
5. A more brilliant manifestation of this kind of painting is rarely seen.
6. It is well for the group worker to keep in mind first the leisure-time experience in the total life situation of young people.
7. At the other extreme are representative bodies made up of constituent groups who react almost wholly as persons in their own right and who act very little as a functioning channel between their own group and the central body.
8. Consumers vary in the proportion of their expenditure spent on the kinds of food which are heavily advertised.
9. The model which we reject, and which represents communication as a process capable of being studied out of context, often gives rise to exaggerated claims about the importance of 'better communication' as a solution to 'social or personal problems', thereby shielding from scrutiny the social structures underlying those 'problems'.

CHAPTER

5

BUSINESS LETTERS—BASICS

After studying this chapter, you will be able to:

- establish your purpose in writing a particular business letter
- write a plan so that the component parts become paragraphs of the letter
- be familiar with the structure and proper setting-out of correspondence
- effectively use the conventions of business letters
- know the general principles of business-writing style
- write a succinct, well-expressed letter which will achieve its aim

Writing letters involves the same basic procedures as any other form of writing. You need to:

1. determine your purpose in writing
2. write down a plan for the letter
3. write the letter
4. check it to make sure it fulfils your purpose

PURPOSES

The importance of stating your purpose or objective—of asking 'What am I trying to do?'—was discussed in Chapter Two. It is worth remembering that one piece of writing will very often have more than one purpose. Most commonly you will have some business to do with the other person but you will also want to communicate something more personal at the same time. You may have to write to someone asking for information about a subject, but you may also want to establish a good relationship with him or her so that they will send you similar material in the future without you asking. You may write to someone asking him to pay an overdue bill but you also want to pressure him so that he won't be overdue again. Or you might want to write to tell an organisation that the material they sent you did arrive and that you are grateful for the speed and efficiency with which they responded. Often your main purpose will be self-evident but you will have to think hard to decide all the other purposes you want to achieve with the letter.

PLANNING

Business letters should avoid side issues. Come straight to the point and stick to it.

Letters should be concise and not waste the time of the reader. So they have to be punchy and direct. The plan should reflect this. Avoid background material and side issues. Come straight to the point and stick to it. If your purposes are to tell someone three things: first, that you have sent the goods that were ordered; second, that they will arrive on a certain date, and third, that you were glad to get the order and would like more; then you need three paragraphs saying just that. Your plan will look like this:

1. The goods were sent September 23.
2. They will arrive September 29.
3. Thanks for the order. Please give us some more.

Each point of the plan should become a paragraph in the letter. In a simple and direct letter like that shown here, this means that each of the first two sentences is a whole paragraph itself, while the last paragraph contains two sentences. In longer and more detailed letters, the same principle should apply. Each of the major points in the plan should comprise a paragraph when the letter is written. Sometimes a paragraph will be only one sentence long. At other times, a paragraph will contain several sentences, depending on what you need to say.

Johnson's Hardware
353 St George's Road
Henley
NSW 2065
Telephone: 443 6678

23 September 1994

George Baker Constructions
21 Cross Street
Henley
NSW 2065

Dear Mr Baker

Timber roof dressing

Today I faxed your order for 3.3 squares of A-Top prefabricated timber roof dressing system to the manufacturer, Murchison Supplies, Newcastle.

They told me they had the stock and they would deliver it to your site on the morning of 29 September.

Thank you for the order. If there are any other hardware supplies you need, please let us know.

Yours sincerely

Keith Johnson

A well-planned business letter

LAYOUT FOR LETTERS

There is a standard format to which almost every type of business letter should conform. This is:

1. Letterhead or sender's address
2. Date
3. Receiver's address
4. Salutation
5. Descriptive heading
6. Body of the letter
7. Signing off
8. Signature and name of writer

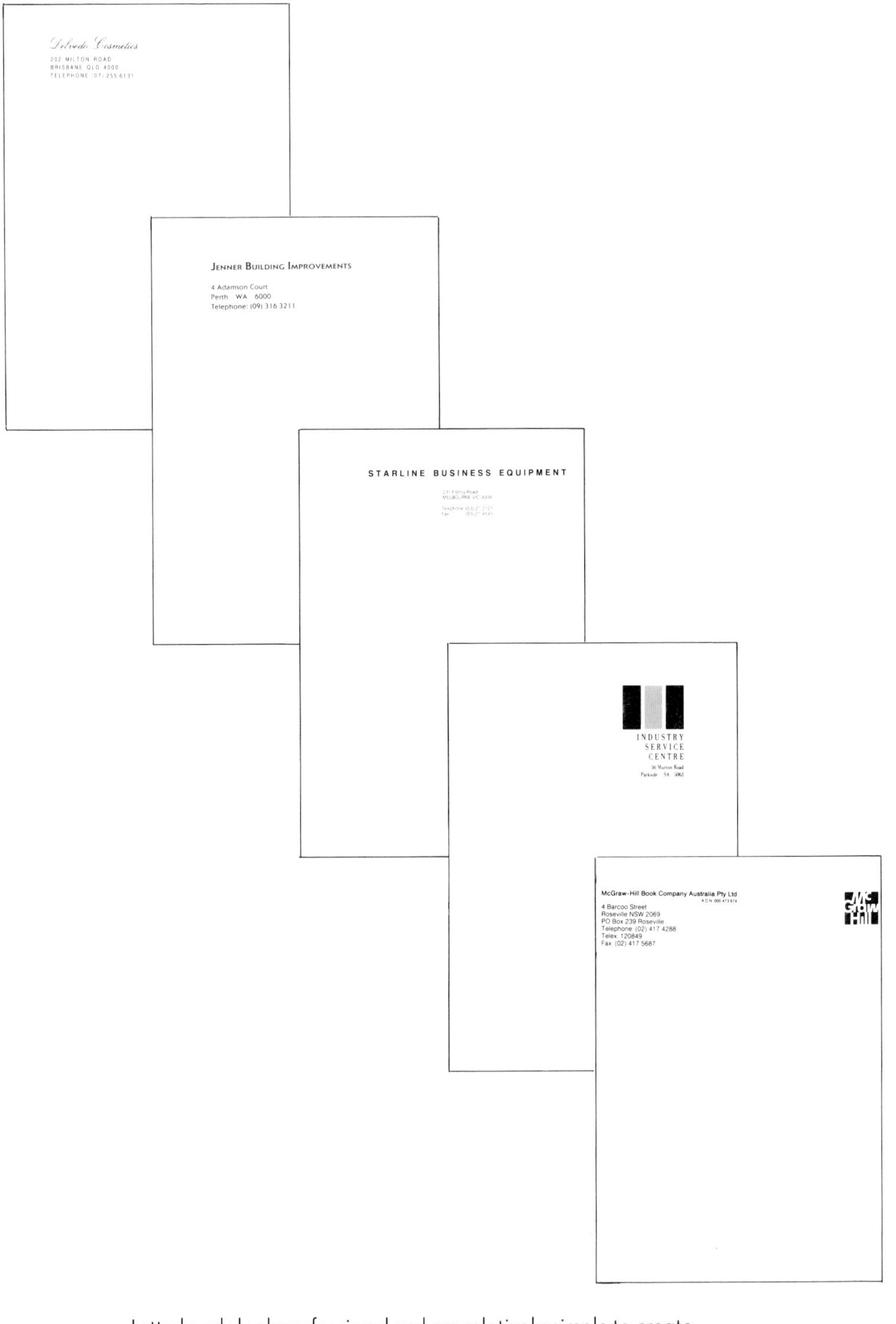

Letterheads look professional and are relatively simple to create

LETTERHEAD

Most organisations have letterheads printed which give at least the name, postal address and telephone number. Any organisation that plans to operate for some time is well advised to have some printed. These days, small 'instant print' shops can do a professional job for little money. Have them printed on A4 sheets of paper. It is far easier for you and everyone who has to handle, copy and file your letters if they are on A4. Don't extend your letterhead design to the very edges of the page. Leave about 2.5 centimetres on both sides for a margin. If your letter is longer than one page, only use a letterhead on the first page, then type onto blank sheets from page two onwards.

If you don't have a letterhead, your address should be typed in the top right-hand corner of the sheet of paper, leaving a margin of at least 2.5 centimetres top and side. The right hand of a sheet of paper, by the way, is always the side that is on your right when you face the sheet, not its right when facing you.

In some large organisations it is useful to include in the letterhead a place for the initials of the author to be typed. This is sometimes needed when the letter, for formal or legal reasons, has to bear the name of the head of the organisation but is actually written by someone else. If there is any further communication about the letter, it is often useful to know who the real author was.

DATE

Place today's date up against the right-hand margin of the page close below the letterhead or sender's address. Never send a letter without a date. If it ever needs to be referred to in the future, the date will tell you very important information about its place in whatever sequence of events surround it. When including the date, use either 'September 29 1995' or '29 September 1995', whichever you prefer. Don't use any punctuation marks when typing the date and don't use the number system, that is, don't type 29/9/95. This system is confusing because some people from other countries (including the United States) use the alternative version 9/29/95. Any potential confusion or dispute will be eliminated if you spell out the name of the month.

RECEIVER'S ADDRESS

Type the receiver's name and address against the left-hand margin of the page, one or two lines below that of the date. Use the same address as you use on the envelope. Some organisations use window face envelopes which means that, if the receiver's name and address is always typed in the same position on the page, there is no need to retype the address on an envelope.

If you know the name and office held by the receiver, then type both together with the name of the organisation. Note that there is no need for any punctuation in an address. For example:

Mr Harold Johnson
Deputy Registrar
University of New South Wales
PO Box 1
Kensington NSW 2033

When you know their names, give people their normal titles, such as Dr, Rev., Professor or Mr. Use Mrs, Miss or Ms depending on the preference of the woman concerned. Using the correct title when dealing with people who are in religious or military organisations is always difficult, so check this out with the organisation rather than make a mistake. A minister in the Commonwealth government or state government is addressed as 'The Honourable ...'. The prime minister and state premiers are addressed as 'The Right Honourable ...'. Other state and commonwealth politicians are simply 'Mr'. Members of local government are titled either 'Alderman', if it is a municipal council, or 'Councillor', if it is a shire council. The mayor of a municipal council is addressed as 'The Mayor' but in a city council is called 'The Lord Mayor'. Again, if you are unsure about any of these, telephone the organisation itself and find the correct form of title.

There is one form of Americanism which is best avoided. This is the use of the word 'Attention:' or 'For attention of:' before the name concerned. This does nothing to help the letter find the receiver and is not normally used in this country.

If you do not know the name of a particular person in an organisation then you will have to use the title only in the address. In general, if the organisation is a company or business of some kind address your letter to 'The Manager'. Don't use phrases like 'Managing Director', 'General Manager', or 'Chief Executive' unless you know that there really is someone in the organisation with that exact title. If the organisation has some form of democratic structure (such as that of a professional association, a club, a society or a trade union), it is normal to address letters to 'The Secretary'. In some public organisations the person designated to accept general letters often has an unusual title. In a university, for instance, this person is 'The Registrar'. In some other organisations it is 'The Director'. The public service these days has as many titles as the military. If in doubt, check it out. The normal form of address in these cases looks like this:

The Secretary
Carlton Football Club
Lygon Parade
Carlton Vic 3053

SALUTATION

We still use phrases like 'Dear Mr Plowman' when we start a letter, even though we might never have met the person and don't hold him 'dearly' at all. The salutation is an archaic form that has persisted to the late twentieth century for reasons that are unclear. There is no reason to get indignant about this, however, like the writers of some books on business communications. There are plenty of other examples of ancient expressions which we still use today without being bothered very much. The phrase 'Dear ...' probably communicates some very mild sense of courtesy. To leave it out would appear discourteous and, as it probably does little harm, it is best retained.

If you are on good terms with the receiver, then the salutation can be his or her first name: 'Dear Margaret'. If you know the name but don't know the receiver personally then use the more formal 'Dear Mr Robbins'.

The issue becomes more difficult when you don't know the name of the receiver. This once posed little problem. A letter addressed to 'The Manager' could always carry the salutation 'Dear Sir'. However, these days there are plenty of women executives within organisations and some tend to be (quite rightly) offended when they are addressed as 'Dear Sir'. You are really telling them you have made no effort to know the person to whom your letter is addressed and that you would not even consider a woman could hold the position. The alternative sometimes recommended is 'Dear Sir or Madam' but this is just as bad because you are once more saying that you haven't got a clue about the person in the job. The best way out is to use the title itself in the salutation. For instance, the secretary of the Carlton Football Club would be addressed as: 'Dear Secretary'. In most cases this will appear perfectly acceptable but even those people who think it looks a little odd would have to agree it is preferable to addressing a football club secretary as 'Dear Sir or Madam'.

DESCRIPTIVE HEADING

It is always useful to give a business letter a heading. This should appear one or two lines down from the salutation and should be underlined and centred on the page. It is always helpful for a receiver to find a heading on a letter. It alerts him or her immediately to the issue concerned and is invaluable when sorting through piles of correspondence. Without a heading, a letter often has to be read partly through for the subject matter to be identified. In a large organisation, headings also help the mail department direct letters more quickly to the right person for action, so you are more likely to get a quicker reply. Further, a heading is a good way for the writer to start a letter because it helps ensure you keep to the point and on the track. A good heading has three or four words. Anything shorter is usually not descriptive enough; anything longer could probably have been shortened. Don't use unnecessary words. For instance, in a job application letter, 'Position Advertised for Construction Division Supervisor' should be cut down to simply 'Construction Division Supervisor'.

A letter's layout should be symmetrical, that is, it should have an even amount of white space at top and bottom and both sides.

BODY OF THE LETTER

The body of the letter is the actual message being sent. It should be typed single spaced with double space between paragraphs. The text should be typed between the margins which, as we said above, should be even and at least 2.5 centimetres on each side. If you are writing a very short letter, it should be typed more towards the middle of the page so that there is no great gap of white space at the bottom, and the margins could be enlarged. The letter's layout should be symmetrical, that is, it should have an even amount of white space at top and bottom and both sides.

As we said earlier, it is quite acceptable to have paragraphs that contain only one sentence. It is just as acceptable to have several sentences in one paragraph. The only rule to follow in paragraphing a letter is that each paragraph should be devoted to one main point. Sometimes this means a paragraph will make one brief statement. At other times it will mean there is a detailed argument made within the one paragraph. When typing paragraphs, there is no need to indent the first word. After the double space, simply start typing up against the left margin.

If the letter continues onto a second page it is best to start that page with the name of the receiver followed by the page number: 'Mr Robert Plowman Page 2'. This should appear at the top, up against the left-hand margin. This practice will help prevent your pages being misplaced at the receiver's office when letters are being copied or filed.

SIGNING OFF

The closing phrase that customarily concludes a letter is another archaic form that some people argue has no place in modern communications practice. Some say we never mean it when we say we are being 'faithful' or 'sincere' and such terminology belongs to an era when the 'master and servant' relationship prevailed. This is probably true but people don't read these words literally. All we are signalling is a small degree of courtesy and some degree of familiarity with the receiver. As such, the signing off phrase probably serves a mildly useful purpose and might as well be preserved.

In general, the phrase 'Yours sincerely' is retained for people we know personally while 'Yours faithfully' is used with those who are strangers to us. Americanisms such as 'Yours truly' or 'Cordially' are best avoided because they look pretentious when used by non-Americans. Some associations and societies have developed signing off phrases of their own for use within their membership, such as 'Fraternally' which is used by trade union officers when writing to members or people in other unions. There is no harm in this and those who feel it serves some meaningful purpose have no reason to drop the practice.

SIGNATURE AND NAME OF WRITER

About four lines below the signing off phrase, the name of the author of the letter should be typed. If you have a title within the organisation on the letterhead then include this as well. The space between the signing off phrase and your typed name should contain your signature. So, the final result should look like this:

Yours sincerely

Jane Mackarell
Marketing Manager

It was once the practice to put the name of the organisation after the signing off phrase. This was thought to make the letter somehow legally binding on the organisation rather than the individual author. But if you have the organisation's name on the letterhead then it is responsible for any arrangements made by the letter writer, provided it was within his responsibility to do so and there was nothing illegal or unethical about the transaction. The addition or removal of the company name at the end of the letter does not make any change to genuine responsibility. It is simply duplication of the name for no good reason.

Always type the name of the person in whose name the letter is written because very few signatures these days are legible. It is also useful to include the author's title so that the receiver will know with whom he or she is dealing and what area and degree of responsibility the author has. If you are writing to someone you know well, however, you might appear to be puffing yourself up to use your title all the time, so some discretion would be in order.

If it is at all possible, sign all your letters yourself. Do not use rubber stamps or similar devices. Avoid asking secretaries or underlings to sign letters for you. Some people think they create the mystique of the super-busy executive when they get their secretary to write 'Signed in his absence by JS'. Nothing could be further from the truth. You look like someone who cares so little about the receiver that you couldn't be bothered reading over your letter; or else you look like someone heading for a big fall, which history shows is a common fate of those who grow too casual about the use of their signature. Even if someone else, such as a secretary, has written a letter for you, if it has your name on it you are being foolish if you don't check it and sign it yourself.

Sign all your letters yourself. History shows that those who grow too casual about the use of their signatures are heading for a fall

In a small number of cases, a letter can usefully contain some additional information after the signature, name and title. Where there are additional documents to be sent with the letter, it is useful to type 'Enclosures:' and then list what is supposed to be enclosed. This is a helpful check if another person has to enclose these documents. It is also useful, where the letter is being sent to more than one person, to include the words 'Copy to:' and then list the names of those who are also receiving the same text. This make the status of the letter clear to everyone concerned. Apart from these two additions, it is best not to clog up the bottom of the letter with a lot of filing and reference data. If these are necessary, they look neater as part of the letterhead and should be kept there.

THE LANGUAGE OF BUSINESS LETTERS

Business letters do not require any special kind of language or jargon. They are like any other form of non-fiction writing designed to be read with a minimum of fuss and effort. The general principles discussed earlier about using simple, concrete and active prose apply in business letters as much as anywhere else. However, because there is usually money and some form of contractual arrangement being discussed in many business letters, the question of accuracy becomes more important. The following general principles should be observed when writing business letters.

Business letters always need six qualities:

- clarity
- completeness
- conciseness
- concreteness
- conviction
- courtesy

CLARITY

A business letter should say exactly what the writer intends. There should be no confusion or ambiguity in expression. Misinterpretation is something neither sender nor receiver can afford.

COMPLETENESS

A business letter should not just say what the author wants, it should say all he wants. There are few things more irritating to a receiver than an incomplete communication which involves chasing up additional information. The usual results are delay and error. A letter should also tell the receiver all he or she needs to know. You can assume a reasonable degree of knowledge about the subject matter when you are both in the same business but it is always best to err on the side of caution. If you are not certain that the receiver will know exactly what you mean by some term, name or expression, then spell it out. Give background information whenever you feel it might be necessary for complete understanding of your message.

CONCISENESS

Few people at their work have the luxury to read slowly and ponderously. You should respect their need not to waste time and write accordingly. Get to the point at the start of the letter and stick to it. Use short sentences to keep your prose punchy. Discard all hackneyed and meaningless clichés, such as: 'Your letter of 5th to hand', 'We acknowledge receipt of', 'Contents duly noted', 'In reply, we wish to state', 'Please find enclosed', 'We beg to', 'In this regard', 'With reference to', 'We wish to advise … inform … state … thank you', 'You are hereby advised', 'For your information', 'Until such time as', 'Trusting this meets with your satisfaction', 'Thanking you in anticipation'.

CONCRETENESS

Because accuracy is at a premium in business letters, they should contain a minimum of abstract phrases and vague generalisations. Don't say 'the great majority of …' or 'an overwhelming number of …'; rather, say '77 per cent of …' or 'a total of 5786 of …'. Give precise dates, times and names. Use concrete examples when you need to illustrate a point. Keep it all as real as possible.

CONVICTION

To persuade someone else to do something you have to be convincing. This means adopting the criteria or expression already suggested here. Most people are convinced by clear, concrete and simple statements. If a subject cannot be reduced to this type of language there is probably something questionable about it anyway and your receivers are probably right to remain uncommitted.

COURTESY

Even when you have to take a strong stand with someone you are better to be courteous than not. Being courteous does not mean being subservient or servile. The person who remains courteous gives himself the best chance of remaining in control of a situation as well as maintaining good-will and civilised behaviour. If a letter is designed to be courteous it will have a generally positive tone. If you have to refuse a request, do it, but at the same time try to suggest an alternative solution. In most conflicts there are two sides to the issue. Even where you have to disagree with someone, try to see things from their point of view and acknowledge the validity of this view before going on to state your own case. This is not being manipulative or deceitful. It is simply recognising the legitimacy of both sides and then insisting on your own. Avoid especially the suggestion that another person is stupid, is whingeing, is badly mistaken or has failed in some way.

It is also undesirable to openly exploit your organisation's strength in some matter. Retain a sense of humility and remember that the relationship of strong to weak might be reversed at some time in the future. In other words, always write to others in the tone of voice in which you would prefer them to address you.

Before we go on to discuss specific kinds of business letters, work your way through the following exercises.

KEY POINTS: Chapter 5 Business letters—basics

- Before beginning a letter, determine your purpose in writing and plan what to write.
- Make sure you conform to the standard format of business letters: letterhead or sender's address, date, receiver's address, salutation, descriptive heading, body of the letter, signing off, signature and name of writer.
- Be clear and concise. Include all necessary information. Use concrete examples to illustrate a point. Show courtesy.

QUESTIONS FOR DISCUSSION

1. Explain how a business letter might be written to serve more than one purpose.
2. What qualities of language are advisable to use when writing for business?
3. List the main differences in structure and style between writing a letter to a friend and writing a letter requesting an order of stationery.
4. List the main parts of a business letter.
5. Why is it important to check names, titles and addresses when sending a business letter?

EXERCISES

Rewrite the following letters in more appropriate and effective language.

1. With reference to yours of the 22nd, we are now in a position to advise that the materials you requested are available. Enclosed please find our order form. Upon completion of same, your materials will be duly forwarded. Hoping this meets with your satisfaction.

2. Your complaint of 22nd January that the wrong colour was supplied on your metal inserts has been investigated by both our quality control and our despatch department. They say there was no way you could have been sent a batch of this kind. However, because you have been a good customer in the past we are prepared to compromise. Send back the batch you received and we will replace them with the silver colour you claim you originally ordered.

3. You are hereby advised that as from next month, this office will be transferring to a new location in Market Street. We wish to inform you that any business remaining to be transacted will be required to be handled through this office. For your information, the move is designed to give better service to worthy and valued customers like yourselves. Assuring you of our best attention at all times.

4. It has come to my attention that your letter of March 1st claimed this society owed you the amount of $45.50. I wish to advise that, at the present time, our records show the amount owing as $35.50. I would be pleased if you would check your records to ascertain the amount. In the event of a dispute arising, we would need to inspect your original records. I trust that we will be able to settle this matter in a satisfactory manner.

5. It has been recognised that a significant proportion of your staff have been encroaching upon the recreation area reserved for our employees in recent weeks. We don't mind a few people wandering in but the situation has now got out of hand and our union delegates are getting upset. It has reached the stage where we feel some kind of action might be necessary. Before this happens, we would be pleased if you could do something to rectify the situation.

CHAPTER

6

TYPES OF BUSINESS LETTERS

After studying this chapter, you will be able to:

- determine which format and style of business letter best fulfils your purpose
- write directly and concisely, making your intentions clear
- write letters of inquiry and answer those who make inquiries of you
- write purchase order letters
- write sales letters
- write and answer complaints

The actual wording of a business letter is largely determined by its purpose. In this chapter, we look at the main objectives that business letters pursue and the appropriate style and content of each type.

LETTERS OF INQUIRY

When you need to make an inquiry, make it short but clear. There are usually two points needed. The first is the question itself which should be as detailed and as specific as possible. The second is the reason you are making the inquiry. The latter is often self-evident but in other cases it helps the receiver sort out what you are really after, especially if the initial question is necessarily vague.

Your tone should be polite but not servile—don't express too much gratitude. Never use that hackneyed phrase, 'Thanking you in anticipation, I remain ...'. If you want to thank someone in advance, simply say 'Thank you.' If you want someone to do something for you, ask them if they 'would' do it, not if they 'could' do it. They might be able but not willing. Here is the text of a typical letter of inquiry.

Marketing Imports
121 George St
Elsewhere NSW 2000

Carrie Foster
Sales Manager
Southeast Dockside Ltd
4 East St
Somewhere NSW 2000

18 September, 1994

Dear Carrie

Tea shipment from India

Would you please advise me when the next shipment of tea from India is expected to be unloaded at your wharf?

Our company normally imports its own supplies direct but our Indian agent has been unable to arrange a shipment to us.

If you are expecting supplies within ten days, we would be interested in having a price quoted for 20 cases.

Yours faithfully

Leslie Warton
Purchasing Officer

ANSWERING INQUIRIES

When answering an inquiry it is best to start by referring to the original inquiry. This reference should be quite specific, in case someone else from within your organisation has been dealing with the same people on a related matter.

You should next say either what action you have taken or will take on the matter. If you cannot answer an inquiry now, it is still best to write immediately anyway saying this and indicating when you will be able to answer. It is far better for the inquirer to be told his letter will be answered later than to be left waiting not knowing if you have ever received the inquiry.

Exotic Adventure Tours
121 George St
Elsewhere QLD 4000

Ken Black
42 Uren St
Somewhere QLD 4000

18 June 1994

Dear Mr Black

May 1995 tour of China

Thank you for your inquiry of September 12 asking about group tours to China in May 1995.

At present we plan to conduct three tours in that month, two going via Hong Kong and the other going direct to Beijing. I have enclosed brochures giving full details of the itineraries and prices.

Yours faithfully

Stephanie West
Tour Manager

Furniture Council of Australia
33 George St
Elsewhere Vic 3000

Mrs J. Jones
64 Westside Cres
Somewhere VIC 3000

18 July 1994

Dear Mrs Jones

Location of Furniture Expo

I am sorry but I cannot yet tell you whether the next Furniture Expo will be held in Sydney or Melbourne.

Our management committee will make a decision on the location on December 15 and I will write with the answer then.

Thank you for your interest.

Yours faithfully

Georgina Best
Project Officer

PURCHASE ORDER LETTERS

The details needed to order something you want to buy are quite specific. The seller must first have a complete description of the goods (quantity, size, style, brand name, model number, colour). If alternative versions, such as a different colour or model, are acceptable to you then include this in the order as well.

Second, the seller needs instructions for delivery, including how the goods are to be shipped (by mail, courier, rail, air and by what company), delivery address and the date by which the goods are required.

Third, the seller needs to know how you will pay for the goods. Will they be charged to your account or a credit card, paid COD, or is a cheque enclosed?

In many organisations, these details have been incorporated into a purchase order form so that a letter is not needed.

You don't need any archaic phrases to ensure the goods are packed properly and delivered in one piece. You don't need any instructions about them being 'in good order and condition'. No one would expect you to order them any other way. Simply say: 'Please send me X.'

Smiths Book Arcade
45 Bourke St
Elsewhere NSW 2000

Mr R. Graham
Book City
55 Olds Place
Somewhere SA 5000

18 January 1994

Dear Mr Graham

Purchase Order: Books

Please send by mail no later than Friday August 12 the following books:

2 copies of A.J.P. Taylor, *A Personal History* at $25 each	$ 50
12 copies of Howard Rolph, *Murray Valley Memories*, at $10 each	$120
1 copy of *Macquarie Dictionary*	$ 40
TOTAL VALUE	$210

I enclose a cheque for $204.50 to cover total value of the order minus your usual terms of 5 per cent discount for payment within seven days, plus $5 for mail cost.

Yours sincerely

Jenny Smith

SALES LETTERS

A sales letter has to double as both a conveyor of information and as an advertisement. If your organisation is engaged in a large-scale selling drive, especially to a consumer market, then it is best to engage an advertising agency or a direct mail organisation to help you draft your letter. Where smaller volumes are involved, however, a personal letter from someone directly involved in calling on customers can be a useful aid.

A sales letter has the advantage that, because it is a letter, the receiver will at least begin to read it. As everyone who has ever received a sales letter knows, however, there is a strong tendency to throw it away once you realise what it is. This makes it imperative that a sales letter gets to the point right at the outset. A number of books about salesmanship overlook this elementary point. They give a lot of advice about 'grabbing the reader's attention' with appeals to their vanity, their curiosity, their sense of excitement or drama or even their insecurity. 'Are you confident of gaining a place at university?' 'Do you know the world's twenty highest mountains are all in the Himalayas?' 'If you were a Hollywood movie star …'

A sales letter should never talk down to the reader. Come to the point in the first sentence.

You don't need extraneous material to persuade people to read a sales letter. Openings like those above are likely to put people off because they are patronising and talk down to the reader. Rather than grabbing readers' interest, they are more likely to signal 'this is an advertisement disguised as a letter' and will be thrown away before the real point of the letter is reached. If you want to tell people you have a new starter motor than uses only half the power of previous models, say that right at the outset. Those readers who have no interest in this development will throw your letter away but those in the business of buying and installing starter motors will be more likely to take notice and to read on.

Let us make the point again. A letter that is trying to sell something does not have to work hard to get people to start reading it. Everyone reads letters that are addressed directly to them and which do not look like advertisements. Most people dislike junk mail and will automatically throw away anything that looks like or is written in the form of an advertisement. A letter is a personal document written from one individual to another. You should respect that individual in a sales letter just as you should in any other type of letter. Don't waste their time, don't talk down to them or try to con them. Write the letter as you would any other business letter. People will read useful information presented in normal business language. A sales letter, like any other, should be clear, complete, concise, concrete and courteous.

The one feature of advertising that a sales letter should incorporate, though, is an appeal to action. Don't end a sales letter with any of the familiar archaic expressions of the 'trusting', 'hoping' or 'thanking' variety. You should tell people who are interested what to do next—fill in the enclosed order form; send a cheque now; telephone for a free brochure today. Where possible enclose a pre-paid self-addressed envelope. Make it as easy as possible for those interested to reply to you.

LETTERS OF COMPLAINT

Every organisation makes mistakes sometimes. In most cases, mistakes are inadvertent. In some cases, they are the result of chronic neglect. In other cases, the organisation concerned is being wilfully exploitative. Nonetheless, if you are the victim of a mistake or you receive bad quality goods or services you should reply in much the same way, whatever your suspicions about the motives of the other firm may be. Your interest is first to have the mistake fixed or the quality rectified. From this perspective, a letter of complaint should achieve three things.

First, it should give a specific description of the goods or services concerned, when they were bought, and any order, invoice or cheque number that might help identify them.

Second, it should say as precisely as possible what is wrong. Don't say goods are 'unsatisfactory' or 'broken' or 'poor quality'. List the faults in terms of concrete attributes of the goods or services concerned: the real speed of the movement compared to that advertised; the names of the part or pieces that are broken; a description of the colour or texture received compared to that expected.

Third, tell the organisation how you want it to respond. If you want a replacement or a refund or a credit or a service call, ask for it directly. Don't leave it open to the firm to suggest how to rectify things. In most cases, your suggestion will be met because the firm will want to minimise any conflict with you. Where it cannot or will not do what you want, it will usually offer the next best thing. The less specific your request is, the less satisfied you will be.

It is also worth remembering that there are few points for you in being angry, rude or abusive. A short, punchy letter saying exactly what is wrong and just what you want done in return carries more power than a righteous denunciation. If the mistake develops into a real conflict and you have to call in help from your legal advisers or some consumer tribunal, they may sympathise with your distress but they will be much more interested in the facts of the case. Don't let any sense of injustice override your adherence to these facts.

Pyrmont Rowing Club
121 Bay Rd
Pyrmont WA 6000

Gordon Simkin
Riverside Boating Supplies
28 High St
Somewhere WA 6000

18 February 1994

Dear Mr Simkin

Perished oar slip guides

On September 12 our club purchased four new Takeo brand oars, size 6B, from your Riverside store. We paid $67.50 for each one on our purchase order form No 867.

Six weeks later, the plastic slip guides on two have perished to the point where they are unusable. We are returning the four oars because we believe it only a matter of time before the remaining two slip guides perish as well.

continued on next page

continued from previous page

We would like you to replace all four slip guides with the rubber material used on previous Takeo oars. We need this done immediately as our team is currently training for next month's championship trials. Thank you.

Yours faithfully

Jeremy Fish

ANSWERING COMPLAINTS

The principles involved in making complaints are similar to those involved in rectifying mistakes. If someone complains and your organisation is at fault, the person does not want an argument about the issue; nor does he or she want an effusive apology. They primarily want you to acknowledge you are in the wrong and to have the mistake rectified quickly. Your letter saying this should be courteous but not excessively apologetic.

Reply to letters of complaint in a polite, civil manner. Future business and the reputation of the firm could rest on your diplomacy.

It should first say you are sorry. The best way to do this is to say 'we are sorry'. Don't 'beg your apology' or say you are 'truly very sorry'. People want you to accept the blame rather than grovel and they prefer a simple, open acceptance above anything else.

Second, try to give some idea of how the mistake occurred. Don't say you have no idea how such a terrible thing could have happened. Even if you don't know precisely what happened, it will give some comfort to the complainant if you can specify the place where it might have happened ('the goods were checked as they left the factory so the damage must have occurred in transit'). Say you will investigate the matter further. If they are confident you have set procedures in motion to ensure the same thing does not happen again, complainants will be more likely to want to do business with you again.

Third, say what you are prepared to do to rectify the mistake. Say you will offer a replacement and by which date or time; say you will send someone at a particular time to inspect the damage and attempt to repair it; or perhaps offer a refund.

Sometimes, however, it is the customer who has made the mistake. They gave you the wrong information, supplied the wrong number or colour or gave the wrong address and the delivery went astray. When replying to complaints based upon their mistakes, you should resist the temptation to be arrogant or dismissive. Tell the customer that you are sorry that he or she has made a mistake. Say this, moreover, at the outset of the letter when you tell them you have to refuse their request to have the mistake rectified. Then give as frank an answer as you can about how the misunderstanding occurred.

General Computer Supplies
125 Smith St
Elsewhere Tas 7001

Ms S. Robinson
Administration Manager
Office Tech Ltd
22 Fox St
Somewhere TAS 7000

18 August 1994

Dear Ms Robinson

Faulty magnetic disks

We are sorry to hear that the Databank magnetic disks supplied by our city warehouse had so many errors recorded on them.

We have tested others from the same batch and found there is an unacceptably high error rate. This particular batch came from a usually reliable supplier in Japan and we are making inquiries to discover the cause of the problem.

We enclose four packets of disks from another brand as replacement. Please return your problem disks to us and we will send them to the manufacturer for further investigation.

Yours sincerely

Dianne Lester

KEY POINTS: Chapter 6 Types of business letters

- Letters of inquiry should be short but clear.
- When replying to inquiries, be prompt. It is better to admit ignorance than not to answer.
- When ordering goods through mail, be specific. Make sure you include all instructions necessary for delivery and payment.
- Sales letters should come straight to the point. They should end with an appeal to action. Make it as easy as possible for those interested to reply to you.
- A letter of complaint should identify the goods or services at fault, say precisely what is wrong and ask for a specific response. It doesn't help to be angry, rude or abusive. The facts of the case are more important than your sense of injury.
- When answering complaints, apologise simply, not effusively. Try and explain what went wrong and say what you are prepared to do to rectify the mistake.

QUESTIONS FOR DISCUSSION

1. What general principles should apply to a letter aimed at getting somebody to buy something or to take part in a 'special offer'?
2. Explain the types of information which should be included in a letter of complaint when you want some action to be taken.
3. If your organisation is in the right, what tone should you adopt when responding to a complaint, and in making complaints? Why?

EXERCISES

1. Mr R. J. Hammond of Deep Valley purchased an expensive roll top desk from your company. It was inspected before shipment and found to be in good condition. Mr Hammond has written complaining that the top won't roll because the desk has been partly damaged. Write a letter in response.

2. Dr John Pope of Broadmeadows rang. He says he ordered some soil, fertiliser and potting mixture from your garden supplies store three weeks ago for delivery last week. He sent a cheque in payment and it has been presented at his bank. You investigate and find the address he gave on his handwritten order, 111 Hargrave Drive, was interpreted by your delivery men as 1/1 Hargrave Drive and that they left the supplies at that address. Write to Dr Pope about the matter.

3. You have just bought and renovated an old run-down motel in a good position in a growing regional centre. It had a bad reputation under the old management and had low occupancy rate. Write a circular letter to individual members of the Commercial Travellers Association telling them that the renovated premises are now open for business and that you are offering a 30 per cent discount for the first month of the new operation.

4. You have just acquired import rights to a new German-designed refrigerator that has a special compartment designed to keep beer and wine at a much colder temperature than the rest of the cooling compartment. It comes in three sizes (1 cubic metre, 1.5 cubic metres and 2 cubic metres) and three colours (white, cream and pale grey). Write a letter to leading retail outlets to persuade them to stock your product.

5. You are a retailer who has received the letter from the above importer. Order two of the small size refrigerators, both coloured white; six of the medium size, four of them white, one cream and one grey; and one in white in the large size.

6. You are the refrigerator importer once more. Acknowledge receipt of the above order, saying you have run out of 1.5 metre coloured refrigerators but that they will be available after December 1.

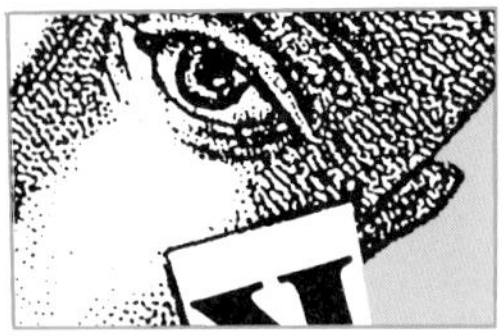

CHAPTER

7

MEMOS, FAXES AND FORMS

After studying this chapter, you will be able to:

- recognise the different types of messages sent within an organisation and their main purpose
- understand why special forms are expected to be used in certain situations
- write an instructive memo to elicit a quick, active response
- prepare a fax cover sheet
- design a variety of forms to be used by staff as efficient means of internal communication

Some of the most important written communications people have with each other are in the form of short informal messages, notes and memos. They are important because they are usually transmitted within an organisation and are part of the lifeblood of that body. The functioning and management of a wide range of operations would come to a sudden halt without these informal communications. So don't treat them with disdain or carelessness. They deserve the same thought, preparation and attention to detail as any more formal piece of writing.

MEMOS

The memo (or memorandum) should be brief and to the point. Its function within an organisation is almost always to get things done. Like a letter, it should be written from an understanding of the perspective of the reader. It should also be just as well planned and well laid out as a letter.

The format for a memo is simple. It needs headings to show to whom the memo is going; from whom it has come; the date it was sent; and the subject. It is not essential but it is helpful to have forms printed for memos. With printed forms, people become accustomed to putting the same things in the same places and finding them there too. This way, people won't forget to date a memo. Also, the subject heading encourages the writer to think through the purpose of the memo carefully. Memos that are sent without a subject line often mean the author could not formulate the subject in his or her mind. If this is the case, the chances of the memo being effective are not good.

When writing the memo, use the following test to make sure it is meaningful. Does the information stand by itself without the use of headings and subheadings? Read the content without referring to the subject line. If it is understandable without this heading then it has passed its main test. If it is not clear then something is probably missing from the first sentence. There is a great temptation when writing brief messages to take too much knowledge on the part of the reader for granted. You have to be even more rigorous about putting yourself in the reader's shoes when writing memos.

Memos should be short but informative. Above all, don't assume that the receiver of the memo has prior knowledge of a situation.

Even though a memo may be short, it still needs to be planned. Don't start writing without thinking. This is the best way to end up writing an obscure, ambiguous or convoluted message. Because a memo has to go straight to the point and be acted upon, it needs more thought and planning than most other written communications. So follow the tactics we have advised in earlier chapters. Jot down a point by point plan for the memo before you start writing. Look at the plan. Decide whether it is the best way to get across what you want to say. When you are satisfied that it is, start writing the memo.

The language of a memo can be more informal, especially in the use of the personal pronouns 'I' or 'we', as in 'I would like ...', or 'We have decided ...'. However, it should also be as punchy and direct as possible. Some people think that in a memo you can clip off a few words here and there and write in a shorthand or note form. We don't agree. Use the normal prose style you would use in any kind of writing. You might want to use lists of numbered points more often in a memo than in other writing but this does not mean you should abandon normal prose conventions. Like a business letter, the language of a memo should be clear, concise, concrete, convincing, complete and courteous.

Guttenburg Publishing Co—Memo

TO: Geoff Williams FROM: Rhonda Hart
SUBJECT: Additional Typing Staff DATE: 7 March 1994

The workload in the editing department has reached the stage where we need two additional typists. I have surveyed the overall requirements of the department and found this need is justified on the following grounds:

1. In the past six months we have employed four additional editors but, so far, no more typists for the department.
2. The workload in the last quarter of 1987 was up by 200 per cent and present indicators are that the first quarter of 1988 will continue this trend.
3. The extra work being generated by our expansion has meant our existing ten typists have each been working an average of eight hours a week overtime. In other words, the department is generating 80 hours of regular overtime per week.
4. Penalty rates mean it costs 50 per cent more to work this much overtime than it would to employ two extra typists.
5. The continued use of overtime cannot continue. Our typists are feeling the pressure in several ways, especially in constant fatigue and tension and in an increase in typing mistakes.
6. Overall, the two extra typists would save the company money and lead to a more efficient and accurate typing output.

A clear, concise memo

Memos should always be sent on the same sized sheet of paper as letters: A4. Some people think that because it is for shorter messages, the memo should be on smaller sized sheets of paper. Few things are more annoying than handling small pieces of paper. Many memos are filed and copied and reproduced. It is far more convenient to do these jobs when the paper is all the same size.

Memos usually signal urgency or the need for a prompt response. They should be designed to galvanise people into action.

As we have already said, a memo is usually designed to get one person or several to do something. It is action oriented, like an advertisement. This means it should, like an advertisement, tell people what action is required of them. You can call for the action at the start of the memo, and then give reasons why it is necessary or desirable (the deductive style); or you can give the reasons or background first and conclude the memo with the call for action (the inductive style).

A final point. If you want people to reply quickly to a memo with little more than a 'yes' or 'no', don't require them to write a whole new piece themselves. Leave space or a special section at the bottom so people can jot down their reply there. You will get faster responses and save work this way.

FAX MESSAGES

The facsimile transmitter, or fax as it is almost everywhere known, has rapidly become one of the most commonly used business communication devices. For the price of a telephone call, you can send exact copies of documents from one location to another, even around the world. There are some protocols you need to follow with fax machines which makes the whole process more efficient.

The most important of these is to use a fax cover sheet. This performs several of the functions that envelopes perform for letters. The fax cover names the person for whom the fax is intended. Few people have personal faxes so, when a fax machine is shared by a number of people, say a whole department, you always need to say which one of them is the receiver. You also need to indicate on the cover sheet who is the sender, just as you do with a letter. At a minimum, give your name, organisation and fax number.

Fax Sheet

To: ____________	**From:** ____________
Company: ____________	**Division:** ____________
Fax: ____________	**Fax:** (02) 417 5687
Date: ____________	**No. of pages to follow:** ______

Subject: ____________________________

A basic fax cover sheet

It is also a good idea to either pre-print fax cover sheets (or store templates of them in your word processor) with a special space left at the bottom of the page for messages. In some cases you will only need to fax the cover sheet with a brief message in this space. In other cases, this message will be important in helping the receiver to understand the rest of the documents you have sent. In this message space, it is quite acceptable to use informal language and drop the salutations and closings that you would use in a letter.

The main thing to watch when writing informal messages on a fax is that you might fail to make your meaning clear. Like memos, the more concise a message, the more you have to think about it and to try to put yourself in the reader's shoes.

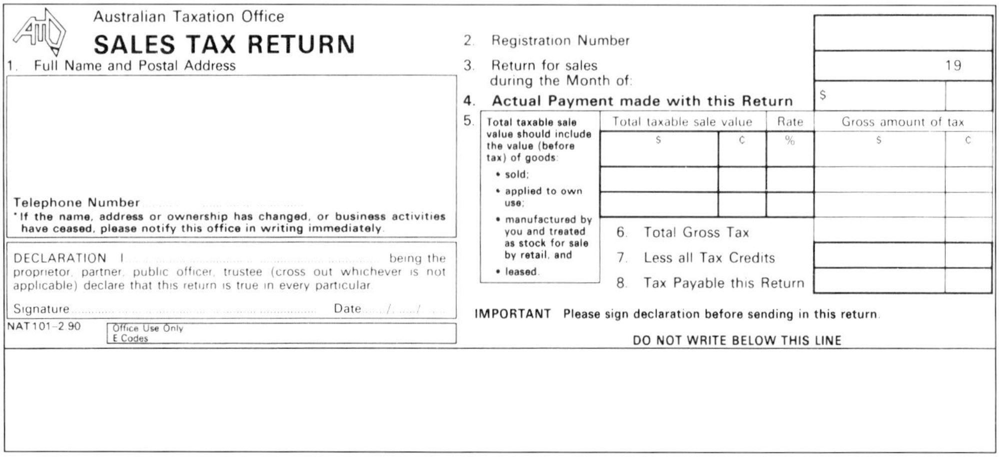
Australian Taxation Office
SALES TAX RETURN
1. Full Name and Postal Address

Telephone Number
*If the name, address or ownership has changed, or business activities have ceased, please notify this office in writing immediately.

DECLARATION I .... being the proprietor, partner, public officer, trustee (cross out whichever is not applicable) declare that this return is true in every particular

Signature .... Date ..../..../....

NAT 101-2.90 Office Use Only E Codes

2. Registration Number
3. Return for sales during the Month of: 19
4. Actual Payment made with this Return $

5. Total taxable sale value should include the value (before tax) of goods:
• sold;
• applied to own use;
• manufactured by you and treated as stock for sale by retail, and
• leased.

Total taxable sale value $	c	Rate %	Gross amount of tax $	c

6. Total Gross Tax
7. Less all Tax Credits
8. Tax Payable this Return

IMPORTANT Please sign declaration before sending in this return.

DO NOT WRITE BELOW THIS LINE

Forms need to be economical and effective communication devices

FORMS DESIGN

If they are not tested first among their intended users, forms will simply extend the dead hand of bureaucracy. If designed with others in mind, however, they can be efficient information gathering devices.

Forms are another type of internal communication device. They generally dictate the sort of information that the organisation wants and leave little room for any creative or detailed response from the people filling them in. Most organisations at some stage in either their internal relations or their relations with clients and the public decide they need a form. People often complain that forms are tiring, long-winded, an invasion of privacy or yet another example of how bureaucratically governed we have become. Yet forms are used because they are highly efficient. You can specify precisely the kind of information you want. You can quickly compile the results by reading off information from one point on each form. Rather than representing unnecessary red tape, forms are usually economical and effective communication devices.

Most of us fill in forms all the time but few of us ever get the chance to design one. The creation of a new form is a difficult job if there is no precedent. It involves four phases:

1. a preliminary planning stage where those people who will use the completed forms should have an input on their needs
2. the form design phase
3. market testing the form, that is, getting a small number of prospective clients to fill it out to see how hard it is for them and whether the form produces the results wanted
4. the final re-design

THE PLANNING PHASE

You need to think about a form from both your own organisation's point of view (what information you want) and from the perspective of those who will fill it out. Who will these people be? Under what conditions will the form be completed? At the office, at home, in the street, with a typewriter, or by pencil? How many people will see the completed forms, how many copies will you need, and how much information does each person handling the completed forms need? Do they all need the total information or only part of it? What precise items of information are you seeking? What is the order or priority of the questions to be? At the planning stage, representatives of all those who will use the information provided by the form should be involved as they will have to ensure that their needs are not overlooked.

The four phases of form design:

1. the planning phase
2. the drafting phase
3. the market testing phase
4. the re-design phase

THE DRAFTING PHASE

Write a draft of the form and then ask yourself the following questions. Does the form have an easily remembered title? Does it need a code number to distinguish it from others like it? Which items can be pre-printed to reduce the amount of writing the form filler will have to do? How can the form be simplified—by expressing the questions better, by reducing the total number of questions? Is the order of the questions logical and does there appear to be a natural progression from one question to the next? Is every question unambiguous? Are there any questions which would draw vague or meaningless answers? Is there enough space left for people with large handwriting to give their answers? Are the instructions on how to fill out the form clear and concise? Is the form in a convenient size for you to process, for your clients to fill in, and for mailing if necessary? Does it need to be printed in different colours to ensure it is followed correctly? Will the quality of the paper stand up to the use expected? Given that many forms are filled out under far from ideal circumstances, is the whole thing clear to someone who is not concentrating hard and who may be distracted by noise or other disturbances in the local environment?

THE MARKET TESTING PHASE

To make sure the form works the way you want it to, you will have to test it under the conditions it will normally expect to find. Take a small cross-section of the kind of people who would be filling in the form and give them a trial with it. Study the results. Then have a round-table discussion with them about how easy or hard they found the task, and whether the answers they could give really expressed their background or their opinion about what was asked.

RE-DESIGN

Finally, have another session with all those involved in the planning phase to consider the results of market testing and to come to a final consensus. Re-design the form in light of this discussion.

KEY POINTS: Chapter 7 Memos, faxes and forms

- Memos should be brief and to the point. They need headings to show for whom they are intended, who they are from, the date and the subject. It's a good idea to have specially printed forms.
- Always send a cover sheet with a fax.
- All forms should be carefully planned from the points of view of both the organisation that issues them and the people who will have to fill them out.
- Testing new forms with a cross-section of people at the drafting stage will improve the final product.

QUESTIONS FOR DISCUSSION

1. Why are memos generally set out in point form?
2. When would a fax be more appropriate to send than a letter?
3. What kinds of forms do you generally find boring, ambiguous or complicated to fill in?
4. If you had to design a form, what aspects of its structure, style and wording would you consider?

EXERCISES

1. You are responsible for organising the distribution of funds for overseas conference travel within your organisation. Your budget is $15 000 and there are twenty people eligible for funding. If they want to apply for these funds they have to fill out a special form. You need this form to be returned within two weeks, which is two days before the conference committee is due to meet to consider how the funds should be allocated and who will have priority. Write a memo that calls for applications for the funds but which tactfully suggests that not everyone will get what they ask for.

2. The photocopier is being abused yet again. The year is only three months old yet two-thirds of the copying budget has already been spent. Yesterday you found someone had inadvertently left the last page of a school P & C meeting newsletter near the machine and you suspect you are subsidising the printing of other outside documents. You walked in on someone last week copying a 150–page book which is against all aspects of the voluntary code which employees agreed to respect. You don't want to restrict use of the copier, nor to install a meter to police the machine. Yet it is getting to the stage where some action will have to be taken to prevent abuse. Write a memo to the staff expressing your concerns.

3. You are manager of a large organisation. Write a memo to one of your executives asking him or her to take care of the arrangements for this year's Christmas party. Staff morale has not been good this year because of a protracted strike which has only just ended with both sides making concessions. You think the Christmas party would be a good opportunity to patch up the relationships within the firm which had previously been good. You authorise the executive to recommend a generous budget and to put on something special.

4. Select a form that is important to the organisation with which you are connected most. Re-design it to make it more effective.

5. Go back to the first question. Design a form on which people could make their bids for grants for overseas conference travel.

CHAPTER

8

INSTRUCTIONS, NOTICES AND BROCHURES

After studying this chapter, you will know how to:

- write a set of detailed, unambiguous instructions
- write an instruction manual for a set of tasks
- write notices that are action oriented and informative
- write and design a detailed brochure about an organisation

INSTRUCTIONS

One of the most difficult of all communication tasks is to write instructions. It is difficult because you know the reader comes to the material ignorant of what to do. When you know how something works or how to perform some operation, it is very hard to place yourself in the position of someone who has none of your knowledge. Yet this is the basic task required—to describe something for someone who is approaching the subject with completely fresh eyes.

Remember when writing instructions that many English words have several different meanings and uses.

Even in simple operations with only two or three steps involved you can make very big mistakes. For example, if you are giving instructions on how to load a camera and you say: 'First take the film out of the packet,' you have overlooked the possibility that some people may read this as an instruction to take the film spool from the box and then, on seeing the end of the film protruding from the spool, to proceed to pull the entire roll of film out of the spool. If they do this, they ruin their chance of ever being able to load this film or take photos with it. What was at fault here was not entirely their stupidity; it was your use of the word 'packet'. You cannot expect a person completely ignorant of film loading to know what you mean when there are two possible objects to which this word could refer.

The best way to avoid mistakes like this is to be aware how easily they can happen. The second best approach is to use illustrations to accompany your text. The illustrations should be as self-contained as possible, that is, someone should be able to follow them without even reading the words. When you use illustrations in this way they should adopt the style of a comic strip. You tell a story in pictures of how people perform the action from the first step to the last. Reinforce the illustrations by placing words describing the action underneath each picture.

There are many occasions, however, when illustrations are either not possible or must be kept to a minimum. In these cases, the words have to carry all the responsibility. You are back with the problem of saying things in such a way that they are unambiguous and completely explanatory to someone fresh to the subject.

There are two approaches you can adopt when you have to write instructions under these conditions. First, you can try to remember yourself what it was like to be completely ignorant of the area in question. If this is possible you may well recall that there were one or two key aspects that had to be learned before you could confidently perform the operation described. Emphasise these in your instructions so that you guide the reader through the same learning process you went through.

When writing about how to operate a machine or assemble some furniture, put yourself in the position of a novice or student.

If your memory does not provide a suitable guide, you can try the second approach. This involves studying the process carefully to understand its basic principles. You have to analyse the process, breaking it down into the smallest detail possible. You then reconstruct these details into a coherent step-by-step description. In this approach, try to ensure each statement you make has only one possible meaning. The next thing you have to ensure is that your description is complete. Your instructions must not leave out any important step or leave a gap in the reader's understanding so that he or she is unsure of what to do next.

Writing instructions is slow and laborious work. Twenty words can take as long to write as 1000 in normal prose. So if you are given this job, allow yourself plenty of time to do it properly.

Finally, all instructions must be field tested. Try to find people who have as little familiarity as possible with the task at hand. Then give them your instructions and watch how they perform. This test phase is absolutely essential. One simple oversight in your instructions can lead people to sometimes make disastrous mistakes. An otherwise valuable and useful product or process can be sunk completely through experiences of this kind.

MANUALS

A manual is a book or folder containing multiple sets of instructions about the operation of a piece of equipment, an organisational procedure, or how the organisation functions. In preparing a manual, the same steps are involved as in writing instructions. The whole operation should be broken down into its smallest components, and instructions written for each. When compiled, all the separate instructions constitute the manual.

One of the difficult decisions to make about a manual is the order in which its contents should be arranged. In some cases, the equipment or the procedure has its own natural point at which beginners can enter, but in most cases this is not so. The most common ways to proceed are as follows.

1. Chronologically—in an organisational procedure this means from tasks that must be done first to those that must be done subsequently. With a machine, it is from the parts or process that begin its operation, through each subsequent movement.
2. From simple tasks to more complex ones.
3. From the base or framework to the periphery (or, to use the analogy of the tree, from the roots, to the trunk, to branches, to leaves).

Like instructions, manuals should be illustrated at every point. They should be produced so they can be understood without any other consultation. They need to be extensively field tested and then modified in light of this experience.

NOTICES

The words used in notices have to be exactly right. The best notices contain both illustrations and words.

There are two kinds of notices. First, they can be action oriented—you want someone to do something or you are telling them not to do something. Or, second, they can be informative, recording that something of importance has occurred or that a place is worthy of note.

Like instructions, they are often difficult to write, even though they may consist of only a handful of words. The words chosen have to be exactly right and to leave no room for doubt or ambiguity. In many cases, the best notice should contain both words and illustration. Designing pictures and symbols that will say vividly and exactly what you want is a task not to be undertaken lightly or by amateurs. If the issue is important, call in a professional designer or artist.

One essential rule about notices is that they should be brief. If your message runs to the length of even a short memo it should not be treated as a notice. Make multiple copies and distribute it in its true form as a memo. One of the most insensitive things management can do is to write a memo and pin it on a notice board for employees to read. Messages of this kind should be distributed to people on an individual basis. Notices are not meant to give people extended information about subjects. Their most common purpose is to cause or prevent action at the point where they are placed, or to record the most basic data (such as names and times) about places and events. Keep them for the jobs they do best.

BROCHURES

Any organisation of substance should produce a brochure about itself. Brochures are designed to give an overview of the organisation to various outside people and groups. Some organisations produce different brochures for different target groups such as shareholders, customers, suppliers and potential employees. However, if carefully thought out, one good brochure can appeal to all these groups.

A brochure is often the most important influence on an organisation's public image. The time and effort put in to produce a good job are usually worth it.

CONTENT:

A brochure should contain the following information:

- aims and objectives of the organisation, and its overall philosophy or set of values
- descriptions of the full scope of its present activities
- its size: this is often measured by number of employees or members and the number of places where it operates
- the names and titles of its principal officers
- its finances: this will vary depending on the nature of the organisation but a statement of the value of assets is a good indicator
- its legal structure: whether it is a private company, a public company, an incorporated association, a registered charity, a club or whatever
- its address: a full list of its headquarters, branches or other places of operation, together with both street and postal addresses, telephone numbers, telex numbers and the like

DESIGN:

Brochures should not be designed or printed on the cheap. Today, the standard materials are at least a glossy cardboard cover and glossy paper inside. Colour printing is desirable.

The main points of design will follow the contents list above. Each of the above points should be illustrated, either in diagram form such as flow charts, or with photographs of activities, locations and principal officers.

More than any other document, brochures about an organisation influence and define its public image. They are worth whatever time and effort it takes to produce a good job.

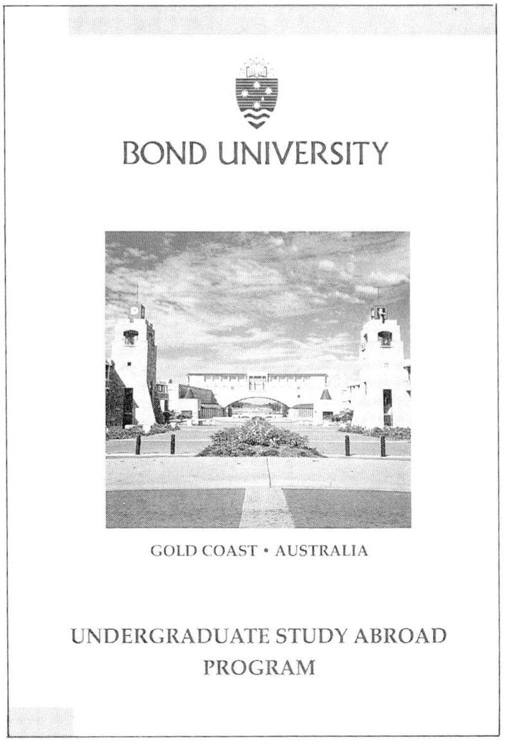

BOND UNIVERSITY

GOLD COAST • AUSTRALIA

UNDERGRADUATE STUDY ABROAD PROGRAM

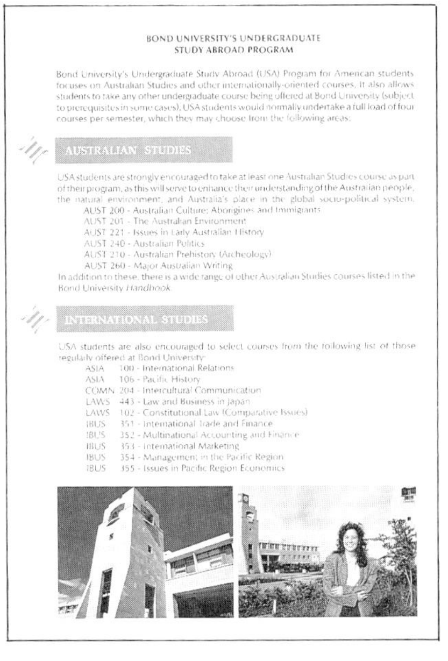

BOND UNIVERSITY'S UNDERGRADUATE STUDY ABROAD PROGRAM

Bond University's Undergraduate Study Abroad (USA) Program for American students focuses on Australian Studies and other internationally-oriented courses. It also allows students to take any other undergraduate course being offered at Bond University (subject to prerequisites in some cases). USA students would normally undertake a full load of four courses per semester, which they may choose from the following areas:

AUSTRALIAN STUDIES

USA students are strongly encouraged to take at least one Australian Studies course as part of their program, as this will serve to enhance their understanding of the Australian people, the natural environment, and Australia's place in the global socio-political system.

AUST 200 - Australian Culture: Aborigines and Immigrants
AUST 201 - The Australian Environment
AUST 221 - Issues in Early Australian History
AUST 240 - Australian Politics
AUST 210 - Australian Prehistory (Archeology)
AUST 260 - Major Australian Writing

In addition to these, there is a wide range of other Australian Studies courses listed in the Bond University *Handbook*.

INTERNATIONAL STUDIES

USA students are also encouraged to select courses from the following list of those regularly offered at Bond University:

ASIA 100 - International Relations
ASIA 106 - Pacific History
COMN 204 - Intercultural Communication
LAWS 443 - Law and Business in Japan
LAWS 102 - Constitutional Law (Comparative Issues)
IBUS 351 - International Trade and Finance
IBUS 352 - Multinational Accounting and Finance
IBUS 353 - International Marketing
IBUS 354 - Management in the Pacific Region
IBUS 355 - Issues in Pacific Region Economics

ACCOMMODATION

All USA students will be accommodated in residence, unless they elect otherwise, since this enables them to maximize their contact with Australian and other overseas students and to participate fully in campus life.

WHY BOND UNIVERSITY ?

Bond University is Australia's first private university. It was created by an act of the Queensland Parliament in 1987 and is a member of the Association of Commonwealth Universities. Its campus and facilities are the newest and most technologically advanced in Australia. Its faculty members are world class and many have substantial teaching experience in the United States. Its programs and courses are designed to be flexible, interdisciplinary, and responsive to current issues. A student-orientated teaching philosophy, and small group instruction, encourages students to be better communicators and to be more analytical. Bond has the best faculty-student ratio, and the highest proportion of overseas students, of any Australian university. These features ensure a valuable and truly international Study Abroad experience.

More than any other document, a brochure about an organisation defines its public image. Brochures should be professionally designed and printed on quality stock.

KEY POINTS: Chapter 8 Instructions, notices and brochures

- Never underestimate how difficult it is to write instructions. Always leave plenty of time for the task.
- Field testing your instructions will help prevent mistakes and misunderstandings.
- Notices should be brief. They should cause or prevent action at the point where they are placed or record the most basic data about places and times.
- A long notice is an insensitive way of issuing a short memo.
- Any organisation of substance should produce a brochure about itself. It should not be designed or printed on the cheap. A brochure will define and influence its public image.

QUESTIONS FOR DISCUSSION

1. What principles should be followed when describing something for someone who is approaching the subject for the first time?
2. What are the main principles involved in writing notices?
3. What are the main objectives an organisation usually pursues when it produces a brochure about itself?

EXERCISES

1. Write instructions on the following tasks.

   How to change a light globe
   How to fix a blown fuse in a household fuse box
   How to change the washer in a leaky tap
   How to replace the ribbon on a typewriter
   How to operate a sewing machine
   How to answer the telephone on behalf of someone else who does not want to be disturbed

2. Write and design a brochure introducing to newcomers your present educational institution, place of work or a club or community organisation with which you are associated.

REVISION LIST FOR PART II

WRITING FOR THE ORGANISATION

- Free exchange of information is vital to the efficient functioning of any modern organisation. This part of the book has dealt with the application of communication skills to the business messages encountered every day.
- The level of communication required in business calls for writing skills at a professional level. A good business style is the same as a good all-purpose prose style—clear, concise and concrete.
- Business letters often make the first impression for an organisation. It should be the best impression possible.
- Letters should be prompt and courteous. They should be laid out correctly. They should include all information necessary. They should make it as easy as possible to respond.
- Generally speaking, memos and forms do not receive the attention they deserve. When a few simple communication principles are applied, these commonplace messages can contribute enormously to the smooth running of an organisation.
- Instructions and manuals are surprisingly difficult to write, and notices and brochures are frequently misused or underutilised.

PART II
KEY TEXTS AND FURTHER READING

Denning, Jim, *Ready-made Business Letters*, Kogan, London, 1986.

Eagleson, Robert D., *Writing in Plain English*, Australian Government Publishing Service, Canberra, 1990.

Gowers, Sir Ernest, *The Complete Plain Words*, Penguin, Hammondsworth, 1980.

Graves, Robert and Hodge, Alan, *The Reader Over Your Shoulder*, Random House, New York, 1979.

Hudson, Nicholas, *Modern Australian Usage*, Oxford University Press, Melbourne, 1993.

Murray-Smith, Stephen, *Right Words: A Guide to English Usage in Australia*, Viking, Melbourne, 1987.

Partridge, Eric, *Usage and Abusage*, Penguin, Hammondsworth, 1982.

Van Alstyne, J., *Professional and Technical Writing Strategies*, Prentice Hall, Englewood Cliffs, 1990.

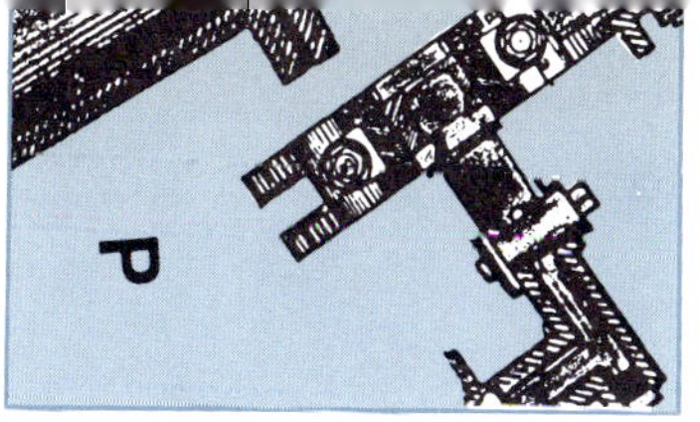

PART

III

WRITING AND RESEARCHING IN EDUCATION

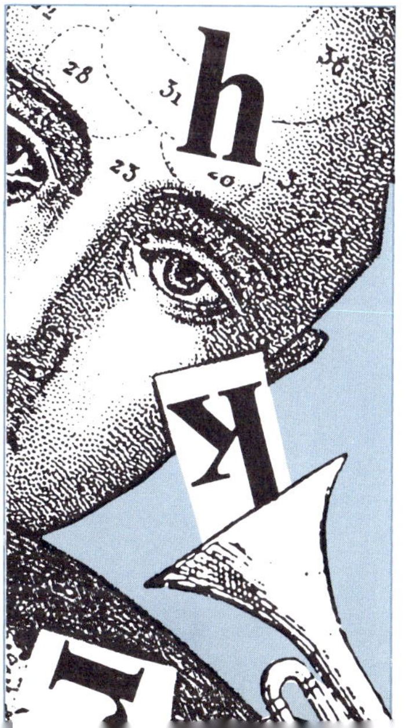

HOW STUDENTS CAN LEARN TO MASTER WRITING

Dr Fred Orr of the University of New South Wales counsels students on developing self-discipline and good work habits.

Essays are an inescapable part of student life. In fact, they continue to be the main assessment tool used by educators worldwide.

If written well, they can demonstrate a student's mastering of the skills of effective written communication. But, if written poorly, they can damage a student's chances at academic success.

Dr Fred Orr, senior psychologist at the University of New South Wales, is eminently qualified to talk about the importance of good essay technique and sensible study habits.

He is the author of several best selling books on these issues, including *How To Pass Exams, How To Succeed At Part-Time Study* and *Study Skills For Successful Students.*

In his role as Acting Head of the university's Counselling and Careers Service, he is constantly counselling students on better ways to organise their time, their tasks and their major submissions.

'Many students don't realise that their main enemy is going to be the clock and that they've got to get started on assignments early. Too many essays are done a night or two before the due date and, consequently, they are frantic, last-minute efforts. Good writing is simply not going to be achieved in that time frame,' he says.

Orr suggests that preparatory work be started as soon as the essay is set. The student should immediately consider the question, weigh it up, clarify it and decide on the angle to be taken.

'One of the skills in tertiary education is learning how to organise oneself and being selective in what you do and how you use your time,' says Orr.

Because students find that they may be working on several essays concurrently, all due at about the same time, he says it is critical to plan wisely and to decide priorities early.

He also recommends that students begin a file or organisational system in which they can keep notes and any other material they will develop in the project.

He feels that many students unfortunately misinterpret essay questions. If they have any doubts at all about the way in which they should approach a particular topic, they should consult their tutor or lecturer.

Another common mistake, according to Orr, is to think that quantity equals quality.

'Many students feel they are assured of high marks if they include large gobs of quotes and excerpts (some of them not totally acknowledged). However, examiners are seldom impressed by the sheer volume of work. Sure, they want to see evidence that the facts and figures are known, but also that they're able to be creatively and critically analysed.'

While anybody can read a large number of books and journals and reproduce the facts, it is the way in which the material is used and structured which shows a higher level of thought, explains Orr.

'Students today should be asking some very incisive questions like: What are the biases and prejudices of the author I'm reading? What is his or her agenda? Why was this research done? Are there any methodological flaws?'

He agrees that, at tertiary level, students may not always be aware of the criteria for evaluation within the marking system.

'Essays are expected to show evidence of critical thinking and analysis. The student must also demonstrate the ability to work logically through a system of facts and quotes, leading to some sort of conclusion,' he adds.

He acknowledges that the essay writing process has inherent stumbling blocks which can paralyse thought and undermine confidence. Despite the extensive number of articles he has written for newspapers and magazines, Orr confesses to feeling anxious when beginning a piece until he finds a structure he can work within.

He tells of a recent time when he received an urgent request to write four articles in one day.

'When the pressure is on and I need some inspiration reasonably quickly, I stretch out in my office, close my eyes and think of the concepts I'm trying to address for about ten minutes. I just let those ideas float and the creative juices stew away. Most times, that relaxed state produces the required results,' he says.

While 'introduction-body-conclusion' is seen as the general structure of an essay, Orr believes that the introduction is often the crucial part and can make or break a piece of writing.

'The introduction is very important because it's setting the stage for what follows and it's establishing a set of expectations in the marker's or reader's mind,' he adds.

He is critical of high schools for not giving pupils enough practice at essay writing and says teachers at every level of education should be responsible for setting regular written tasks and marking assignments comprehensively and diligently. Feedback is critical so that students can learn from their mistakes, hone their skills and elevate their morale by obtaining positive reinforcement, says Orr.

While incorrect spelling, bad grammar and poor punctuation do little for the credibility of the essay writer, he says the more difficult skill of interpreting factual matter and presenting it in a logically based system, is also hard for most people to master.

'The more sophisticated essay techniques can only be developed through a lot of practice, consultation and feedback,' he says.

Being certain about the key terms of the question is also important. Terms like 'assess', 'describe', 'analyse', 'define' and 'give evidence of' all require students to respond differently, advises Orr.

He warns that students should also be aware of the conventions governing the way in which references are cited in certain subjects.

'For example, a student doing a major history essay is generally expected to include footnotes. However, in most psychology essays, footnotes aren't used at all and different methods of citation are preferred. Students should know these rules for the different academic disciplines,' he says.

Orr is also a firm believer in what he calls 'mental maintenance' activities, or psychologically warming up the mind before each academic task. This is the mental equivalent of an athlete preparing for a strenuous work-out.

'If you walk into class having done some pre-reading, your mind is naturally sensitised to particular ideas of concepts. When these ideas are mentioned, your learning is facilitated and your understanding is enhanced. Better essays will result from this process,' he says.

Setting practical, realistic goals on a weekly basis will also keep students feeling that they are constantly achieving.

However, he stresses that it is necessary to have a break from the study routine by always having something positive and pleasant to look forward to—a sporting activity, a favourite television show or a meal out.

'The secret with all study and major writing tasks is to start early and progress with a systematic plan, well in advance of the submission date. This period of intense concentration should also be interspersed with enjoyable activities. Above all, you've got to be well organised.'

CHAPTER

9

ESSAYS–PLANNING AND RESEARCH

After studying this chapter, you will be able to:

- implement an effective, time-saving research plan
- critically analyse an essay question
- organise collected resources into a useful filing system
- make better use of library research services
- improve your reading and comprehension skills

There is a wide range of handbooks and pamphlets available to students at all levels of the education system telling them how to research and write essays. Large numbers of students follow the advice given in these publications and carry the habits they develop at school, university or college into their working lives. These guides to essay research and writing therefore eventually become important contributors to the way the nation as a whole develops its skills in studying itself—its markets, its industrial output, work practices, business affairs and the overall social environment.

A great many of them, however, are based on concepts and methods that belong to another era. In particular, their advice on research is based on practices developed in the nineteenth century and hardly revised since. Most still advise hand-written techniques in the era of the photocopier, modern filing systems and computerised databases. These old techniques keep the research process at a slow pace and inhibit our ability to study and report on the rapidly changing world around us. This chapter sets out an approach to researching and writing essays which is both a faster and more thorough approach than the traditional methods.

ANALYSE THE QUESTION

Before attempting to answer any essay question, analyse and break it down into logical segments. Only then can you evolve a plan.

Research for a topic cannot be done aimlessly. You cannot simply wade into the subject matter hoping that your reading will make everything fall into place sooner or later. You need to organise your research from the outset. Before you start, you need a plan—a set of headings under which the various pieces of information you turn up in the research can be placed. You will get this first set of headings by analysing the question. Take the following question as an example.

> What are the causes of strikes? Examine the different relations between employers and trade unions in various countries and suggest reasons why some countries have high levels and others low levels of strikes.

In drawing up a research plan from this question, you would take the first part first—the causes of strikes. Write down the heading: 'Causes of strikes'. The second part asks you look at employer–union relations in various countries. In considering how to do this you look at the last part of the question and you decide to have two lists of countries—one with high strike levels, the other with low strike levels. So you write down two more headings: 'Industrial relations in countries with high strike rates' and 'Industrial relations in countries with low strike rates'. You already know a little about the topic and that Britain and Australia have high rates of strikes and Japan and the United States have low rates. So you add two subheadings to each of your second and third headings. Your plan now looks like this.

1. Causes of strikes
2. Industrial relations in countries with high strike rates
   2.1 Britain
   2.2 Australia

3. Industrial relations in countries with low strike rates
   3.2 Japan
   3.3 USA

This is a fairly broad set of headings. After looking at it and thinking again about the question, you decide it would be more useful if it was divided into some additional categories. You already have a rough idea of the things that might cause strikes. The daily press has reported people going on strike for higher wages. There have also been reports about strikes over a shorter working week and other issues concerning the hours people work. One further issue that comes to you is the widespread action in Victoria in 1992 over the issue of retrenchments in the public service. Each of these issues would be a factor in each of the countries you have already listed. So you re-draw your plan to look like this.

1. Causes of strikes
   1.1 Wages
   1.2 Hours
   1.3 Retrenchments
2. Industrial relations in countries with high strike rates
   2.1.1 Britain—wages
   2.1.2 Britain—hours
   2.1.3 Britain—retrenchments
   2.2.1 Australia—wages
   2.2.2 Australia—hours
   2.2.3 Australia—retrenchments
3. Industrial relations in countries with low strike rates
   3.1.1 Japan—wages
   3.1.2 Japan—hours
   3.1.3 Japan—retrenchments
   3.2.1 USA—wages
   3.2.2 USA—hours
   3.2.3 USA—retrenchments

This now looks like a fairly comprehensive plan from which you can make a start.

THE RESEARCH PROCESS

The next thing to do is buy or otherwise acquire a good supply of manila folders. Write each of the eighteen headings from the above plan onto one manila folder. These eighteen folders are the start of your filing system for the essay. They will house the material you gather during your research. Once you have written the headings on them, the folders themselves become the plan of the essay. If you want to rearrange the plan, you change the order of the folders. If you want to add additional sections to the plan, you add another folder bearing the heading of the new section. If you want to delete a section, remove the folder and transfer the material in it to a more appropriate one.

Let's assume that the question you are given is accompanied by a reading list. The basic research task of the essay is to read through this list, extracting the information you think is relevant to answering the question. This research stage is critical to the quality of the work you do and the speed with which you can do it.

Traditional guides to the research process tell you the best way to capture information is to make a note of each relevant point or opinion on a single sheet of paper or on a card. Give each sheet or card a brief heading and add the name of the book, author and page number of the source. When you feel you have collected enough information, you shuffle the sheets or cards into an appropriate order and then begin writing from them.

Take few handwritten notes from books. Instead use a photocopier to copy information you want and then mark important passages on your copy. Keep your copied pages in manila folders. Arrange your folders in the order in which you will structure the essay.

This is a very time-consuming and arduous operation. There is a large amount of sheer physical effort involved in hand-writing the notes alone. People who adopt this method often find that, when they come to write from the facts and opinions, they wish they had recorded a few more details, or some of the context surrounding the information. If they want to do this, they have to go back and look up the original source again. The method goes back to Sydney and Beatrice Webb, the British social reformers and historians, who did their best work in the 1890s and 1900s. Beatrice gave a good account of the method in her autobiography, *Our Partnership*, and it has been recommended ever since. The Webbs were expert researchers and good writers. But they lived in the pre-typewriter era and pre-photocopier era when authors did all their research and writing in long hand.

Research today should make use of the technology now available, especially the photocopier. There is no need to write out information, opinions and theories by hand. Choose a library where there is ready access to a photocopier and use it liberally. Copy a whole page or several pages of material you want to collect. Then mark on the copy the particular passages that are important with a luminous, transparent marking pen.

Make all your copies on the one size of paper, A4. Make sure the source of each page is identified by author and title. Then file the marked copy in your appropriate manila folder. Never mark the original library book or journal. This does nothing to reinforce a point in your mind and only serves to annoy the next person who has to use that material.

Sometimes you will want to copy a whole article from a journal or a chapter from a book. Be wary of collecting too much information from one source but, if it is desirable, go ahead. Use your marking pen to save you time in the future by highlighting the sentence or parts of the text you want to keep for reference.

If you adopt this method you will make very few hand-written notes. The only hand-written notes you should make and file (again on A4 sheets) will be memos and notices you write to yourself about bright ideas you have had on the subject or reminders not to overlook certain points.

Making liberal use of a photocopier in this way might at first seem expensive but is justified on two grounds. First, you cut the time you take to do a proper research job by between 50 and 70 per cent. Second, you get much better information. You can copy long passages and whole tables of statistics and, in doing this, ensure that your final essay is more accurate. At the writing stage you will not only be able to draw on the quoted opinions of an authority on the subject, you will still have in front of you the overall context in which the statement was made. You will not only have a statistic on a point, you will still be able to see other statistics in the table from which your original one came.

As you read on the subject, you will gradually fill your manila folders with copies. You might also add to your collection, filed in their appropriate folders, a few whole documents such as bulletins of labour statistics published by the government. At the end of your reading program, you have two tasks: first, to arrange the material within each folder in the order you will deal with it when writing; second, to arrange the folders themselves in the best order for the writing stage.

During the reading stage, you will probably feel the need to revise the headings of your original plan. In the example discussed here, you might find the heading 'Hours' is too narrow so you expand it to 'Working conditions'. The same is true of 'Retrenchments' which you expand to 'Job security'. There are two additional influences on strikes that you discover as you go along. These are 'Trade union strength' and 'Government policy' which get folders of their own. You also discover good information on Italy and Sweden but you can't find much on Japan. You make the necessary additions and deletions.

Before you start writing, there is one procedure you should always adopt. Give yourself time to take one final overview of your plan. Go through the headings and order of the folders. Sift through all the material you have collected within each folder. This procedure puts the whole of the project within your head at the one time, giving you a 'holistic' view of the work so far and the likely shape of the finished essay. This is the stage at which any major fault with the structure will be discovered and where the process of synthesising all your material may often generate good new ideas. In the example here, the final review leads you to discard the idea of writing about one country after another on each separate topic. You decide it will be better to group countries together under the major topics. You reshuffle your folders to get the following final plan.

1. Causes of strikes
   1.1 Wages
   1.2 Working conditions
   1.3 Job security
   1.4 Union strength
   1.5 Government policy
2. Industrial relations in countries with high strike rates
   2.1 Wages—Britain, Australia, Italy
   2.2 Working conditions—Britain, Australia, Italy
   2.3 Job security—Britain, Australia, Italy
   2.4 Union strength—Britain, Australia, Italy
   2.5 Government policy—Britain, Australia, Italy
3. Industrial relations in countries with low strike rates
   3.1 Wages—USA, Sweden

3.2 Working conditions—USA, Sweden
3.3 Job security—USA, Sweden
3.4 Union strength—USA, Sweden
3.5 Government policy—USA, Sweden
4. Conclusions

These will be the eighteen folders from which you write the essay. Keep the three major heading folders (1. Causes of strikes; 2. Industrial relations in countries with high strike rates; 3. Industrial relations in countries with low strike rates) for introductory or more general material.

The folders can be simply kept in a pile of their own but a more efficient method is to put each one into a separate suspension file, with its own index tag, and then place the suspension files into a filing cabinet or, better still, an archive box. Archive boxes are ideal for students and anyone who needs a cheap, portable filing system. They are made of cardboard and cost only a few dollars each. Suspension files sit within the rims of archive boxes. With their lids on, several archive boxes will sit steadily on top of one another. They are easily lifted and carried from room to room or transported from home to library or classroom. All the research for even a very long essay can be fitted in one box. By scanning the headings visible on the index tabs of an open box you can always see before you the total plan for the essay.

Overall, the first key to successful essay writing is to have a proper filing system and good organisation of your material. The aids suggested here—manila folders, suspension files and archive boxes—provide a cheap, portable but very effective way of achieving this.

USING BOOKS AND LIBRARIES

The impression conveyed to most people by books and libraries is usually one of calm and studied quietude where scholars take their time to reflect

Efficient researchers take a selective approach when using library resources

on the subject matter. Good researchers, however, approach books and libraries in the opposite manner. They take an aggressive approach, plundering and mining the information they want. When writing a research essay you rarely have the time to read any book all the way through. In most cases the best approach is to look at the table of contents and see which parts of which chapters seem relevant to your task and then read only them. Do the same with a book's index: find the key words in the index that fit your topic or plan and read only those passages in the text where these words occur. This method will weed out a great deal of inessential material from your reading list. Only when this process of plundering the table of contents and index has left you satisfied that the book has something important to say about the topic should you then sit down and read large parts of it.

Become familiar with the reference services your library provides. Knowing how to use these services is an important research skill.

Adopt a similar approach to articles in journals and magazines. Read the introduction and conclusion of each article first. Only where these contribute to your plan or answer some of your questions should you go on and read the whole of the article. This is a ruthless method but, at a time when information on all topics is exploding everywhere, it is the only way to cover a wide range of opinion on a subject and still leave yourself time to complete the essay within its deadline.

Similarly, don't treat libraries as hallowed repositories of learning. Go in with the aim of extracting what you can. All libraries have catalogues of the books and journals they keep. Some of these are held on cards in old wooden drawers but increasingly today catalogues are stored on computer which you have to read on a computer terminal. If you are unsure how to use any of these, go straight to the librarian and ask for help. They are paid to assist you.

There are three types of library catalogue:
- authors
- serials (for journals)
- subject

There are three types of catalogue. The first is a list of everything in the library listed in alphabetical order by author's name. The second is a serials catalogue, sometimes called a periodicals catalogue, which is a list of all the journals and magazines held. The third is a subject catalogue which lists both books and journals under headings determined by subject matter. Under each subject heading is a list of all the relevant books and journals on the topic that the library holds.

COMPILING READING LISTS

If you are starting on a subject new to you, go to the subject catalogue first and look through it. Then go to the serials catalogue and see which journals related to your area are in the library. Once you have a fair idea of how much the library holds on the topic go and talk to the librarian about your subject and the way you plan to tackle it. The librarian will show you bibliographies on the broad area in which your topic is located. Bibliographies are published lists of books and magazines on various topics. From the library catalogues and bibliographies, the librarian will help you draw up a reading list from which to start work. If you can't find a librarian willing to help, then simply go through the process described here on your own. Whichever way you go, the reading list is an essential tool. It acts as a guide to your own reading in the research phase and you can publish it in the completed essay as your bibliography.

COMPUTER DATABASE SYSTEMS

One of the greatest developments for researchers in recent years has been the computer database. If you are engaged on a piece of work that is important to you, consider consulting one of these services. Most big university and college libraries now make them available for a modest fee. They involve a very fast computer search through all the books and articles held in Australian libraries on a topic you nominate.

The computer database is a very much updated version of the old subject catalogue. It allows you to key in the name of a topic and will then tell you how many items on that subject there are. If you key in another related word the system will tell you how many items there are that combine the two subjects.

For instance, you are interested in the level of crime committed by psychiatric patients. If you key in the word 'psychiatry', the computer will tell you there are X number of works on the subject (in this case there would be thousands). If you key in the word 'crime', you will get the same result. But when you ask the system to tell you how many items there are that contain information about *both* psychiatry and crime, the number will shrink considerably. You can then ask the system for abstracts of the, say, 75 items on psychiatry and crime. It will print out for you the author, title and publication date of each of these items. In some databases, the printout gives you a summary of each item held. Using this technique by combining three or four words can direct you right to the precise books and articles you need.

Those few who are familiar with computer database systems wouldn't be without them.

Australian databases are relatively inexpensive to use. International databases, which are now available to this country through telephone-satellite link, cost more (around $100 for an hour or so's work on the computer plus a reasonably lengthy printout) but are often worth it. Computers now mean we have direct access to the subject catalogues of the world's libraries. This is an incredibly valuable resource which is still not appreciated enough by most researchers. Those few who have become familiar with the system wouldn't be without it.

PRIMARY AND SECONDARY SOURCES

It is often useful when drawing up a reading list to distinguish between primary and secondary sources. Secondary sources are books and articles written by people who have only a second-hand knowledge of the subject. They compile all the work done by those who have direct experience and they describe the topic in a kind of overview or synthesis. Sometimes this is called a 'literature review'. In science, primary sources are those written by scientists describing directly their experiments. In history, primary sources are the documents left by people actually living at the time the history was made. Secondary sources in science can be written by scientists or more general authors and are summaries and analyses of a range of experiments conducted in a field. Secondary sources in history are those written by historians in our own times. It is always best to read the secondary sources first before honing in on the primary sources to get down to the fine details.

READING AND ABSORBING

Most people would like to make their research more effective by being able to read more quickly and to absorb more of what they read. These two aims, however, usually run counter to each other. The faster you read, the less you absorb; the more slowly you read the better you concentrate and remember.

There are three techniques that will improve your reading speed:
- more practice
- better comprehension
- selective reading

It is possible, nonetheless, to increase the speed of your overall or average reading rate while absorbing more of what you read. Your aim should not be to read everything quickly. Some important documents will still need a great deal of time and attention while, on the other hand, leisure material can be quickly browsed through. These differences should remain even if you can increase your average reading time.

There are three techniques we want to put forward to improve your reading speed: more practice, better comprehension and selective reading.

PRACTICE

Reading is like any other physical or mental skill, the more you practice the better. Try to increase the volume of material you read each week. If you are not already in the habit of reading a quality morning newspaper every day then start now. Beginning the day with a brisk read is a good form of mental exercise. You bring your mind into focus and clear away the overnight cobwebs. It is a healthy habit to become addicted to—and once you get started properly you will soon become addicted. You won't feel really awake until you have read the paper. If you are in an occupation where there are professional, trade or specialist magazines, subscribe to them and read them thoroughly when they arrive. Make a point also of looking for book reviews or advertisements for new books in your area of work or interest. Make the reading of non-fiction books in your field a high priority. As a general rule, non-fiction books are better reading practice and better for you than works of fiction, even on long plane or train journeys. Work out how much you read now each week and try to increase it by 50 per cent in the short term and by double in the longer run. The more you read the better reader you will be.

One approach we regard as unhelpful is speed reading. From time to time, organisations appear which, for a large fee, claim they can teach you how to read great volumes of material very quickly. The techniques most of these courses are based on are simply those of skimming, that is, running through passages picking up key words. Skimming is not reading, it is simply looking for words. Reading is the act of engaging your mind with that of the author and to do this you need to read all the words in the passage in front of you. You can read some material, especially fiction, fairly quickly because the meaning is easy to grasp and flows on readily from one point to the next. Where the meaning is harder to understand and there are new concepts to consider or new ways of looking at something discussed, then you must slow down to carefully consider what the author is saying. Skimming is OK if you want to run quickly through a text to find the place where you want to actually start reading, but skimming can never take the place of reading because it does not take in meaning.

COMPREHENSION

This leads us to the second approach to better reading, to increase your powers of comprehension. People can read shallowly and they can read deeply. When reading deeply you take the author's meaning into your mind, absorb it, consider how much you agree or disagree with it and commit it to memory. The best way to increase your reading speed and ability is to increase your powers of comprehension or your powers of reading deeply. This again is a matter of practice.

Students at high school are sometimes given comprehension exercises in English classes. A number of textbooks have been published in the area. They reprint a passage of text, usually from a newspaper or magazine article, and then ask a series of questions about the article. If you are not used to doing comprehension exercises, it is surprising how difficult these questions can be, even for people who have a fair amount of reading to do in their jobs. If you are in the latter category then your comprehension skills need more exercise than we have space to provide in this book. Buy one of those high school comprehension textbooks and work your way through the exercises until you develop your ability to a level you are satisfied with.

There are some general points about comprehension that you should remember.

1. All questions must be answered from the text itself. Don't bring in outside knowledge of your own to answer any question and don't make assumptions about what the writer has said. Check the original text for the exact wording if you are in any doubt. If you follow this rule you will develop your powers of concentration and your ability to pinpoint the precise meaning expressed by a writer.
2. Try to determine the writer's intention. In other words, think about not just what the writer has said but why he or she said it. What is the writer trying to make you think or to get you to do?
3. Be aware of the techniques used by the writer. Many words that writers use are persuasive rather than factual. An apple may be a bright red colour and have a high water content but when someone describes it as 'rich and juicy' they are not giving you an objective description. They are trying to give you some idea of what it would be like to taste the apple and are therefore trying to persuade you to buy it.
4. Be aware of your own reactions. If you are attracted to a message or turned off by it, try to understand why this is. What is it about the writer's words, intentions and techniques that make you feel this way?
5. What is the logic used in the text? Do the conclusions really follow from the case presented? Is the evidence sound? Is the reasoning sufficient to be convincing? In other words, try to bring a critical response to every claim made and to the article as a whole, even when you think you agree.

SELECTIVE READING

To increase your reading speed, a much better approach than skimming is selective reading. This means you do not read everything in an article or a book before you. You make selections depending on your needs. As we emphasised earlier in this chapter, you should not necessarily regard non-fiction articles or books as things to be read from start to finish or from cover to cover. Sometimes you will want to do this, but in most cases you will want to get only what you need from them. Most good non-fiction articles and books have introductions which tell you why they have chosen the subject concerned and the approach they will adopt. Most have conclusions which summarise their findings. In many cases, you will find it sufficient to read only the introduction and conclusion, especially if you are not in a position to criticise the argument or evidence presented.

Selective reading minimises your research time, focuses your mind and develops your capacity for reading deeply.

Another feature of good non-fiction writing is that it is usually divided into sections by means of descriptive headings. Often you need only read through the headings to find the section you want. Reading all the headings gives you an idea of the overall context and you can then settle down to a careful reading of the part that interests you. When you open a non-fiction book, go to the table of contents and read it through. If the author has considered the way that most non-fiction readers use books, the contents will be detailed and say what they refer to. Unfortunately, some authors still have the mistaken idea that chapter and section headings need to be cryptic or poetic and so they are impossible to understand. An author who is so insensitive to the demands of non-fiction readers is generally not worth reading anyway and can usually be ignored without much loss. If you cannot find what you want in the table of contents, turn next to the index. Look up the categories you want. Sometimes you might want to read through the whole index. This way you will often turn up categories you hadn't thought of but which might contain material you need. Any non-fiction book that lacks an index is not worth buying or borrowing and, again, is best ignored.

Selective reading is the way that most experienced researchers approach non-fiction writing, especially long works such as books and reports. Rather than being a short-cut or sloppy method, it is actually a good habit to develop. The process of hunting through a book or report for the passages that interest you most is an act that focuses the mind. It gives your reading purpose and increases your ability to absorb reading material. It is a good way to develop the capacity for reading deeply.

KEY POINTS: Chapter 9 Essays—planning and research

- Most handbooks on researching and writing essays are based on techniques developed in the nineteenth century. Faster and more effective technology is now available.
- The question should be analysed and broken up into manageable parts.
- Choose a library where there is ready access to a photocopier and use it liberally. Copy a page or pages onto A4 paper, identify the source by author and title and use a fluorescent pen to highlight references.
- Keep the photocopies in manila folders. Shuffle the folders to get your final essay plan. They can be stored cheaply in cardboard suspension files and archive boxes.
- Use libraries aggressively. Compile reading lists and explore the possibilities of computer database systems. Begin with secondary sources and overviews.
- Reading, like any skill, improves with practice. To read more effectively, read more.
- Speed reading courses generally don't work. Selective reading is much more effective. Read introductions and conclusions. Find the section on your special interest in the table of contents or the index. Read no more than you have to, but read what you read thoroughly.

QUESTIONS FOR DISCUSSION

1. What is the purpose of information headings when condensing an essay question?
2. Explain how an information filing system can be built up.
3. What kind of information can a library computer database give you?
4. Outline the difference between a primary source and a secondary source.
5. How can selective reading be achieved?

EXERCISES

1. Obviously, the best exercise anyone could do to practise the advice in this chapter is to write some real essays set for real subjects, using all of our guidelines. Apart from that, try the following exercises.
2. Before you write your next essay, draw up a plan for research, as described in this chapter, take it to your subject lecturer and discuss how well the plan approaches the topic.
3. Take two key words from the title of your most recent essay. Go to your library and use these words to conduct a database search for a bibliography for the essay. Compare the result you gain from the computer with the reading list given to you by your subject lecturer.

CHAPTER

10

ESSAY AND THESIS WRITING

After studying this chapter, you will be able to:

- structure an essay in a logical, coherent manner
- write the introduction, body and conclusion of a research essay
- justify your arguments with evidence
- make proper use of essay conventions such as footnotes
- prepare a bibliography and an abstract

In the research phase described in the last chapter, you have done all the work of organising the essay, deciding how you will make your case and what evidence you will use to back your claims. The order of the folder headings and the actual contents of the folder now form the framework within which the essay will be written. The eventual list of headings on your manila folders will be the final plan for the essay itself. In other words, being organised during the research phase means you will have already done a great deal of the work. Writing each section of the essay is a matter of opening each folder, going through the material in it, writing a plan for the section itself and its paragraphs, and then writing the actual text.

THE INTRODUCTION

Introductions are often difficult to write and one thing we strongly advise you to avoid is a slow, agonising start to writing an essay because you can't write the introduction. A number of professional writers always write the introduction last—when they have got the final version of what it is they are introducing. If the introduction gives you any trouble, put it off until later and start writing the essay at the easiest part. When you have built up a momentum in the writing process, you might want to come back and do the introduction.

If the introduction gives you trouble, put it off until later and start writing the essay at the easiest part.

The purpose of the introduction is to say what you are going to do in an essay. Because there is a question already set, this means your introduction will be telling how you plan to answer the question. Don't give the actual answers or conclusions, though. In the question we chose as our example in the previous chapter, the causes of strikes, you could start by saying you will examine the role of the major sources of industrial disagreement—wages, conditions, job security—and then look at the influence of union strength and government policy on the issue. You will do this in relation to countries with high levels of strike activity, such as Australia, Britain and Italy, and countries with low levels of strikes, such as the United States and Sweden. In other words, an introduction can simply be an outline of the structure of the essay.

Another way to introduce an essay is to state the problem you are going to solve. You can give a brief description of current views on the subject and show how they are deficient in answering it. You then say that your approach hopes to fill in the gap in our understanding. Above all, whatever type of introduction you adopt, use it to show that you are answering the question. A common complaint by markers of essays is that students have not answered the question. The introduction should be a means of telling both the marker and yourself how you have actually tried to answer it.

There are other types of introduction that you might want to use. In some cases they will suggest themselves as you are doing your research. You will have an idea that clarifies the problem in an illuminating way and you will want to start with it. As you are doing your research, you might find it useful to keep a folder called 'Introduction' in which to make notes about points like these that you want to make there.

USING EVIDENCE

The more evidence you can bring to support your case the better. This means citing the opinions of a wide range of authors. But never use the words of another author as if they were your own.

The sections of the main body of the essay should all be composed of evidence that goes to support the overall case you are making. Evidence can be of two kinds: it can be the opinions of people who are recognised as authorities in the area concerned; or it can be factual material derived from research and statistics. The more evidence you can bring to support your case the better. This means citing the opinions of a wide range of authors. Whether you are giving a direct speech quotation or you are putting the author's views in your own words, make sure you always cite the name of the person concerned: 'Arthur Lloyd-Jones claims that X is Y'; 'In studying ABC, R. F. Bogart found that DEF.' A good essay will have a generous quantity of names sprinkled throughout it. When you cite an author, you should always give a reference or a footnote to show exactly where the author's point was made. We discuss how to do this in a section later in this chapter.

Sometimes it is useful to conduct a debate between authors in order to establish one point and to demonstrate that you have considered other views on the issue. For instance: 'In the 1970s, most opinion on Topic X held that A was always B. The main authority, Margaret Harris, maintained there could be no exceptions to this. However, in 1980 E. T. Clark argued that this was true only if one defined A very narrowly. Two years later he discovered examples of A1 which were obviously C.'

One word of warning: never use the words of another author as if they were your own work. This practice works against you in two ways: first, the marker will probably be familiar with the words anyway and will mentally accuse you of plagiarism, that is, of stealing the words or ideas of someone else without acknowledging it (and which we discuss further below); second, by naming the author who wrote the words or ideas you give evidence of the range of your reading and this will win you more points than omitting the name.

Numerical evidence is often more convincing than other kinds. Use precise measurements of:
- totals
- quantities
- averages
- proportions
- dimensions
- distances
- statistics

The sort of factual material you bring to an essay will depend on the subject matter but one point always worth remembering is that numerical evidence is often more convincing than other kinds. If you can give precise measurements of totals, quantities, averages, proportions, dimensions, distances and statistics, you will usually have strong evidence. Measurements like these are never perfect or absolute in any sense but they do indicate that you or the person you are citing as your authority has gone into the issue in a close and detailed way. Evidence that cites statistics is always taken more seriously than that which doesn't.

The practice of citing numerical evidence is one good way of avoiding one of the great temptations and weaknesses of student essays, the tendency to make unsupported generalisations. One often finds statements like the following: 'In these days, when the divorce rate has never been higher…', 'Doctors have a higher suicide rate than other occupation groups.' Both these statements should be supported by the appropriate statistics: actual divorce rates for this year compared to some previous years; the actual suicide rates for doctors compared to other people. (In both these examples, the student who bothered to look up the statistics would find that both these generalisations turn out to be wrong—look them up for yourself.) Unsupported generalisations—the type of statements that are easy to make without much thought—are indicators of laziness and will always draw criticism from essay markers.

When you have completed the main sections of the essay put it away, preferably overnight, and then return to re-read it the next day. In this checking phase, try to read at two levels: one, at the level of close detail, looking for spelling mistakes and poor expression; two, at a very broad level to consider how the main ideas of the essay relate to one another. At this second level be on the lookout for inconsistencies, that is, for points in your case that might contradict or work against each other. It is easy to allow one or two points to slip into your work that, if you think about it, tend to support views that are not yours. Reading the essay with fresh eyes is the best way of picking up any inconsistencies like this.

HEADINGS

There are still some teachers who discourage their students from using headings within essays. Many of these are people with a background in English Literature who regard the essay as an art form. They think that headings interrupt the flow and momentum of the essay and that such interruptions are not elegant. They often believe that the text of the essay should itself be sufficient to convey its structure or direction. From this view, only weak or insecure writers have to resort to headings. We disagree with this view very strongly. While we acknowledge that a good essay will have its own momentum and direction irrespective of any headings, we still believe that headings improve the work for both the reader and writer.

Headings in an essay do two things:
1. they allow the reader to see the overall structure of the essay
2. they make writing easier

For the reader, headings do two things. First, they allow the reader to see the overall structure of the essay and, at any stage, to know where he or she is. That is, at any point within the essay, headings tell where it has been and where it is going. This way they maintain a broad focus on the overall case being made. The reader might be absorbed with particular detail at any point but headings keep reminding him or her of the total perspective. Second, they make it much easier for the reader to go back over sections to check a passage or a point. Essays are works of non-fiction prose and non-fiction is not read once only for its story. It is often read and re-read several times so the reader can glean the information or study the argumentation. Without headings, this re-reading process would be more difficult and much slower.

The use of headings also makes writing easier. Writing the essay is a matter of following closely the final plan. The research folders should be organised in the order in which the essay is to be written. Each section of the essay should start with its own heading taken directly from the final heading written on the folder. With the heading already decided and the scope of each section determined by the contents of the folder, much of the difficulty is removed from the final writing process. When you are well organised this way, writing can become a pleasure.

THE CONCLUSION

The conclusion is a summary of the main points of your argument. You should also use the conclusion to show that you have answered the question and to summarise the method through which you have answered it. In a good essay, the introduction and conclusion should stand on their own two feet. They should be all someone needs to read to know what you were trying to do and how you have done it.

PRESENTATION

A good essay is always well presented. Few education institutions actually insist on typing but essays always look better if they are typed. Whether typed or written, the text should be on one side only of A4 sheets of paper. If typed, the lines should be double-spaced or one-and-a-half spaced. Pages should have generous margins of at least 3 centimetres on both sides and top and bottom. They should have a title page at the front with your name and the question or essay title in the centre.

FOOTNOTES AND REFERENCES

Whenever you mention an author's name or rely on his or her work in the text of an essay, you should include a reference or a footnote which gives the full name of the author, the particular book or article involved, the page number and publishing details. This information would normally clutter up the text so two alternative systems have been developed. In the Harvard reference system, after the author's name is mentioned, the year the work was published and the page number/s are given in brackets at that point in the text; a complete reference to the same work is given in the bibliography, or reading list, at the end of the essay. For example:

> In his study of inland exploration, Clark (1987:27) shows that the official parties often followed tracks already made by squatters.

Readers especially interested in Clark's views can turn to the bibliography, look up Clark's name and see the name of the book or article he wrote in 1987. On page 27 is the point made above.

If the author's name does not appear in the text but you still want to rely on his or her authority, then give surname, date and page number.

> Several studies of school participation rates in Australia (Bland, 1989:47; Mitchell, 1990:155–6; Roberts, 1992b:49–51) have found them affected by youth unemployment levels.

Note that in the example of Roberts' work, the date '1976b' refers to the fact that in th bibliography, Roberts has three publications listed for 1976, designated a, b and c. Where there are several authors for one book you only use the first surname followed by the phrase 'et al'. For example: (Bailey et al., 1985:254).

The second method of indicating the source of a work is the footnote. In this system, a small number is placed in the text at the point where the reference is made. At the bottom of the same page, the number is repeated and the full details of authorship, title and publication details are given. For example:

> Television has become a dominating and corrupting influence on sport, Turner claims in his new book.[5]
>
> ....
>
> 5. Graeme Turner, *Sport, Money and the Media*, Penguin, Melbourne, 1992, p. 56.

The advantage of footnotes is that they allow the reader to glance down the page and immediately see the work that is referenced. In some books you will see footnotes are actually 'endnotes' because they are published either at the end of the chapter or at the back of the book itself. The disadvantage of footnotes is that they involve more typing than the Harvard system, although once a book or article has been noted once in the footnotes abbreviated forms are accepted. If the second reference follows immediately after the first, then the Latin word 'ibid.' indicates this. If other footnotes intervene between references to the one book, then the author's surname and the words 'op. cit.' will do. If we are following the above example, the footnotes would read:

> 6. ibid., p. 78
>
> ....
>
> 15. Turner, op. cit., p. 183

The acceptable ways to cite articles from journals and chapters from collected editions of books are as follows:

> Frank Stilwell, 'Towards an alternative economic strategy', *Journal of Australian Political Economy*, 12, June 1982.
>
> K. E. Mitchell, 'Bodgies, Rockers and Punks', in R. Wilson (ed.), *Deviance in Urban Society*, Macmillan, 1984, p. 256.

Note that the titles of books and journals are in italics (or would be underlined if typed) while the titles of articles and chapters are enclosed in inverted commas.

We prefer the footnote method to the Harvard reference system because, while it involves a little more work for the writer, it involves much less for the reader who is saved the trouble of hunting through the bibliography to find the full reference each time. Footnotes also allow you the opportunity to make additional comments and asides that would otherwise interrupt the flow of the text.

You should try to become proficient at including either footnotes or references in essays. They are not merely pedantic, unnecessary additions to a text. They have several important roles. They allow readers to be certain what you are referring to, down to the page number, when you cite an author, a book or journal article. This avoids any confusion about which opinion of an author you are talking about. They also allow readers to find

Footnotes and references are not mere academic glosses. They assist readers in three ways.

- They allow readers to be certain about what you are referring to.
- They inform readers of material they might not have known existed.
- They allow readers to build their own reading lists on a subject.

material they had not known existed before they saw your reference to it. Further, they allow readers to build up their own reading lists on a subject. Your footnotes and references can guide the reading and research of many people. Overall, they are an important part of the communication between communities of people interested in a particular field. For this reason alone, you should make an effort to use them.

PLAGIARISM

Research essays, by their very nature, rely heavily on ideas and information provided by books and articles written by other people. The essay writer has to handle this material in a careful way. The essay must be constructed largely on the work of others but it must avoid claiming the work of others to be the author's own. If you present the same ideas, the words or the phraseology of other people as if they were yours, you will be guilty of plagiarism which is a serious form of academic misconduct. Professors have lost their jobs after being accused of it, and students have been stood down.

Plagiarism is a failure to acknowledge that the ideas or information being presented derive from the work of others. It is a serious form of academic misconduct.

Essentially, plagiarism is a failure to acknowledge that the ideas or information being presented derive from the work of others. The best way to avoid it is to be completely open and frank about the sources used in researching the essay. Develop the custom of citing and acknowledging the authors you have read, and of conducting debates between them. We described how to do this in the earlier section of this chapter on using evidence. There is nothing wrong or second-hand about writing this way. Most of the ideas anyone has, most of the questions we all ask and the frameworks in which we channel our thoughts, derive from other people who have broached the subject before us. Intellectual work, though it goes on inside the heads of individuals, is very much a collective effort. The proper acknowledgment of those from whom you have learned is an essential part of the intellectual process.

THE BIBLIOGRAPHY

A bibliography is an alphabetical list by author's surname of books and journals that have been read for an essay or a longer piece of work. Articles, chapters and books are cited in the same way as in footnotes except that the surname is usually listed before the initials or given name of an author. The numbers immediately after a journal article refer to its volume number and/or serial number. Page numbers are included for articles and chapters but not for books. The following is an example of a typical bibliography.

Andrews, John, 'Energy and Employment in Australia', *Chain Reaction*, Friends of the Earth, Melbourne, 3, 2, 1977, pp. 54–7.
Commoner, Barry, *The Poverty of Power*, Bantam, New York, 1977.
Future Lobby, *The Right to Share Work*, Prospect, Sydney, 1978.
Grossman, Richard, 'A solar solution to unemployment', in G. Daniker (ed.) *Positive Economic Policies*, Greenpeace, Auckland, 1985, pp. 189–207.
Illich, Ivan, *The Right to Useful Unemployment*, Boyars, London, 1978.

Nicholls, Jeff, 'Jobs and Energy', paper to conference on Jobs for Use—Not Waste, Macquarie University, Sydney, September 1977.

ABSTRACTS, PRÉCIS AND SUMMARIES

Some teachers require students to submit a brief abstract, a précis or a summary with their essays. In a growing number of academic journals this is now a formal requirement. It is a good idea to get used to doing this as the habit is a valuable one. With the growth of computerised databases, as we mentioned earlier, it is now possible to compile lists of almost all the written material done on a particular subject in English. The typical database cannot store the whole content of every article in its memory but it can store full details of the author and the publication and it does have room for a short abstract or summary. For other researchers in the field, it is so valuable to have the abstract available on the computer printout, that the practice of including abstracts in all journal articles will continue to grow. Students should adopt the practice as a matter of course.

If you have written your introduction and conclusion carefully, then preparing an abstract will come easily. It is simply a short version of the aims and method of the essay (from the introduction) and the conclusions it reached (from the conclusion). In other words, put together a combined and shortened version of the introduction and conclusion and you have an abstract.

KEY POINTS: Chapter 10 Essay and thesis writing

- If the introduction gives you any trouble, put it off until later. It need be little more than a prose outline of the structure.

- Support assertions with evidence. Evidence can be of two kinds: first, the opinions of authorities in the field; and second, factual material derived from research and statistics.

- Always name your sources. Plagiarism is serious academic misconduct.

- Summarise your findings in the conclusion. In a good essay, the introduction and conclusion stand alone.

- A good essay is always well presented.

- Understand and be able to use the Harvard and footnote systems of citing references. Be familiar with the conventions for a bibliography.

- Abstracts, précis and summaries are invaluable for researchers, and students should include them as a matter of course. Put together a combined and shortened version of the introduction and conclusion and you have an abstract.

- Submit essays typed, on single-sided A4 paper, with double or one-and-a-half spacing, and with at least 3 centimetre margins all round.

QUESTIONS FOR DISCUSSION

1. What are the main differences between an essay and a piece of creative writing?
2. What are the inconsistencies in essays which examiners would be on the look-out for?
3. What is plagiarism and how can it be avoided?
4. What are the advantages of headings in essays?
5. Why should essay writers use footnotes and references?

EXERCISES

1. As we noted at the end of the last chapter, the best exercise for essay writing is to actually write some essays, following all our guidelines. However, in lieu of that, try the following.
2. Take your most recent essay and write a new introduction for it and a new conclusion, following the guidelines in this chapter.
3. Retrieve some of your old essays which were not organised under section headings. Go back through them and add section headings where appropriate.
4. Go through your most recent essay and tidy up all your references. Make them all consistent with the conventions of either the footnote method or the Harvard system. Ensure all titles are italicised or underlined, all page numbers are included, and all the other conventions are followed precisely.
5. Take your most recent essay and give it a proper bibliography, following precisely the guidelines in this chapter.
6. Take your most recent essay and write an abstract for it.

REVISION LIST FOR PART III

WRITING AND RESEARCHING IN EDUCATION

- While there is a range of handbooks and brochures available to the student and researcher on essay writing, the majority are based on techniques developed in the nineteenth century. Technology now available can halve the time required to research a major piece of work. Students should exploit modern techniques for reproducing and storing information.

- However advanced it might be, technology is no substitute for reading. There are simple ways of improving your speed and comprehension, and of making the most of a limited amount of reading time.

- As with any major work, thoughtful planning of an essay eases the burden at the writing stage.

- The question should be analysed and broken up into manageable parts.

- Choose a library where there is ready access to a photocopier and use it liberally. Copy a page or pages onto A4 paper, identify the source by author and title and use a fluorescent pen to highlight references.

- Keep the photocopies in manila folders. Shuffle them to get your final essay plan. They can be stored cheaply in a cardboard suspension folder.

- Use libraries aggressively. Compile reading lists and explore the possibilities of computer database systems. Begin with secondary sources and overviews.

- Become adept at selective reading. Read introductions and conclusions. Find the section on your special interest in the table of contents or the index. Read no more than you have to, but read what you read thoroughly.

- If the introduction gives you any trouble, put it off until later. It need be little more than a prose outline of the structure.

continued on next page

continued from previous page

- Always support your assertions with evidence. Evidence can be of two kinds: first, the opinions of authorities in the field; and second, factual material derived from research and statistics.
- Always name your sources. Plagiarism is serious academic misconduct.
- Summarise your findings in the conclusion. In a good essay, the introduction and conclusion stand alone.
- Understand and use the Harvard and footnote systems of citing references. Be familiar with the conventions for a bibliography.
- Abstracts, précis and summaries are invaluable for researchers, and students should include them as a matter of course. Put together a combined and shortened version of the introduction and conclusion and you have an abstract.

PART III
KEY TEXTS AND FURTHER READING

Clanchy, John and Ballard, Brigit, *Essay Writing for Students*, Longman Cheshire, Melbourne, 1991.

Fletcher, Charles, *Essay Clinic: A Structural Guide to Essay Writing*, Macmillan, Melbourne, 1990.

Howard, K. and Sharp, J. A., *The Management of a Student Research Report*, Gower, London, 1983.

Orr, F., *How to Succeed at Part-Time Study*, Allen & Unwin, Sydney, 1988.

—— *Study Skills for Successful Students*, Allen & Unwin, Sydney, 1992.

Taylor, Gordon, *The Student's Writing Guide for the Arts and Social Sciences*, Cambridge University Press, Cambridge, 1989.

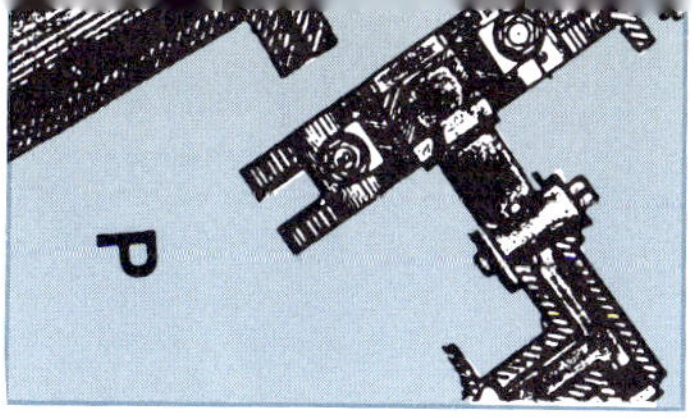

PART

IV

INTERPERSONAL SKILLS AND CLIENT RELATIONS

HOW TO NEGOTIATE TO WIN

Michael Hudson teaches people how to mediate disputes, how to deal with sensitive issues and how to conduct effective negotiations.

Australians once regarded handling clients, consulting with staff and negotiating with suppliers as the soft end of the business scale. The real stuff was thought to be making the products, transporting the goods, getting things done. Dealing with people came a very poor second.

Today, all that has changed. Most businesses recognise that the way they relate to the most important people that they have to deal with—their customers, their managers and employees, their financiers as well as their suppliers—are among the most critical factors that will determine their survival.

Skills of this kind have become so important that they have bred a new group of specialists who now make a living out of advising and training organisations in these fields.

One of these specialists is Michael Hudson of Sydney who is co-founder of Effective Negotiation Services, an international company which provides professional negotiation-based advice to the private and public sector.

'I'm hired by clients to assist in the management of negotiations or "how" the process is conducted, rather than advising on the content or "what" is covered,' he explains.

Formed in Sydney and Melbourne in 1979, the company licenses negotiation practitioners in countries such as Belgium, Canada, Germany, the United Kingdom, Hong Kong and Singapore. ENS courses and consulting techniques have been used in over thirty countries and are conducted in English, German, Spanish and Basic Chinese.

The company defines its philosophy in the following way: 'The future of individuals and their organisations depends less and less on the positional power of their champions and more and more on the influencing skills of their negotiators.'

ENS is involved in running workshops which teach and counsel in such areas as: intra-group dispute management, pre-negotiation rehearsal, how to mediate successfully and how to deal with sensitive issues.

'A lot of our training activities require the participants to get inside the other person's shoes, so if we're conducting a combined supervisor and union worker negotiation, the results can be extremely interesting.'

Though he prefers to sit in on negotiations from the outset, Hudson often receives calls to salvage talks which have become deadlocked. He concedes that this can be a difficult situation to rectify and delicate handling is needed.

'Breakdowns in discussions are often caused by failure to understand the other party, not only in terms of what they say, but what they don't say, and that can be disastrous. The hidden agendas are probably a large component of what's influenced their decision-making,' he says.

If discussions have reached the stalemate stage, Hudson says he might suggest a 'process intervention', a mechanism to relieve the stress or tension. This could often be a break or adjournment which serves as a cooling-off period.

He is especially interested in the way control is achieved in negotiation and gives examples of two approaches used to get the 'upper hand'.

First, he states that leverage might be gained by the actual material and the bearing it has on a decision. 'It may be a case of "My facts are right and yours are wrong," or "I've got the money and you don't," or "I've got the law on my side and you're on shaky legal ground,"' he says. Less skilled negotiators consider this is sufficient to achieve their point.

Second, and more important, he believes that more skilled negotiators have the ability to achieve process power. This can be the way a person establishes rapport with the other party, and the way he or she performs or undertakes the interaction which may include everything from body language to tactical manoeuvres hinting at incentives, threats or promises.

'For instance, a person might say: "If you work with me on this basis, then I can promise there'll be a big future for you." Whether that eventuates or not is another matter, but the other person would probably be attracted by the power of the picture painted. Some people are great at levels of puffery which may be close to untruths,' Hudson explains.

ENS literature also refers to the findings of modern research which suggests that managers and professionals they spend at least half their time negotiating. Given the amount of time they spend in discussions, the firm realises they have a natural tendency for them to want to compete and beat the other party (a win-lose approach), but it also understands and may advise them that working with the other side can produce an outcome of mutual benefit (a win-win approach).

Hudson likens the 'win at any cost' approach to divorce negotiations in which the pain of separation pushes husband and wife into a protracted battle. But he says the situation could be made less traumatic by a degree of consensus, co-operation and, perhaps, compromise.

After ten years of corporate experience in Australia, Canada and the United States and twenty years of consultancy work, Hudson's advice has been sought on hundreds of issues. He mentions a recent request for his help by an American company concerned with the implications of land-ownership rights on an island near Papua New Guinea. Hudson is also considering a proposal to go to Brunei where the government is looking at how to best conduct business ventures beyond oil.

'The great variance in cross-cultural differences makes it absolutely critical for negotiators to have knowledge of other societies and to know why people behave and react in different ways,' he says.

He refers to the Eastern need to safeguard a person's own reputation or self-esteem. He says it is interesting how this need is being used strategically by the Japanese in business.

'The Japanese negotiator might say they couldn't agree with a request because they would lose face if they were to accept the proposal. So the Australian or American would be led into thinking this philosophy is especially significant in an Asian context, without really thinking that the same applies to them,' explains Hudson.

In general terms, Hudson likes to think of the practice of negotiations as creatively offering options, rather than bullying or undermining the other party.

'If you want a child to take a bath, you might ask them it they would like it before or after dinner. The secret in negotiations is to offer people a sense of choice and a feeling that they're calling the shots, but always within the framework of your own options,' he states.

CHAPTER

11

CLIENT SERVICE AND RELATIONS

After studying this chapter, you will be able to:

- understand the basic principles involved in communicating with clientele
- send clear messages to others
- send non-verbal messages
- listen carefully
- handle inquiries
- handle complaints
- handle problems with difficult clients
- handle compliments

The most important group of people for any organisation, whether public or private sector, profit or non-profit, is its clientele. In some cases the clientele will be paying customers and, if you do not attract enough of them, the whole business will fold and you will be out of a job. In other cases, the clientele is virtually a captive audience, such as school students, and their numbers will not vary greatly whether the service is good, bad or indifferent. Nonetheless, everyone who is employed has a clientele of some kind and has an obligation to do the best job they can for them. We all have clients of some kind and we are all ultimately dependent upon them for our livelihood. Moreover, the basic principles of client service and client relations do not vary, no matter who the clientele is, as this chapter will demonstrate.

HOW TO COMMUNICATE WITH CLIENTS

The basis of relations with clients is actually the development of the kinds of communication practice that are advocated throughout this book. Good client relations start with good communication. Communications with clients are usually in three forms:

- written—letters, memos, signs, procedures manuals, checklists
- verbal—announcements, conversations, speeches
- non-verbal—gestures, body language, appearance, posture, facial expressions

In each of these forms, there are three ways you can improve the way you communicate with your clientele:

- make sure the message you send is clear
- listen carefully
- watch for non-verbal messages from your client

SENDING CLEAR MESSAGES

Communication does not flow straight from one person to another without interruptions. It passes through the filter of our attitudes and emotions and is interpreted in the context of our own experience. You might think you have given very clear instructions to a new client about how to fill out a certain set of forms. But the condition of being in a new environment is likely to generate its own anxieties and confusions. You might interpret the client's inability to complete the forms properly as a sign of stupidity, whereas it is really unfamiliarity. If you go on to treat the person as some kind of dimwit, you will only compound the problem. The factual content of a message is only part of the total communication. The way in which those facts are perceived and interpreted is equally important.

To ensure the message you send is clear, you first need to think about the person to whom you are talking. How are they likely to react to you? How much background information do they need? How much will they already know about the topic? You then need to determine exactly what it is you want to say. Identify the topic and stick to it. Whether you are writing or speaking, make the message as short as possible. If necessary, break it into digestible pieces and deliver one at a time.

SENDING ACTION MESSAGES

Often you will want a client to do something in response to your communication. You can do this in an officious authoritarian way which is almost guaranteed to make the client suspicious and to get him or her off side. Or you can try to express yourself in terms of the listener's point of view. If a change of policy was done partly to serve your client's interests, you cannot assume that the client will automatically see it that way. What is in the change for the client has to be explained at the same time as the new policy is announced.

LISTEN CAREFULLY

Good communication with clients also involves listening to them carefully. Hearing what they say is one thing, but listening to them is another. Listening requires effort. It involves paying attention all the way through, without interrupting. When the client has finished, you should ask questions to make sure you understand the point. If the issue is complicated, repeat or restate what the client has said to ensure you have got it right. In restaurants, for instance, it is normal practice for waiters to repeat an order to the customer who has just made it. Every service organisation should learn from this example.

NON-VERBAL MESSAGES

As well as listening to the words, it is just as important to listen to the feelings of a client. Feelings are most often expressed through non-verbal communication such as gestures and body language. For instance, the client who checks her watch is sending a very deliberate signal—she thinks you are taking too long. Acknowledge the point by letting her know you will serve her as soon as possible. People are often happy to wait as long as they know they are not being ignored. Non-verbal messages include:

- tone of voice
- speed of speech
- the way someone stands or sits
- expression on a face
- eye contact, or lack of it
- gestures and movements
- dress
- physical distance between people

Learn to use non-verbal communication and to respond to it in others.

HANDLING INQUIRIES

You can look upon inquiries made by clients either as annoyances or opportunities. When someone comes to you with an inquiry, he or she is handing you an opportunity to provide service and to create a good impression for your establishment. In some industries, an inquiry provides an ideal sales opportunity. You can respond to the inquiry by selling a product or service.

Many people fail to recognise the connection between casual inquirers and future clientele. If they are not already legitimate clients, or customers with cash in hand, it is easy to keep them waiting, put them on hold or sound annoyed. If you do this, you can be sure they will never bother you again, for most will take an instant dislike to your organisation. Inquirers should always be treated as potential clientele, either as customers who will spend money with your firm or as people whose needs you will be called upon to fulfil. When an inquirer approaches you, the proper way to respond is as follows:

- smile and offer to help
- ask questions to find out exactly what the inquirer wants
- try to make positive suggestions
- if you do not know the answer, find it out

HANDLING COMPLAINTS

The real test of client relations skills is the way you handle difficult situations. This is especially true when the problem is not your fault but has been caused by someone else. A complaint should be treated as an early warning sign, telling you that some aspect of your product or service has a problem. Never assume that someone who complains is a crank who does not have to be taken seriously. Treat a complaint as an opportunity to put things right. Always try to do so while the complainant is still on the premises. After they've left is usually too late.

Most people actually hate to complain. They will put up with a lot before they will say something. When they do complain, it might sometimes sound as if the matter is trivial but, more often than not, it is the result of an accumulation of small problems which have reached the point where the client is driven to action. The challenge is to resolve the problem on the spot and turn the complainant back into a client again. If you fail to do this, the complainant will never return and will bad mouth you to all his or her friends.

For most service organisations, good word-of-mouth is the best and most reliable source of clientele, and bad word-of-mouth will lose you clients. If you succeed in turning complainants back into clients, they will probably be impressed and tell others about how well their complaints were handled. Most people realise that all organisations are only human and will make mistakes or let their standards slip at times. By responding immediately to resolve a complaint, you actually prove that the problem itself is not one that normally occurs and can leave someone with a better feeling than if they had not had reason to complain at all.

Follow these step-by-step procedures when responding to a complaint.

- Watch for signs of discontent before they become explosions.
- Keep calm and listen.

- Thank the client for bringing the matter to your attention.
- Apologise.
- Never argue or disagree, even if the complainant is wrong.
- Ask questions and note the facts.
- Decide what to do and take action.
- Explain what you are doing and why.
- Make a record of the complaint and pass it on to those responsible.
- Follow up to ensure the matter was rectified.

Front office personnel are the interface between a hotel and its clientele and therefore must be able to handle problems, including difficult guests, in an efficient and friendly manner. Pictured is Mira Protruder, concierge at one of Sydney's best international hotels, the Park Hyatt at Circular Quay.

HANDLING PROBLEMS AND DIFFICULT CLIENTS

Some clients will approach you with a problem that is not a complaint but which is something important that they need your help to resolve. Dealing with a problem is similar to dealing with an inquiry, except that the situation is likely to be more urgent and to require greater sensitivity and initiative on your part.

Follow these step-by-step procedures.

- Ask questions to clarify the problem.
- Solve the problem yourself if you can.
- If you cannot solve it, try to find someone who can.
- Do not ignore or dismiss the problem.
- Do not blame the client. ('Didn't you read the instructions you were given?')
- Do not laugh, even if you think it's funny.

- Do not say 'It's not my job,' or 'We can't help you,' or 'We don't deal with that here.' If any of these is true, say that you know someone who can be of more help and help the client to find that person.

Every organisation comes across awkward clients who will try the patience of everyone on the staff. Respond in the following way.

- Smile and keep cool—do not take anything personally.
- Try to understand what is really bothering the client—some need nothing more than some attention.
- Try to respond as quickly as possible.
- If the customer is drunk or abusive, you will probably need to call on some help, either in the form of a colleague, which will normally change the client's attitude, or security, but only as a last resort.

HANDLING COMPLIMENTS

As well as learning how to deal with the difficult situations, you should also know how to handle the positive ones. If a client gives you a compliment you should respond in the following way.

- Smile and say thank you.
- Ask the customer to write a letter or complete a compliments form, if one exists.
- Find out exactly what the client appreciated.
- Pass the compliment on to the specific personnel or department.
- Keep a record of compliments received.

KEY POINTS: Chapter 11 Client service and relations

- Good relations with clients are based on good communications.
- Sending clear messages involves understanding things from the client's point of view.
- When you require action from clients, couch your request in positive terms that explain the client's interests.
- Listening to clients is vital for communicating. In complicated situations, repeat what they have told you to ensure you have got it right.
- Pay as much attention to non-verbal signals as to verbal ones.
- An inquiry from a non-client should be regarded as a chance to turn the inquirer into a client.
- Treat a complaint both as a signal that your establishment needs to lift its game and as an opportunity to win the complainant over by responding quickly and rectifying the situation.
- Treat a client with a problem not of your making in the same way as you would an inquirer.
- If you are given a compliment, thank the client and ask for more details.

QUESTIONS FOR DISCUSSION

How would you deal with the following situations?

1. You work for a hotel and a client from out of town asks what he should visit while in the city.

2. You work for a hospital, and someone asks if you know a good dentist.

3. You work in a restaurant and someone complains that the wine is not cold enough.

4. You work for a welfare agency and a client pushes in ahead of others and demands to be served first because she is in a hurry.

EXERCISES

1. What do the following non-verbal clues tell you about a client's state of mind?

   - tapping fingers on counter
   - glancing at watch
   - arms crossed over chest
   - chewing on fingernail
   - smiling
   - frowning
   - closed eyes
   - clenched teeth or mouth
   - staring
   - does not look at you

2. If you are employed, respond to the following:

   (a) Make a list of all the products or services your company provides for its clients, including anything that differentiates it from your competitors.

   (b) Make a list of the most common inquiries you receive in your place of work and the appropriate answers, or where to find the answers.

   (c) Make a list of the questions that you most dislike to be asked in your place of work. Provide answers to all of them.

   (d) Think of the most recent occasion when you made a complaint about something. Write down some good points and some bad points about the way your complaint was handled.

CHAPTER

12

INSTRUCTIONS AND REQUESTS

After studying this chapter, you will be able to:

- give clear face-to-face instructions to colleagues
- make successful verbal requests within an organisation
- respond to telephone inquiries in a professional manner
- make telephone inquiries of others

Apart from the personal greetings and conversations we use to establish and maintain good relations with the people we work with, the most common verbal communications within an organisation are instructions and requests. These are, in fact, the lifeblood of an organisation. Without them, most of us would not know what we should do nor when to do it. The pace of modern work is usually such that we do not have time to write down our instructions and requests. We tell people face-to-face or over the telephone. This type of communication is usually short and direct but is often done badly. Few of us take the time to think about the process. However, because this form of communicating is so central to our working lives, we should take it more seriously and try to improve our techniques.

The underlying principles of giving good instructions are the same as those for other forms of communication. You should try to put yourself in the position of the receiver and ask yourself how much knowledge of the subject he or she has and needs. You should also plan your message before you deliver it.

GIVING INSTRUCTIONS

The underlying principles of giving good instructions are the same as those for other forms of communication. You should try to put yourself in the position of the receiver and ask yourself how much knowledge of the subject he or she has and needs. You should also plan your message before you deliver it. However, because instructions are so crucial to the operation of an office or factory process or the functioning of an entire organisation, and because, if they are misunderstood, accidents or disasters can sometimes eventuate, they involve some special criteria of their own.

PREPARATIONS

These are as important as the instructions themselves.

1. Know or find out the background of the people concerned, especially their qualifications, level of skill and experience in the area to be instructed.
2. Formulate a plan for the instructions. This will involve dividing the process to be instructed into a series of small steps. Each step should be placed in its proper sequence, from start to finish.
3. In your plan, make a note to especially emphasise key points such as safety or quality issues.
4. Gather all materials and equipment relevant to the job, as well as any written or visual instruction material, and have them on hand when the instructions are to be given.
5. Find a site to give the instructions that is (a) near to the job to be performed, but (b) at a reasonable distance from any distractions such as noise which might prevent complete attention, and (c) make sure nothing will interrupt you during the instruction phase.

INSTRUCTION PROCEDURE

There are ten points to be observed.

1. Assemble the person or persons and put them at ease with a friendly or amusing comment.
2. Give a one or two sentence overview of the complete task to be instructed.

The most important points in giving instructions are:
- give a one or two sentence overview of the complete task
- describe its importance
- name all the materials and equipment to be used
- give a step-by-step description of procedures, accompanied by physical demonstrations
- describe all problems that will arise if the task is not done properly
- ask for questions and/or discussions
- ask instructees to perform the task while you watch

3. Describe its importance to the immediate task and the organisation as a whole.
4. Name all materials and equipment you will be discussing.
5. Give the instructions that you have prepared, step-by-step, with physical demonstrations where appropriate.
6. Describe all problems, accidents, losses of quality and the like that will emerge if the task is not done correctly.
7. Ask for questions of any points about which the listeners are not clear. Give plenty of time and encouragement for those who might be reluctant to come forward.
8. If necessary, repeat the instructions and demonstration.
9. Where appropriate, ask the people to perform the task in front of you. Correct any mistakes in a constructive rather than negative way.
10. Tell the people where they can get help if anything goes wrong.

HANDLING PROBLEMS

The most common problems in giving instructions are in giving too little information or too much. Anyone who has been doing a job for a long time finds it difficult to place themselves in the position of someone completely new to it. There are usually basic points you take for granted and which you assume everyone must know. This is why it is important to draw up your plan carefully, uncovering the key assumptions and principles of the process involved. It is especially important when dealing with people from other cultures. For this reason, you should also observe people handling the task at least once to ensure that nothing fundamental has been overlooked.

The opposite mistake is to give too much information. There are times when so much detail about a process is provided that the whole task becomes too much to learn at one sitting. There are two possible responses to this problem.

A common problem is in giving too little information: to avoid this, put yourself in the position of someone completely new to the field.

Equally common is giving too much information: to avoid this, eliminate all extraneous instruction apart from that needed to perform the task itself.

1. Break the task up into a number of components and give instructions on each at separate stages.
2. Eliminate all extraneous instruction. For instance, when teaching someone to drive a car or to use a word processor, they don't need to understand the principles of the internal combustion engine or of the microprocessor. Once they have mastered the initial task, it may be useful to go on to the inner workings of the process to improve their understanding and performance. But, at the start, concentrate on physical expertise alone to get the task up and running.

A third problem for which you should prepare will come from the nature of the people concerned. Some will be reluctant or slow learners; some might resent being instructed at all; others might have difficulties in understanding because of cultural or language problems. There are two ways to minimise problems of this kind.

1. In the preparation stage, find out as much as possible about the personal and occupational background of the people.

2. If this is not practical, add one more step to the instruction phase by getting them to describe their own background, especially that related to experience or aspirations for the job or task at hand. If there are a large number of people, this might mean going round the circle asking each to state their name and background. This might seem like wasting a little time but by making your instruction more effective it will be worth it.

MAKING REQUESTS

Making a request within an organisation is the verbal equivalent of writing a submission (discussed in Chapter Twenty-five). Similar principles govern each.

PLANNING AND DEFINING OBJECTIVES

Plan the request in your mind or on paper before you make it. The first thing to work out and the main point to keep in mind is the ultimate objective of the request. The objective actually has two components: what you want to achieve; and the means through which you hope to achieve it. For example:

> To get the enrolment forms completed on time by seconding two extra people from other departments to help with the photocopying.

Once the objectives have been defined, the principal tasks should be broken down step-by-step so that you are sure of two things: first, the complete process and all that needs to be done, and, second, that the request can actually be fulfilled or achieved, that is, that you are not asking for the impossible. You should also identify at this stage any major problems that may emerge or changes that will have to be made, in order to anticipate any objections others might make to the request.

THE REQUEST PHASE

There are two things to consider here: the structure of the request (what you will actually say), and the way you deliver the request. The structure of the request should have three components which you will have determined in the planning phase and which incorporate your objectives. In most cases, the structure will go like this:

1. the nature and dimensions of the issue or problem
2. current approaches to it
3. what you want to do about it

How to make a request:
1. Explain the nature and dimensions of the issue.
2. Describe current approaches towards it.
3. Say what you want done about it.

This is the same framework we recommend for submission writing.

The nature and dimensions of the issue should focus on causes and effects: why the issue or problem has arisen and the results, good and bad, that have emerged.

Current approaches to the issue should give a description of what is presently being done about the issue. If nothing is being done, make this clear at this point nonetheless.

What you want to do about the issue should be a statement of the objective you have formulated and your plan for action. In some cases, you might want to describe the plan for action in terms of a series of options: we could do this, alternatively we could do that, or again perhaps another thing. The options should each be feasible and, from among them, you should choose your own main priority and prepare reasons to support it.

If you take the trouble to formulate a request in the way we have described here, the question of the way to deliver it will partly resolve itself. A request should never be made in an obsequious or deferential manner. This is a sure recipe for a knock-back. The best way to deliver a request is through a firm statement of the issues described above. People respond to reasoned arguments rather than deference. Properly prepared, a request can be delivered with confidence. A confident tone is by far the most appropriate and the most likely to succeed.

COMMUNICATING BY TELEPHONE

Instructions and requests are very often delivered by telephone and there are some principles of telephone use that it is appropriate to describe at this stage. The points made here apply to all forms of telephone communication. Most of us use the telephone so often that we are not aware of any special needs. Well-prepared telephone communication, however, is so much more effective than the unprepared variety that a program of practice and training will be found useful by many people.

ANSWERING CALLS

Telephonists, or anyone answering the telephone for an organisation, should first give the name of the organisation.

No business telephone should be allowed to ring more than six times. If you do not have the staff to answer your calls this quickly, you need another telephonist. The caller normally asks to speak to an individual or an extension. The telephonist should repeat the extension number or name, to give the caller the opportunity to correct it if misheard. At the extension, the receiver should answer with the extension number or the department name, and then their own name.

No business telephone should be allowed to ring more than six times. If you do not have the staff to answer your calls this quickly, you need another telephonist.

Use a courteous but not deferential tone of voice, pitched low rather than high. At all costs, avoid the rising terminal (finishing a sentence by raising your voice pitch), even if you are asking a question. This is a signal of insecurity. Finish each sentence on a low pitch.

Good telephonists always record on a piece of paper the extension number requested and the connecting circuit number on which a caller is waiting for a busy extension. They also record details of staff movements so they know who is available at the desk and who is not.

Extension users should leave a notepad for messages when absent for short periods. They should tell a nearby colleague, or the telephonist, when they are likely to return and where they can be located.

One of the most overdone practices in answering calls is to ask who is calling before transferring a call. If you are in, but do not want to be interrupted, then apply this to all callers except obvious emergencies. Leave a message with the switchboard operator to get the name and number of all callers so you can call them back when it suits you. It is unnecessarily rude for a caller to be asked for his or her name and then, after enough time for the operator to check with you, to be told you are in a meeting or given some other excuse. It is much more courteous for the operator to tell all callers at the outset that you are not available and *then* ask each their name and number. This way, you are not insulting or making obvious discriminations between callers. If there are some special callers to whom you *do* want to speak, the telephonist can be informed and, after they have given their names, the telephonist can then inform them they will be put through.

MAKING CALLS

Extension users should make their own calls. The switchboard operator's efficiency is greatly reduced by requests to dial calls by extension users. This makes the operator's more important job of giving a proper response to incoming calls difficult and, at times, impossible.

Executives who regard their time as too valuable to spend calling up others should employ a secretary. If they or their firm cannot afford a secretary they should do their own dialling.

When making a call, you should start by giving your name (that is, your first and last names without any Mister or Miss as a prefix). Then make clear at once the reason for your call. Avoid any roundabout approach to the topic. State it directly at the outset. If there are important qualifying or secondary points, go straight on to make them. Then seek some response from the other party which will indicate which way the conversation is next likely to go.

Executives who regard their time as too valuable to spend calling up others should employ a secretary. If they or their firm cannot afford a secretary, they should do their own dialling.

To be able to do this smoothly often means you will have to plan your call before you make it. Think about or jot down notes about what you want to say and the essential points you need to cover. If you need to, tick each point off as you make it.

Because the telephone is a vocal medium only, we lose a great many of the signals that we add when talking face-to-face: gestures, movements, facial expressions, nods and the like. This makes it more important to ensure the receiver understands what you are saying. It is often necessary to repeat details or instructions. Do this in a courteous way by asking the receiver if you may repeat what you said.

Similarly, when the other person is talking, you should let him or her know you are listening and that you understand. For instance, when agreeing with someone, say 'Yes' down the phone at about the same frequency as you would nod your head if you were face-to-face. If you are receiving instructions or requests, repeat them to double check you have got the message right.

If you have to leave the line for a while to look something up, give the other party a rough idea how long you will take. If you find you need longer than this, keep the caller advised by returning to the phone to report how you are going. If the search takes a very long time, excuse yourself, take the other person's number and say you will call back immediately you have the required information. In other words, don't

The best overall rule is to telephone as you would be telephoned. Your telephone manner and voice reflect not only your own personality but your organisation's standards of courtesy and efficiency.

leave someone hanging on the line without knowing how long you will be or what has happened to you.

COMPLETING CALLS

The person terminating the call should observe the courtesy of ensuring that the conversation has been completed to the satisfaction of both parties. In other words, don't hang up if you feel the other party still has something to say. Wait until you both know you agree the conversation is over.

If you are accidentally cut off, it is up to the person who originally rang to re-establish the call. This is true irrespective of who was responsible for the cut off. If you both try to ring back at the same time, of course, all you will get is an engaged signal. The person who was called should hang up and await the recall.

The best overall rule is to telephone as you would be telephoned. Your telephone manner and voice reflects not only your own personality but your organisation's standards of courtesy and efficiency. It pays to put in the effort to train staff to handle the telephone properly.

KEY POINTS: Chapter 12 Instructions and requests

- Do not issue instructions without adequate preparation. Give the right amount of background, neither too little nor too much.
- Making a request is the verbal equivalent of writing a submission. Define objectives and formulate a plan for action. A confident tone is by far the most likely to succeed.
- No business telephone should be allowed to ring more than six times.
- When speaking on the telephone be courteous but not deferential. Don't forget to replace body language (like nodding agreement) with appropriate verbal cues.

QUESTIONS FOR DISCUSSION

1. When giving instructions, how can you know how much background knowledge people have of the issue concerned?
2. Why is it important to spell out your objectives before you make a request? What are the possible consequences of not doing this?
3. Discuss the rudest behaviour you have encountered from someone on the telephone. How should they have acted?

EXERCISES

1. Prepare a plan to give instructions on how to perform your present job, that is, to allow someone to take over as your successor.
2. If you are a student, plan to give instructions to someone on how to contact your educational institution, enrol in your classes and prepare the materials needed for the course.
3. In a group or classroom situation, have each member of the group instruct the rest on either Exercise 1 or 2 above. The participants should give an assessment on how successful they thought each instruction to be.
4. If you are employed, plan a request to your boss to either (a) employ an additional person to help you with your job, or (b) buy a new version of the piece of equipment you use most.
5. If you are a student, plan a request to do either (a) one less written assignment for your course, or (b) one more written assignment for your course.
6. In a group or classroom situation, have each member of the group make the request in either Exercise 4 or 5 above to another person. Have the group assess each request.
7. In light of the assessments, repeat Exercise 6 but this time via a simulated telephone call with you as the caller and another class member as the receiver.
8. From the classified advertising columns of your local newspaper, select a job you would like to apply for. Plan what you will say (using some of the guidelines for job application letters discussed in Chapter Sixteen) and simulate in the classroom a telephone call to the organisation to apply for the job. Other members of the class should assess your call..

CHAPTER

13

INTERVIEWS

After studying this chapter, you will be able to:

- be better prepared to be interviewed by others
- be better prepared to interview others
- make the most effective case for yourself at an interview
- interview others in ways that bring out their best

Interviews are one of the most important types of verbal communications in the careers of most people. Most of us are the subjects of interviews at the start of, and throughout, our careers. Many of us reach positions where we have to conduct interviews ourselves. A discussion of the interviewing process, therefore, should see it from both sides. This chapter describes the principal aspects from the perspectives of both interviewee and interviewer. In both cases, it should be emphasised, being effective means nothing more than implementing the basic techniques of good communication that underlie the other chapters of this book—listening to and working at understanding others, and sending clear and direct messages of your own. Like other forms of communication, interviewing is a skill that may be learned and practised, and the more of this you do the more successful will be the outcome.

PREPARATIONS

FOR INTERVIEWEES

The first part of preparing for an interview is actually securing it. In many cases, the interviewee is sent an invitation to attend but in some important instances, especially job interviews, actually getting the interview is half the battle. When applying for a job, through either a telephone call or a letter, place considerable emphasis on gaining the interview. Emphasise your availability at any suitable time and make sure the employer has at least one telephone number through which you can be contacted quickly.

Once you have an appointment, double check the time, the date and the place where the interview will take place. If it is to be in a building with which you are unfamiliar, find out the floor number and the name or number of the room.

When arranging the appointment, take the opportunity to discuss the interview with your contact. The three main points to discover are:

1. the objective of the interview
2. the amount of time it will take
3. the number of people doing the interviewing and, if possible, their names

If you don't already know it, finding out the objective of the interview will help in researching the subject and in preparing answers. The amount of time allocated to an interview is an important piece of information because it allows you to prepare appropriate answers—either short and punchy in a brief interview, or more discursive and explanatory in a longer one. It is a good idea to know the number of people who will do the interviewing—it can be an unnerving experience to find yourself facing a panel when you expected an individual. If you know the names of the interviewers, you have the opportunity to find out some background on them. It is easier to talk to people when you know something about them. Sometimes you might also be able to anticipate the line of questioning they would be likely to follow.

The three main points to discover are:
1. the objective of the interview
2. the amount of time it will take
3. the number of people doing the interviewing and, if possible, their names

Depending on the subject matter, you should be able to prepare answers to a range of questions. Don't make the imagined questions and answers too precise because, if you do, you are likely to be thrown if you don't get the exact wording on the day. Rather, work on broad subject areas likely to come up and try to articulate to yourself your views on them.

FOR INTERVIEWERS

Those conducting an interview should agree on the kind of information they want to gain and on the goals they hope to reach by the end of the interview session. Once these objectives have been established, they can then formulate specific questions.

The main point that the interviewer or interviewing panel must have clear from the outset is the objective or objectives of the interview. They should agree on the kind of information they want to gain and on the goals they hope to reach by the end of the interview session. Once these objectives have been established, they can then formulate specific questions. In some cases the questions will be direct, aiming at specific information, but in others they will be more explorative and designed to bring out the attitudes or personality of the interviewee. In all cases, questions should be clear, unambiguous and free of jargon and obscurities. There is little point in asking for one kind of information if the interviewee interprets you as seeking another kind. This is confusing for both sides. This is why questions should be formulated and discussed beforehand.

The nature of the interview and the questions to be asked should be the main factors in determining the amount of time allocated. It is usually valuable to provide a certain length of time and keep to it. Interviewees should be told the length of the interview at the outset.

The location of the interview is an important consideration. The surroundings should reflect the character of the organisation and the nature of the interview—relaxed or imposing, as the case may be. Most interviews are private affairs so the premises should be able to guarantee confidentiality by being reasonably soundproof. There should be a minimum of distraction from people and noises nearby and the interview should be free from interruptions.

Interviewers should also do some background research on the interviewee. In job applications, candidates provide this background themselves but in other types of interviews it is usually necessary to search out information. It is not unknown for an interviewer to get such basic facts as the person's name wrong. So each interviewer needs to create a small dossier on the person concerned containing, at a minimum, basic personal information, plus other data relevant to the purpose at hand.

CONDUCT OF INTERVIEWS

GUIDELINES FOR INTERVIEWEES

Body language and other forms of non-verbal communication are important elements in the way an interviewee performs. Most advice tells you to appear relaxed and act naturally, but this is usually easier said than done. Good appearance is mostly a matter of avoiding some bad and unsettling habits. You should sit up straight with a slight forward lean. This will make you appear interested, in contrast to a far backward lean which appears too casual, or a hunched forward pose which appears nervous. Place both feet on the floor and keep them there. You may cross your legs at the ankles but don't sling one leg across the other thigh or knee—again this looks as though you are not serious. For most of the interview your hands should be on the table, lightly clasped. This will stop you from such awkward and nervous mannerisms as putting your hand in front of your mouth or scratching yourself. Don't play with or pick at anything, especially hair, nails or items of clothing. Never smoke at an interview, even if invited; it looks ungainly and always puts off non-smokers.

Try and use a natural tone of voice. Don't try to speak in a way that does not come naturally to you—it will always be detected. Be conscious of the loudness and pitch of your voice and try to make both appropriate for the environment and the distance between you and the interviewer(s). Avoid being too loud, too soft or too shrill. Don't speak too quickly. Again, this makes you sound nervous.

It is important to maintain good eye contact with the interviewer or panel. You maintain their interest in you and show your interest in them. Good eye contact helps establish character and promotes confidence.

In answering questions, you should be direct and frank. Being direct means:
1. answering the question and not skirting around or avoiding it
2. talking in plain language without using jargon or obscure terminology

In answering questions, you should be direct and frank. Being direct means, first, answering the question and not skirting around or avoiding it, and, second, talking in plain language without using jargon or obscure terminology. Where interviewers ask deliberate questions, they are listening for certain kinds of answers. If you evade the issue or use jargon to cloak your inability to answer, this will always be recognised for what it is. Being frank is a matter of being straightforward and honest. Again, evasions, half-truths and omissions will be detected more by interviewers than the interviewee realises. In an interview, because you are the focus of attention, you become more transparent than you normally are and if you start being less than straightforward, it usually shows.

Another important point about answering questions is to make sure you have understood the question. Don't be concerned about telling interviewers that you are not certain what they mean and asking them to repeat some questions. They may not have formulated the question in a clear way so you are entitled to ask for a re-phrasing. If you answer without being sure what the question means you will look much worse than if you had asked for an explanation.

Usually at the end of the interview, the interviewee will be asked if he or she has some questions. Be definite at this stage. If you have no questions simply answer 'No'. In some circumstances you will have formulated some questions before you arrived so, at this stage, ask them in a direct manner. Don't ask questions simply for the sake of it, especially if all you have are obvious and/or lame queries. Whichever way you respond, do it with confidence because this is the close of the interview and this discussion will create impressions that last.

GUIDELINES FOR INTERVIEWERS

Whatever the purpose of the interview, those conducting it should observe some basic rules. The main one is to recognise how vulnerable the interviewee feels and to act in a way that brings out his or her best. The most effective way of doing this is to show a real interest in the interviewee and

A relaxed appearance, good eye contact and a direct and honest approach are all important elements in an interview

Interviewers should recognise how vulnerable the interviewee feels and act in a way that brings out his or her best. The most effective way of doing this is to show a real interest in the interviewee and the subject matter. This is done mainly by formulating relevant questions in a clear way and expressing them directly to interviewees.

the subject matter. This is done mainly by formulating relevant questions in a clear way and expressing them directly to interviewees. All non-verbal communications—such as the way the interviewer(s) appear, sit and gesture—should be positive and comfortable, without being too casual.

The timing of the interview should show consideration. All interviews should start on time, even if there are several to conduct within a given period and even if some that might profitably take longer have to be cut back. It is also unnerving for interviews to be either too short or too long. For instance, to conduct a fifteen minute interview on subject matter that would be better handled in forty-five or sixty minutes is not an effective way to proceed. Similarly, an overlong interview can be extremely wearing for the interviewee. In an interviewing panel, individual members may not feel this pressure to anything like the extent that the interviewee does because they are not the centre of attention and they are not called upon to respond to every issue. The length of time scheduled for the interview should take the interviewee's position fully into account.

Distractions and interruptions should be minimal, as noted earlier. Interviewers should make themselves unavailable to anyone else at the time. This rule should be more strictly adhered to than in the case of meetings where people are often willing to be interrupted for an important call. The momentum of an interview is an important factor in establishing relationships and in drawing out the information and attitudes of the interviewee. This can be lost by an unnecessary interruption.

Questions, as noted earlier, should be clear and direct. If an interviewee asks for clarification of a question this should be done willingly. It is most likely due to a genuine difficulty in the expression of the question.

Note-taking is necessary in some interviews but it should be avoided where possible. The relationship between interviewer and interviewee is distracted when one has to take notes. Tape recorders—the small, portable variety—are better because they allow the questions and answers to flow more readily. However, some people freeze at the sight of a tape recorder. The use of recording devices should be carefully considered in light of the nature of the interview and the response of the interviewee. Generally, the best time to make notes is immediately after the interview has concluded and the interviewee has left the room. The points made are still fresh in the minds of interviewers and any chance of distraction has passed.

Finally, the interview should be closed effectively. If it is appropriate, summarise and review the information presented to ensure both sides agree what has been discussed and that nothing major has been omitted. Ask the interviewee if there are any questions that he or she has. After responding to these, thank the person for attending and give a firm statement about any follow up that will be made.

KEY POINTS: Chapter 13 Interviews

- Interviews are perhaps the most important verbal communications of peoples' careers.
- Avoid negative body language. Sit up straight and lean forward slightly. This will make you appear interested. Don't play, pick or scratch.
- When conducting an interview make allowances for the vulnerability of the interviewee. Try to bring out his or her best. Questions should be clear and direct and distractions kept down to a minimum.
- If you are given a job interview, do some background research on the organisation and industry. This will give you confidence.
- Certain questions are asked frequently. Be prepared to discuss your qualifications, experience and reasons for applying, your career objectives and your approach to crisis management.
- If you are in charge of recruiting, remember it is only fair to inform unsuccessful candidates promptly.

QUESTIONS FOR DISCUSSION

1. Why should an interviewee try to find out the backgrounds and number of people conducting the interview? What might happen if he or she does not find this out?
2. Why should those conducting an interview agree beforehand on what they will ask?
3. How should an interviewee respond if asked a question that might be embarrassing? Why?
4. What are the basic rules that interviewers should observe?

EXERCISES

Interviews are an ideal situation for role play exercises involving from five to eight people. Three or four of the group should constitute the panel members for an interview. The others, from two to four people, should be the interviewees.

Appraisal interviews are probably the most useful kind for this exercise since the interviewees can respond realistically about themselves. Make the exercise an appraisal of how interviewees have progressed in either the course they are undertaking or the job they are currently performing. Each member of the panel should have a specialist area about which questions should be asked.

After each interview, each panel member should fill out an evaluation sheet on each candidate. The evaluation should be related to how well each person answered the specific questions and should also have space for general comments on attitude and presentation. Each space in the evaluation sheet should have room for both comments and a score. Interviewees should have their overall score totalled from the evaluation sheets. Both comments and scores should be made available to the candidates.

After this exercise is complete, the roles can be reversed. The former candidates now become the interviewers and the members of the former panel become the interviewees.

CHAPTER

14

CONSULTING, LISTENING AND NEGOTIATING

After studying this chapter, you will be able to:

- consult with others in an organisation
- reach a decision based on consultation
- set up permanent consultative mechanisms
- listen critically to what others say
- negotiate with others in an organisation
- reach a decision based on negotiation

In the organisations of the 1990s, where the authoritarian management practices of the past are waning, interpersonal skills are assuming a new importance. People no longer respond to heavy-handed approaches. Partly as a result, there has been a noticeable growth in courses to teach interpersonal skills to people in administrative positions. Some of these involve learning the latest fashionable human relations techniques such as 'transactional analysis' and 'conflict resolution'. Underneath all such techniques, however, lie some basic principles about the way human beings relate to one another which have not changed much over the centuries.

Fundamental to interpersonal skills is the ability to put yourself in the other person's position and to see a situation from their point of view. Learning how to consult, to listen and to interpret other people's needs are among the most valuable skills that any of us can learn.

Understanding another person's point of view does not necessarily mean you have to agree with it. Often you will have your own perspectives and interests to pursue, and these may have to modify or override those of others. In these cases, the process involved becomes one of negotiation where the various interests involved are bargained and traded. This chapter is a discussion of the two central skills of interpersonal relations—consulting and negotiating.

CONSULTING

Consultation is not a process of joint decision-making. Once the views of all have been heard, only those with the authority take the decision.

Consulting others within an organisation on a subject is a means of using all the information and experience available to come to a decision. It is also a means of involving the members of the organisation in the decisions that affect them. Consultation is not, however, a process of joint decision-making nor an abrogation of responsibility by the person doing the consulting. Once all the views have been heard, a decision has to be made by the individual or group with the authority to do so.

Consulting can be a process undertaken to inform a single decision on a specific issue, or it can be a mechanism set in place through which a range of issues are discussed on a regular basis.

CONSULTING ON A SPECIFIC ISSUE

Consulting with small groups involves:
- personal interviews
- small group meetings

Consulting with larger numbers involves:
- publicity on the issue
- meetings with major interest groups
- invitations for written submissions

Consulting on an issue involves discussing it with those who have a concern or an interest. Where the number of people involved is small, consultation can take the form of a series of personal interviews or meetings.

Where the numbers are large, however, some more formal procedures need to be set up. There are three aspects to these procedures.

1. The issue needs to be publicised widely so that all concerned will be informed that consultations are being made. The publicity needs to be wide, rather than directed at those you know are interested, because often there are groups who you might not have considered who believe they have an interest in the matter. If there are already firm proposals on the issue (such as plans drawn for a new layout or building, or a range of options for change defined) these should be included as part of the publicity.

2. There should be meetings with the major interest groups. This involves, first, identifying who these groups are in relation to the issue at hand, and second, contacting the representatives of the groups. If a group is large, it is only feasible to meet with its representatives. Sometimes these will be people formally elected to designated positions; with less clearly defined groups who lack formal structures, you may have to contact people who seem to you to be representative of the group. Obviously, the latter course can be a sensitive issue and it is important to ensure that those you contact are genuinely representative types.
3. As part of publicising the consultative process, you should invite written submissions from anyone who wants to make them. It is better to allow people to express themselves in their own words rather than providing a questionnaire or form to be filled in. The latter approach restricts responses to what you think is important rather than taking into account what those being consulted think ought to be discussed. Give a deadline for written submissions that provides enough time for them to be written properly.

CREATING CONSULTATIVE MECHANISMS

A growing number of organisations are finding that a permanent system of consultation can be valuable for promoting harmony, resolving conflict before it arises and, overall, for developing a more effective environment. The general principles involved in establishing consultative mechanisms are as follows.

1. The management of the organisation needs to make a public commitment to consultative procedures.
2. Within commercial concerns, there should be company-wide management, employee and union steering committees to overlook consultation and participation.
3. There is a need for an organisation information sharing plan to be developed.
4. Representative committees should be set up to handle ongoing negotiations for change in those areas that are defined as the most important in terms of their effects on the organisation and the people involved in it.

Most of the work in consulting others on either specific issues or on a regular basis will involve face-to-face discussions. Since the main objective of the exercise is to be able to see the other person's point of view, one of the most important skills to bring to the process is that of listening to what others have to say. Many people assume listening is a straightforward matter but, as the following sections discuss, it is a skill in which most of us have room for improvement.

LISTENING CRITICALLY

Listening is a dual process. On the one hand, the good listener is open-minded to the points he or she is hearing. On the other hand, good listening is not a passive activity in which you accept everything you are told.

You need to be both open and critical, to make an active engagement with the mind of the speaker.

Staying open-minded is often difficult but it is necessary. At any time in a discussion a point might be made, or one might occur to you, that you will find valuable. So being open-minded is an essential part of being a good listener. It is often difficult to listen to viewpoints with which you disagree, or which you have heard plenty of times before. It is easy to develop the tendency to mentally shut out the speaker, to pretend to be listening but really be spending your time composing your reply and waiting for a chance to interrupt. Being open-minded means you suspend your own case for the time being. You wait until the speaker has made his or her point fully. The act of mentally arguing with a speaker, and concentrating not on the speaker's message but on the best opportunity to interrupt, is one of the main reasons many people never really hear what others have to say. The act of listening properly will leave you with the ability to repeat the message to the speaker's satisfaction. If you develop this practice you will not only be listening better but be in a stronger position to agree or disagree if you want to.

Being open-minded means you suspend your own case for the time being. You wait until the speaker has made his or her point fully.

It is also a good practice to prevent yourself from jumping to conclusions. Often when listening, we prejudge a message by thinking we know what is coming from the appearance or the personality of the speaker. At other times we hear the first part of a message and assume how it will conclude. Good listening involves delaying judgment. Try to make yourself avoid the tendency to make up your mind too early. Rushing to judgment is rarely a profitable way to listen to someone.

However, suspending or delaying judgment does not mean that you put off making up your mind indefinitely. On the contrary, the good listener will always go on to judge and assess the assumptions, evidence, argument and logic that is put across. While there are many people who make judgments too quickly there are many more who remain passive, spoon-fed listeners who believe whatever they hear. The best listeners go through a process that involves:

- delaying judgment about the personal characteristics of the speaker
- waiting until the speaker has fully elaborated the message
- determining what are the main points of a message (saying them either to himself or aloud)
- assessing whether these points are supported by the evidence in a logical way
- finally, making a judgment whether to accept all, part or none of the overall message

Listening is not only a process of passing judgments on the opinions of others, it is also one in which new messages confront our own biases and assumptions. We should be as open to ourselves as we are to others. To listen well we need to recognise our own value judgments so that they don't blind us to new and different information. We are always in danger of tuning out those messages that don't fit our preconceptions. We usually prefer information that comes from certain sources, or certain types of people or which are couched in certain types of phraseology. We should try to be as aware as possible of these biases so that they don't lead us to reject messages from which we might genuinely learn something. Everyone has their own biases and, while it is probably impossible to examine them all, we need to be actively alert to what they are. There are many people in society, especially in politics, advertising and the media, who have become very powerful by telling us what we want to hear. If we are not to be easily led, we need to remain constantly aware of our own biases and prejudices so that we hear everything that is being said, and not simply what we would like to hear. Good listening is an essential part of being an active and alert citizen of a modern society.

Good listening practice involves:

- delaying judgment about the speaker's personal character
- waiting until the speaker has fully elaborated the case
- determining the main points
- assessing whether the main points are supported by evidence
- making a judgment on the whole or part

LISTENER FEEDBACK

One of the important roles of a listener is to give some response to the speaker so, whatever judgments are being made, the speaker knows he or she is being heard and understood. Responses can also convey the information that listeners are interested in what is being said and would like the speaker to continue. There are four basic kinds of listener feedback:

- an attentive look at the speaker, with eyes alert and an expectant facial expression
- nodding the head in agreement from time to time
- brief remarks of acknowledgment such as 'I see', 'Really', 'Very interesting', 'Hm mm'
- summarising the case just put ('You think that…') or repeating the last few words that have been said

Most listener feedback is designed to be encouraging rather than discouraging and lets the speaker know you have a positive response of some kind. When you want to provide negative feedback you should be more cautious. Interruptions should be avoided even when you disagree with the speaker. Remember that listening is not debating. You are not there to defeat the speaker. It is best to give speakers the benefit of the doubt when they pause. Avoid the temptation to use a pause as an opportunity to jump in with your own opinion. Try not to interrupt, even during a long pause. When you think the message is complete, leave a little time before responding.

You will also want to make some kinds of feedback to indicate that you might have missed something or that you are unclear or unconvinced about a point. If you don't understand something and you want some more explanation, use a reflecting phrase such as 'You think that...', 'You said...', 'You mentioned...'. A reflecting phrase can give you a second chance to pick up a point you missed, to ask for additional evidence or to test the logic of the speaker. Sometimes you will want the speaker to comment on a point that he or she has not made, especially a point that runs counter to the case being put. A reflecting phrase, put in question form, is also useful in this situation. You might ask 'What about...?' or 'What do you think about Person X's claim that...?' or 'Don't you think that...?' If politely done, this is a perfectly legitimate form of feedback that may actually assist

A reflecting phrase can give you a second chance to pick up a point you missed, to ask for additional evidence or to test the logic of the speaker.

the speaker to present his or her case in a better way and to clear up any misunderstandings.

NEGOTIATING

Like consulting, negotiating is a procedure aimed at reaching a decision on an issue. It usually involves bargaining and trading by both sides and is often the scene of tension and conflict. It often carries considerable responsibility and a great deal can be won or lost through the personal interaction that occurs across the negotiating table.

The first principle any negotiator should establish is to gain authority to bargain on behalf of his or her side. A negotiator who cannot do a deal on the spot, but who has to refer everything back to a higher authority or management, is not really negotiating at all.

The first principle any negotiator should establish is to gain authority to bargain on behalf of his or her side. 'Authority' here means, of course, that there are limits beyond which a negotiator cannot go on behalf of an organisation. But within these limits, the negotiator needs free rein and the ability to make his or her own bargain. A negotiator who cannot do a deal on the spot, but who has to refer everything back to a higher authority or management, is not really negotiating at all. It is the higher management that is negotiating through a front, which is generally an unsatisfactory way to proceed for all parties. It leaves room for the other side to go over the negotiator's head and thus develop a divide-and-conquer strategy.

If you are in a situation where the other side does not have real authority to take its own decisions, you should call off the negotiation and insist on talking to the person who makes the real decisions.

Negotiations can be conducted by one person per side or by several per side. Having more than one person can be helpful to reinforce morale and

In negotiations, a written agenda gives all those involved a clear idea of what will be discussed. Often a number of people participate, to offer support or a different slant on a particular situation

provide different perspectives, but too many can lead to confusion and division. In a situation that calls for more than one person, two or three, but no more, is desirable.

You should establish from the start whether you intend to negotiate a piece-by-piece agreement or whether there will be no agreement in part until the whole deal is settled. Generally, the latter approach gives you a more flexible hand at all stages.

It is also advisable to agree to put all agreements in writing. Understandings that are not spelled out are likely to lead to misunderstandings in the future and to render the negotiating procedure void.

Once the negotiations have begun, the first item up for discussion should be the agenda. It is advisable to have your own position on what you will discuss, and what you will not, carefully prepared and in writing. It is common practice in industrial relations for these documents to be exchanged in advance of the personal negotiations beginning.

The discipline of setting down your own proposals on paper should give you a clear idea of the realities of the situation. You will have a firmer idea of the outcome you want and what is realistically obtainable. If you have exchanged agendas in advance, you may have the opportunity to cost the other side's proposals. If you want to reject or modify these proposals you can put your case in a persuasive way by showing on paper exactly what they will cost you.

Have your own position on what you will discuss, and what you will not, carefully prepared and in writing.

ASSERTION AND AGGRESSION

Because you are bargaining face-to-face, personal relations that develop across a table become a significant factor in the outcome. The more you let your emotions take charge, the less valuable job you will do for your side. Inflammatory remarks or patronising attitudes are usually counterproductive. You are not at the negotiating table to assert any imagined superiority but to get a job done. There will often be the case where one or both sides will contain someone with a barely controllable aggressive temperament. You should avoid having such people on your side at all costs. If someone on the other side loses his or her temper, respond in a cool and controlled manner. Make it clear that you are negotiating on the basis of issues, not personalities and that you will not tolerate personal abuse. If the problem continues, you should break off negotiations until the other side sorts out the problem for itself.

A distinction to keep in mind in situations of conflict is that between assertion and aggression. Aggression is an attempt to force a position on another person and usually leaves them feeling angry, defensive or deflated. Assertion, on the other hand, is a way of acting forcefully without diminishing the other party and without attempting to deny the other side any influence in the outcome. Aggression is characterised by abusive language and derogatory comments and an attempt to win at all costs. Assertion tries to win over rather than defeat the other side. The assertive negotiator will often:

The more you let your emotions take charge, the less valuable job you will do for your side. Inflammatory remarks or patronising attitudes are counterproductive.

1. examine the situation from the other person's point of view, not to capitulate to it but to try to find common ground for bargaining

2. take the time to describe the relations between the parties that have emerged and to express the impact the other side's behaviour is having
3. detail the changes he or she feels are necessary and offer to negotiate on them
4. describe, in an objective and non-threatening way, the likely results if this change does not take place

Controlling negotiations includes communicating just what you are willing to give up.

Treat all demands with respect and reject those which are unacceptable with calm, rational reasoning. One of the greatest difficulties found in negotiating is deciding how to reject a proposal, knowing that you may have to accept it at a later stage. You also need to learn to say 'No' in a way that shows you mean it. Do not use your firmest tone of rejection on petty items. Surround your rejection of less important items with supporting information ('Wage rates in that section are already 10 per cent higher than the rest of the industry') and invite further discussion on items you are willing to give way on later ('Why should that be so? You will have to offer more evidence before we could accept'). Controlling negotiations includes communicating just what you are willing to give up.

CAUCUSING

One valuable tool of the negotiator is the caucus in which you take time off to have a private discussion with the members of your own team. It is important not to abuse the caucus process so that negotiations degenerate into a series of alternate position-takings instead of a real dialogue.

The time to caucus is:

- when things start moving too fast for you and you do not want to make a mistake on an important issue
- in response to a major initiative proposed by the other side

The time to caucus is:
- when things start moving too fast for you and you do not want to make a mistake on an important issue
- in response to a major initiative proposed by the other side

Caucusing implies that you are giving a proposal serious study, so do not use it lightly. A caucus also means that, when you reconvene with the other side, your side will take the initiative. Whether you decide to accept, reject or modify, the next move is up to you. Teams that caucus on every small point give the impression they are stalling, or that they don't have the confidence to settle right there at the table. They become defensive in fact as well as appearance and they let control of the negotiations pass to the other side.

TIMING

The pace of negotiations is another important determinant of their outcome. There are various tactics that can be adopted.

1. Begin slowly, spending hours on the most minor items and, usually, rejecting them all. This approach is often adopted by the ultra-cautious and more often than not ends up with a wild rush at the end when thoughtless concessions can be easily made by either side.
2. Alternatively, you can keep the pace brisk from the outset. If there are some items that are not of major significance, settle them immediately.

However, save the points on which you won't move, and those which you intend to use as levers to secure your own demands, until the end when they count.

3. Some negotiators like to use fatigue as a bargaining lever. By taking discussion late into the night, they try to make the other side make concessions out of exhaustion. This, however, is a two-way weapon. Sometimes the opponent can prove less subject to fatigue than the protagonist. It might make some people willing to change their minds but it can make others stubborn and immovable.
4. The best course is to limit bargaining time to normal business hours. Do not make the timing so inflexible, however, that you are compelled to break off just when you are on the verge of agreement on an important point.
5. Another useful timing tactic is to take an adjournment. Adjournments provide an opportunity for stepping back to refocus on a problem. If both parties are locked on a position, a night's sleep can often make it appear in a different light and can thus break the deadlock.

Overall, negotiations should be conducted on a professional basis. This means remaining objective, cool and well paced. This is the best way to maintain a good negotiating hand.

KEY POINTS: Chapter 14 Consulting, listening and negotiating

- Learning to consult, listen and interpret other people's needs are among the most valuable skills we can learn.
- Understanding another person's point of view does not mean you have to agree with it.
- Consultation means involving all members of a group or an organisation in the decisions that affect them.
- However, consultation doesn't mean consensus or democratic decision-making. After consulting, those with authority still take the decisions.
- When dealing with small groups, consult through meetings with all affected. When dealing with large numbers, invite submissions and meetings with major interest groups.
- Good listening is not a passive activity in which you accept everything you are told. You need to make an active engagement with the mind of the speaker, being open-minded but critical where necessary.
- Good listening involves waiting until the speaker has fully elaborated the case and then deciding what were the main points made.
- Negotiating involves bargaining and trading by both sides.
- A negotiator should always have the authority to bargain for his or her side within well defined limits.
- Always start a negotiation with an agenda that both sides accept.
- People who lose their temper or who want to assert their personal superiority always make bad negotiators.

QUESTIONS FOR DISCUSSION

1. Why is it important to take seriously the other person's point of view, even when you don't agree with it?

2. What are the advantages of creating a permanent consultative body within an organisation? What are the disadvantages?

3. Why should you, when listening to others, delay judgment about them and what they are saying?

4. Why is it valuable to provide feedback when you are listening to others?

5. What are the dangers of not having an agenda when negotiating?

EXERCISES

1. Choose a simple issue which needs reforming at either your place of education or employment. Set up a consultative process with all relevant persons to reach a solution.

2. Choose another simple issue which needs reforming at either your place of education or employment. Set in train a process of negotiation to reach a solution.

REVISION LIST FOR PART IV

INTERPERSONAL SKILLS AND CLIENT RELATIONS

- Effective communication is the key to interpersonal skills and client relations, perhaps more than in any other area.
- Client relations involves some sensitive communication skills—especially those involved in active listening and looking for non-verbal signals—as well as handling inquiries, making recommendations, handling complaints and taking compliments.
- Consulting, listening and interpreting others' needs are among the most valuable skills that can be learned. The processes of consultation and negotiation are both subtle and complex.
- A negotiator should always have the authority to bargain for his or her side within well defined limits.
- Always start a negotiation with an agenda that both sides accept.
- People who lose their temper or who want to assert their personal superiority always make bad negotiators.
- Instructions, requests and communication by telephone are integral parts of any work environment, and should be accorded the same care and attention as given to other tasks.
- Interviews can be the most important verbal communications of many people's careers. Technique can make or break an interview. It pays to be prepared.

PART IV
KEY TEXTS AND FURTHER READING

Albrecht, Karl and Zemke, Ron, *Service America!* Dow Jones-Irwin, Homewood, 1985.

Apps, Roy, *Customercraft: Keeping the Customers Satisfied*, Macmillan, London, 1989.

Bolton, Robert, *People Skills: How to Assert Yourself, Listen to Others, and Resolve Conflicts*, Simon & Schuster Australia, Sydney, 1987.

Cornelius, H. and Faire, S., *Everyone Can Win: How to Resolve Conflict*, Simon & Schuster Australia, Sydney, 1989.

Dooley, Cheryl, *Telephone Technique*, Simon & Schuster Australia, Sydney, 1993.

Fisher, R. and Ury, W., *Getting to Yes: Negotiating Agreement Without Giving In*, Hutchinson, London, 1981.

Francis, Dave, *Organisational Communication*, Gower, London, 1987.

Hunt, G. T. and Eadie, W. F., *Interviewing: A Communication Approach*, Holt, Rinehart and Winston, New York, 1987.

Japan Human Relations Association, *The Service Industry Idea Book: Employee Involvement in Retail and Office Improvement*, Productivity Press, Cambridge, 1990.

Johnson, D. W. and F. P., *Joining Together: Group Theory and Group Skills*, Prentice Hall, New York, 1982.

Lash, Linda M., *The Complete Guide to Customer Service*, John Wiley and Sons, New York, 1989.

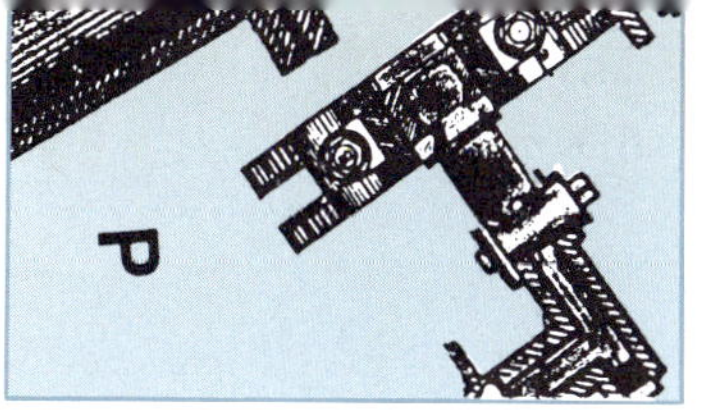

PART

V

EMPLOYMENT COMMUNICATIONS

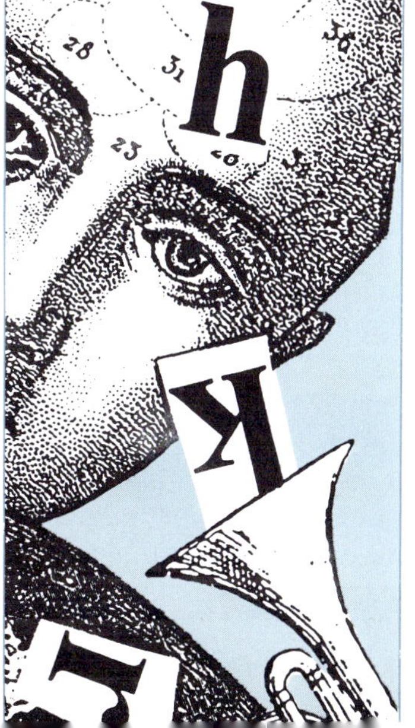

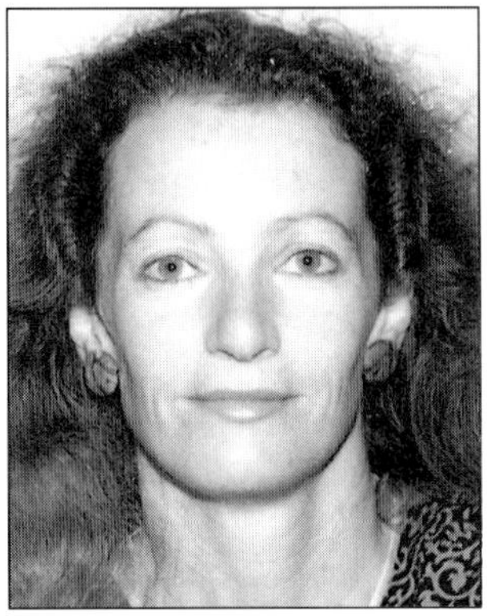

HOW EMPLOYERS CHOOSE THE PERSON FOR THE JOB

Human resources consultant, Marilyn Smith, tells how employers match job applicants to the positions available.

In today's competitive economic climate, even reaching the interview stage is a major feat for any job applicant. Then there is the test of performing well in order to impress a potential employer. But the employer is also faced with the challenging task of choosing the right person for the job.

Consequently, the importance of the job interview has taken on new dimensions for both parties in the area of employment communications.

Enter Marilyn Smith, a management consultant with Mentor Human Resource Group, in Sydney's Gordon. She specialises in the area of behavioural-based interviews. These are designed to work out the best applicants for particular jobs, through a series of planned questions targeting specific qualities, abilities and skills. The applicants' responses are then matched to the requirements of these jobs, so that a fair, correct and legitimate choice of employee can be made by the interviewer.

Smith teaches the method at three-day workshops attended by managers in the public and private sector. They work through several steps: reviewing the job and the competencies required, drawing up a list of questions to elicit the needed skills, evaluating the interviewees' responses, making a final decision on the successful applicant and allowing for feedback .

Smith explains that this process of 'targeted selection' has been popular in some Australian companies for fifteen years, but its advantages are only now being fully realised.

'This system has two basic premises: first, if you look at any job, you can define it in terms of the abilities expected of a person. You examine the job and the person to see how they fit. Second, this type of interview makes it easier for employers to justify that their decisions are based on fair concepts, at a time when equal employment opportunity is an important issue.'

While primarily training interviewers, Mentor Human Resource Group also works indirectly with people on community training programs who act as interviewees in simulated interviews. These exercises help the people on both sides to understand the pressures of obtaining a position and the responsibility of management to choose people well suited to a particular line of work.

Smith says she understands the stress of the unemployed, as well as the struggles of management when faced with re-structuring: demoting, promoting, retrenching or hiring new staff. Smith's own background has included fifteen years in the human resources field in the retail and manufacturing industries, where she was mainly responsible for recruiting decisions.

She feels that management today is trying to be more humane in its decision-making mechanisms and has welcomed the philosophies of behavioural-based interviews.

'Targeted Selection interviews work because the same questions are asked of all candidates in the running for a specific job. As a result, the interviewee can be assured that the same basis for analysis or evaluation is used and that the final decision is an objective one,' says Smith.

These special types of interviews operate on the principle that behaviour exhibited by people in their past job or life experiences is extremely important in determining how they will cope in similar circumstances in the future.

'For example, if an employer wants to measure decisiveness in a person, he or she may say: "This job requires spur-of-the-moment decisions. Can you tell me about some you've made in the past?" ' explains Smith.

The qualities or characteristics targeted will differ from job to job, but the most common are:

- the need for good oral and written communication
- customer-service proficiency
- the ability to analyse, judge and make decisions
- the capacity to cope with a certain level of stress
- 'motivation fit' (whether the job suits the applicant's nature or temperament)

In order to prepare as comprehensively as possible for an interview, Smith advises job-seekers to research the company and the job thoroughly. She emphasises that this preparation is crucial given that harsh economic times force employers to weed out non-starters from the outset.

She also agrees that people are the best assets available to a company or business and employers can't afford to make mistakes in their selection.

'It is important to talk to managers about their selection criteria before an interview, to know the exact demands of a job and its specifications,' she says.

Being familiar with the reasons the previous incumbent left or was fired might also be useful background knowledge, believes Smith. Talking to other people in the company can give a person insight into the qualities admired by the hierarchy, as well as the attitudes to avoid, she adds.

Smith says an applicant's self-esteem can also be boosted by mentally dwelling on the worthy things achieved in the past, such as coping well with a difficult situation or submitting some quality work on time.

'Go to an interview prepared to talk about what you've done in the past in specific terms and relate those examples with confidence,' she states.

Since an applicant can generally assume that some degree of 'targeted selection' will be used in an interview, Smith feels a positive frame of mind is vital.

'Communicating in a natural manner and being confident and credible are the most important issues, regardless of which side of the table you're on,' she declares.

CHAPTER

15

MAKING JOB APPLICATIONS

After studying this chapter, you will be able to:

- adopt a strategy to govern the search for employment
- write an effective job application letter
- spell out in detail your particular abilities

It is no secret that the employment market for many people today poses some enormous problems. Yet it is nonetheless true that the great majority who qualify through the education system and who go to seek employment do gain jobs. Unemployment is high but it is still only a minority of the tertiary qualified who cannot find work. What has changed for everyone, however, is that it now takes a great deal more time and effort to find a position.

The labour market today is much more competitive and everyone has been forced to become much more active, indeed more aggressive, in the search for employment.

What has also changed is the attitude towards job seeking that many people have been forced to adopt. Twenty years ago, few people did much more than scan the classified advertising section of the newspapers, register with an employment agency or, most commonly, inquire through friends about any positions they might know were available. Today, the labour market is much more competitive and everyone has been forced to become much more active, indeed more aggressive, in the search for employment.

In this environment, people who are unfamiliar with the process of looking for work—that is, those who have recently completed their education and are looking for their first job, or those who have not changed jobs for many years but who now need to do so, either because they have become unemployed or because they are looking for a career change—clearly need some advice. If you have access to a careers advisor, you would be well advised to take advantage of it. Many people, however, are not connected to institutions where such advice is available, so they are more dependent upon their own resources. If you are in this category, you need, first, to do some serious reading on the subject and, second, to develop some skills in job applications. The best reading we can recommend is published in America but is widely available in Australian bookshops and contains a wealth of advice and information which is applicable anywhere. This is *What Color is Your Parachute?* by Richard Nelson Bolles. The book is published in an updated edition each year and has been on the American best-selling lists since it first appeared in 1972.

You don't just apply for employment, you need to conduct a campaign to get a job.

Bolles advises his readers to adopt the attitude that you don't just apply for employment, you need to conduct a *campaign* to get a job. The campaign he advises is divided into ten strategies which are:

1. At the start of the campaign, you have to mentally prepare yourself to contact up to 200 employers, if necessary, in person.
2. You need to spend between twenty and thirty hours a week on your job hunt.
3. You need to decide where you would like to work and then visit these places to talk to employers, the people who have the power to hire you. Confining yourself to sending letters and résumés, or to talking to officers of the personnel department, is not enough.
4. Most of the search should be directed at small companies, with twenty or fewer employees, rather than the large organisations whom everyone else thinks of first.
5. You should visit a minimum of two employers a day.
6. You can also make use of relatives and friends. Tell at least thirty-five of these what kind of job you are looking for.

7. Don't think solely in terms of one kind of job. Think of what else you can do and would enjoy doing, and develop an alternative job plan.
8. Visit the careers advisor or job placement office of your old high school, college or university.
9. Don't confine the search to one type of organisation or one type of place. Develop an alternative employer plan.
10. Use many different avenues for job hunting. Don't confine yourself to looking in the newspapers, visiting local employment agencies, or sending out résumés. Be creative in developing alternative job seeking approaches.

Use many different avenues for job hunting. Don't confine yourself to looking in the newspapers, visiting local employment agencies, or sending out résumés. Be creative in developing alternative job seeking approaches.

JOB APPLICATION LETTERS

Before many employers will give you an interview, they want to see a written application for employment. One of the main skills anyone should develop is learning to write an effective job application that presents your abilities and qualifications in the best possible light.

A written application for a job should contain at least two things: a letter applying for the job and a personal résumé which summarises your qualifications and experience.

In this section we will discuss the letter first (and the résumé in Chapter Seventeen) but, in practice, you should prepare your personal résumé first and then write the letter based on its details. The résumé makes you evaluate yourself in relation to the job. You are then in a good position to write the letter.

The prospective employer, however, reads the other way around. If the employer is impressed after reading the letter, then he or she will move on to look at the résumé. After that, you might get a call to come in for a personal interview. It is crucial, therefore, that your letter does the job you want it to.

If the employer is impressed after reading the letter, then he or she will move on to look at the résumé. After that, you might get a call to come in for a personal interview. It is crucial, therefore, that your letter does the job you want it to.

It needs to do two things. First, it should demonstrate that you are a good candidate for the job and deserve an interview. Second, it should look professional and make a good impression for you. It should be expressed in a clear, concise and convincing language and should appear neat and tidy. Its spelling should all be correct. It should be laid out like a good business letter, with generous white space and no sense of being cramped. Early in a person's career, job application letters should fit onto one A4 page. They should always be produced on a good quality typewriter or computer printer. If you cannot type or haven't got access to at least a good electric typewriter, then pay a secretarial service to type both your application letter and your résumé. There are six criteria your letter should fulfil.

1. It should name the position you are applying for.
2. It should state where you saw the advertisement or how you heard of the job.
3. It should say why you are applying for the job.
4. It should pick out the main points from your résumé that are relevant to the position.

5. It should say why your qualifications make you a good candidate for the job.
6. It should tell the reader where to contact you and when you would be available for a personal interview.

First, try to put yourself in the position of the employer. Would this letter make you put yourself on the short list for the job?
Second, have you fulfilled all the details required by the job advertisement?

Once you have drafted the letter, read it critically with two aims in mind. First, try to put yourself in the position of the employer. Would this letter make you put yourself on the short list for the job? Does it show you are interested in the position? How do you come across personally—arrogant, modest, aggressive, confident? Second, have you fulfilled all the details required by the advertisement? Will the application be submitted well within the deadline set? Have you mentioned that you have all or most of the qualities the advertisement is seeking? Is there any other information sought by the advertisement that you have neglected?

Some large organisations, especially government departments, ask you to fill in an application form. Do this, but then go ahead and write your letter and résumé as if the form did not exist. Then submit all three as your application.

IMPORTANT DETAILS

In the top right-hand corner, type your name, address and telephone number(s). Also type your name at the end of the letter after your closing and signature.

Be specific about your abilities and experience. Do not use generalisations. For example:

Skills

Weak: I have learnt typing, shorthand and word processing.

Strong: As my enclosed certificate shows, I can type at 40 words per minute with 98 per cent accuracy.
I take shorthand at 75 words per minute.
I can write and print stories on a computer using Microsoft Word or WordPerfect. Because I know how to use two systems, I can pick up any other word processor quickly.

Experience

Weak: I was in the air cadets at school.

Strong: At Davidson High School, I was a member of the Air Training Corps for four years and gained the rank of trainee commander. I learned the controls of the cockpit in a Beechcraft simulator. I also understand the basics of air defence strategy and the particular tactics used in the Falklands War.

Weak: I have had work experience at a magazine and a radio station.

Strong: As part of my work experience, I spent one week with Cumberland Press. This involved accompanying staff reporters on visits to:

- Parramatta Courthouse
- Blacktown Police Station
- Fairfield City Council meetings

I spent two days on the subeditors' table and was given three stories to subedit.

My work experience in radio comprised four days at 2SER-FM's Sydney studios. I did background research for stories that staff reporters used on 2SER's hourly news bulletins. These stories were:

- interview with Dr John McBride over scientific controversy
- investigation of Sydney housing prices
- personality background of author Paul Theroux

Interests

Weak: My hobbies are football, tennis and bushwalking.

Strong: I am active in three sports:

1. Rugby Union: I was a member of the grade rugby team at Davidson High from 1984–87 and now play for Briars Club, Burwood.
2. Tennis: I have played tennis socially for the past eight years.
3. Bushwalking: I am a member of the Friends of the National Parks Society and am an active bushwalker. I have walked the following parks:
   - Barrington Tops
   - Lower and Upper Blue Mountains
   - Colligo Wilderness
   - Frenchman's Cap, Tasmania

KEY POINTS: Chapter 15 Making job applications

- The employment market might be difficult for many people today, but the great majority still gain jobs.
- You need to see your job search as a matter of conducting a campaign. There are at least ten strategies that this campaign can adopt.
- A written application for a job should contain both a letter of application and a résumé.
- An application should do two things for you: it should demonstrate that you are a good candidate for the job and deserve an interview; it should look professional and make a good impression.
- Many young people describe their background in vague terms that sell themselves short. Be specific and give concrete details.

QUESTIONS FOR DISCUSSION

- In what ways has the climate for gaining employment changed in the last twenty years?
- What are the three types of alternative plans that Richard Bolles advises you to adopt when job searching? Why would he recommend this?
- What are the two main things a letter applying for employment needs to accomplish?
- Why is it important to be specific about your abilities and experience?

EXERCISES

1. From the classified pages of your local newspaper, select two advertisements for jobs for which you are fairly well qualified. Write a letter of application for each job.
2. Select another two advertisements for jobs for which you have some, but not all, the qualifications. Write a letter of application for each job, emphasising your strengths.
3. Write unsolicited letters to two organisations applying for two different jobs that you would really like. Be realistic and choose jobs that you would have some chance of gaining.

CHAPTER

16

EMPLOYMENT INTERVIEWS

After studying this chapter, you will be able to:

- undertake preparations for an interview for a job
- know the likely questions that employers ask in interviews
- know how best to reply to employer questions
- know what questions to ask an employer yourself
- see a job interview from the employer's point of view

EMPLOYMENT INTERVIEWS

APPLICANTS' PERSPECTIVES

When an employer decides to recruit someone for a job, the normal procedure is to compile a short list of about four to six people who will be personally interviewed. Sometimes interviews are conducted by individuals but they are normally conducted by a small panel of from three to five people to handle the task. Models for job application letters were given in Chapter Fifteen. This chapter assumes you have sent the letter and have been invited to attend for an interview.

Some days before you go, read over the application letter and think about every piece of relevant experience you have described. Employers are very often looking for personal qualities and potential as much as for experience and formal skills. Experiences you have had which you might think to be of too minor a scale—being cast in a school musical, being secretary of a youth club, producing a newsletter for a community group—might be highly relevant to the job at hand and any of them could be the one item which, from an array of similar candidates, tips the scales in your favour.

If you are serious about the job, you will find out as much as possible about the organisation and the industry it is in.

If you are serious about the job, you will find out as much as possible about the organisation and the industry it is in. This usually means one evening's research in a library where you will read, say, a company report, an industry or state year book and similar references. When the appointment is being made, ask how many people will be on the panel and ask for their names. If the names are available, look them up in the organisation's annual report so that you go to the interview with a good idea of who you will be talking to. There may be no chance in the interview to tell people you know their background but it will certainly make you more confident when talking to them.

There are a series of questions most asked in job interviews and you should prepare answers to them. Don't expect that they will be asked in exactly the wording that follows, or that all of them will be asked, but do be prepared to discuss these issues.

A specific question may be asked about why the applicant thinks he or she is qualified for *this* position. This is very often the question that will land or lose the job.

1. *General background* One of the first questions is often a request for a summary of the candidate's background, even though this information has been presented in the application letter. Someone applying for their first job would obviously focus on their education, the qualifications they gained and any extracurricular activities in which they participated. Someone with work experience would focus on both their employment and educational backgrounds. In answering this question, it is acceptable to repeat and emphasise points made in the application letter.
2. *Qualifications* A specific question may be asked about why the applicant thinks he or she is qualified for *this* position. This is a different question to the one on general background. It is really asking for a succinct argument on the way the candidate's qualifications make him or her well suited to the job. 'Qualifications' in this context means all qualifications—educational, employment-based and personal. This is very often the question that will land or lose the job. The answer has to be

clear and memorable and it would pay candidates to work out their best answer well beforehand and discuss it with friends to see how convincing it sounds.

3. *Experience* Candidates are sometimes asked for the relevance of their experience to the position. This is where some prior research can be put to effective use. The answer can be a summary of the candidate's relevant employment, community or educational experience (that is, what you have done rather than what you have learned), combined with a discussion of the nature of the industry, the organisation and the position itself. This is also a critical question on which the job can be won or lost.

4. *Reasons for applying* Candidates are often asked why they want the job. Always have an answer prepared for this one. If you are applying for your first or one of your first jobs, you should have an answer that describes:

   - why the career is attractive to you
   - how long you have wanted to work in this area
   - how you have prepared yourself for the career
   - how you believe the present job fits your career aspirations

In some organisations and in some types of occupation, employers give candidates questions designed to test their ability in situations of crisis

5. *Career objectives* Another common question is to ask people what are their long-term career objectives. The main point about this question is to ensure that people can actually think and plan ahead, in other words, that they have the capacity for long-term vision. The most appropriate answer is one that indicates you have thought in these terms about yourself and have taken some actions towards realising your ambitions.

6. *Crisis management* In some organisations and in some types of occupation, employers give candidates questions designed to test their ability in situations of crisis. For instance, applicants for a position as a teacher in charge of young children might be asked what they would do if the estranged father of a child demanded to take the child away from school when there had been no word from the mother that this was to happen. Or other candidates in service occupations might be asked how they would respond to strong but unjustified criticism from a customer. You should try to find out during your research what are the most common types of conflict or dilemmas for employees in the job you are seeking. Formulate a response to this kind of crisis that describes you acting in a calm and reasoned manner that works to minimise the conflict and prevent a greater crisis from emerging.

Finally, you should have some questions of your own. Do not be reticent in asking how much you will be paid—no one expects you to work for nothing and someone who did not ask about this would be considered a little strange. Ask also about working conditions and other benefits of the organisation—but ask about conditions related to productive effort rather than about holidays or sick leave. Use some questions to make additional points in your favour—by asking, for instance, about any support the organisation might provide if you wanted to do further training or how well it responds to employee suggestions and participation in decision-making.

You should have some questions of your own. Do not be reticent in asking about how much you will be paid—no one expects you to work for nothing.

EMPLOYERS' PERSPECTIVES

While all job interviews are different, there are some common approaches that most employers will adopt for an interview. They centre primarily on gathering data about the job itself and on relating questions to this data. The interviewer needs to ensure that a proper analysis of the task itself is done as part of pre-recruiting planning. This job description should include the qualifications and experience needed, and the actual tasks to be performed. The information should be summarised on a job description sheet which is provided to each person on the interviewing panel. The sheet will serve as a reminder of what is involved and as a guide to the initial formulation of questions.

Standard questions should cover areas such as:

- the candidate's qualifications and experience
- suitability for the position concerned
- attitudes towards the organisation and the industry
- the candidate's career ambitions and objectives

The panel needs to meet before the interview to decide on the standard questions they will ask. There should be a list of common questions which are put to each candidate. The panel should also leave itself time to ask unprepared questions to follow up any interesting comments that individuals may make. The standard questions should cover areas such as:

- the candidate's qualifications and experience
- suitability for the position concerned
- attitudes towards the organisation and the industry
- the candidate's career ambitions and objectives

There are two final stages in the job interview. First, the employer should ask the candidate if he or she has any questions of the organisation. Second, give a clear statement of when the outcome will be known and communicated. If possible, give the exact date the successful candidate will be notified and when the unsuccessful will be told as well. Do not keep the people who have taken the trouble of applying and interviewing in a state of uncertainty any longer than necessary.

KEY POINTS: Chapter 16 Employment interviews

- Before you go for an interview, read over your application letter and think about the experience you describe.
- Find out as much as possible about the organisation and its industry.
- Young people applying for their first job should focus both on their education and their extracurricular activities.
- Describe your qualifications in clear and memorable terms.
- Have an answer prepared about why you applied for the job and about your long-term career objectives.
- Prepare answers to a question on crisis management, if this is appropriate.
- Prepare questions of your own to ask.

QUESTIONS FOR DISCUSSION

- What kind of information about an organisation should a candidate have before a job interview?
- Discuss the kind of qualifications you should emphasise at a job interview.
- If asked your reasons for applying for the job, how should you reply?
- If asked a question about how you would handle a crisis on the job, how would you reply?
- What kind of questions should you ask at a job interview? Why?

EXERCISES

Interviews are an ideal situation for role play exercises involving from five to eight people. Three or four of the group should constitute the panel members for an interview for an invented position of a kind familiar to all. The others, from two to four people, should be the candidates for the position. Each member of the panel should have a specialist area about which questions should be asked.

After each interview, each panel member should fill out an evaluation sheet on each candidate. The evaluation should be related to how well each person answered the specific questions and should also have space for general comments on attitude and presentation. Each space in the evaluation sheet should have room for both comments and a score. Interviewees should have their overall score totalled from the evaluation sheets. Both comments and scores should be made available to the candidates.

After this exercise is complete, another job position should be selected and the roles reversed. The former candidates now become the interviewers and the members of the former panel become the interviewees.

CHAPTER 17

PREPARING AND WRITING A RÉSUMÉ

After studying this chapter, you will be able to:

- prepare a personal résumé to accompany a job application letter
- describe to employers your educational background, work experience, extracurricular activities, and references

The personal résumé is also called a 'personal inventory', 'curriculum vitae' (or CV), 'personal data sheet', 'personal profile' or 'qualification sheet'. Whatever its name, it is essential to have one these days when you are applying for a job. It is a summary of your experience and qualifications. It is a list of jobs you have had, formal qualifications you have acquired, and informal experiences that would be relevant to your employment.

It should be updated or amended before each new application. You will nearly always have done something or achieved something between one application and another. Also, you will probably want the list to emphasise different aspects of your background that are more relevant to one position than another. The résumé should contain five main sections: the heading, education, work experience, extracurricular activities, and references. Optional sections are special interests, special skills and membership of groups and societies. Whether you include all or any of these will depend on the job you are applying for.

A résumé should be updated or amended before each new application.

You can vary the order in which you present these sections. If you have just finished school, college or university, and have little work experience, your biggest selling point will be your education. You should therefore list education qualifications before work experience. If you have a solid work history, your outstanding qualification is your experience, so you might decide to list the section on your work immediately after your personal details.

You can also vary the order you list information within the sections on education and work experience. You can list education in reverse chronological order, with your most recent qualification at the beginning of the section. This format is optional, however. Many applicants prefer to put secondary education before tertiary education. By and large, it is best to list your work history in reverse chronological order with your most recent job first. Applicants with a long work history in two or more different fields sometimes list their work experience under separate headings, such as teaching, secretarial and publishing. Those with a range of work experiences have an advantage. They can select work experiences most relevant to the job they are applying for, and omit others. Later we will look at examples of different formats of résumés.

HEADING

The heading lists the title (résumé, curriculum vitae, data sheet, or whatever description you choose) plus personal information about yourself such as your name, home address, telephone numbers at home and work, and date of birth. You can also list marital status, children and state of health, but these items are optional. You may not want, or need, to include this information.

EDUCATION

In this section you will describe your formal education at school, technical or business college, a college of advanced education or university.

Your work history and the job for which you are applying will determine the format you adopt. If you have a short work history you should list all your educational background and qualifications, including subjects or courses relevant to the job. Divide the section into two parts—secondary and tertiary. Under secondary education, list the school/s and years you attended, the final school certificate you obtained, subjects you majored in, your HSC or final school results and any academic prizes or distinctions you won. In addition, list meritorious achievements such as being a school prefect or captain, and extracurricular distinctions in writing, music, drama, debating and sporting competitions.

Under tertiary education (technical or business college, training school such as mothercraft nursing, college of advanced education, university), you should list the degree, diploma or certificate awarded, the institution you attended and the date you received the degree, diploma or certificate. List courses you majored in and any special distinctions or prizes you won.

You might also include under this heading special certificates or expertise you have acquired, such as secretarial skills or fluency in a language, short courses you have completed, such as retail management or computer programming, or accreditation to practise in various fields such as nursing and real estate. Some applicants prefer to list this type of information towards the end of the résumé under the heading 'special skills'. If you are currently undertaking a course of study, list that as well and state when you are due to finish. Applicants with extensive work experience usually refer only to their educational qualifications and the institutions they attended, but again this is optional.

WORK EXPERIENCE

As we noted earlier, there are two ways of categorising your work experience. One is to list your work history in reverse chronological order with your most recent job at the top of the list. The other is to group your work experience into categories. Most people adopt the chronological format but if you have an extensive work history in different fields the second method is preferable.

Your work history should list a number of details about each of the jobs you have held. List first the period you held each position, in years only if you have been in the workforce for some time, but in months and years if you have had only a short work history. Next, list the title of the position you held. If a job did not have an official title then describe it in simple terms such as administrative officer or assistant store manager. Next, include the name of your employer, their address, telephone number and a contact if appropriate. You might also want to list your responsibilities and to whom you reported. This is a useful inclusion if you have only had a small number of jobs. It can lead to fruitful discussion in the interview. If you had a large number of casual jobs while a student, include those which had some responsibility or some relevance to the present job. Some employers prefer students who worked their way through their studies. Later in your career these could be dropped from the list.

You might also want to list your responsibilities and to whom you reported. This is a useful inclusion if you have only had a small number of jobs.

EXTRACURRICULAR ACTIVITIES

These will include interests you pursue outside your studies or your current employment. They include sporting, community activities and, if you are a student, positions in student clubs and societies. They provide some additional information about you and do have some bearing on how you will fit the job and the organisation. These often become a talking point in the interview, so make sure you list them and are prepared to discuss them. You might also include at this point any special memberships you hold of societies or organisations related to your occupation or profession. Your interest at this level will demonstrate a commitment beyond simply carrying out a job and will create a favourable impression.

REFEREES

You should provide a list of two or three referees who will verify your suitability for the job. Each referee should give a different version of your qualifications and abilities, so include at least one who will describe your educational or professional qualifications and at least one who will testify to your work capabilities. Use only those referees who will give a position evaluation. It is usual to include past employers or senior staff members familiar with your course work at school, college or university. It is wise to ring a referee to check if he or she agrees to be named in your job application.

Most students or people with little work experience when asked to prepare a résumé for the first time will tell you that they cannot. However, it can often be surprising to see the information mount up.

RÉSUMÉS FOR STUDENTS OR PEOPLE WITH LITTLE WORK EXPERIENCE

When asked to prepare a résumé for the first time, most students or people with little work experience will tell you that they cannot. Asked why, they invariably answer that they have nothing to say about themselves. The most common reasons are that they have just left school, they have not completed any tertiary education and they have had little work experience.

The first step for someone like this to write an effective résumé is to answer some questions about themselves. It can often be surprising to see the information mount up.

EDUCATION

Under the heading of education, answer these questions.

- Were you a member of a sporting team?
- Did you win any special prizes for sport?
- Did you have a position at school, such as prefect?
- Did you win a scholarship?
- Did you perform in school plays, musicals or the orchestra?
- Were you a member of a debating team?
- Did you help edit the school newspaper or make a video or a film?
- Were you a member of the school cadets?
- Did you win prizes or distinctions for competitions in writing or mathematics?
- If you left school early, did you train at technical or business college?

Even if you didn't do well compared to other students, it is still worth listing the subjects in which you did best, or liked the most, so that employers will know in what direction your interest and abilities lie. If you dropped out of a course, you should include your limited study, especially if it related to a job you performed. An example would be an apprentice in motor mechanics who attended a certificate course in motor mechanics at the local technical college.

WORK EXPERIENCE

On the question of work experience, include every type of job, casual or part-time, no matter how menial, nor how long you did it. You might not think it worth noting that you worked as a cashier at the local supermarket every Saturday for two years. But this job will have given you an insight into retail management. You will have developed interpersonal skills relating to a wide cross-section of people, mastered a range of retail technology, learned something of the rigors of the workplace and developed a clearer perspective of what you want to achieve in your career. Put in this light, your job in the supermarket should never be discounted.

EXTRACURRICULAR ACTIVITIES

Next, list all the activities you consider as community-oriented, or extracurricular hobbies.

- Are you a member of a local netball, soccer, surf life-saving, basketball, tennis or karate club?
- Are you a subscriber to any group or association?
- Are you interested in photography, bush-walking, boating?
- Have you been active in your local church or Police Citizens Youth Club?
- Have you been a helper in any voluntary community organisations?

You might not think it worth noting that you worked as a cashier at the local supermarket every Saturday for two years. But this job will have given you an insight into retail management.

These kind of details give a more rounded picture of the person you are. They will help you be more objective about your abilities, and they help a perspective employer judge qualities such as personality, character, initiative and enthusiasm.

WRITING THE RÉSUMÉ

You should prepare your résumé *before* you write any job application letter.

1. A well-ordered relevant résumé will demonstrate your ability to organise. You will have a permanent database about yourself. You can add or delete or change information at any time to suit the particular job. A good résumé will save you a lot of time and worry.
2. Preparing a résumé first will force you to draw up a complete list of details about your background, education, qualifications, work experience, extracurricular activities, membership and hobbies. Until you do this you will entertain only vague ideas about yourself and you will tend to underestimate your abilities and experience. Once you have completed a résumé you will have something concrete to work from when you write up your job application letter.
3. Put another way, the résumé is a *summary* of your background, qualifications and experience. The job application letter is an *interpretation* of

The résumé is a *summary* of your background, qualifications and experience. The job application letter is an *interpretation* of the résumé.

the résumé. Each job will call for a slightly different interpretation of the résumé. You will select the most appropriate information to suit the particular job. In some applications you will emphasise some details more or less or delete others altogether because they may prejudice your chances. With practice, you will become quite clever at manipulating the information to give the best picture of your personality, abilities and expertise.

Instead of a large amount of written detail on how to write a résumé, we prefer to give you concrete examples of résumés for people of quite different backgrounds, education and experience. They range from people with little formal education and work experience to those with extensive qualifications and long work histories.

RÉSUMÉS AND JOB APPLICATION LETTERS

1. This is a résumé in a *chronological* format of a nineteen-year-old young man who left school at the age of sixteen and has worked in a variety of jobs. His selling points are that he has recently completed a course in motor mechanics, has worked in motor repairs for two years and has just enrolled in a course in panel beating. His continuous work history since leaving school and his extracurricular interest in the restoration of vintage cars will create a favourable impression. (See the covering job application letter that follows.)

RÉSUMÉ

NAME	John Edward Morrison 4 Sterling Crescent KOGARAH NSW 2217 Telephone: 543 4456
DATE OF BIRTH	20 August 1968
WORK EXPERIENCE	
1987–93	Executive Motors 239 Brown Street Kogarah NSW 2217 Responsibilities: General motor repairs and maintenance and some clerical duties.
1986	Artist Supplies Pty Ltd 389 Railway Parade Cronulla NSW 2230 Responsibilities: Worked as sales assistant and driver, selling art supplies over the counter and by telephone, and delivering art supplies.

continued on next page

continued from previous page

1984–86 Donald Worton Landscapes
345 Prahan Street
Oatley NSW 2223
Responsibilities: Planting of trees, shrubs and flowers, building rockeries and laying lawn.

1984 Gino's Restaurant
239 Bridge Street
Kogarah NSW 2217
Responsibilities: Management of coffee lounge, preparation of food and clerical duties.

EDUCATION

Kogarah High School, 1980–83
completed Year 10

St George Technical College, Kogarah 1986–87
completed Motor Maintenance Certificate course.

St George Technical College, Kogarah, 1993–94:
currently undertaking course in panel beating.

EXTRACURRICULAR ACTIVITIES

Kogarah Police Citizens Youth Club, 1983–84
Gained certificates in weight lifting and karate

Kogarah United Soccer Team, 1983–84
Second grade full back

Member, Salvation Army Youth Legion,
Kogarah, 1983–84

INTERESTS Secretary, NSW Rover Car Club, 1987
soccer, swimming, weight lifting, and restoring vintage cars

REFEREES

Malcolm White
Managing Director
Artist Supplies Pty Ltd
389 Railway Parade
Cronulla NSW 2230
Telephone: 523 5660

Peter Barron
Police Citizens Youth Club
99 Martin Street
Kogarah NSW 2217
Telephone: 546 3349

Stanley Docker
33 Illawarra Road
Glebe NSW 2037

2. Job application letter to accompany preceding résumé.

4 Sterling Crescent
Kogarah NSW 2217

23 April 1993

Mr Reginald Wright
Manager
Acme Motors
34 Darling Street
Cronulla NSW 2330

Dear Mr Wright,

Assistant Mechanic

I wish to apply for the job of Assistant Manager with Acme Motors advertised in the *Sydney Morning Herald* on 2 April 1993.

I believe I have the necessary qualifications and experience to satisfy your requirements.

As my résumé shows, I have a certificate in Motor Maintenance from St George Technical College and I am currently undertaking a second course at the College in Panel beating which I expect to complete this year. Since 1985 I have worked as a mechanic with Executive Motors in Kogarah.

Your advertisement specified an interest in and knowledge of European cars. During my period with Executive Motors I have carried out maintenance work on a range of European cars including Saab, BMW, Volvo, Audi and Mercedes models. I am also an owner of a vintage model Rover car which I have restored and maintained myself. I am presently the secretary of the NSW Rover Car Club.

I look forward to hearing from you about an interview. My telephone number at work is 560 9987 and home 543 4456.

Yours sincerely,

John Morrison

3. This is a résumé in a *chronological* format of a twenty-five-year-old woman who has recently completed a degree in social work. She has a short work history in her field of interest. Her strengths are an above average academic ability, the social work placements she completed as part of her course work requirements, an extracurricular commitment to community work and a continuous part-time work history as a sales assistant and nursing aide while undertaking university studies. (See covering job application letter that follows.)

RÉSUMÉ

NAME: Wendy Martin
6 Garran Close
GARRAN ACT 2605
Telephone: 06 269 9882

DATE OF BIRTH: 20 October 1967

TERTIARY EDUCATION

1986–91 University of New South Wales
Kensington NSW
Faculty of Professional Studies,
Bachelor of Social Work
(Second class honours, first division)
Majors in Social Work, Research Methods, Human Behaviour and Social Work Practice

AWARDS Charlotte Brereton Prize in Social Work, Practice 3, 1990
Distinction in Social Work Practice 1, 2, 3

SOCIAL WORK PLACEMENTS

1990 Westmead Women's Refuge, NSW
Position: Trainee social worker
Duties included planning, development and execution of training course for volunteers, media publicity, design of course literature, submission writing. Experience in leadership, team work, group work, financial management, meetings, public relations.

1989 Moree Health Centre, NSW
Position: Trainee social worker
Duties included family counselling and intake assessment. Experience in interviewing, case management, team work and report writing.

1988 Prince Henry Hospital, NSW
Position: Trainee social worker
Duties included design, execution and publication of research which quantified the experience of patients undergoing radiotherapy treatment for cancer, and casework. Experience in research design, research analysis, report writing and interviewing.

SECONDARY EDUCATION

1980–85 Sydney Girls High School
Moore Park NSW
Higher School Certificate, 1980
Aggregate 437/500
Percentile ranking 95–100 per cent

School Captain, 1985

continued on next page

continued from previous page

	Member, Debating Team, NSW Debating Competition 1983–84
	Honours, Grade 7 Piano, Australian Music Examinations Board

EMPLOYMENT

1992	Department of Territories PO Box 30 CANBERRA ACT 2601 Telephone: (06) 262 1334 Office of Substitute Care Position: Social Worker Responsibilities presently include assessment and follow-up of adoption and foster care applicants; preparation and presentation of reports, casework plans and submissions to delegated officers, committees and the courts. Other duties include crisis counselling of adoptees, personnel management, personnel training and statistical analysis. Experience in assessment, interviewing, counselling, report writing, analysis, leadership and management.
1989	Chevron Nursing Home, Mt Druitt, NSW; Buona Vista Nursing Home, Liverpool, NSW Position: Part-time nursing aide Nursing assistant to psychiatric geriatric patients.
1985–88	Newman Jewellers Pty Ltd 390 Pitt Street Sydney NSW Position: Part-time store manager and sales assistant Duties: Part-time selling to customers and some stocktaking

EXTRACURRICULAR ACTIVITIES

1987–89	Member, Students' Representative Council, University of NSW
1986–87	Voluntary part-time worker, Senior Citizens Support Group; Tempe Women's Refuge, Tempe, NSW: assisted on survey of 100 women on child-care needs in local community.
	St John Ambulance certificate
	Fluency in French language

REFEREES

Dr Deborah Houghton Senior Project Officer Office of Substitute Care Department of Territories PO Box 30 CANBERRA ACT 2601 Telephone: (06) 262 1334	Professor John Whitehead School of Social Work University of New South Wales PO Box 1 KENSINGTON NSW 2033 Telephone: (02) 697 7777, ext. 49

continued on next page

continued from previous page

Dr Genevieve Burton
Senior Lecturer
School of Social Work
University of New South Wales
PO Box 1
KENSINGTON NSW 2033
Telephone: (02) 697 7777, ext. 50

4. Job application letter to accompany preceding résumé.

6 Garran Close
GARRAN ACT 2605
23 April 1993

Dr Jane Lynton
Principal Research Officer
Research School of Social Sciences
Australian National University
Canberra ACT 2601

Dear Dr Lynton,

Research Assistant, Grade 2 Reference No. 667.902

I am most interested in applying for the position of Research Assistant, Grade 2, with the Research School of Social Sciences, as advertised in the *Canberra Times* on 2 April 1993.

I have worked for the past twelve months in social welfare research projects utilising analytical and organisational skills and I am keen to further diversify my interest and experience in research.

My professional and personal qualities have equipped me well for the position advertised. The enclosed résumé detailing my degree in Social Work (second class honours, first division) illustrates a solid theoretical and practical grounding in human relations and social research.

As a student, I studied Research Methods 1 and 2, and designed and implemented a variety of methods of research as follows.

1. Constructed a questionnaire to identify the career development and training needs of staff of non-English-speaking backgrounds.

continued on next page

continued from previous page

2. Directed community consultations with Sydney group of mothers on need to provide child care services.
3. Designed, executed and published research which quantified the experience of patients undergoing radiotherapy treatment for cancer.

I have developed organisational skills in the day-to-day management of research in the Substitute Care Unit and have been responsible for the design and publication of a special research manual.

I believe I have a number of strengths to offer:

- a methodical and exacting approach to tasks
- an ability to take a balanced view of evidence and opinion on subjects, then determine the most relevant information
- a strong sense of self-motivation, energy and drive to complete tasks
- a proven ability to work without supervision

My commitment to my area of interest is such that I am prepared to work outside normally expected hours if necessary.

My two referees are as follows:

Professor John Whitehead
School of Social Work
University of New South Wales
PO Box 1
Kensington NSW 2033
Telephone: (02) 697 7777, ext. 49

Dr Genevieve Burton
School of Social Work
University of New South Wales
PO Box 1
Kensington NSW 2033
(02) 697 7777, ext. 50

You are also welcome to contact my present employer as a referee. She is:

Dr Deborah Houghton
Senior Project Officer
Department of Territories
PO Box 30
Canberra ACT 2601
(06) 262 1334

I will be available for employment from 6 May 1993 and look forward to hearing from you about an interview. My home telephone number is (06) 269 9882.

Yours sincerely,

Wendy Martin

5. This is a résumé in a *chronological* format of a twenty-two-year-old man who has completed a degree in business studies but has little experience in his field of work. His strengths are a solid history of part-time work in office and managerial tasks while undertaking tertiary studies and a strong extracurricular commitment to sporting activities which would appeal to some employers. (See covering job application letter that follows.)

RÉSUMÉ

NAME: Harvey Cecil Carlton
220 Amethyst Avenue
Bondi Beach NSW 2026
Telephone: (02) 398 6678

DATE OF BIRTH: 10 May 1970

SECONDARY EDUCATION

1982–88 Barkly College
Pacific Highway
Hornsby NSW
Higher School Certificate
Aggregate 340/500
1st Grade Rugby Union, 1986–88
House monitor, 1987–88
A Grade Competition Tennis, 1985–88

TERTIARY EDUCATION

1989–93 University of Technology, Sydney
Broadway, NSW
Bachelor of Business, 1993
Majors in Accounting, Business Administration, Marketing. High distinction in Accounting 2 and 3; Editor, *Monitor*, student union newsletter, 1988–92

WORK EXPERIENCE

1991–92 Koala Hotel, Belmore Road
Randwick NSW 2031
Position: Clerk
Duties included registering hotel patrons, recording reservations, ordering of food and room delivery.

1989–90 Carle Associates
Research Consultants,
133 Olive Street
Paddington NSW 2021
Position: Office assistant
Duties included bookkeeping and general clerical tasks.

continued on next page

continued from previous page

Experience with telephone interviewing, research and computers.

EXTRACURRICULAR ACTIVITIES

1991–92 Eastern Suburbs Rugby Union 2nd Grade Competition
1990–91 Eastern Suburbs B Grade Tennis Competition
Honorary Treasurer, Uniting Church, Bondi Beach Community Centre
Other interests include abseiling, computers and numismatics

REFEREES

Dr James Carson
Acting Head
Faculty of Business Studies
University of Technology, Sydney
PO Box 123
Broadway NSW 2007
Telephone: (02) 2 0930, ext. 314

Mr Arthur Barratt
Principal
Barkly College
Pacific Highway
Hornsby NSW 2077
Telephone: (02) 41 7789

John Carle
Carle Associates
Research Consultants
133 Olive Street
Paddington NSW 2021
Telephone: (02) 331 4456

6. Job application letter to accompany previous résumé.

220 Amethyst Avenue
Bondi Beach NSW 2026

23 April 1994

Mr John Wilton
Personnel Manager
Sporting Equipment Pty Ltd
987 Waterloo Street
Surry Hills NSW 2010

Dear Mr Wilton,

Marketing Research Manager

I am replying to your advertisement for a Marketing Research Manager in the *Australian* on Saturday, 2 April 1994.

continued on next page

continued from previous page

As you can see from my résumé, I recently graduated from the University of Technology, Sydney, with a Bachelor of Business Studies. I majored in Marketing, Business Administration and Accounting.

I have had considerable experience in market research. For two years I worked as a part-time research assistant with Carle Associates, Market Research Consultants in Paddington. My responsibilities involved market research on a number of accounts, including two sporting organisations, Gym Equipment Incorporated and Athletico Pty Ltd.

You specified an extracurricular interest in sport. My credentials in this area are excellent. Since secondary school I have been involved in a wide range of sporting activities and, as you will see from my résumé, I have achieved a high level of performance in NSW competition Rugby Union and tennis. I am a member of the Sydney Abseiling Club and during my editorship of *Monitor*, the University of Technology Student Union newsletter, I contributed numerous articles on campus sporting activities (see appendixes). In my capacity as honorary treasurer of the Uniting Church Bondi Beach Community Centre, I am responsible for financial matters relating to the Centre's classes in judo, karate and aerobics.

I look forward to hearing from you for an interview and can be contacted by telephone at 398 6678.

Yours sincerely,

Harvey Carlton

7. This is a résumé in a *categorical* format (that is, divided by category). It belongs to a thirty-seven-year-old woman who has a long work history in three different fields: publishing, teaching and administration. Instead of being list chronologically, work experience is categorised under three separate headings. This makes it easier for the prospective employer to identify and assess both the applicant's overall capabilities and those skills most appropriate to the job she is applying for. The job requirements determine the order of the headings. (See covering job application letter that follows.)

RÉSUMÉ

NAME Janice Letitia Collingwood
34 Larson Road
Petersham NSW 2049
Telephone: (02) 560 9987

continued on next page

continued from previous page

DATE OF BIRTH 20 August 1956

EDUCATION

1968–72	Fort Street Girls High School, Higher School Certificate
1973	Hales Secretarial College, Sydney, Secretarial Diploma
1974–77	University of Sydney, Bachelor of Arts (Honours: Second Class Honours, First Division)
1978	University of Sydney Diploma of Education
1989–93	University of New South Wales Currently candidate for doctorate in Australian history

EMPLOYMENT: PUBLISHING

1991–93	Manager, Bunya Books, Parramatta NSW

EMPLOYMENT: TEACHING

1986–91	Lecturer in History, University of Technology, Sydney Broadway, NSW
1984–85	Lecturer, Communications for Social Welfare Macarthur Institute of Advanced Education (now University of Western Sydney, Macarthur)
1980–83	Teacher of History and English, NSW Department of Education

EMPLOYMENT: ADMINISTRATION

1978–79	Co-ordinator, *History News*, journal of Professional Historians Association
1979–80	Publicity officer, Australia Council, North Sydney

PUBLICATIONS

See Appendix 1, list of publications

MEMBERSHIP OF GROUPS AND SOCIETIES

1990–93	Member, Professional Historians of NSW
1983–93	Friend of the Library of NSW
1984–93	National Trust
1982–93	Royal Australian Historical Society
1977–93	Australian Historical Association

continued on next page

continued from previous page

REFEREES

Professor Janis Norton
School of History
University of New South Wales
PO Box 1
Kensington NSW 2033
Telephone: (02) 697 7777, ext. 345

Dr William Ashton
Senior Lecturer
Faculty of Humanities
University of Technology, Sydney
Broadway NSW 2007
Telephone: (02) 2 0930, ext. 234

Dr Brian Neilson
Senior Lecturer
School of History
University of New South Wales
PO Box 1
Kensington NSW 2033
Telephone: (02) 697 7777, ext. 342

8. Job application letter to accompany preceding résumé.

34 Larson Road
Petersham NSW 2049

5 April 1993

Dr Gillian McCredie
Chief Executive Officer
Royal Australian Historical Institute
13 Bridge Street
Sydney NSW 2000

Dear Dr McCredie,

Editor of Australian Educational Publications,
Royal Australian Historical Institute

I wish to be considered for the position of Editor of Australian Educational Publications with the Royal Australian Historical Institute advertised in the *Sydney Morning Herald* on Saturday, 2 April 1993.

I have a sound background in Australian History. I graduated with a Bachelor of Arts (Honours) from the University of Sydney in 1977, majoring in History and English, and a Diploma of Education from the University of Sydney in 1978. I am currently completing a doctorate in Australian history at the University of New South Wales, and have a substantial publications list in Australian history (see résumé, Appendix 1).

continued on next page

continued from previous page

I have taught Australian history at both secondary and tertiary levels and am thus familiar with most educational material on Australian history.

I have a thorough knowledge of the publishing industry in the capacities of publisher, editor and writer. Since 1991 I have worked as manager and editor with a small publishing company which has produced several bicentenary historical works. In 1978–79 I was co-ordinator of the history journal, *History News*, which is distributed throughout Australia.

Over the years I have established contact with historians at all levels of the academic field and among popular historians and journalists. I am a member of many historical groups and societies including the Royal Australian Historical Society and the Australian Historical Society and I am a Member of the Professional Historians of New South Wales.

As referees, I would like to nominate the following:

Ms Margaret Blake
Managing Director
Bunya Books Pty Ltd
56 Hargrave Street
Parramatta, NSW 2150
Telephone: (02) 645 9098

Professor Janis Norton
School of History
University of New South Wales
PO Box 1
Kensington NSW 2033
Telephone: (02) 697 7777, ext. 345

I look forward to hearing from you about an interview. Please contact me at work (645 9098) or at home (560 9987).

I would be available to start from 11 May.

Yours sincerely,

Janice Collingwood

9. This is another résumé in a *categorical* format. It belongs to a forty-year-old woman who has a long work history in three related areas of the health profession. Instead of being listed chronologically, work experience is listed under three separate headings: nursing, medical research and teaching. Nursing is further divided into five categories: renal, intensive care, cardio-thoracic, psychiatric and general. Although she has worked in the one field, her qualifications and experience are diverse. Separating her abilities into categories makes it easier for the prospective employer to identify and assess both her overall capabilities and those skills most appropriate to the job she is applying for. The job requirements determine the order in which to list headings. (See covering job application letter that follows.)

RÉSUMÉ

Anna Lucinda Trimble
3/89 Underwood Street
Gladesville NSW 2111
Telephone: (02) 810 5564

DATE OF BIRTH 8 March 1952

TERTIARY EDUCATION

Psychiatric Nursing Certificate, North Ryde Psychiatric Centre, North Ryde NSW, 1970
Nursing Administration Certificate, Department of Health, Sydney, 1973

General Nursing Certificate, Prince of Wales Hospital, Randwick, NSW, 1975

Postgraduate Renal Nursing Certificate, Royal North Shore Hospital, St Leonards, NSW, 1979

Postgraduate Intensive Therapy Nursing Certificate, Royal Prince Alfred Hospital, Camperdown, NSW, 1981

Advanced Human Physiology Certificate, Sydney Technical College, Ultimo, NSW, 1985

Diploma of Teaching, Sydney Institute of Advanced Education, 1987

Bachelor of Education, Sydney Institute of Advanced Education, 1989

Nursing Scholarship: NSW Health Commission, Sydney, 1985–86

SECONDARY

School Certificate, St Anne's College, Dubbo, NSW, 1967

EMPLOYMENT: NURSING

Renal
1990 Concord Repatriation Hospital, Concord, NSW
Registered part-time nurse in renal unit

continued on next page

continued from previous page

1979–80	Concord Repatriation Hospital, Concord, NSW Charge Nurse, Haemodialysis, Home Training Centre, responsible for developing and implementing the haemodialysis home training program
1978–79	Royal North Shore Hospital, St Leonards, NSW Registered nurse and postgraduate student in Renal Nursing Course
1976–78	Concord Repatriation Hospital, Concord, NSW Senior registered nurse in renal/haemodialysis unit
Intensive Care	
1986–88	St Luke's Hospital, Potts Point, NSW Senior registered nurse, part-time, intensive care unit
1983–84	Prince of Wales Hospital, Randwick, NSW Relieving charge nurse, intensive care unit, responsible for management of unit which involved knowledge of the most recent technology and some training of staff
1980–81	Royal Prince Alfred Hospital, Camperdown, NSW Registered nurse and postgraduate student, intensive therapy course
Cardio-Thoracic	
1981–83	St Joseph's Hospital, Ealing, London, United Kingdom Staff Nurse, Intensive Care Unit, Cardio-thoracic Surgery Unit
Psychiatric	
1970–74	North Ryde Psychiatric Centre, North Ryde, NSW Registered Psychiatric Nurse, promoted to Charge Sister, 1973
1968–70	North Ryde Psychiatric Centre, North Ryde, NSW Trainee Psychiatric Nurse
General	
1974–76	Prince of Wales Hospital, Randwick, NSW Trainee general nurse

<u>EMPLOYMENT: MEDICAL RESEARCH</u>

1988–90	Royal North Shore Hospital, St Leonards, NSW Research Officer responsible for developing and implementing a drug research program

EMPLOYMENT: TEACHING

1984–86	NSW College of Nursing, Glebe, NSW Program Director, Acute Care Course responsible for the planning, implementation and co-ordination of a program in acute care; development of health education seminars for remote areas of NSW

continued on next page

continued from previous page

PROFESSIONAL MEMBERSHIPS

Member, NSW Nurses Association, 1979–93
Member, Royal Australian Nursing Federation, 1968–93
Member, Clinical Nurse Specialist Association, 1983–93

EXTRACURRICULAR ACTIVITIES

Health Advisor, NSW Consumer Goods Standards Association, 1983–90
Student Representative, Social Committee, Sydney Institute of Advanced Education, 1987–89
Honorary Secretary, Body Corporate, Strata Plan 78823, Sydney, 1986–90

REFEREES

Dr Quentin Madgwick
Renal Unit
Prince of Wales Hospital
Randwick NSW 2031
Telephone: (02) 398 4325

Ms Rowena Morrison
Executive Director
NSW College of Nursing
55 Heresford Street
Glebe NSW 2037
Telephone: (02) 660 6785

Dr Janelle Brunswick
Principal
Sydney College of Advanced Education
PO Box 63
Camperdown NSW 2050
Telephone: (02) 51 4523

10. Job application letter to accompany the preceding résumé.

14 May 1993

Mrs J. L. English
Director of Nursing
The Prince Henry Hospital
Little Bay NSW 2036

Dear Mrs English,

Renal Nursing Co-ordinator, Hospital and Eastern Health Service

I wish to apply for the position of Renal Nursing Co-ordinator, Hospital and Eastern Health Service, advertised in the *Sydney Morning Herald* on Thursday, 14 May 1993.

Your advertisement asked for a highly experienced registered nurse with a background in renal clinical work, nurse education and medical research. I believe I have the qualifications and experience to fulfil your requirements.

continued on next page

continued from previous page

Renal unit management

I gained post-basic qualifications in renal nursing in 1979 and have worked for six years at Concord Repatriation and Royal North Shore Hospitals.

For two years I was nursing unit manager at the Home Training Centre at Concord Repatriation Hospital where my main responsibility was to develop and implement the haemodialysis home training program. The program catered for renal patients who were suitable for self-care at home and referred from the main renal unit. Treatment included haemodialysis and continuous ambulatory peritoneal dialysis and involved the participation of relatives. We provided full support and supervision for patients and relatives in their homes and our outreach service operated on a 24-hour on-call roster.

As nursing unit manager, I was responsible for liaison with a multi-disciplinary team in renal care and for the management and organisation of the unit. Because of staff shortages I often supervised in other areas such as the Outpatients Clinic, Transplant Unit and the Inpatient Unit. These units treated patients for acute and chronic renal disease involving a range of peritoneal dialysis techniques.

Nurse education

I believe I have a strong background in nurse education. As well as my general certificate in nursing which I gained at Prince of Wales Hospital at Randwick in 1975, I have post-basic qualifications in four specialities: renal nursing (Royal North Shore Hospital, 1979); psychiatric nursing (North Ryde Psychiatric Centre, 1970); intensive care nursing (Royal Prince Alfred Hospital, 1981), and cardio-thoracic nursing (St Joseph's Hospital, Ealing, London, 1981–82).

I hold a Nursing Administration Certificate from NSW Department of Health (1973), an Advanced Human Physiology Certificate from the Sydney Technical College (1985), a Diploma of Teaching from the Sydney Institute of Advanced Education (1987), and a Bachelor of Education from the Sydney Institute of Advanced Education (1989).

For two years I was the Program Director of an Acute Care Course at the NSW College of Nursing. This involved the planning, implementation and co-ordination of a teaching program in acute care and development of health education seminars in remote areas of New South Wales.

Medical research

As the principal research officer for two years of a drug and alcohol program at Royal North Shore Hospital, I gained experience in a wide range of research capabilities. Working with a staff of four assistants, I developed and implemented a research program, supervised the survey, data entry and statistical analysis, and prepared and published the final report.

Overall, I am widely knowledgeable in the areas central to the job of co-ordinator of the Renal Nursing Unit. Throughout my career I have demonstrated an ability as

continued on next page

continued from previous page

manager and organiser, a willingness to adapt to new situations and a thorough understanding of interpersonal skills necessary in the sensitive area of renal nursing. I am a highly motivated person with a strong commitment to the profession of nursing and health management.

My referees are:

Dr Quentin Madgwick
Renal Unit
Prince of Wales Hospital
Randwick NSW 2031
Telephone: (02) 398 4325

Dr Janelle Brunswick
Principal
Sydney College of Advanced Education
PO Box 63
Camperdown NSW 2050
Telephone: (02) 51 4523

Ms Rowena Morrison
Executive Director
NSW College of Nursing
55 Heresford Street
Glebe NSW 2037
Telephone: (02) 660 6785

My telephone number at home is 810 5564. I look forward to discussing this job with you further.

Yours sincerely

Anna Trimble

KEY POINTS: Chapter 17 Preparing and writing a résumé

- The main points to list in a résumé are: your education, work experience, extra-curricular activities and references.
- You might also include special interests, special skills, memberships of groups and societies.
- Even young people with little or no work history can develop a detailed résumé if they apply themselves to the detail of their backgrounds.

QUESTIONS FOR DISCUSSION

- Why should you list things in your résumé, like extracurricular activities, that have little or nothing of direct relevance to the job you are applying for?
- If your only employment has been in part-time, menial jobs while you have been a student, are they worth listing in a résumé?
- Why should you update your résumé at regular intervals? What happens if you don't?
- If work experience and educational qualifications are listed in your résumé, should you repeat the details in a letter of application?

EXERCISES

1. Write your own résumé, giving full details about yourself. Use the conventions of layout and categorisation recommended in this chapter.
2. Look at one of the jobs for which you wrote an application in Exercise 1 of Chapter Fifteen. Prepare a modified version of your résumé to emphasise the abilities and qualifications that you have for this job.
3. Look at one of the jobs for which you wrote an application in Exercise 3 of Chapter Fifteen. Prepare a modified version of your résumé to emphasise the abilities and qualifications that you have for this job.

REVISION LIST FOR PART V

EMPLOYMENT COMMUNICATIONS

- The employment market might be difficult for many people today, but the great majority still gain jobs.
- You need to see your job search as a matter of conducting a campaign. There are at least ten strategies that this campaign can adopt.
- A written application for a job should contain both a letter of application and a résumé.
- An application should do two things for you: it should demonstrate that you are a good candidate for the job and deserve an interview; it should look professional and make a good impression.
- Many young people describe their background in vague terms that sell themselves short. Be specific and give concrete details.
- Before you go for an interview, read over your application letter and think about the experience you describe.
- Find out as much as possible about the organisation and its industry.
- Young people applying for their first job should focus both on their education and their extracurricular activities.
- Describe your qualifications in clear and memorable terms.
- Have an answer prepared about why you applied for the job and about your long-term career objectives.
- Prepare answers to a question about crisis management, if this is appropriate.
- Prepare questions of your own to ask.
- The main points to list in a résumé are: your education, work experience, extracurricular activities and references.
- You might also include special interests, special skills, memberships of groups and societies.
- Even young people with little or no work history can develop a detailed résumé if they apply themselves to the detail of their backgrounds.

PART V
KEY TEXTS AND FURTHER READING

Bisdee, Bob, *Successful Job Hunting in the 1990s*, Macmillan, Melbourne, 1992.

Bolles, Richard Nelson, *What Color Is Your Parachute?* Ten Speed Press, Berkeley, 1993.

Frank, William S., *200 Letters for Job Hunters*, Ten Speed Press, Berkeley, 1990.

Lewis, Adele, *How to Write Better Resumes*, Barrons, New York, 1983.

McLaughlin, Shirley, *Making a Living: The Job Seeker's Manual*, Allen & Unwin, Sydney, 1992.

Nicholson, John and Clemie, Susan, *The Good Interview Guide*, Wright Books, Melbourne, 1990.

Stevens, Paul, *The Australian Resume Guide*, Worklife, Sydney, 1990.

—— *Making Job Applications Work*, Ashton Scholastic, Sydney, 1982.

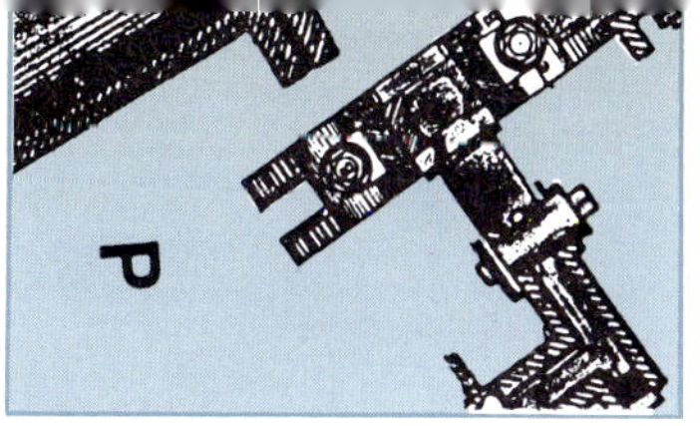

PART

VI

WRITING FOR THE MEDIA

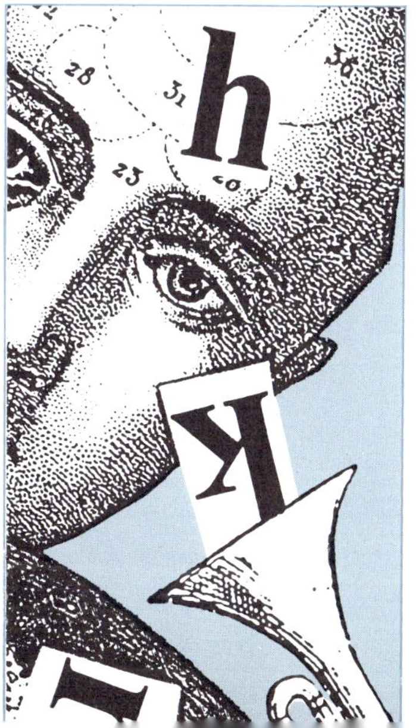

PUTTING SCIENCE INTO THE SUNDAY PAPERS

Peter Pockley is one of Australia's few full-time science journalists. Here he explains his approach to writing and tells how he is trying to build a more scientifically literate newspaper readership.

Despite Australia's status as a world leader in some areas of the sciences (notably in astronomy, medical research, biology and chemistry), Dr Peter Pockley remains one of the few full-time science journalists working in the print media in this country. It is an irony which this former science academic turned writer is painfully aware of.

'We don't have any newspaper anywhere in this country publishing a comprehensive weekly science section. These major features are very popular in all the quality newspapers in the United Kingdom and in the United States. At last count there were about 100 newspapers running such sections in the United States,' he says.

He concedes that the editors of newspapers in Australia are still not particularly receptive to scientific articles which are regarded as dealing with specialised content beyond the understanding or interest of the general public.

In his role as science and technology writer for the *Sun-Herald*, a mass-market tabloid newspaper since 1989, Pockley hopes he has de-mystified science as something abstract and foreboding.

'When I tackle my writing I try not to be too erudite or sophisticated in the language I use. At the same time, because of the editor's support, I'm able to cover topics which are fairly abstruse. I like to think I can help to set the agenda of information and debate among the general community in intellectual matters, which otherwise wouldn't come to their attention.'

Pockley also writes freelance articles for the *Canberra Times*, the *Age* and the *West Australian* but admits it is not always easy to convince editors of the newsworthiness of scientific subjects.

'Our papers have not capitalised on the advantages the press does have of considered scientific writing with diagrams and graphics which can illustrate and expand people's minds and ideas, more than just a snippet of news or that quick flash across the television screen,' he states.

While topicality and practical access to issues most often govern his choice of topics, his varied readership compels him to produce up-to-date and stimulating matter, which will satisfy a broad range of interests.

His own formal qualifications are in the physical sciences, including a PhD in Geology from Oxford University, but his writing crosses all boundaries. 'I write about the physical, biological and social sciences, as well as commenting on government policy on science and education,' says Pockley.

His first inclination is to always cover a local story because of immediate access to sources such as contacts, interviews and photos and to heighten the natural interest of readers. However, being comprehensive isn't always an easy task, as Australia only produces about 2 per cent of the world's scientific output.

'It's natural when an Australian publishes an article in a prestigious journal like *Nature* or the American journal, *Science*, to see if I can make a story out of it,' he says.

He feels it is important to travel overseas in his position as a science writer, even at considerable personal expense.

'If you stay in Australia you become very limited in your views. I write and broadcast overseas in areas where Australian science and technology can stand up in a world sense and be counted. In order to know where Australia rates, you have to travel, otherwise you cannot place in context people and institutions claiming they are doing world-class research. There are some groups that have grossly over-played their self-appointed status and the local media has swallowed that,' he says.

Pockley has been at the forefront of scientific debate for many years. He was the first qualified scientist to work in the media in Australia when he was appointed to the directorship of ABC science programs in 1964, a position he held until 1973.

He believes that scientists have to 'unlearn' a great deal when they address a general audience, as they tend to reinforce the stereotyping of science by the way they write and speak. For instance, he says they are so used to depersonalising, or taking the 'first person' out of their writing, that it can be extremely difficult for them to adopt a simpler, less formal approach.

'Even the general journalistic principle of putting the most important points early in an article is difficult for scientists and academics to grasp, as they have been used to placing their key facts in the conclusion, as in essay style,' he says.

Pockley advises that concise, simple and direct language should be used in technical articles. Interestingly, he believes that scientific terminology isn't a barrier in itself, but that convoluted, passive syntax can be more of an obstacle to easy reading and comprehension.

'I'm perpetually having to re-interpret the writings of people. I make it a practice to ask them for a copy of their scientific paper or a summary, but I'll also interview them as well. People, whoever they are, do talk in conversational terms face-to-face or over the phone when they are much more accessible,' he states.

CHAPTER

18

WRITING NEWS AND FEATURE STORIES

After studying this chapter, you will be able to:

- write news prose suitable for publication in the press
- report speeches and opinions of public figures
- write lead sentences for news stories
- write lead sentences for feature stories
- structure both news and feature stories
- present copy in a form suitable for publication

The daily press is frequently criticised for its low standards—for publishing stories that are sensational or trivial or in poor taste. While some of these criticisms are certainly justified, we nonetheless want to argue that newspaper journalism remains one of our most important forms of communications. In particular, we think the prose style of journalists is one of the best models for others to follow.

Over the past hundred years, the newspaper industry has always been fiercely competitive. To survive in this climate, news reporting has been forced to closely monitor the demands, tastes and needs of its customers, the readers. Newspapers have to be sold out on the streets every day of the week.

The daily practice of writing for mass audiences within a competitive environment has meant journalism has been refined over time to perform its task well. In terms of reaching large numbers of people in a style which is widely understood and appreciated, journalists must be recognised as highly successful communicators. Anyone else who wants to appeal to a similarly wide audience should learn from their experience. This chapter is a study of the basic elements of newspaper journalism.

THE READER OVER YOUR SHOULDER

Of all forms of writing, journalism is the one where the readers are least known to the author. The typical newspaper in the major capital cities has between half a million and one million readers a day. When writing for an audience of this size, the journalist cannot know how much information each audience member has about the story he or she is writing. This is in contrast to a personal letter to a friend or an office memo to a colleague where the writer generally knows how much the reader knows about the subject in question. For the large audience of a newspaper, the journalist has to assume the reader has little knowledge of the subject. Writing this way is difficult. When you are familiar with the details of a story yourself, it is very easy to work on the unstated assumption that readers will know at least some of the basic information.

The journalist has to assume the newspaper reader has little knowledge of the subject. Writing this way is difficult. When you are familiar with the details of a story yourself, it is very easy to work on the unstated assumption that readers will know at least some of the basic information.

For example, one of the most familiar mistakes made by secretaries of sporting clubs when they send in their weekend results to the local suburban or country newspaper is to forget to include the name of the sport itself. A typical story written under these circumstances may begin: 'Kingston defeated Western Districts three to nil in a thrilling semi-final yesterday.' The writer is so wrapped up in the details of the event that he or she fails to appreciate that there are large numbers of people who will read the newspaper and who have never heard of Kingston or Western Districts nor have any idea what sport they play.

Professional journalists have to be continually awake to the basic information that readers need to have to make sense of a story. Even stories involving very famous people have to assume that there may be some people in the audience who are not quite certain who the person in question might be. Journalists do not begin a story: 'Paul Keating yesterday signed the contract for the purchase of a third domestic satellite.' Rather, they would begin: 'Prime Minister Paul Keating yesterday signed the contract ...'

People who are public figures are always identified by their public title at least once in a story about them. Even when a publication circulates only to a small community, this principle should still be upheld. A school newspaper should not begin: 'Mrs Turner last week suspended six girls for smoking.' Rather it should read: 'Barcoo High headmistress, Mrs Dorothy Turner, last week suspended six girls for smoking.' While most readers of this newspaper would know the lady in question, student journalists should work on the assumption that there may be some readers (perhaps parents or other people outside the school) who would be uncertain of her position.

Every time a journalist writes a sentence he or she has to ask the all-important question: 'Is there enough information here to make it perfectly understandable to the reader over my shoulder?' This 'reader' should be assumed to be someone who is unfamiliar with the subject in question. At first, the habit of asking this question is a difficult one to acquire and the journalist has to work hard at it. You have to be particularly aware of the situation when gathering information for a story, especially if there is no opportunity to go back at a later time to collect any essential information you might have initially missed.

To identify a public figure, report:
- name
- title
- organisation

To identify an ordinary citizen, report:
- name
- age
- occupation
- location

One way to check whether your story is intelligible to a reader unfamiliar with the subject is to write it and then put it away, preferably overnight. This gives you a chance to distance yourself somewhat from the topic and, when you come to read the story the next day, you look at it with fresh eyes. This makes it more likely that you will pick up obvious omissions which you have overlooked in the initial writing stage. Unfortunately, journalists working on daily newspapers do not have the luxury of being able to take an extra day to double check their stories. They have to try to develop the skill of reading their material from a 'fresh' perspective as soon as it has been written. To do this they need a continual awareness of 'the reader over your shoulder'.

In some types of story, the basic information needed follows a well-tried formula, particularly in the way to identify people. When dealing with public figures, their title is the basic information needed: 'the Archbishop of Canterbury, Dr Robert Runcie'; 'the head of Joint Intelligence, Major-General Harold Wright'; 'the Minister for Labour, Mr Robert McKinnon'; 'lead singer of The Tramps, Bob Hoon'. Where ordinary citizens who are not public figures are involved, it is normal to include enough information to 'place' the person within their social context: 'Mr John Harris, 35, an accountant of Strathfield, was killed in a three-car collision at Bankstown yesterday.' Here the identifying information tells us a great deal about the person. The name tells us he is a male of Anglo-Saxon background. The addition of information about his age, occupation and the suburb where he lives gives us a sufficient overview of the person to provide a fair idea of his economic standing and social status. The same details tell us a great deal about the next person: 'Ms Helen Mouskouri, a 28-year-old social worker from Newtown, is standing as an independent candidate for Mayor.' In most other cases, there are no formulas to guide the journalist. You have to put yourself in the position of the reader and continually ask yourself how much you need to know to make sense of the situation you are describing.

SHORT SENTENCES

Journalism is meant to be read quickly and easily. One of the ways it achieves this is through the use of short sentences. Some newspapers actually impose a maximum word length on sentences used in their stories. Some specify as few as twenty words per sentence; others allow up to thirty. But even those which don't have fixed word limits still demand that sentences be kept short. The aim of this is to limit each sentence to one idea. News reports aim to be both clear and punchy. Sentences that contain a number of different ideas work against both these aims. Consider the following.

> The high percentage of informal votes was due to a failure by many voters to realise that under the new system there were different requirements for the House and the Senate and that although they had followed their party's advice and numbered only one choice in the House they had to place 15 numbers in sequence on their Senate ballot paper.

There are a number on ideas here contained within the one sentence. Broken into short sentences, the meaning is clearer and the whole communication is easier to read.

> The high percentage of informal votes occurred because many voters failed to understand the new system. They did not realise there were different requirements for the House and the Senate. Many followed their party's advice and numbered only one choice in the House. However, they still had to place 15 numbers in sequence on their Senate ballot paper.

Short sentences are also more dramatic. When giving a narrative of events, it is possible to convey information accurately in one-sentence passages.

> Although there was little chance of finding the trapped boy alive, rescue workers toiled throughout the night and by 5 am the next day they had tunnelled to a small chamber beneath the rubble where they found him still breathing.

However, broken up into short sentences, the same news report can convey some of the drama of the events themselves.

> There was little chance of finding the trapped boy alive. Rescue workers, however, toiled throughout the night. By 5 am the next day they had tunnelled to a small chamber beneath the rubble. There they found him. He was still breathing.

Apart from their impact on the reader, short sentences have one more enormous advantage. They are easier to write. As we noted in Chapter Two, there is nothing more guaranteed to slow down the writing process than starting a sentence without knowing how it will end. If you are in the habit of writing in short sentences you can test various versions of a sentence inside your head before you put a word on paper. This way you avoid the false starts and the convoluted endings that always accompany long, involved sentences. It is also easier to follow a plan when writing short sentences. If the plan is done carefully it will consist of a series of single ideas which tell a story or argue a case. Each idea should be put into a sentence of its own.

When writing to the formula of one idea per sentence, it is often difficult to decide what constitutes 'one idea'. For practical usage, the simplest form of 'one idea' will usually be a subject and object connected by a verb: 'The car crossed the bridge.' There are other cases, however, where you will want to include two ideas in one sentence. One common case is in a conditional statement, 'If ..., then ...', such as: 'If the strikers do not return to work, the Premier will sack them.' This is still a short enough sentence for newspaper usage. It illustrates that the one idea per sentence rule is best regarded as a loose guide rather than anything hard and fast. The best way to think about the issue is that sentences should be kept short where possible, and the number of ideas within each sentence should be kept to a minimum.

The main thing is to make a serious effort to learn to write in short sentences. It is one of the keys, not just to journalism, but to becoming a successful writer of any kind. It allows you to write quickly and clearly and to express complex relationships in a coherent way. It is a simple device and it takes so much of the agony out of writing that it is worth practising whenever possible.

NEWS PARAGRAPHS

Newspaper journalists generally limit each paragraph to only one sentence. This is not a technical device that aids writing like the use of short sentences. It is a practice that has grown out of the needs of newspaper layout. Most news stories have to be cut at the layout stage in order to fit the space available for them. Paragraphs are kept to the minimum length, that is, one sentence long, so that when typeset they each form a compact unit that makes it easier to cut a story to fit more precisely. It is also easier to rearrange the order of sentences if they are typeset in self-contained small paragraphs. If you are writing a news story then follow this style, but if not, write longer paragraphs which contain several sentences that fit together to make one point.

ACTIVE SENTENCES

Newspaper journalism prefers active sentences to passive sentences (or active voice to passive voice). We discussed this in Chapter Four but it is worth emphasising again. Active sentences are direct and rhythmic and carry the reader forward with a definite momentum. Passive sentences tend to hold things up and slow them down.

Active: The detective shot him dead.
Passive: He was shot dead by the detective.

The verb 'to be' (taking the form above as the word 'was') turns an active sentence into a passive one. Avoid using it where possible. Unlike all other verbs, it does not actually 'do' anything in a sentence. In the example above, the passive form is suitable only if you want to place some emphasis on the last word. ('Who shot him?' 'He was shot by the detective.')

ADJECTIVES AND DESCRIPTIVE TERMS

In journalism there is one simple rule about the use of adjectives—keep them to a minimum. If you want to describe a scene, don't tag an adjective or a colourful descriptive phrase onto the object concerned. Don't write:

> John loved his first day at the warm and friendly school.

Instead, compose two sentences:

> John loved his first day at school. It felt warm and friendly.

Similarly, avoid:

> The bright, sparkling river carried them downstream.

Instead, write:

> The river was bright and sparkling. It carried them downstream.

To write this way is not to break up scenes and feelings into short sentences just for the sake of it. The descriptions are actually enhanced and emphasised by being recorded separately. This technique forces the writer to be more sparse with descriptions. It leads you to use adjectives and descriptive terms only when they add an impact to the subject matter. Your writing is less flowery and ornamental. When you do include a description it has a real purpose in the text and stands out in the reader's perception.

CONCRETE DETAILS

Sentences in news stories should contain concrete information that describes real things and actions. They should describe things so that they may be seen, felt or otherwise picked up by readers' senses. Journalism should provide the names and dimensions of objects, people, colours, movements and sounds to allow readers to experience the reality of the scenes being described.

Dimensions are particularly important. They include such measurements as the size of an object, the age of a person, the distance between things, the time taken for something to happen. Numbers like these help readers put details into a perspective and allow them to more vividly picture a scene or event. Consider the following story from a Sydney newspaper.

> Two seamen were killed and five others injured when a huge explosion and fire ripped through an oil tanker anchored at the Shell terminal at Gore Cove early today.

> Frantic crew members jumped 25 m from the deck of the 26 000 tonne *Cellana* into the water as flames spread to the cabin section.
>
> More than 40 men trapped in their cabins battled the blaze with extinguishers as firemen fought to rescue them.
>
> Residents of the area ran from their homes wearing only pyjamas when the fire broke out.
>
> Able Seaman Peter Maiden, 35, from Victoria, said he heard 'an explosion like an atomic bomb' as he worked on the bow of the ship.
>
> 'I saw balls of flame leaping 40 m into the air and another explosion followed,' he said ....
>
> — *Daily Mirror*, Sydney

Note the concrete details in the above example: the number of seamen hurt; the name, size and precise location of the ship; the distance from the deck to the water; the number of seamen fighting the fire; the clothing worn by onlookers; the name, age, title and address of the seaman witness; the sound and size of the explosion and flames. Other details given further down in the story (not published here) include the precise time the explosion occurred, the number of fire brigades and fire floats at the scene and more information about how the two died and about those injured.

This is a fairly conventional disaster story in a down-market tabloid newspaper but it still illustrates many of the principles of good journalism. It involves the gathering of a great deal of information under probably difficult conditions. Few non-journalists would be able to describe this scene as vividly because they would not realise how much on-the-spot research they would need to do, especially in gathering the numbers upon which so much of the story depends. How many, for instance, would think to ask a stunned or excited eyewitness how old he was or his address?

There are many other types of news story that don't offer the same opportunity for graphic details as an explosion and fire. Political speeches, for instance, are very often full of vague or cautious promises and abstract concepts. A story reporting a political speech will of necessity report the words delivered but, in the process of selecting parts of the speech to report, most journalists will still try to focus on the more concrete concepts that the speaker uses. Politicians who speak more in concrete than abstract terms will tend to be reported more often and more prominently. The same is true for anyone else who wants coverage in the news media. The use of concrete language should therefore be a rule-of-thumb for both journalists and those who want to be reported in the news.

DIRECT SPEECH

News stories contain a high proportion of direct quotations. This can range from 20 to 40 per cent of the total volume of the story. In the example above, the eyewitness account of the sound and size of the explosion and flames could have been reported directly by the journalist. By placing the description in the mouth of the eyewitness, the story allows the reader both to get the information and to gain some impression of the feelings of one who was there. News stories that do not have direct speech from people involved lack the feeling of human presence in what happened.

Stories that report speeches, talks or interviews given by some public figure or expert usually contain more direct quotations than stories whose main aim is to record events. They generally contain more than 50 per cent as direct speech. The non-direct speech in these cases is made up of the reporter's summary or paraphrase of part of what was said, descriptions of the surroundings and conditions under which the talk was made, and some personal details about the speaker.

REPORTING OPINIONS

In general, the rule about reporting opinions is that it is normal to report the opinions of others but unusual to include those of the journalist. The function of a news story is not to argue a particular case but to present views which the newspaper judges are in its readers' interests. In news stories, journalists do not write 'I believe ...' or 'In my opinion ...'. Nor do they express any ethical or moral views: 'How unjust ...' or 'What an outrage ...'.

When reporting opinions, journalists should record those of their subjects but keep their own opinions to themselves. Pictured is a background briefing at Parliament House, Sydney

News stories, however, can be quite opinionated even when appearing to be presenting 'just the facts'. Writing any story always involves selecting information. You can never tell everything there is to know, or even all that you know, about a subject. You have to choose those details that will tell the story best. This involves selecting some details and omitting many others. It is impossible to be completely objective in this process so news stories are inevitably biased in one way or another. The degree of bias can vary greatly, however. Some details can be presented from a deliberately moral or ethical position. The journalist does not have to say 'How unfair ...'—the journalist can present information in such a way that most readers will automatically react with this exclamation themselves.

The important ethical issue is not bias but honesty. A journalist can report only one side of a contentious issue yet act in a perfectly ethical manner if it is clear that he or she is reporting the newsworthy views of a public figure or someone well qualified in the subject. The next day it would be just as ethical to report the opposing views on the same subject of another public figure or expert who, a day later, had replied to the first. This is all normal practice and is quite honest and open. Dishonesty arises when there is suppression or distortion. If the journalist knew that a really newsworthy reply had been made by the opponent above within an hour of the first opinion being expressed, yet did not report this as part of the original story, that would be dishonest and misleading.

While expressions of opinion are generally unacceptable for news reporters, they are often expected in feature stories, commentaries and columns. Some journalists in these types of articles are well received *because* they are highly opinionated.

JOURNALESE AND CLICHÉS

One of the occupational hazards of writing quickly is to fall back on overused and abused words and phrases. Use of such journalese and clichés is bad writing because they are usually vague and don't pin down your meaning precisely enough; and because they are so familiar that readers' eyes tend to glaze over and they give no substance to what you have written. Here are some familiar examples.

> Employers claim the union demand is the thin edge of the wedge in the campaign for shorter hours.

> The police chief is leaving no stone unturned in his search for the culprits.

> The conventional wisdom is that interest rates rise following a large budget deficit.

When first used, many of these phrases had originality and freshness, such as 'conventional wisdom', coined by the American economist J. K. Galbraith as an acid put-down of tradition-bound thinking about economic problems. His phrase, however, has now been so overused that it has itself become part of our tradition-bound language. Clichés like these are lazy writing and should be edited out whenever they find their way into an article. Here are some additional examples. Which one of them has crept into our discussion in the paragraph below the subheading above?

- the acid test
- holding to ransom
- stop stone dead
- ballpark figure
- the bottom line

- at the coalface
- the current malaise
- hired gun
- the penny has dropped
- move centre-stage
- pinpoints the concern
- colourful character
- the right psychological moment
- gung-ho style
- where the action is
- law and order
- failed to materialise
- white elephant
- make the supreme sacrifice
- occupational hazard
- conspicuous by his absence
- tough times ahead
- one school of thought
- tailor-made for it
- leave to the tender mercy of
- flair and enthusiasm
- exploring every avenue
- magnetic personality
- the long arm of the law
- ripe for plucking
- meticulous attention to detail
- to hold out no hope
- common or garden variety
- winning ways
- a matter of cold, hard fact
- the proof of the pudding is in the eating

NEWS STORIES—LEADS

The first sentence of a news story is its most important. This lead sentence should be able to tell the basis of the story on its own. Readers should find out what has happened by reading it alone. The rest of the story provides background or elaboration to the lead. The traditional requirement of news is that it should tell the *who, what, when, where* and *why* of a story. If the lead is to stand alone, include as much of this information as is reasonable in the lead itself.

IDEAS

Where possible, the lead should contain one idea. Too many ideas in a sentence detract attention from one another and the central point is weakened. The idea should also be easy to grasp. This does not mean that, in a complex subject, the lead should simplify the issue. Any complex idea can be expressed clearly if the journalist searches for the right words. Overall, the lead should aim to express an idea clearly and succinctly.

SENTENCE ORDER

The subject–verb–object construction is the most direct and easiest to understand. Most leads will say that an agent (subject of the sentence) performed an action (the verb) upon something (the object).

WORD CHOICE

Since the impact made by the lead depends upon the subject and verb, the choice of nouns and verbs is crucial. Wherever possible, the subject should be a concrete noun that the reader can see, hear, taste, feel or smell. It should stand for a name or a thing. The verb should be a vivid action verb that connects the reader to the object or which makes the reader pause and mentally remark the news conveyed.

LENGTH

The lead can be slightly longer than other sentences in a news report but should still be short—less than 35 words.

READER'S PERSPECTIVE

The most important point about a lead is that it should be written from the reader's point of view. Organisations often write their own news stories and send them to newspapers in the form of press releases. The leads on these stories often make their point from the perspective of the organisation itself rather than from that of the readers of the newspaper. Journalists have to rewrite these press releases to make sure they interest their readers. Consider the following two examples from each perspective.

> *Organisation's perspective*
> The Metropolitan Water, Sewerage and Drainage Board today announced a new capital works program to supply fresh reticulated water to domestic consumers in the Peninsula District by November 1994.

> *Reader's perspective*
> People living on the Peninsula will have fresh water connected to their homes by November 1994, the Water Board said today.

In the above examples the Board's emphasis is on the fact that it is embarking on a new capital works program. The newspaper, however, emphasises the impact of the announcement on the lives of its readers. Note also that the Board treats itself rather seriously and includes its full title in the lead. The newspaper, however, uses the name which most people call the organisation. The same is true of the area affected. The Board's lead uses the formal title 'Peninsula District' whereas the newspaper uses the more familiar 'the Peninsula'. Here are two more examples of the same sort of thing.

> *Organisation's perspective*
> The Leader of the Opposition today announced the Centre Party's new industrial relations policy to deregulate the labour market and reform the Conciliation and Arbitration Commission.

Reader's perspective
Workers should have more freedom to negotiate with their own employers on wages and conditions, the Leader of the Opposition said today in releasing the Centre Party's new industrial relations policy.

In both the examples given here we have assumed that the readers would be the general audience of a large, popular daily newspaper. If, however, the newspapers concerned had been more specialised journals aimed at, say, business readers, they would have taken a different slant in their leads. For example:

Pipe-laying contracts worth $30 million dollars will be offered by the Metropolitan Water Sewerage and Drainage Board under its program to extend fresh water supplies to the Peninsula District by 1994.

A Centre Party government would free employers from the directives of the Arbitration Commission and allow them to negotiate directly with unions, the Opposition Leader said today when launching his new industrial relations policy.

FEATURE STORIES—LEADS

In most newspapers there is a clear distinction between news stories and feature stories. News stories are those which make announcements or report new developments in events. Feature stories are those which give background to stories that have already been published as news; which cover issues that are important but not as urgent as the main daily news; or which refer to issues and events which take a much longer time span than one day to unfold.

News stories have direct leads while feature stories generally have indirect leads. Feature stories do not normally start with the main point. They lead up to it from some preliminary descriptive material. There are a great variety of styles that are used as these indirect leads but there are two that are very common and relatively easy to write.

The first is, in a story on a social issue, to focus on one or two individuals who are subject to the issue, to tell their story in a brief but dramatic way, and then make the main point or the real lead in broader social terms. For instance:

The high cost of treating a sick child has brought Keith and Helen Barnes to their knees.

Four years ago they were a prosperous young professional couple, both in well-paid positions and enjoying all the trappings that high salary and generous fringe benefits can bring. Their young son, Andrew, was cared for in their harbourside home by a full-time live-in nurse.

Then, for his third birthday, Andrew was given a three-wheel bike by his parents. A week later he fell off and bumped his head on a back garden path. It was the normal sort of bump that any three-year-old is likely to get but it began a financial nightmare for his parents.

The bump was diagnosed by the Barnes' family doctor as a mild case of concussion. The next day the boy's head was visibly swollen and, after being rushed to hospital, his skull was drilled to relieve hydrocephalus, or 'water on the brain'.

Since then, water build-up has occurred regularly inside Andrew's head and he has just as regularly had operations to relieve the condition. He has spent a total of eighteen months in hospital and had his head drilled twenty times. He has had over one hundred X-rays, countless brain scans and a wide range of test equipment strapped to his head for long periods of time by a variety of specialists. None have been able to explain why his head acts the way it does but they have still charged highly for the advice.

Medical insurance has covered most of their costs but Andrew's parents have still had to pay out over $100 000 in hospital, medical and ambulance bills and for at-home nursing care.

Doctors tell them the next four years will probably be much like the last four—a continual battle to keep Andrew alive and a continued struggle to pay the increasing costs involved.

The Barnes family has fallen victim to a 'catastrophic illness'—a mysterious, incurable, recurring ailment that inflicts one member with a physically devastating disability and the rest of the family with a financial burden that is overwhelming.

At least 10 per cent of all illness in this country has been defined as 'catastrophic'. This form of ill health wreaks havoc not just on its immediate victims but on a much wider circle of family, relatives and friends. It costs families huge sums of money and eats up vast quantities of their time …

The 'direct' lead in this story is the last paragraph. From this point, the story goes on to talk in more general terms about the issue. The personal drama of the individual family is designed to personalise the question so that readers will both grasp the implications better and identify more closely with people who are victims of the condition described.

A second type of indirect lead is the one which again personalises the issue under discussion but which does so by creating a vivid scene or picture within the reader's mind. This lead is something like the description of a scene given at the start of a stage play and it performs many of the same functions. Consider the following.

The scene is the cedar-panelled board room of the country's biggest mining organisation.

Corporate executives, trade union representatives and a university professor file into the room. They take their places around the huge polished table.

Each has an engraved cream folder containing a copy of the agenda for the latest meeting of the board of directors.

The gathering looks like the kind of formal meeting that is typical of a large wealthy organisation, except for one thing. It is an all-male meeting. There are no women members of the board.

Although women make up nearly 40 per cent of the workforce; and even though over 50 per cent of the major private shareholders in the country are female, women are all but excluded from the boards of our large private corporations.

Here again, the real lead is the last sentence. The indirect introduction acts to set a highly visual scene which underlines the point made in the real lead in a dramatic way. The real lead could have been:

Few women serve as directors on the boards of our major private corporations, a survey by this newspaper revealed today.

But in this form, most readers would probably have asked 'So what? We all know that.' The indirect lead used in this story is designed to make readers reflect on a fairly normal situation and see it in a different way, that is, as something abnormal.

Indirect leads are sometimes also used in news stories. When the actual announcement has been made by another source, such as the previous night's television news, then a morning newspaper will often run the basic story but with an indirect lead rather than a direct one. This practice is also followed in weekly news magazines which provide a round-up of news already published that week.

NEWS STORIES—STRUCTURE

The basic structure of a news story is as follows

1. The lead
2. Explanatory and/or amplifying material for the lead
3. Background (if necessary)
4. Secondary points, each self-contained

As we said above, the lead in a news story should be able to stand on its own. It should make its point and contain sufficient information to constitute a story in its own right even if no other sentence follows it. Many stories in the press, and in news headlines broadcast on television and radio, are published just like this, especially in sections that give 'news briefs' or 'round-ups'.

Explanatory or background material is often contained in the second, third and fourth sentences of a news story. This material fills out the information provided in the lead, adding more points to the basic story.

Background material is sometimes given in the fourth, fifth and sixth sentences. Where an event or situation has been running for some time, background information may be useful for people coming to the story for the first time or for those who may be unsure of the original details. Not all stories are appropriate for background material so this is an optional part of the structure.

Secondary points follow next. These are pieces of information that add to and round out the original story. They should be included in descending order of importance or interest. Each sentence should be self-contained and expendable. That is, it should be possible to leave it out and not affect the rest of the story. News stories are written so that they can be cut from the bottom upwards to fit the space available for them. They do not have a conclusion. The last sentence should be the least important or interesting. If the last paragraph is removed, the story should still make sense. If the last, second last and third last points are cut, it should make no difference, and so on.

Here is a typical news story with its structure highlighted.

Lead: The National Farmers Federation has been advised by the major banks that they will not foreclose on farmers hard hit by the recent rise in interest rates.

Amplifying material: This guarantee was given during talks last week between representatives of the Federation and the five major banks.
Explanatory material: The banks advised that although there was a liquidity problem in the farm sector, problems of loan repayment were no worse than in other periods of tight liquidity during the past three decades.
Background: A report on last week's discussions issued yesterday by the Federation shows that predictions of imminent financial disaster in the rural sector are unfounded.

According to the banks the level of foreclosure among Australia's 170 000 farmers was negligible and consistent with the rate of foreclosure over many years.
Secondary points: The banks acknowledged that there was a liquidity problem in the farm sector.

They said there would be no foreclosing on any client whose liquidity problems related primarily to the recent rise in interest rates and fall in commodity prices.

The banks confirmed that the rice and sugar industries and parts of the West Australian grain belt were in the worst position to cope with a continuation of these pressures.

Most farmers have responded to the squeeze on cash flows by increasing overdrafts and running down bank deposits where available.

The latest Bureau of Agricultural Economics projections show an overall decline of 22 per cent in the real net value of rural production over last year.

Sydney Morning Herald

FEATURE STORIES—STRUCTURE

News stories can be any length but tend to be short. Feature stories, on the other hand, are generally longer—often from 1000 to 2000 words. Because they have this additional length, feature stories have a more formal structure. After an indirect lead they usually state their main point. Then they present the evidence for their case. They usually have a conclusion. The prose can flow more smoothly as each point can be regarded as part of a larger whole rather than something self-contained.

The principles involved in the structure of a feature story cannot be laid out in advance any more than we have offered here. Each story will have its own needs and hence its own structure. However, we still want to insist on the importance of planning a feature article. You should have a point-by-point plan for the whole article, as we recommended in our discussion of planning in Chapter Two. Then, as you come to write each point, you should first work out a plan of the way it will go.

A feature story will usually try to take the reader from one place to another. It could be an informative kind of journey, from a position where the reader does not know much about a subject to one where he or she is much better informed at the end. Or it could be from where the reader starts with one opinion on a matter to where the feature article has persuaded him or her to have another opinion or some deeper understanding. The planning of the structure should be done after purposes like these have been sorted out clearly in the writer's mind.

As we said in Chapter Two, the first thing to do when approaching any writing job is to ask yourself to define your purpose. The structure you will decide on and the kind of evidence you will present will be based on how you answer this question.

PRESENTATION

If you are writing a piece of journalism to submit to a newspaper or magazine there are some principles to follow in the way you present your work.

1. Make sure you are familiar with the publication and that you know the nature of its audience. Is it a newspaper selling to the general public, a magazine selling to working women on high incomes, a journal aimed at men with a strong interest in sport? Understanding this audience and the way the publication wants to appeal to it will tell you a great deal about the type of articles the publication will be looking for and the style in which it should be written.
2. Your writing must be typed, in double spacing or one-and-a-half spacing. The quality should be at least that of an electric typewriter. Handwritten material, poor quality manual typewriter standard and dot matrix output from a computer printer are not acceptable.
3. Type on one side only of a white sheet of A4 paper.
4. Leave at least a 3 centimetre margin on both sides of the page as well as the top and bottom.
5. Never break up a word with a hyphen between one line and the next. Keep all words intact. The final version published for readers might have hyphens but at the editing stage it is very annoying to find words broken up this way.
6. Number every page consecutively at either the top or bottom of the page.
7. Add a title page to the front. This should contain the article's title, the author's name, the author's title or job position if this is relevant to the article, the author's address and telephone number, the date the article was submitted.
8. Fasten the pages together with a paper clip, not staples or a pin.
9. Enclose the article flat in a good quality A4 envelope. Don't fold it up and send it in a letter sized envelope, even if it is only a few pages long.
10. If you want the article back if it is not accepted, enclose a stamped self-addressed envelope.
11. Make a photocopy of everything you write and do not submit anything until you have this copy. Send the original and keep the copy for yourself.
12. Telephone the person responsible for accepting articles—the editor, the news editor, the features editor or whatever—and tell him or her that you have an article that might be suitable for the publication and that you are sending it in.
13. Deliver the article yourself or send it by courier the same day as you telephone. The mail is usually too slow and unreliable.

KEY POINTS: Chapter 18 Writing news and feature stories

- The prose style of journalists, developed over a century of fierce competition for readers, is one of the best models for others to follow.
- It's important to put yourself in the position of the reader. Remember not to assume knowledge.
- Short sentences are clear, punchy and dramatic. Keep the number of ideas per sentence to a minimum.
- Use active rather than passive sentences. Where possible, avoid adjectives. Include concrete details and report direct speech.
- It is normal to report the opinions of others but, except in feature stories, rare to include those of the journalist. However, the selection process always involves some degree of bias. Such a bias is ethical as long as no relevant information is suppressed or distorted.
- The basic structure of a news story is as follows.
  1. the lead
  2. explanatory and/or amplifying text for the lead
  3. background (if necessary)
  4. secondary points, each self-contained
- Submit articles typed, on single-sided A4 paper, with double or one-and-a-half spacing, and with at least 3 centimetre margins all round.

QUESTIONS FOR DISCUSSION

1. Describe the main components of the prose style of journalism.
2. Does the prose style of newspaper journalism serve the needs of its readers?
3. Is a feature story lead which focuses on an individual the best way to start an article about large numbers of people?

EXERCISES

Rewrite the following three leads for news stories. Write two leads in each case: one for a popular daily newspaper and the other for a business magazine.

1. Telecom today announced a new scale of telephone charges which include the following increases: the price of domestic calls up by 10 per cent from 20 cents to 22 cents per call; the cost of long distance calls between major capital cities between 9 am and 5 pm will rise by 30 per cent from $1.00 per minute to $1.30 per minute. The cost of long distance calls outside business hours, however, will be reduced from 80 cents to 60 cents per minute.

continued on next page

continued from previous page

2. The state government today accepted the recommendations from the House Committee report into the regulation of prostitution. The report argued that prostitution should be illegal within areas zoned as residential but legal in all commercial and shopping zones in the city, the suburbs and the major country towns.

3. The Commonwealth government has approved a public holiday on Monday, 4 September to commemorate International Women's Day. The holiday will be celebrated in all states and will affect six million workers and two million school children.

In the following exercises, it will be helpful to find similar kinds of news stories or feature articles in newspapers or magazines, and to study carefully the way they treat the issues concerned.

4. Attend a graduation ceremony, a school speech day, a building opening or some other similar commemorative occasion where a public speech is to be made. Take notes of the speech and write a news report based on it.

5. Attend a meeting of your local shire, municipal or city council. Take notes on the debates and discussion that occur during the meeting. Select three items that would interest local citizens and write a news story on each. The stories should be based only on what transpired at the meeting and should not include any information gathered from outside sources.

6. Watch a television current affairs program which covers a topical issue in some depth (such as ABC-TV's 'Four Corners' or 'Quantum'). Write (a) a news story, and (b) a feature article on the issue.

7. Choose a person you know who has recently made some notable achievement such as reaching a certain age, completing a course of study or gaining a desirable position (the achievement does not have to be one that would normally attract media attention). Interview the person about the significance of the achievement and the person's plans for the future. Write (a) a news story, and (b) a feature article based on the interview.

8. Select an issue that is presently the subject of some controversy in your local area. Gather information and interview people with strong views on the subject from at least two (desirably more) opposing perspectives. Write a feature article on the subject.

CHAPTER

19

TECHNICAL AND SCIENTIFIC ARTICLES

After studying this chapter, you will be able to:

- write technical articles for non-specialist readers
- tailor a prose style to a particular audience
- preserve technical terms but avoid jargon
- adopt a prose style that is both precise and concise
- develop a structure for a technical article from the research process

Technical and scientific articles written for magazines and journals are usually different from journalism aimed at the general public. The writer can assume a greater knowledge of the subject matter and a greater interest in it among readers than in mass-market newspapers and magazines. Technical and scientific articles are usually published in specialist publications. People buy them because they either work in that field or because it is an important part of their leisure and recreation interests. This defines the audience at the outset and shifts the task of the writer to a different level. On the one hand, the writer can assume an intelligent interest in the subject by the reader. This means that you only need to define once the key terms of the vocabulary and the concepts discussed. There is no need to spell out every point every time it is raised. You don't need to spoon-feed the reader or to lower the intellectual force of the discussion to accommodate slow or disinterested readers. On the other hand, technical terms and language need to be used sparingly. It is essential that the discussion does not descend to jargon or shop talk which excludes all but the most dedicated professional.

It is also important in technical writing not to be overly dramatic nor to beat-up the story you have to tell. Those who know the subject are most unlikely to be taken in by such tactics. However, there is still pressure on the writer to be interesting, to give readers familiar with the subject new information and to introduce new developments and new approaches to the subject. In other words, technical writing should always try to avoid the stereotype that it is dry and boring.

DEFINING THE AUDIENCE

As in any form of writing, the audience is the main consideration in a technical article. However, the type of reader is probably more important to consider here than in almost any other area because they can vary so much. The audience could be composed entirely of highly skilled specialists in a narrow field. Or they could be people in related professions who might be indirectly but still significantly affected by a new development. Or the audience might be a wide range of readers who have only a moderate interest or curiosity in the subject. Before you do anything else, you need to specify quite clearly to yourself what kind of audience your article will try to attract and how your article will relate to them.

For general audiences, write either:

- background articles—history of the subject plus its purpose or function
- instructional articles—step-by-step, how-to-do-it guide

The nature of the research, the structure of the article and the way you conceive the entire task will follow from this last question. If the audience is of a general kind then there are two kinds of articles that are more likely to be written for them. The first is a background article. This will itself have two aspects: first, the history of the subject and, second, an explanation of its purpose or function within your broad field. The second is the instructional article. This gives the reader who is unfamiliar with the subject a step-by-step, how-to-do-it guide. It should not only tell how something is done but why. The purpose of an operation or part is an important part of the instruction because it gives the reader reasons for doing what he is instructed and this makes it more likely that the instructions will be actually followed.

If the audience is a specialised group which is knowledgeable about the general subject matter then an article will usually be one of two other kinds. The first is a descriptive article aimed at giving specialists information about a new product or process. The second is the persuasive article aiming to persuade readers to adopt a particular point of view or to get the specialists to adopt a product or procedure as part of their operations. Often, a technical article can combine descriptive and persuasive elements.

Once you have defined the audience, the scope of the article and the nature of the research task will begin to fall into place. As part of the process of thinking about the article, you also need to consider the type of language in which it will be written. More problems with technical articles occur over questions of language, especially the use of technical terms and the level of complexity required, than in any other type of writing. For this reason, the next two sections take up this question. Part of the planning process should be devoted to determining the language that the article will adopt.

For specialist readers, write either:
- descriptive articles—information on new developments
- persuasive articles—an argument for a point of view or action desired

THE VOCABULARY OF TECHNOLOGY

It is important to be able to distinguish between technical terms and jargon. Technical terms should have two characteristics. First, they should be restricted to those objects, processes, measurements and actions that cannot be described in normal English—items that are unique to the particular technical field being discussed. Second, technical terms must have precise meanings. There should be a clear definition of what they refer to. The definition should make it clear that the term has strict limitations and excludes shifts of meaning that might produce ambiguities.

When employed in these ways, technical terms improve the communication process between people working in the field. People are quite clear what the term refers to and what it does not mean. Technical terms of this kind are also readily explainable to those outside the field. It is often important for someone in one area to be able to communicate with people in others. On a construction site, the electrical contractor needs to be able to explain his needs to the architect and to the structural engineer. He can do this if his own range of specialist terms are kept to a minimum and are very precise.

Instead of a wide range of jargon, technical writing should adopt a restricted number of specialist terms which have precise meanings.

Jargon is a specialised language that does more harm than good. It often begins as a series of technical terms but degenerates into a whole language of its own. People adopt abbreviations, nicknames and other short-cuts to describe objects and operations in their work and before long it is impossible for anyone outside the field to understand what they are saying. In some fields, such as the law, a language has grown up to protect the employment of the profession. Concepts about the way people relate to one another which, in a democratic society, should be widely accessible to everyone have been shrouded in words and phraseology that are frequently unintelligible. Lawyers often argue that this is because of the need to give precise meaning but one only has to look at the archaic phrases employed in the law, or to read a legal opinion or judgment interpreting words or phrases, to see that the law is, of necessity, a fairly imprecise body of knowledge that is constantly changing. The only reason for its obscure language is to create a demand for legal practitioners to interpret it. This makes a mockery of the notion that ignorance of the law is no excuse for not keeping it. Much of the language of the law is deliberately designed to keep people uncertain of it and to make them dependent on lawyers.

Another of the worst offenders is the computer profession. Computers certainly need a range of technical terms because they have parts, processes, dimensions and speeds that do not occur in any other area of business or industry. In the early years of the industry, computer professionals communicated largely with one another and had little to do with outsiders. The traditions of poor expression and jargon that grew up in this period are still with us and actually hinder the ability of people to make the most benefit of computers. The situation in an office is like that on a construction site. People in, for example, accounting, marketing and computers need to talk to each other about the way their operations integrate. Instead of a wide range of jargon, computing should have a restricted number of technical terms which have precise meanings and which can be readily communicated to people in other departments.

People who are very familiar with a subject often find it difficult to explain the basics because they have lived with them for so long they take them for granted.

These considerations are important for anyone thinking about writing technical and scientific articles. You cannot avoid using some technical terms but you should never allow the article to descend into jargon. This means making a conscious effort to limit the number of technical terms in an article. This way everyone who knows the field will know the precise meaning of these terms and there will be a minimum risk of confusion.

If the audience for the article is likely to include outsiders or people unfamiliar with the field then you should maintain the above practice. Do not drop technical terms altogether in order to put your words into everyday English. Instead, make sure that each technical term is explained the first time it is used, either in the text itself or in a footnote. If the explanation has to be more than three sentences it is better placed as a footnote so that readers who do know what it means will not be bored. In some cases, it will be desirable to explain the technical term by a diagram or illustration. In these cases, you might prefer to include the explanation as part of an appendix at the end of the article.

People who are very familiar with a subject often find it difficult to explain the basics because they have lived with them for so long they take them for granted. If you are in this position, keep a dictionary or glossary of standard terms and use it to help you define them. If you are writing a long article, a paper or a short book on the subject which is designed to be read by outsiders, it might be helpful to include a glossary at the end of the text. If you do this, you still need to explain your terms in the text the first time you use them.

THE STYLE OF TECHNICAL WRITING

PRECISION

Technical and scientific articles should be precise. There should be a greater degree of certainty about what is meant in these kinds of articles than in any others. Precision in the technical sense is not the same as precision in the legal sense. Lawyers, as we noted above, believe the way to be precise is to define terms at great length and to have a range of subordinate clauses including some meanings and excluding others. Technical articles, in contrast, should be precise by being concrete.

As a rule of thumb, this involves focusing on names and numbers. Instead of vague indicators, the exact name of equipment, parts, operations and procedures should be used at all times. Dimensions are even more important in these articles than in more conventional journalism. Precise measurements of size, distance and time taken should be given. While newspaper journalists might write: 'More than 1000 people were affected,' a technical article should say: 'A total of 1076 people were affected.' Times should also be precise: not 'about 3 am', but '2.57 am'. Like other journalism, technical articles should use concrete language at all times and, even in passages that contain no strictly technical terms, should focus on things that may be seen, felt or otherwise picked up by the senses. They should describe colours, movements, sounds and textures in realistic terms wherever possible.

CONCISENESS

Technical articles should also be concise and punchy. This means writing in a direct manner without wasting words, without wandering off the point into unnecessary asides, and without trying to impress anyone with a literary writing style. More than anywhere else, technical writing should communicate ideas between writer and reader with as little distraction from the written page as possible. It is the ideas that should be impressive, not the writing.

The best single device to use to be concise is the short sentence. A sentence that contains only one or two ideas in less than thirty words—better still, less than twenty—is too short to contain any waffle or unnecessary diversions. It imposes its own discipline simply by its length. More important, technical articles frequently have to explain complicated or sophisticated equipment or procedures. These are best made clear by breaking up their complexity into a series of separate steps or ideas and devoting one sentence to each.

Technical articles frequently have to explain complicated or sophisticated equipment or procedures. These are best made clear by breaking up their complexity into a series of separate steps or ideas and devoting one sentence to each.

Let's take an example of a good piece of scientific writing to illustrate some of the points made so far in this chapter. The following passage is from Richard Bergland's excellent book, *The Fabric of Mind* (Penguin, 1985), a study of the human brain and a history of scientific theories about the brain. He is describing experiments into the ventricles, the hollow, fluid-filled centre of the brain, done by William Dandy in Baltimore in 1911.

> Dandy's experiments were performed in dogs and were designed to learn more about the disease of 'hydrocephalus'. In those days, before antibiotics, meningitis was commonplace and those who survived were often left with 'water on the brain' or hydrocephalus. The understanding of hydrocephalus, he reasoned, would lead to an answer to the question, 'Why is the brain hollow?'
>
> In Dr Halsted's general surgical practice [where Dandy was training as a brain surgeon], operations for obstructed stomachs and obstructed bladders were

commonplace and, as a medical student, Dandy could not have escaped the lesson that 'outlet obstruction' caused ballooning of hollow organs.

Dandy quite naturally asked, 'Could outlet obstruction cause the ballooned-up ventricles of hydrocephalus?' and designed experiments to test that possibility. In dogs, he placed a 'cork' in the aqueduct that linked the third and fourth ventricles.

After this operation the ventricles were much larger, very similar to those seen in hydrocephalus. To Dandy, this development meant that the ventricles had been blown up like a balloon as a consequence of outlet obstruction.

Dandy's next question, 'Where could the water come from?', also prompted an experimental approach. He opened one half of the brain, the left cerebrum, like a clam in order to remove the choroid plexus that lay in the floor of the ventricle. Then he inserted his 'cork' in the aqueduct as he had done before. Now he found that only the right ventricle became swollen, the one that still contained the choroid plexus.

Dandy concluded that the water in the ventricles that caused hydrocephalus came from the choroid plexus. It appeared to him that water was continually coming from the choroid plexus and needed to get out of the brain. If it could not pass through the outlets, the brain would swell like a balloon, in every way like the stomach and the bladder.

There are a number of points to observe and note in this passage. First, Bergland's sentences are short, with most containing only one or two ideas. Second, the structure of the passage is important. It tells the story, step-by-step, in a narrative form. This is a method that has long been recognised as highly effective by people in a number of fields. In documentary film-making, for example, one of the traditional pieces of advice is that if you want to make a film about the manufacture of glass bottles, you tell a narrative story of the way that one bottle is made, from its beginning as sand and other raw materials, then step-by-step through each stage of the manufacturing process, to its emergence as the finished product.

Third, the passage uses technical terms very sparingly. It uses the technical names of the two main parts of the brain it is discussing, the ventricles and the choroid plexus. But parts that are less important to the story are described in words drawn from ordinary English. The link between the third and fourth ventricles (in paragraphs 3 and 5 above) is not called by any technical name but simply described as an 'aqueduct'. The material used to obstruct this aqueduct is treated the same. No technical term is employed; it is simply called a 'cork'. We realise, however, that it would not be really made of cork but is performing the function of a cork.

Fourth, Bergland talks of organs 'ballooning', an effective metaphor which readers readily imagine and which he uses several times. He also gives a vivid picture of one half of the brain being opened 'like a clam'. The author here makes an effective use of an analogy by comparing one unfamiliar object or process to one that is familiar to the lay reader. This is a technique he employs several times in this passage and throughout the book. It is one of the key techniques of successful technical writing. At the end of the passage he makes another vivid comparison but this time he links it to Dandy's own surgical experience. He describes the brain swelling like the stomach and the bladder, which recalls the picture he has already painted in paragraph two.

In the book, this passage is accompanied by two drawings (which we have not reproduced here) which show side views of the split dog's brain with (1) the cork in place and (2) the choroid plexus being severed in surgery. Drawings of this kind are very useful supports to the text but they should be used with care. The text should stand on its own and be understandable without the drawing. The drawing should have a caption which allows it, too, to stand on its own and be clear to someone who has not read the main text.

Bergland's book is aimed at a wide audience. It is written for surgeons of the brain, for doctors in general practice, for biochemists, for psychologists, for psychiatrists and for the intelligent lay reader. He wants to convince them that traditional theories of the brain as an electrically driven computer are wrong and that the brain is a gland and is run by hormones and chemical fluids. In presenting this theory to a wide audience, he assumes his readers have little knowledge of the parts of the brain or of the existing theories about how it functions, even though he knows some readers have a great deal more of this knowledge than others. He reserves technical terms for the key concepts he wants to discuss. He makes sure that the first time he uses a technical term he defines it and provides a drawing of the part of the brain or the process it refers to. The end result is a book that successfully addresses both scientists and medical professionals on the one hand, and general readers on the other. It is an excellent handbook for anyone interested in technical and scientific writing.

Reserve technical terms for the essential concepts under discussion. For the rest, use familiar English terminology. The first time a technical term is used, it should be defined and, preferably, an illustration of it provided.

One readily available source of both good and bad examples of technical writing is the computer magazine field. Some of the popular personal computer magazines sold in newsagents contain articles of both kinds, often in the same issue.

On the one hand, some of their articles address the reader in an open, unpretentious manner like Bergland in the passage above. On the other hand, some are examples of the very worst kind of jargon and unintelligible in-talk. As an exercise, buy two or three copies of these magazines and pick out examples of each type.

Two other writers who provide good models of style for technical and scientific articles are Stephen Toulmin and June Goodfield who together have written three widely acclaimed books on the history of science, *The Fabric of the Heavens, The Architecture of Matter* and *The Discovery of Time.*

Another marvellous scientific writer is the evolutionary biologist, Stephen Jay Gould, who has lifted the popular scientific essay to new heights. Five volumes of his collected articles are readily available in paperback.

THE RESEARCH PROCESS

Research for a technical article should be done in clearly defined stages.

1. Analyse the subject or the problem you intend writing about. Under the earlier section 'Defining the audience' we suggested there were four types of technical article:

(a) background (historical and explanatory)
(b) instructional
(c) descriptive
(d) persuasive

The first two, we said, were more suited to newcomers to the subject; the last two were appropriate for those knowledgeable in the field. Sometimes, technical writers are advised to make a distinction between 'classification' and 'analysis'. By classification, you build up a description of a field by listing in logical categories all the varieties of the field. This is a common method of describing the range of animals that come within a particular species. In analysis, the opposite procedure is adopted. A field or a subject is broken down from a whole into the parts that make it up. This classification–analysis approach can be useful for scientific procedures in certain subject areas but we think it is essential that it be viewed in terms of the audience for whom the approach is being done. The classification–analysis distinction fits into articles for both audience types we have identified. It may be employed as part of a background article for newcomers or as part of a descriptive article for old hands.

2. Draw up a research plan from your analysis of the issue. This research plan will be similar to that described in Chapter Nine. It will be a set of headings under which various pieces of researched information will be filed. Be prepared to expand, contract or modify this list of headings as you proceed with your research. When the research is complete, this list will be the framework for the article itself. Its headings will correspond to the headings you actually use in the article and will be the plan that you follow in the writing phase.
3. Allocate one manila folder to each heading in the research plan and put all your notes and photocopies appropriate to the heading into its manila folder. Follow the procedures recommended in Chapter Nine for making liberal use of photocopying and minimum use of direct, handwritten note-taking. Keep one folder for the introduction and one for the conclusion and file material in these as you think appropriate.
4. When you decide you have done enough research, take a holistic view of the overall list of headings in the research plan and the contents of the folders. Ask yourself whether this final version is the best possible arrangement of material ready for writing. If necessary, re-shuffle the order of some of the folders and rearrange the contents of some of them. This is an important phase because, most of the time when you are engaged in research or writing, you concentrate on the details in front of you and don't think enough about the total picture. Make sure you give yourself the chance to take a total perspective on your work.

THE WRITING PHASE

If you have been well organised in your research and have a good plan for the article, the writing phase will not be daunting. You will already have decided the type of article it will be and the order in which it will be written. As we advised earlier, technical terms should be used sparingly and defined the first time they are used. The degree of familiarity you take with the subject matter will depend on your interpretation of the audience's needs. Your prose should be precise and concise. Use analogies or comparisons whenever you need to describe an unfamiliar object or process. Employ illustrations generously if this is possible, even if it means doing them yourself.

Divide the article into sections and take the headings for each section from the final plan. Within each section, each point should be made by its own paragraph. Most paragraphs will be from three to six sentences long. Try to plan each paragraph before you start writing it. The normal plan for a paragraph will follow either the inductive or deductive model. In the inductive model, you put down each piece of information that goes to make up your point. Then, in the last sentence of the paragraph, you draw from these points the conclusion you want. In the deductive model, you begin the paragraph by asserting your main point. You then use the rest of the paragraph to write down the evidence that goes to support this first sentence. Not all paragraphs follow these models. Some will be straightforward descriptions, starting at one point and finishing at another.

The introduction and the conclusion will probably be the hardest to write. If you find this is so, leave both until last and begin writing the article from a more comfortable place. The introduction can be one of two kinds. First, it can be a statement of what you are intending to prove or describe or establish in the article. Don't make a formal declaration in this statement; try and write in a relaxed manner. Second, you could try the sort of introduction used in newspaper feature stories. As we wrote in the previous chapter, two common types of introduction on these lines are: (1) describing one or more individuals who are involved with or subject to the issue, and using their experience to lead into a general statement about the question; or (2) creating a vivid scene in the mind of the reader by a closely detailed description of the object or setting, in much the same manner as a playwright would describe the scene for the start of a play.

Many technical articles finish with a conclusion that brings together all the points made and gives an overview of the whole subject. In some cases, though, this is neither possible nor desirable. If the article is of the descriptive or instructive type, a conclusion will often not be necessary. You can leave it to the reader to have followed the article through its stages and to have absorbed each section. In these cases, the article can simply stop when you reach the end of the description. Like all other forms of writing, you can tell whether this is a satisfactory way to end by putting the article away overnight. When you return the next day with a 'fresh' perspective, you can tell if it needs a summary type of conclusion or not.

PRESENTATION

Any article submitted for publication should observe minimum standards of presentation. For full details of these, read the thirteen points recommended for journalism published at the end of the previous chapter. A brief summary follows.

1. A submitted article should be typed on a good quality computer printer, or, at least, on an electric typewriter, on one side only of A4 paper.
2. It should be formatted in one-and-a-half or double spacing and have generous margins on both sides plus top and bottom.
3. The pages should be consecutively numbered and held together by paper clip, not a pin or staples.
4. The article should have a title page containing your name, address, telephone number and the date.
5. Before you let the article out of your hands, make sure you have a photocopy of it.
6. Send the original, placed flat in an A4 envelope, to the editor of the publication and keep the copy for yourself.

KEY POINTS: Chapter 19 Technical and scientific articles

- Writers of articles in specialist publications can assume an intelligent interest on the part of their audience. They do not need to spoonfeed slow or uninterested readers.
- The use of precise technical terms should not be allowed to degenerate into jargon. Use footnotes or a glossary to make yourself clear.
- Technical and scientific articles should be both precise and concise. Details should be exact and the style should not distract the reader from the content.
- Use headings and illustrations to make your points as clearly as possible.
- Submit articles typed, on single-sided A4 paper, with double or one-and-a-half spacing, and with at least 3 centimetre margins all round.

QUESTIONS FOR DISCUSSION

1. Is it really possible to communicate with both specialist and lay audiences in the one piece of writing?
2. Does the work of scientists who are also popular science writers, such as Stephen Jay Gould, Paul Davies or Paul Feynman, fit the analysis offered in this chapter?

EXERCISES

Most readers of this chapter will be people with a scientific or technical background who will have their own individual area of expertise. Given this, please attempt one or all of the following exercises.

1. Write an article suitable for professionals in your field on one of the following topics:

   (a) the most exciting recent development in your area
   (b) a deplorable recent issue in your area
   (c) a human interest biography on a particular individual who works in your field (even if he or she is not well known)
   (d) a 'personality' profile of an organisation of department in your area (even if the organisation is not well-known)
   (e) an article which explains clearly the workings of a particular process in your area

2. Write any of the above articles for the intelligent lay reader who would be interested in your field.

REVISION LIST FOR PART VI

WRITING FOR THE MEDIA

- Developed over a century of fierce competition for readers, the prose style of the press remains one of the best models for writers of all kinds to follow.

- Journalistic prose is a very good example of the techniques needed to write to a large audience who cannot be expected to have very much background knowledge of the subject at issue.

- It's important to put yourself in the position of the reader. Remember not to assume knowledge.

- Short sentences are clear, punchy and dramatic. Keep the number of ideas per sentence to a minimum.

- Use active rather than passive sentences. Where possible, avoid adjectives. Include concrete details and report direct speech.

- It is normal to report the opinions of others but, except in feature stories, rare to include those of the journalist. However, the selection process always involves some degree of bias. Such a bias is ethical as long as no relevant information is suppressed or distorted.

- Writers of articles in technical and specialist publications can assume an intelligent interest on the part of their audience. They do not need to spoonfeed slow or uninterested readers.

- The use of precise technical terms should not be allowed to degenerate into jargon. Use footnotes or a glossary to make yourself clear.

- Technical and scientific articles should be both precise and concise. Details should be exact and the style should not distract the reader from the content.

PART VI
KEY TEXTS AND FURTHER READING

Bergland, Richard, *The Fabric of Mind*, Penguin, Harmondsworth, 1985.

Blicq, Ron S., *Technically-Write*, 4th ed, Prentice Hall, Englewood Cliffs, 1992.

Boyd, Andrew, *Broadcast Journalism: Techniques of Radio and TV News*, Focal Press, Oxford, 1993.

Cappon, Rene J., *The Word: An Associated Press Guide to Good News Writing*, Associated Press, New York, 1992.

Gould, Stephen Jay, *Bully for Brontosaurus*, W.W. Norton, New York, 1991.

Granato, Len, *Reporting and Writing News*, Prentice Hall, Sydney, 1991.

Hines, John, *The Way to Write Magazine Articles*, Elm Tree Books, London, 1987.

Jervis, Bob, *News Sense*, Advertiser Newspapers, Adelaide, 1989.

Kinross-Smith, Graeme, *Writer: A Working Guide for New Writers*, Oxford University Press, Melbourne, 1992.

Morris, Jill and Lancaster, Mary, *Writing Freelance Articles for Newspapers and Magazines*, Interface Publications, London, 1985.

Newson, Doug and Wollert, James A., *Media Writing: News for the Mass Media*, Wadsworth, Belmont, 1985.

Purchase, Shirley (ed.), *The Australian Writers' and Editors' Guide*, Oxford University Press, Melbourne, 1991.

Weiss, E. H., T*he Writing System for Engineers and Scientists*, Prentice Hall, Englewood Cliffs, 1982.

White, Sally, *Reporting in Australia*, Macmillan, Melbourne, 1991.

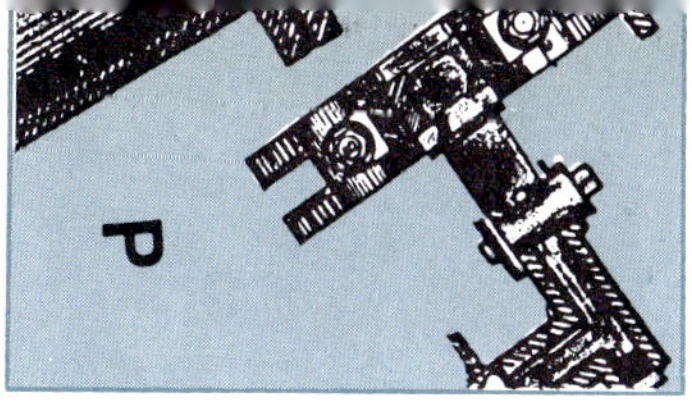

PART VII

REPORTS AND SUBMISSIONS

HOW TO GAIN THE EDGE IN RESEARCH

Elizabeth Swan and the State Library of New South Wales are breaking new grounds using electronic systems for corporate research.

You are writing a report for an organisation that wants to expand its market by exporting to other countries. You would like to know how many other companies like yours are competing in the international market, what volumes of sales they make each year, and which countries provide the biggest markets for your line of goods. This all sounds like something that would take months of work and cost tens of thousands of dollars. Wrong. A good library can now give you all this information within days and at a fraction of the cost you thought possible.

Thanks to computers and satellite communications systems, libraries are making dramatic changes to their traditional services. Some of the leading libraries now act as information brokers for today's competitive business environment. Just ask Elizabeth Swan. In a joint venture with the State Library of New South Wales, she set up Information Edge, a corporate information service, in 1989. The service has since established itself as a valuable asset to all types of businesses.

'At Information Edge, we use our knowledge of how to use libraries and how to use on-line databases to do research for companies,' she explains.

Swan worked in the corporate world for twenty years, partly with a publisher in the Netherlands which was developing databases to provide information to doctors. Later she had a similar role with ACI in Australia.

'I knew there was a lot of information available which was very relevant to companies,' she says.

Through the use of sophisticated on-line technology, Information Edge provides details of published literature on a variety of topics worldwide: market-share statistics, hazards related to chemicals, occupational health issues, how to improve productivity, how to motivate staff, corporate structure and industry growth trends.

And it seems busy executives are starting to realise that access to up-to-date, timely and reliable data is crucial to their companies' success. This is a trend which Swan hopes will increase.

She says that people to date have not been information literate, but that businesses are now understanding that if they pay for information resources, they will have more control over them.

Information Edge receives a staggering variety of requests from major companies, law firms, government departments and even individuals.

Swan cites the example of a man who wanted to sell print posters in the United States and needed to find out what were the best distribution outlets. Through the expertise of her team of researchers, they were able to get him a contact list of ten potential companies that he could approach as distributors.

'By identifying his needs and matching them with electronic sources, we were able to give him some very valuable leads,' she enthuses.

She stresses that she and her staff were using on-line technology at ACI as early as 1977, but that there are still many people who do not understand its strengths and cost-effectiveness.

Swan is adamant that business information should be available to people at all levels of a company, including blue-collar workers. During a recent visit to a factory in Western Sydney, Swan spoke to a manager who wanted to know the dangers associated with a particular solvent used in the plant and if it could affect his staff.

'He had no idea that Information Edge could help him easily and quickly. For about $200 we could find out everything that had been published over the last twenty years about the possible carcinogenic effects of the solvent,' she says. 'What is different about Information Edge is that we've said we will sell our skills at using databases to all people, including those who don't have access to a library.'

At its Macquarie Street Sydney headquarters, the State Library provides free on-line searches and access to CD-ROM databases, which give important lists of published references, but Swan says there is an added dimension to the services provided by Information Edge.

She gives the example of a client who wanted to know about the images created by packaging. For instance, what was it that made an after-shave package look macho or a certain perfume package appear to be very feminine?

The client asked Swan to do an electronic search and got a list of titles and summaries of articles that had been published on the topic around the world. He then chose the particular material he wanted and Swan's team also obtained full-text copies of the documents required from international libraries.

At present, it is possible to download summaries or abstracts of articles from most international databases. Only a minority of databases facilitate direct access to the full text of the articles. In the near future, however, there will be rapid development of full-text facilities. Swan predicts that experiments with fibre-optics are making sending of pictures a possibility. Given the extraordinary advances in information technology, she acknowledges there is no limit to what may come about.

She excitedly talks of Information Edge's access to Tradstat, a trade statistics database, operated from Switzerland, which monitors the volume and prices of products into and out of the major trading countries—the

EEC members, the United States, Canada, Japan, Korea, Taiwan and Hong Kong. As Australia and some major South-East Asian countries are not yet contributing, a system of 'deduced reports' must be used for these countries.

'If the data from these countries say, for instance, that they have imported a certain volume of apples from Australia, then it is deduced that Australia has exported the same number,' Swan explains.

Tradstat is only one of many international database hosts used by Information Edge. One of the most comprehensive is Dialog, operated from the United States, which has over 250 databases and over 200 million records relating to science, medicine, technology, law, chemistry and business. Swan speaks proudly of one of the most spectacular responses by Information Edge to a difficult request. 'A man phoned who wanted to know what kind of concrete was used in the wharves in Singapore. We did a search on Dialog on 158 databases at once and found the answer in six minutes.'

The information was found in an article published by Port of Singapore Authority engineers based on a paper they'd presented at a conference in Beijing, China. It had been indexed on a database in Paris and was available on Dialog in California, from which the Sydney librarians were able to access it.

'The world is our oyster,' concludes Swan. 'The same satellite technology used in television broadcasts is being used to bring us unlimited knowledge on an international basis.'

CHAPTER

20

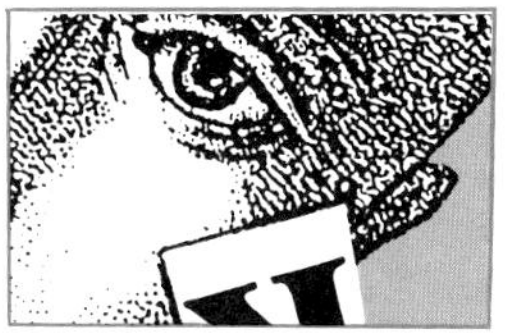

REPORTS—RESEARCH AND ANALYSIS

After studying this chapter, you will be able to:

- distinguish between information reports and analytic reports
- draft a plan for a report, including its purpose, audience and costs
- define the major issues to be addressed by a report
- determine the major types of appropriate research sources
- organise evidence uncovered by the research process

TYPES OF REPORTS AND THEIR SIGNIFICANCE

Reports are the lifeblood of any system of managing an organisation. Reports provide basic information about what is going on inside the organisation and about its relationships with the outside world. They form the basis of most of the serious decisions that are made about the directions the organisation should take and the future it should pursue for itself. On the one hand, they can focus on small details and, on the other, they can take a total view. They come in various lengths and they have different purposes.

So, when someone in an organisation is asked to prepare a report on a subject, the first thing to do is to establish exactly what kind of report is wanted. In many cases, the main purpose is to put together certain pieces of information so that the person or group who has requested the report can make their own decisions. In this case, an *information report* is appropriate. In some organisations, information reports are produced on a periodic or routine basis. These can involve as little effort as filling in a standard form or style sheet, such as in many performance, attendance or inspection reports. Increasingly, routine information of this kind is being produced with the aid of computers.

We discuss the principles of writing these shorter reports in Chapter Twenty-Three. The information reports that are more challenging are those that involve discovering new facts rather than simply pulling together known ones. This means that they have to go through a process of research and investigation.

The major types of reports are:
- information
- analytic
- integrated

A distinction is sometimes made between an information report and an *analytic report*. The latter is often depicted as more difficult to write, involving not only research and investigation but an analysis of the issues involved combined with recommendations for action. Examples of analytic reports are studies of the growth prospects of a firm or an industry, research into the markets for new products, examination of the employment prospects within an occupation or trade.

While the distinction between an information report and an analytical report is still a useful one to make, especially when asking for clarification about exactly what kind of report is being requested, in practice today it is often hard to tell the difference. As they move more into the realm of research and investigation, information reports are requiring more thought and organisation of data from the writer. Often, both types involve a similar degree of investigation and the only difference between the two is that one stops short of making recommendations for action. In other words, the *integrated report* which combines both information and analysis is today the most common.

Report writing is one of the most valuable of communication skills. Reports are important in two ways: first, in supplying an organisation with the intelligence necessary for it to function effectively and take decisions; second, in fostering the skills of report writers themselves and thereby enhancing their career growth and development. The effort needed to master report writing will pay for itself many times over.

DEFINING THE REPORTING TASK

Once given an assignment, the report writer needs to make some important decisions about the project. These decisions should not be taken lightly because they will determine the whole direction of the report and, ultimately, whether it achieves its goals or not. While some of these decisions can be modified as work on the report progresses, they should be regarded as the relatively permanent definitions of the shape of the project.

DEFINE THE TYPE AND PURPOSE OF THE REPORT

Establish clearly the subject and purpose of the report, and get it clear from the outset what type of report this will be. Write them down in a brief sentence and check them with the person who has requested the report. Determine exactly what you are expected to produce. Are you:

- to present specific or general information?
- to suggest new approaches and ideas?
- to report findings?
- to recommend a course of action?

DEFINE TERMS CLEARLY

Most reports are based on some key concepts or terms. If there is any misunderstanding about what these are, the whole project can go astray at the outset. Take the time to define these key terms and check them with others to ensure your interpretation is correct. Most major reports of investigation for government go through this exercise in which they take their 'terms of reference' and, one by one, they describe what they understand these terms to mean.

Decisions to be made at the start:

- type and purpose of the report
- key concepts and terms
- audience and its needs
- time and money available
- major issues to be addressed

DEFINE THE REPORT'S READERS

The reader's knowledge of the subject matter and interest in it will influence the content and language of a report and the level of research that goes into it. Ask yourself the following questions.

- Is the person, group or department inside or outside your organisation?
- What is their level of familiarity with technical details? Are the likely readers initiated in the subject, its terminology or jargon?
- Who has commissioned the report and why? Are there internal political ramifications?
- What use will the reader make of the report?

The report needs to be structured to incorporate the reader's needs and expectations. If readers are likely to be relatively unfamiliar with the subject matter, you will have to explain all the technical terms and concepts before you can discuss them, and you will have to keep jargon to a minimum. Above all, you must start with the attitude that the research must be competent and its facts incontrovertible.

DETERMINE THE TIME AND MONEY TO BE SPENT

No one should simply wade into a report-writing exercise without giving proper consideration for the amount of time and effort to be devoted to each of its aspects. Most reports have a deadline when they are due to be complete but, within this framework, you still need to work out a timetable for the completion of each stage of the project. The best approach is to write out a work plan, showing at least the following:

- time to be devoted to research and investigation
- time to be devoted to writing
- time for circulating first draft and revising
- time for typing, copying and other production aspects of publishing the final version

This is but a bare sketch of a work plan and, in practice, it should be much more detailed. You will need to allow leeway within the plan for unexpected problems that will delay the job longer than you anticipated. You should also identify difficult areas where the amount of work to be completed cannot be determined until you have actually started on it.

DEFINE THE MAJOR ISSUES

In many cases, the nature of the project will be defined when it is given to you. In some cases this will involve a formal set of terms of reference, in other cases it will be less formal but still spelt out in some detail. If, however, the job is posed in very broad terms, as it often is likely to be, then you will have to define the major issues yourself. One way to do this is to adopt a familiar approach and pose the traditional questions: *who*, *what*, *when*, *where* and *why*. This kind of analysis allows you to break down a large problem into several smaller ones. It also gives you the basis for a research program and for devising a work plan.

Take the following example. Your organisation is having difficulties in recruiting secretaries and you are required to write a report on secretarial salary levels to see if the rates offered by your organisation are compatible with market rates. The difficulty is that there are thousands of people employed as secretaries across a wide range of industries. To define the topic more precisely and to reduce the issue to reasonable proportions, use the *who*, *what*, *when*, *where* and *why* questions.

Who:	Secretaries with at least five years experience and high levels of shorthand and typing skills
What:	A study of their salary levels
When:	Present
Where:	Within our metropolitan recruiting area of Western Sydney
Why:	To determine whether salaries in our organisation are competitive

After answering the questions you can phrase the issue this way. 'The purpose of this study is to survey salaries for experienced and highly skilled secretaries in Western Sydney to determine whether our current salary scales are competitive.' This procedure has reduced the problem to a workable size—you do not have to survey secretarial salaries in all states or even all of your own state because the study is now confined to those you are likely to recruit; further, you do not have to study all types of secretaries, only those who fulfil your fairly specific requirements. Perhaps the most important of the above questions was *'why?'* Very often, once this question has been posed and answered, you have stated the main purpose of the research and many other elements in formulating the question will fall into place.

DRAFTING A PRELIMINARY PLAN

Once you have prepared a work plan, you should draw up a preliminary plan of the written report itself. This is useful for three reasons:

1. It gives you a total picture of the task and this allows you to balance your time and resources more efficiently as you proceed.
2. By showing you all the sections that have to be covered by the report, it reduces the chance that you will inadvertently omit an important section or issue.
3. It provides you with a plan for the research phase of the report, providing signposts for the investigation and giving you an initial set of categories under which you should file the material you gather.

A preliminary plan usually contains three major divisions and a number of subdivisions, such as:

Introductory material
Necessary background information
Reason for the investigation
Present conditions
Reasons for considering changes

Investigative material
Findings of previous investigations
Methodology and work done in present investigation
Results obtained from present investigation

Analytical material
Discussion of significance of investigative material
Relation to present practices
Recommendations based on the above

Objectives of a research plan:
- to provide a total picture of the task
- to reduce the chance that you will omit something important
- to define the categories under which to file evidence

Let us see how this abstract framework fits a real preliminary plan. The subject is whether a firm of accountants and a computer software writer who have successfully marketed an accountancy software package 'Accountpac' to medium- and large- scale businesses in Australia should adapt their package for use on personal computers for sale to small businesses.

ADAPTATION OF ACCOUNTPAC FOR PC USERS

Introduction—Background to Accountpac
History of Accountpac development
Size of current market
Significance of Accountpac for firm
Reasons for extending market to small business PC users

Market potential and costs of adaptation
Size of PC accountancy market
Existing contenders in market
Methodology and results of survey of software dealers
Problems of retail software market
Likely market share of Accountpac
Costs of adaptation for PC use
Costs of back-up service for retail sales

Analysis of costs and benefits of adaptation
New market revenues versus new market costs
Benefits of expansion of client base
Benefits of entering PC market
Recommendations about adaptation

THE RESEARCH PHASE

Once you have established your framework for research, you can begin the investigation proper. There are a number of techniques that have been developed by professional researchers and you should take advantage of them wherever appropriate. (Some have already been discussed in Chapter Nine on research essays. This chapter repeats and adapts some of that material.) Used with intelligence they can turn the most daunting research project into something manageable and even enjoyable.

ORGANISING YOUR MATERIAL

Major types of sources:
- primary—witnesses, direct reports
- secondary—books, articles, analysis
- business files
- personal experience
- written submissions
- library research
- literature reviews
- statistics

Start by preparing a series of manila folders, each labelled with one of the subheadings from your preliminary plan. As you gather information, file it in its appropriate folder. If you come across something too big to be filed this way, such as a book or a lengthy report, photocopy the relevant sections and put the photocopies in its right folder. If you come across a document that could be placed in two different folders, make a copy and place the original in one folder and the copy in the other. As you proceed, you may feel the need to modify or expand your original plan. This is normal and should be expected. Do it by writing new headings on additional manila folders and slotting them into their appropriate place in your filing system.

When your research is complete, the headings of your manila folders should comprise the headings and subheadings under which the final report will be written. In other words, you should consider the research phase as simultaneously a process of investigation and a process of organising your material into the plan of the report itself. If you proceed this way, you will not be faced at the end with an overwhelming bulk of unsorted information. You will always have your material under control. You will be able to see where you are going and be better placed to make intelligent judgments about the information you progressively uncover.

SOURCES

It is useful when thinking about sources of information to divide them into primary sources and secondary sources.

PRIMARY SOURCES

These are taken from first-hand experience with the subject or event in question. They can be personal observations by witnesses to an event, diaries, letters, newspaper reports, television and radio reports, speeches, photographs, autobiographical data and contemporary publications containing direct first-hand observations. Two other forms of primary sources are findings from interviews and questionnaires.

SECONDARY SOURCES

These are sources which interpret events, which make observations or comment upon them at a later time. They include books, articles published in journals, documentary films and anything else that analyses the first-hand information after the event.

Here are examples of primary and secondary sources in a well-known book, Blanche d'Alpuget's biography of former prime minister, Bob Hawke.

Primary sources

Newspaper reports in the *Sydney Morning Herald*, the *Age*
Hawke's personal diaries from 1967 to 1981
Hawke's speeches as president of the Australian Council of Trade Unions
Minutes of ACTU meetings
TV and radio news reports about Hawke
Letters Hawke wrote to his mother and father in 1955

Secondary Sources

J. Hagan, *The History of the ACTU*, Longman Cheshire, Melbourne, 1981
J. Hurst, *Hawke: The Definitive Biography*, Angus and Robertson, Sydney, 1979
'Four Corners', ABC-TV, 11 September 1982 (analysing Hawke's period as ACTU President and giving background to his rise to Labor leadership)

Where do you go looking for information for a report? The following are some of the most important sources.

ORGANISATION RECORDS OR COMPANY FILES AND ARCHIVES

Much of the information you need may be in your organisation's or company's records, files or archives. Look here first. Someone else may have done a lot of legwork for you. These records may contain past reports written on similar topics which could be useful background material.

PERSONAL EXPERIENCE

If the topic is one on which you have had personal experience then you are a valuable source of information yourself. To translate this experience into something that will be convincing to others, it is little use saying something like: 'My long experience in this area leads me to think that ...' You need to record facts, dates, measurements, records of conversations and other kinds of hard data that give others confidence you know what you are talking about.

WRITTEN SUBMISSIONS

A good principle on which to operate is to try to get others to do as much of your work for you. Most public inquiries make a call through advertisements for written submissions from any interested party. Whenever appropriate, and through a suitable form of communication, you should do the same. Some people are glad of the chance to put their views or concerns about a subject in this way. They see the process not as one of you avoiding work but as one of them being properly consulted on the issue. Some submissions are good enough to be included verbatim in a report.

LIBRARY RESEARCH

Organisation or company libraries, municipal and state libraries, university and college libraries, and specialist collections such as medical libraries or law libraries—any of these are worth a visit, if only to comb through their subject files on your topic. One of the most useful reference sources held by most big libraries is Australian Public Affairs Information Service (known to libraries as APAIS) which is a listing of articles published in newspapers, magazines and journals each year. Its subject index is an extremely valuable resource and it is a good place to start your research.

LITERATURE REVIEWS

In library research, one of the most useful pieces of work to look for is a literature review. This is a survey of the 'literature' on a certain subject, that is, a survey of a large number of the writings on it. Often, you will find, your own subject or one close to it has been surveyed by one or two authors in this way. This is often indicated in indexes of articles published in journals where commentaries (or annotations) on each article are included ('...Jones has written a literature review of the last ten years of debate on Subject X.'). They are a very helpful way of getting an overview of the topic and of seeing how the various contributions relate or are in conflict with one another. If there are no existing literature reviews, and you have the time, writing a literature review of your own is one very good way of getting on top of an issue. It not only helps you understand the topic but can provide a useful chapter for your report.

STATISTICAL BULLETINS

There are a great many issues now covered by surveys by the Australian Bureau of Statistics (ABS). In many pieces of research, the ABS should be an early port of call. There is a telephone information service available in most capital cities employing information officers specifically to deal with public inquiries. A wide range of selected ABS statistics are available on Discovery, the videotext computer system accessed over telephone lines. In fact, the cost of a Discovery subscription is usually worth it for access to the ABS statistics alone. Most of the statistics that people need are available either on the telephone or on Discovery. If you need more detail than these services provide, you can request ABS statistical bulletins which are publicly available for a small charge. You can also become a subscriber to the regular publication of many of these bulletins.

As well as these six sources of information, there are the techniques of interviews, questionnaires and surveys that are used by professional research organisations. These techniques are discussed in detail in the next chapter.

INTERPRETING THE DATA

As we emphasised earlier, if you are well organised you will organise most of your data as you go through the process of researching and filing information under the headings drawn up in your preliminary plan. If you do this, making appropriate modifications to your headings and folders as you go, you will not be faced with a major job of analysis at the end of the research phase. In other words, the research phase will also be the analysis phase. Some of your data, however, will require special analysis, especially where you are trying, first, to find the causes of a problem or, second, to make a recommendation for action.

ANALYSIS OF CAUSES

To establish a cause you need two kinds of data:

1. some numerical data showing a change in some factor at about the same time as the event you are trying to explain occurred
2. an understanding of the relationships and motivations involved in the events you are describing

To establish a cause you need:
- numerical data showing change
- an understanding of the motives of those involved

For instance, you are trying to find the cause of a sudden increase in resignations from your firm. You find that it occurred after mid-May when a new personnel manager was appointed. So you have a correlation between an increased rate of resignation and the new personnel manager. You might now conclude that the former was caused by the latter. However, you should always remember that correlations never amount to a cause on their own. If you go on to consider the relationships and motivations of the people who resigned, however, you might reconsider your conclusion. It is unlikely, even if he or she rubbed many people up the wrong way, that one new appointee would lead a large number of people to resign. One or two might have a dispute and leave, but most employees are motivated by more serious concerns. You discuss the question with the personnel manager and interview by phone a number of those who resigned. You find instead that the real cause was the maturation of a superannuation scheme the company had started ten years earlier. All employees over sixty had become eligible on the date in question for a lump sum benefit if they chose to retire, and a significant number took the option. The real cause was thus not the obvious one indicated by a simple correlation but a far more plausible one.

MAKING RECOMMENDATIONS

Another aspect of the interpretation phase comes when you have to ask, 'On the basis of these facts, what is the most appropriate course of action to recommend?' In most cases, you should avoid rushing in with the most obvious suggestion. Rather, you should think of several possible lines of action and then compare them for effectiveness, weighing the advantages and disadvantages of each in the light of the information you have before you. You should try to establish a range of priorities including such considerations as cost, time, effort and morale. For instance, if you discover that one solution is inexpensive to implement but not so good for morale whereas another is good for morale but is expensive and time-consuming, you will need to decide which is the most important priority, morale or cost? Faced with such a dilemma, the best way to proceed is to break down the options and measure their impact as closely as possible in order to weigh the balance as finely as possible.

By the time you have completed all the stages described here—defined and planned your project, researched and organised the relevant information, analysed the data, determined the causes and decided upon your recommendations—it is time to start writing. Before we discuss report writing, though, we want to examine in some detail one more group of research methods—the professional techniques of interviews, questionnaires and surveys—which are taken up in the next chapter.

KEY POINTS: Chapter 20 Reports—research and analysis

- Reports provide basic information about what is going on inside an organisation and in the outside world.
- It is important to define the type and purpose of the report. An information report is appropriate for most purposes. When recommendations are added to research and investigation, the result is an analytic report.
- Define your terms clearly. Define the report's intended readers and the major issues to be addressed. Determine the amount of time and money to be spent.
- Draft a preliminary plan.
- There are six important sources for compiling reports:
  1. organisation records or company files and archives
  2. personal experience
  3. written submissions
  4. library research
  5. literature reviews
  6. statistical bulletins
- Analyse causes thoughtfully. Weigh up recommendations with care.

QUESTIONS FOR DISCUSSION

1. What would be the consequences of *not* defining objectives, audiences and issues before beginning any research project?

2. What would be the consequences of *not* drafting a preliminary plan before beginning research?

3. Discuss the traps involved in using correlations to show causes.

EXERCISES

1. Get a copy of a recent report written for the state or the Commonwealth government. Identify and list the full range of sources used in the report.

2. Assume you have been asked to write a report on the adequacy of eating and recreational facilities at your organisation. Draft a plan for this report and identify the kind of research you would need to undertake.

3. Assume you have been asked to write a report on the adequacy of parking facilities at your organisation. Draft a plan for this report and identify the kind of research you would need to undertake.

4. Assume you have been asked to write a report on how your organisation can increase the numbers of its clientele. Draft a plan for this report and identify the kind of research you would need to undertake.

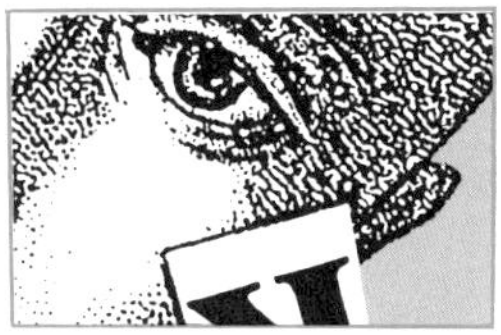

CHAPTER

21

INTERVIEWS, QUESTIONNAIRES AND SURVEY RESEARCH

After studying this chapter, you will be able to:

- distinguish between the major types of interviews that are used in research
- write a questionnaire suitable to be administered to a group of people
- analyse the data provided by a group of completed questionnaires
- distinguish between various kinds of survey research

When a professional research firm takes on a project, there are a number of now well-known methods to apply. Some of these—such as library searches, literature reviews and requests for submissions—were discussed in the last chapter. Here we want to focus on the principal ways of gaining information about the attitudes and behaviour of significant numbers of people. In most projects undertaken by professional researchers, one or more of the methods described in this chapter are usually adopted. These methods are within the capacity and the ability of non-professionals who might be given the responsibility to research a subject for their own organisation.

INTERVIEWS

Interviews are one of the most common forms of gathering information. They consist of the researcher asking one person at a time a series of questions. Interviews are sometimes classed as 'structured' or 'unstructured', although often they are a combination of the two.

UNSTRUCTURED INTERVIEWS

- Unstructured interviews are like conversations about a subject. They provide qualitative information.
- Structured interviews ask precise questions. They are used to provide numerical or quantitative data.

Unstructured interviews are very much like conversations on a subject. The interviewer knows what areas he or she wants to cover but will have one or two specific questions prepared to ask. The advantage of this approach is that the interviewer is free to pick up interesting, useful or surprising answers and to follow them up with more questions. In other cases, the unstructured interview allows for ambiguous or hesitant responses to be cleared up by a little probing. One of the problems of this method, however, is that because the questions are not usually asked in the same way of all interviewees, it is possible that any differences found between interviewees are due to differences in wording or the way the questions were asked or in the relationships that emerge during the interviews. In some unstructured interviews, the interviewer may get along well with the interviewee and this will colour the answers given. Alternatively, a tense or hostile relationship between the two may generate answers of an altogether different kind.

Unstructured interviews are usually adopted when the 'quality' of the information, rather than the 'quantity', is paramount. For example, when a vocational guidance counsellor questions a student about long-term career goals in an effort to help that individual student decide on a career path, the interview is usually a probing one to gain qualitative data. When the same counsellor interviews students in order to draw up a profile of the career goals of the whole school population, the data sought is quantitative and a structured interview would be more appropriate. When surveying attitudes to complex issues, unstructured interviews are usually the most appropriate. Attitudes to issues such as the way an organisation works, job satisfaction or appreciation of a product or service are usually found to be complex. For this reason, two groups of frequent users of unstructured interviews are market researchers when they are trying to determine why interviewees like or dislike a product; and management consultants when they are trying to analyse the way an organisation functions.

STRUCTURED INTERVIEWS

Findings from structured interviews are regarded by most researchers as more rigorous. The questions are written down as a list (a questionnaire) and the wording and order of the questions are put in the same way to all interviewees. Therefore, they all respond to the same thing. Different answers to the same series of questions should indicate real differences between those answering, and not simply differences in the way the questions are put, as might be the case in unstructured interviews. A structured interview allows more accurate comparisons to be made among all respondents and gives more reliability to results for a large group of people.

In general, structured interviews are appropriate for gathering quantitative data about issues of fact such as the interviewee's gender, age, occupation, country of birth and educational qualifications. They take less time and are less expensive than unstructured interviews. This makes them more appropriate for a larger group of interviewees.

INTERVIEW SAMPLES

Both the structured and unstructured interview are expensive and time-consuming compared to other methods of surveying people which we discuss below. This means that the size of the group of people interviewed, or the interview sample, must be limited. Even a brief research interview can take thirty minutes and covering a number of points can take at least double this time. If the interviews are to be conducted at a number of different locations, it is usually difficult for one person to get through more than four a day. The size of interview samples should reflect these timing realities and the costs involved.

Interview research in industry will normally be based on small samples. This means researchers should take the trouble to ensure the sample is

A random sample can be formed from people the interviewer finds in a public place, such as a shopping centre

representative. If you are examining the attitudes of firms in the computer industry to new government taxation policies, the survey will be inaccurate if you only interview large firms for whom the allowance means big annual savings, and if you omit small companies who hardly stand to benefit at all. You need to include some representatives from across the whole of the industry—large, medium and small firms; manufacturers and importers; service providers and equipment suppliers. Usually the size of the sample you need to interview will be determined by the number of categories of representatives you select. In the case of the computer industry, for example, there are hardware companies, software companies, service providers; local producers; importers; and retailers. If you decide to divide these six types into large and small firms, you have twelve categories. If you then decide to interview three firms in each category, you have thirty-six interviews to do—a sizeable job but almost the minimum needed to get a good cross-section of opinion within the industry.

This method of dividing the total 'population' to be questioned into categories and then ensuring you get more than one interview from each category is a procedure that can be followed for most kinds of interview research within business and industry. In questionnaire-based research it is often called 'stratified sampling'. We discuss this further below.

GROUP INTERVIEWS AND SEMINARS

If the logistics of arranging a large number of interviews are difficult, yet you still feel that unstructured interviews are the best way to elicit the information you need, then group interviews and seminars may be the answer.

Seminars are sometimes held as part of research into proposed government policy changes. Representatives of those people who would be affected by the change are mailed information about the foreshadowed policies and then brought together by the department concerned to air their views on the proposals. One advantage of this method is that, by hearing the views of others, people often refine their own opinions to a more useful level. Another advantage is that if the people affected are geographically dispersed a seminar is a fast way of gaining feedback on the policies.

This is also a method widely used in market research. A selected group, usually housewives, is given the opportunity to try out a new product. They then attend a group interview (unstructured) where they are asked about their attitudes towards the product. This situation often stimulates more informative discussion than would be available in a one-to-one interview.

INTERVIEWER BIAS

Interviewers will normally have views of their own on the subject being researched. Even if they try to disguise their own values and attitudes, they will communicate something to the person they are questioning. It is now well known that during interviews, the majority of people will, if they do not have strong opinions on a subject, lean towards telling interviewers what they think they want to hear. Interviews are interactive situations in which both the people concerned affect one another. In sociology, research has found that black American children give different answers to interviewers depending on whether they are white or black. Many people are more ready to acknowledge personal qualities and attitudes to some interviewers rather than others.

Some researchers have responded to the lack of objectivity in the interview by calling for the abandonment of personal interviews altogether. However, were this advice followed, a great deal of very useful and revealing qualitative information would be unavailable. One way to minimise the problems is to bring the issue itself into the open during the interview, by asking the interviewee whether he or she would answer differently to a another interviewer.

It also needs to be recognised that there are many interviews where interviewer bias is not an important issue. This is mostly where the research topic has less to do with personal attitudes and beliefs and is more concerned with behaviour, actual responses and facts about people such as their occupation or educational qualifications. The more objective the issues being probed ('What did you actually do?' rather than 'How do you feel about this?'), the more objective the interview itself will be.

This section has examined interviewing only in its use for research purposes. There are many other kinds of interviews. Their nature and the ways to handle them are discussed in more extensive detail in Chapter Thirteen.

QUESTIONNAIRES

Open-ended questions are used in unstructured, qualitative interviews. Closed or fixed-choice questions are used in questionnaires for fact gathering.

Questionnaires are a familiar technique for gathering data. They consist of a list of questions which are asked of all people in a survey. Questionnaires can be administered as part of a personal interview (in which case the situation constitutes a structured interview), over the telephone or through the mail. The advantages of questionnaires are the same as those of structured interviews: they are an effective method of gathering large amounts of quantitative data. When used over the telephone or through the mail, they take on the extra advantages of being inexpensive and fast. When contemplating questionnaires as a research tool, it is worth considering the merits of the two main types of question: open-ended and closed or fixed-choice.

OPEN-ENDED QUESTIONS

These are not the same as the questions asked in an unstructured interview. In the open-ended variety, the questions are always the same; it is the answers that vary. The open-ended question allows respondents the opportunity to compose their own answers instead of being forced to choose between a fixed set of answers written on the questionnaire. An example of an open-ended question would be: 'The firm is now conducting 30 per cent less research and development than it was five years ago. What factors have led to this?'

The advantage of open-ended questions is that they allow respondents to express their opinions in their own words. In many cases, especially complex ones, this is the only feasible way to proceed since the interviewer cannot anticipate the full range of possible answers.

The disadvantages come when you try to analyse the answers. Because they are all different, they are difficult to categorise and analyse. You cannot simply say that a certain percentage of respondents answered in one way. The analysis has to be very sensitive and usually heavily qualified. The results will inevitably be less precise than those from closed questions. However, where the reality of the situation is itself complex and not easily defined in shades of black and white, the results from open-ended questions may be closer to the truth, for all their imprecision.

CLOSED OR FIXED-CHOICE QUESTIONS

A fixed-choice question is one where respondents are asked to confine their answers to terms chosen by the interviewer. In some fact-gathering cases, for example, where you are asked what was the highest level of secondary schooling you completed ('Year 9', 'Year 10', 'Year 11', 'Year 12'), it is the most effective way to proceed. If you did not specify exactly what you wanted, some might answer in terms of the certificate they gained or even their own age, and you would have no consistent basis on which to analyse the data.

Where they analyse opinions and beliefs, however, fixed-choice questions are on weaker ground. A typical question of this kind would be: 'Trade unions exercise too much power. Indicate your attitude to this statement by circling one of the following: Strongly agree, Agree, Disagree, Strongly Disagree, No opinion.' In this range of possible answers there is no room for the person who believes that, say, a small number of trade unions exercise too much power, but that most will act in a responsible way as long as management does as well. Nor is there any room for the person who is not certain what the question means by 'too much power': is this power over employers, over the public, over the government or all three?

Further, there is unlikely to be much agreement among respondents about what 'too much' means. Some will regard any influence trade unions have as 'too much'. Others will believe the unions have power only when they can enforce major social change. The published results of a question like this may appear precise, for instance, '52.1 per cent of Australians agree that the unions have too much power'. However, because the opinions included differ so greatly over the meaning of both 'too much' and 'power', the finding is fairly worthless.

Most people's attitudes to complex social institutions like trade unions involve a range of perspectives and qualifications. Hence, it is clear that fixed-choice answers are not the most accurate way to test opinions, unless the interviewer is clear that the opinion being tested is of a very elementary kind, for example, 'Do you believe in God?' or 'Who do you think would make the best prime minister—A, B or C?'

WRITING A QUESTIONNAIRE

The first place to start in preparing a questionnaire is to define the issue as clearly as possible. You then need to list the points you want to cover. Once the list is written, points that are of a similar kind should be categorised and grouped. Then start writing the questions. As far as

Principles of questionnaire design:
- questions must ask for precise information, exact numbers
- for opinions, state the issue then ask if interviewee either: strongly agrees, agrees, disagrees, strongly disagrees, or no opinion
- avoid leading questions with inbuilt answers
- keep them brief—use the minimum number of questions needed to gain the information wanted
- start with an introduction saying who is sponsoring the research and why
- always do a pilot survey, then rewrite the questionnaire

possible, place yourself in the position of the respondent to see if the question is intelligible, unambiguous and is really asking what you want. There are some types of questions that you should avoid. In general, keep to the following principles.

1. Questions must be clear. It is unclear to ask a question like: 'Do you visit the dentist regularly?' (What do you mean by 'regular'?) The right way to ask this question is:

   How often do you go to the dentist?
      Once a year?
      Twice a year?
      Once a month?
      More often than once a month?

2. Where the issue is a straightforward one and not subject to a wide range of interpretations (such as those we discussed above in the case of opinions on trade unions), then five options should be acceptable. Make a statement of opinion and then ask whether respondents: (a) Strongly agree, (b) Agree, (c) Disagree, (d) Strongly Disagree, (e) No opinion.
3. Avoid leading questions. These are questions that have inbuilt answers or which push people towards one answer rather than another. They often find their way into public opinion polls. For example:

   Do you think trashy magazines should be banned from supermarkets?
   Do you think vicious murderers should receive longer jail sentences?

4. Keep questionnaires brief. This is not only to keep down your interviewing time but, more importantly, to minimise the amount of work involved in analysing the results.
5. Start a questionnaire with a very brief introduction, saying who you are or what your organisation or department is, and stating your purpose in seeking the information. Try to keep the introduction to two or three sentences.
6. You should always pilot a questionnaire. This means testing it on a small sample of people to see how they answer, whether they understand what you mean, and whether you will get the type of answers you are seeking. In particular, you need to ensure that the respondents share your interpretation of the terms in each question and what its overall meaning is. Analyse the results of the pilot and then rewrite the questionnaire before administering it to the main group for whom it is intended.

ADMINISTERING QUESTIONNAIRES

There are three principal ways to administer questionnaires: in person, by telephone and by mail.

IN PERSON

In this method the interviewers fill out the questionnaires themselves, thereby ensuring they are completed according to instructions. In some cases, of which the Australian Census is the best known, the questionnaire is left with respondents and they are asked to fill it out. If the respondent needs help, the interviewer will later go through the questions personally. The Census is something of a special case, though, and in most commercial interview research, such as market research, the interviewer is the one who fills out the questionnaire. This method is the best for getting the complete schedule of questions answered and for getting the maximum response from the targeted group. However, it is also the most expensive.

Three ways to administer surveys:
- in person
- by telephone
- by mail

BY TELEPHONE

It is less expensive to telephone people than to visit them and, in the case of most straightforward questionnaires, a telephone interview will get almost as good a result as a personal visit. This method is also effective in getting questionnaires filled out completely and in getting answers from a high proportion of the targeted group.

BY MAIL

A postal questionnaire is the least expensive method of gathering data through a questionnaire. You should mail it with an accompanying letter explaining the reason for the survey and asking for co-operation. You should also enclose a return envelope with a Freepost number (available at the local Post Office) so that the respondent does not have to pay for the stamp. Postal surveys get the lowest return rate and the highest number of unfilled questions of the three methods. The return rate regarded as good by professional researchers is 50 per cent though in some cases where the issue is not directly relevant to many people, 20 per cent will do. Normally, if you get less than 30 per cent on the first mail-out, you should write a second letter (enclosing another questionnaire) asking for co-operation. Very often, the people who are motivated to complete questionnaires have a reason to do so—they have some grievance or some enthusiasm for the project. You need to carefully analyse your returns to determine what proportion of them reflect these special interests and how much your sample reflects the overall group. This often involves intelligent guesswork rather than precision analysis. As long as you are aware of the likely biases that occur in a mail survey, you can still make an acceptable analysis of the returns you do get.

ANALYSING THE DATA

Questionnaire analysis involves compiling numerical tables of the answers and interpreting the tables in an accompanying commentary. It is customary to start by describing how the questionnaire was administered, to how many people and what proportion of returns were received. An uncompleted copy of the questionnaire and accompanying letters are usually included in an appendix at the back of the report. There are two stages in analysing a questionnaire: an analysis of totals and a relational analysis.

ANALYSIS OF TOTALS

This involves totalling the answers to each question and presenting the results in tables. Where the questions deal with straightforward facts, such as the gender, age and country of birth of respondents, the results may be grouped in one table. The accompanying commentary should point out all significant, unusual or surprising findings in these totals.

RELATIONAL ANALYSIS

This is usually the main interest in the results—how answers to one group of questions relate to others. For example, in a survey of a company's workforce, it might be important to know how many tradespeople have formal, tertiary qualifications and how many do not. To determine this, you would need to pull out all the questionnaires which have trades listed under occupation, and then go through them to count the totals of the answers relating to educational qualifications. In even a small questionnaire, all the mathematically possible relationships among the returns could never be counted. This means you have to select the relationships you think might be significant and count them. What you select is very much a matter of judgment based on the conclusions you are hoping to find and the general 'feel' you have gained about the answers as the project has progressed. In other words, there is as much art as mathematics in analysing questionnaires.

Counting the totals and making relations between them is made vastly easier by the use of computers. For surveys involving up to several hundred questionnaires, personal computers are quite adequate for the task. For questionnaire research to university standards, the software package SPSS/PC (Statistical Packages for the Social Sciences) is the most commonly used. However, for the great majority of users, the newer commercial database software for personal computers do most that is needed. This is particularly true of packages which have the ability to calculate totals of questionnaire data as well as 'cross-tabulated' views of the data. Database packages like these can also produce graphical views of the results. These graphs can be printed and included in the final report. Today, anyone doing questionnaire research should take advantage of the speed and efficiency offered by database applications.

SURVEY RESEARCH

Interviews and questionnaires are methods employed in what is generally known as survey research or social surveys. Survey research involves the collection of standardised data from a sample of people who are identified as representative of a social group or a population. A population may be the citizens of a whole country, an age group, an ethnic group, people within a geographic location, with the same occupation or with some characteristics in common—the poor, the rich, single mothers, college students and the like. The population will be defined by the objectives of the research—for example, a study to investigate income distribution of parents of preschool children. Here, 'parents of preschool children' constitutes the population group. Standardised data is collected when the same set of interview questions or questionnaire is administered to all members of the group. Survey research is divided by some practitioners into two categories: descriptive surveys and analytical surveys.

DESCRIPTIVE SURVEYS

These focus more on description than explanation. They aim at arriving at an accurate measurement of various characteristics of a population group. The Census is the best example. It aims at giving a description of the personal characteristics and standard of living of the population of Australia.

ANALYTICAL SURVEYS

These are concerned with analysing and explaining social relationships. For example, one way to analyse the educational retention rates of young people (how many drop out of school early, how many complete secondary school, how many go on to tertiary education and so on) would be to do a survey among a representative group of youth, and then work out what characteristics accompany both high and low retention rates. Characteristics that might be relevant would be the educational level of their parents, the income available to their families, their attitudes to school and work, and the influence of their peers and siblings.

Because there are so many possible factors involved in an issue like this, and you cannot test everything, the researcher has to have an idea of the significant relationships before he or she starts. The survey will therefore be testing a preconceived hypothesis or set of hypotheses.

With random samples, a small number of interviewees is chosen at random from within a large population.

With stratified samples, interviewees are chosen from a large population to ensure that there are representatives from each of the groups within it.

SAMPLE SURVEYS

The Census is one of the few surveys that actually questions the whole of its population target group. For most surveys it is too expensive and impractical to get to everyone in the group selected. Instead, a sample is chosen to represent the whole group. One way to select a sample is on a 'random' basis. If you want to draw a sample of 100 students from a total school population of 1000, you could put all their names in a hat and, blindfolded, draw out 100. This 'random sample' has not been biased by any of your own assumptions. However, it is not the most satisfactory way to proceed. You might just happen to draw a sample that has a high proportion of boys from older age groups who are high achievers. Any further surveys you conduct with this group will contain biases that reflect these characteristics. You will omit data from younger and less successful students.

A more refined procedure is to produce a 'stratified sample'. This reduces the likelihood of your 'random' selection producing an unrepresentative group. A stratified selection in a school population would contain representatives from each age group. It would also have a fair cross-section of ability and achievement, and, if the school is co-educational, it would have an even number of boys and girls. A stratified sample of this kind is more likely to be representative of the whole school population and any further research you do will be better balanced for it.

In general, if you are drawing a sample from a closed population such as a school or workplace, then you should use the stratified sample technique. If you are drawing a sample from a much larger population group, such as a suburb or country town, then a random sample could be used. To draw a random sample from a suburb, you would choose, say, every tenth house in every fifth street. But you would have to ensure that you selected from the whole suburb and not just from the areas that are better off, or, alternatively, only from those that contain people on lower incomes, for this would introduce a bias to the sample.

MULTIVARIATE ANALYSIS

As we noted above, an analytical survey of a sample population is a means of testing preconceived hypotheses of the researcher. This means, in other words, finding some data that backs up the researcher's initial hunches about the group. In some cases, the data will not confirm these hunches but will point in other directions to other relationships being the important ones. In this case, the researcher has to accept a new hypothesis.

Testing the relationships found in survey data is usually called testing the significance of the 'variables' involved in the issue being researched. For example, the variables we discussed above in education retention were parental education, family income, attitudes towards school, peer influence and sibling influence. If you found that 80 per cent of early school drop-outs had parents who never completed school themselves, and that 70 per cent of university students had parents who went to university, then you can record the first variable as being highly significant in education. In reality, you don't need figures anywhere near as high as 80 per cent or 70 per cent to show a relationship is significant. There are statistical techniques to measure much finer degrees of significance in relation to sample size. We don't go into these in this book but they are standard techniques which are described in most textbooks on statistics.

If we go on to test the relationship of the other four variables above in a similar way, then we are engaged in 'variable analysis', or what is more commonly called 'multivariate analysis'. This means measuring the effects of a number of variables on each other. Although there are statistical techniques available, as well as computer software such as SPSS/PC to handle very sophisticated multivariate analysis, many people can draw intelligent relationships between variables without going this far. In most small surveys, especially those conducted within one organisation or within one industry, the significant relationships between the variables stand out clearly. Careful commentary on the figures produced from survey tables, and a clear eye on the graphs produced from these tables, will indicate which relationships are meaningful and which hypotheses are confirmed or denied.

KEY POINTS: Chapter 21 Interviews, questionnaires and survey research

- Unstructured interviews are effective for gathering qualitative information. More rigorous structured interviews are better for quantitative data.
- A stratified sample is better than a random selection for obtaining a broad range of views.
- Open-ended questions are by nature imprecise, but where the issues are complex and opinions are being sought, they may be closer to the truth.
- Fixed-choice questions yield consistently reliable information but are ineffective for testing all but the most elementary beliefs.
- Questionnaires should be clear and brief. They can be administered in person, over the telephone or by mail. Bear in mind that mail-outs are likely to be biased.
- Numerical analysis is greatly simplified by the use of computer software such as SPSS/PC, but relational analysis remains a matter of judgment and 'feel'.

QUESTIONS FOR DISCUSSION

1. Why is it hard to be objective in personal interviews? Is this reason to abandon this method of inquiry?
2. How do open-ended and fixed-choice questions differ? Give examples of your own of each type.
3. How do descriptive and analytical surveys differ? Give examples of your own of each type.
4. What is a stratified sample? How does it differ from a random sample?
5. What is multivariate analysis? Give an example of your own.

EXERCISES

1. Sales of newspapers are not expanding, even though the population is growing. As part of a study into people's attitudes towards newspapers, draw up a plan for an unstructured interview suitable to be administered to your student or work colleagues. You are interested to know what kind of newspapers they buy; why they buy them, or if they don't, why not; whether they find them reliable and if not why not, and any other factors that affect their purchase of newspapers. The plan should describe the areas to be discussed and two firm questions.

2. As part of a survey into the way that young people in the 1990s perceive their future employment prospects, draw up a plan for an unstructured interview on the subject. You are particularly interested in how they feel their education has left them prepared or unprepared for their future employment. You also want to know the factors that lead young men and women into different career choices. The plan should describe the areas to be discussed and two firm questions.

3. You are conducting a survey of the plans for further education of your student or work colleagues. You want to determine what proportion of them expect to continue their studies and to what eventual level; and you want to relate their propensity to study to background factors such as their existing education level, employment history, age, gender, parental education, and current family status (single, married, children, etc.). Draw up a questionnaire suitable to be administered during a structured interview on the topic.

4. As part of a study on the effectiveness of advertising for fast food, draw up a questionnaire suitable to be administered to your fellow students or work colleagues during a structured interview. You want to know what brand advertising they recall and on what medium; how often they eat fast food, if at all; their consumption of non-advertised versus advertised fast food; whether advertising influences their behaviour; whether there are any age or gender differences in response; and any other factors you might believe significant.

5. Pilot test each of the above four plans and questionnaires on your fellow students or work colleagues. Rewrite them in light of the experience of the piloting.

6. Draw up a questionnaire to test how your student or work colleagues would vote at the next Federal election. You are interested to know what party they will vote for; which party either they or their family have traditionally supported; if their intended vote is different to their

continued on next page

continued from previous page

traditional support, why they are switching; what issues they perceive as the most important; their age, gender and ethnic background; plus other factors you believe to be important.

The questionnaire should be suitable to be mailed—that is, respondents should be able to complete it unaided. It should gather its data in as few questions as possible. Pilot this questionnaire on a small number of subjects, rewrite it, and then administer it to a group of your student or work colleagues. Analyse the results.

Write a report describing your methodology, the nature of your sample and the results you found.

CHAPTER

22

REPORTS—WRITING AND PRESENTATION

After studying this chapter, you will be able to:

- define the structure of a typical report used by business or government
- write the introduction and body of a report
- use an appropriate prose style when writing a report
- draw conclusions and make recommendations from the information presented in a report
- provide appropriate references for information you have gathered
- adopt an attractive form of presentation

In a long piece of writing like a report, readers need as much help as they can get to follow the case being made and to comprehend the whole thing. No one can be expected to keep the entire contents of a report inside their head at the one time. Writers should not only say what has to be said but provide assistance to their readers to know what has been said. Some writers think this task can be accomplished by a summary of the main points. This is sometimes true but very often summaries are so condensed that their meaning is obscured. A far more effective means of help is a well-designed outline and layout.

OUTLINE AND CONTENTS

Providing people with information and persuading them to your point of view is a matter of taking them on a journey of investigation. Like any journey, you need a definite starting point and a clear destination. From the outset, there should be signs pointing the way and naming the final goal. At regular intervals and at forks in the road, there should be legible and understandable directions. From time to time, the traveller should be able to glance back down the road, to see where he has come from and to reorient himself. At the end of the road, it should be clear that the destination has been reached.

The most effective way to include these kinds of signposts and directions in a report is through the use of chapter headings, text headings and subheadings which clearly define each passage. These headings tell the reader where he is, where he has been and where he is going. When these headings are brought together as an outline of the report, they provide a map of the whole work which anyone can follow far more readily than through a summary. The most useful place to bring the headings together is as a table of contents which precedes the report and which both indicates the scope of the overall piece and shows exactly how many pages are devoted to the whole and to its parts.

The most effective way to include the kinds of signposts and directions needed to follow a report is through the use of chapter headings, text headings and subheadings which clearly define each passage. When brought together in a detailed table of contents, they provide a map of the whole document.

Some guides to report writing advise authors to first do their research, then arrange the main points into order and finally write a plan based on these points. However, in the procedures recommended in Chapter Twenty, the place to define main points is during the research phase itself. If you have followed these procedures, you should have a file of manila folders each named with a descriptive heading and each containing the documentary material relevant to that heading. By the time the research is complete, the folders should have been arranged in the order in which the report will be written. The folders, in other words, constitute the plan of the report and their headings are its outline. The table of contents should be readable directly from the folders.

As you write the report, and as you see new relationships within the material you have brought together, the order of these headings may change. Some will be combined with others, and some sections will be expanded and given additional headings. These changes should be expected. In most cases, however, they will be modifications rather than any fundamental revision of the plan that emerges from the research phase. An example of an outline of a report presented in the form of a table of contents is given below. However, for a more detailed example turn to the contents page of this book where you will see the headings that indicate the outline, the complete scope and all the signposts needed to understand what this book is about.

PRESENTATION AND LAYOUT

The way a report is presented is as important as its message. This is not a matter of trying to impress people through the quality of the printing, the binding or any other aspect of appearance. Presentation should be regarded as a means to understanding. As we emphasised above, one part of the presentation, the outline or table of contents, is an essential contribution to understanding by allowing the reader to see the report as a whole. Other aspects of presentation should be regarded as essential guides to take the reader through the text itself and to help ensure that the reader comes to a full understanding of the case that has been made and the evidence for it. What follows in this section is an account of the way a long, analytic report should be presented. In a shorter report, some may be omitted, such as appendixes and bibliography. A major report would normally have the following components.

1. Letter of transmittal
2. Title page
3. Table of contents
4. Summary and recommendations
5. Introduction
6. Body of report (which comprises as many sections as you need to use)
7. Conclusion/s
8. Appendixes
9. Bibliography

LETTER OF TRANSMITTAL

This is a brief letter addressed to the person who asked for the report. If the report is internal to an organisation, the letter can be in memo form. It should tell who authorised the report and, briefly, why the report was written and where you obtained the information. If there are formal terms of reference for the report, these can be included in the letter of transmittal. The letter may be bound as part of the report itself or attached to it.

Some points that may be included in the letter of transmittal:

- convey a greeting to the recipient
- open quickly with a tone such as 'here is the report you requested'
- establish the subject in the first sentence
- in some cases you might include an *extremely* brief summary of the study
- acknowledge the assistance of those who helped in the report (although this can sometimes be done better in the introduction, especially if there are several people to acknowledge)
- close with a 'thank you' and a forward look

The structure of a report:
1. Letter of transmittal
2. Title page
3. Table of contents
4. Summary and recommendations
5. Introduction
6. Body of report (which comprises as many sections as you need to use)
7. Conclusion/s
8. Appendixes
9. Bibliography

TITLE PAGE

The following information should be included on the title page: title of the report, full identification of who authorised the report, name and title of the author and date completed. Make the layout attractive with major lines centred (and in bold if you have a word processor) and perhaps underlined. In small reports, the title page will be the cover page. In large reports which are bound include the title page inside the cover, the same as books do. If a separate cover is made, it should give the report's title and the author's name.

TABLE OF CONTENTS

This should give the contents of all parts of the report, including *all* headings and subheadings (but not the letter of transmittal and title page). It should also give page numbers of every section and subsection adjacent to their headings. The headings should be the same as those in the final outline and, if a numbering system is used (see discussion below), the contents should include the same system as that used in the report proper.

SUMMARY AND RECOMMENDATIONS

The summary (or 'executive summary' as the combination of summary and recommendations is often called) is designed to be read by people who will not have the time to read the whole report. It is undesirable for the summary to be longer than two pages. It should briefly state the problem, the scope of the investigation, the methods used to research the issue, the principal arguments and important issues raised in the discussion.

If the brief for the report called for you to make recommendations, these should be made in the text itself, where they naturally fall, and then gathered together and repeated here, immediately after the summary.

The summary should be written at the very last, after every other part of the report is complete and you know exactly what you have produced. The language should be punchy but written in prose, not note form. Almost every reader will go to the summary first, before reading the body of the text. Many do not read anything but the summary, making up their minds on both the issues and the quality of the report on this alone.

The introduction should cover:

- authorisation
- objectives
- scope
- sources
- acknowledgments

INTRODUCTION

The introduction should be the second-last thing you write because, like the summary, you need to know what you have said before you introduce it. The introduction presents the background to the issue and makes several important points which help the reader understand the whole report. It contains the following elements.

THE AUTHORISATION

This names the person who requested the report and the date the request was made. It may also contain some background explanation to the authorisation and perhaps some extracts from any authorising document.

OBJECTIVES

The purpose and aims of the report should be stated clearly. There should be a precise definition of the issue or problem which the author intends to discuss or resolve. If there are formal terms of reference covering the report these should be stated here and, if interpretation of these terms is needed, this is the place to do it.

SCOPE

This defines the boundaries of the investigation. It describes the extent of the research and explains why certain topics have been omitted. The writer should explain why some issues not investigated were beyond the limits of the report. This often means referring back to the terms of reference.

SOURCES

The writer should discuss the range of sources used, including primary and secondary sources, from which the information in the report originated. There is no need here to list all the books or reports consulted (that is the role of the bibliography) but there should be an indication of how widely the author did read. Other sources such as personal investigation, interviews, statistics and questionnaires should also be mentioned.

ACKNOWLEDGMENTS

If the writer has received valuable assistance from some people in the preparation of the report, they can be acknowledged towards the end of the introduction. Only include those who have genuinely helped on this project, however, and cut out any mushy 'acceptance speech' references to people 'who have always been an inspiration to me'.

BODY OF THE REPORT

Inductive sequence: for longer reports
1. method of investigation
2. evidence found
3. conclusions

Deductive sequence: short reports only
1. conclusion
2. method of investigation
3. evidence found

This is where the writer discusses his or her investigations in full and presents the findings in a coherent form. It is sometimes desirable to present the findings first and then go on to discuss them by analysing the data, bringing out implications and deducing the appropriate action. In other cases, however, the reverse process might be adopted, that of discussing the method of investigation and then presenting the findings. These two approaches are respectively the *deductive* and the *inductive* sequences.

The inductive sequence follows the approach the writer used to address the issue. It first presents its methods of investigation, then discusses its findings, then draws conclusions and makes recommendations. The reader must proceed through the report before arriving at the conclusion.

The deductive sequence places the conclusion first and then justifies it by describing the method of investigation and findings. The reader comes to the conclusion from the outset.

As a general rule, deductive sequences are suitable for short reports where the investigation is fairly straightforward. In longer reports, where the reader will only be convinced of the conclusions if they are preceded by sound investigation and logical analysis, the inductive method is best. In a long report with an inductive sequence, readers who want to know the conclusion first will have the summary available to them anyway.

The overall shape of the body of the report will be determined by the outline or plan developed during the research phase. As you write, ensure that the plan contains a logical development of ideas. Each paragraph must be clearly related to the one before it. There should be no gaps in the argument.

Include in the text all your headings and subheadings from the outline. Headings make each part of the text easier to follow and make the whole more comprehensible. It is acceptable to have as many as one subheading for every paragraph, if this is what the text requires. In a long report, however, one would normally expect to find a subheading every three, four or more paragraphs.

NUMBERING SYSTEMS

In short reports, the various sections and subsections can be divided by their headings. In long reports, however, it is sometimes desirable to use a numbering system as a means of categorising all chapters, sections and paragraphs. This is useful when you are reasonably sure the report will itself be subject to a fair degree of analysis when people will want to be able to easily refer to particular paragraphs.

There are several different ways of numbering written text but the one adopted almost universally in Australia for reports is the decimal system. Under this system, each chapter bears a major number, then each section bears a decimal point of its chapter, each subsection a lower decimal point, and each paragraph another point lower. For example, a Chapter 4 would be divided as follows.

Chapter	4
Section	4.1
Subsection	4.11
Paragraph	4.111
Paragraph	4.112
Paragraph	4.113
Subsection	4.12
Paragraph	4.121
Paragraph	4.122
Section	4.2
Subsection	4.21
Paragraph	4.211
Paragraph	4.212
Subsection	4.22
Paragraph	4.221
Paragraph	4.222
Paragraph	4.223

Do not automatically assume, however, that because you are writing a long report you need to use a numbering system like this. In most cases, the normal page numbering system works quite well enough for most people to refer to the information they want. Only use numbering systems like this when you know that information will need to be retrieved from the report to a greater than usual extent. Some writers compromise and do not number paragraphs but do use the decimal system for numbering chapters, sections and subsections.

RECOMMENDATIONS

At each point in the body of the report where it seems appropriate to make a recommendation, make one. Use underlining or some other type of emphasis to make it stand out and, if there are several of them, give each a number in sequence. When you are ready to write the section of the report headed 'Summary and recommendations' simply retype each of your recommendations in the order it appeared in the text. Recommendations are written for action so they should be as concrete and specific as possible. Avoid the tendency to run them together. Break each down into as many component parts as seems natural. Spell out clearly exactly what you want to happen.

CONCLUSIONS

The conclusions should be an extension, a summary or a restatement of your findings. If necessary, the conclusion can be a collection of findings already presented. (Note that this is different from the summary which restates not only findings but aims, method and recommendations as well.) The conclusions should be stated carefully and clearly. Although conclusions are normally short compared to the rest of the report it is worth spending more time writing them than normal because they will be scrutinised more closely by readers. Avoid the tendency that many people have towards making vague generalisations and ensure your words are as precise and concrete as possible.

APPENDIXES

Any additional information which is relevant but which is a diversion from the main arguments in the body of the report can be usefully accommodated in an appendix. Long tables of statistics, examples of questionnaires used, or explanations of procedures which are interesting but not essential are the usual candidates for the appendix of a report. Appendixes are usually designated by letters rather than numbers to distinguish them clearly from chapters: Appendix A, Appendix B, and so on. Each appendix should be presented as a separate entity and given a separate line in the table of contents, the same as a chapter.

BIBLIOGRAPHY

The bibliography is a list of the written sources you used when researching the report. It is presented at the end of the report in alphabetical order by author's surname. Most short reports do not have a bibliography because the few books or articles you read are mentioned prominently in the text and it is unnecessary to repeat them. In a long report, or an important one, a bibliography is essential for two reasons: first, it demonstrates how widely you have read and thus how many viewpoints you have considered on the issue, and, second, it will be a useful research tool for others inquiring into this field. If you include a thorough bibliography, you will find other people will regard your work as a valuable resource and thus come to regard you as a valuable resource person. An example of how to present a bibliography was shown in Chapter Ten on Essay and Thesis Writing.

PHYSICAL PRESENTATION

The physical appearance of a report should be practical and businesslike. Do not be too elaborate or people will start questioning the cost. Above all, though, do not allow the presentation to look sloppy or careless. Typing should be at least electric typewriter quality and, if copies are made, they should be high quality with no marks or blemishes. If the report is very long, have it bound commercially with glossy cardboard or plastic covers in bright colours to avoid that drab public service look. This can be done relatively inexpensively these days. Additional points you should remember follow.

- Use A4 bond paper consistently.
- Leave space for big margins, top, bottom and both sides.
- Be generous with layout: have double spacing between paragraphs and before new sections and subsections.
- Spacing between lines should be one and a half or double spacing, whatever your preference, with quotations and footnotes/endnotes in single spacing.
- Chapters should start on new pages.
- Most headings should be ranged left on the page but chapter titles and other important headings can be centred.
- Number all pages consecutively throughout the report, including any appendixes and bibliographies.
- Always make at least one copy of the report for yourself and never let a manuscript out of your possession until you have made a copy.

LANGUAGE AND STYLE

Reports should abide by all the guidelines for prose style that we have advocated throughout this book. There are, however, some special points about language and style that are worth emphasising for those engaged in report writing.

IMPERSONAL TONE

Most of the time you should avoid the use of personal terms 'I', 'we', 'my' and 'me'. Especially avoid that redundant phrase 'in my opinion'. If you hold the opinion that x is y, then simply state 'x is y'. By making the statement alone you tell the reader you have this opinion. Another way to annoy readers is to refer to yourself awkwardly as 'the author' or 'this writer'. It is possible to adopt an impersonal tone and write very long reports, full of your own opinions, without referring to yourself at all. Do not make this too hard and fast a rule, though. On occasions, a modest reference to yourself can add a valuable emphasis, especially when describing things you have personally seen or done. These personal references will only carry weight, however, if they are used sparingly.

OBJECTIVITY AND IMPARTIALITY

It is impossible to be purely objective in a report. If you argue for one point of view rather than another you necessarily lose your objectivity. Your aim, however, should be to get as near to objectivity as possible, or to use a better term, to be as impartial as possible. You should give the appearance of approaching the subject without having made up your mind and without taking sides. You should also appear to be as cool, as reasoning and as unemotional about the subject as possible. Avoid emotive terms, distinguish assumptions from opinions and minimise unsupported judgments and inferences. Avoid moralistic judgmental language such as 'right', 'wrong', 'good' and 'bad' until you have amassed enough evidence to make the use of such terms convincing. Here are two descriptions of the same scene with emotive words emphasised.

> When we questioned the manager of William Minter and Co. about the quality of the carpentry, he *obstinately* refused to recognise my comments as a fair assessment. Together, we inspected the work where he launched into a *tirade of abuse*. In the face of this *disgraceful* performance I left the site.

Give the appearance of approaching the subject without having made up your mind and without taking sides. You should also appear to be as cool, as reasoning and as unemotional about the subject as possible.

A more impartial account would be:

> I informed the manager of William Minter and Co. that the quality of the carpentry was not to the standard originally specified. He told me the work had been performed by qualified tradesmen who 'always perform to standard'. Together we inspected the work. He then became emotional and told me I was unqualified to make an assessment, adding: 'You wouldn't know a quality job if it hit you in the face.' Seeing negotiation was impossible, I decided to leave.

PRECISION

The language of a report should say exactly what you mean and should be coherent and unambiguous. Most reports are designed to recommend some course of action, so there is real pressure on the report writer to tell others precisely what has to be done. There are three principles to observe which are particularly relevant to report writing.

1. Put yourself in the reader's shoes and try to read every sentence you write from that perspective. Keep asking yourself: 'What does the reader need to know to understand exactly what I am saying?'
2. Use short, active sentences. Keep most sentences to within twenty-five words. Write as simply and directly as possible, using the active voice ('He prevented the damage,' rather than 'The damage was prevented by him.'). Avoid useless or redundant phrases, such as 'as of this date', 'in this regard', 'at the present time', 'for the purpose of', 'in view of the fact that', 'until such time', 'whether or not', and so on.
3. Use simple, concrete terms. Avoid abstract and obscure words. Avoid metaphors, similes and other figures of speech. Avoid clichés, jargon and hackneyed expressions.

TABULATED LISTS

Most reports contain quantities of facts and figures. Tabulation assists both reader and writer comprehend a passage quickly. Be careful, though, not to overdo it. A report that is completely full of tabulation looks like a list of notes rather than a prose composition. Within a basic essay framework, tabulation is a useful aid to understanding and remembering. Take the following example:

> Efficiency increased last year because of better stock control, computerisation of employee records, more flexible use of casual staff and more strict accountability for materials.

To make this sentence easier to read you could tabulate its contents like this:

> Efficiency increased last year for four reasons:
> 1. better stock control
> 2. computerisation of employee records
> 3. more flexible use of casual staff
> 4. more strict accountability for materials

Three ways to record references
1. at the foot of a page—footnotes
2. at the end of the document—endnotes
3. in brackets immediately after the point made

DOCUMENTATION AND REFERENCES

A report that relies on other written sources should make reference to them so that others can, if they wish, see where your information comes from and follow up points you have made. By citing these reference sources you give confidence to others that you know what you are writing about and that you have consulted the work of others who have investigated the same topic or aspects of it. We discussed the use of references in Chapter Ten on Essay and Thesis Writing but let us go over some of this ground again in relation to report writing.

There are three ways to record references:

1. at the foot of a page—these are called footnotes
2. at the end of the document—these are called endnotes
3. in brackets immediately after the point made

It is always more convenient for the reader to be able to see the reference on the page where its point is made. If there are only two or three references in a report, they can be made on the spot in brackets. Where there are several references they are better to read as footnotes but it is difficult and time-consuming to type references in this position, unless you are using a word processor with software that will handle footnotes automatically. For reports prepared on conventional typewriters, it is more efficient to include references as endnotes. The ideal, fairly obviously, is the word processor. Some writers who use references frequently have found the purchase of a word processing system is justified on these grounds alone.

As well as citing books and articles consulted, footnotes and endnotes can be used to document verbal or unwritten information (for example, to cite the name of an interviewee and the date of the interview). They can also be used to include detailed information that would distract the reader if included in the body of the text. Do not overdo this, however, by placing all explanatory or background information in footnotes. It can become tedious if the reader has to constantly shift from text to footnotes and back again simply to understand what is being written. The text should be self-contained and should include all the essential background and explanatory material. Such material that is not essential to understanding the text is all that should go into footnotes or endnotes.

FROM DRAFT TO FINAL VERSION

Because they are relatively long documents, few people can compose reports directly. Most need to go through draft stages. An experienced report writer should be able to go from first draft to final version with one editing process in the middle. The job of editing involves checking for mistakes but should be regarded, most importantly, as a process of checking for intelligibility. Here is a checklist on which to test the report.

1. Are any facts misstated or misinterpreted?
2. Are any points exaggerated?
3. Are there instances where opinions have been presented as facts?
4. Are there any contradictions or inconsistencies?
5. Are all findings properly drawn from the evidence?
6. Are all numbers and dates accurate?
7. Are there any gaps in the argument or evidence that have not been considered?
8. Is there any material out of place?
9. Are there any irrelevancies or unnecessary digressions?
10. Are there any sentences or paragraphs that are too long?
11. Are there any concepts left unexplained?
12. Are there too many abstract words or any unintelligible jargon?
13. Above all, is the report convincing?

KEY POINTS: Chapter 22 Reports—writing and presentation

- Well-designed outlines and layout help readers follow the case.
- The table of contents should reflect the original plan of the report.
- Begin with a letter of transmittal, a title page and an introduction which includes acknowledgments.
- Include appendixes and a bibliography after the conclusion.
- Present reports typed, on single-sided A4 bond paper, with double or one-and-a-half spacing, and with at least 3 centimetre margins all round.
- Use an objective, impartial and impersonal style. Tabulate lists. Include references. Always check for intelligibility before your final draft.

QUESTIONS FOR DISCUSSION

1. Why is it important to use headings and subheadings liberally throughout a report?
2. Explain the difference between an inductive and a deductive sequence in a report. Why is the inductive sequence more suitable for longer reports?
3. How can you achieve objectivity and impartiality in a report when you are trying to persuade your readers to a particular point of view?

EXERCISES

These exercises are designed for students who completed those at the end of Chapter Twenty. Write reports based on the following briefs.

1. You have been asked to write a report on the adequacy of eating and recreational facilities at your organisation. After drafting a plan for the report and undertaking the research, write a report on the whole project.
2. You have been asked to write a report on the adequacy of parking facilities at your organisation. After drafting a plan for the report and undertaking the research, write a report on the whole project.
3. You have been asked to write a report on how your organisation can increase the numbers of its clientele. After drafting a plan for the report and undertaking the research, write a report on the whole project.

CHAPTER

23

ADMINISTRATIVE AND MANAGEMENT REPORTS

After studying this chapter, you will be able to:

- plan a strategy for the production of regular reports within an organisation
- define the periodic reports needed by an organisation
- produce progress reports
- produce reports of inquiries
- produce proposals and recommendations

The reports discussed in the previous three chapters were mainly concerned with gathering, investigating and analysing information. Another important kind of report is needed where people have a responsibility to report back to others about an organisation's progress. These can be periodic reports produced at various times during the year.

A REPORTING STRATEGY

A person or group at the centre of an organisation normally presents a formal report once a year to all those with a direct interest in its operation. These can include employees and shareholders of a company, members of an association, a union or a club, or anyone else with a similar relationship to the organisation. The annual report is an important document for both readers and writers. It is a summary of the status of the organisation and a pointer to its future directions. Producing it forces all those involved to think about what they have been doing, to evaluate their success or otherwise, and to readdress their objectives. We discuss the principles that should be incorporated into an annual report in the next chapter.

The establishment of a formal, comprehensive and regular reporting procedure should be one aspect of an overall communications strategy.

While there is a formal obligation for almost all organisations to produce a set of annual accounts, many see little need to go beyond the bare minimum of legal requirements. However, any organisation that wants to succeed in the long run will take the issue of communications far more seriously than this. The establishment of a formal, comprehensive and regular reporting procedure by management should be one aspect of an overall communications strategy. Objectives need to be set and strategies implemented and systematically managed. This will promote a greater sense of involvement by all employees, members and shareholders. If there is no such strategy, the vacuum left will be quickly filled with information of a different kind. Rumour, hearsay and gossip will become the main form of communication. The probability of inaccuracy and distortion will multiply and a sense of alienation may well develop among people who should be the organisation's most stalwart supporters.

The principles behind a well-thought-out strategy for reporting from management should include the following.

RELEVANCE

The information presented should be relevant to the audience and their relationship to the organisation. Employees, for instance, are interested in job security, payment and the day-to-day decisions that affect their working conditions. Shareholders have more interest in financial issues. Members are often most interested in services provided. To ensure that the information is relevant, it is useful to set up some form of participatory procedure so that representatives of the report's audience can comment on and contribute to the shaping of the report.

RELIABILITY

Information should be accurate and complete. Good reasons should be given when particular information cannot be disclosed. Vague or obscure references to problems are always unsatisfactory. There is little point in playing down real problems by reporting in terms such as: 'Difficulties in the accounting division affected overall profitability,' when the reality was that the chief accountant embezzled $2 million that reduced company profits by two-thirds. You will get more support from both shareholders and employees by being open (partly because in this case they would recognise the loss as an unusual and one-off occurrence.) Reports that appear to have something to hide will only generate distrust.

CLARITY

Management reports should be:
- relevant
- reliable
- clear
- explanatory
- punctual
- readable

The knowledge and understanding of the audience needs to be taken into account in an annual report, as in any other form of written communication. This may require that technical details of new equipment or accounting procedures be explained in non-technical terms. Time and effort should also be put into explaining more complex concepts and issues to readers. It may also mean that special arrangements be made for certain groups such as non-English-speaking employees. Reports should be very careful, however, not to descend to paternalism nor treat the reader like an idiot, something which readers always recognise and resent.

BACKGROUND

The report should not be confined to the raw data or information produced but should be accompanied by an explanation of its meaning and significance. It should also describe how this information was collected, measured and distributed. Readers always dislike vast quantities of uninterpreted data being dumped on them. They are likely to view proper backgrounding as a good indicator of how serious the report's producers are in undertaking the communication process.

PUNCTUALITY

Periodic information should be published on time, when it is due, and not just when things are especially good or bad, that is, not for propaganda purposes. This is always recognised for what it is. Producing reports on time engenders confidence and helps an organisation gather supporters to either share its problems or take advantage of its opportunities.

VOLUME

Care should be taken not to swamp readers with irrelevant detail. Too much information is as bad as too little and will be counterproductive to the aims of informative communication.

ADMINISTRATIVE REPORTS

To properly monitor its own activities, every organisation needs to produce a regular series of reports. These are usually relatively short and they perform a range of different functions—compiling information, analysing data and making recommendations for action. They are part of the feedback loop of information without which most organisations would be ignorant of their own current condition or status. This kind of administrative reporting is essential if there is to be any kind of effective management. It is from these shorter, more frequent, internal reports that the organisation's major public documents, such as the annual report, are compiled. Some of these reports are very brief, just a few tables of statistics or accounts. Most, however, need some prose analysis to point out trends, to explain peculiarities and to summarise the overall status of the function being monitored.

PERIODIC REPORTS

Periodic reports:
- divide activities into intelligible categories
- provide totals of activities within each category

Most organisations need to keep informed of the operation of their various sections or departments. The most common type of report to perform this task is the periodic administrative report. Periodic reports are produced at regular intervals according to the organisation's needs but, commonly, they appear once a month or once a quarter. With the increased use of computerised information, some large organisations in highly competitive areas will insist on weekly reports.

Periodic reports do two things: first, they divide the activities concerned into intelligible categories, and, second, they provide the totals of the activities performed within each category. Hence a sales report could be divided into the categories of:

- product—which lists sales of items of a similar kind
- department—which lists sales by the department, division or section of the organisation
- region—which lists sales made by particular regions, cities or localities

In many cases, categories like this are broken down into their relation to one another. Sales by region, for example, could be broken down into regional sales by product and regional sales by department. Under each of these categories, total sales for the period concerned—the week, the month, the quarter or whatever is chosen—are calculated. In some cases, the totals and categories are all the report needs but, in most cases, a written analysis of the major findings produced by the figures needs to be added.

Another kind of periodic report is produced when the executive officers of an organisation report to the board of directors. This is normally written in prose but contains precise figures, sometimes listed in tables; at other times discussed in the body of the text. An executive officer may be the general manager of a company, the secretary of a trade union, the manager of a club. They have the responsibility for the day-to-day running of the organisation and part of that job is to periodically report on its total operations. The basic format is the same as that discussed above: first, the division of the operations into appropriate categories, and, second, a measure of the volume or status of the activities. However, all the operations may not be of the kind that can be measured, so some prose discussion about each category is usually in order. These reports can be short and pithy (like the general manager's report from WorkVentures, a community-based computer training centre, published here) and assume a fairly high level of knowledge and interest on the part of the readers. The points made are written under the assumption that there will be discussion during the board's meeting where the manager or secretary will have the chance to clarify or elaborate on any points.

WORKVENTURES BOARD—NOVEMBER 1992 GENERAL MANAGER'S REPORT

A. STAFFING

Over the last month:

- **Craig Henshaw** has been employed as Sales and Marketing Manager for ITeC Training Services, our joint venture business with Western Sydney ITeC.
- **Alex Olivera**, a Jobskills participant has started work at Surry Hills as cleaner/handyperson. He will be based at SBEC and be supervised by Phil.
- **Astrid Keys** has been engaged on a temporary basis by ITeC Division as Admin Officer while permanent staffing arrangements are clarified.
- **Louise Tarrant** has been engaged as a consultant to help clarify staffing and management arrangements in the ITeC Division.
- **Janet Green** and the **ITeC Administration team** were awarded the September staff award for a superb effort in producing over 20 Jobtrain tender proposals and winning nine in tough competition.

B. FUNDING AND SPONSORSHIP

- A substantial amount of our 1998 government grant funding should become clear in the next month. Ministerial decisions on Skillshare funding levels are due on 26 November with some supplementary program funding decisions being due Friday 20 November 1992.
- The staff executive group met with Paul Baker, new head of **DIRETFE Employment Programs** branch on Tuesday 17 November to discuss program directions, funding cutbacks and other issues. This was a useful session and a followup visit is to be organised to inspect our premises.
- We were awarded ten **Jobtrain** contracts for January-March 1993—nine in ITeC, one for Peninsula division.
- I met with Max Dumais, Executive Director of the **Australian Association for Philanthropy** in Melbourne on 12 November 1992. In the past this group has been principally concerned with foundations (mostly Melbourne-based) but is now looking at ways to encourage enterprise among non-profits and 'corporate citizenship' by business. Max is keen for WorkVentures to be involved in this new thrust—as a model for non-profit/business partnerships. He is proposing a National Corporate Citizenship Award program as one way of giving attention to businesses showing leadership in the community in areas such as corporate philanthropy, the environment, employee relations, etc. I think this could be a useful link for us.
- I have written to the **Public Interest Advocacy Centre** asking for their help in finding a law firm to help us with legal services on a 'pro bono' basis. This will include help in assessing the desirability of a WorkVentures foundation and its formation if approved.

C. STAFF EXECUTIVE MATTERS

- We are planning a review of **Insurance** held by the company in the wake of a new Insurance Package for Skillshare. We will report on findings and recommendations after a meeting with the brokers—Sedgewicks.

continued on next page

continued from previous page

- Occupational Health and Safety—We plan to consider a draft OH&S policy from our committee next month and bring it for board approval as soon as possible.
- Other matters for consideration next month include:
  - — use of staff development funds, trainer qualifications and payment of HECs fees
  - — a standard format for policy and procedures documents
  - — ethical and policy issues for clarification as part of VETAB training accreditation requirements.

D. OTHER MATTERS

- **Colin Ball TEC Workshop**—seems to have been a useful session but I don't think we are very clear what further action WorkVentures should take at this stage. I am to follow up Liberals to try to contact their policy development person in this area. We have also agreed to continue efforts to organise visits by Liberal leaders to Surry Hills, to seek a review of the policy to scrap NEIS and discuss the Local Industry Advisory Boards they propose.
- Heather Middleton is planning a **WorkVentures** newsletter issue before Christmas.
- Action is proceeding on the **Public Relations Strategy**—consultants are being briefed and a promotions committee meeting is being arranged. Does the board want a representative on this committee?

ACTION For decision on board committee representative

- Inquiries are growing for our Internship program with some good applicants very likely by the December 18 closing date

OTHER ACTIVITIES LAST MONTH

- Skillshare Accreditation working party meetings (19/10, 27/10)
- Meeting with Western Sydney ITeC re ITS joint venture (27/10)
- Performance Information Project meetings (28/10)
- Staff Review completion with Phil (2/11)
- Visit by Anglican archdeacon from Warwick, Queensland (3/11)
- Skillshare NSW conference (5 & 6/11)
- SBEC meeting with Sydney City Council Tourism and Business Development Officer (9/11)
- St Saviour's parish presentation (18/11)
- Meetings with Alan re Vocational Training Research Project (10/11, 17/11)
- ITeC Australia meetings Melbourne (11 & 12/11)
- Botany BEC dinner (12/11)
- Planning workshop with NSW Fairshare Committee (16/11)
- Skillshare OH&S workshop (19/11)
- Peninsula Division PAC event (20/11)

SOME ACTIVITIES PROPOSED NEXT MONTH

- Robyn McCarthy staff review (24/11)
- Appointment of superannuation consultant (25/11)

continued on next page

continued from previous page

- Rowena's induction (30/11)
- Skillshare NSW Accreditation committees (30/11, 3/12)
- Division draft budget review meetings (various)
- Skillshare OH&S Workshop (2/12)
- NSW NSA Branch committee meeting (2/12, 9/12)
- SBEC council (3/12)
- Skillshare City Eastern Hospitality training meeting (4/12)
- SBEC staff meeting (7/12)

A periodic administrative report, like this one from the general manager of Work Ventures, Steve Lawrence, to his board, can assume a fairly high level of knowledge and interest among its readers

PROGRESS REPORTS

Aims of a progress report:
- what was completed and by whom
- whether it was completed on schedule
- whether the rest of the project needs any consequent adjustment

These resemble periodic reports in that they are made on a regular basis. They report progress in any developing operation but are most common in the building industry and other areas where a number of tasks need to be combined in a certain order to complete a project. They are usually related to a preconceived project schedule or timetable for the completion of the individual tasks that go to make up the whole job.

The progress report normally tells three things:

1. what has been completed and by whom
2. whether it was completed on schedule or not
3. whether the rest of the project needs any rearrangement in the light of progress, or lack of it, to date

Progress reporting on projects is one task in which computer techniques have been involved since the 1960s. Complex construction projects were one of the first to adopt these techniques to schedule projects, to decide which was the optimum way to proceed (the 'critical path') and to monitor and reschedule progress as the construction advanced. Today, sophisticated project management software is available for personal computers. Database programs are also suitable for this kind of reporting. A progress report from one of these programs would look like this.

EXEL HOUSING CONSTRUCTION
TASK SUMMARY REPORT
Project Schedule—Gillford House No. 54

Schedule start	*Actual start*	*Responsibility*	*Status*	*Description*
2/2/94	3/2/94	KJC Architect	Complete	Draft plans
1/3/94	3/3/94	Geoff Jones	Complete	Obtain build permit
5/3/94	4/3/94	Jim Egan	Complete	Contract electrical
7/3/94	9/3/94	Harry Baker	Complete	Prepare lot
9/3/94	10/3/94	AGS Plumbers	Complete	Lay water pipes
12/3/94	12/3/94	Peter Ko	Complete	Foundation mould
14/3/94	16/3/94	Geoff Jones	Complete	First inspection
17/3/94	17/3/94	Peter Ko	Complete	Foundation inspect
20/3/94		Transcons	No start—critical	Side framework
20/3/94	23/3/94	Wall Bros	Late	Build base frame
23/3/94		Transcons	No start — critical	Build roof frame
25/3/94		Bruce Spring		Connect electrical
25/3/94		AGS Plumbers		Extend water pipes
1/9/94		Geoff Jones		Final inspection

To flesh out this progress report, a written commentary on the critical late starter, Transcons, would be needed, including discussion of why the firm is late, what contact has been made with it, how the lack of a start affects other parts of the project, and so on.

REPORTS OF INQUIRIES

Major inquiries require the kind of investigation and reporting described in Chapter Twenty-Two. However, there are many kinds of more limited inquiries that need shorter reporting procedures. In general, a brief report of an inquiry to gather information on a particular subject should include the following:

- a title which describes the subject matter, and records who commissioned the report, when it was commissioned, and the name of the author
- a brief statement of the objectives of the inquiry
- description of the methodology of inquiry, that is, sources consulted, persons interviewed, practices observed and the like
- findings of the inquiry, divided into categories, and discussed within those categories
- recommendations for action

There is often no need for a summary because the report itself is virtually a summary. There is no need for a conclusion because the recommendations for action fulfil this role.

Structure of a report from an inquiry:
- title
- objectives
- method of inquiry
- findings
- recommendations

The report should be written in prose, not note form, but should be brief and should come to the point in all sections. Its style should be objective and there should be enough detailed information conveyed for readers to make up their own minds about whether the recommendations are sound.

PROPOSALS AND RECOMMENDATIONS

In some cases, proposals and recommendations for action arise not from inquiries but from people's direct experience of the way an organisation is functioning. A report making recommendations on the basis of this experience should have the following components:

- background to, and nature of the issue or problem
- description of the existing responses to the situation
- problems with the existing responses
- information, data and logical support for change
- recommendation or proposal for action

Where the issue is a simple one, a brief report with the type of structure on page 276 will suffice. Where there is more at stake, a full-scale submission might be in order. We discuss the nature of submissions in Chapter Twenty-Five.

KEY POINTS: Chapter 23—Administrative and management reports

- Any organisation that wants to succeed in the long run will do more than produce the minimum number of legally required reports. Regular, comprehensive reporting will promote a greater sense of involvement by all employees, members and shareholders.
- Reports should be relevant to the audience, reliable, clear and punctual. They should provide neither too little information nor too much.
- Quality of presentation, while important, is no substitute for content.
- Brief administrative reports are essential to effective management. They need be no more than a few tables of statistics or accounts, with some prose analysis to point out trends.

QUESTIONS FOR DISCUSSION

1. What are the advantages of developing a plan for regular reports to be produced by an organisation? What are the possible consequences of *not* making these regular reports?
2. Why do organisations produce periodic administrative reports?
3. Why do projects need progress reports?

EXERCISES

1. Design a form which would be suitable to produce a progress report on a project in an area with which you are familiar. If you are in an educational institution, the project could be to redraft the syllabus for each subject taught at the institution. If you are employed by an organisation, the project could be to modernise or upgrade all its departments. You will need to draw the form and to specify the headings for its various columns.

2. Conduct a simple inquiry into an area with which you are familiar. Produce a report specifying your objectives, methodology, findings and recommendations.

3. Make a series of recommendations for improvements in an area with which you are familiar. Specify the nature of the issue, the existing responses to the situation, reasons for change, and specific proposals for action.

CHAPTER 24

ANNUAL REPORTS

After studying this chapter, you will be able to:

- act as co-ordinator of a team producing an annual report
- act as editor of an annual report
- establish a style guide for authors of an annual report
- define the preliminary pages of an annual report
- determine the contents of an annual report

Many organisations are legally obliged to publish an annual report, especially to provide information about their financial status. This data is, of course, important but it should be recognised that the relationships between an organisation and its employees, members and even shareholders is always more than financial. An annual report that aims to establish good communications with these varied audiences will present a range of other information as well.

The report will be a portrait of a year in the life of the organisation and will provide as much detail about its human face as about its economics. Conceived this way, an annual report is a major undertaking which becomes the most important single definition of what the organisation has done and what it aims to be. Like any other form of communication, an annual report needs to be well planned but, because it brings together information from a wide range of sources, the whole effort needs to be well co-ordinated too. Large organisations often appoint two people to be responsible for it, one to act as co-ordinator, the other as editor. Even if you can afford only one such person, these two distinct roles still need to be clearly defined in advance.

The following sections discuss what is involved in co-ordinating and editing an annual report.

ROLE OF THE CO-ORDINATOR

An annual report needs a co-ordinator to act as the one central point from which all instructions originate and to which all the various contents of the report are directed.

The work of the co-ordinator is to both plan and organise the report. He or she must:

- draw up a plan or schedule to oversee the production of the report—including time allocated, money available, people responsible and locations needed
- gain a commitment from all the people involved to adhere to the plan before it is implemented
- assign tasks and brief all personnel involved, including authors, editor, designer and printer, before they begin work and keep all informed of any changes or updates to the schedule
- become the central receiving and distribution point for all data and other types of information which are needed to write the report

The qualities the co-ordinator needs are those of a strategic planner. The co-ordinator must:

- organise and deliver the resources needed to produce the report
- organise the activities of a group of people over a lengthy period and in a number of different locations
- keep well-organised, up-to-date and easily accessible records of all work in progress
- stay calm as deadlines draw nearer

The co-ordinator also needs to make a range of contingency plans because, in a large, complex job of this kind, some original arrangements are bound to fall through at the critical moment. The co-ordinator must:

Role of co-ordinator is to:
- draw up a schedule for writing and production
- gain commitments from all involved to adhere to deadlines
- assign tasks to authors, editor, designer and printer
- act as the central receiving and distribution point for information

- organise alternative authors to replace those who leave or who are unavailable when they are needed most
- organise alternative computer systems to handle the job in case the existing system breaks down
- keep a back-up of all work that is on computer
- organise alternative printers in case those selected have a last minute problem which prevents them meeting the deadline set

The work of the co-ordinator is complete when all the information for the report has been provided and when all the sections have been written by their appointed authors. The co-ordinator then passes this collection of material to the editor.

ROLE OF THE EDITOR

The editor has two roles:
1. Substantive editing
- checking overall consistency
- ensuring logical flow of arguments
- looking for inaccuracies and omissions
- checking support for conclusions
2. Copy editing
- checking style and consistency
- checking grammar and usage
- checking references and continuity
- assigning headings and subheadings
- determining design

Editors of annual reports need to divide their task into two divisions and to treat each separately.

SUBSTANTIVE EDITING

The first task is what is normally called substantive editing. The job of substantive editing is to take a total view of the report and, in particular, to check five aspects:

- the consistency of the overall story being presented
- the logical flow of arguments
- the quality of the evidence provided
- inaccuracies and omissions
- the support provided to the conclusions that are drawn

The substantive editing process often involves going back to some of the original authors and asking them to do more work. The schedule for the production of the report needs to allow enough time for this to occur.

COPY EDITING

The second task the editor must perform is that of copy editing. This involves making a close check of the text to ensure that its style is clear and that its grammar, spelling and punctuation are accurate and consistent. Copy editing involves checking for all the following.

1. *Style* Editors should ensure the text is written in simple, direct prose and is free of pretentious language and bureaucratic phraseology.
2. *Jargon and hidden assumptions* Since the report is intended for an outside audience, it should be free of jargon and local terminology which can only be understood by those within the organisation. The text should not assume readers have a detailed knowledge of the internal

workings or facilities of the organisation but should describe these things clearly for those who are not in the know.

3. *Consistency* The editor should ensure that the same style is adopted for quotation marks, capitalisation, italics and numbers throughout the text.
4. *Grammar and usage* The editor is responsible for ensuring that correct grammar is adopted throughout the report and that usage of words and phrases is both sensible and up-to-date.
5. *References* The copy editor needs to check every reference in the text to ensure there is a corresponding footnote or bibliographical entry.
6. *Continuity* Any reference in a text to a previous or subsequent chapter or section should be checked by the editor. The structure of chapters often gets rearranged and internal references to them can easily become misdirected. The editor should also check all numerical sequences, such as page numbers, numbered headings, footnotes, numbers identifying tables and graphs, and simple lists, to ensure there are no omissions.
7. *Headings and subheadings* The copy editor is responsible for assigning the levels of headings and subheadings to a report.
8. *Design* Large organisations often employ specialist designers for their reports but, today, with desktop publishing software available on computers, the copy editor can readily double as designer as well. Most of these software packages contain templates for reports which make most of the design decisions (such as typeface styles, sizes and spacing) for you. They are perfectly acceptable and allow an untrained editor to turn out a job that looks professional.

With so many things to look for, the copy editor will normally need to read the text several times, focusing on a different issue each time. This is the typical practice in the book publishing business where the manuscript editor will read once for grammar, spelling and punctuation, read a second time to check tables and graphs, read a third time for consistency of headings, subheadings and other sequences, and so on. Editors of annual reports should adopt the same procedure.

The copy editor also needs some references to assist in correcting style and usage. The two most useful are: *Style Manual for Authors, Editors and Printers*, published by the Australian Government Publishing Service, Canberra, 1988; and Stephen Murray-Smith's *Right Words: A Guide to English Usage in Australia*, Viking, Melbourne, 1987.

USE OF A STYLE GUIDE

Editors can help reduce the amount of corrections they need to make by drawing up a style guide and presenting it to all authors before they submit their work. A style guide allows you to determine a consistent presentation for all text and to decide how to present common elements such as dates, numbers and acronyms. Most Australian editors will find it best to follow the *Style Manual for Authors, Editors and Printers* cited above, but individual authors will probably not want to wade through it all. The editor should help out by providing one or two sheets of paper which summarise the 'house style' for the report. It should provide directions such as:

- present lists using bullets rather than numbers
- use capitals only for proper names, not for titles
- use single quotation marks when reporting speech
- indent any quotation that contains more than two sentences

A style guide might look like the following.

NUMBERS, DATES, TIMES 22 March 1995, *not* Mar. 22 or 22nd 1980s, *not* 1980's 1992–93, *not* 1992/3 6 am, *not* 6 a.m. (02) 123 4567	ACRONYMS, ABBREVIATIONS BHP, *not* B.H.P. for example, *not* e.g. that is, *not* i.e. per cent, *not* % South-East Asia, *not* SE Asia
SPELLING appendixes, *not* appendices organise, *not* organize disc, *not* disk, except in reference to computers program, *not* programme Australian Labor Party, *not* Labour	STYLE 'Let me begin', *not* "Let me begin" Lists: itemise with bullets, *not* numbers Tables and graphs: each needs a heading and its source Pictures: each needs a caption
CAPITALS, PUNCTUATION chief executive, *not* Chief Executive board of directors, *not* Board of Directors taxation policy, *not* Taxation Policy co-ordinate, *not* coordinate minimal use of semicolons and colons	USAGE IBM has reduced, *not* have reduced sales representatives, *not* salesmen air steward, *not* air hostess about, *not* with reference to, *nor* in regard to

Style guides are usually short summaries of 'house style'

PRELIMINARY PAGES

The text of an annual report starts with the beginning of the first chapter and continues through to the end of the report, including appendixes and the index. The first page number is given on the first page of the first chapter and is in arabic numerals. The text is preceded by the preliminary pages which includes the title, table of contents and preface. The preliminary pages are usually prepared last and take a different numbering system, normally in roman numerals. The preliminary pages can include the following, though not all these items would appear in an annual report.

The title, on the first right-hand page inside the cover
Copyright notice, printer's name and ISBN/ISSN number, first left-hand page
Letter of transmittal
Terms of reference
Membership of reporting body
Table of contents, starting on a right-hand page
Executive summary (conclusions plus action recommendations)
Preface
Acknowledgments
Introduction

TITLE

The title of an annual report should be brief, clear and unambiguous. It should have a strong emphasis on the name of the organisation and should include the words 'Annual Report' and the period covered. If the report is for less than a year then state the precise dates covered. Avoid pretentious literary efforts like 'A Year of Transition' or 'Confronting Change'.

CONTENTS OF ANNUAL REPORTS

STRUCTURE AND RESPONSIBILITIES

The range of activities within an organisation are best organised into categories that indicate the duties and responsibilities of key personnel and major divisions. The information included here might be presented as a list or lists, or in the form of organisational charts, and can include:

- the range of activities, services provided and products
- a list of the major divisions or departments within the organisation, showing their relationship to each other
- the management structure, including the names, photographs and functions of key personnel
- a list of associated organisations, subsidiaries and their activities
- the major customers and suppliers
- the structure of membership, or the major shareholders
- the broad economic and political environment within which the organisation operates

Contents of a typical annual report:

- preliminary pages
- structure and responsibilities of organisation
- future plans and prospects
- financial status
- personnel and staff development
- reports from key personnel

FUTURE PLANS AND PROSPECTS

Plans for the future of an organisation are an important discussion point for all those involved with it. People may not only want to contribute to new developments but their confidence in an organisation is often bound up in the knowledge of its plans and objectives. They can be discussed as two types, external and internal.

External
- new links, mergers or takeovers
- export performance

Internal
- production and investment programs
- research and development
- new services and activities
- new products and technologies
- sales performance
- changes in location

FINANCIAL STATUS

Everyone connected with an organisation needs to have a good understanding of the financial environment within which it operates. The promotion of this understanding, rather than the simple fulfilment of legal accounting responsibility, should be a major goal of an annual report. The areas to discuss should include:

- composition of capital and the ratio of debt to equity
- profits—before and after tax
- turnover
- sales performance, overall and by market sectors or geographic divisions
- output, orders, prices and market requirements
- wages and salaries
- dividends
- the effects of inflation

Use personal reports from key personnel to:
- summarise the main points made by the document as a whole
- report on changes within each major division
- note a landmark achievement of the previous year
- announce a major new development

PERSONNEL AND STAFF DEVELOPMENT

There should be clear and detailed accounts of the people employed by the organisation, their conditions and the provisions made for them. This can include:

- profile of the workforce, including occupation, sex, age and department—accompanied by estimates of future requirements for staff
- methods and policies of recruiting and promotion
- the past year's appointments, promotions and transfers
- obituaries
- employee amenities
- induction and staff development policies
- training and retraining provisions
- introduction of new working methods
- policies for redeployment, reclassification, redundancy and dismissal
- procedures governing grievances and discipline
- safety and occupational health policies and programs
- equal opportunity policy
- rights of unionists

- industrial relations and disputes
- coverage and application of awards and industrial agreements
- retirement provisions, pension schemes and superannuation
- profit-sharing, stock options and bonus arrangements

PERSONAL REPORTS FROM KEY PERSONNEL

Some of the sections within an annual report should be presented in the form of personal reports. One of these is normally written by the formal head of the organisation (such as the president or chairman) and is preferably very brief. A more detailed personal report may be presented by the executive head (the secretary or managing director) which summarises the main points made by the document as a whole. If the organisation has a small number of large departments, it is normal to invite the heads of each to provide a report on the changes and developments within their own area over the past year. Photographs should accompany each personal report so the reader will be able to better identify the author.

Other key personnel might also be invited to contribute a personal report if they have something worth saying, such as noting a landmark achievement of the previous year or announcing a major new development. Personal reports should not be overdone, however. A document full of them usually smacks of paternalism and ego boosting rather than good communication. The majority of the text should be written in the third person, objective prose style found in quality journalism.

THE INDEX

Because it is a historic document, an annual report should have an index. Readers will need to refer to different parts of it at various times and, as a service to them, an alphabetical index at the end of the publication should always be included. Indexing takes considerable skill and there is a professional body, the Australian Society of Indexers, which provides contacts of those with experience in the field. If you cannot afford a professional indexer and have to do the job yourself, then you must, at a minimum, index all the proper names mentioned in the report. A subject index, however, is also highly desirable. At a minimum, this should cover all the subject areas listed in the chapter titles, section headings and subsections.

PRESENTATION

The quality of the presentation of an annual report is important but it should never be a substitute for content. No one is misled by expensive paper, artwork and printing if very little of value is actually written in a report. Content should always have priority over form—the message is more important than the medium. This is not to say that you should not contract an expensive job with artists, photographers and quality printing. Often this level of effort can provide a fitting environment for what is, after all, one of the important symbols of the organisation.

Although it may look environmentally friendly, recycled paper is not suitable for annual reports. They are documents which should be designed to provide a historic record of their organisations. Recycled paper has a shelf life of only twenty years. After this it deteriorates. Annual reports should be printed on paper that will be preserved in perpetuity.

Another good reason to use high quality paper and printing is to reproduce photographs. If you can afford it, try to accompany each of the sections described above with at least one photograph. It should be taken by a professional and reproduced either on gloss art paper or on high quality matt art paper. Good black and white photography, well reproduced, can be as effective as colour. Photographs are often an essential addition to the text to give readers a better sense of the nature and scale of the activities concerned than is possible through written prose.

It often proves worthwhile to engage a commercial artist to prepare charts, graphs and diagrams, which can explain some of the more complex and detailed aspects of your operations. If you cannot afford this, then at least try to present your statistical and financial data in graphic form. Most of the leading computer spreadsheet programs have built-in graphic facilities which can produce perfectly acceptable illustrations.

Today, the majority of annual reports are produced on computer desktop publishing programs. When the editing is complete, you simply deliver a copy on disk to a printer or computer service bureau. It is not only cheaper to do it this way but more convenient. Last-minute corrections can be handled quickly in-house without taking days for changes to be made by an outside typesetter. Anyone contemplating producing an annual report should investigate this kind of software.

KEY POINTS: Chapter 24 Annual reports

Annual reports should cover:

- the structure of the organisation and responsibilities of key personnel
- future plans and prospects
- financial status of the company
- staff development
- personal reports from key personnel

QUESTIONS FOR DISCUSSION

1. Why should you separate the work of the co-ordinator from that of the editor of an annual report?
2. What are the advantages of establishing a style guide for the production of an annual report?
3. Why would you need to produce the preliminary pages only after the main chapters of an annual report have been written and set in type?

EXERCISES

1. Acting as co-ordinator, draw up a schedule and assign all the tasks needed to produce an annual report for an organisation with which you are familiar such as your place of education or employment.

2. Become involved in either writing or editing at least part of the actual annual report for this organisation.

CHAPTER

25

SUBMISSIONS

After studying this chapter, you will be able to:

- define the objectives of a submission to government
- prepare a budget for the activities sought in the submission
- draw up a schedule for the completion of a project
- write a submission to gain funding for a project

Submissions have become one of the most important forms of communication within both business and government organisations and between the private and the public sectors. Increasingly, someone who wants to make a major change in the operations of any large organisation will be asked to write a submission on the subject. Anyone who wants access to financial grants, subsidies or contracts within government programs will need to be able to write a good submission before their application will be considered.

If you want to influence an investigation or an inquiry into a subject that is important to you, the best way to do it is through a submission. Writing submissions has become one of the most important ways to develop opinion and to make things happen.

Submissions today, however, are being written within an increasingly competitive environment where the skill of the author is often the factor that determines who will succeed or not. So simply writing submissions is often not enough; the goal should be the production of quality submissions. This chapter is a guide to help achieve this.

DEFINING OBJECTIVES AND TASKS

The submission' s objective should be written in one or two sentences and should be as self-contained as possible.

Submissions should always be written for a purpose: normally to get some action taken or to change someone's mind about an issue. It is important that the submission writer has this purpose fixed firmly in his or her mind from the start. This aim or objective should permeate every aspect of the submission from its title and its overall structure, down to the smallest detail of a budget. So the first step to take in preparing a submission is to define this objective very clearly and concisely.

The objective should be written in one or two sentences and should be as self-contained as possible. It should say in concrete terms what your purpose is, but be expressed so that someone who knows nothing about you or the project will get a clear idea of what you want to achieve. For example, a suburban progress association might define an objective in the following terms:

> *Objective:* To persuade the State Rail Authority to build a stone retaining wall adjacent to the station at Point Clare; to reclaim, fill and level the enclosed waste ground; and to construct a commuter car park for 100 vehicles.

This definition describes the two most important components of any objective: first, the result you want to achieve (construction of a car park for 100 commuter vehicles), and, second, how you will do it (building a stone wall, etc.). In some cases, you might want to be even more specific by adding the total of the budget for the job, but in most cases an objective comprising these two components will be sufficient.

Although an objective, when finally written, may seem simple enough, it will nearly always take some time to write. It is rarely an easy matter to spell out precisely what a task entails. This is not just a matter of getting the words right. It also involves thinking through what you really want and what you are willing to do to get it.

The act of writing out the objectives forces you to go from vague wishes (to be able to leave your car near the railway station while you take the train to work) to a concrete proposal for the solution. It makes you consider alternative solutions and reject those that are impractical or unlikely (say, in this example, allowing all-day street parking in front of the shops near the station). In some cases, it may also make you put forward solutions that others might not think of and which are not immediately apparent (say, building a retaining wall to level an otherwise unusable tract of steeply sloping land).

Once the overall objective has been defined, the project on which the submission is to be based can be broken down into its principal tasks. The point of this is to provide the initial structure for writing the submission. A breakdown of the objective into principal tasks should be done by a logical, step-by-step analysis of the separate tasks that need to be done. The tasks defined should be distinct enough for a different person to do each of them or for one person to do them at different times. In the example of the objective given above, the separate tasks involved would be as follows.

1. To appoint a small committee from the association to supervise the project.
2. To conduct a feasibility study into physical construction aspects of the proposed car park.
3. To conduct a survey among residents of Point Clare to see how the existence of a car park would affect their use of rail transport.
4. To research State Rail Authority data on existing volume of traffic through the station.
5. From the resident survey and from calculations of existing commuter travel patterns, to estimate the likely use of the proposed car park and its impact on the volume of rail passengers from Point Clare.
6. To write up a draft submission on the proposal.

The next stage should be to divide these into action tasks. This procedure should follow directly from each of the above principal tasks. In Task 3 above, a breakdown would look like this.

1. To appoint someone to supervise the survey.
2. To draw up a questionnaire.
3. To pilot the questionnaire on a small sample of residents and make any necessary corrections.
4. To recruit interviewers.
5. To question residents through street interviews at the railway station and by door-knocking households.

When each of the principal tasks has been broken down into action tasks, you should be able to schedule the whole project in terms of every action that needs to be taken. You can then work out the cost of each action and so derive an overall budget. Both scheduling and budgeting are discussed in more detail later in this chapter. Let's now go to the stage of actual submission writing.

WRITING THE SUBMISSION

Every submission should be written around three core points:

- the nature and dimensions of the problem
- the current approaches to the problem
- what you want to do about it

Every submission should be written around three core points:
- the nature and dimensions of the problem
- the current approaches to the problem
- what you want to do about it

In drawing up a submission's structure, these should be the basis on which other material is built. The first point, the nature and dimensions of the problem, should be based on as much concrete information as possible. It should focus on cause and effect: why the problem has occurred or why the issue has arisen, and the results both good and bad that have been found.

This section should include numerical and statistical data and/or the opinions of people who know about the subject, including opinions that have been published in articles and books and opinions expressed in interviews to the submission writer and through questionnaire research. Wherever it is appropriate, these people should be named and direct quotations given of their views on the subject.

Current approaches to the problem should be a description of what is presently being done about the issue. This section may describe the existing policies of government or other responsible organisations and will often be critical of them, though in a non-emotive and objective way. Where nothing is being done about an issue it is not enough to simply write 'Nothing is being done.' Use this section to describe the possible alternative courses of action and point out during each description that this course is not being followed. This will give you a persuasive lead-in to the reforms you want to advocate.

The section that discusses how you will solve the problem should have two subsections. One will be based on your objectives and the other on your methods. It is worth describing these separately because it allows you the opportunity to see clearly whether your methods are really appropriate for the objectives or not. This also allows the reader of the submission the same opportunity to examine this connection and, more than anything else, this will be the factor that convinces the reader or not that you have a genuine solution to the problem.

Around this three-point core should be other supporting material. This should include some mention of where the impetus for the submission began (such as a public meeting called in response to the problem; a research project that revealed the breakdown of some existing arrangement; a newspaper advertisement by an inquiry calling for submissions, and so on).

In some submissions you should not only propose a solution or a method of response to an issue but you should suggest means by which your response can itself be tested or evaluated. This could be a proposal for monitoring—that is, for reporting on results continuously as they occur. Monitoring is usually an on-going process of recording and publishing fairly simple numerical data, such as the total number of people recruited to a program each month, or the total cash receipts for each performance, etc. Or you might propose a more formal evaluation. An evaluation is usually a one-off but substantial research project in which the underlying principles or philosophies of the activity are examined in light of the results. Sometimes this will lead you to change your methods to reach your original goals; in other cases you will want to modify your objectives if you find they are not realisable; in further cases, you might find your original goals were too modest and much more can be accomplished than you originally thought.

It is often important to describe the expertise of the writer and organisation as if you were applying for a job.

If an evaluation is appropriate, it is normal to do it after a specific period has elapsed in which the activity has had a fair trial, say six months, one year or three years. Monitoring and evaluations are usually designed to provide constructive criticisms of your approach. When you have the results, you can both review your procedures to make them better fit your objectives and reconsider your objectives in the light of what you now know is possible to achieve.

It is also important in many submissions, especially where they are advocating that the submission writer be given a job in response to the issue, to describe the expertise of the writer and organisation. In other words, some submissions are like applying for a job and therefore they need a concise but detailed account of the qualifications, the skills and the relevant experience of the people involved. In some cases, this will involve naming specific people to work on the job and listing their responsibilities and qualifications.

Costing involves:
- estimating how much money you need to spend
- calculating how much time will be taken for particular tasks

Another important section of a submission is its budget. This is essential if you are asking someone for money to do a job but it is also worth doing even if you are paying expenses yourself. It lets you know what you are in for and lets you define limits you do not want to exceed.

A schedule of tasks to be completed, and their timing, is another essential component. This should include a firm starting and a firm finishing date, with the precise day of each stated. Even where the start date is uncertain and depends on the response the submission receives, you should write an 'if … then …' time schedule: 'If the project starts on 30 May 1995, it will be complete by 30 November 1995.'

In some submissions, you will want to include the names, addresses and telephone numbers of referees who can testify to your ability to handle the job concerned.

With these points in mind, the following represents the structure of the body of a typical submission.

1. Origins of the writing of the submission
2. Causes, effects and dimensions of the issue
3. Current responses to the question, their adequacy and inadequacy
4. How you propose to solve the problem or respond to the issue
5. Methods of evaluating, monitoring and reviewing your solution
6. Qualifications, skills and experience of your organisation
7. Names of personnel, their specific responsibilities and qualifications
8. Budget
9. Timetable and schedule of tasks and events
10. Referees

COSTING AND BUDGETING

If your submission is asking for money to conduct a project then you need to be able to make a fairly reliable estimate of the costs involved. You should take this costing process fairly seriously because, if you are successful, you will have to live within these costs for at least the first year of the project's life. If you underestimate the real costs involved, you will either be limited in your ability to fulfil your objectives, or else you will be out of pocket.

BUDGET ESTIMATES

A. Professional fees

Position	Charge-out rate per day (days)	Time on project	Total fee $
			Subtotal $

B. Direct costs

1. Equipment and materials (specify)	Subtotal $
2. Data processing (if necessary)	Subtotal $
3. Travel (fares, accommodation)	Subtotal $
4. Stationery, copying, postage, telephone	Subtotal $
5. Miscellaneous (specify)	Subtotal $
TOTAL BUDGET	$

Costing is not only a matter of estimating how much money you need to spend. It also involves calculating how much time will be taken by particular tasks. The biggest expense in almost any paid activity is that of wages and salaries, and costs in this area are directly related to the amount of time people spend on the tasks concerned. You need to calculate very carefully how much time this will be. Even the best planned estimates, however, will invariably turn out to be significantly astray from the actual time eventually spent, simply because there will always be unexpected events intervening. One piece of advice sometimes given to people in working out wages and salary costs for projects is to work out what you think it will cost and then double it. This, however, is risky advice. If successful, you are bound to earn more for the task than it costs you, but, if there is any competition for the job, you are not very likely to win. It is better to try to be as accurate as possible and then allow yourself a small margin for error.

The following is a budget form taken from tender documents for a contract research project for the Commonwealth Government. Would-be contractors are asked to fill in their details under these headings. This is typical of the level of detail that a sponsoring organisation wants from a budget. This budget, it should be noted, does not call for extremely minute details. It recognises that all costings of this kind are estimates and does not require every single item to be named or calculated to the last cent.

Professional costs in a budget of this kind are usually based on a combination of wages and salaries of the people who will do the work plus the overheads of the organisation employing them. The normal way to work out overhead costs is to take the sum total of non-wage expenditure of the organisation (all rent, insurances, power, cleaning, telephone, etc.) and divide it by the number of weeks and hours the place operates, which is normally 50 weeks a year at 40 hours a week. From this you will arrive at an hourly overhead rate. You need to perform the same operation to arrive at the hourly salary rates of the people to be employed on the job. Add the hourly overhead rate to the hourly salary rate and you have a figure that counts as an hourly 'Professional Fee' described in the form above. When you have worked out how many hours it will take to do the job concerned, you multiply this by the hourly professional fee to get the total budget for professional fees.

Headings such as 'Equipment and materials', 'Data processing' and 'Travel' can only be filled in when you have specific plans for a project. However, recurring costs such as stationery, telephone and postage can be worked out on a similar basis to overheads. Calculate the total annual spending by the organisation on these items and divide it by the time the project will take. Strictly speaking, stationery, copying, postage and telephone costs have already been included in the budget as part of the overheads component of professional fees. Adding them as an extra item allows a little flexibility in the budget to take account of unexpected costs.

As well as costs, a budget should also include revenues. If your submission is to a government or other major institution, this sponsoring body will be the major source of revenue. In some cases, a budget will request a particular schedule of payments, say, 25 per cent of the total on the signing of an agreement and the rest in three instalments of 25 per cent each. In other cases, the budget will simply list the amount requested as a lump sum and wait until an agreement in principle is reached before discussing the timing of payments. Any other sources of revenue the project is likely to attract should be included in the budget so that sponsors are aware of the full financial picture. Finally, some budgets will contain a provision for accountability. This means that they guarantee to provide regular (say, monthly or quarterly) financial reports of incomes and expenditures.

It is often desirable to include a work plan in which the relationships between tasks is spelt out and the timing of each one is indicated.

SCHEDULING AND TIMING

A submission needs to be based not only on the total amount of time its project will take but also the scheduling of that time. Scheduling a project involves deciding the dates when its component tasks will start and finish. Some tasks may be conducted concurrently but others cannot start until something else has finished. It is often desirable to include a work plan in which the relationships between tasks is spelt out and the timing of each one is indicated.

This type of scheduling has been common in the construction industry for many years where managers need to make sure they remember that one job has to be finished before the next stage can start or that a particular machine or tradesman is needed on the site on a certain day. Two types of chart developed in the construction industry have been found widely useful and, where a work plan is needed in a submission, they can be readily drawn up.

The first is a Gantt chart of which Figure 25.1 provides an example. The activities which make up the project are listed down the left-hand side of the chart, and a line across the top of the chart shows the date. The symbols under the date line show when each activity is scheduled. A number of different symbols can be used: to show when the activities should take place; when they may take place without making the project as a whole run late; and which are the critical activities, the ones which are setting the pace for the project. Any delay in a critical activity will make the whole project late.

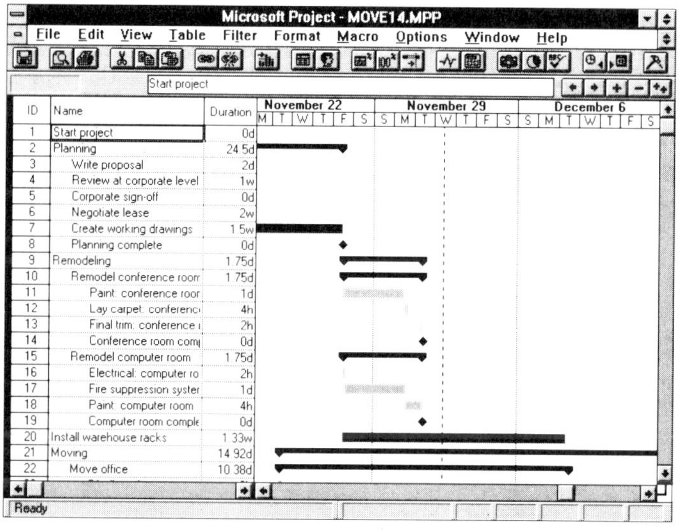

An example of a Gantt chart

The other type of chart used is a PERT chart which is illustrated as Figure 25.2. This shows the relationship of all activities. For example, the first must be completed before the second and third can start. Similarly, the second and third must be completed before later ones can start. Using charts like these, it is possible to schedule and keep track of very complex relationships, timings and costings.

THE LANGUAGE OF SUBMISSIONS

We have said enough about style and language in earlier chapters of this book and here we simply urge writers of submissions to adopt the conventions of normal businesslike prose. This means avoiding all the faults we

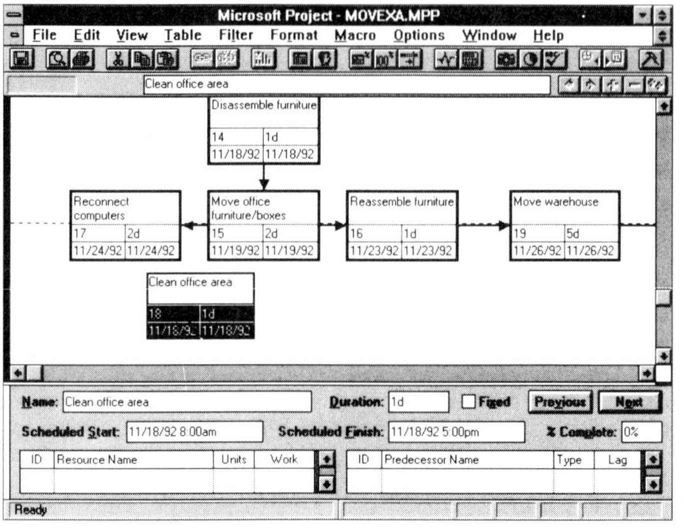

An example of a PERT chart

have discussed in the forms of officialese, jargon and obscure writing that still, unfortunately, plague so much of our society's written communication. The language of submissions should be simple, direct and objective. It should never be obsequious or contain even a hint of pleading or begging for favours. Address the receiver of the submission as an equal and as someone who will gain from your contribution.

In the following article, the writer gives an appropriate warning about the problems of jargon often found in welfare industry submissions.

The Obscure Language of Welfare

by Tony Vinson[1]

Criticising other people's prose is always a dangerous game. The transparent deficiencies in one's own writing invite retaliatory ones. Yet the recent experience of chairing a government inquiry[2] compels me to draw attention to the incomprehensible jargon that is constantly used by those working in the Australian welfare industry to describe community problems. The same jargon is commonplace in social work and welfare courses.

First I must confess that I have long been conditioned to the use of the type of prose of which I am now strongly critical. I have sometimes taken refuge in it. It was the obligation placed on members of the government inquiry to translate jargon-riddled submissions to the professionally uninitiated, that jolted me into realising how much of what was presented to us was devoid of meaning. At times, all one could do was try to reconstruct what had been written in an attempt to give it meaning. Here are a few examples of submissions that, upon closer inspection than they usually receive, leave one puzzled as to the intended message:

- 'Where expensive equipment lies idle after public demand for its provision, it is often the case of activism on the part of the providers.'
- 'Consumer advice can only be achieved if there is proper provision for

community access. Community access alone, however, will not guarantee adequate consumer consultation.'

- 'The basic aim of the advisory committee would be to provide the most integrated form of co-ordination and liaison...'
- 'Lack of co-ordination between institutional and community based services results in lack of access to ongoing services in which there is continuity of care.'

Once I had realised how difficult it sometimes is to understand what welfare practitioners are trying to say, it dawned on me that the same shortcomings are tolerated in places where every effort should be made to correct them. Tertiary courses in welfare studies and the editorial standards of professional journals do little to discourage reliance on welfare jargon.

I do not mean to confuse jargon with technical language. The latter is a necessary aid to professional thought and expression. The problem is that when it is necessary to understand the meaning of many technical sounding statements, such as those submitted to welfare inquiries, all too often the technical language is bogus. It is pretentious and interferes with the process of communication instead of improving it. It is deliberately or accidentally mystifying. Kenneth Hudson[3] has suggested the following simple test for jargon:

> Could this have been expressed more simply without communication suffering in the process?

If the answer is 'yes' then the probability is that one is faced with a piece of jargon. Much of what was submitted to our welfare inquiry would certainly have failed Hudson's test.

Hudson believes that the type of language I am suggesting is now characteristic of the welfare industry is anodyne. Therein, perhaps, lies part of the explanation for why we get away with it. 'Far from having a mutually bracing effect and making one concentrate, it [the language] paralyses the brain. Not only is one unable to devote one's energy to it, in order to extract whatever meaning it may contain, one has no desire to do so.' It was when I was obliged to try and penetrate the meaning of statements like those I have cited, that I noticed the dulling rhythm of chains of polysyllables, an effect that can be relied upon to anaesthetise the critical faculty of less motivated readers. To break the monotony, I tried reading obscure passages out loud and discovered that, with suitably affected variations of emphasis, they can be made to sound deceptively impressive.

In the unnaturally compressed language of welfare, nouns are glued together ('service delivery', 'co-ordination mechanism', 'consumer access', 'knowledge base'), and prepositions are left out. In Marcuse's terms[4], a syntax is created in which the structure of the sentence is abridged and condensed in such a way that no tension, no 'space' is left between the parts of the sentence. This linguistic form militates against a development of meaning. The result is that the mind glides towards oblivion and within fifteen minutes, sleep or a state of waking bliss may be induced.

1. Professor Tony Vinson is in the School of Social Work at the University of New South Wales. This is an extract from his article 'The Obscure Language of Welfare', in *Advances in Social Work Education*, University of New South Wales, December 1986.
2. T. Vinson, V. Couli and R. Walmsley, *Beyond the Image: Review of Welfare Services and Policies in the ACT*, AGPS, Canberra, 1985.
3. K. Hudson, *The Jargon of the Professions*, Macmillan, London, 1978.
4. H. Marcuse, *One Dimensional Man: Studies in the Ideology of Advanced Industrial Society*, Routledge, London, 1964.

PRESENTATION

The presentation of a submission should follow closely the principles laid down for reports. The main aim in presentation should be to help the reader understand what you have written. This is far more important than trying to impress people with expensive printing and binding. There are, however, minimum standards of quality that should be maintained. The type should be at least to the standard produced by a good electric typewriter. Cheap dot matrix printing from word processors are unacceptable but letter quality dot matrix type is now good enough. The paper should be good quality bond. If the submission is long it will be handled better if it is bound between plastic or cardboard covers, of the kind available at newsagents. Like a report, a submission may be composed of the following sections, depending on its length.

Letter of transmittal
Title page
Table of contents
Summary and recommendations
Introduction
Body of the submission (which contains the main structure of the submission that has been discussed in this chapter)
Conclusion/s
Appendixes

For more details on each of these sections, see Chapter Twenty-Two where they are discussed in relation to reports. Some submissions will eliminate the introduction and conclusion listed here since these sections will be handled as part of the main body.

One final aspect of the presentation should not be overlooked. This is getting the submission in on time. If the sponsoring body has set a deadline, make sure you submit your work on the day or earlier. There is inevitably a proportion of submissions that arrive one or two days late and, just as inevitably, they do not make a good impression. They convey very strongly the idea that anything else you were required to do would be late as well. If there is some reason why you will be late, telephone the sponsoring organisation and let them know this and give them the date when you will actually submit. Getting your submission in on time is a good signal that you will conduct the whole project in the same way. It is the first prerequisite of success.

KEY POINTS: Chapter 25 Submissions

- If you want to influence an investigation or inquiry, the best way to do it is through a submission.
- Increasingly, the skill of the author determines who will succeed.
- Submissions should always be written for a purpose. The first step is to define the objective clearly and concisely.
- Every submission should be written around three core points:
  1. the nature and dimensions of the issue
  2. the current approaches to the issue
  3. what you want to do about it
- When asking for money you need to be able to make a fairly reliable estimate of the costs involved.
- It is often desirable to include a work plan in which the relationships between tasks are spelt out and the timing of each is indicated.
- Adopt the conventions of normal businesslike prose.
- Getting your submission in on time is a good signal that you will conduct the whole project in the same way.

QUESTIONS FOR DISCUSSION

1. When making a submission, you need to describe the existing responses to the issue concerned. Discuss the ways this might be done.
2. When a submission proposes a solution to a problem, it is common to also propose a means of evaluating the success of the solution. Why is this important?

EXERCISES

1. Take a problem with which you are familiar and prepare an outline of a submission for a plan of action to respond to it. The outline should give a clear indication of the total contents (including letter of transmittal, title page, etc.) as well as a detailed structure of the body of the submission itself.
2. Using this outline, write either the whole or part of this submission.

REVISION LIST FOR PART VII

REPORTS AND SUBMISSIONS

- Because reports provide basic information to an organisation about itself and its relations with the outside world, they have become increasingly important forms of communication.
- This section introduces the information report and the analytic report and advises on how to consult sources for research.
- Several common ways of gathering information involve dealing with numbers of people. The most effective methods are by interview, questionnaire and survey. Each method has its own strengths and weaknesses, and its own pitfalls for the unwary.
- There are certain kinds of presentation that help readers find their way through a document. Other kinds of presentation help lose them. Careful planning can ensure your reports help readers.
- There is a formal obligation for almost all organisations to produce a set of annual accounts. But regular, comprehensive reporting can do much more than this. It can promote a sense of involvement by all employees, members and shareholders.
- Submissions are coming to rely on the skill of the author to ensure their success. Is the objective clearly defined? Are the budget estimates realistic? Was the submission in on time?

PART VII
KEY TEXTS AND FURTHER READING

Australian Government Publishing Service, *The Annual Report Kit*, AGPS, Canberra, 1991.

—— *Style Manual for Authors, Editors and Printers*, 4th ed, AGPS, Canberra, 1988.

Blicq, Ron S., *Guidelines for Report Writing*, Prentice Hall, Scarborough, 1982.

Purchase, Shirley (ed), *The Australian Writers' and Editors' Guide*, Oxford University Press, Melbourne, 1991.

Roberts, Jean, *Successful Submission Writing*, Information Australia-Margaret Gee, Melbourne, 1985.

Weiss, E. H., *The Writing System for Engineers and Scientists*, Prentice Hall, Englewood Cliffs, 1982.

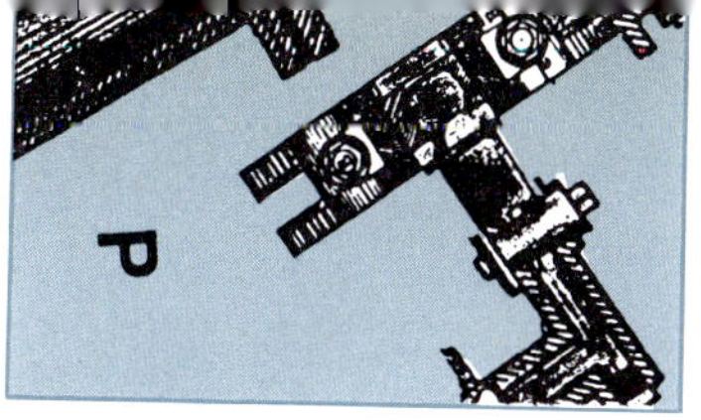

PART

VIII

LOGIC AND REASONING

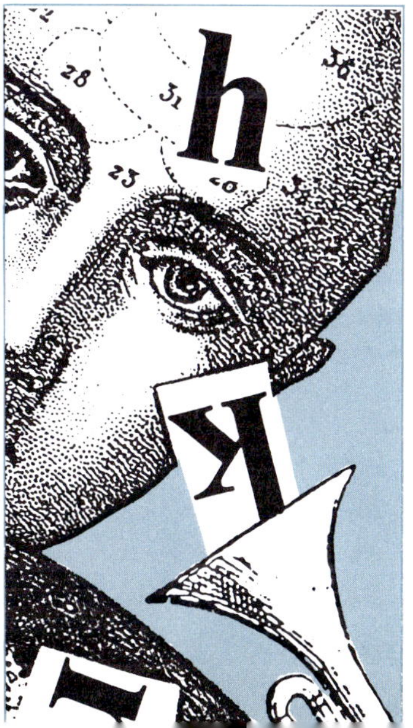

HALLMARK OF INTELLIGENCE

How Phillip Staines uses logic to develop students' ability to make critical judgments.

Every day, we are bombarded by statements from political figures, celebrities and advertisements that try to persuade us to take a certain point of view. One of the marks of an intelligent person is that he or she can analyse these statements for the quality of their reasoning and make up his or her own mind about their value.

Similarly, when an intelligent person presents a case for others to hear or read, one of its hallmarks should be that it is expressed in a logical pattern of thought and argument.

Dr Phillip Staines is co-author with Philip Bell of the book *Reasoning and Argument in Psychology*, University of New South Wales Press, 1983, and has taught in the School of Philosophy at the University of New South Wales since 1985. Prior to that, he taught a course entitled 'Rationality and Critical Thought' in the School of General Studies at the same university.

In his view, many people make mistakes in accepting the arguments of others and in presenting arguments of their own through a lack of understanding of how ideas may be cohesively linked to support a conclusion.

'When you look at someone else's argument, there are two issues: first, whether you have understood the question that the argument is directed at answering; second, whether you have understood the structure of the argument,' he says.

He has found that students, when examining pieces of writing, often have difficulty in distinguishing the conclusion from the premises. The 'premises' are the components, or the building blocks, that go to construct the final case or 'conclusion'. He explains this confusion by the fact that arguments often have a tree structure: certain premises may support an intermediate conclusion. Then that conclusion, together with another premise, go together to advance the final conclusion.

While he acknowledges that, because of their complexity, some arguments may be harder to follow than others, he says that even established writers don't always make the structure of their reasoning clear.

'Reasoning is to do with going logically from one thing to another. Communicating your reasoning is what you do when you're arguing (if you ignore the popular sense of "arguing" meaning to get hot under the collar),' he says.

He advises that reasoning can be made clearer to an audience or a reader by starting with certain propositions that they can readily identify, and then moving to a conclusion via a sequence of short steps. This progression aids comprehension. It is the best way to get the audience to accept that a certain conclusion logically follows.

'When you present a case, you always have an audience in mind which wants to see your reasoning. You can help them follow you by, first, stating clearly the premises from which you are starting, and, second, by tracing carefully each of the steps you take in building your argument. 'It's also useful to remember that, although arguments start with premises, as a matter of logical necessity, you must leave some of your assertions unsupported. For example, I might say, "It's now Friday, so tomorrow is Saturday." I'm taking it for granted that everybody would agree that today was Friday,' he says.

Staines defines this type of argument ('P... so necessarily ... Q') as a *deductive* argument. In deductive arguments the conclusion is intended to follow necessarily. So if their reasoning is done properly, they are watertight.

However, we do not always think we have conclusive reasons or proof. Where the premises purport to support the conclusion without proving it, the argument is *inductive*. In an inductive argument the conclusion should be supported by the premises but it does not necessarily follow. Instead of arguing 'P, so necessarily Q,' we say 'P, so it is likely that Q.'

'For example, I might say, "Smith's car is in the university car park, so it's likely that he's here today." Of course, he may have flown off interstate for the day and decided it was cheaper to leave his car at the university. But it's still not a bad bet to assume that he would be on campus somewhere,' says Staines.

Staines concedes that the use of persuasive devices to prop up arguments is widespread. Two of the most common are 'appeals to authority' and 'appeals to fact'.

The former suggests that because a certain 'expert' has asserted something, or a number of 'eminent scholars' have asserted a view, then it must be necessarily true. What may be overlooked here is that it is the arguments, rather than their proponents, that need to be evaluated.

The second strategy involves making a bald statement such as 'it is a widely accepted fact that ... ' without making any attempt to present a worthwhile argument to justify or discredit a particular view.

Staines appreciates the reasons for verbal or written embellishment and agrees that, as social beings, we can't be expected to know everything through first-hand experience.

'If I know to avoid a red-bellied black snake, it's not because I've been bitten and been poisoned. It's because I've read about it and I've trusted what I've read. But that's not to say we should uncritically accept everything we read. It's a matter of balance,' he says.

Staines also advises about the pitfalls of automatically labelling different points of view under headings such as 'sexist' or 'conservative' or 'trendy'. When we classify arguments according to their political correctness and reject them on these grounds alone, we are falling into one of the most common traps. We should try to understand each argument in terms of what it is saying, rather than who already supports it or who is against it.

'Part of our mental apparatus is the urge to classify. We do this even when we say, "It's a fine day" or "It's not a fine day." Our very nature involves us in distinguishing one thing from another, by grouping like things together. However, thinking that the classifications are watertight can be a mistake,' he says.

He also explains that he finds it interesting that we are sometimes more willing to be receptive to arguments if they are couched in a jargon or style of language with which we are familiar.

'As rational creatures, we're surprisingly dependent on how things are put. It's odd that we seem to be cognitively structured so that we might reject an idea from the outset, but when it is put in different words, we might accept it. This may also be to do with our own conditioning and life-experience,' he says.

He believes that a student essay must show evidence of logical thought and reasoning, through which arguments should be well supported.

'Sometimes it seems that statements are included in written pieces merely via association. It may be that an idea occurs to the writer, he or she likes the sound of it, and becomes determined to use it, but it does not advance the argument,' he states.

Staines declares that formal logicians believe there are patterns of argument that do not depend at all on the meaning of the particular words. They think these form the criteria for good argument, regardless of the subject.

'For example:

All dogs are mammals.
All mammals are warm-blooded.
So all dogs are warm-blooded.

can be translated into:

All As are Bs.
All Bs are Cs.
So all As are Cs.

Now, A, B and C could stand for anything at all and it would still be a good, valid argument,' he says.

He explains it was an ancient Greek, Aristotle, who discovered that patterns of this kind (their technical name is 'syllogism') could be applied to all types of arguments.

However, he points out that the A–B–C pattern doesn't remain valid when you use a word with varying meanings such as 'desirable'.

'In some situations, "desirable" could mean that "I want it to be the case," or it could mean, more objectively, that "It ought to be." In using a word which could be variously interpreted, an equivocal argument has been created. Instead of something definite, the argument has changed to: "All As are Bs, or something else",' he says.

Staines thinks students should use critical judgment when reading information and, rather than mindlessly copying other people's arguments, they should always ask themselves two questions: 'What reason is there for thinking this is true?' and 'How likely is this to be true?'

CHAPTER

26

LOGIC AND ARGUMENT

After studying this chapter, you will be able to:

- understand the basic principles of logic
- sort out the premises of an argument from its conclusion
- identify some forms of valid and invalid arguments
- identify deductive and inductive arguments

All the communication skills discussed in this book will amount to very little if writers and speakers fail to put across their points of view in ways that are logical; or if readers and listeners cannot discriminate between logical and illogical statements. To speak and write logically means to use correct reasoning in your arguments. The word 'argument' used here, and used in most discussions of logic and reasoning, does not mean some kind of disagreement or exchange of opposing views (the sort of thing we have at home). An 'argument' in its technical sense is a group of statements which advance a point of view or which support that point of view. If you want to persuade or convince someone to take a point of view then you should present them with a well-reasoned argument, that is, a logical argument. Of course, many people (advertisers and politicians are well-known examples) do not make logical arguments to persuade others—they make emotional appeals or forceful assertions. If we want to be intelligent and reasoning in the face of these kinds of appeals, we need to be able to examine the logic behind them. Very often, we will find that people who try to convince us this way are using spurious reasoning that deserves to be rejected. Here are two examples of faulty logic.

Not everyone who smokes gets lung cancer.
Some people who do not smoke get lung cancer.
Therefore, smoking does not cause lung cancer.

Every communist and every anarchist in Australia opposes nuclear weapons.
Bob Browning opposes nuclear weapons.
Therefore Bob Browning is either a communist or an anarchist.

Logic is the study of correct and incorrect reasoning. It is a study which clarifies the distinctions between good and bad arguments, telling us why some arguments are strong and should be accepted and why some arguments are weak or worthless.

We will look at what is wrong with both these arguments shortly. Before we go any further we should define some of our terms.

Logic is the study of correct and incorrect reasoning. It is a study which clarifies the distinctions between good and bad arguments, telling us why some arguments are strong and should be accepted and why some arguments are weak or worthless. Logic is a subject that can be studied at colleges and universities to a very high degree of sophistication. This chapter is an introduction to some of its basic points.

An *argument*, as we noted above, is a group of statements that advance a point of view.

A *statement* is a sentence which makes a factual claim. Statements can be either true or false. 'Kangaroos eat grass' and 'All swans are white' are both statements, whereas expressions that do things, such as give orders, make requests or express approval—'Don't touch it,' 'Let's play cricket,' 'Thank you, darling'—are not.

In an argument, the statements come to a *conclusion*. Every argument has one conclusion. In the two examples above, the last sentences are the conclusions. As in these cases, conclusions are often preceded by the word 'therefore', or perhaps the word 'so'. However conclusions are not always the last sentence in an argument. Some arguments can start with the conclusion, such as:

The baby cannot have whooping cough. The whooping cough vaccine is known to be 100 per cent effective and the baby has been vaccinated.

The statements that lead to a conclusion are usually called its *premises*. In the argument above, the premises are that the whooping cough vaccine is known to be 100 per cent effective, and that the baby has been vaccinated. And the conclusion is (therefore) the baby cannot have whooping cough.

The first step in analysing an argument is to sort out its premises from its conclusions. The next thing to do is to consider whether its premises are true or false. If one or both of the premises are false then the argument cannot be accepted.

The first step in analysing an argument is to sort out its premises from its conclusions. The next thing to do is to consider whether its premises are true or false.

Sometimes it is difficult to assess statements of fact and you have to take them on trust, or perhaps make a conditional assessment—if the premises are true, then the conclusion follows. Once we have determined if the premises are true, we still need to consider whether they give proper support to the conclusion. For instance, it is easy to construct an argument in which the premises are true but which nonetheless give no support to the conclusion. Here is one.

All dogs are mammals.
Some women are doctors.
Therefore, Australia is a dry country.

In this case, both premises are true and the conclusion is true. However, the premises have no relationship to each other nor to the conclusion. So they cannot support the conclusion.

Logic is not about whether the premises are true or false. Logic is concerned with the way that, within arguments, premises do or do not lend support to conclusions. Statements can be true or false but arguments cannot be true or false. Arguments can be strong or weak, valid or invalid. The tests we apply to the logic of an argument depend on the kind of argument it is. There are two basic kinds of arguments: deductive and inductive.

Logic is not about whether the premises are true or false. Logic is concerned with the way that, within arguments, premises do or do not lend support to conclusions.

We will discuss each kind of argument in the next two sections but here we should emphasise a point that may be worth remembering when using this book. In other chapters, we sometimes recommend that the plans you work out for your essays, letters, reports and speeches follow either a deductive or inductive pattern. When we do this, we explain how this would work in the context of an essay, report or whatever.

While you do not need to remember the details of this chapter to understand the others, we think the points made here are still very relevant and worth repeating. The study of the principles of logic is not just something that will help you become clearer in your own thinking and wording of small groups of statements like the examples in this chapter. It actually underpins the major pieces of work that you will eventually do. To be convincing, an essay, report or any other type of communication should be based on an underlying logic. This means that one of the basic requirements of writers and speakers is that they learn to think from a logical point of view.

DEDUCTIVE ARGUMENTS

A deductive argument is either valid or invalid. If the truth of the premises guarantees the truth of the conclusion, then the argument is valid.

A deductive argument is one in which the conclusion follows from the premises. You state the premises and you deduce the conclusion from them. Moreover, the conclusion is already expressed in the premises. You gain no additional knowledge from a deductive argument; you are simply working out something that is already inherent in what the premises say. The traditional argument that demonstrates this is:

All men are mortal.
Socrates is a man.
Therefore, Socrates is mortal.

A deductive argument is either valid or invalid. It cannot be something in between. If the truth of the premises guarantees the truth of the conclusion, then the argument is valid. If it is possible for the premises to be true but the conclusion still to be false, then the argument is invalid. We are not saying that the argument itself is true or false. Truth and validity are quite different things. It is possible for an argument to be valid but have false premises and a false conclusion. For example:

All men are white.
Archbishop Tutu is a man.
Therefore, Archbishop Tutu is white.

The argument is valid. If it were true that all men are white then any man, Archbishop Tutu included, would indeed be white. The false conclusion follows from the false first premise. An invalid argument is one in which the conclusion does not necessarily follow, even though it may, in fact, be true. Let us rearrange our argument about Socrates:

All men are mortal.
Socrates is mortal.
Therefore, Socrates is a man.

In this case, both premises are true and the conclusion is true, but the argument is invalid. We can see this if we use the same argument form with a different character involved. Let us substitute Rover the dog for Socrates the man:

All men are mortal.
Rover is mortal.
Therefore, Rover is a man.

In this case, our two true premises gave us a false conclusion. A valid argument, as we said, is one in which the premises guarantee the conclusion, and in this case it is not so. This is because the category of 'mortal' is much wider than the category of 'man'. The argument is invalid because it is possible that someone who is 'mortal' is located in that part of the 'mortal' category that extends beyond the category of 'man', as indeed Rover is. Because the form of this argument is invalid, it makes the previous argument about Socrates invalid since it has precisely the same form. Our earlier argument about 'Bob Browning' is in the same boat. It went:

In a valid argument, true premises always guarantee a true conclusion. An invalid argument can have any combination of truth and falsity.

Every communist and every anarchist in Australia opposes nuclear weapons.
Bob Browning opposes nuclear weapons.
Therefore, Bob Browning is either an anarchist or a communist.

This is a very common form of political argument which is sometimes called 'guilt by association'. We can see it is invalid if we consider that the category of people who 'oppose nuclear weapons' is a much wider category than that of 'communists and anarchists'. Bob Browning may well be one of those people against nuclear weapons who are outside the communist–anarchist circle. Note that even if Bob turned out to be a closet anarchist, this still does not make the argument valid. If there is a possibility that the conclusion does not follow from the premises, then the argument cannot be valid.

This means that, in a valid argument, true premises always guarantee a true conclusion. However, an invalid argument can have any combination of truth and falsity among its premises and conclusions.

The way to assess the validity of most deductive arguments is to try to think whether or not you can find an example which makes the premises true but the conclusion false. This is not foolproof—just because you cannot think of an example does not prove the argument is valid—but it is a quick rule of thumb. In the Bob Browning case above, for example, you might think it is possible for someone like him to be against nuclear weapons and at the same time be a member of the Australian Democrats political party (and therefore certainly not a communist or anarchist). As long as this possibility, or one like it, exists, then the argument is invalid, it does not necessarily follow.

Logicians have compiled a very sophisticated set of rules that govern valid arguments. The subject is far more complex than we have space to go into here but one practice of logicians is sometimes worth adopting. This is to translate arguments into symbols in order to avoid any confusion that might arise from our existing opinions about a subject. If we take the above arguments about Socrates, one of which was valid and the other invalid for reasons we discussed, then our symbol translations would look like: Let 'men' equal 'A'. Let 'mortal' equal 'B'. Let 'Socrates' equal 'S'. Our arguments would look like this.

Valid	Invalid
All men are mortal	All men are mortal
Socrates is a man	Socrates is mortal
Therefore, Socrates is mortal	Therefore, Socrates is a man
All A are B	All A are B
S is A	S is B
Therefore, S is B	Therefore, S is A

We know that any argument that takes the logical form of the one on the right is invalid, so if we are finding it difficult to work out validity from the words on the page, it might help to translate the terms in the premises into symbols and then test them with the models presented here.

When we are faced with an argument, what we are ultimately interested in is whether or not we should accept the conclusion. In the case of deductive arguments, we will accept the conclusion only if we are convinced all the premises are true and that the argument is valid. As we saw above with Archbishop Tutu, it is perfectly possible to have a valid argument but a conclusion which we cannot accept because one of its premises is wrong. As we said before, truth and validity are quite separate things. To test the truth of the conclusion, you have to test both the truth of all the premises and the validity or logic of the argument. If you are convinced of both of these, then you can have confidence in the conclusion.

INDUCTIVE ARGUMENTS

In inductive arguments, we do not deduce the conclusion from the premises. Rather, the premises act as evidence that goes to build up a case for the conclusion. The test of an inductive argument is not whether it is valid or invalid but whether it is strong or weak. This is because the conclusion is never entirely contained within the premises, as it is in a deductive argument, so we do not have the same kind of absolute certainty. At best, the evidence can be so overwhelming that we can say we know a conclusion is true. Or we can suspend judgment about a conclusion because there is insufficient evidence to persuade us. Let us go back to the argument about smoking at the start of this chapter.

> Not everyone who smokes gets lung cancer.
> Some people who do not smoke get lung cancer.
> Therefore, smoking does not cause lung cancer.

In inductive arguments, we do not deduce the conclusion from the premises. Rather, the premises act as evidence that goes to build up a case for the conclusion.

The two premises of this argument happen to be true, and cigarette companies often use these facts to cast doubts on the medical authorities who claim that smoking is a cause of lung cancer. The case against cigarettes is not proved, the companies say. It is true that the case is not 'proved' in the sense of a deductive argument. However, the criteria for much of our knowledge about the world does not have to be that certain for us to accept it and act upon it. For example, if it were true that two-thirds of the people who smoked twenty cigarettes a day for thirty years contracted lung cancer, and if only about one-sixth of those people who get lung cancer are non-smokers, then most reasonable people would agree with some confidence that, first, smoking does cause lung cancer for a high proportion of long-term smokers, and second, most, but not all, lung cancer victims are smokers. In other words, the inductive argument against smoking turns out to be a pretty strong one.

This is in the nature of our factual knowledge about the world. In logic classes, students are usually given the statement 'All ravens are black' as an example of a statement for which we have inductive evidence. This means

Necessary statements carry absolute certainty but they are often not very interesting because they tell us what we already know. Contingent statements, on the other hand, while less certain, are more interesting because they are dependent on our discovery of the world about us.

that all the sightings of ravens we have made so far have been of black ones. In other words, the evidence is piling up all the time that all ravens are this colour but it always remains possible that, in some remote place, a colony of grey or white ravens will turn up. A statement of this kind is sometimes called 'contingent'—it could be found to be false at any time by a new discovery. This is in contrast to statements that are called 'necessary' such as 'A father is a male parent,' which, by definition, is always true as long as words mean what they do now. It is logically impossible to find a male parent who is not a father. 'Necessary' statements correspond to deductive arguments in the same way that 'contingent' statements correspond to inductive arguments. Necessary statements carry absolute certainty but they are often not very interesting because they tell us what we already know. Contingent statements, on the other hand, while less certain, are more interesting because they are dependent on our discovery of the world about us.

Until the end of the eighteenth century, classes in logic used a different example to 'All ravens are black' when they discussed contingent statements. The usual statement was 'All swans are white.' The logicians who said this was a contingent (inductive) rather than a necessary (deductive) statement were proved correct when black swans turned up during the discovery of Australia (although some initially thought the birds' colour was faked by the early natural scientists as a joke against their logic teachers). Australia also posed some problems for the definition of mammals. 'Mammals give birth to live young' had once been regarded as a defining statement which, like 'A father is a male parent,' was necessarily true. The discovery of two Australian egg-laying mammals, the platypus and the echidna, changed the status of this statement from necessary to contingent and made naturalists rewrite their definition of a mammal.

Let us look at another example of an inductive argument.

> The intra-uterine device, Proof, was used by one hundred women in North America for six months.
> None of them complained of any side-effects.
> Therefore, it is safe for women to use Proof.

In this argument, the conclusion goes far beyond the facts contained in the premises. It takes evidence that applies to one hundred women in a particular country and draws a conclusion that applies to all women everywhere. Its evidence is confined to experience over six months yet the conclusion applies to all time. The evidence also is confined to side-effects about which the tested women complained, yet the conclusion asserts Proof is safe under any conditions.

If we think about it, we can apply our test of a valid argument to the Proof argument. We need to find ways in which these premises could be true and yet the conclusion false. For a start, the physical characteristics of North American women might be different to women in other, especially Third World, countries and what might be true in America might not hold true elsewhere. The one hundred women form only a tiny sample of all women and they might have characteristics that make them atypical. For instance, if none of them had any family history of cancer, the fact that they felt no side-effects tells us nothing about what might happen to other women more prone to develop cancers. The premise says none complained of any side-effects. This does not necessarily mean that they had no side-effects. They might have developed problems of which they were not aware but which medical testing, for instance, might have discovered. The premises do not tell us whether any medical testing was actually done, so all the evidence we have is on the women's own testimony of the side-effects they felt. This is not the strongest evidence on which to determine safety. Further, evidence gathered over a six months period is not enough to give us a strong belief that the product is safe for all times. Side-effects, such as the development of cancers, may take some years to become apparent. Overall, we should conclude the above inductive argument is a weak one.

By comparison, let us look at a stronger inductive argument along similar lines.

A chemical spermicide is used by four thousand women who have no history of major health problems and who are aged between nineteen and forty-five.
They are tested annually by medical practitioners for the next five years without any health problems being found.
Therefore, in healthy women between nineteen and forty-five, the spermicide will not produce health problems over a five year period.

This is a strong inductive argument because it does not generalise beyond the conditions of the experiment. It overcomes the more obvious fallacies of the previous argument. It is not a deductive argument because the conclusion does go further than the premises. We are generalising from the experience of a fairly large sample of four thousand women to the likely experience of all women who use the product. Although strong, the conclusion does not amount to absolute proof because it always remains possible that if we had examined more cases we might have found one or more women who were badly affected by the product. This is the uncertainty we usually accept in inductive arguments.

To re-emphasise the point. We can look at one million ravens and find they are all black but this does not guarantee that a white raven will not turn up somewhere, sometime. If one white raven did turn up, it would be enough to discredit the statement 'All ravens are black.' In an inductive argument, all it takes is one counter-example to discredit the conclusion. A counter-example is any one that contradicts the conclusion of an inductive argument.

Most of the time, it does not matter very much if we do not have absolute proof about an inductive argument. People are quite happy to accept that all ravens are probably black, even though it remains possible that a counter-example will turn up. Absolute certainty is not the kind of thing that matters in our knowledge about bird colours. However, there are other cases where it is more important that we do not make mistakes. If we consider the above argument about intra-uterine devices we can see why this is so. IUDs were tested on relatively small numbers of women in their early days and no apparent side-effects were found. However, once they became used by a wide variety of women over long periods, it became clear that several types were associated with high incidences of cancer in their users. Even though the majority of users did not develop cancer, it is now generally accepted that the risks are too high and that IUDs are not a safe form of contraception, as the early inductive arguments had concluded. Health officials in many countries now discourage their use.

Inductive arguments lead to strong or weak conclusions or, in other words, to conclusions with varying degrees of probability rather than to logical certainty. By their nature, they do not constitute proof in the deductive sense but this is no reason to reject outright this form of argument. Unlike deductive arguments which find conclusions that are already embedded in our definitions or premises, inductive arguments take us beyond what we already know. They are part of the process of discovery and of the building of our knowledge of the real world.

In this chapter we have dealt with the fairly formal characteristics of arguments. In everyday writing, thinking and speaking, however, we are much more informal than this. The next chapter looks at a range of arguments, and several varieties of faulty logic, that arise in our more familiar use of language.

KEY POINTS: Chapter 26 Logic and argument

- Logic is the study of correct and incorrect reasoning. Communication skills amount to very little if writers, speakers, readers and listeners cannot reason correctly.
- An *argument* is a group of statements (or *premises*) leading to a *conclusion*. If the premises are false or if the argument is invalid, the conclusion is likely to be incorrect.
- A *deductive* argument is one which arrives at a conclusion that is inherent in the premises. By contrast, an *inductive* argument examines the real world to find evidence towards a conclusion.
- Deductive arguments are either valid or invalid. Inductive arguments should be assessed according to whether they are weak or strong.

QUESTIONS FOR DISCUSSION

- What do we mean by these terms: 'argument', 'statement', 'conclusion'?
- What do we mean by 'logic'? Does logic tell us whether a conclusion is true?
- What is a deductive argument? Give an example of your own.
- What is an inductive argument? Give an example of your own, not one taken from this book.

EXERCISES

1. What are the premises and conclusions in the following three arguments?

   (a) Australia cannot win the next cricket test series. Tests are only won by strong batting sides. Australia has no batsmen that are equal to the task.
   (b) The contraceptive pill is 100 per cent effective. Emily cannot be pregnant since she is on the pill.
   (c) It is illogical to reason thus, 'I am richer than you, therefore I am superior to you,' 'I am more eloquent than you, therefore I am superior to you.' It is more logical to reason, 'I am richer than you, therefore my property is superior to yours,' 'I am more eloquent than you, therefore my speech is superior to yours.' You are something more than property or speech. (Epictetus, *Discourses*.)

2. Identify the premises and conclusions in the following arguments, then determine which ones are valid and which invalid. If necessary, translate the terms of the premises and conclusions into symbolic form.

   a) Everyone who is really fit eats a high fibre diet and exercises often. Jenny must be fit because she eats plenty of high fibre and gets lots of exercise.
   (b) All teenagers are persuaded by advertisements promising them an exciting social life. Wine cooler advertisements show teenagers who drink the product have a really exciting social life. These advertisements will certainly sell wine coolers.
   (c) I think Rhonda is a single mother. She is receiving a pension and all single mothers are eligible for pensions.
   (d) Anyone who enjoys really hard-core pornography must have a contemptuous, violent attitude towards women. Robert has committed violent sex crimes against women which I am sure stem from his enjoyment of hard-core porn.

CHAPTER

27

RATIONAL DEBATE AND COMMON FALLACIES

After studying this chapter, you will be able to:

- identify some common fallacies used in arguments
- expose irrational arguments used by others
- avoid using these fallacies in your own arguments

The premises of an argument, as we have shown in the previous chapter, must support the conclusion or else the argument is worthless. Flaws in arguments of this kind are called fallacies. In some cases fallacies are of the strictly logical kind, as we saw in the last chapter's discussion of deductive arguments. There are other kinds of fallacies, however, which are more informal and which occur because of carelessness or lack of attention to the argument or through people misleading themselves or others. We consider some of the main kinds of informal fallacy in this section, although we emphasise that the list is far from being complete.

BEGGING THE QUESTION

An argument that contains the conclusion as one of the premises commits the fallacy of begging the question. This seems an obvious enough mistake but it is often difficult to detect. If the conclusion is couched in much the same words in both premise and conclusion then the fallacy will stand out clearly. But often the wording in the two cases is so different that it is hard to see what has happened. Take the following case.

> Patriotism is the basis of national existence and this explains why people everywhere are loyal to their own countries.

Here, the premise 'patriotism is the basis of national existence' makes almost the same statement as the conclusion 'people everywhere are loyal to their own countries'. In this case, begging the question does not make the conclusion false. Rather it means that there is no real argument involved—simply the repetition of the one sentiment in different words. The conclusion is not explained by the premise at all, it simply repeats it. The 'argument' starts by assuming what it wants to establish.

Many kinds of circular arguments are examples of begging the question. Someone may argue that Dickens was a great writer because he is read by people with refined judgment. How do we tell they have refined judgment? We tell by the fact that they read Dickens. Or: People who watch a great deal of television are mindless idiots. How do we know they are mindless idiots? Well, just look at how much television they watch. Many arguments about questions of taste in literature, music and culture generally are longer than these but, when examined carefully, turn out to have the same underlying structure of circularity and commit the same fallacy of begging the question.

AD HOMINEM ARGUMENT

An *ad hominem* argument translates from the Latin as an 'argument directed to the man'. There are a number of varieties of this fallacy. Often it is used to attack the truth of what someone has said. This often happens in a court of law when a barrister may argue that a person's evidence is worthless because the person has a record of dishonesty or is untrustworthy. It was once common for barristers to question a rape victim about her previous sexual experience in order to establish that she was a person of slack morals who was probably a willing party. This kind of argument is fallacious because the personal character of a witness is logically irrelevant to the truth or falsehood of what she or he says, or to the correctness or otherwise of his or her argument. To argue that a proposal for government action is bad because it is supported by the Communists or the New Right is to commit the same fallacy. Such arguments are often persuasive but this is because of emotional or psychological factors not those of logic. Each argument needs to be examined on its own merits, not on the character of its proponent.

Each argument needs to be examined on its own merits, not on the character of its proponent.

Another version of *ad hominem* argument is where someone argues that a proposition ought to be accepted or rejected because of the special circumstances of the person advancing it. Someone may argue that a police investigation of police corruption should be rejected because the police have a vested interest in finding the force is incorruptible; or that research done by teachers into education standards is unreliable because teachers would not want to cast doubts on the education system. Again, though persuasive, these arguments deserve to be rejected on logical grounds. The only way to proceed is to closely examine the strengths and weaknesses of the case put by the police or the teachers.

FALSE DILEMMA

A dilemma is an argument which holds up two alternatives, and states that only one of them can be true. A false dilemma occurs when there are actually more than two alternatives but the argument suppresses all but two of them. For example:

> If we don't continue logging the forest, the timber-cutters will be unemployed. So take your pick: trees or jobs.

This is a familiar type of argument in the debate over conserving the environment. It is by now clear that this is a false dilemma and that there are several other alternatives to either cutting down the trees or leaving the workers unemployed. For example, if the trees are preserved and the environment protected, there may be more employment generated through other forms of investment, such as tourism. A fourth possibility is that if the logging is continued and all the trees are cut out, the timber-cutters will eventually be unemployed anyway.

False dilemmas are one example of a wider kind of fallacy which has to do with suppressing evidence. If all the evidence relevant to making a decision is not brought forward then the argument should fail by omission, although again this kind of approach is frequently persuasive to those who don't think carefully about the issues.

False dilemmas are examples of suppressing evidence or introducing hidden premises.

Take another instance of suppressing relevant evidence or introducing hidden premises. The old question 'Have you stopped beating your wife?' is usually not susceptible to a simple 'yes' or 'no' answer (unless, of course, you are actually a wife-beater). The question assumes that a definite answer has already been given to a previous but unasked question, in this case, 'Have you ever beaten your wife?' Asking whether you have stopped beating her is a trick question which implies that you have already answered 'yes' to the unasked question. In court, lawyers often ask these kinds of questions to get a witness to incriminate himself, such as: 'Where did you put the money you stole?' The question assumes an affirmative answer to the unasked question, 'Did you steal the money?'

Even though a reasonably attentive witness or jury may not fall for this trick, these questions are often asked in a more sophisticated form in political debate. 'Why should we tolerate Asians coming here and taking our jobs?' is a familiar kind of racist appeal. The hidden assumption, that Asians are actually taking our jobs is very questionable since most studies of migration and employment have found that migrants increase economic demand and generate more jobs than they occupy. Or a private developer who wants to take over part of the activities of a profitable public utility may ask: 'Why is private management of resources always so much more efficient than government control?'

The best way to respond to hidden questions is to break them down into their component parts. Often, when the implied prior question is correctly asked, the second or explicit one simply dissolves. In the question above, we would state the implicit question as: 'Is private management always more efficient than government?' We would then ask if we can find exceptions to it. It is very doubtful, for example, that private management would do a better job of operating our water supply system or our roads or any other resource where it makes sense to have only one supplier who is dedicated to the public interest. If we accept this, then the explicit question of 'why' private management is always better is one we cannot sustain or which we would want to rephrase.

ARGUMENT FROM IGNORANCE

Two examples that illustrate this type of fallacy are sometimes heard in heated debates over religion. God does not exist, one side will argue, because no one can prove He does. The other side will counter that God does exist because no one has been able to prove He does not. The argument from ignorance is committed when anyone argues that something is true simply on the basis that it has not been proved false, or that it is false because it has not been proved true. Clearly though, our ignorance of how to prove or disprove a statement hardly makes a strong case about either its truth or its falsehood. Nonetheless this kind of argument is often found in debates about religion, psychic phenomena, UFOs, mental telepathy and the like, where there is no clear evidence to base knowledge upon.

The argument from ignorance is committed when anyone argues that something is true simply on the basis that it has not been proved false, or that it is false because it has not been proved true.

In Western judicial systems, however, this mode of argument has a special status. These systems hold that a person is presumed innocent until proven guilty. If the prosecution is judged as not establishing a person's guilt, he or she is found 'not guilty'. From a logical point of view, 'not guilty' does not equal 'innocent', it simply means the case has not been proven, but not that the accused did not commit the offence. The legal system has to make the 'presumption' that 'not guilty' equals 'innocent' from the point of view of being seen to be just. Making such a presumption is a leap in the logical dark that suits the system's own needs rather than the canons of strict reasoning.

APPEAL TO AUTHORITY

Appeals to authority become fallacies when the authority is speaking outside his or her own province.

By appealing to the opinions of someone who is a well-known expert in a particular field, you can sometimes lend weight to an argument. In a debate over history or literature, for example, you can quote the views of a highly respected historian or writer or literary critic and your opponents will usually have to take these views seriously. When historians or critics get together, however, their debates are not conducted through appeals to other learned texts but to the evidence and to reason. It is also worth remembering some famous recent court cases in which forensic scientists disagreed quite dramatically over the same material. Appeals to authority by one side in a case have been contradicted by appeals to authority by the other side. In such cases, lay people have to weigh up the evidence as they see it.

Appeals to authority become fallacies when the authority is speaking outside his or her own province. This is, however, a very common kind of appeal. Testimonials from sporting stars about the value of various brands of deodorant or toothpaste carry no logical weight at all. The same is true if a famous actor or singer takes a public stand about a controversial social issue. If we agree or disagree with them it should be on the facts and the reasoning they offer, not just because they are famous or because many people like and admire them. A common version of this fallacy occurs in the case of the scientist expressing religious opinions. Some will argue that a famous scientist has studied the world and the universe and does/does not believe in God. This is then counted as weight for the side the advocate is taking. Science and religious belief, however, are different kinds of thought processes with their own criteria of strength and weakness and one should not appeal from expertise in one to expertise in another.

POPULAR APPEAL

Popular appeal usually signals that a propagandist has not done the hard work of marshalling evidence and reason in support of a case.

A similar fallacy to the one discussed above is the emotional appeal 'to the people'. This is a familiar device used by political demagogues, propagandists and advertisers. A particular belief or a particular brand is said to be right because it is popular, or because it is the number one best seller. This device is usually adopted when the propagandist cannot be bothered or does not have the resources to do the hard work of marshalling evidence and reason in support of a case. 'All these people act this way,' the propagandist says, 'so you should too.'

Sometimes the appeal to the popular is couched in terms of 'common sense'. This is frequently used to argue against intellectualised views of a subject. Theory says one thing, this argument often goes, but people's common sense, recognised through their 'gut reactions' or their experience of life, tells them something else. In some cases, this can be a useful corrective. History is full of cases where intellectuals have put forward views of how society should be run which have run counter to the lived experience of ordinary people and which, after costly civil wars and conflict, have turned out to be disastrous failures. However, we should also remember that 'common sense' is that which tells us the world is flat and that the sun and stars revolve around the Earth. The great achievements of human beings have not come by sticking to common sense but by leaving it behind and by examining the evidence carefully and reasoning logically.

One of the favourite arguments of politicians who appear to have a great deal of opposition to their measures is to use another version of the appeal to the popular. This is the appeal to the 'silent majority'. 'A small but vocal minority might be getting a great deal of media exposure for opposing me,' the politician will say, 'but I know the vast, silent majority of people support me. I will press on.' This is often an effective, but nonetheless fallacious, argument. A 'majority' that cannot be observed or measured because it is 'silent' is hard to argue against, so no one can easily deny the claim. People who have no opinion or who are wavering on the issue may come around to support the politician because they believe, without any evidence, that most other people already support him.

IRRELEVANCE

A common fallacy occurs when the premises of an argument appear to be related to the conclusion but actually have no connection with it. This is common in court trials where the prosecutor may go to lengths to establish that the crime committed was a nasty or horrible one. This may arouse great indignation in the hearts of the jury but it is actually irrelevant to whether the accused committed the crime or not.

Advertisers also frequently base their appeals on arguments of this kind. The sugar industry, for instance, has conducted a campaign against cyclamate sweeteners, describing them as 'artificial' and full of chemicals, whereas sugar is 'natural' because it comes from a plant. In reality, however, highly refined white sugar remains a chemical substance and its origins in plant life do not give it any special status as being more 'natural' than anything else that human beings produce and consume. By using the word 'natural', the sugar industry is trying to associate its product with 'raw' or 'unrefined' foods which nutritionists generally regard as being superior to highly processed and refined foods. As white sugar falls squarely into the latter category, the evidence of its plant origins is beside the point, or misleadingly irrelevant, in the nutrition debate.

This common fallacy occurs when the premises of an argument appear to be related to the conclusion but actually have no connection with it.

ARGUMENT BY ANALOGY

This is a common form of argument and just as common a source of fallacious reasoning. It generally holds that X is like Y and, since the conclusion drawn from X was Z, therefore Y is like Z. It is a familiar type of argument used by politicians and political journalists who wish to predict the future from their reading of history. One common version goes like this: 'Licentious sexual behaviour preceded the fall of the Roman Empire. Therefore, the sexual permissiveness of our own times threatens the basis of Western society.' The problem with analogies on this scale is that they focus on one element within a very complex social situation, and shut out consideration of other factors that may well have had much greater influence on the event.

Very often analogies fail because they are so selective. They pick out comparisons that suit their conclusion but suppress all the other evidence of a similar kind which might contradict them.

Economics is another example. Some commentators today draw comparisons between selected economic indicators, such as debt levels and the prices of commodities, and to argue that because there were indicators of a similar kind just prior to the economic crash of 1929 which preceded the Great Depression, we are headed today for the same fate. Again, this overlooks the myriad of other indicators which today appear quite different to those of the late 1920s. It also ignores a vast array of changes to the world economy over the past sixty years and to the greatly expanded role of national governments and international organisations.

Another common analogy is made between animal and human behaviour. The fact that some male apes and canines are fiercely competitive over territory has been used by some psychologists to try to explain warfare between humans. Apart from the fact that these analogies usually don't fit—there is little resemblance between fighting behaviour of individual animals and the forms of organisation and relations involved in warfare—they conveniently ignore comparisons with different apes and other animals that are not territorially acquisitive or aggressive. Very often analogies like this fail because they are so selective. They pick out comparisons that suit their conclusion but suppress all the other evidence of a similar kind which might contradict them.

This is not to say that all analogies are false nor that it is fallacious to make comparisons between past and present or between animal and human behaviour. Sometimes analogies can reveal interesting things and lead us to conclusions we might have missed. But, in most cases, they are a weak form of argument because of the great difficulty of making close-fitting comparisons between subjects that are basically dissimilar.

ANECDOTAL EVIDENCE

This occurs when a person offers the story of a single experience, or an anecdote, as evidence of a general proposition. It is a very popular and common way of arguing but is basically flawed by the fact that a sample of one may be a completely misleading guide to the general situation. Anecdotal evidence is frequently heard in debates about the welfare system. Someone may know one or two neighbours who are receiving a pension as single mothers, yet they have men who visit their houses and sometimes stay overnight. From this, the person concludes that all single mothers are fiddling the system. If someone disagrees with this general statement, the person replies, 'Well, I know at least two ...'.

Anecdotal evidence is a very popular and common way of arguing but is basically flawed because a sample of one may be a completely misleading guide to the general situation.

Another form of anecdotal evidence comes from our own direct experience. We might respond to something in a certain way and conclude that everyone will respond to it the same. Much money has been lost in business by someone thinking that large numbers of people will share his or her appreciation of a product. In a later chapter on statistics there is a discussion about sample sizes—how you need to take a fairly good and sizeable cross-section of people and ask their taste or opinion before you can have confidence that most of the population will think or react in similar ways. Anecdotal evidence—the experience of one—is simply too small a sample upon which to make generalisations.

FALSE CAUSE

It is often easy to relate coincidence with cause. What we mean is that people often see two things happening together, one before the other, and assume from this that the first causes the second. In its most extreme form, this type of coincidence is obviously fallacious, such as in the fable of the foolish rooster who thought it was his crowing that made the sun rise. Every morning, just before dawn, he would crow and, sure enough, the sun rose every time. But there are many arguments and strongly held beliefs in our society that are basically no sounder than this in their logic.

For much of the past two decades, economists believed that an increase in the money supply—governments printing money—was the cause of the inflation that ravaged most Western economies in the 1970s and 1980s. Milton Friedman won a Nobel Prize for showing the statistical relationship between the two, just as one could establish a statistical relationship between a rooster's crowing and the sun rising. These days, the more astute economists recognise that the situation is much more complex than this and that underlying factors, such as increases in the terms of trade, can lead to both money supply and inflation increasing at the same time. In other words, money supply increases do not cause inflation. Both increase at the same time but they are caused by something else.

People often see two things happening together, one before the other, and assume from this that the first causes the second.

GENERALISATIONS

We should conclude from several of the above types of fallacy that it is wise to be cautious when making generalisations. Before making a general statement about some kind of social phenomenon, make sure there is good evidence of the behaviour of a fair number of people. Also make sure there is not evidence of the contrary behaviour of a large group of other people. It is very unusual in our complex society for *all* people to have similar reactions to anything at all. People are divided in their beliefs and behaviours and generalisations are easier to knock down than to put up.

Nonetheless, do not take this as a warning against making any generalisation at all. We need to make generalisations to make sense of the society around us. In fact, we will probably make mental generalisations whether we want to or not. Generalisations are necessary components of our understanding but we should always be cautious when making them.

Perhaps the most obvious fallacy of which to be aware is that of considering only exceptional cases. For example, if you witness the effects of alcohol only on those who indulge in it to excess, you may conclude that its sale should be banned. But one should also consider the large number of adults for whom alcohol is not very harmful at all. Similarly, from observing the behaviour of some members of an ethnic minority group, one cannot conclude that all people of the same background act in the same way, any more than someone else should consider that all people of an Anglo-Saxon background are the same. Within our own social groupings we recognise and tolerate great diversity, and—to make a fairly safe generalisation—we should realise that other social groups will have a similar breadth of personalities and activities, and similar quotas of deviants and conformists.

KEY POINTS: Chapter 27 Rational debate and common fallacies

- A flawed argument is called a *fallacy*. There are numerous kinds of informal fallacy.
- If the conclusion merely restates one of the premises, an argument is *begging the question*.
- Attacking a proposition not for its own sake but because of the person who put it forward is an *ad hominem* argument.
- In a *false dilemma*, two propositions are put forward, of which only one may be accepted as true. Other alternatives are suppressed.
- An *argument from ignorance* is one in which a proposition is believed to be true because it cannot be proved false, or vice versa.
- An *appeal to authority* is a fallacy when an authority in one field is held to be an authority in all fields.
- *Popular appeal* is a fallacy when something is held to be true simply because it is widely believed.
- *Irrelevance* occurs when the premises of an argument appear to be related to the conclusion but in fact have no connection to it.
- An *argument by analogy* is one in which a proposition is held to be true because something similar once happened, somewhere.
- *Anecdotal evidence* is a fallacy when a proposition is held to be true in all cases simply because it is true in one person's experience.
- *False cause*, in which one thing is held to have caused another because they happened one after the other, is a fallacy when both events may be attributable to other causes.
- *Generalisation* is a fallacy when a thing that is true in many cases is held to be true in all.

QUESTIONS FOR DISCUSSION

- Why does a circular argument beg the question?
- What is wrong with rejecting an argument because of the reputation of the person speaking?
- If we cannot prove something to be false, does this make it true?
- If a book is a best seller, does this mean it is good?
- Why is it unwise to use anecdotes as the basis of generalisations?

EXERCISES

Identify the fallacies in the following passages and explain why each is a fallacy. Some contain more than one fallacy.

1. Using a team of doctors to investigate medical incompetence is like asking the army to investigate its own wartime atrocities.
2. I am confident the headmaster will re-examine your mark in a fair manner. One of the basic inclinations of human beings is, after all, to be just.
3. John is the best candidate for this position because he has the best reputation in the department. We know he has the best reputation because he is a certainty to get the position. He deserves the position because he is the best candidate.
4. Howard has been in Parliament for twenty years without anyone ever accusing him of being corrupt. He must be as honest as the day he was born.
5. The drug squad has detected over one hundred major drug traffickers through telephone taps. It should have the right to tap everyone's phones.
6. This toy is made of flimsy material. Our tests have shown it takes an average three-year-old just two days to break it. It will obviously be a commercial failure in the shops this Christmas.
7. The wives of all the top executives in town spend most of their time at the Country Club. If you want your husband to be a success, you had better join.
8. John Lennon became a transcendental meditationist. There must be something in it.
9. Kids today just don't try. I interviewed five today for a job with my firm and they all looked scruffy. No wonder there is so much unemployment.
10. I am sure UFOs visit Earth. No one has ever been able to refute their existence.
11. There is a groundswell of public opinion which is not yet reflected in the opinion polls but come election day I am confident it will be there.

continued on next page

continued from previous page

12. Children never see Santa Claus because he knows when they are awake and he won't come into their houses until they go off to sleep.

13. High school examinations should be banned. No one ever does exams once they join the workforce so they are useless in preparing us for our careers.

14. Outside Russia, no one has ever died in a nuclear accident. Compare this to the high rate of death among coal miners. Nuclear power stations in the West are perfectly safe.

15. Women live longer than men. They must be made of genetically sounder material.

16. Of course all businessmen cheat on their taxes. You should see the fiddles my boss gets up to.

17. Trade unions are ruining the country. We have had stock waiting on the docks for two weeks but the wharfies are on strike. There should be laws passed banning unions.

18. To allow all citizens absolute freedom of speech must be in the national interest; because it is always advantageous for a community to have people untrammelled in their right to express themselves in an unlimited manner.

19. Fellow citizens, I ask you. Why are most people now recognising that we need fundamental changes to our taxation system? Last week we saw Australia's leading yachtsman take up the cause.

20. Boss, I deserve a pay rise. Interest rates are up and my mortgage payments are going through the roof.

REVISION LIST FOR PART VIII

LOGIC AND REASONING

- The best communication skills in the world will not amount to much if writers and speakers, and their readers and listeners, cannot reason correctly. Logic is the application of correct reasoning.
- An *argument* is a group of statements (or *premises*) leading to a *conclusion*. If the premises are false or if the argument is invalid, the conclusion is likely to be incorrect.
- A *deductive* argument is one which arrives at a conclusion that is inherent in the premises. An *inductive* argument does not prove its case logically, but provides evidence towards a conclusion.
- Deductive arguments are either valid or invalid. Inductive arguments should be assessed according to whether they are weak or strong.
- A flawed argument is called a *fallacy*. There are many kinds of informal fallacy.
- If the conclusion merely restates one of the premises, an argument is begging the question.
- Attacking a proposition not for its own sake but because of the person who put it forward is an *ad hominem* argument.
- In a *false dilemma*, two propositions are put forward, of which only one may be accepted as true. Other alternatives are deliberately suppressed.
- An *argument from ignorance* is one in which a proposition is believed to be true simply because it cannot be proved false, or vice versa.
- An *appeal to authority* is a fallacy when an authority in one field is held to be an authority in all fields.
- *Popular appeal* is a fallacy when something is held to be true simply because it is widely believed.
- *Irrelevance* occurs when the premises of an argument appear to be related to the conclusion but in fact have no connection to it.

continued on next page

continued from previous page

- An *argument by analogy* is one in which a proposition is held to be true because something similar once happened, somewhere.
- *Anecdotal evidence* is a fallacy when a proposition is held to be true in all cases because it is true in one person's experience.
- *False cause*, in which one thing is held to have caused another because they happened one after the other, is a fallacy when both events may be attributable to other causes.
- *Generalisation* is a fallacy when a thing that is true in many cases is held to be true in all.

PART VIII
KEY TEXTS AND FURTHER READING

Barry, V. N. T. and Rudinow, J., *Invitation to Critical Thinking*, 2nd ed, Holt, Rinehart and Winston, New York, 1990.

Bell, Philip and Staines, Phillip, *Reasoning and Argument in Psychology*, University of New South Wales Press, Sydney, 1983.

Copi, Irving M., *Introduction to Logic*, Macmillan, London, 1961 and subsequent editions.

Fogelin, R. J., *Understanding Arguments: An Introduction to Informal Logic*, 3rd ed, Harcourt Brace Jovanovich, New York, 1987.

Gilhooly, K. J., *Thinking*, Academic Press, New York, 1988.

Hodges, Wilfred, *An Introduction to Elementary Logic*, Penguin, London, 1975.

Wright, L., *Better Reasoning: Techniques for Handling Argument, Evidence and Abstraction*, Holt, Rinehart and Winston, New York, 1982.

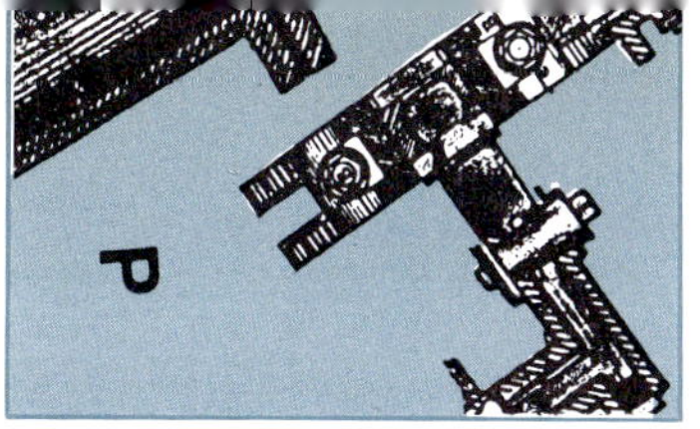

PART

IX

PUBLIC SPEAKING

HOW TO WIN OVER AN AUDIENCE

Bryce Courtenay, ad man and best selling novelist, tells how he became a public speaker.

Bryce Courtenay is a man of multiple talents. He first made his career in advertising, becoming one of the industry's leading figures as creative director of George Patterson, Sydney. Then, in his fifties, he changed direction and became one of our most successful writers with the highly acclaimed novel *The Power of One*, followed by *Tandia* and *April Fool's Day*. Since then he has become one of the highlights of the celebrity guest speaker circuit.

When you meet him, you quickly see why he has made such a success of his latest field. Although he talks in a natural, unpretentious way, you can tell he has given a lot of thought to his subject matter. In this case, we were discussing the topic of public speaking.

Given his wide experience of subjects such as business, psychology, marketing, English literature and self-improvement, he concedes he probably has a repertoire of about fifteen topics on which he can speak with authority. But he is at pains to point out that his speeches are never rehearsed or word perfect.

'Too many speakers have a set number of speeches which are fixed in granite, when the clever speaker should be flexible to change. The ability to ad-lib is important,' he says.

Courtenay's comments are frequently heard on television and radio. After his first novel was published, he became keenly sought after as a guest speaker. He talks to special interest groups, schools, women's groups and business conferences and consequently he encounters a wide variety of people.

'It is essential to always speak in terms of your audience. I always look on it as talking from eye to eye, at a straight level. You should never talk up or down to a group, you should talk out to your listeners,' he advises.

He has no time for motivational speeches in which the rhetoric of goal-setting is down pat. While he agrees that they may be stirring at the time, they are never very memorable.

'I aim to plant a single indelible idea in the heads of my audience and all my material will work to that. I'll return to that point again and again until I've convinced the group that they are not only capable of grasping it, but acting on it,' he says with purpose.

Courtenay firmly believes that anybody can communicate well if they remind themselves that certain principles never change. He feels the key to success lies in asking three questions: What am I trying to say? To whom am I trying to say it? How best do I communicate with these people?

Technical correctness in delivery, timing, syntax, grammar and structure, he believes, will not necessarily make for an absorbing speech.

He mentions the capacity of the late Australian ophthalmologist and former Father of the Year Professor Fred Hollows to enthrall a crowd. 'He was a great speaker because he spoke from the heart. He was funny, sad, dynamic, humble and able to change a listener's mood. You should never be afraid of showing your emotions,' he adds.

Courtenay acknowledges that clarity, simplicity and sincerity in a speech are important, but thinks there is another vital factor which cannot be overlooked.

'The human being responds to one thing above all, the story-teller.' He quickly qualifies that he is not talking about the anecdotal raconteur, somebody who merely strings together a series of incidents. 'I'm talking about a person who says "Gather round, I'm going to tell you a tale," and then illustrates a point by transporting the audience to another place and time,' he says.

He stresses it is absolutely vital for humans to hear stories that enliven the mind to a range of possibilities.

'If I were offered the choice of twenty-five years in prison or death by shooting, I'd take the latter instantly,' he affirms with passion. 'People don't respond well to isolation. Unless we hear stories, we lose our morale and our minds die,' he says.

Courtenay is extremely interested in the dynamics of establishing a rapport with an audience and will go to extraordinary lengths to do so.

In fact, he admits he regularly challenges and confronts an audience and has no hesitation in moving them to extremes of emotion.

'I set out to capture and captivate the audience. If I haven't made them angry or uncomfortable, or haven't made them laugh or cry and taken them through the whole gamut of emotions, I've failed,' he says.

He is equally insistent about his strategies for ending a speech. 'I must leave them on a high, on a note of enormous hope, and they must walk away with something they can use.'

He observes that every speaker should adopt a personal style with which he or she is comfortable. In fostering that style, Courtenay thinks that there are no golden rules, but that certain attitudes must be adopted.

1. He emphasises that a person should speak in the audience's own idiom, according to the listeners' ages, backgrounds, cultures and beliefs.
2. Linked with this is his abhorrence of technical terms when used simply for their own sake. 'Technical jargon should only ever be used when a literal translation is not available,' he states.

3. He says it is important for an orator to trust the mind implicitly and the relevance of what is being spoken about.
4. Added to this, Courtenay says that a speaker should know the material well. The speech should never be read. 'It should almost sound conversational,' he advises.
5. An understanding of who the audience is also helps the speaker target the sentiments and language of the speech.
6. Finally, he feels it is imperative to show emotion in a very human way. 'People respond to those who are sincere,' he says simply.

CHAPTER

28

PUBLIC SPEAKING—PREPARATION

After studying this chapter, you will be able to:

- prepare notes for speeches to be given at both formal and informal occasions
- prepare speeches for different audiences and different settings
- adapt speech notes to varying times available for delivery
- ask appropriate questions to determine the nature of an audience
- decide on the type of speech that is appropriate for different audiences in various settings
- use a range of research techniques and sources in preparing speech notes

Television debates and interviews have changed the way audiences expect speakers to perform. Pictured is 'Geoffrey Robertson's Hypothetical' program, screened on the ABC

The ability to speak in public, that is, in front of a group of ten or more people, is growing in importance in the workplace, the education system and within the community generally. The growth of information-based occupations and the increasing need for information-related skills in all jobs has affected the demand for speaking just as much as writing. Few Australians, however, are really good at speaking in public, not from any lack of inherent ability but primarily because of lack of practice. Many people who should be speaking publicly avoid it because they believe they lack the talent. We are confident, however, that most people, and certainly the great majority who progress to the later levels of the education system, can learn to become effective public speakers. They can learn to speak competently before a classroom, an audience in an assembly hall, at a formal occasion, on television and on radio. This chapter and the following two are designed to help develop the skills needed. Before we start on these techniques, we should note the new environment in which speakers have to operate.

Television and radio have changed the way audiences expect speakers to perform. This is because audiences have learned to absorb larger amounts of information in shorter periods of time. Audiences will no longer listen to long-winded speeches. They expect the speaker to get to the point quickly and to allow others to put their case. With some notable exceptions, such as the academic lecture or the speech on a formal occasion, the old, rigid traditions of debating style advocated by Oxford-style debators and the like have given way to a more relaxed and more direct communication between speaker and audience.

Another result of the media's influence is the higher standard of debate that audiences now expect. Television programs are based on the proposition that the audience will switch to another channel unless it receives an appropriate mix of content and variety. Whether you have been invited to make a speech or have volunteered to give one, the cardinal rule is that you must have something of value or interest to say. This means you should adopt the practice of speaking only on subjects you know well or in which you are deeply interested. To speak well on a topic, you need first-hand experience or to have researched the subject thoroughly. The days when people were satisfied to be entertained by a speaker with a few jokes and a few wise sayings from the classics are long gone. If you presume to monopolise the time of others, you should be informative, entertaining, convincing and brief. And, like good prose, your speech must be simple, direct and clear.

WHY PREPARATION IS IMPORTANT

For all speakers, the key to success is preparation. Good speakers always prepare everything they are going to say before they say it. This applies to even quite minor speeches. One of the greatest writers in the English language, Mark Twain, once said, 'It usually takes more than three weeks to prepare a good impromptu speech.' Twain's comment was, of course, exaggerated, but the point he made is still valid. Nothing comes without effort, and your speech is only as good as the amount of work you are willing to put into it. You should always try to maintain this standard, no matter how unimportant the occasion may seem.

Your speech is only as good as the amount of work you are willing to put into it.

Take, for example, a small meeting in the local community about traffic hazards in your street. Even if you intend making only a few suggestions, you should prepare yourself beforehand. Simply jot down the three, four or five points you wish to make. Back them up if possible with some facts and figures. Then arrange the points in a logical fashion to present to the meeting. It will be obvious to your audience that you have considered the matter properly and that you are not just talking off the top of your head. With practice, you will learn to prepare your speeches more quickly. The time you take will of course vary according to the amount of experience you have had and the type of speech you are going to make. But the time you spend on preparation will be rewarded.

- You will gain the respect of your audience. There is nothing people at meetings dislike more than someone waffling on, obviously making it up as they go along.
- You will be more likely to change the audience's views because you will give a clearly prepared and structured case rather than a random delivery.
- You will be more likely to satisfy the audience's expectations because you will give a logical development of an argument, explanation or story which they will more easily understand and remember.

- You will satisfy the audience's need to mentally picture your speech. When a speech is ill-prepared and badly structured, audiences find it difficult to 'see' your point of view.

NERVOUSNESS

For beginners, preparation is the best single defence in the battle against nerves. If you speak on a subject about which you feel strongly, and if you prepare a number of things to say about it, you can then concentrate on your subject to the exclusion of everything else. You may not be able to completely eradicate the sort of problems everyone experiences at first, but you will have your notes in front of you to lean on. If you start to panic you can quickly glance at them to refresh your memory and to tide you over the awkward moment.

Preparation is the best single defence in the battle against nerves.

Well-prepared notes backed up by visual material are essential aids for the beginner. With practice, you will learn to use these aids in a manner that is relaxed and casual and which does not detract from your overall performance. In the next two chapters we discuss the preparation of notes and aids to presentation. Here we want to focus on what you need to know about the occasion at which you are to speak.

RESEARCHING THE OCCASION AND THE VENUE

To speak effectively, you need to learn as much as you can about the occasion. You find out exactly what you are expected to say, and to whom. You will also need to investigate the physical setting in which your speech will take place. The more experienced a speaker you become, the more background information you will expect to acquire beforehand.

TYPE OF SPEECH

First, be clear about the type of speech you are to give. Establish whether the setting is formal or informal. If you are giving a lecture, address, conference paper, after-dinner speech, thank-you speech or toast, the occasion is formal. But if you are participating in a workshop or giving a discussion paper, you need to take a more flexible approach.

Below, we list four types of speeches. You should decide which type suits the particular occasion.

SPEECHES THAT ARE READ

This method is used when the speaker wants to communicate important, complicated or statistical information where every word is under scrutiny and where even the slightest error will generate criticism. This applies particularly if the speech is being reported by the media. Examples would be a politician's speech in parliament or an academic's speech to a conference. Beginners should avoid this method because they are invariably bad at it. They have a tendency to fix their gaze undeviatingly at their notes and to ignore their audience. Experienced speakers such as radio and television announcers are practised at this art and it is usually difficult to tell whether they are speaking from notes or reading their material direct.

SPEECHES THAT ARE REHEARSED AND MEMORISED

There are two schools of thought as to whether beginners should use this method. One is that beginners should never memorise their lines because they are more likely than anyone else to forget them. Stage fright is capable of erasing an entire speech from the speaker's mind. The other school of thought believes that all speakers are performers and, as such, must learn their lines and rehearse them. We recommend a modified version of the second approach, but only if the speaker qualifies in two ways: first, they know they have a very reliable memory, and, second, they have practised the speech aloud, preferably in front of others, until they have a good grasp of the material and how to deliver it.

The extemporaneous speech gives the flexibility to alter content and style to suit the occasion and gives more room for the speaker's personality to come through

THE EXTEMPORANEOUS SPEECH

Among all speakers, this is the most popular. We recommend it for beginners. The speech is thoroughly prepared beforehand, but the speaker performs as if he or she were talking spontaneously about the subject. The technique is that the speaker has written out the speech in full, has condensed it into well-structured notes, has learned by heart the plan or outline of the speech and then speaks only to the major points and not to the exact word. This approach is the most suitable for learners because it provides the necessary practice of talking on your feet, and incurs less risk of forgetting material than is the case in the memorised speech. The good extemporaneous speaker may have also prepared selected quotations, anecdotes and visual material to add colour and variety to the performance. The speaker may also have completely memorised and rehearsed the opening and closing parts of the speech. This style of public speaking offers the speaker flexibility to alter the content and style of the speech according to the occasion and the audience's response. It also allows more room for the speaker to impose his or her own personality.

THE IMPROMPTU SPEECH

This is a speech delivered without preparation. It is recommended only for the experienced orator. Beginners should never attempt this method. Yet, for some unknown reason, many beginners think that this approach is the one most suited to them. They think that the best speakers are those who do not need to prepare their material beforehand, and that a speech will be better if it is left to the moment of inspiration. This idea originates from the belief that gifted speakers, writers, painters and so on are born and not made. (The true artist is not supposed to stoop to anything as workmanlike as preparation and practice.) The truth is that even experienced speakers are wary of the impromptu speech and will attempt it only when they are confident that the speech they are called upon to make is the same or almost the same as a speech they have given before and with which they are familiar. In other words, they are not really giving a completely impromptu speech but rather a version of a previous one.

Even experienced speakers are wary of the impromptu speech.

SPEAKING IN A PANEL

If you are speaking as a member of a panel, find out how many are on the panel, the positions or opinions each panel member represents, the topic each panel member will speak to and the order in which panel members will speak. Group presentations need contrast and variety, so be careful not to duplicate other speakers' contributions.

THE TOPIC

Ascertain precisely the topic of your speech. Get a careful reply to this question, as a misunderstanding could spell disaster. If the audience has come hear about AIDS in South-East Asia but you have prepared a speech on aid to South-East Asia, you will see them become restless rather quickly. The best thing is to get confirmation in writing from the person organising the talk. You should also know to what depth the organisers expect you to explore the topic. Ask if you are required to give a brief overview, a summary, a comprehensive explanation or a detailed argument.

TIMING

Establish clearly how long you are expected to speak (one hour, 30 minutes, 10 minutes, or two minutes). This is also a very important question, particularly if you are a member of a panel, or in a television or radio interview or discussion. Consider the problem you would face if you prepared a speech lasting 30 minutes and you found you had only three minutes in which to give it. The amount of time allocated to your speech will determine what you have to say. Restrict yourself to what can be covered comfortably. Don't race to get it all in. Be ahead of your audience so that if time is closing in, you can omit large portions of your speech. You should always prepare for such emergencies. Seasoned speakers constantly vary their speeches without their audiences' knowledge. They know that there is a time in every speech when the audience has had enough. Being able to recognise that point is an art form in itself. Remember, short, pithy speeches that make three to five points are the memorable ones.

Restrict yourself to what can be covered comfortably. Don't rush to get it all in.

Also find out at what point of the meeting/conference/occasion you are expected to speak, for example in the opening session, during workshops, or plenary session.

PHYSICAL SETTING

Learn as much as you can about the physical setting for the speech, whether it is in a large or small hall, or in a small board room, in a studio or on location. Find out seating numbers, the type of stage, arrangement of panel seating, availability of a microphone and visual aids. All these factors will condition the way you approach the task, the materials you will bring (for instance, you cannot show overhead transparencies if there is no projector or screen) and what you will actually say.

GIVING A PAPER

There are other questions that may determine the way you prepare your speech. These relate mainly to speeches given at seminars, workshops and conferences. Instead of giving a whole speech, you may be asked to summarise its contents to the audience in a given amount of time. This is called 'speaking to your paper'. A 'paper' is an essay or piece of writing that is read to the audience. Thus, to speak to your paper is to give a speech that is a condensed version of the paper or essay. You may be asked to write up your speech after you have given it. These are some of the questions you should ask the organisers.

- Find out if you are expected to write up your speech into a paper. If so, ask in what form it is expected and how long it should be. Conference and seminar papers are often published. Ask whether your paper is going to be published and in what form. The conference organisers may need your approval in writing. Sometimes speeches are written up into papers and distributed to people attending a conference or seminar before it is held. You will need to know if this is going to happen because you will tailor the style and delivery of your speech accordingly.
- Find out whether the speakers are expected to be available to talk to the media. This is quite common if you are giving a speech at a conference, and more so if your speech is topical or controversial.
- Find out whether you are to receive payment for the speech or whether you will be reimbursed for travel and accommodation expenses. The more experienced a speaker you are, the more likely you will want clarification of these matters, preferably in writing.

RESEARCHING THE AUDIENCE

When you are researching your audience, there are a number of basic things you will need to know.

Six questions to ask about the audience.

1. How many people are there?
2. What is the age range?
3. What is the ratio of males to females?
4. What are the educational backgrounds?
5. What are the occupational backgrounds?
6. Are there any special interests or knowledge?

- Find out how many people will be in the audience. With a large number there is little room for audience feedback, but with a small group you should provide opportunity for questions and comments.
- Find out the age of your audience. The age range of your audience will be an important determinant of the content and style of your speech. Consider the difference between the speech you would give to an assembly of primary school children and the speech you would give to an assembly of the parents of the same children.
- Ascertain the composition of your audience. For example, you may want to know if it is predominantly male or female. In most cases this will be irrelevant, but there are times when it will matter. If you were invited to speak on health issues to a local senior citizens' association comprising mostly women, you would tailor your speech to suit the needs of women, mostly widows, in the age group of 60 onwards.
- Find out the educational or professional background of the audience. This is usually easy to judge but you should consider the audience's level of interest. They may be experts, interested amateurs or beginners with little or no introduction to the subject. Your speech has to strike a fine balance. You have to avoid patronising your audience on the one hand, and talking over their heads on the other. Traversing familiar ground may bore them, yet to assume a level of knowledge or interest they do not have will leave them bemused.
- Find out if your audience has special interests in political, community, religious, philanthropic, educational or technical issues. They may be

Discover which aspect of the subject will interest the audience most.

members of a professional association, trade union, church, pensioners' organisation, youth group or educational institution.

- Discover which aspect of the subject will interest the audience most. It is difficult to achieve a balance between what you want to speak about and what your audience wants to hear. However, an audience respects enthusiasm and will usually forgive a speaker's momentary indulgence on an aspect of his or her special interest.

ESTABLISHING THE PURPOSE OF THE SPEECH

So far we have discussed why you should prepare certain aspects of your speech before others. By now you have determined three preliminaries:

1. the type of speech you are expected to give
2. the nature of the audience
3. the physical setting in which the speech will take place

Once you have answered these questions you can move onto the next step, which is to analyse the purpose of your speech. People often think the purpose is obvious but this is rarely the case. As part of your preparation, it is essential to get the purpose firmly in your mind. Some of the main purposes of public speeches are discussed next.

EXPOSITION: TO TEACH OR INFORM YOUR AUDIENCE

This type of speech may be a lesson, lecture, or training exercise designed to impart information. It may involve a number of approaches. The speaker may describe, explain or discuss ideas, issues or events, or instruct the audience how to do something. The style of this speech is simple and clear and the speaker will often employ audio-visual aids such as an overhead projector, films, graphs, charts, illustrations, tape recordings and exhibits. Exhibits are items the speaker shows the audience to give a concrete example about the subject being discussed or how a certain thing is done, such as a working model, equipment or ingredients.

ARGUMENT: TO PERSUADE OR CONVINCE YOUR AUDIENCE

To gain maximum impact, you should present logical argument backed by clearly presented evidence.

This may be a sales talk, political meeting, courtroom presentation, church sermon, local resident action group rally, protest meeting, parents' association meeting. In these cases, the speaker aims to change the views of the audience and sometimes to get the audience to take action on a certain issue or event. The speaker may appeal to a variety of responses in the audience: emotional, logical or intellectual. The speech may be highly organised and the speaker will normally have calculated the effect of every word of the speech.

To gain maximum impact, the speech will present a sound and logical argument backed up by clearly presented evidence such as facts, statistics and the liberal use of audio-visual material. This type of speech is a good training ground for beginners. The speaker is often deeply involved in the subject and can usually draw on personal knowledge and experience. The problem for the beginner may be not how to gather information but how to know what to leave out.

CEREMONIAL: TO PERFORM A RITUAL

This can be a wedding speech, funeral oration, memorial speech, a school speech day address or a thank-you speech. The speaker invites the audience to celebrate or commemorate an event and to consider its special meaning and significance. It does not attempt to alter the audience's beliefs but rather to strengthen them, and to inspire greater effort and a sense of achievement. Usually this is a positive speech in which the speaker praises or rewards the subject or event. The speaker appeals primarily to emotion and may use poetry, drama, music, lighting and other aids to accentuate the emotional character of the ritual.

ENTERTAINMENT: TO ENTERTAIN OR AMUSE

This is a popular lecture designed to appeal to a general audience. It may be given in clubs or similar organisations, usually part of a lecture tour, an after-dinner speech or professional performer's speech. This type of speech is designed to amuse the audience, usually in contrast to less entertaining presentations on the same occasion, and so draws on the speaker's ability as a raconteur and purveyor of the unusual, witty and humorous. Beginners should avoid this type of speech. It is the preserve of the veteran or gifted speaker. In recent years this style of public speaking has become an increasingly attractive source of income for former celebrities from all walks of life (prime ministers, film stars, sporting champions, artists and adventurers). In these cases, the speech is often written by a professional speech writer and read or memorised by the performer.

The list above is not exhaustive and there are other types that fall between or overlap our categories. Further, many speeches may serve more than one function. For example, a church sermon can perform four distinct functions.

1. It is designed to teach the congregation something.
2. It is designed to persuade the congregation to accept a particular point of view.
3. It is designed to stir the congregation to act on a particular matter.
4. It performs a ceremonial ritual.

There is no reason why a good sermon should not also include a certain amount of wit and humour. The best speeches will normally be found to pursue several functions.

Once you have determined the purpose of your speech, it is time to start thinking about the topic you are going to speak on. The next section takes up this issue.

CHOOSING A TOPIC

We have just considered the three main things a speaker should consider before making a speech: the occasion and venue, the nature of the audience, and the purpose of the speech. By now you have firmly established what you are expected to do. In most cases, the topic has nearly always been decided for you. However, there will be occasions when you will have to choose a topic yourself. The main point to remember, as we have said already, is that you choose a topic which you know well and in which you are keenly interested. With this in mind, there are several possibilities you can consider.

1. School experiences. Beginners will find this is the surest ground if they have just left school.
2. Work experiences. These can include part-time, casual and holiday jobs that students often perform while carrying on their studies.
3. Voluntary work experience. This is another useful category for beginners or students.
4. Sporting interests and hobbies.
5. Study of a field of knowledge.
6. How to make something.
7. Issues or projects of topical interest, issues in the news.

THE RESEARCH PHASE

Condensing research material to manageable proportions can be a major stumbling block.

Many speakers agree that their biggest problem is knowing what to do with all the information they accumulate in their research. Condensing research material to manageable proportions can be a major stumbling block for even the most experienced researcher. If, however, you carefully answer the preliminary questions discussed at the start of this chapter, you will find that the worst part of the job has already been done. You will see that some areas of investigation are irrelevant, some are less important than others, some will be inappropriate to the type of audience, and so on.

The research phase in preparing for a speech is similar to research for a written presentation. We have already discussed research techniques in two chapters, Chapter Nine on Essays—Planning and Research and Chapter Twenty-One on Interviews, Questionnaires and Survey Research. These chapters will give you most of the information you need to know on research for a speech. Speeches normally contain more generalised information than the fine detail and more precise argumentation found in writing. If you need to do research for a speech, you will go to secondary sources (the commentaries of general observers) rather than to primary sources (such as raw statistics or original documents). Below we give a few pointers on where to locate research material of this kind.

INDEXES

One of the most useful reference sources held by most big libraries is APAIS, which is a listing of Australian articles published in newspapers, magazines and journals each year. Its subject index is an extremely valuable resource and it is a good place to start your research. Don't hesitate to ask a librarian for assistance to use this reference. Other very useful indexes are those of major newspapers such as the *Age*, the *Sydney Morning Herald*, the *Australian* and the *Australian Financial Review* which are now accessible through the major libraries.

THE MEDIA

Speech writing often demands access to highly topical material and you can find this in the media. Most big libraries have up-to-date files of the most recent newspapers and magazines. As we noted above, indexes are available for some of these and they provide a more efficient way of looking for items on your topic than searching through all the back issues yourself. If you are quoting news or current affairs items from radio and television programs, be careful to note the station or channel, name and date of the program.

LIBRARIES

There are central reference libraries in the major capital cities which are open to the public mostly on a walk-in basis. Others also open to the public are municipal and shire council libraries, university and college libraries, technical libraries such as legal or medical libraries. Large organisations often have their own libraries with technical information experts and librarians to assist you.

GOVERNMENT

One of the services state and federal government departments must provide is reference literature describing their roles and functions. They will also provide information on items of public interest, such as statistical information on population, national income, welfare benefits and so on. Some departments provide newsletters and bulletins containing the most recent information on government policy and statistics. The Australian Bureau of Statistics has offices in the major capitals where sales of a vast array of statistical bulletins and publications are available. The Bureau's offices also provides a library open to the public, a telephone inquiry service that anyone can use, a Dial-A-Statistic recorded information telephone service and a fairly comprehensive range of data through computer information services. The Australian Government Publishing Service operates its own bookshop in several capital cities where all major government publications are available. There is material at these bookshops you will not find anywhere else.

The Australian Bureau of Statistics provides a vast array of bulletins and publications.

PERSONAL EXPERIENCE

One of the most useful and interesting sources for reference material is the speaker's personal experience. In using this to add authenticity to your information, you need to record accurate facts, dates, measurements, records of conversations and other kinds of hard data that give others confidence you know what you are talking about. Well-prepared speeches based on personal experiences can be among the most convincing and moving of all forms of communication.

Well-prepared speeches based on personal experience can be among the most convincing and moving of all forms of communication.

So far, we have discussed the first part of the preparation needed for public speaking. The second part is actually writing the speech. This is a topic in itself, which we take up in the next chapter.

KEY POINTS: Chapter 28 Public speaking—preparation

- Audiences today are saturated by talking heads in the media so they are more demanding of people who speak in public, even at the local community level.
- Preparation of a speech is just as important as delivery.
- The best way to win the battle against nerves about public speaking is to be well prepared.
- Avoid giving public speeches where you simply read aloud a prepared script.
- For formal occasions, prepare a full script, then condense it into notes that list the main points, then speak to the notes.
- There are no real impromptu speeches.
- There are six things you need to know when preparing a speech:

  1. whether you're speaking alone or with others
  2. your precise topic
  3. exactly how long you have to talk
  4. the physical setting
  5. the nature of your audience: its numbers, their ages, sex, education and employment background
  6. the purpose of your speech: whether it is to inform, persuade, entertain or perform a ritual

- There are five main sources of research for speeches about current topics:

  1. newspaper and magazine indexes
  2. newspaper and magazine stories
  3. reference libraries
  4. government information services, especially the Australian Bureau of Statistics
  5. personal experience

QUESTIONS FOR DISCUSSION

1. Why is it important to find out the backgrounds of the people who are the audience for a public address? What might happen if you failed to find out their backgrounds?
2. If a speaker is a beginner or nervous, what are the tactics he or she can adopt to minimise the effects?
3. When should you allow time for discussion and questions from the audience? What are the advantages of doing this?
4. Discuss four major advantages of a prepared speech versus an unprepared one.
5. How can the physical setting of a speech (the size of the room, its seating arrangements and the like) affect the way you deliver it?

EXERCISES

1. You have been asked by a local services club to give a lunchtime talk to its members on the major problems facing young people today. Decide which particular problems you would discuss and describe how you would prepare yourself to give this talk.

2. You have been asked to join a panel of five speakers at a school speech day in a forum to discuss the 'real world' that youth will encounter after they leave school. You are asked to speak on one aspect of your choice. Describe how you would prepare yourself for this panel discussion.

3. You have been asked to address a group of twenty people who have just become Australian citizens at a naturalisation ceremony. Your topic is broadly defined as the benefits and problems of being an Australian. Describe which issues you would discuss and how you would prepare yourself to give this address.

4. A public meeting has been called by your local council to discuss the possibility of applying for a licence to start up a community radio station. You have some firm opinions about such a venture. Describe how you would prepare yourself to make a short speech to the meeting on the issue.

5. The same council has called another public meeting to debate its proposal to demolish an historic building and construct a much-needed sporting complex in its place. Take a side in the debate and describe how you would prepare to persuade the meeting you are right.

CHAPTER

29

WRITING FOR THE SPOKEN WORD

After studying this chapter, you will be able to:

- ☐ draw up a plan for a speech that will allow an audience to follow you clearly
- ☐ write a speech so that it can be delivered effectively
- ☐ use some of the techniques of professional speech writers
- ☐ write a speech to inform and instruct an audience
- ☐ write a speech to persuade and convince an audience

WHY A PLAN IS IMPORTANT

The plan or outline is the single most important step in writing a speech. Once you have completed the plan, the actual words fall into place far more easily. Beginners are sometimes reluctant to write a plan. They think it is unnecessary and tedious. Yet making the effort to prepare a plan properly is the best way to gain confidence in writing a speech. A plan will help you compile your research material into a manageable form. It will help you clarify your ideas about the speech and impose a logical development on your ideas.

A plan gives you a 'visual' sense of the whole speech. To some people this is very important. They can 'see' what needs to be included or deleted. It is a good idea to draw up your plan on a large piece of paper or cardboard and pin it up in front of you before you start to write the speech. If you have a word processor with an 'outlining' facility, this is even better. In the same way, a plan allows the audience to mentally 'see' the structure of your speech as you give it. Because your material is clear and well organised, it is easier for your audience to follow your line of argument and to remember the main points.

Let's now look at the structure or framework of a plan for a speech.

STRUCTURE OF THE SPEECH

The structure of the speech is the way the plan has been put together—the arrangement of the main points or subsections. The most useful way to approach the structure is the simplest:

1. the beginning or introduction of the speech
2. the middle or body of the speech
3. the end or conclusion of the speech

There is an old maxim that describes the structure of a speech better than anything else: tell them, tell them, tell them. First, you tell the audience what you are going to tell them (the beginning), then you tell them (the middle), then you tell them what you have told them (the end). The beginning and the end of the speech are simply devices to help the audience follow the speaker's line of argument. They are guideposts that show the audience the direction the speech will take (the beginning) or has taken (the end). So we will look at these two parts of the speech first before going on to examine the middle or body of the speech.

Don't keep the audience waiting too long to get to the main point.

THE BEGINNING

In most speeches, the beginning is a statement of what the speaker intends to say in the body of the speech. It usually consists of one or two sentences. A slightly longer introduction may describe the theme or argument with reference to the main points or subsections. Looking at it another way, the introduction is a short summary of the contents of the speech. This is why veteran speech writers usually write the beginning of a speech last.

A dramatic opening drawn from anecdotes can stir an audience to action.

Keep the beginning as short as is appropriate. Don't keep the audience waiting too long for you to get to the main point. If you are writing a speech to inform or instruct (exposition), restrict the introduction to a simple statement of intent. The audience's main concern will be to learn something, so be brief and direct. For example:

> 'I am going to discuss the social effects of alcohol consumption and I will look particularly at the growing incidence in Australia of drinking among women and young people. I believe there are five important issues. These are ...'

In a speech to convince or persuade, or to stir your audience to action (argument), use a dramatic opening drawn from anecdotes, human interest stories, quotations, the rhetorical question or statistics as introductory devices to capture the audience's attention. For example, if you wanted to convince your audience of the harmful effects of smoking, you might start with an account of a recently publicised case in which a 38-year-old woman who contracted lung cancer sued the company whose cigarettes she had smoked for some twenty years. Or you might take a more academic approach and present statistical evidence showing the correlation between death and smoking in Australia. But, again, the structure should be simple and succinct and no more than a few sentences.

THE END

The end or conclusion of a speech will usually be similar to the introduction. The end should be a summary of the main points of the speech and, again, is best kept to a small number of sentences. Brevity does not mean you don't need to prepare the end of the speech. Careful preparation of the end or conclusion is important. The end is the last thing the audience remembers of your speech, so you should make sure the end relates to the total content of the speech, not just some parts or the last part.

Beginners who make a point of carefully preparing the end of their speech will avoid common mistakes such as finishing abruptly and catching everyone by surprise, or finding oneself at the end of the speech with the comment, 'oh, that's all I have to say'. Avoid clichés such as 'in conclusion', 'to sum up', 'in closing', since all such endings are self-evident and detract from what should be an eloquent finish. Finish with the words 'thank you' to let the audience know it is the end, but do not go into any elaborate thanking ritual to the audience for listening to your speech. If you have done your job properly, it is the audience who should thank you.

THE MIDDLE OR BODY

In the middle of the speech, make only three to five major points.

The middle will vary according to the type of speech. Before we look at the different structures a speech may have, we will examine some general principles about this sector.

The middle or body of the speech is where the speaker develops the theme or argument of the presentation. It is best to keep to three to five major points. Each point becomes a subsection of the middle part of the speech, and each point or subsection may have its own internal structure of introduction and development of points.

Each point or subsection is joined by transitional devices that hold the speech together and help the audience move from one part of a speech to the next. They can be ideas, sentences or words. A transitional device is when you say something like this:

> A few moments ago, I discussed the statistics about women and smoking. The next thing I want to discuss is how these statistics have been interpreted by the medical profession ...

Three types of structures for a speech are:

- chronological
- comparative
- causal

In this example, you have recalled something you have said earlier to link it to the point you want to make next. Transitional devices are guide-posts that help the audience follow your train of thought. They give the audience time to prepare for the next point and give the speaker room to gather his or her thoughts. They help the audience make sense of a mass of information. You should use them liberally.

The middle of a speech is not always the same, but will vary according to the type. This applies particularly to a speech to inform or instruct. To illustrate these different structures we will use the example of a speech on motor vehicle safety.

CHRONOLOGICAL OR HISTORICAL STRUCTURE

In this structure, you might look at the history of motor accidents and motor safety since the beginning of the twentieth century until now. This structure is usually called a narrative because it tells a story. You might look at the design of early cars, the conditions of the roads they drove on, and relate traffic accident and death rates. You could then trace the history of the social roles of motor cars. You could perhaps highlight periods of dramatic accident increases such as occurred after World War II. You could finish by examining the impact of reforms in vehicle design, compulsory seat belt legislation and random breath testing.

COMPARATIVE STRUCTURE

Here you might compare the incidence of accidents and safety factors in contemporary Western societies that are similar to Australia (for example, the United States and New Zealand) and draw some conclusions between various characteristics of these societies and the accident rate.

CAUSAL STRUCTURE

Here you would focus on the causes of accidents today, the types of vehicles responsible for most accidents, the type of road conditions on which accidents occur, what drivers were doing when they had accidents (overtaking, speeding, etc.), and analyse which are most responsible and what reforms are most likely to be effective to reduce these causes.

WRITING THE SPEECH

Good speech writing should aim to get the audience to listen, understand and remember. To be effective your speech writing has to be clear, simple, pictorial, repetitious and free of clichés and jargon.

The hardest thing to learn is to write the way you speak.

We speak one way and write another. The hardest thing to learn is to write the speech the way you speak. The temptation to write a speech the way you write is very hard to avoid. Although the spoken word is less complicated, most people, ironically, find it harder to write. This is one reason why politicians employ speech writers.

The most eloquent speeches are brief and unadorned. Paring a speech to its barest essence is an art form and, for the beginner, laborious. With practice, however, you can discipline yourself. You can learn to edit your work ruthlessly—to take out, cut down and reduce all.

Do not make the mistake of trying to impress by dishing up large slabs of information. The audience's preoccupation is to learn something new, not how much you know. Limit your ideas. Don't try to condense ten years' experience into ten minutes. Most speeches, we emphasise, should be restricted to three to five points. In a ten-minute speech, for example, you can deal with only one or two points thoroughly. Simplify your prose. Slash compound sentences to simple sentences of a subject and predicate. Eliminate elaborate phrases and long words. Delete all unnecessary words, foreign phrases and jargon. Most importantly, read the speech aloud to yourself as you write, constantly checking that you can say it in a comfortable manner, as you would in an informal conversation to a friend. This way your speech will take on your personal mannerisms.

Professional speech writers tailor their words to the speaker's individual style and personality.

Professional speech writers are adept at tailoring speeches to reflect a speaker's individual style and personality. To the novice their speeches may look odd, less than perfect English, full of half-sentences, colloquialisms, and the repetition of ideas and thoughts disguised in different examples. All good speeches should be individualised in this way, but take one word of caution: don't go to the point where you use words and expressions that sit awkwardly with your personality. If you don't say it, don't use it. This applies particularly to the use of colloquialisms, technical jargon, buzz words and currently fashionable phrases.

INFORMING AND INSTRUCTING

Put yourself in the audience's position and listen to the speech from their point of view.

In an earlier section we considered various purposes of public speaking. A speech to inform or instruct may take many forms, such as a school lesson, an academic lecture, a technical instruction or a training exercise. Your main concern is to impart information by describing, explaining or discussing ideas, issues or events, or instructing the audience how to do something. The style must be simple and clear.

You want to tell your listeners in as few words as possible who, what, why, when, where, and how. Ask yourself: is the audience familiar with the subject or is this subject new to them? Take, for example, a speech on the effects of narcotic drugs on the human body. It would take a qualified medical researcher only a few minutes to explain the effects to a group of doctors, but it would take far more time for the same researcher to explain lucidly the same results to a lay audience. Put yourself into the audience's position and listen to your speech from the audience's point of view.

In your introduction, outline briefly the aim of your speech. The audience will now expect that every point you make in the middle or body of your speech will relate to this objective. Present your evidence so that each point follows on logically. Use transitional devices liberally to give a sense of smooth progression.

Back up your statements with quotations and statistics from recognised authorities. Use statistics in a pictorial way. Avoid raw statistics in the form: 'The average Australian family today has 1.89 children.' While true in a statistical sense, most people don't use the word 'average' in the way that statisticians do. Presenting figures this way may sound ridiculous to an audience unused to statistics, and laughter in the wrong place can be singularly off-putting, especially for a beginner. Numbers are always best presented in graphic form where the comparisons and trends are much clearer.

Avoid vague generalisations. Clearly define your terms.

Avoid vague generalisations. Clearly define your terms. If, for example, you use the expression the 'middle class of Australia', explain what you mean by middle class. Avoid unsubstantiated claims (or points for which you lack evidence), although, of course, the spoken word allows you far more licence than print. We speak to achieve immediate communication, but we write for eventual comprehension and so need better proof to support our case. Nevertheless, if you use contentious material that members of your audience may dispute, be two steps ahead and acknowledge this.

Back up your statements with quotations and statistics from recognised authorities.

Remember always that people listening cannot revise or recap and cannot research your meaning on the spot. Back up your statements with quotations and statistics from recognised authorities. Use visual aids liberally: graphs, diagrams, illustrations, photographs, drawings, recordings, transparencies on overhead projectors, films and exhibits. Exhibits are items the speaker shows the audience to give a concrete example about the subject being discussed or how a certain thing is done.

PERSUADING AND CONVINCING

Speeches to convince or persuade or to stir an audience to action can vary widely—a lawyer's statement to the jury, a politician's speech on the hustings, a school principal's exhortation to a student assembly, a local resident in a debate at a community meeting. In these cases, the speaker aims to change the views of the audience and at times to get the audience to take action on a certain issue or event, usually to vote in a certain way in the jury room or at the meeting.

Four stylistic devices for persuasive speeches are:

- rhetorical questions
- quotations
- anecdotes
- personal testimony

This type of speech appeals to a variety of responses in the audience: intellectual, logical, but most of all emotional. The speaker often resorts to stylistic devices to mould the audience's response, such as rhetorical questions (which answer themselves), quotations (pithy or witty sayings—find them in a dictionary of quotations), anecdotes (a brief story about someone's experience which is relevant to the issue), and personal testimony (often similar to an anecdote but with a statement about how the individual feels about the issue). The speaker is often deeply involved in the subject (for example, politician, clergyman, activist) and can usually draw on personal knowledge and experience to support his or her case. Emotional appeals usually work by reminding the audience of their allegiances to other people ('We, as Australians, have always stood up for ...' ; 'The people of the southern suburbs have had enough of ...' , 'We know how much all of us here have respected ...'). If the appeal is a phoney one—

that is, people have never really felt the way the speaker claims they have—then neither the emotion nor the speech will work. Emotional appeals can only be effective if they genuinely capture the experience of their audiences.

Persuasive speaking may also usefully call up factual and numerical information in its support. All your facts must be accurate and you must know their source. An opponent can demolish your whole case by refuting just one of your facts ('If he can get this point so wrong, how can we trust anything else he says?') If someone does challenge you, you need to be able to say where your information came from and how reliable it is. This means there is no substitute for personal research to enable you to cite recognised authorities and the opinions and arguments of others who support your case.

People like to think they are acting from noble rather than selfish motives. State their self-interest in a way that encompasses the group of which they are part.

Argue logically and anticipate counter-arguments. Consider beforehand the opposition you are likely to encounter so you have all the opposing arguments ready. A willingness to recognise, if not concede, your opponent's point of view need not appear as weakness, and lets the audience see you as a person of broad rather than narrow vision.

Finally, remember that to win over your audience, your reasoning must be based on benefits to the listeners if they are to be persuaded to act in the way that you advocate. It is easy to overdo this approach, however. People like to think they are acting from noble rather than selfish motives. State their self-interest in a way that encompasses those of the group (wide or narrow) of which they are part.

Writing for the spoken word is never easy, but it always repays the effort. To be successful at it, we cannot emphasise too much the value of research into the occasion, the venue and the audience as well as the subject matter itself. Above all, it needs an ability to put yourself in the position of the audience, to hear yourself as others will hear you. To do this needs a willingness to be self-critical and a capacity to learn from experience. People who can develop these qualities, and who have the opportunity to practise them, have what it takes to become effective speech writers.

KEY POINTS: Chapter 29 Writing for the spoken word

- Preparing an outline or a plan of a speech before you start writing is important for three reasons.

  1. It helps you to compile your research material into a manageable form.
  2. It helps you clarify your ideas about your speech.
  3. It helps you impose a logical development onto your ideas so you will be more likely to draw your audience to the conclusions you want it to reach.

- In a speech to inform or instruct, the opening should state clearly the subject matter of the talk and what you hope to achieve in it.

- In a speech to convince or persuade, use a dramatic opening drawn from one of the following:

  1. an anecdote
  2. a human interest story
  3. a rhetorical question
  4. some dramatic contrast, made with evidence such as statistics comparing one group with another

- In the middle or body of any speech, develop your theme or argument, but keep to between three and five major points. To introduce a new main point you can help the audience follow you by using a 'transitional device' that recalls something you have already said and links it to the next point you want to make.

- The end of a speech is the last thing the audience remembers. Summarise your main conclusions but make them brief and punchy.

- The structure of a speech can have one of three patterns: chronological, comparative or causal.

- A chronological structure examines developments or trends over time.

- A comparative structure looks at one type of event as it occurs in several places at the same time.

- A causal structure focuses on the reasons why something happens.

QUESTIONS FOR DISCUSSION

1. How does writing a speech on a given subject compare to writing an essay on the same topic? What are the main differences?

2. In a speech designed to instruct and inform, what are the principal factors that will help it succeed? Give some examples.

3. In a speech designed to persuade and convince, what are the principal factors that will help it succeed? Give some examples.

4. Why are audiences helped by the use of transitional devices between main points?

5. To persuade people to your point of view, is it best to appeal directly to their self-interest?

EXERCISES

Write a ten-minute speech for you to deliver to an inexpert lay audience on one or more of the following topics.

1. The advantages and disadvantages of your present employment
2. The advantages and disadvantages of your present course of study
3. The Australian attitude to sport
4. Television—a social benefit or a social problem?
5. Aboriginal land rights
6. Government intervention: too much or too little?
7. The education system—is it good enough?
8. Who runs Australia—government, business, unions, someone else?
9. Should Australia base more or less of its economy on tourism?
10. Work—do we take it too easily or too seriously?
11. Should we buy Australian or buy overseas?
12. How to control illegal drugs
13. Should we reintroduce capital punishment?
14. Youth—the major problems
15. The Australian welfare system
16. A topic that currently consumes your interest

CHAPTER

30

PUBLIC SPEAKING—DELIVERY

After studying this chapter, you will be able to:

- use different voice signals to communicate meaning
- use body language to communicate meaning
- reduce nervousness when speaking in public
- use various audio-visual aids both as stage props and communication devices

Preparation represents 75 per cent of the effort that goes into the typical speech. However, the components of preparation discussed in the previous two chapters—planning, writing, making notes and rehearsing—are all dependent on the eventual delivery. If the delivery does not measure up, then the potential of the preparatory work has not been realised.

Speaking is a performance and, like actors or teachers, speakers are expected by their audiences to be both informative and engaging. The constant scrutiny of an audience means there is not a single moment when the speaker can turn off. There is no opportunity for relaxing or taking time off. Good delivery requires the development of its own kinds of skills.

This all goes to make public speaking a fairly daunting prospect for the inexperienced. There are, however, a range of techniques that can improve any delivery and that, with practice, can turn most people into competent speakers. In this chapter we discuss these basic elements of delivering a speech.

USING YOUR VOICE

SIGNALS THROUGH SPEECH

Most people are aware that they can say the same words in different tones of voice and convey radically different meanings. It is important for the public speaker to be conscious of this possibility and to be in control of its potential.

There are a wide range of voice qualities involved in signalling this way—speed, pitch, loudness and rhythm. An anxious person usually talks faster than normal and at a higher pitch. To communicate less anxiety, therefore, you need to lower your pitch and slow down the pace. Significant pauses between major points also indicate confidence and authority. The best way to signal insecurity and submissiveness is to end sentences with a rising terminal, that is, a raised pitch on the last word (one of the most unfortunate current speech habits of adolescents). Speakers who sound most authoritative are those who have a downward inflection in their voice at the end of each statement.

Few people have a naturally strong and pleasant speaking voice. As public speakers, most people face the prospect of having to improve the quality, tone and projection of their voices. Following are some techniques which can assist your delivery. But first, get a tape recorder and record yourself making some statements. When you play the tape back, note down points you need to improve and to practice.

1. Do you clearly pronounce your words?
2. Do you say your vowels roundly?
3. Do you vary the pitch of your voice?
4. Do you use words grammatically?

PROJECTION

While it may be difficult to alter the nasal or grating sound of a voice, one major weakness that practice can improve is softness. When you learn to project your voice, it becomes louder. Because your voice is louder, you begin to take more notice of other qualities such as pronunciation, pitch, grammar, accent, vowels and consonants. The well-tried method of improving voice projection used in acting training is to try to speak to a person in the back row of the audience. Good projection takes time, and in the long run has less to do with loudness than it does with improved pronunciation and pitch.

One way to improve voice projection is to learn your lines like an actor. Write your speech out in full, condense it into notes, then rehearse it out loud, preferably with a tape recorder. Practising it aloud will force you to impart a more dramatic quality to the lines.

You can improve voice projection by learning your lines like an actor:

- write your speech out in full
- condense it into notes
- rehearse out loud into a tape recorder

TIMING

Learn to speak slowly and precisely, using your natural voice. It is better to speak slower than faster, and the bigger your audience the slower you should speak. Learn to use pauses. Listeners are usually pleased to get the chance to catch up with you. Most speakers have a tendency to speak faster than they should, especially if they are nervous. A well-placed pause is as effective as any emphasis, for example:

> ... and the fault lies here (pause), right in this meeting (much longer pause).

Do not, however, overdo things by exaggerations and unnecessary emphasis on words that do not deserve it. Save any emphasis—raising the voice, gesticulation of hands—for the climax of the argument or the telling statistics where it will be twice as effective.

TONE OR INTONATION

Vary the intonation of your voice. Some speakers know how to vary their voice tone. Others speak in a monotone that follows the same tone and rhythm. This is very boring for the audience, no matter what the content of the speech. To avoid a flat and monotonous voice, vary the depth and height of voice tone. Inject some drama and emotion into the meaning of your words.

PRONUNCIATION

This improves if you speak slowly and clearly. Practise pronouncing your vowels (*a*, *e*, *i*, *o* and *u*) fully. Pay special attention to the clarity of consonants (the 'hard' parts of words that are not vowels—*b*, *c*, *d*, *f*, etc.) especially at the ends of words. Consonants rather than vowels set words apart. Australians have a tendency to slide over consonants, which gives rise to the ocker mumble.

It is more important to speak clearly and pronounce your words well than to worry about your accent.

ACCENT

Most Australian accents fall into one of two categories: general or broad pronunciation. Most Australian radio and television newsreaders speak with a general pronunciation. Broad pronunciation is more nasal, that is, much of the sound comes out through the nose and less from the mouth and chest. There is nothing wrong with a broad accent. Its most famous exponent is Paul Hogan, who became an international celebrity. Bob

Hawke showed that someone with a broad accent could become prime minister. It is more important to speak clearly and to pronounce your words well than to worry about your accent.

BODY LANGUAGE

As well as words and illustrative material, a public speaker also communicates through postures, gestures and expressions. In the last decade there has been a good deal of attention paid to these latter types of signals through the study of 'body language'. Experienced public speakers, especially politicians, draw on a wide range of body language to make their words more effective. Unfortunately, less experienced speakers can sometimes be unaware of the signals they are giving through their posture and gestures. Their body language can then be saying something quite different to their actual words. This is an area worth studying closely.

POSITION

If a speaker is placed on a rostrum or stage at a higher level than the audience, this puts the speaker in a position of dominance. This is common when a speaker is addressing a large audience and needs to command their attention. Before a large audience, speakers should always stand. In a smaller seminar, when audience feedback is required, a setting of greater equality, where people are on the same level and perhaps all facing one another, is a more effective arrangement of position.

POSTURE

Posture
- to express confidence: stand erect with the head up and chin out
- to show submission: round the shoulders and lower the head and chin
- to appear friendly: hold the hands out in front of the body
- to look aggressive: put the hands on the hips
- to be assertive: lean forward on a table

This is another means of communicating important relationships with an audience. There are distinctive postures that signal confidence and dominance, and others that signal insecurity and submissiveness. Confidence is expressed by standing erect with head up and chin out. A submissive posture is signalled by rounded shoulders and a lowered head and chin. There are also friendly and hostile postures. Hands held out in front of the body signals a warmth towards and an appeal to the audience. Hands on hips can add an aggressive streak. Folded arms can suggest either relaxation or lack of confidence (especially if accompanied by a lowered chin), depending on other gestures. At a table, leaning forward generally signals assertiveness, slumping in a seat can indicate submission and lack of confidence, while leaning back a long way can either indicate relaxation or indifference, again depending on the circumstances.

Movement is also a part of the posture you strike. In most cases, movement should be minimal, deliberate, controlled and done only for a purpose—to give theatrical emphasis to an important point or to operate audio-visual equipment. Too much movement indicates insecurity and tends to generate tension. On the other hand, no movement at all can look unnatural. Only practice will give you certainty in this area. Accept any offer to see yourself on videotape. This is by far the best way to improve movement on stage.

If you are a member of a panel of speakers and have to wait for your turn, you should be aware that you are already being observed. Arrange yourself in your seat comfortably. If you want to cross your legs, cross them at the knee rather than at the ankles or by placing one ankle over a knee. The last two gestures signify a lack of assertiveness. Avoid fiddling with your clothes, hair, glasses or notes. Fidgeting of any kind is perceived as nervousness and detracts from your performance and your co-speakers' performances.

GESTURES

The movement of hands, feet and other parts of the body communicate a diverse range of messages. If a speaker is emotional, he or she may send a number of signals: fist clenching (assertion or aggression); face touching (anxiety); scratching (uncertainty, guilt); face or forehead wiping (tiredness).

Gestures are also related to the words being used. The speaker may point to people or objects to indicate who or what the words refer to. Hand gestures may illustrate shapes, sizes or movements that relate to the subject matter. Other gestures can indicate numbers or show how items are grouped. These kinds of gestures are normal and expected by audiences. Most of us use them involuntarily all the time. Practice and experience in public speaking should allow you to become aware of what gestures you are making so that you can control them and use them to say exactly what you want.

Be extremely conscious of your body. Habitual movements irk and alienate audiences. Nod your head only when you need to make a point (nodding usually signals agreement). When seated, don't jig your legs or tap your feet. Avoid exaggerated gesticulations such as table thumping and pointing. Do not scratch face, ears, beard, or pull ears or hair. Don't fiddle with objects such as pens, notes, keys, buttons, jewellery and audio-visual aids, before or after you have used them.

Hand gestures
- to show aggression: clench the fists
- to express anxiety: touch the face
- to expose uncertainty: scratch yourself
- to appear tired: wipe face or forehead

FACIAL EXPRESSIONS

We use our facial expressions to communicate a wide range of emotions. For a public speaker, the most effective expression in the great majority of situations is the broad smile that says the speaker is very well disposed to the audience. Other common messages sent by the mouth are displeasure (closed and turned down), surprise (slightly open) and pleasure or agreement (turned up).

The eyebrows usually combine with the mouth to make a gesture. Eyebrows, however, most frequently work when listening to someone else. Fully raised, they signal disbelief. Half raised, they indicate surprise. Half lowered, they show the listener is puzzled. Fully lowered, they can indicate disbelief or anger.

Facial expressions
- to win an audience: smile broadly
- to show displeasure: mouth closed and turned down
- to show surprise: mouth slightly open
- to show pleasure or agreement: mouth turned up
- to signal disbelief: eyebrows fully raised
- to show anger eyebrows: fully lowered

EYE CONTACT

This is another important part of communicating with an audience. Watch your audience throughout. Try not to ignore one part of the audience. From time to time, deliberately move your eyes from section to section. The worst possible fault is to read a speech from notes or papers without looking up at the audience.

CLOTHING

Clothes are another part of the way you express yourself and your relation to the audience. The clothes you wear when you speak in public should be chosen with this in mind. Most speakers will want to wear clothes similar to their audience, which is one more reason why the kind of audience research recommended in Chapter Twenty-Eight is necessary. At a casual convention with a holiday atmosphere, you would probably be out of place in business clothes, although some may choose this if they want to make a special effect. Casual clothing at a formal occasion would be rejected (or sometimes chosen) for similar reasons.

When you don't know what to expect, the general rule is to dress up rather than down. It is also true that if you look good, you feel good. Clothes can impart confidence.

NERVOUSNESS

Unless they are politicians who speak for a living, most public speakers have some sense of nervousness before they begin. Generally the larger the audience, the more acute the nerves. There is nothing unusual about this and, in fact, it may be welcomed. A mild case of nervousness works to sharpen your mind and focuses it on the task before you. Problems arise if nervousness gets out of hand and rises to the point where it prevents you from thinking clearly so you end up saying things you did not intend or you freeze up altogether.

The best way to prevent nerves getting out of hand is to do a thorough job of preparation, as we explained in the previous two chapters. You will control your nerves if you have:

1. written your speech out beforehand
2. made notes of your major points
3. practised or rehearsed what you intend to say
4. gained a clear idea of the audience and its needs

Effective relaxation techniques
- become aware of tense muscles and relax each individually
- deep breathing

Some people benefit from relaxation techniques before they start. The most effective are the most direct. Be aware of any clenching or tightening of your muscles, especially your hands, arms, legs and facial muscles. Think about these muscles and consciously relax them if they are tense. Another highly beneficial therapy is deep breathing. If you can take some deep breaths unobtrusively before you start, you will usually perform better.

One of the most effective antidotes to nerves, especially for inexperienced speakers, is to use what they call on the stage a prop. In public speaking it is now widely recognised that the best type of prop is an audio-visual presentation.

The following sections of this chapter take a detailed look at the use of audio-visual aids, a technique that assists all speakers but one which is especially useful in helping to overcome the problems that all beginners inevitably face.

AUDIO-VISUAL AIDS

It is easy to see why audio-visuals are a comfort to the inexperienced public speaker. They have the psychological effect of diverting the audience's attention away from the speaker to the illustration, the graph or the slide, thus giving the speaker a few moments in which to relax, to gather thoughts and to prepare for the next point. For this reason, we strongly recommend audio-visual aids for people who have little or no experience in public speaking. They are the most helpful supplement to the speaker's notes. If properly arranged beforehand, audio-visual material will guide the speech along its prepared path. In cases of total memory blank to which beginners are unfortunately prone, the sight of material related to the topic will always jog the speaker's memory.

Audio-visual aids take much of the tension out of a speech. They allow the beginner to gain the experience of standing up in front of an audience, but they reduce the close personal scrutiny that a words-only presentation invites. The more experience you gain this way, the less you will gradually need to rely on the audio-visuals as confidence builds in other areas of the performance.

Audio-visual aids add interest, amplify the message and give the speaker confidence

The catch with audio-visuals is that they also involve quite a lot of work. They must be of a high standard—good artwork, legible print, clear photographs, stimulating film—well prepared, and perhaps even rehearsed before the speech. This may involve trips to the library to find relevant statistics or pictorial information; to requisition cassettes, slides or film; a visit to the media centre of your institution to book film and slide projectors or cassette players; and, in your research time, effort in preparing tables, graphs, charts, diagrams, captions on pictures, transparencies or whatever else you decide to use.

USE: WHEN AND WHY

Audio-visuals can be used on almost every occasion. The belief that they belong only in schoolrooms and lecture halls no longer holds. Today audio-visual presentations are employed widely in large and small meetings in all areas of government, the public service, industry, business, education, tourism and entertainment. Their use can probably be justified 90 per cent of the time.

ADDING INTEREST AND VARIETY

Earlier we discussed the effect television has had on public speaking and the way it has reduced our tolerance for 'talking heads'. Audiences accustomed to television want greater diversity in speeches and one way to achieve this is to use audio-visual aids. Today an enormous range of audio-visual accessories is available (which we discuss later in this chapter). Their scope and variety encourages speakers to develop imaginative presentations.

SIMPLIFYING THE MESSAGE

Audio-visuals are useful when you want to explain difficult concepts—a complicated story, complex ideas, statistics or analytical material. They allow you to say the same thing more than once without boring the audience. The speaker presents the information verbally, then repeats it in pictorial or other form. Simplifying complex information is very important when you are speaking to an audience with a wide cross-section of age and ability.

BETTER COMPREHENSION

Audio-visuals help the audience as well as the speaker. Audiences usually find listening hard work, regardless of how good the speaker is. Anything that adds contrast and variety to a speech makes the audience's job easier. Audio-visuals also help the audience comprehend information more quickly.

Television has heightened this visual bias. Television audiences have learned to comprehend larger amounts of information in shorter periods of time. The speaker who uses audio-visuals can take advantage of this audience predisposition.

THE RANGE OF AUDIO-VISUAL AIDS

There are a wide variety of audio-visual aids. They can be divided into two categories: aural, such as the microphone and cassette player, and visual, such as pictures, slides, film and video. There are two types of visual aid—those that can be shown in normal light and those that need a darkened setting. Films and slides are excellent aids but because they are shown in darkness, they restrict communication between speaker and audience. They also inhibit note-taking, and have a habit of inducing sleep. So you must have a good reason for using this type of audio-visual aid in a one-off speech. Naturally, teachers and students welcome films and slides to break the monotony of a long series of lectures or seminars.

The range of audio-visuals includes:

- microphone
- blackboard, chartboard or whiteboard, using chalk or felt pens
- overhead projector, using transparencies
- slide projector, using slides
- film projector, using films
- cassette player, using tape cassettes
- video player, using video cassettes
- pictures that include items prepared beforehand such as:
  photographs
  drawings
  diagrams
  tables
  graphs
  maps
- handouts for distribution to members of the audience
- exhibits for display by the speaker in front of the audience or for circulation among the audience

PREPARATION AND TESTING

Well beforehand you should familiarise yourself with projection equipment or other audio-visual material. Check all items beforehand.

1. Test the microphone thoroughly to see that it works.
2. Make sure the blackboard or chartboard is clean.
3. Look to see that there are power outlets and that power points and light globes are working.
4. Set up the film, slide or overhead projector in advance.
5. Make sure that films and cassettes are wound the way you need them (a previous user might not have rewound the film); that pictures, diagrams, charts, tables or slides are in the order you want to use them and, importantly, that items unrelated to your talk are eliminated from the kit or package.

Apologising for brokendown equipment, leaving the audience while you find help, fumbling over the mechanics of your equipment, searching for a slide or picture out of order or including material which does not relate to your talk—all these diminish your performance immediately. Don't use audio-visual aids you cannot comfortably operate. Use only those aids you can easily transport to and from the location. In many cases audio-visual aids will already be in place. It is your responsibility to check on their condition and availability. Personally test them on the premises.

THE MICROPHONE

The microphone is the most common audio aid. But, like radio broadcasting, speaking into a microphone requires special techniques. Your prose should be punchy, with short sentences, succinct phrases and plenty of pauses. There are also a number of technical things to remember and, in some cases, to rehearse before the day.

- Don't place your mouth close to the microphone.
- Don't let the microphone block the audience's view of you.
- Don't talk to the microphone instead of the audience.
- Remember to look at the audience.
- Don't touch the microphone while you are speaking. It will amplify the lightest tap into a loud noise.
- Don't rustle notes near the microphone.
- Don't hold notes or papers between you and the microphone, as this will warp the sound.

If a microphone breaks down during a performance, stop using it immediately. How many times have you watched speakers continue who are unable to be heard? Forget the microphone but remember to project your voice to the back row.

BLACKBOARD, CHARTBOARD AND WHITEBOARD

These are still popular. Most people have had some experience with them so they are probably the best all-round aids for a wide cross-section of speakers. Boards have a number of advantages.

- They are the visual aid you are most likely to find in educational institutions.
- All you require is chalk for blackboards and felt pens for chartboards and whiteboards.
- You can easily change writing or drawing on them. When a number of presentations are to be given, you can erase information after each presentation and start afresh for the next.
- You can build up a story, case, hypothesis or argument as you explain it. This is important when you want to conceal information until the right moment.
- You can write or draw freehand to illustrate specific items during your speech.
- You can invite members of your audience who are being instructed to contribute information on the board too.

Overall, boards are versatile aids. However, there are disadvantages. There are two important rules for the effective use of blackboards, chartboards or whiteboards.

1. Avoid working on the board longer than necessary with your back to the audience. Eye contact should be maintained as much as possible, so you should regularly turn to face the audience. Better still, prepare your material on the board before your audience assembles. If this is not possible, the best alternative may be to prepare transparencies for an overhead projector.
2. Write legibly and draw accurately. Substandard presentations are counterproductive. If you can't write or draw well, you should consider alternative audio-visual aids.

OVERHEAD PROJECTOR

The overhead projector is the most versatile and useful of all visual aids. It is commonly found as a permanent fixture in educational institutions. It is quite heavy and cumbersome so it is usually not recommended unless already in place.

You can prepare almost any type of material for the overhead projector: handwritten or typed notes, drawings, tables, diagrams, charts, maps. To project an image with an overhead projector, you use transparencies which can be bought at any good stationers. To transfer your written, drawn or typed material onto the transparency, simply use a felt pen, a whiteboard pen or a typewriter. Whiteboard pens are the best because you can wipe any mark off with a tissue if you want to make changes. Most copiers today can reproduce material on transparent film. This is a quick and useful process for anyone who needs transparencies at short notice or if you have illustrations you want to show.

The overhead projector has a number of advantages.

- It can be used in normal lighting. A darkened room restricts communication between speaker and audience.
- It is simple to use. You turn on the power switch and put your transparency onto the projector. The material will then be projected onto a screen. When you have finished with the transparency, you replace it with the next one and so on. When you have shown all your material, you turn the projector off.
- It is inexpensive and easy to prepare transparencies. All work can be done beforehand.
- It is easier for the audience to see the information because it is projected onto a screen and is clearer and larger than information on a blackboard or chartboard.
- It is easy to conceal information from the audience, to reveal material in steps or to direct the audience's attention to specific items. This is a useful ploy in speeches to inform or instruct. The speaker simply covers the transparency and then uncovers the wanted parts.
- It is useful for complex explanations, especially when you want to build up a story, theory or case. You simply place one transparency over another. If, for example, you wanted to illustrate human anatomy, you would use the first transparency to show the skeleton and the second to show the muscle groups.

SLIDE PROJECTORS

Photographic slides are useful because they are small and portable, and you can take the photographs yourself of the person, object, place, event, illustration, photograph, chart, table, map or whatever else you decide to use. However, today's discriminating audiences expect a high standard of photography, so slides can be expensive and laborious to prepare. They may involve several photographic sessions and time-consuming processing. Commercially produced slides are available which may be perfectly suitable for your needs.

Disadvantages are that slides must be used in a darkened room, thus reducing contact between speaker and audience. It is best to use an automatic remote-controlled slide projector. Manual models are too fussy for speech presentations.

FILM PROJECTORS

A wide range of professional feature, commercial and educational films are available from film libraries. Most institutional libraries stock the most popular educational films and tapes. Few speakers are in the position of preparing their own film. Film has the drawback that it must be shown in a darkened setting.

VIDEO PLAYERS

Increasingly larger numbers of people have access to facilities for preparing videotape recordings. Videotape is particularly useful as an instructional aid. The presenter prepares tape of actual events which can be replayed to the audience as part of a discussion. Typical would be a film shown to school leavers on how to get a job. Included in the film might be a brief discussion of techniques for preparing a job application, and a role playing exercise on job interviews.

A videotape made on the spot with a low-cost portable camera-recorder system is increasingly used as a basis for discussion. An example relevant to public speaking would be the use of videotape to record students giving a speech in a seminar on speech presentation. Students view themselves and quickly assess how to improve their speaking skills.

Videotape also has the added attraction of being able to be used in normal daylight.

PHOTOGRAPHS, DRAWINGS, DIAGRAMS, TABLES, GRAPHS, MAPS

A good way to illustrate material is to prepare visual aids beforehand. There are a number of techniques you should employ.

1. They should be large enough to be clearly seen by people in the back row of the audience. If not, then you should use some form of projection, overhead, slide or film.
2. For text and numbers, use simple, block lettering.
3. Eliminate all but the most necessary information. An audience should be able to comprehend the whole thing in five seconds or less.

EXHIBITS

These are items the speaker shows the audience to give a concrete example about the subject being discussed or how a certain thing is done, such as a working model, equipment or ingredients. A talk about rock-climbing, for example, is enhanced by a demonstration of the gear the climber uses.

Exhibits must be large enough for people in the back row to see clearly. If this is not possible, it is better to use an illustration of the material on a slide, overhead or film projector. A moving exhibit is worth much more than one that does not move. Audiences enjoy demonstrations of how a thing works.

There are some problems in using exhibits, however. Interesting objects have a tendency to take over from the speaker. Three important rules are:

1. Keep exhibits out of sight until you are ready to use them and put them out of sight when you have finished.
2. Never circulate an exhibit, handout or any other item among an audience while you are speaking. This is disruptive, promotes talking and competes with you.
3. Don't stare at an exhibit while you discuss it. Remember, your eyes should be in contact with the audience.

KEY POINTS: Chapter 30 Public speaking—delivery

- It is not only the words you choose but the way you use your voice that communicates meaning. To speak well, you need to be able to use

  1. projection
  2. timing
  3. tone
  4. pronunciation

- Body language is also an important way in which you express meaning, particulularly through

  1. position in relation to the audience
  2. posture
  3. gestures
  4. facial expressions
  5. eye contact
  6. clothing

- To overcome nervousness in delivery you need to have

  1. written out your speech beforehand
  2. made notes from the full text
  3. rehearsed what you intend to say
  4. gained a clear idea of the audience and its needs
  5. learned some relaxation techniques
  6. prepared some audio-visual aids to use as props

- Audio-visual aids are always useful because they
  1. add interest and variety
  2. help simplify a message
  3. assist the audience to better comprehension

- The range of audio-visual aids includes
  1. microphones
  2. blackboards, whiteboards and chart-boards
  3. overhead projectors
  4. slide projectors
  5. film projectors
  6. cassette players
  7. video players
  8. photographs, illustrations and graphs
  9. handouts
  10. exhibits

QUESTIONS FOR DISCUSSION

- When giving a speech, what is the most likely way to signal that you are feeling insecure?
- Is the Australian accent a handicap or an advantage when giving a speech? What about other accents?
- What is body language? What would you do to express the following emotions: confidence, submission, friendship, aggression, assertiveness?
- What are the main techniques that will help you overcome nervousness when speaking?
- What are the advantages of using audio-visual aids in a speech?

EXERCISES

Once you have studied the previous three chapters, the most useful exercise left to do is actually perform some public speaking. If you worked through Chapter Twenty-Nine, you will now have a ten-minute speech ready to deliver. If not, go back to the end of that chapter, select one of the sixteen topics suggested as exercises, and write your speech now. When you are ready, take your notes, assemble your props and audio-visual aids and deliver the speech to your class.

REVISION LIST FOR PART IX

PUBLIC SPEAKING

- Audiences today are saturated by talking heads in the media so they are more demanding of people who speak in public, even at the local community level.
- Preparation of a speech is just as important as delivery.
- The best way to win the battle against nerves about public speaking is to be well prepared.
- Avoid giving public speeches where you simply read aloud a prepared script.
- For formal occasions, prepare a full script, then condense it into notes which list the main points, then speak to the notes.
- There are no real impromptu speeches—even with the shortest notice, an experienced speaker will draw up a quick plan.
- There are six things you need to know when preparing a speech.

  1. Are you speaking alone or with others?
  2. What is your precise topic?
  3. Exactly how long do you have to talk?
  4. What is the physical setting?
  5. What is the nature of your audience: its numbers, their ages, sex, education and employment background?
  6. What is the purpose of your speech? Is it to inform, persuade, entertain or perform a ritual?

- Preparing an outline or a plan of a speech before you start writing the actual words is important for three reasons.

  1. It helps you to compile your research material into a manageable form.
  2. It helps you clarify your ideas about your speech.
  3. It helps you impose a logical development onto your ideas so you will be more likely to draw your audience to the conclusions you want it to reach.

- In a speech to inform or instruct, the opening should state clearly the subject matter of the talk and what you hope to achieve in it.

continued on next page

continued from previous page

- In a speech to convince or persuade, use a dramatic opening drawn from one of the following:

  1. an anecdote
  2. a human interest story
  3. a rhetorical question
  4. some dramatic contrast, made with evidence such as statistics comparing one group with another

- In the middle or body of any speech, develop your theme or argument but keep to between three and five major points. To introduce a new main point you can help the audience follow you by using a 'transitional device' which recalls something you have already said and links it to the next point you want to make.

- The end of a speech is the last thing the audience remembers. Summarise your main conclusions but make them brief and punchy.

- The structure of a speech can have one of three patterns: chronological, comparative or causal.

  1. A chronological structure examines developments or trends over time.
  2. A comparative structure looks at one type of event as it occurs in several places at the same time.
  3. A causal structure focuses on the reasons why something happens.

- It is not only the words you choose but the way you use your voice that communicates meaning. To speak well, you need to be able to use

  projection
  timing
  tone
  pronunciation

- Body language is also an important way in which you express meaning, especially through your

  position in relation to the audience
  posture
  gestures

continued on next page

continued from previous page

facial expressions
eye contact
clothing

- To overcome nerves in delivery you need to have

written out your speech beforehand
made notes from the full text
rehearsed what you intend to say
gained a clear idea of the audience and its needs
learned some relaxation techniques
prepared some audio-visual aids to use as props

- Audio-visual aids are always useful because they

add interest and variety
help simplify a message
assist the audience to better comprehension

- The range of audio-visual aids includes

microphones
blackboards, whiteboards and chartboards
overhead projectors
slide projectors
film projectors
video players
photographs, illustrations and graphs
handouts
exhibits

PART IX
KEY TEXTS AND FURTHER READING

Bolton, Robert, *People Skills: How to Assert Yourself, Listen to Others, and Resolve Conflicts*, Simon & Schuster Australia, Sydney, 1987.

Gunther, N., *The Art of Effective Speaking*, Reed, Sydney, 1982.

Leeds, D., *Powerspeak: The Complete Guide to Public Speaking and Presentation*, Piatkus, London, 1989.

Malouf, D., *How to Create and Deliver a Dynamic Presentation*, Simon & Schuster Australia, Sydney, 1988.

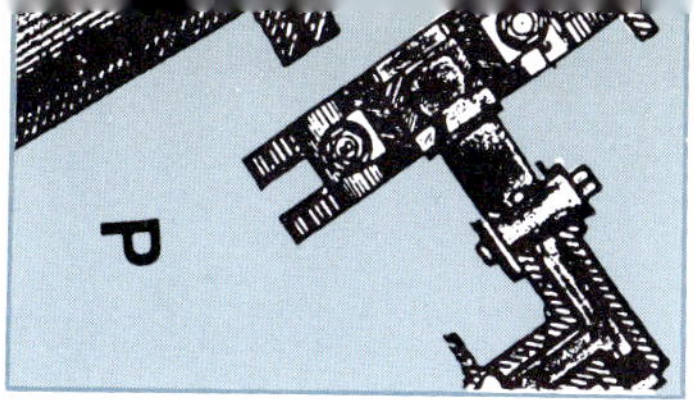

PART

X

COMMUNICATING IN THE ORGANISATION

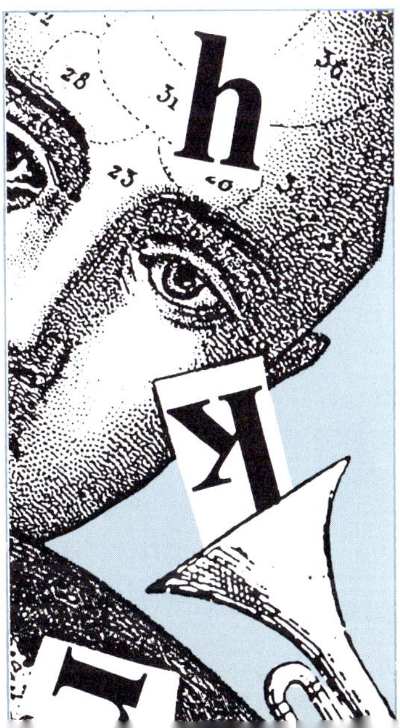

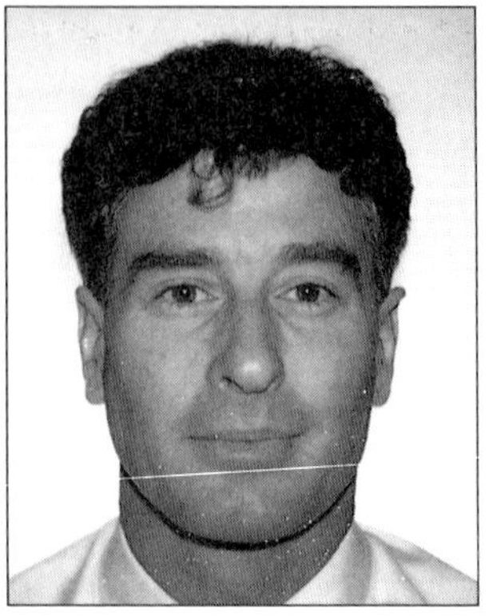

DEVELOPING AN EFFECTIVE COMMUNICATIONS STRATEGY

In a competitive world environment, Australian companies need to open their lines of communications to both staff and clients, argues management consultant Brett Morris.

Not so long ago, the chief executive or managing director of any organisation was an inaccessible, all-powerful figure whose word was law. He ruled a hierarchy made up of successive levels of department heads, middle managers, supervisors and, at the bottom, the employees who actually produced the goods or provided the services. Most staff deferred to those above them and went in fear of putting a foot wrong.

Management practices today are changing rapidly. 'Communication', 'consultation' and 'employee participation' are now key concepts used by corporations with visions for the future.

Brett Morris, managing director of Fortune GBA, heads a team of management and training consultants in North Sydney. He welcomes the trend towards developing communication processes that cut across the outmoded, hierarchical structures of many companies. 'Running businesses along vertical functional lines may have been feasible in the 1950s and 1960s with low inflation, little technical change and high consumer demand, but it doesn't work now. The belief used to be that you could run a company with a few smart people at the top who told everyone else what to do and who had all the answers. Today, in an era of global competition, management needs to tap into its best resource—people,' he says.

Morris believes it is vital for companies to re-examine the roles managers perform. 'Managers,' he says, 'should become problem givers rather than problem solvers; that is, they don't have to have all the answers. The need for feedback, for understanding staff perspectives and for involving them in the decision-making process are crucial factors in motivating managers to harness the energy and brain-power of their employees.

'Communication is essential for humans. Money is not the main reason why people work. Certainly, if you don't pay them, they won't turn up, but they have much stronger psychological needs, such as social interaction and being made to feel that their work really matters,' he says.

Morris designs processes and runs workshops aimed at developing managers' facilitative, coaching, counselling and leadership skills. He believes it is imperative for managers to get off their pedestals to create an environment that allows for staff integration across all levels of responsibility.

He is also adamant that poor communication in any organisation can destroy the belief that people have in the business, in what they do and in themselves.

His first critique of current practices is that management make mistakes in recruiting or promoting people primarily for their experience or technical skills. He sees facilitative, interpersonal and conflict-resolution skills as being equally important, but overlooked by management because they are harder to assess.

Secondly, he is critical of management for only recognising outstanding performance rather than looking at the operation of the whole team effort.

'Most of the people in any organisation who provide services are often the lowest paid and the least recognised. They are often distrustful of management because it has ignored them in the past,' he declares.

Finally, he disagrees with the usual procedures through which the chief executive communicates new management strategies for a business—through slick videos or the hype and fanfare of speeches delivering the 'grand plan'.

'Nobody believes all that. It's artificial and sounds like the flavour of the month. The staff are the ones who should be approached, consulted and listened to by management,' he says.

Morris strongly believes that corporations that are not integrating their lines of communication with their business processes will not be around in a few years' time.

'The demise of most businesses can be picked up three to five years before it happens. Our philosophy at Fortune GBA is to guide companies to self-discover where their problems lie, rather than being the experts on a temporary visit who come in from the outside. We find that many of the answers to their problems can be found by creating better lines of communication,' he explains.

He stresses that efficient communication is not just linked with improving the morale of employees and streamlining internal operations, but that organisations must also talk constantly with their clients and customers.

'It is vital that managers are in regular contact with their customers to understand their needs and problems, so that they can be identified and solved,' he adds.

He argues that, strategically, the prime way in which most organisations have tended to compete over the past thirty to fifty years has been through focusing on products and markets. But today's successful global competitors are now shifting the balance of their attention from 'where' they compete to 'how' they compete.

'This move essentially means they're looking at how to integrate their communication processes across the business and top-down, bottom-up. They're analysing how people work and co-operate with each other, making effective communication a competitive advantage in its own right,' he says.

Morris cites some strategies or ways in which an effective communications policy could be implemented by management.

1. Management should show an interest in employees on a one-to-one basis.
2. The chief executive should be a facilitator of human potential by recognising that all employees can contribute, and should encourage its expression.
3. Management must be flexible and adaptable to cope with the speed of change in business procedures, technology and market fluctuations.
4. Management should listen to and understand the concerns of staff and the pressures they encounter, so that it will have more empathy with them.
5. Business must be more customer-centred at every level of its operations.

Morris says that despite his twelve years in the management consultant field working with some top companies, he is still astounded at how pervasive the need for communication is, even among well-established and proven performers.

'You can have as much capital as you like, you can have the best technology and a long, dominant market share, but the real source of productivity is people,' he declares fervently.

He therefore strongly urges management to develop a human face and to foster enduring, trusting relationships throughout the whole company.

'When it comes to leadership, the most important job a manager has is to communicate and ensure that everyone at every level has a sense of accountability and emotional attachment to what the business is trying to do, and is aware of how their contribution helps in achieving the overall result.'

CHAPTER

31

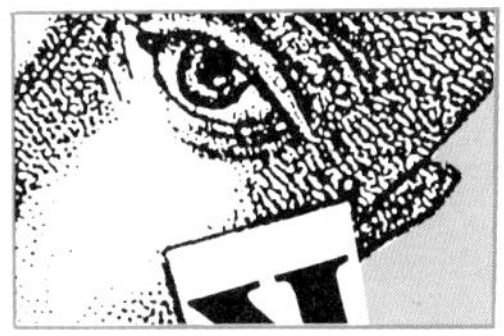

MANAGEMENT THEORY AND COMMUNICATION STRUCTURES

After studying this chapter, you will :

- understand the basis of the management theories developed for manufacturing industry in the twentieth century
- understand the reasons new theories have emerged in the 1980s and 1990s in the wake of the growth of the service economy and the Information Age
- know the techniques that are fostering employee conceptual thinking and initiatives in the management of organisations
- understand the rationale and basic techniques of total quality management
- understand the techniques of the new service management
- identify the role of communications in the new organisational environment

In the 1990s there is a revolution under way in the way we theorise about organisations and in the communication systems that we set up within them.

Communication within organisations is not something that is merely done by individuals. The very nature of the communications that occur can be strongly influenced by the context in which they occur. In other words, the working environment can have a great influence on what is said and how it is said. Theories of communication have always been an important part of management theory. As a result, the structures of organisations, or the way that relationships between people are fixed in place, is partly determined by the structure of their communication networks. Hence we cannot think seriously about communicating within an organisation without having some views about the structures of that same organisation.

In the 1990s there is a revolution under way in how we theorise about organisations and in the communication systems we set up within them. This chapter is a survey of the major developments in the field.

MANAGEMENT THEORY AND THE INDUSTRIAL ECONOMY

For most of the twentieth century, theories about how to manage organisations have been strongly influenced by the writings of two men, both Americans: Frederick Taylor and Peter Drucker. Both were theorists of the era when manufacturing industry dominated the economy and both were best known for developing and implementing theories for the management of large industrial corporations. Moreover, both made their names and had their greatest successes in the car manufacturing industry. Taylor is best known for developing the techniques that allowed the mass production of cheap motor cars by Henry Ford in the 1910s; Drucker wrote his first best selling book about his work for General Motors in the 1940s. A crucial aspect of both theories was the way in which management communicated with its industrial workforce.

Under the influence of Taylor, the communication process became entirely top-down, from management, who now had all the knowledge, to employees who did only what they were told by managers, and who had little need to communicate with one another.

TAYLOR ON SCIENTIFIC MANAGEMENT

Frederick W. Taylor's early career was in the steel industry in the late nineteenth century where production was in the hands of artisans who kept the knowledge of their skills to themselves. Taylor observed the range of tasks the artisans performed, then broke each task down into a description of its basic components or smallest movements. Taylor's methods of observation later became known as 'time and motion studies' and his theories were called 'scientific management'.[1] From his descriptions, management was able to determine new ways of performing the job by defining small tasks and engaging unskilled employees who had no knowledge of steel-making apart from the simple movements they were given and which they repeated throughout their shifts. Jobs in steel shifted from being the province of skilled artisans who performed a range of tasks to the work of unskilled workers who each performed a very limited number of small tasks. Hence the communication process became entirely top-down, from management, who now had all the knowledge, to employees who did only what they

1. F. W. Taylor, *The Principles and Methods of Scientific Management*, New York, 1911, Harper & Row, London, 1964

were told by managers, and who had little need to communicate with one another. When Taylor's methods were applied by Henry Ford to the mass production of motor cars, scientific management quickly became enshrined as the dominant method for the rapidly expanding industrial world.

DRUCKER ON MANAGEMENT BY OBJECTIVES

Peter F. Drucker was a management consultant employed by General Motors in Detroit in the 1940s to study the problems managers were experiencing with workers who were employed under the methods Taylor had instituted. By this time, mass production of standardised products had grown to huge proportions and manufacturing firms had developed large bureaucracies that had become subject to inefficiencies and low morale. Drucker focused on issues such as the centralisation and decentralisation of authority, co-ordination of activities between departments and divisions, and the definition of missions and direction. These issues led him eventually to write twenty-four books on management theory and practice between the 1940s and 1980s. All became best sellers and made Drucker the doyen of management theorists in the second half of the twentieth century.

His major theoretical contribution was the concept of 'management by objectives'.[2] He criticised Taylor's methods because their concentration on individual tasks often left the worker with no overall knowledge of how his own performance related to the whole output of the firm. In some factories, for instance, he found some workers who were not even sure what it was they were making. He found similar ignorance of the total picture in a number of the large bureaucracies of US public utilities. Drucker's theories of MBO, as they became familiarly known, stressed the importance to employees of having objectives to work towards. People worked more effectively and produced greater output, he argued, when they knew what they were supposed to accomplish. With clear and shared goals to work towards, people employed in a wide range of activities—from sales, to engineering, to administration—would become more motivated, more responsible for the efficiency and quality of their work, and more self-directing. Even though MBO allowed employees to set their own objectives in some cases, the communication model on which it was based was little different from that of Taylor. It was a top-down model in which management gave virtually all the directions. Management's role was still to define what was to be done and how it was to be done. Under MBO, workers were no longer treated like unthinking robots, but their job was still to take orders without question and to communicate little or nothing themselves to the system.

Under MBO, workers were no longer treated like unthinking robots but their job was still to take orders without question and to communicate little or nothing themselves to the system.

THEORIES OF THE INFORMATION AND SERVICE ECONOMY

By the 1980s, American management techniques had lost their former dominant position. This occurred partly because Japanese manufacturers, who had developed quite different management theories of their own,

2. Peter Drucker, *The Practice of Management*, Harper & Row, New York, 1954; *Managing for Results*, Harper & Row, New York, 1964.

out-performed and outsold their American counterparts. Everyone wanted to know the secrets of the winner's success. But at the same time it became apparent that the economy had moved into a different phase of activity. In most developed countries, employment in manufacturing peaked in the 1960s. Thereafter, manufacturing shrank in importance to be replaced by the service sector and the information industries, as we discussed in Chapter One. The 1980s saw the emergence of post-industrial society and the Information Age.

Management theory of this new era is not, as yet, dominated by individual gurus such as Taylor and Drucker. There are a wide range of ideas and influences that now compete for attention. The two countries that have contributed most have been Sweden and Japan. Both introduced radical new concepts into motor car manufacture in the 1970s and, following that example, they both became pioneers of new ways of managing service industries in the 1980s. The new concepts can be divided into three main areas:

- employee initiatives
- quality
- service

In each case, new theories have involved new structures and new ways of communicating within organisations. Let us summarise developments in each of these three areas.

EMPLOYEE INITIATIVES

Organisations are now being urged to recognise that their continued existence depends less upon the genius of their management and much more upon the continuous origination of employee ideas about how to satisfy existing clientele, find new customers, generate efficiency and reduce costs.

Organisational structure should allow for the origination of ideas. The Japanese were the first to emphasise that most organisations are the site for the generation of huge numbers of ideas about improving the way things are done. Most of these ideas are not solicited; they simply occur to people in the course of doing their job. The problem was that the structure of older organisations did not allow any means for these ideas to be communicated, apart from token gestures such as suggestion boxes which were rarely taken seriously by either managers or employees. A number of firms came to recognise that the only way to tap this resource of ideas was through a much freer organisational structure. Some of the forms that these new structures have taken are the following.

The Japanese were the first to emphasise that most organisations are the site for the generation of huge numbers of ideas about improving the way things are done. Most of these ideas are not solicited; they simply occur to people in the course of doing their job. The issue became: how to tap this resource.

JOB ROTATION

This is one of the simplest forms of organisational restructuring. It means that employees are moved from one division to another on a regular basis to learn how things operate and to add to their range of skills. One familiar form of job rotation is a management trainee program in which new recruits are given a carefully monitored program of job placements in different positions within the organisation. They might spend from six months to one year in one division, then spend a similar period in another, until they have covered all the major divisions within the organisation. At the end, the trainee is promoted to a supervisory position.

Another kind of job rotation occurs with more senior personnel. In order to qualify for promotion, an employee is required to spend a specified time, say from one year to three years, in a front-line position in one of several divisions of the firm. Many companies now use job rotation with two aims in mind: first, to induce people to fill the positions that have greater than normal stress pressures and that, if not subject to rotation, would regularly induce burnout among permanent employees, and, second, to strengthen the pool of their potential middle managers.

JOB ENGINEERING

In most cases, people have to adapt their own skills and abilities to fit the requirements of the job. Under job engineering, however, the organisation adapts the job to fit the skills and abilities of the people available to do it. It is not something that happens as a one-time adjustment but is a continuing activity that changes both as people come and go and as the skills of individuals develop over time. Job engineering requires a critical input from the organisation's personnel department, which needs to provide creative solutions to work with the human resources available.

JOB ENRICHMENT

This is one of the key concepts of the post-industrial era. In direct contrast to the Taylor method of breaking down tasks into small components, job enrichment involves adding tasks and responsibilities to existing jobs. The most famous advocates of this method have been the management of Volvo cars in Sweden. The company replaced the production line, where individuals had previously performed the same routine tasks, with a series of locations at which a team of employees would be responsible for producing either a whole vehicle or major parts of a vehicle. Job enrichment often involves more expense in training but is usually cost-effective in terms of higher levels of productivity, lower turnover of staff and higher quality of work.

CONCEPTUAL SKILLS

While previous management theories have focused on technical skills and behavioural skills, the new methods often emphasise the need to develop the conceptual skills of employees. Conceptual skills involve the ability to understand how one's own activities relate to the changing objectives and strategies of the organisation. In this, the approach is the same as that of management by objectives. However, the new emphasis also includes the need for an employee to make decisions and take actions that further the organisation's objectives. Conceptual skills are therefore not simply an internalised set of motivating principles but a guide to how to act. This assumes, of course, that the organisational structure is one in which employees actually have the ability to make decisions themselves. In many

In direct contrast to the Taylor method of breaking down tasks into small components, job enrichment involves adding tasks and responsibilities to existing jobs.

front-line service positions, this is being recognised as increasingly important. Employees are given a broad range of responsibilities and within this framework are permitted to make their own decisions about how to respond to customers, as long as this accords with the overall strategy.

INVERTED PYRAMID STRUCTURE

The most publicised example of employees being required to exercise conceptual skills occurred at Scandinavian Airlines System (SAS) during the 1980s. A new management team under president Jan Carlzon took over what was in 1980 an unprofitable airline, weighed down by the bureaucracy of its six owners, which included three governments. They transformed what had been a largely local carrier into an operation with a high reputation among international business travellers, and at the same time restored it to profitability.

One of the keys was what Carlzon called an 'inverted pyramid structure'. This structure involved not merely taking advice from front-line staff with direct customer contact about how to improve service, but actually giving those staff the responsibility for devising and delivering the improved service themselves. It placed authority in the hands of the service deliverers to select a course of action that would satisfy their customers. Instead of management developing guidelines on how staff should handle every conceivable situation, then spending much time and money in training staff to internalise the guidelines, SAS gave their employees the right to exercise their own conceptual skills to devise policies and backed them with the finances to bring the policies to fruition. Their freedom to act was given within a framework of a broad, overall strategy about service delivery and operating profits. The inverted pyramid structure worked. It found that, rather than running riot with expenses, employees acted responsibly in devising new services while at the same time containing costs within the company's profit objectives.

The inverted pyramid structure involved not merely taking advice from front-line staff with direct customer contact about how to improve service, but actually giving those staff the responsibility for devising and delivering the improved service themselves.

QUALITY

One of the reasons for the Japanese success in manufacturing in the last twenty years has been the widespread perception that their products are superior in quality to those of the English-speaking countries. This is particularly so in the motor car industry where buyers of low-cost Japanese cars have persistently reported lower levels of defects than in similarly priced products from other countries. Japanese techniques of quality control in manufacturing have now been widely emulated under the concept known as Total Quality Management. These TQM techniques, as they are now known, have also been adapted to the needs of service industries. It is common today to find TQM techniques being advocated in service industries such as hospitality, transport and communications. Techniques of modern quality management include the following.

QUALITY CIRCLES

This is a form of organisation that provides an organised procedure to develop and implement ideas for quality improvement. Small groups of employees from within one department or division meet at regular intervals for sessions devoted to problem-spotting and problem-solving. They discuss problems that are either currently affecting or are likely to affect quality in their own work area or their own job. The group itself both identifies and takes responsibility for applying solutions to the problems it uncovers. In some cases, a quality circle will contain a management representative who can take recommendations for action to the wider management structure. However, this is usually necessary only when the recommendation requires a major financial commitment. In most cases, the quality circle acts as a self-contained unit, responding to and responsible to its own department alone.

In a quality circle, the group itself both identifies and takes responsibility for applying solutions to the problems it uncovers.

QUALITY ASSURANCE TEAMS

Quality assurance teams are usually less self-directed and more management-oriented than quality circles. The role of most quality assurance teams in a service organisation is to inspect the quality of service delivery to customers. They normally have a set of standards or ideal levels of service against which to measure their findings. After their inspection, they usually produce a set of reports or statistics that indicate how each customer contact point measures up against the standard. The reports produced by quality assurance teams are normally distributed both to management and to the personnel at each location that has been inspected. This way, they can not only make their own recommendations but elicit suggestions for improved performance from those in the front line whom they have been measuring.

SELF-AUDITING

Whether or not an organisation measures service by a quality assurance team, it should still ensure that front-line delivery staff and supervisors are clear about the standards upon which they are being evaluated. One device for front-line staff that many organisations have found effective is the use of self-audits or self-audit checklists. These should be carried out on a regular basis and should comprise the same set of standard measurements as would be used by a quality assurance team if it existed. Supervisors and staff can use them to check the service delivery standards at their own location. The aim of this device is to implant the concept of regular checking of quality into the jobs of front-line staff and their supervisors and to hold them accountable for maintaining their own standards. Of course, self-assessment of any kind offers a natural invitation for people to overlook some of their faults and to exaggerate their virtues. To counteract this, some firms link self-audits with the (less frequent) reports of quality assurance teams, and invite the personnel concerned to discuss any inconsistencies that may arise.

The aim of a self-audit is to implant the concept of regular checking of quality into the jobs of front-line staff and their supervisors and to hold them accountable for maintaining their own standards.

SERVICE

Although the service sector is now the largest part of the economy of all Western countries, to many of its customers this sector in the past has been characterised more by lack of service than by its delivery. This is largely due to the historic fact that some of our most common, traditional services have been the province of very large-scale organisations. Any large organisation, by nature, slips easily into a bureaucratic mode in which internal procedures become more important than service delivery and in which the interests of the staff often prevail over those of the customers. Although some of our largest service-delivering bureaucracies, such as the post office, are government instrumentalities, there have been just as many cumbersome and inefficient bureaucracies in the private sector. We notice the public bureaucracies more because, despite our complaints, most survive. In the private sector, they simply lose their clientele and disappear, either by going broke or being bought out. The last few years, however, have seen a new emphasis on service in organisations of all kinds. This has been partly the influence of the TQM methods discussed above, but has also come from a range of theories and techniques recently developed specifically for service industries, including the following.

Karl Albrecht, chairman of the TQS Group and creator of the Total Quality Service model, is one of the leading American writers in the area of service

SERVICE STRATEGY

A service strategy is a written program, available to all in the organisation, that combines the results of surveys of what customers want with the overall objectives and the value system of the organisation. It is a strategy that provides a framework within which ideas can be developed for service delivery. The core of a service strategy is the means by which it is communicated. It has to be communicated to staff on a continual basis to reinforce the need to maintain the standards that it defines. It forms the basis of training programs for new staff. It also needs to be continually communicated to customers, for it constitutes the basis of the organisation's marketing, the generation of new business and the stimulation of repeat business. For both personnel and clientele, it amounts in sum to the total image of the organisation in terms of the standards by which it is known and which it has to live up to.

CUSTOMER SERVICE UNITS

Most service strategies place a great deal of emphasis on measuring customer satisfaction. One of these measures comes from data prepared by a customer service department or an organisation's complaint and inquiry unit. These departments or units provide reports of the number and kind of compliments, inquiries and complaints the organisation receives. Most firms that set up units of this kind also regard them as service delivery points. They normally regard their role in handling complaints as one of turning a complaint into repeat business. If a complaint is handled quickly, directly and without fuss, a complaining client can often be turned into one who is more than satisfied with the response and who is likely to be a returning customer. Hence the measurement of the value of a customer service or complaints department is the service it provides to those who approach it and which leads them to either spread favourable word-of-mouth advertising or to purchase the service again.

The core of a service strategy is the means by which it is communicated. It has to be communicated to staff on a continual basis to reinforce the need to maintain the standards that it defines.

CUSTOMER AUDITS AND TRACKING SYSTEMS

Some customer service units also conduct customer audits and maintain customer satisfaction tracking systems. A customer audit is normally conducted by asking selected clients to audit actual service delivery. A hotel, for example, would ask customers to complete a checklist about the quality of service delivery while they are still on the premises. Some organisations require a sample of clients to provide these audits in return for discounts on accounts or for free services. A customer satisfaction tracking system is normally maintained among clients who have used the service and left the establishment. This involves conducting surveys of a sample of clients on an annual, quarterly or some other regular basis. Surveys can be done by mail or telephone. Some firms offer incentives such as discounts for clients who take the survey. They normally ask how satisfied the client is with the quality of service, what problems have been experienced, whether assistance was sought to answer a query or solve a problem, how many people the customer told about the experience, and whether the client will return. In organisations strongly committed to their service strategy, customer tracking of this kind is often done on a continuous basis.

VISIBLE MANAGEMENT

Another technique sometimes adopted by service-conscious firms is called 'visible management'. This is designed to keep senior management, middle management and back office personnel in contact with clientele. At Disney World in the United States, for example, senior executives spend several days each year performing routine service delivery tasks such as selling tickets or serving food and drinks. This not only keeps managers in touch with customers but it demonstrates to all employees that senior management are committed to maintaining standards of service delivery.

Visible management not only keeps managers in touch with customers but it demonstrates to all employees that senior management are committed to maintaining standards of service delivery

An adaptation of this technique is sometimes called 'management by walking about'. This is simply a process in which managers visit service delivery sites. It can also be called 'field visiting' or 'walking the shop floor'. Its objectives are for front-line staff to see and talk to members of the management team with whom they would not otherwise come into contact. It also helps to provide management with concrete experience for decisions they might have to make about staffing levels, renovations needed and capital expenditure.

All these developments amount to what many management theorists now recognise as the new organisational culture of the 1990s. As we noted in Chapter One, they all depend on organisations paying a great deal of attention to the means by which they communicate with one another. They also mean, as we noted, that in the Information Age the old passive systems of communication are being rapidly eroded. Everyone who is employed today has to become a communicator.

KEY POINTS: Chapter 31 Management theory and communication structures

- For most of the twentieth century, management theory was dominated by the writings of the Americans Frederick Taylor and Peter Drucker. Both developed their ideas within a manufacturing environment and both had a top-down model of communication.

- The 1980s saw the emergence of post-industrial society and the Information Age in which most people worked in service organisations.

- Management theories for the new era have emerged from Sweden and Japan. They have replaced the old top-down model of communication with concepts based on employee initiatives, quality and service.

- Organisations now recognise that their survival depends less on the genius of their management and more upon the origination of ideas from employees in the front line.

- Structures designed to foster employee initiative include job rotation, job engineering, job enrichment and conceptual skills.

- In some service organisations, the top-down model has been replaced by an inverted pyramid.

- Japanese concepts of Total Quality Management include techniques such as quality circles, quality assurance teams and self-auditing.

- New techniques for the delivery of service are derived from TQM methods and include service strategy, customer service units, customer audits and visible management.

- The chief implication of this organisational revolution for the individual is that everyone who is employed today needs to become a communicator.

QUESTIONS FOR DISCUSSION

1. Why does 'scientific management' imply a top-down communications model?

2. Why have ideas and initiatives from employees become more important in an economy dominated by service industries?

3. Discuss the benefits and limitations of the inverted pyramid structure.

4. What is the connection between the renewed emphasis on techniques for quality control and the growing recognition of the importance of customer service?

EXERCISES

Read and summarise the work of one or more of the leading writers in the new fields of Total Quality Management and service management. Some of these authors and their books are listed in Key Texts and Further Reading for Part X, p. 436.

CHAPTER

32

GROUP DECISION-MAKING

After studying this chapter, you will be able to:

- determine when a decision needs group input
- understand the dynamics of small group interaction
- chair a small group meeting
- avoid the problems that often arise when small groups meet

WHY GROUPS SHOULD MAKE DECISIONS

Decision-making meetings are normally held for specific purposes: to make a decision, to solve a problem, to share information or to get something accomplished. Rather than having a regular schedule (like the formal meetings discussed in the next chapter), they are often held at fairly short notice whenever an important issue arises. They are not confined to commerce and industry—any type of organisation can and does hold them. Essentially, they are used to gain collective opinion on the issues involved.

A familiar complaint about meetings is that there are too many of them and they take up too much time. Most of us have seen examples of expensive but ungainly corporate and public buildings which, it is explained, were designed in committee meetings.

A familiar complaint about meetings is that there are too many of them and they take up too much time. Some estimates claim that executives and officers of organisations spend between 60 and 70 per cent of their working hours attending them. Another familiar complaint is that they produce compromise decisions that satisfy no one. Most of us have seen examples of expensive but ungainly corporate and public buildings which, it is explained, were designed in committee meetings. People often complain that policies determined by groups are just as unattractive.

Meetings, however, have become part of our organisational culture for some sound reasons. Decision-making is, on balance, more effective in groups than individually. Research has indicated that ordinary people in groups in many cases make better decisions than brilliant people acting on their own. This is because most groups have a wider range of information and perspectives available to them than do individuals. Most organisational groups are made up of people who are specialists in their own fields. This means they have one perspective that they bring to the meeting. The meeting is the place where specialist expertise and interests merge. Rather than being the scene of weak compromises, meetings should primarily be viewed as the place where knowledge and expertise are pooled for the benefit of all.

Each participant in a meeting has his or her own perspective on the issues raised. By sharing these views, the meeting enlarges the number of possible approaches. More options will be available for consideration. With a variety of perspectives and knowledge, a more critical examination of ideas and proposals can be made. Very often, instead of making a compromise that satisfies no one, a meeting will choose one of the options presented and decide against others. This way, it can both have before it a wide range of possibilities and can choose the most effective path. In other words, rather than ruling out individual brilliance, the meeting is potentially the place where the best products of individual minds are aired and where the best paths from among them may be chosen.

Rather than being the scene of weak compromises, meetings should primarily be viewed as the place where knowledge and expertise are pooled for the benefit of all.

There is also the question of an organisation's commitment to act on decisions taken. This commitment is always likely to be stronger when it is the subject of group deliberation rather than the views of one or two people. A well-organised meeting can be a forum for structured discussion that fosters cohesiveness, improves the relationships between the members of the organisation and provides an opportunity to maximise the involvement of those who take part in deciding the course of action to be followed. Without commitment of this kind, people feel less responsible towards the outcomes of the organisation and bring less energy and enthusiasm to their work.

Of course, as every one who has attended them knows, meetings can also be the source of destructive relationships, petty and needless conflict, patronage and nepotism, as well as the wasting of enormous quantities of time. The effectiveness of meetings depends very much on the ability of those leading and participating in them. The rest of this chapter discusses techniques for maximising the benefits of meetings and minimising their destructive potential.

Meetings can also be the source of destructive relationships, petty and needless conflict, patronage and nepotism, as well as the wasting of enormous quantities of time. The effectiveness of meetings depends very much on the ability of those leading and participating in them.

SMALL GROUP INTERACTION

The first thing to recognise about meetings is that people will have different perspectives on the issues raised and there will be degrees of conflict between these perspectives. A meeting that does not have some conflict has probably not brought out the real views of participants. The test of an effective meeting is the way it handles conflict—whether it turns it to destructive or creative outcomes.

There has been a wide range of research into the way that members of small groups relate and interact with each other. A number of stages of this interaction have been identified as follow.

FAMILIARISATION

If participants in the meeting are not known to each other, they use this stage to get acquainted, to see where each person stands on relevant issues and to size each other up. If members do know each other, it is the issues before the meeting that are the subject of familiarisation. Participants put forward their views on the subject cautiously, hoping to draw others out.

CONFLICT

Once members are confident they have the measure of others, they tend to argue strongly for their own positions, hoping to sway the meeting to their viewpoint. But as each person does this from their own perspective, there is an inevitable conflict when these views clash with those held by others. In some cases, strong disagreements may emerge.

RECONCILIATION

This is the most delicate stage of a meeting which can make or break it. The meeting needs one person or one small group to take responsibility for reconciling the differences and building on the points of agreement. This role is often taken by the chair, but any member of the meeting may do it. It needs to be recognised as a highly political role that will confer leadership status on the person or persons who take it up. It means examining the conflicts to find an area of common ground and to develop that ground in a way that is acceptable to the group. The timing of this stage is often crucial. It must not be taken up too early. The conflict stage must have emerged fully and be somewhat exhausted. At this stage, reconciliation will be welcomed by most participants, but not before. Sometimes, the reconciliation will not be acceptable to a small minority of members. The meeting then has to express its disagreement with them, which it usually does by a formal vote on the issue.

The meeting usually needs one person or one small group to take responsibility for reconciling the differences and building on the points of agreement. This means examining the conflicts to find an area of common ground and to develop that ground in a way that is acceptable to the group.

REINFORCEMENT

At this stage, the meeting accepts that a decision has been made to which all, or nearly all, members are committed. A proposal for further action is now very appropriate. This action should have the agreement of all concerned and should give most some role in bringing it about. This develops commitment and a sense of responsibility which acts to further the unity and cohesiveness of the group.

PROBLEM SOLVING IN GROUPS

The stages of debate during meetings need to respond to the issues of group psychology described above, but they also need to discuss the actual issues involved. Meetings need to ensure that they are not diverted by personality relations and they cover the main areas. The principal points that should be raised are:

Principal points to cover in a small meeting are:
- the nature of the issue
- the dimensions of the issue
- the current approaches to it
- action for the future

1. the nature of the issue, a clear expression of its meaning and limits, an agreement on the definition of its central terms
2. the dimensions of the issue, which means quantifying it in an appropriate way through an acceptable set of measurements—if the issue is a problem that needs to be solved then the incidence of the problem and the number of people affected would be minimum measures to put to the meeting
3. the current approaches to the issue—what, if anything, is currently being done and the philosophies underlying each approach
4. action for the future, which should be the main subject of the group's discussion, even if it is not raised until towards the end of the meeting

Within this framework, it is necessary to recognise a number of other aspects of group decision-making. Some of the decisions taken will be routine, highly structured and based upon mainly technical aspects of the organisation. These are the easiest kind. Others are based on problems that are less structured and in which personal relationships greatly influence the decision-making process. In these cases technical considerations become less important and relationships between people more so.

It is also important for meetings to consider the long-term implications of the solutions they propose. The decisions of one meeting can have effects on the rest of the organisation, sometimes in unintended ways. Co-ordination with other parts of the organisational structure should therefore be an essential aspect of the factors a meeting considers before taking any decision. As well as its own participants' responsibility and commitment, the meeting should also consider the likely commitment of the other members of the organisation.

ROLES OF PARTICIPANTS

People who participate in meetings have their own responsibilities towards their success. Most of these are the normal courtesies we owe to anyone in a public situation, but meetings add some conditions of their own.

Before the meeting, each participant should put in some preparatory work. This should involve familiarisation with the agenda and some research into the items on the agenda. Where research is not practical, the participant should at least think about agenda items and try to formulate an early position. This means that discussion can be on a basis of at least some evidence and reasoning and not simply consist of off-the-top-of-the-head comments that are often irrelevant and which usually waste everyone's time.

At the start of the meeting, the chair should ensure that people know one another. If there are new members to a group that has met before, the chair should announce this, giving a brief background of the new person or persons. If the group is small enough, say up to ten members, the existing members can be personally introduced to the new one. With a large group, only the new member is introduced. Where all the members are new to each other and the group is a modest size, say up to twenty people, it is often very useful to have everyone introduce themselves. This is done by seating everyone facing each other in a circle or semicircle, and, in clockwise order, asking each person to state their name, their relevant background and their reason for attending. These statements should be no more than two or three sentences each.

During the meeting, participants should speak with consideration for the attitudes and feelings of others. They should make their points firmly but not dogmatically. This is in each participant's own interest because they may find they want to adapt or change their views later in the proceedings and it is often hard to modify a position that has been laid down in very absolute terms. It is perfectly acceptable to disagree with others, even in strong language, but the conflict should never be personalised through personal abuse or by ascribing personal motives to others. Other speakers should be heard without interruption—in other words, treat others the way you would like to be treated yourself. Humour may be used to relieve tension for the whole group but not to ridicule or humiliate opponents.

It is perfectly acceptable to disagree with others, even in strong language, but the conflict should never be personalised through personal abuse or by ascribing personal motives to others. Humour may be used to relieve tension for the whole group but not to ridicule or humiliate opponents.

ROLE OF THE CHAIR

The role of the chair is, first, to ensure that the above guidelines for decorum are maintained and, second, to guide the discussion towards achieving the meeting's goals. The act of guidance should not be conceived as one of dominance. In fact, the first thing that will happen should the chair attempt to dominate the meeting is that most participants will freeze up and not contribute to the best of their ability. Rather, the chair should keep track of the arguments and evidence presented and point out to participants where the discussion has been going and where it might be headed. This is best handled by taking the opportunity of summing up the progress of the debate at appropriate times and relating this to the initial question or problem.

The most critical stage in a meeting or in debate on an issue is that situation described in the earlier section when leadership is needed to transform a conflict into an agreement about outcomes. The chair is the key person, though not the only one, in working this transformation and gaining commitment to the decision that the meeting needs to take.

In terms of maintaining decorum, the chair should intervene diplomatically but firmly whenever speakers become irrelevant, long-winded or aggressive. The chair should also keep interjections to a minimum and encourage contributions by some of the more reticent members of the group.

There are two kinds of behaviour that call for intervention by the chair:
- where one person talks too much and tries to monopolise the meeting
- where one person is acting aggressively or unpleasantly to others

Meetings can be subject to a range of negative or obstructive behaviour which both the chair and individual participants should work to correct. There are many forms of objectionable meeting behaviour, but the two main kinds are:

- where one person talks too much and tries to monopolise the meeting—in this case, the chair or other members are entitled to tell that person that he or she has had their say and someone else deserves a turn
- where one person is acting aggressively or unpleasantly to others—this is difficult to handle but one way of disarming such people is to ask them why they are behaving this way

Finally, there are a number of individual responsibilities that participants should take upon themselves to ensure that the meeting realises its potential. The chair needs to provide a lead in these roles but all those attending should take them up. They include the following.

1. *Promotion of discussion* This is primarily achieved when participants proffer information and opinions to which others are stimulated to respond, but it can also include the seeking of information and opinions by asking for evidence and ideas from others in the group.
2. *Summarising* This involves re-ordering the main points made and listing them in ways that show how they are related (or unrelated). It is often a helpful way of proceeding if the discussion has reached a stalemate or deadlock.
3. *Diagnosis* This involves trying to analyse the problems that have emerged within the group, in either its personal relationships or in the way it has defined the subject it is tackling, and seeking to unblock them.
4. *Focus on reality* Sometimes meetings concentrate so intensely on an issue that the real world tends to take second place to the dynamics between group members about the subject matter. Reminding members that their ideas have, in the end, to be practical and workable, and drawing comparisons with real situations can be an extremely useful function to keep the meeting on the rails.
5. *Goal direction* It is sometimes necessary for comments to be made on the progress the meeting is making towards the achievement of the objectives it originally set. Meetings can often be diverted or simply lose sight of their initial goals so, by raising this issue, a member can perform a valuable function.
6. *Release of tension* A hard-working meeting, especially if there is disagreement or conflict involved, can be tense and stressful in ways that impair best results. Tension release mechanisms should be adopted in these cases, including humour about the subject matter (not about

All members should take responsibility for:
- promoting discussion
- summarising
- diagnosing
- focusing on reality
- keeping to the goal
- releasing tension

individual participants), to bring discussion down to earth and, the most simple and effective method, taking a coffee break or another kind of adjournment to allow a cooling off period and a reappraisal.

One last point: a record should be kept of every meeting. This means taking minutes of the major points made (not the fine details) and of decisions reached. Minute taking can be a job for a secretary brought in just for this purpose. Alternatively, the meeting can delegate one of its members to take minutes, or else the chair can take the responsibility. Minutes are always valuable documents for any organisation and care should be taken in both recording them and filing them for future reference.

KEY POINTS: Chapter 32 Group decision-making

- Ordinary people in groups make better decisions than brilliant people acting on their own.
- Rather than being the scene of weak compromises, decision-making meetings are places where the best products of individual minds are aired and the best paths chosen.
- An organisation's commitment to act on a decision is stronger when it has been the subject of group deliberation.
- Petty conflict and time wasting can be avoided if those leading the group understand its dynamics.
- Each meeting, no matter how small, goes through these four stages: familiarisation, conflict, reconciliation and reinforcement.
- To keep to the point, a small group meeting should focus on the nature of the issue at hand, the dimensions of the issue, current approaches to it and action for the future.
- The chair has two roles: first, to ensure that decorum is maintained among participants, and, second, to guide discussion towards achieving the meeting's goals.
- Individual members of the group all have a responsibility to ensure the meeting reaches its potential.
- Minutes should be kept of every meeting, usually by one member appointed by the group.

QUESTIONS FOR DISCUSSION

1. In a small group meeting, what are the most objectionable kinds of behaviour? Why? Give examples from your own experience.
2. Discuss the qualities of a good chair of a small group meeting.
3. What are the responsibilities of individual participants in a small group? Why? Give some examples from your own experience.

EXERCISES

This is an exercise for a classroom group of between five and twenty members. Choose a topic that has been in the news recently. Establish an objective of making a decision about an aspect of this topic. Schedule a meeting of between thirty and sixty minutes on the subject and give participants time to prepare for it. The goal is to reach a consensual decision, that is, one to which all members can have a commitment, not a simple majority. Determine your own method of electing or nominating a chair. As soon as the meeting is over, each member should complete a response form with comments recorded under the following headings.

- participation of individual members of the group
- functioning of the chair
- quality of the decision
- group effectiveness
- group commitment to the decision

Make further comments on the relationships between:

1. participation and commitment to the decision
2. quality of the decision and individual participation
3. role of the chair and group effectiveness

If possible, record the meeting on videotape and, alternatively, make the above comments in light of a replay of the videotape. This will make the meeting a more objective vehicle for participants' judgments and should allow better assessment.

CHAPTER

33

FORMAL MEETINGS

After studying this chapter, you will be able to:

- understand the formal requirements of meetings held by an organisation with a democratic structure
- give notice that a meeting is to be held
- arrange for minutes to be taken
- draw up an agenda for a meeting
- act as chair of a meeting
- accept motions and amendments and take votes on them
- conduct elections for official positions
- maintain order and make rulings

Any organisation that has a democratic structure, such as a club, a society, an association, a trade union or a public company, uses formal meetings as the basis of its major decisions and policy guidelines. The minimum legal requirement for most organisations of this kind is that they hold at least a general meeting once a year but most hold them more frequently, normally once a month. The rules or standing orders that govern these meetings often seem antiquated and unnecessarily rigid. They have, however, evolved over a long period and embody a great deal of human experience in the way that organisations of this kind can hold themselves together, contain conflict and get things done. They deserve to be taken seriously, even if many organisations want to modify and adapt them to their own purposes. In this chapter, we go through the basic principles of conducting a traditional, formal meeting.

Normally, you should give at least one week's notice before a meeting is held. The notice should tell:

- where and when the meeting is to be held
- the agenda
- a contact name, normally the meeting's secretary

GIVING NOTICE OF THE MEETING

The first process involved in a meeting is to inform people that it is to be held. This is giving notice of the meeting. The length of time by which notice must be given is often stated in the organisation's standing orders or constitution but, even if it is not, try to give people at least one week's notice. If they get the document at the last minute, few people will be able to come and, of those that do, few will have had time to properly consider the issues on the agenda, with the result that discussion will be less informed and less relevant than it needs to be.

The notice can be in the form of a letter which says when and where the meeting is to be held. Write in normal style, avoiding archaic phrases such as 'Notice is hereby given ...' and the like.

The notice should also include the agenda. This is the list of items to be discussed at the meeting. The list is in the order in which items will be heard. Some people list only the main items on the agenda:

1. Manager's report
2. Treasurer's report
3. New building project
4. Equipment purchase
5. Election of delegates to regional association

To be more formal, you would list the full agenda, that is, all the business that will be handled, as follows:

1. Apologies for absence
2. Minutes of the previous meeting (attached)
3. Matters arising from the minutes
4. Correspondence
5. Reports
   (a) Manager
   (b) Treasurer
6. New building project
7. Equipment purchase (see attached paper)

8. Election of delegates to regional association
9. General business
10. Date of next meeting

The second version of the agenda mentions two attached papers—the minutes from the previous meeting and a document about the equipment purchase. In some organisations, notices of meeting contain a variety of background papers that inform participants about the matters that the meeting will discuss. In these cases, the notice of meeting should be sent out in plenty of time for participants to read the background papers. Participants, for their part, have a responsibility to read this material before they attend.

All meetings, no matter how routine, should have their proceedings recorded in the form of minutes. This is usually a job for the organisation's secretary. If there is no secretary, ask for volunteers or appoint a participant to do the job.

The minutes of the last meeting are the notes made about the discussion and decisions at that meeting. As the previous chapter emphasised, all meetings, no matter how routine, should have their proceedings recorded in the form of minutes. Every meeting should ensure that someone will take its minutes. This is usually a job for the organisation's secretary. If there is no secretary, ask for volunteers or appoint a participant to do the job. The minutes of the last meeting are often sent out with the notice of the coming meeting. Some organisations hand out the previous minutes as people arrive for the current meeting but this does not leave much time to read over them. It was once the practice for secretaries to spend time laboriously reading out the minutes of the last meeting. But this was a habit developed in the days before cheap means of reproducing documents were available; today it is a waste of time and should be dropped.

Depending on their standing orders, some groups will include copies of the main reports to be delivered with the notice of meeting. They may also present a list of nominees for any elected position to be decided at the meeting and in some cases will provide background information and policy statements from candidates for election. It is also common for important items of general business, including the wording of proposed motions, to be notified before the meeting and, where this is the case, they should also be included in the notice of meeting. If all these requirements are adhered to, it should be recognised that the notice of meeting can become a very thick document and can be expensive to reproduce and mail. Organisations have to strike their own balance between their desire for participants to be well informed before a meeting and the costs involved.

It is also common for important items of general business, including the wording of proposed motions, to be notified before the meeting and, where this is the case, they should also be included in the notice of meeting.

THE MEETING IN PRACTICE

Meetings of some organisations, such as public companies, trade unions and political parties, require participants to show their credentials at the door. This may be a statement of shareholdings, a current financial membership ticket, or a form sent out with the notice of meeting. Where the decision taken will be important, such as the preselection of a political candidate or the election of a board of directors, it is usually important to check credentials to make sure that only those eligible get inside to vote. In most cases, however, checking credentials is not necessary and should be waived.

Any organisation with a democratic structure must use formal meetings as the basis of its major decisions and policy guidelines

The meeting should not start until there is a quorum. This is a fixed number of participants determined by the organisation's constitution or standing orders. Quorums are used to ensure that a small, unrepresentative group cannot take over the meeting (and, in some cases, the whole organisation). They are also a useful basis on which to decide that enough people are in attendance to make the meeting worthwhile. Once there is a quorum present, the chair declares the meeting open and the proceedings begin.

THE AGENDA

If an agenda has already been circulated, the chair raises items as they are listed. The second of the two agendas printed above is a fairly typical example of the working agenda of most formal meetings. Some will wait until the start of the meeting itself to arrange the items on the agenda in a specific order. If a participant wants to change the order of the initial agenda, say, to discuss one item early in the proceedings to make sure it gets a full hearing, then this is the time to do it. If the agenda is not preprinted, it is often helpful at this stage to write it on a board or piece of paper where all can see it.

APOLOGIES

Minutes of the previous meeting should be either circulated beforehand or else available on paper to those who attend.

This is usually the first formal item of business raised. The chair calls for apologies and those who have already submitted them are read out by the secretary. Those attending can also offer late apologies for others. Apologies are made to a meeting partly out of courtesy but mainly because some committees have rules that persistent lack of attendance without apology will make a member ineligible to remain in the group.

MINUTES

As noted earlier, minutes of the previous meeting should be either circulated beforehand or else available on paper to those who attend. This saves the boring task of reading them aloud. The chair normally asks whether the minutes are a correct record of the previous meeting. Unless someone spots a serious typing error or someone else claims the minutes misrepresented their position on some issue, then the chair should simply declare them to be correct and sign them as such. In most cases, the precise accuracy of the minutes is not important and much time can be wasted if people insist on their previous comments being recorded exactly as they made them. It is good practice to only insist on strict rigour in the minutes when there is a controversial issue or an organisational conflict with legal implications.

MATTERS ARISING FROM THE MINUTES

Often a meeting will have some work to be carried over in the interim period. Someone has to take some action, or members have to think about an issue and come back to it next time. Discussion of matters arising from the minutes is the place where these issues are raised. Those delegated to do jobs should report back on them and carry-over business may also be raised at this point. Normally, the chair asks whether there are any matters of this kind and participants answer in the order in which they catch the chair's eye. If there are several items to be discussed which will take some time, the chair might make a list of them, a mini-agenda, and give the meeting the chance to approve some of them without hearing discussion.

In matters arising from the minutes, those who were delegated to do jobs at the previous meeting should report back on them. Carry-over business may also be raised at this point.

CORRESPONDENCE

This is where letters received by the organisation since the last meeting are discussed. They can be circulated as part of the notice of meeting or may be copied and handed out at the meeting. Like the previous meeting's minutes, it is best to avoid taking up the meeting's time by the secretary or chair reading out all correspondence received. Much of it is routine material or junk mail and not worth airing publicly. If it is not possible to copy correspondence, read out only the most important pieces. Because correspondence is discussed early in the meeting, there is often a tendency for some people to dwell on items, making interesting but unnecessary comments. It is up to the chair to keep things moving at this stage. If a piece of correspondence looks like leading to a major debate, it may be a good idea to reschedule it as part of the main items of the agenda. This will allow the meeting to put the matter into perspective with the other major issues before it.

If a piece of correspondence looks like leading to a major debate, it may be a good idea to reschedule it as part of the main items of the agenda.

REPORTS

In the agenda listed earlier, the main reports for the meeting were those of the manager and the treasurer. These are normal reports to meetings of organisations where there is a committee or board with overall responsibility and executive officers who handle day-to-day administration. The committee meetings are the place where the executive reports to the board and so these reports are the main business of the meeting. This arrangement is common in companies, trade unions and voluntary organisations. Another type of report is that from a subcommittee that has been appointed by a previous meeting to investigate a matter or perform a task. In other cases, reports are from delegates the group has appointed to undertake tasks or attend other meetings on its behalf.

Either way, there are some common principles that underlie reports. Important reports should be typed, copied and circulated beforehand, preferably with the notice of meeting. Where this occurs, there is little point in the reporter then reading the document aloud at the meeting itself. Rather, he or she should 'speak to' the report, that is, summarise it or point out its main implications. Where people are reporting back from other meetings they have attended, they should be as objective as possible and report the main resolutions and debates with a minimum of personal commentary. In the case of subcommittees, the meeting has the right to expect a formal report on the subject involved and the subcommittee normally has the right to expect that report to be accepted, provided there are no objections to the subcommittee's interpretation of what it should have done. It is not usually appropriate for the main meeting to object to a subcommittee's recommendation if the subcommittee has done what it was asked to do. In other words, having passed the responsibility over to the subcommittee, the main meeting is obliged to act on its findings unless there are extraordinary reasons not to.

Important reports should be typed, copied and circulated beforehand, preferably with the notice of meeting. Where this occurs, there is little point in the reporter then reading the document aloud at the meeting itself. Rather, he or she should 'speak to' the report, that is, summarise it or point out its main implications.

MAJOR AGENDA ITEMS

These are usually based on motions which are proposals put to the meeting for debate and voting. Once a motion has been voted on and the vote won, the motion becomes a resolution of the meeting. Usually, agenda items of this kind are to authorise the spending of money, to take action of a certain kind or to adopt a certain policy stance, that is, they represent important commitments for both the meeting and the organisation. The mechanisms of motions and resolutions are discussed in more detail in the next section. Some meetings adopt the practice of automatically agreeing with non-contentious issues. They do this by asking the meeting if any items on the agenda are to be 'starred'. Those issues that any participant wants to discuss or debate are named and a star placed beside them on the agenda paper. The meeting resolves to agree to all 'non-starred' items. It then turns to debate those that are starred.

ELECTIONS

Most officers of democratic organisations are elected at annual general meetings. At other meetings, one or two elections may be needed because someone has unexpectedly resigned from a subcommittee or because delegates must be sent to a special conference. The election takes place with the chair calling for nominations. Someone names a participant at the meeting and another person seconds the name. The person named is then asked whether he or she accepts the nomination. If the answer is yes, the chair calls for further nominations. If only one name is put forward, the chair declares that person elected. If there is more than one name, an election has to be held under the rules for elections of the organisation. Notice of an impending election should be given in the notice of meeting.

GENERAL BUSINESS

This is for items not named on the agenda that are generally of less importance than the major agenda items. If an issue is a major one for the group, the person proposing it should not leave it until general business but should inform the chair at the start of the meeting, when the order for the agenda is being discussed. This means that a matter of this kind becomes a major agenda item rather than something sprung on people under the heading of general business. Announcements of coming events that are of interest to the meeting and similar issues are the proper province of general business. If someone raises a really important issue at this time (which some people do because they want to take the meeting by surprise and push through something that would otherwise have difficulties), some chairs will not accept it for discussion and will suggest it be held over until the next meeting.

If someone tries to take the meeting by surprise and raises an important issue without notice under general business, the chair should either reject the item for discussion or hold it over until the next meeting.

DATE OF NEXT MEETING

You should always decide when to have your next meeting before you finish the present one. This gives people a chance to check their diaries and to change a proposed date if it clashes with other existing commitments that too many people have.

MOTIONS, DEBATES AND RESOLUTIONS

MOTIONS

A motion, as noted earlier, is a proposal for some kind of action or for the meeting to adopt a certain attitude on a matter. It is a proposal put up for debate by the meeting. It needs a mover (someone to actually put it forward) and a seconder (another person to endorse it). The mover, therefore, should arrange before the meeting for someone to second the motion and preferably to speak to it as well. Motions that lack a seconder usually lapse.

Motions should be written as succinctly as possible. The gist of the motion should be the proposed action, rather than justification for it. Long-winded motions put people off. In some organisations, motions can only be accepted by a meeting if advance notice of them has been given. Usually, however, there is a provision in these organisations for special urgency motions to be debated if the matter is of a special kind.

Motions should be written as succinctly as possible. The gist of the motion should be the proposed action, rather than justification for it. Long-winded motions put people off.

In large conferences, all the above procedures will be fairly strictly adhered to. In smaller meetings, however, there is usually less formality. A person may raise a point for debate, and only after it has been discussed for some time by the meeting will a motion be formulated and voted on.

AMENDMENTS

An amendment is a modification of the motion. It is a proposal for a slightly different wording or form of action to the original. An amendment also needs a mover and a seconder before the meeting will accept it. The chair should insist that an amendment does not directly contradict the

Normally, amendments should work to improve motions by taking into account perspectives that the mover might have missed. Nonetheless, some opponents are not willing to tackle the mover head on but adopt the tactic of proposing an amendment that has the effect of nullifying the original motion.

original motion because those who oppose a motion should vote against it rather than try to amend it. Nonetheless, some opponents are not willing to tackle the mover head on but adopt the tactic of proposing an amendment that has the effect of nullifying the original motion. Normally, amendments should work to improve motions by taking into account perspectives that the mover might have missed. Amendments are voted on before the vote is taken on the original motion. If there are several amendments to a motion, some of them are likely to overlap by containing points that say the same thing. It is usually up to the chair to sort all this out and to reject some amendments (that is, refuse to put them to the vote) on the grounds of duplication. It is rarely possible to consider and vote on more than two amendments per motion. The chair will suggest that those amendments that are not suitable to put to the vote be withdrawn and, in most cases, their proposers will agree to withdraw.

Politicians make their living out of debating and over centuries have evolved formal procedures to govern what they say and how they say it. Pictured is Prime Minister Paul Keating in the House of Representatives, September 1992

THE ETIQUETTE OF DEBATE

During debate on a motion, the chair decides who has the right to speak. Would-be speakers try to catch the eye of the chair by raising their hands. The chair indicates by gesture who will speak and in what order. It is preferable that people stand while speaking. This is a signal to everyone else that one person 'has the floor' and that no one else should speak at the same time. If the meeting is one where not everyone knows each other, it is a normal courtesy for speakers to start by stating their names and the organisation they belong to. At large meetings, the chair normally reserves the right to set a time limit on individual speeches.

When people are speaking they should not be interrupted or subject to interjections. Of course, as anyone who has listened to parliamentary broadcasts well knows, this rule of debating etiquette is honoured more in the breach than the observance. However, meetings are better for everyone concerned when speakers are heard in silence. The rules of debate of most large organisations provide for interruptions only under specific conditions. This is when someone takes a 'point of order' to draw attention to a breach in the procedure of the meeting, that is, to claim the rules laid down for meetings are not being followed. It is then up to the chair to rule on the point of order, to accept or reject it. Points of order are normally acceptable forms of interruption if the speaker is not addressing the issue of the motion but is rambling onto other unrelated topics, or if the speaker is using 'unparliamentary' or abusive language.

Points of order are normally acceptable forms of interruption if the speaker is not addressing the issue of the motion but is rambling onto other unrelated topics, or if the speaker is using 'unparliamentary' or abusive language.

In a debate on a motion, each speaker is normally allowed to make only one speech. Of course, in smaller, less formal meetings this rule is often waived but for large organisations it is common. The main exception is accorded to the person who moved the initial motion. This person usually speaks first and then, after every one else has made their contributions, the mover has the final right of reply.

TAKING THE VOTE

If there are amendments to a motion, the amendments are put to the vote first. This is usually done by the chair putting it to the voices. For some reason, people see nothing unusual in using archaic terms at this stage of a debate. Most chairs will ask: 'All those in favour say "aye",' to which people will respond with a hearty Old English 'Aye', although these days most say 'No' instead of 'Nay'. If the result is at all unclear from the voices, the chair will request a 'show of hands' and will take a more accurate count of who is for and who is against the amendment. If an amendment is lost, no more is heard about it. If it is won, it becomes incorporated into the original motion. The chair then reads out the final version of the motion and puts it to the vote. In the overwhelming majority of cases, a vote can be decided either on the voices or by a show of hands. In a few special cases, such as elections, a secret ballot is more appropriate.

ROLE OF THE CHAIR

The role of the chair is:

- to maintain order and decorum
- to ensure that all speakers are treated fairly
- to ensure that decisions are made in the proper way
- to keep the meeting moving along without bogging down on one issue

As the accounts of the various stages of meetings make clear, the chair has an important role and considerable power throughout. Basically, the chair is there to maintain order and decorum, to ensure that all speakers are treated fairly, to ensure that decisions are made in the proper way, and to keep the meeting moving along without bogging down on one issue.

KEEPING ORDER

Only one person should speak at a time in a meeting and the chair should ensure that this rule is maintained. The chair should not allow interruptions or interjections, except on points of order described above. By accepting a list of speakers (usually acknowledged by gestures during the debate) the chair ensures that all have a chance to make their points in an orderly

Normally, the chair does not vote on any issue (nor speak for or against any motion) since the chair is supposed to be impartial on all issues before the meeting. If, however, a vote is tied, the chair will make a casting vote which will, of course, decide the issue.

manner. The chair should also intervene to prevent chat among participants which can be very disconcerting to the speaker who has the floor, especially to those not used to speaking in public.

MAKING RULINGS

It is up to the chair to make rulings on whether to accept or reject motions and amendments. Sometimes the chair will reject a motion because it is not relevant to the purpose of the meeting or because it contravenes the standing orders or the constitution of the organisation. The chair will also reject some amendments that are not relevant or that directly contradict the original motion. The chair also makes rulings on whether to allow a point of order or other procedural interventions such as a 'point of information' (a correction of fact to a point made by a speaker in a debate) or a 'personal explanation' that any participant can make if he or she claims to have been misrepresented or maligned unfairly by another speaker.

If someone disagrees with a ruling made by the chair, a participant at the meeting usually has the right to challenge that ruling if there is a seconder for the challenge. In these cases, the chair abdicates the position, the secretary becomes the chair and conducts a vote of the whole meeting on the ruling. British convention is that a two-thirds majority of the meeting is needed to overturn a ruling of the chair. After the vote, the chair resumes his or her position, unless the chair is so affronted by the vote that he or she decides it represents 'no confidence' in the chair and then resigns the position altogether.

CASTING VOTE BY THE CHAIR

Normally, the chair does not vote on any issue (nor speak for or against any motion) since the chair is supposed to be impartial on all issues before the meeting. If, however, a vote is tied, the chair will make a casting vote which will, of course, decide the issue. Some chairs are reluctant to use their casting vote this way, feeling it is undemocratic, and will ask for more debate and another vote by the whole meeting. However, in an important situation, the casting vote is there to be used.

Once a motion has been passed in its original or amended form, it becomes a resolution of the meeting. Theoretically, everyone attending the meeting is committed to all its resolutions, even those who voted against them. In some cases, such as Cabinet or a company board, this concept is maintained and, under the principle of board solidarity, those who disagreed with a decision at the meeting will keep this to themselves and defend the decision publicly. In most cases, however, people who disagree with a point within a meeting continue to disagree outside and, on this point, they act like a 'loyal opposition'.

The role of the secretary is to:

- make preparations for the meeting
- keep the minutes
- handle correspondence and other records

ROLE OF THE SECRETARY

The secretary normally has three main roles to perform.

1. Making preparations for the meeting, in particular compiling the notice of meeting and sending it to participants.

2. Keeping the minutes of the meeting, including noting who attended, who apologised, the major points made in various debates, recording the exact wording of motions and amendments put and lost, election results and other important aspects of the meeting.
3. Answering correspondence, filing correspondence, minutes and other documents, writing any letters required by the meeting, and following up other correspondence.

The secretary is also an adviser to the chair on matters of procedure. The secretary should be familiar with the organisation's constitution and, if it has them, the standing orders or regulations that govern its meetings. It is advisable that, in important meetings, the secretary should keep copies of the constitution and standing orders handy for reference if needed. As noted earlier, if the chair has to stand aside for some reason, the secretary may become chair until that issue is resolved. The secretary, in other words, has a valuable role to play and needs to be well informed about the responsibilities involved in the position.

The task of making preparations for a meeting is another important job that usually falls to the secretary. It is the secretary who books the conference room or hall where it will be held. The secretary chases up the relevant officers to get their background papers and reports for inclusion in the notice of meeting. As well as writing up the minutes of the previous meeting, the secretary makes copies and either sends them out with the notice of meeting or keeps enough copies on hand for distribution at the meeting. It is also advisable to keep enough spare copies of the agenda and major documents for those participants who forget to bring theirs along. Where major reports are to be delivered or guest speakers are to attend, it is the secretary's responsibility to remind these people in advance of the date and venue. Finally, the secretary should arrive at the meeting early, preferably before anyone else, to open the meeting place and make sure its facilities are suitable and that all is prepared. All meetings function better if there is someone to make the effort to get everything ready in advance.

KEY POINTS: Chapter 33 Formal meetings

- Though they may seem antiquated and restrictive, formal meetings have evolved over a long period and embody a great deal of human experience in how to conduct meetings.
- A formal meeting is preceded by a notice of meeting, provided usually one week before the meeting is to be held.
- The notice of meeting should contain at least an agenda.
- It may also contain copies of important reports and correspondence to be discussed at the meeting.
- The normal order of business at a formal meeting is:
  order of agenda
  apologies
  minutes of the previous meeting
  matters arising from the minutes
  correspondence
  reports
  major agenda items
  elections
  general business
  date of next meeting
- A motion is a proposal for action to be taken or a policy decision to be made; it needs a mover and seconder.
- An amendment should modify a motion but not contradict it.
- In ideal conditions, speakers should be heard in silence, interrupted only by formal points of order made to the chair.
- For votes, the chair should call for a show of hands but if the result is at all close, the chair should insist on either a formal count of heads or a secret ballot.
- The role of the chair is to maintain order and decorum and to ensure decisions are taken in the proper way.
- The role of the secretary is to make preparations for the meeting, keep the minutes and handle correspondence.

QUESTIONS FOR DISCUSSION

1. Why should you give notice of a meeting?
2. What should be included in the notice of meeting, and why?
3. What are matters arising from the minutes?
4. Who gives reports to meetings?
5. What qualifies as a major agenda item?
6. What should be conducted under general business?
7. What is a motion and how does it get before the meeting?
8. What is the proper role of an amendment to a motion? What would be an improper role for an amendment?
9. Who can make a point of order and why would one be made?
10. Does the chair speak for or against motions? Does the chair vote on motions?

EXERCISES

This is an exercise for a student group of between five and twenty. Conduct a formal meeting of your group to discuss the nature of your course. You may discuss the communications strand or, if this is part of a wider body of study, the whole course structure. Ensure that the following aspects are covered.

1. Set a date for the meeting.
2. Elect a chair and a secretary.
3. Determine (informally) the main agenda items.
4. Prepare a notice of meeting that includes the agenda.
5. Conduct the meeting according to formal principles.
6. Make resolutions about the course.
7. Elect delegates to communicate resolutions to the appropriate authorities, preferably through personal meetings with them.
8. Conduct a second formal meeting to consider the responses to the initial resolutions..

CHAPTER

34

HUMANISING MEETINGS AND DISCUSSIONS

After studying this chapter, you will be able to:

- adapt the physical setting of a meeting, especially its seating, to suit the nature of the meeting
- appreciate the value of introducing participants
- adopt practices that will foster discussion among even the most reticent participants
- understand the hidden structures that can inhibit group meetings and know how to work to overcome them

The formal practices of meetings described in the previous chapter have evolved in an environment in which one of the main roles of the chair was to preserve order and to contain conflict. Politics has had the most influence on shaping these rules, especially Parliament, where two ostensibly opposite sides sit in the same chamber, but as verbal 'enemies'. Within political parties, faction feuds have often been even more antagonistic than in Parliament itself, and the procedures and rules of meetings have at times been important vehicles through which power has been challenged, won and lost.

Most meetings, however, are not the site of conflicts of the political kind. In most cases, people have mutual rather than antagonistic interests and they want meetings to further those interests. They find some of the traditional formalities either irrelevant or inhibiting. Further, the formal procedures take some time to understand and people new to an organisation can find that they restrict their participation for a considerable period of time. Overall, most kinds of organisations will find they want to modify the formal rules and adapt meeting procedures to be more suitable for their own ends. This chapter looks at how this can be achieved and at the ways that meetings can be made more congenial and more comfortable.

THE PHYSICAL SETTING

The physical setting of a meeting has important effects on the relationships between people. A very large meeting or conference usually has a small table of officials or speakers raised on a platform or stage where they can be seen. They face a large number of people who are looking not at each other but at the centre stage. This is a situation in which the chair and other officials have a great deal of control over the proceedings, and the seating reflects this. The more equal people want their relationships at a meeting to be, the more they will sit on the same level and the more they will face each other. Although some community groups have regarded themselves as radical for rearranging the chairs at the meetings in a circle, this practice is actually centuries old. The 'knights of the round table' is one well-known example of a meeting of equals and many other ancient cultures make distinctions between circular and front-facing meetings.

The more equal people want their relationships at a meeting to be, the more they will sit on the same level and the more they will face each other.

Seating arrangements both affect relationships and reflect them. The more relaxed and uninhibiting you want a meeting to be, the more you should choose to arrange your chairs in ways that make everyone equal. In this position, the chair becomes a servant of the meeting rather than its controller. You may want tables for people to write on for convenience but, if you do, you should recognise that this will place something of a physical and visual barrier between people. There is a trade-off to be made here between the most open physical setting and one that allows people a facility to take notes. Make the choice after considering the kind of meeting it will be and the relationships you want to foster.

The appearance of the meeting room or hall also makes an important contribution to any meeting. Lighting, decor and factors such as the hardness and softness of seating can have an impact on the degree of concentration participants pay to speakers and on the degree of alertness they bring to their deliberation. If the meeting is on your own premises, you can tailor meeting rooms to suit the personality of the organisation. Styles of decor that reflect fast-paced modernism, rock-solid conservatism or practical utilitarianism are not difficult to achieve. If you are using someone else's premises, you can still go some of the way towards creating an appropriate environment through items such as banners, posters, flowers and utensils.

Refreshments are also a factor to consider. Iced water in quality glassware placed on tables for all participants can be a minor luxury that many people appreciate. Tea or coffee served between one and a half and two hours after a meeting starts can be a refresher that gives new life to people's attention spans and learning curves. Providing alcohol is usually a bad idea as it makes some people talkative and argumentative, and puts others to sleep. Save the grog until the meeting is over.

If it is relevant to the purpose or operation of the meeting, participants can introduce themselves by describing in a few words their reasons for being there, their interests, special expertise or whatever. In large groups such as conferences, people normally wear name tags.

INTRODUCING PARTICIPANTS

If the meeting is relatively small, it will function better if all members are introduced to one another. If people are meeting for the first time or if a reasonable number of new people are present, take the time for everyone to introduce themselves to the whole meeting by name and by title or some other identifying label. At large conferences, participants normally wear name tags. This is a good idea even for small groups where most people are not known to each other.

If it is relevant to the purpose or operation of the meeting, participants can introduce themselves by describing in a few words their reasons for being there, their interests, special expertise or whatever. Even shy people can usually handle this kind of introduction and it is a good way to break the ice and prepare for more fruitful discussions later. If a group has been meeting for some time but on one occasion there is a new member present, the chair should make a point of welcoming the new person and of describing some of his or her background.

PROMOTING PARTICIPATION

INDIVIDUAL RESPONSIBILITY

A good contribution is responsive to the opinions of others at the meeting and relates to the points they make.

To a large extent, the degree of participation and the level of contribution that individuals make to a meeting depends largely on them. No amount of environment-setting or motivation can promote participation if people are not willing to put in the effort. Members make real contributions to meetings when they prepare well in advance by researching the subjects on the agenda and having meaningful opinions about them, rather than simply talking off the top of their heads on the spur of the moment. There is, however, a balance to be struck here. One of the worst, and one of the most familiar, members of a meeting is the person who comes with a prepared speech, either written or memorised, who delivers it and takes no account of what anyone else has said. These set pieces are very common in political meetings but, because they do not engage anyone in discussion or debate, they usually end up being a waste of time for both meeting and speaker alike. A good contribution is responsive to the opinions of others at the meeting and relates to the points they make.

ROLE OF THE CHAIR

The second most important factor is the way the chair performs. A chair can be too strong or too weak. A strong chair will dominate the proceedings and thereby stifle them. The chair who sees it as his or her responsibility to do most of the talking is abusing the power the position naturally confers. Others will feel reluctant to contribute. A nervous chair can also be a dominating one. Some who are unsure of themselves feel the slightest gap in discussion as an embarrassing silence and they fill it with their own voice rather than waiting to see if others will use the opportunity to make a contribution to the meeting. Weak chairs also permit the loudest voices and the biggest egos to dominate proceedings, and this can be as bad as a dominating chair.

SMALL GROUPS

As a general rule, the smaller the group, the greater the level of individual contributions. If fostering participation is a major aim of the meeting, one tactic frequently adopted is for a large meeting to break into small groups for particular discussions. Within a group of five or six people, everyone can be invited to have his or her own say. Once the members of the various groups have shared their views or arrived at their decisions, they then come together again and each group reports to a 'plenary' of the whole meeting.

If fostering participation is a major aim of the meeting then one tactic frequently adopted is for a large meeting to break into small groups for particular discussions. Within a group of five or six people, everyone can be invited to have his or her own say.

It is easy to overdo the small group tactic, though. Very often, the groups duplicate each other's efforts. Members of each group also miss out on the discussions that go on in the other groups. Overall, the small groups may actually make fewer or less advanced decisions than the meeting as a whole would have. For a meeting of twenty people to break into four groups can often be a waste of time. The objective of maximising participation, it should be recognised, may not be the best one for the meeting to pursue. Again, a balance of judgment is needed here to weigh the advantages of high participation against the costs of effective decision-making.

SHARING TASKS

One of the best ways to increase participation is to give people tasks to perform. People become much more involved in an organisation when they feel some degree of responsibility for its success. A group that divides its tasks, no matter how menial, among all its members will be better for it. As an example of job-sharing, for instance, three of the tasks of the secretary—recording the minutes, generating and answering correspondence, and preparing the notice of next meeting—may be split among three people. When a meeting passes a resolution, it may decide to give the mover and perhaps the seconder the responsibility of following up the action called for. This is not only a good way of generating participation, it also makes people consider their motions from both a more serious and a more practical perspective.

A group that divides its tasks, no matter how menial, among all its members will be better for it.

A number of organisations, faced with some people occupying the key positions year after year and thereby dominating and inhibiting their operation, have introduced systems of rotating the positions.

ROTATING POSITIONS

A number of organisations, faced with some people occupying the key positions year after year and thereby dominating and inhibiting their operation, have introduced systems of rotating the positions. The most important job is that of chair. Some believe that the chair requires a certain kind of personality or energy that not everyone has but, in most cases where job rotation has been tried, it has been found that people usually rise to the task. Obviously, not all chairs perform equally successfully. In general, however, the organisation itself performs better when the positions are shared around and what it loses in individual performance it more than makes up from the overall boost to morale and the gain in total experience. The normal periods of tenure for each position under a rotation scheme are either six months or one year. Anything longer and the impact of the reform is rapidly diluted.

The positions of secretary and treasurer also benefit from rotation. Both involve more hard work and less appreciation than the chair and rotation is justified simply because it is fair that the onerous tasks should be shared around. Some members will claim they are unfit for these positions because they cannot type or because they don't understand anything about keeping books. However, taking on these jobs should be regarded as a good opportunity for people like this to learn by doing. Any group is strengthened when the skills needed for its operation are distributed widely throughout its membership.

HIDDEN STRUCTURES

The abandonment of formal structures often means that informal or hidden structures take their place and, in fact, become much harder to regulate because they are below the surface. Non-structured relationships can quickly become dominated by those with the strongest wills and the loudest voices.

One of the temptations for groups who want to humanise their meetings and get away from formal procedures is to abandon procedures, positions and structures altogether. They can then, they believe, simply relate as human beings and make genuinely collective and egalitarian decisions. Over the past decade, however, the experience of a number of organisations who have tried this has been that good intentions are not enough. The abandonment of formal structures often meant that informal or hidden structures took their place and, in fact, became much harder to regulate because they were below the surface. For example, some women's groups and environmentalist groups, whose philosophies were strongly anti-authoritarian, found that non-structured relationships quickly became dominated by those with the strongest wills and the loudest voices. Those members whose principles made them unwilling to join in the competition to make themselves heard found they lacked the means to put forward views that ran counter to the most vocal of their colleagues. There was no chair to whom they could appeal for equal time and no ground rules to limit or share out discussion time. Many simply dropped out, disillusioned and cynical.

One of the reasons that the archaic forms and language of traditional meetings procedure have lasted so long is that they are a response to the kind of problems that will arise in any form of human relationship. They confronted the issues of the dominance of personalities and loud voices, as well as a great many other potential problems within meetings, long ago.

Although their language may be out of date, many of the principles enshrined within formal procedures are universal and represent some of the accumulated wisdom of the species.

All this does not mean that attempts to humanise meetings by reducing their formality are doomed. Rather, people making the effort should recognise what they are up against and act accordingly. They should work to retain the most useful aspects of formal procedures while adapting them to their own needs and adding their own brand of informality. Once again, the exercise should be regarded as a balancing act—trading off a few losses in order to make the maximum gain.

Although their language may be out of date, many of the principles enshrined within formal procedures are universal and represent some of the accumulated wisdom of the species.

KEY POINTS: Chapter 34 Humanising meetings and discussions

- A physical setting can have an important effect on relationships between people.
- Small meetings normally dispense with a platform and chairs facing the front. Instead, participants sit at the same level and their chairs face each other.
- Small meetings function better if people know one another. Initial introductions are therefore very important.
- Individual participants should prepare for even a small meeting, but not to the point of bringing a prepared speech and reading it out.
- The chair of a small meeting needs to strike a balance between doing too much talking and giving free rein to those with big egos and loud voices.
- Medium to large groups often find it useful to break into smaller groups to focus on specific issues.
- Sharing tasks, such as taking minutes or preparing for the next meeting, is a good way to promote participation.
- Rotating positions, especially that of the chair, can prevent some people from dominating and inhibiting the operation of a group.
- Abandoning all formal structures often means that hidden structures take their place, with the loudest voices and strongest wills taking over at the expense of the rest.

QUESTIONS FOR DISCUSSION

1. How does a physical setting, such as placing chairs at the same level facing each other, affect the relationships between people at a meeting? Describe other kinds of chair arrangements and the relationships they would promote.

2. Discuss the role of the chair of a small group with which you are familiar.

3. If you have had experience of meetings which have broken into small groups, discuss both the advantages and disadvantages of this approach to humanising meetings.

4. What are the advantages and disadvantages of rotating the positions of chair and secretary of a meeting which convenes on a regular basis?

5. What are the consequences of abandoning all formal structures of meetings? Discuss any small group with which you are familiar.

EXERCISES

Arrange a series of small group meetings to discuss and perhaps reform the course you are presently undertaking. Arrange the physical setting and make introductions in ways that will encourage everyone to have an equal voice. Rotate the chair and other responsibilities at different meetings. Write a description of this series of meetings with a focus on the effects of the directions given here.

CHAPTER

35

WRITING OBJECTIVES, TERMS AND POLICIES

After studying this chapter, you will be able to:

- define the objectives of an organisation and write them down in clear prose
- write a mission statement for an organisation
- write a statement of philosophy
- write a set of terms of reference to govern an inquiry or a newly formed group
- define and write policies for the activities of an organisation
- write procedures to accompany these policies

Most organisations at some time in their lives find they need to define and publish a set of objectives or a series of policies and procedures. Objectives can range from a simple set of goals written down by a small team to help focus its attention on a task in front of it, to an organisation's mission statement that provides a very broad set of objectives to be pursued over the long term. Policies and procedures amount to a set of rules that can be consulted by anyone in an organisation about how to proceed in a particular situation.

A variation on the same theme is a set of terms and references. If an organisation sets up an inquiry or a new group to undertake a particular role, it may define their terms and references so that the members will know what they can and cannot do.

Objectives, policies, terms and references appear to cover a great deal of ground and to be appropriate to quite different circumstances. This is true, but the main point this chapter wants to make is that, when it comes to defining and writing them, their authors should ensure that they pursue a number of essential and common elements.

DEFINING OBJECTIVES

Defining objectives:
- First, indicate who, apart from yourself, will benefit from what you intend to do.
- Second, give a clear idea of how you intend to actually perform the task.

At its most basic, a set of objectives is a statement of what you intend to do. However, because nothing can be done in a vacuum, any set of objectives needs two more essential components. First, you should always indicate who, apart from yourself, will benefit from what you intend to do. Second, you should give a clear idea of how you intend to actually perform the task before you. Let us state this in point form to make it a little more memorable. A set of objectives should always encompass at least:

1. what you intend to accomplish
2. who will be the target of your activities
3. how you will achieve the outcome

The degree of emphasis given to each of these three will vary considerably. In some cases, say, when an organisation targets a new market segment for its products, the 'who' will need to be spelt out in considerable detail. But in others, say in defining the objectives of a subject to be taught as part of an educational program, the 'who' can be given a minimal mention because the context makes it obvious that you are talking about students. The same is true of the 'how'—in some cases it will be so obvious that it deserves only passing reference, but in others, such as when you are introducing a new method of proceeding, it may be important to dwell on it.

Let us now introduce the most important set of questions that you need to consider when making any of the definitions discussed in this chapter.

Who? What? When? Where? Why? and *How?*

These are the standard questions that need to be posed in any form of inquiry. They are, for example, taught to journalists as the basic questions to ask when researching any story, and they provide the guidelines for historians to pursue when trying to explain any event.

In the definitions discussed in this chapter, they provide a range to *consider* but not necessarily to answer in all cases. In the case of defining objectives, the most important questions to ask are *who? what?* and *how?* In many cases, the *when? where?* and *why?* will be so obvious that they are not worth saying at all. For instance, if an organisation has only one location, the 'where' becomes redundant. Nonetheless, anyone writing a set of objectives should at least go through the ritual of considering whether all these questions need to be answered.

Useful tip When writing objectives or mission statements, it is always very helpful to see an example of the way someone else has attempted a similar task. Try to get hold of a set of objectives written by one of your predecessors, or even one of your competitors, and then build on their work by applying it to your own situation.

MISSION STATEMENT

A mission statement is a set of objectives, very broad and long-term as noted above, which is intended to do three things:

- to provide a framework which will guide the behaviour of management and staff
- to set standards by which the organisation can judge its progress
- to provide a source from which other, more immediate objectives can be derived

A mission statement is normally, however, a set of worthy principles rather than a collection of direct goals from which everything else can be directly deduced. It should be treated with respect, but few members of the organisation will take it literally all the time. The most valuable role a mission statement can perform is to bring an organisation back onto the rails from which it might have strayed. The history of the 1980s is littered with numerous corporate casualties who diversified in often weird and ultimately damaging ways. In many of these cases, a mission statement, had it existed, might have been the means through which those responsible were hauled up and asked to justify how their actions were contributing to longer-term objectives.

Mission statement:
- write in simple, direct and succinct prose
- start by defining the value the organisation will provide to its principal clientele
- without being too specific, state what it will do to serve this clientele—focus on action
- explain broadly how it will accomplish its goals

Like other objectives, a mission statement should focus primarily on the *who, what* and *how*. The most useful question to ask when formulating a mission statement is *who*. Ensuring that your clientele take a prominent place within a mission statement is probably the single most useful principle you can enshrine in the document. Focus on how you will serve your clients and then state what you will do to bring this about.

A mission statement should be written and published. Guidelines for its composition include the following.

- It should be written in simple, direct prose and should avoid vague abstractions.
- It should be as brief as is reasonable.
- It should start by defining the value the organisation will provide to its principal clientele.

> **MISSION STATEMENT**
>
> **AUSTRALIAN BROADCASTING CORPORATION**
>
> The Australian Broadcasting Corporation Act 1983 requires the ABC to:
>
> - provide within Australia innovative and comprehensive radio and television services of a high standard
> - provide programs that contribute to a sense of national identity, inform and entertain, and reflect the cultural diversity of the Australian community
> - provide radio and television programs of an educational nature
> - promote Australia's musical, dramatic and other performing arts
> - transmit to other countries radio and television programs of news, current affairs, entertainment and cultural enrichment.
>
> *Source:* Australian Broadcasting Corporation, *Annual Report 1990/1991*

- Without being too specific, it should state what it will do to serve this clientele—in other words, it should focus on action.
- Again without being too specific, the statement should explain how it will accomplish its goals.

STATEMENT OF PHILOSOPHY

Some organisations are required to back a set of objectives or a mission statement with an explanation of their philosophy. A statement of philosophy can often be difficult to produce—people may understand intuitively their philosophies but will still have difficulty in articulating them. When trying to write them, many slip into the tendency to utter a number of worthy sentiments and leave it at that. But if these sentiments are so conventional that no one would disagree with them or are so bland that they commit the organisation to very little, there is little point in undertaking the exercise at all.

There are two points of reference for a statement of philosophy. The first is the mission statement itself. The broad objectives of *who, what* and *how* can be supplemented by an expression of what the authors determine are the *dominant values* they want to see adopted by all within the organisation. The second could well be an opposition or competitive organisation. If you are operating within a competitive environment in which there are some practices of which you disapprove, a statement of philosophy can be a useful opportunity to distinguish yourself from your opponents. This does not mean that you can adopt such a definition only when there is corruption or malpractice abroad. You might want to say, for instance, that your values are customer-oriented rather than staff-oriented, or that your

MISSION STATEMENT

UNIVERSITY OF QUEENSLAND

The University of Queensland is a major Australian University with international standing in many fields. Its mission is to:

- maintain its position as the leading provider in Queensland, and one of the leading providers in Australia of higher education in a wide range of professional, scientific and cultural disciplines
- promote the extension of knowledge through research, and the preservation and evaluation of knowledge through scholarship of the highest international standard
- transmit knowledge through excellence in teaching and publication
- produce high quality graduates who are well equipped to meet the professional needs and the scientific, technological, economic, and cultural and social challenges of Queensland and the wider Australian community
- foster interaction between the University and the community in order to facilitate the application, exploitation and transfer of University scholarship for the benefit of the nation
- provide a leadership role in the cultural and intellectual life of the Australian community by encouraging objective critical assessment of current ideas and beliefs.

Source: University of Queensland, *Calendar 1991*

front-line staff are your most valuable employees. In the first version you send a message to staff about what should be their priorities; in the second, you send a similar message to management. Like a mission statement, the way you write your statement of philosophy is important. Avoid abstract terms, try to eliminate ambiguities and write simply and briefly.

TERMS OF REFERENCE

The first thing the members of any government inquiry normally do when they are given a set of terms of reference is to sit down together to interpret them. They then produce a document of their own explaining to themselves the meaning and limits of each of the terms. In most cases, they need to do this because the politicians who have drafted the terms have left them in a vague and abstract state.

There is a long a tradition in Australian politics that regards this way of operating as the norm; few other organisations, however, can afford such a luxury. If they give a group of people a set of terms of reference to follow, they should expect the group to do just what it is asked to do and not to set a different agenda of its own. The moral of all this is: write terms of reference in simple, direct and clear English and be particularly precise about dimensions. For instance, if you want someone to investigate the kinds of jobs young people gain after they leave school, spell out the precise age groups you want, or the precise period after they have left school—'eighteen-and nineteen-year-olds' rather than 'recent school leavers'; 'within six months of completing Year 12' rather than 'soon after they leave school'.

Apart from being as clear and precise as possible, terms of reference should fulfil the same role as the objectives of an organisation. The people who define terms of reference for an inquiry are really setting the objectives for the inquiry. So the principles discussed above prevail here as well, though usually in finer detail.

Most terms of reference will answer the following.

Terms of reference should fulfil the same role as the objectives of an organisation. They should state:
1. what you intend to accomplish
2. who will be the target of your activities
3. how you will achieve the outcome

Who? The name or a precise description of the clientele or the target group of people concerned

What? An open inquiry, an in-house investigation, a brief to set up a new department or to take over from an existing committee, or the like

When? Precise date to start and absolute deadline to finish

Where? The precise geographic scope of the study

Why? The reasons that led the commissioning body to appoint the group

How? An inquiry taking verbal evidence; a sample survey; a piece of historical research or the like

TERMS OF REFERENCE

YOUNG PEOPLE'S PARTICIPATION IN EDUCATION AND TRAINING

Having regard to the findings of previous relevant studies and reviews, and having regard to current reviews and working parties and initiatives being implemented in each of the States and Territories, to report to the Australian Education Council and to Ministers of Vocational Education, Employment and Training on the future development of post-compulsory education and training in Australia, with particular reference to those young people who have left school and are not participating in a formal education or training program. The Review would consider:

a. the appropriate form and level of a new national target for participation in post-compulsory education and training, an appropriate

continued on next page

continued from previous page

basis of measurement of that target, and a recommended time-table and strategies for its achievement;

b. appropriate national curriculum principles designed to enable all young people, including those with special needs, to develop key competencies, with the associated implications for curriculum development, initial teacher preparation and continuing professional development;

c. the means by which links can be drawn between different education and training pathways and sectors to expand the options available to all young people, including those with special needs, and to achieve national coherence in entry and exit points between education, training and employment;

d. the appropriate roles and responsibilities of schools, TAFE and higher education in the provision of post-compulsory education and training for young people consistent with the principles and objectives identified in (b) and (c) above, and the roles of private and industry providers;

e. current barriers to the effective participation of disadvantaged young people, including those with disabilities, in post-compulsory education and training, and strategies for increasing their participation and improving their educational and labour market outcomes;

f. the implications of current and prospective changes in post-compulsory education and training for the provision of careers education, information and counselling to students, including the requirements for information on educational pathways and associated career paths; and

g. the likely resource and funding implications of existing trends in, and further strategies for, post-compulsory education and training.

Source: Report of the Australian Education Council Review Committee on *Young People's Participation in Post-compulsory Education and Training*, AGPS, Canberra, July 1991

TERMS OF REFERENCE

ABORIGINAL EMPLOYMENT AND TRAINING PROGRAMS

Having regard to:

- the Government's objectives to increase the number of Aborigines employed; to raise the level of skills of the Aboriginal community; and, to broaden the range of occupation in which Aborigines are employed;
- the current levels of Aboriginal unemployment and those likely to apply in the foreseeable future;
- the needs and demands of the Aboriginal community;
- the need to provide an integrated and comprehensive set of programs for Aborigines maximising cost-effectiveness and minimising overlap;
- the need for continuing restraint in the growth of public expenditure;
- the desire of the Government and Aboriginal organisations for maximum Aboriginal management of their own affairs;

assess whether the existing Commonwealth funded Aboriginal employment and training programs meet the Government's objectives and make recommendations for changes as and when required.

The Review should in particular:

- examine the objectives, cost-effectiveness, delivery and impact of existing programs specifically directed at providing employment and training for Aborigines [other than the Community Employment Program (CEP) which has only recently been initiated];
- assess the adequacy of the existing balance of employment and training opportunities provided to Aborigines in the private, public and community sectors having regard to the varying needs of different Aboriginal communities, including the needs of Aboriginal women;
- consider the adequacy of existing arrangements for the co-ordination of program activity for Aborigines (including the CEP) and means for better integrating such programs; and
- assess the outcomes of the National Employment Strategy for Aboriginals.

Source: Report of the Committee of Review, *Aboriginal Employment and Training Programs*, AGPS, Canberra, 1985

POLICIES AND PROCEDURES

In the past, documents specifying policies and procedures were a common feature of large bureaucracies. Some managers thought that the way to run a large department, especially one which had a large clientele with a range of different demands, was to prepare a policies and procedures manual. This handbook would be given to employees and contained a description of all the situations that could conceivably arise and all the questions that could conceivably be asked, and the appropriate response that staff were supposed to give to each one. On this line of thinking, the policies and procedures manual became the central tool of staff training and the central reference point for all activity. Training new staff consisted primarily in giving them exercises that would help them to remember the details of the manual.

This whole approach, however, generated four major problems.

1. In any large and complex operation, the manuals took a great deal of time to write and to revise—sometimes years. By the time they were finished, many of the situations they described were no longer relevant and the responses they advocated were out of date. The world did not stand still waiting for the manual to be finished.
2. No matter how ingenious were the committees who drew up these manuals, clients always managed to find exceptions to the rules. It became apparent that the range of human activities would always remain too variable to be confined to handbook descriptions.
3. The manual became an excuse for bureaucratic inflexibility. Because there were so many exceptions, front-line staff could tell clients that their particular requests or needs didn't fit the rules and there was nothing that could be done for them. This helped generate an arrogance among some staff towards the clientele, but also fostered inertia. Lazy staff could hide behind the manual's prescriptions and do as little as possible.
4. The older the bureaucracy, the larger grew its manual. Some reached the point where there was no one on staff who knew all the contents. These voluminous manuals were increasingly left unread, even by management personnel.

Problems with policies and procedures manuals:
- by the time they are written they are out of date
- client behaviour is too variable to comprehensively describe
- the manual can become an excuse for bureaucratic inflexibility, arrogance and inertia
- some become so large that no one can read them all

Solution:
- give front-line staff broad guidelines of customer service and trust their intelligence and sensitivity

As we noted in Chapter Thirty-One, the 1980s produced some powerful models of alternative approaches to the relationship between front-line staff and clientele. At Scandinavian Airlines System, the old bureaucracy and its policies were replaced by an approach that gave front-line staff a great deal of flexibility to decide themselves the best way of handling the enormous number of variable problems that customers present when travelling by air. The new model provided staff with broad objectives defined in terms of customer service and satisfaction, but left the fine detail to the intelligence and sensitivity of front-line staff themselves, with enormously improved results.

Today, those forward-looking organisations that still use policies and procedures documents limit their scope to a narrow range of critical issues.

In client relations, these are often restricted to matters dealing with the extension of credit and payment of bills. In staff relations they are confined to wages and conditions, promotions, occupational health and safety, and equal employment opportunity issues. For people writing policies and procedures in these areas, the following guidelines should be observed.

Policies

A policy resembles an objective, and in many cases, is little more than a detailed and more concrete version of one aspect of a broad objective. For example:

Objective	To foster a recognition of the importance of occupational health and safety among staff.
Policies	Ergonomic chairs are to be used by all computer operators; no smoking is permitted inside the building.

Procedures

A procedure is a guide to action that explains how a policy is to be interpreted in a real-life situation. For example:

Policy	All new staff positions are to be filled after being openly advertised.
Procedure	Positions for training personnel should be advertised in the Employment section of the Saturday edition of the *Sydney Morning Herald* and in the Higher Education Supplement of Wednesday's edition of the *Australian*.
Policy	Students are not to be absent without notice and without a satisfactory explanation.
Procedure	An absent student must telephone the administration office before 9 am on the day concerned; when the student returns after the absence he or she has to complete an absentee form in the Bursar's office and accompany it with either a medical certificate or a letter of explanation from a parent or guardian.

As we noted above, policies and procedures should be as narrowly defined as possible and should provide guidelines for as small a part of the organisation's operations as makes sense. This approach should ensure that they are as brief and succinct as possible—one or two pages is much better than three or four. Any organisation is looking for trouble if it feels it needs to produce something the size of a small handbook.

The principle to follow in writing is the same as that of objectives: answer the *who, what, when, where, why*, and *how* questions. Since policies are similar to objectives, they can usually be described in terms of *who, what*, and *how*. Since procedures are more action-oriented, they normally require answers to all six of these questions. Procedures resemble terms of reference and should be written with the same guidelines in mind: simple and direct English, concrete rather than abstract words and precise numbers, dates and dimensions.

KEY POINTS: Chapter 35 Writing objectives, terms and policies

- Objectives should be defined as what you intend to accomplish, who will be the target of your activities, and how you will achieve the outcome.
- The standard questions of any system of inquiry: *who, what, when, where, why* and *how* should be asked when writing objectives, with an emphasis on the *who, what,* and *how*.
- A mission statement is written to provide a framework that will guide the behaviour of management and staff, to set standards by which the organisation can judge its progress, and to provide a source from which other more immediate objectives can be derived.
- A statement of philosophy is similar to a mission statement but it adds a description of the dominant values that prevail within an organisation.
- Terms of reference are written in a similar way to objectives, with a focus on what the inquiry or group is required to accomplish, who will be its target, and how it will achieve its outcome.
- Policies and procedures manuals these days are avoided by forward-looking organisations. In those areas where they are essential, they should be brief, to the point and expressed in concrete language and precise terms.

QUESTIONS FOR DISCUSSION

1. What is the relationship between a mission statement and a statement of philosophy?
2. What are the differences between objectives and policies?
3. What is the relationship between terms of references and procedures?
4. Why are progressive organisations abandoning the use of policies and procedures manuals?

EXERCISES

1. Look up the mission statement or a statement of the philosophy of an education institution with which you are familiar (these statements are usually published in the Calendar or the Prospectus). Point out passages in either statement that could be improved. Present your own rewritten version of these passages.

2. Look at some of the rules and regulations or policies and procedures of an educational institution with which you are familiar. Critically analyse the document, pointing out obsolete or irrelevant conditions, if any. Rewrite one or more pages of the document, putting its prose into more succinct and precise language.

3. Choose an example of an activity that recurs over a long period, say a year (such as attendance at an education institution or annual holidays). Define and write the policy that currently prevails about it.

4. Think of an activity that you have to perform in education or at work on most days of the week. Write a set of procedures so that someone unfamiliar with this activity would know what to do.

REVISION LIST FOR PART X

COMMUNICATING IN THE ORGANISATION

- The 1980s witnessed the emergence of post-industrial society and the Information Age in which most people worked in service organisations.
- Management theories for the new era have emerged from Sweden and Japan. They have replaced the old top-down model of communication with concepts based on employee initiatives, quality and service.
- Organisations now recognise that their survival depends less on the genius of their management and more upon the origination of ideas from employees in the front line.
- Structures designed to foster employee initiative include job rotation, job engineering, job enrichment and conceptual skills.
- Japanese concepts of Total Quality Management include techniques such as quality circles, quality assurance teams and self-auditing.
- New techniques for the delivery of service are derived from TQM methods and include service strategy, customer service units, customer audits and visible management.
- The chief implication of this organisational revolution for the individual is that everyone who is employed today needs to become a communicator.
- Ordinary people in groups make better decisions than brilliant people acting on their own.
- Rather than being the scene of weak compromises, decision-making meetings are places where the best products of individual minds are aired and the best paths chosen.
- An organisation's commitment to act on a decision is stronger when it has been the subject of group deliberation.
- Each meeting, no matter how small, goes through four stages: familiarisation, conflict, reconciliation, and reinforcement.

continued on next page

continued from previous page

- To keep to the point, a small group meeting should focus on the nature of the issue at hand, the dimensions of the issue, current approaches to it and action for the future.
- The chair has two roles: first, to ensure that decorum is maintained among participants, and, second, to guide discussion towards achieving the meeting's goals.
- Individual members of the group all have a responsibility to ensure the meeting reaches its potential.
- Though they may seem antiquated and restrictive, formal meetings have evolved over a long period and embody a great deal of human experience in how to conduct organisations.
- The role of the chair at a formal meeting is to maintain order and decorum and to ensure decisions are taken in the proper way, but not to enter debates or to vote unless a casting vote is required.
- The role of the secretary at a formal meeting is to make preparations for the meeting, to keep the minutes and to handle correspondence.
- A physical setting can have an important effect on relationships between people.
- Small meetings normally dispense with a platform and chairs facing the front. Instead, participants sit at the same level and their chairs face each other.
- Small meetings function better if people know one another. Initial introductions are therefore very important.
- Individual participants should prepare for even a small meeting, but not to the point of bringing a prepared speech and reading it out.
- The chair of a small meeting needs to strike a balance between doing too much talking and giving free rein to those with big egos and loud voices.
- Medium to large groups often find it useful to break into smaller groups to focus on specific issues.

continued on next page

continued from previous page

- Sharing tasks, such as taking minutes or preparing for the next meeting, is a good way to promote participation.
- Rotating positions, especially that of the chair, can prevent some people from dominating and inhibiting the operation of a group.
- Abandoning all formal structures often means that hidden structures take their place, with the loudest voices and strongest wills taking over at the expense of the rest.
- When writing objectives for an activity you need to define what you intend to accomplish, who will be the target of your activities and how you will achieve the outcome.
- A mission statement is written to provide a framework which will guide the behaviour of management and staff, to set standards by which the organisation can judge its progress and to provide a source from which other more immediate objectives can be derived.
- A statement of philosophy is similar to a mission statement but it adds a description of the dominant values that prevail within an organisation.
- Terms of reference are written in a similar way to objectives, with a focus on what the inquiry or group is required to accomplish, who will be its target, and how it will achieve its outcome.
- Policies and procedures manuals these days are avoided by forward-looking organisations. In those areas where they are essential, they should be brief, to the point and expressed in concrete language and precise terms.

PART X
KEY TEXTS AND FURTHER READING

Albrecht, Karl, *Service Within*, Irwin, Homewood, 1990.

Albrecht, Karl and Zemke, Ron, *Service America!* Dow Jones-Irwin, Homewood, 1985.

Carnes, W., *Effective Meetings for Busy People: Let's Decide It and Go*, IEEE Press, New York, 1987.

Crosby, Philip, *Quality Without Tears*, McGraw-Hill, New York, 1984.

Drucker, Peter, *Post-Capitalist Society*, Butterworth-Heinemann, Oxford, 1993.

— *The Practice of Management*, Harper & Row, New York, 1954.

Francis, Dave, *Organisational Communication*, Gower, London, 1987.

Ishikawa, Kaoru, *What is Total Quality Control?—The Japanese Way*, Prentice Hall, Englewood Cliffs, 1985.

Kreps, G., *Organisational Communication*, Longman, New York, 1990.

More, E. and Laird, R., *Organisations in the Communications Age*, Pergamon Press, Sydney, 1985.

Normann, Richard, *Service Management*, Heinemann Professional, Chichester, 1984.

Oakland, John S., *Total Quality Management*, Heinemann Professional, Oxford, 1989.

Pugh, D. S. (ed), *Organisation Theory: Selected Readings*, 3rd ed, Penguin, London, 1990.

Renton, N. E., *Guide for Meetings*, 5th ed, Law Book Company, Sydney, 1990.

Ross, R. S., *Small Groups in Organisational Settings*, Prentice Hall, Englewood Cliffs, 1989.

Taylor, F. W., *Scientific Management*, Harper & Row, New York, 1947.

Ward, Sue, *The A-Z of Meetings: How They Work, How to Run Them*, Pluto Press, London, 1985.

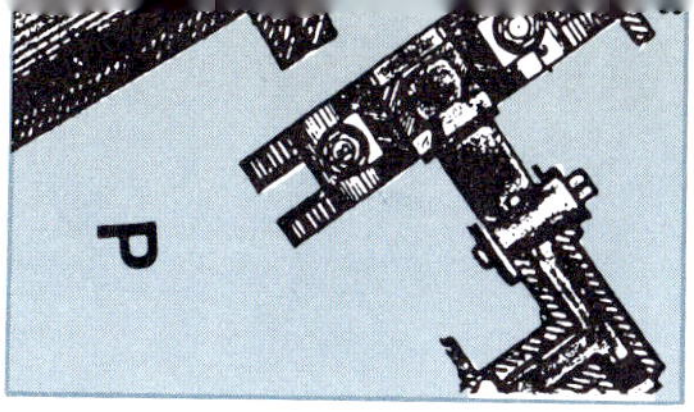

PART

XI

PUBLIC RELATIONS

FROM PR CONSULTANT TO 'PEOPLE BROKER'

One of Australia's most successful public relations people, Jan Murray, tells of the range of tasks that now go on behind the scenes.

The popular perception of a public relations practitioner is that of a publicist—someone who organises glamorous cocktail parties, well-orchestrated press conferences and glitzy product launches. But this is only one dimension of an increasingly demanding and exacting business which depends upon consummate communication skills.

Jan Murray, who has run JMA Advertising/Public Relations for ten years, prefers to be considered a marketing consultant. 'Marketing is the basis of what we do—promoting an idea, a cause or a product and placing it in front of the public in the best possible light,' she says.

From her cosy offices in Cremorne, Sydney, she also speaks of the importance of the research, thinking and planning that go into facilitating a dialogue among interested parties. In her role as a 'people broker', she puts people with ideas together with people with money, to set up initial lines of communication.

She mentions her company's involvement in a recent development project, the building of a new lyric theatre for Sydney.

'A client came to us, wanting investors and equity partners to develop some old wool stores at Darling Harbour, Sydney, for the proposed theatre. We sat down with their architects and brought in the movers and shakers from the ballet, opera and theatre worlds to discuss views on how the project should be developed.'

At the same time, Murray was trying to help finance the undertaking by raising the image of the company and the project concerned, so that people would be willing to invest.

The next step involved getting busy with the property writers in the media and organising meetings with them and the client to generate some positive publicity. This was followed by the designing of the marketing tools—the leaflets, brochures and the prospectus.

Murray's experience and understanding of how to use the media was also put to the test in 1988 during Australia's bicentennial celebrations.

'We were told after agreeing to promote the First Fleet Re-enactment Voyage that the organisers had run into serious money problems and negative publicity,' she remembers.

Things got so bad that the twelve captains in the First Fleet re-enactment sailed as far as Rio de Janeiro and then refused to go any further until they were paid. Murray put an associate on a plane to assure them the money was coming.

'I then orchestrated a campaign on the Macquarie radio network to get pledges of financial support from members of the public. It took off like a bushfire as the station ran with it all weekend. We raised the money and the show went on,' she laughs with relief.

Murray is very aware of the media's hidden agendas and ruthless selectivity. She says that journalists can see through the propaganda of press releases and will never run anything as an unpaid advertisement.

'It's best to be honest and raise both sides of an issue. You may even have to mention a competitor's name to get your story published, but if you have confidence in your product or idea, the risk is worth taking,' she says.

Interestingly, her company studies the styles of particular journalists, presenters and commentators and liaises with them.

'We rarely send out a broad press release, because that is like dropping it into a black hole. We service particular journalists and provide them with everything they require, from facts sheets to photos. It is also a good idea to maintain contact with them to make sure they haven't misinterpreted anything. If that happened and a story went to press, it would be a disaster,' she states.

Murray has many political contacts whom she also regards as friends. (Her husband, John Brown, was Federal Minister for the Arts, Sport, the Environment, Tourism and the Territories, from 1983 to 1988 under the Hawke government.)

Thanks to her inside knowledge of the political process and the workings of the public service, her company receives requests for help from people seeking government funding, bringing issues to the notice of politicians and representing the interests of industries whose representatives want to have their say about proposed changes to legislation.

'I see myself as a minder of both sides, because I'm coming from within the political process and I'm representing my client. I know the limits of possibility and that's the telling point. By now, I feel I can get inside the heads of politicians and clients.'

Murray is the first to admit that she constantly monitors government legislation through its various points of passage, right through to the committee stages when outside groups can have an impact upon its final drafting.

She stresses that she would not be effective if she were constantly going to Canberra, but will make personal representations on behalf of clients over important issues in the community.

'Politicians can be quite isolated. The personal approach is often the best way to inform them of the aims and aspirations of industry and pressure groups,' she comments.

She dislikes the term 'lobbyist' because it has pejorative overtones of somebody badgering politicians to do something against their will.

'We're there to mesh with their political aims and agenda to get the best result for our client,' she explains.

She is adamant that a sharp learning curve is vital in the public relations business and that you need to have an excellent general knowledge.

'You also need to know how to find answers through research and consultation. You must do your homework on your client's product or issue. People come to us about dealing with waste disposal one day and then, the next day, it may be how to get film finance or arrange to have a road gazetted. You have to be on top of each subject,' she advises.

Murray cites good writing skills, a network of contacts, self-confidence and an understanding of how the media works as necessary qualities to survive in public relations.

Public relations is a career you grow into through developing your own personal resources and awareness of how society operates, according to Murray.

'The best advice I can give to young people interested in the PR game is to go out and first experience life—that says it all,' she concludes.

CHAPTER

36

PUBLIC RELATIONS— STRATEGIES AND TECHNIQUES

After studying this chapter, you will:

- know the reasons for the growth of public relations over the last two decades
- understand the principal objectives of public relations
- know who engages in public relations
- know the techniques they use
- know the various audiences they try to influence
- understand the difference between public relations and publicity, advertising, propaganda, marketing and sales promotion
- be able to draft the outline of a public relations campaign

Public relations is about using communication to generate goodwill for an organisation with the several publics it needs to influence to survive. These include its customers, its employees, the government, its financial investors, the media and the public at large.

Public relations has emerged in the past decade as one of the fastest growing areas of the professions. Until the 1960s, almost the only people who engaged public relations consultants were entertainers and politicians who had a natural interest in gaining favourable publicity in the media. They were followed by a few large corporations whose main aim was to get publicity, but for their products and services. In the more communication-conscious 1980s and 1990s, public relations—or 'PR' as its practitioners almost always call it—has come to be recognised as one of the most important areas in which an organisation can become engaged. Handled well, public relations can have valuable consequences in terms of marketing, government policy, industrial relations and community respect. Handled badly, an organisation can quickly run up losses in each of these areas, as well as several others.

PUBLIC RELATIONS—WHAT IT DOES

Public relations is about using communication to generate goodwill for an organisation with the several publics it needs to influence to survive. These include its customers, employees and financial investors, and the government, its financial investors, the media and the community at large. The list of the types of organisations that use public relations today is enormous. It not only includes business corporations and government, but extends to educational institutions such as universities and technical colleges, to hospitals and health centres, community service organisations, religious and welfare bodies and even media organisations themselves. It has become more important because the whole of society has become better informed, more communication-conscious and more particular about the quality of information it demands. Moreover, many organisations have realised that, whether they engage in public relations or not, their reputations invariably go before them. In other words, whether they like it or not, most organisations have some kind of public image that can serve them well or ill. Rather than having a reputation derived from misinformation and innuendo, these firms have now realised that they should be out in the community trying to communicate what they are really trying to achieve.

Public relations is not simply about trying to create a favourable 'image' with the community. Its main, long-term aim is to communicate real information about its clients' objectives, policies, standards, products and services.

Public relations is not simply about trying to create a favourable 'image' with the community. Any organisation will, naturally, prefer to generate goodwill rather than bad publicity. But the main, long-term aim of public relations today is to communicate real information about its clients' objectives, policies, standards, products and services. Public relations concerns itself with how and why people have opinions and attitudes and the sources of their information. It also uses communication techniques of varying kinds to try to generate favourable attitudes towards its clientele. However, one thing is clear from the experience of the last twenty years: people today are not easily persuaded and a good reputation cannot be bought or turned on by publicity alone. Goodwill needs to be cultivated, built up and earned.

There are two main ways through which people in public relations are employed. Some organisations, usually large, employ their own public relations departments. This will normally include one PR manager, another senior practitioner and several young public relations assistants. Smaller organisations will normally engage a public relations agent, as they would an advertising agent. In this second arrangement, a PR agency will work for several clients at a time, devoting different degrees of attention to them, according to their budgets. In either case, their overall roles include the following:

People today are not easily persuaded and a good reputation cannot be bought or turned on by publicity alone. Goodwill needs to be cultivated, built up and earned.

- to establish and maintain communication with the media and its audiences
- to prevent unwarranted conflict and misunderstanding
- to promote respect and goodwill
- to establish a good name with employees, suppliers and clientele
- to improve industrial relations
- to promote a firm's products or services
- to project its corporate identity
- to foster a public understanding of its objectives and standards
- to research public opinion and advise on how to influence it
- to analyse future trends and advise on their consequences.

In the two chapters that follow, we discuss in some detail how to engage in public relations with the media and with government. At this point we want to indicate just how broad is the range of audiences that now fall within the field.

COMMUNITY RELATIONS

Most organisations will benefit from good relations with their communities. They should develop programs to demonstrate their good citizenship, not only at the immediate local level of their suburb or country town but also as contributors to the state and the nation. Most firms that are aware of this need will develop and publicise policies to contribute to community, educational, sporting and cultural activities, to contribute to improving the environment, and to foster social equity through a range of employment policies and programs.

EMPLOYEE RELATIONS

One of the most important audiences of any organisation is its own staff. Generating understanding between employees and management is now one of the most common goals of a public relations program. This ranges from the writing and production of in-house magazines and newsletters, to contributing to policy reviews on issues such as recruiting, training, industrial relations, equal employment opportunity and even social activities.

The financial reputation of any organisation can be one of its most valuable assets or, if it is not good, can be one of its greatest liabilities. Companies need good relations with the investing public to maintain their share price and guarantee their capital and credit.

RELATIONS WITH FINANCIAL INSTITUTIONS

The financial reputation of any organisation can be one of its most valuable assets or, if it is not good, one of its greatest liabilities. Public companies need good relations with the investing public to maintain their share price and guarantee their capital and credit. Private companies also need a good reputation with banks and other suppliers of credit. Public relations can play a very important role in generating approval for management or for minimising disapproval. For many organisations, shareholders and the investing public are crucial audiences because, at critical times, their votes can approve or fail to approve major management plans, or they can support or reject a takeover bid. Reputation is often the one factor that can turn the tide at times like this.

MEDIA RELATIONS

Most organisations at some time have a good news story they would like communicated to the world at large. Public relations practitioners will handle this through news releases and/or news conferences.

Because most people in our society gain most of their knowledge about current issues through the news media, newspapers, radio and television news reports are the keys to influencing public opinion. Most organisations at some time have a good news story they would like communicated to the world at large. Public relations practitioners will handle this through news releases and/or news conferences. At the opposite scale is the role of public relations in media damage control. The media can sometimes get hold of a story, that, if not handled properly, can make an organisation look bad. The role of public relations in these cases is to tell the truth about the situation (if you tell lies you will usually be found out, especially if the media is keen to pursue the story, and you will end up looking twice as bad) but also to try to get the media and its audiences to see the situation from the client's point of view.

GOVERNMENT RELATIONS

Whether they are in business or in community services, most organisations today have a vital interest in government policy, both in following its changes and in trying to influence them. Before it can put its point of view, an organisation needs to know what government is planning to do, and who are the relevant people concerned. Public relations practitioners who work primarily in government relations are usually known as lobbyists. Today, there are a large number of them working in Canberra and in the major state capitals. Their main role is to try to have input into legislation, regulations and government programs that affect their clients. Other public relations people will often, nonetheless, be engaged in relating to government. This can occur at local and state government levels, where they are more likely to gain faster and more direct results than in the rarefied atmosphere of Canberra.

PR AND OTHER FORMS OF COMMUNICATION

Public relations today is generally regarded as part of both the communications and the marketing aspects of organisational life. It relates to, but differs from, other aspects in the following ways.

PUBLICITY

Public relations began simply as publicity. The aim was to get free 'plugs' or favourable stories in the news media. The first public relations people were former journalists who used their contacts in the news media to generate publicity for their clients. Publicity remains one important part of public relations but, today, the practice has moved on to much wider territory.

ADVERTISING

When a firm advertises, it pays for space in a newspaper or magazine, or for time on radio or television. By paying it gains almost complete control over how its message is published or broadcast. This is in contrast to publicity where the editors and journalists decide what is said and how favourably or unfavourably the firm is treated.

PROPAGANDA

Propaganda today means statements that are one-sided, false or greatly exaggerated. What differentiates propaganda from publicity is the criterion of truth. Any public relations consultant who has his or her client's interests at heart will tell the truth on behalf of that client. Propaganda, on the other hand, disregards the idea of truth completely and seeks to persuade people by any means at hand.

Any public relations consultant who has his or her client's interests at heart will tell the truth on behalf of that client.
Propaganda, on the other hand, disregards the idea of truth completely and seeks to persuade people by any means at hand.

MARKETING

Marketing is involved not only in the promotion, distribution and sale of goods and services but also, today, in their production. Most products are produced only after their likely success has been tested in the market place by a range of techniques in market research. Advertising is one part of the marketing function and so is that part of public relations which has to do with publicity and promotion. When a car manufacturer launches a new vehicle, for instance, it will not only spend a lot of money on advertising but will try to influence motoring writers to review it favourably.

SALES PROMOTION

Sales promotion normally relates to generating attention and interest in a product at the point of sale in a retail store. The range of techniques includes packaging and displays, discounts, contests and stunts. Public relations people sometimes become involved in the publicity aspects of sales promotion but, in general, this is a peripheral aspect of their work.

PUBLIC RELATIONS CAMPAIGNS

When a public relations manager or agent is advising an organisation, he or she will normally recommend the need for a campaign to be planned and conducted over a sustained period of time. The campaign usually involves the following components.

- *Setting objectives* This involves defining why the campaign is being conducted and what its ultimate goals will be.
- *Targeting audiences* This involves defining in order of priority those people who the campaign is aimed at influencing.
- *Establishing current attitudes* This involves a research program to establish firmly the current opinions of the target audiences.
- *Redefining objectives* In light of this research, a more precise set of objectives for the campaign can now be established.
- *Selecting the media* This not only involves deciding how best to reach the audience through the mass media of press, radio and television, but

what other kinds of media—mailouts, brochures, booklets, conferences, stunts and so on—are also likely to be most effective.

- *Preparing a budget* All public relations costs money and the client will need to have a firm idea of the likely cost of gaining the objectives that have been set.
- *Implementing the plan* At this stage the campaign can be put into the field.
- *Evaluating the results* Monitoring and evaluating the outcomes should be done on a continuous basis. Because public relations often deals with very difficult areas, initial plans do not always work as expected. A good campaign will continually assess itself and, where necessary, change tactics or directions.

This survey of the field of public relations is designed to indicate how extensive and sophisticated it has become. Public relations practitioners need to be able to deploy a wide range of skills including researching, writing, editing, speaking and broadcasting. Almost every skill discussed in this book will be part of the repertoire. The growth of the field, which in Australia alone now generates more than $200 million worth of business a year, provides a good indication of how important these skills have become in an era where information and communication have become central to modern organisational practice.

KEY POINTS: Chapter 36 Public relations—strategies and techniques

- A wide range of organisations now engage in public relations, including business, government, educational institutions, hospitals, community service organisations and religious bodies.
- They are trying to generate goodwill among several of their publics, including their customers, employees, the government, financial investors, their local communities, the media and the public at large.
- Whether they engage in public relations or not, most organisations have a public image that can serve them well or ill.
- The long-term aim of public relations is to communicate real information about clients' objectives, policies, standards, products and services.
- Public relations personnel are employed either in specialist departments within large organisations or in agencies who have a number of clients.
- Their role includes: preventing conflict and misunderstanding, promoting goodwill and respect, improving industrial relations, projecting a corporate identity, researching public opinion, analysing and advising on future trends.

QUESTIONS FOR DISCUSSION

1. Why have organisations given a more important role to public relations in the last twenty years?
2. When is damage control needed? Give some examples with which you are familiar.
3. Why is it important to maintain good relations with the government?
4. Why is it important to maintain good relations with the finance sector?
5. What is the difference between public relations and publicity?
6. What is the difference between public relations and propaganda?

EXERCISES

Take one aspect or one division of the organisation where you work or where you are studying. Draw up the outline of a campaign to improve its goodwill and public image. In doing this exercise, follow each of the stages recommended above under the heading 'Public relations campaigns'.

CHAPTER

37

POLITICAL LOBBYING

After studying this chapter, you will be able to:

- communicate effectively with your local members of Parliament
- prepare a small delegation to meet a politician
- conduct a campaign to influence politicians on an issue that concerns you
- understand the advantages and disadvantages of various means of lobbying, including letters, petitions and demonstrations
- choose a suitable legal structure to incorporate a political lobbying group

To lobby is to make an effort to get your point of view across to others and to have it acted upon. Most lobbying is directed at politicians. People who are concerned about a matter on which a political decision is important—the introduction of a new law, the repeal of an existing one, the granting of funds or the raising or reduction of taxes—try to influence politicians to take the same view as they do. Lobbying is not confined, however, to politics and may be found in a wide range of human activities. Citizens may lobby a big corporation which is making a decision that will affect their locality. Students may lobby their principal to change some aspect of school regulations. People may lobby government departments or statutory authorities on a wide range of issues.

Lobbyists sometimes go to dramatic lengths to demonstrate their point of view

The skills involved in lobbying include a wide range of writing, researching, illustrating and speaking. If you want to change the world, you need a full array of communication skills.

The essential point about lobbying is that it seeks to make things happen through persuasion rather than through orders or coercion. Those who are lobbying do not have direct power over those who are lobbied. The former cannot tell the latter what to do; they have to persuade them to do it. They have to let them know what it is they want and then convince them to give their support. The skills involved in lobbying, moreover, encompass virtually all those that this book has discussed—a wide range of writing, researching, illustrating and speaking. In other words, if you want to change the world, you need a full array of communication skills.

Even though politicians in democratic systems are elected by their constituents and are beholden to them, on a great many individual issues politicians do not necessarily see things in the same way as voters. Almost every day, political issues arise on which there are conflicting views. If you as a citizen or as a member of an organisation want to get an individual politician or a whole political party to take your side in one of these conflicts, you will have to undertake a campaign of lobbying.

POLITICIANS AS PEOPLE

Before approaching any politician, you might care to reflect on your attitude towards politicians in general. A great many Australians have a low opinion of politicians as a breed. It is common for them to be viewed as either cunning, ruthless, corrupt and dedicated solely to their own advancement, or incompetent, lazy and only in parliament to have a good bludge. Dare we suggest that both views are gross exaggerations? If you get involved in a serious campaign of lobbying and spend some time with your local member and perhaps a minister or two, you will find politicians are not ogres but are pretty much the same as other people. Because it is their job, they are reasonably well informed about the people and concerns of their local electorate and the attitudes of their party colleagues. Few have access to any information that is denied to the rest of us. In fact, they get most of their information from the same place as the rest of us: the news media.

All this means that you can talk to politicians in ordinary language. You should not assume they have a great deal of knowledge about the subject that concerns you. Therefore you will have to communicate with them as if they were lay people rather than experts on your topic. If your views are representative of others in your community, you can assume that a local politician will see most issues as you do and will share your concerns. If your concerns appear to the politician to represent those of a large number of voters, you can also assume that you will be taken seriously and get a reasonable hearing.

If you get involved in a serious campaign of lobbying and spend some time with your local member and perhaps a minister or two, you will find politicians are not ogres but are pretty much the same as other people.

Politicians in Australia are nearly all members of political parties. In lobbying, it does not matter if you vote for or support the same party. Members of parliament have a responsibility to all their electors, irrespective of their political views. When lobbying on a single issue, you may be surprised to find your local member will put party attitudes to one side and will focus on the issue itself.

THE LOCAL MEMBER

The first step to take in lobbying is to find whom you should approach. The local member is the best place to start. It is his or her duty to see you if you are in the electorate. Find out the names of the politicians elected for your state and federal electorate plus the representatives of the local council. The library or post office can tell you, or there is a Government Information Service in capital cities which can be found in the government pages at the front of the telephone book. Local members have electorate offices where they regularly interview their electors. They often advertise their address and times available in the local newspaper.

Local members have electorate offices where they regularly interview their electors. They often advertise their address and times available in the local newspaper.

It is sometimes difficult to know beforehand whether an issue is one for local, state or Commonwealth government. In general, education, police and health care issues are state matters, while social security and health insurance are Commonwealth issues. Some areas, such as the environment and the arts, involve all three tiers of government. If you can work out the appropriate level for your issue, well and good, but if you cannot, simply go to the most convenient local member, who will soon put you right. Sometimes a state politician will approach a federal one for you, and vice versa, if they are in the same party.

To get to see a local member, you should make an appointment. Politicians have electorate secretaries who will make the appointment for you. Because politicians have a large number of people to see, their secretaries usually guard their time jealously. It will pay you to get on well with the electorate secretary.

THE DELEGATION

When you get an appointment with a politician, you should prepare a delegation. The best number of people to attend is two or three. Unless it is a personal matter, two people are better than one because they support one another and back each other up. Most appointments are relatively short—fifteen to thirty minutes—so there is not enough time for more than three people to talk. Also, more than three appears unnecessarily intimidating to the politician concerned.

Because delegations have limited time, they should be well prepared. Work out beforehand who will say what and in which order. Rehearse if you feel you need to. It is also a good idea to bring information and documents that you can leave. Avoid leaving large, daunting collections of papers that take a lot of working through. At a minimum, leave a one-page summary describing your view of the issue. Attach any supporting material to the summary. Politicians usually see a large number of people on their interview days and they have to cover a wide variety of issues. A good, punchy summary is the most likely to be effective.

Because delegations have limited time, they should be well prepared. Work out beforehand who will say what and in which order. Rehearse if you feel you need to. It is also a good idea to bring information and documents that you can leave.

THE CAMPAIGN

On issues that go beyond your local area, you will probably have to lobby many politicians, perhaps even all major parties. To do this, you need to carefully consider two fundamental aspects of conducting a campaign: first, the approach you will use and what you will say, and, second, the means (such as letters, telegrams, petitions) through which you will say it.

In deciding your approach, the first thing to assume is that politicians are like average members of the public. If your issue has not yet surfaced in public debate or the media, you should assume they know little about your cause. You will therefore need to explain the basics and work out all your arguments in full. You cannot take any attitudes for granted. Even when you know that some politicians do have a knowledge of the subject, the exercise of going back to basics will be a useful one for both of you.

Politicians are like average members of the public. If your issue has not yet surfaced in public debate or the media, you should assume they know little about your cause. You will therefore need to explain the basics and work out all your arguments in full.

The second aspect of your approach should be to try to see the issue from the politician's point of view. Naturally enough, they have a propensity to want to keep their jobs and to get promoted if they can. Keep this in mind when working out what to say. Without appealing too obviously to naked self-interest, work out what ways in which support for you would be popular, how it would gain kudos or votes, how expensive or inexpensive it is likely to prove, how it could be implemented.

Political parties have platforms on many issues. A platform is a statement of intent usually made at a party conference. Contact the party and get a copy of its platform. If your issue fits in with it, this will colour your approach. If your issue is the opposite of the platform, do not despair too much. Platforms are not binding on the party once it is in government. There are many cases where platforms, drawn up in one period, are ignored or contradicted by government at another time. You will, however, have to work hard to demonstrate that there are more votes for the party in overriding its platform than in keeping to it. In particular, you will need to take your campaign into the media to influence public opinion, an issue we take up in the following chapter.

Once you have determined the shape of your message and approach, there are a number of means through which you can express it. These include using professional lobbyists, petitions, letters, telegrams and public demonstrations.

PROFESSIONAL LOBBYISTS

A number of people, located mainly in Canberra, make a living out of lobbying. They know how the government and the public service work and they know many politicians and public servants personally. They are usually employed on contract by large organisations, and they are expensive—charging between $100 and $500 an hour for their services. They can be effective, but the expense rules them out for many groups.

PETITIONS

Sending petitions to parliament is a traditional way of lobbying that has been practised for hundreds of years. There is a special way of wording them if they are to be sent to state or federal parliaments (see the accompanying boxes, where the required wording is in bold). This archaic, servile form of language should be out of place today. A petition to local government, or any other organisation, does not have these requirements and may be couched in modern English.

PETITION TO STATE PARLIAMENT

To the Honourable the Speaker and Members of the Legislative Assembly of New South Wales, in Parliament assembled: The humble petition of the undersigned citizens of Australia, New South Wales, respectfully showeth:

That we residents of Cunningham strongly object to the proposals to turn over state government land at nearby Wallaroo Point for the use as an Army firing range.

continued on next page

continued from previous page

The land has a long tradition of use by the public for recreation, surfing and fishing and its alienation will mean the permanent loss of these activities.

Business in Cunningham is strongly dependent on the tourist trade attracted to the beaches at Wallaroo Point and an Army takeover will mean a permanent loss to the local community.

We also believe that the noise and pollution from Army vehicles on public roads, as well as the firing range itself, will lead to a marked deterioration in the quality of our environment and our lives.

Your petitioners therefore humbly pray that your honourable House will vote against the forthcoming legislation which would transfer control of the land from the State government to the Army.

And your petitioners, as in duty bound, will ever pray.

SIGNATURE ADDRESS

Petition to a state parliament

PETITION TO COMMONWEALTH PARLIAMENT

To the Honourable the Speaker and Members of the House of Representatives in Parliament assembled: The humble petition of the undersigned citizens of Australia respectfully showeth:

That we support your efforts to introduce a National Identity Card, especially as a vehicle for the reduction of tax evasion. We believe tax evasion has now reached such a scale in the so-called 'cash economy' that ... etc. etc.

Your petitioners therefore humbly pray that you will persist with your efforts to introduce a National Identity Card.

And your petitioners, as in duty bound, will ever pray.

SIGNATURE ADDRESS

Petition to the Commonwealth parliament

There are now so many petitions on so many issues that another one simply gets lost in the crowd.

Petitions purport to show how many people support or oppose an issue. However, today they are not a highly effective means of influencing politicians. Listen to the opening sessions of Federal Parliament on the radio when the petitions are read and you can tell this for yourself. There are so many petitions on so many issues that another one simply gets lost in the crowd. Also, politicians know that many people who sign them are not strongly committed to the issue concerned.

LETTERS

Of all the written material that politicians receive from voters, a personally written letter is the most effective.

Of all the written material that politicians receive from voters, a personally written letter is the most effective. When they weigh up how much influence to give to lobbying devices, politicians generally give one letter the same weight as one petition, even if the petition has many names on it. To give a campaign the feeling of having widespread community support, you need a large number of individual letters to be written. Of course, if you can persuade a large number of people to write letters, you really do represent a substantial community movement. For this reason, politicians take letters seriously.

Some organisations in the past have prepared standard letters and asked their supporters to copy them out, and sign and mail them. This ploy, however, is so obviously detectable that it is usually a waste of time because it becomes no more effective than a petition. You may want to suggest to your supporters some points to make or some lines of argument. But they must compose and write or type the letter themselves.

Letters should ideally take up one page and be typed, though a few handwritten ones will add authenticity. A wave of such letters from electors will make any politician think more seriously about an issue. Most recognise that people who write letters are committed to the issue and are the types most likely to change their vote if they don't get the political response they want.

Faxes carry almost as much weight as letters for the same reasons. Because they convey a sense of urgency, they are best kept as weapons to be used at the last minute. If a stream of them arrive the night before a crucial vote is to be taken, any politician will think twice about the issue, especially when they have been preceded by lobbying in the form of delegations and letters. The main problem with using faxes for lobbying is that, if your group wants to send a large number of them, you will tie up the politician's fax machine for an extended period. This means most of your own supporters will not be able to get through. Hence, if sending faxes, do it at night or very early morning when there will be very few other calls.

DEMONSTRATIONS

These can be powerful weapons but they can just as easily backfire. Demonstrations should be held to get media coverage that shows that people are so disaffected by an issue they are willing to take to the streets. Demonstrations need a long lead time and have to be well organised and well publicised beforehand. If you put on a demonstration and not many people turn up, you will do your cause much more harm than good because it will look as if you have no public support. Also, if there is any violence, even if just a bit of mild pushing and shoving, the media will seize on this and will report nothing else. You will look like a bunch of hooligans and your opponents will easily discredit you.

Demonstrations need a long lead time and have to be well organised and well publicised beforehand. If you put on a demonstration and not many people turn up, you will do your cause much more harm than good because it will look as if you have no public support.

The nuclear disarmament marches of the early 1980s attracted thousands of participants

The most effective demonstrations have celebrities as speakers or march leaders. The media will almost always give them favourable coverage. If you don't have someone famous to support you, however, do not worry too much. Someone who is articulate and passionate about an issue can do just as good a job. It is also a good idea to have witty slogans on posters, colourful clothing, some interesting activity for the television cameras and, in many cases, small children. Try to ensure you appear not as unrepresentative ratbags but as confident, civilised people with whom others can identify.

Because they are so two-edged, demonstrations are best kept until last, when you have gone up all the other channels of lobbying but have got nowhere. If your demonstration is then a flop you have not lost much, but, if it is a success, it may be the vehicle to turn defeat into victory.

FORMING A LOBBYING GROUP

If you intend to run a sustained campaign of lobbying in which you will raise and spend a reasonable sum of money, and if you are going to make public statements, you should consider some form of organisational structure that will give legal protection to both yourselves and the people who deal with you. Laws in Australia recognise some forms of association as having a separate existence from the people who are members of them. The advantages of legal recognition as a separate 'legal person' are that the association is liable for its debts and other legal obligations. A structured association may hold property, enter contracts in its own name and sue and be sued in its own name, rather than that of individual members.

The four most likely forms of association a lobbying group could adopt are incorporated association, proprietary company, company limited by guarantee or a co-operative.

INCORPORATED ASSOCIATION

Non-profit associations can be incorporated and thus limit the liability of their general members and committee members. This is probably the most common form for community groups. Incorporation is restricted to associations that are not carried on for the main purpose of trading. You can still raise funds from donations, bazaars and the like, and spend it on rent, telephones, printing and such, but if the element of trading becomes the principal activity or objective, it becomes ineligible for this type of structure.

If you intend to run a sustained campaign of lobbying in which you will raise and spend a reasonable sum of money, and if you are going to make public statements, then you should consider some form of organisational structure which will give legal protection to both yourselves and the people who deal with you.

On incorporation, an association becomes capable of acquiring property and of acting legally in its own name. All property is held on behalf of the association by its incorporated body. The name, objectives and rules of the association must be lodged with the Corporate Affairs Commission in its state or territory and any changes to these must be approved by the Commission. Associations are only recognised as incorporated in their own state or territory.

The members of an incorporated association are not liable to contribute to the debts and liabilities of the association if it is wound up, except to the extent, if any, provided in the association's rules.

PROPRIETARY COMPANY

This is the most common form of company for a small business. Some community organisations choose this structure because it imposes few restrictions on the internal conduct of the organisation. It needs a minimum of two shareholders and can have up to a maximum of fifty shareholders. It must also have at least two directors. It cannot be listed on the stock exchange, nor invite the public to subscribe for shares in the company.

Because they are carried on for private profit, proprietary companies are restricted in the government funds they can attract. Most government programs make direct grants and subsidies to non-profit organisations.

COMPANY LIMITED BY GUARANTEE

A company limited by guarantee is a non-profit organisation with a number of advantages as a structure for community organisations.

- Members are not required to invest in shares or capital of the company.
- The liability of members is limited to the amount of their guarantee.
- It has perpetual succession, that is, the company continues indefinitely and is independent of the particular individuals who are its members from time to time.
- As a non-profit body, it is eligible for direct grants and subsidies from government programs.
- Compared to other non-profit bodies, such as incorporated associations, companies limited by guarantee permit much greater freedom in trading and managing finances.

The memorandum of association of a company limited by guarantee usually provides that any surplus of assets or property remaining after the company is dissolved shall not be distributed among the members, but rather transferred to some other institution having similar objectives and structure.

CO-OPERATIVE

All states have legislation governing the establishment of co-operatives but some are much more suited to community groups than others. Where the legislation is suitable, a co-operative can be an attractive legal structure for community associations. It allows a flexible internal structure, with members writing their own rules about how it will operate, who will make decisions and so on. As a non-profit organisation, a co-operative is eligible for programs offering direct government grants and subsidies.

Members of a co-operative usually buy shares in it and their liability is limited to their shareholding. The rules of the co-operative may be written, however, to allow authority and decision-making to be shared in a variety of ways not related to the actual ownership structure.

Before deciding which legal structure is the most appropriate, an organisation should make a decision on at least four issues:

- its objectives, that is, the scope of what it will attempt in the foreseeable future, and the amount of trading it will engage in
- the size of its operation and whether this will involve raising money and investing capital funds
- the relations between the people working within the organisation, and
- whether it wants to be eligible for direct grants from government bodies

Once these decisions have been made and recorded in document form, the organisation can approach others for advice on the appropriate form of legal structure.

KEY POINTS: Chapter 37 Political lobbying

- Citizens in a democracy can lobby politicians to change the law and can lobby government departments and statutory authorities on a range of issues that affect their locality.
- Do not assume a politician has a great deal of knowledge of the subject about which you are lobbying. Politicians are ordinary people who get most of their information from the media, like everyone else.
- Your local member is obliged to give you a personal interview. Make an appointment through his or her electorate secretary.
- Politicians can be elected to Commonwealth, state or local governments. Try to decide which is the most relevant to your issue.
- A delegation of two or three people is more effective than one or more than three. Delegations have limited time and so should be well prepared.
- Try to persuade a politician on an issue in the same way you would an ordinary member of the public. But try, also, to see how the issue affects the politician's chances of being re-elected.
- Petitions today are largely ineffective means of lobbying politicians. Personal letters written by individuals are far more effective.
- Demonstrations can be effective but can also backfire if not enough people turn up. Save them for the last stage of a campaign but use them only if you have nothing to lose.
- Lobbying involves risks in terms of finance and the law, so it is best to form a legal structure to handle both. The best legal structure for a lobbying group is either an incorporated association or a company limited by guarantee.

QUESTIONS FOR DISCUSSION

1. If you are approaching a politician to try to get changes made to your local environment, what types of issues would be most influential?
2. How would you plan a delegation to the politician to lobby on this issue?
3. How would a looming election affect your chances of success on this issue? Why?

EXERCISES

1. A community welfare organisation elects you to visit your state member of parliament with a submission to open a new refuge for homeless youth. Describe:

   (a) how you would prepare yourself for the deputation
   (b) how you would initiate the interview
   (c) what you would present to the MP
   (d) how you would conduct yourself in the interview
   (e) what strategy you would employ to extract a firm answer from the politician

2. The only after-school child-care centre in your area is threatened by closure. A parents' body gives you the responsibility to conduct a campaign in the local community to generate support to forestall the closure. Describe how you would go about this task, including:

   (a) how you would enlist help
   (b) what authorities you would approach for help and support, both moral and financial
   (c) in particular, how you would lobby local and state government bodies concerned with child welfare
   (d) whom you would approach in these organisations

3. You are one of three people who have been elected by the local community to form a delegation to see the Minister for Defence about a decision to give a contract once held by the local small arms factory to an overseas firm. Members of the delegation include the managing director of the factory, the head of a local business who supplies parts to the factory and the head of the local branch of the main trade union involved. Describe how the delegation would carry out this mission. Describe stages in planning, preparation and presentation of your project.

4. Take an issue about which you, as a citizen, feel concerned. Plan a campaign of lobbying to make present government policy conform more closely to what you believe to be right.

CHAPTER

38

HOW TO USE THE MEDIA

After studying this chapter, you will be able to:

- write a news release
- distribute a news release to the news editors of newspapers, radio stations and television stations
- understand the requirements of radio or television interviews
- conduct a news conference

If you can get good publicity in the news media, half your public relations or lobbying battle is won. It is worth taking a great deal of trouble to try to influence the media. A large part of the knowledge and opinions that most people have about current issues comes from the media. However, it is not true that bad publicity is better than no publicity. Film stars and rock singers can thrive on bad publicity, but few other people can. A bad press can leave a PR or lobbying campaign dispirited and demoralised and your chance of influencing others can be reduced to zero. So treat the media carefully to get the best publicity you can.

THE NEWS RELEASE

These are often called 'press releases' but since the most influential medium today is television, the older term is now out of date. The news release is the first means through which organisations contact the media. Its aim is not to be published or broadcast as it is (though it should be written so that it could be) but to interest editors and journalists in taking up the story it tells. It should be sent to all the media you want to influence—newspapers, magazines, radio stations and television stations.

Minimum criteria for a news release:
- good quality typing on A4 paper, double spaced
- succinct and accurate points
- date written
- name, address and telephone of contact person

Each type of medium has a person with a different title responsible for assigning journalists to cover stories. If you cannot find out this person's name or title, address your news release to 'The News Editor' of the paper or station concerned. There are commercial publications available which list the names, positions, addresses and other information about people in the media. These publications, such as the *B&T Year Book*, are expensive but they are available in the major public libraries. If your organisation is serious about lobbying, it will produce and maintain its own media contact list.

Minimum criteria for a news release are as follows

- It should look professional. It should be on one side only of A4 paper and must be typed with a good quality typewriter or computer printer. A letterhead is desirable but not essential. It may be one or two and, in a few cases, three pages long.
- It should make your points and put your case succinctly and accurately, with correct grammar and no spelling mistakes.
- It should contain the date it was written.
- It should include the name, address and telephone numbers (work and home) of contact persons who can be followed up by journalists.

Send the news release to everyone you think might run the item. There is no point in giving anyone an 'exclusive' copy. If the item is newsworthy, it will be covered. If it is not newsworthy, it will not get a run, no matter how 'exclusive' you try to make it.

You should realise that news offices are very ruthless places and, no matter how good your story is, it might not be published because there is a similar story on another page or because, at the last minute, the space it was allocated is given over to something of higher priority. This is the nature of the game. If you miss out once, it is probably because of factors like this rather than the intrinsic merit of your cause. Don't take an initial failure personally—simply keep trying.

If your story is timely or urgent, deliver news releases by hand rather than by post. By the time the mail is delivered, events may have overtaken your news release and made it redundant. No one day is better than others for generating news. Sunday was once known as a 'quiet' day when news releases had less competition from other news. These days, however, politicians are awake to this and often time important statements for Sunday in order to get better coverage in Monday morning's papers. The only rule to follow is to send out the news release immediately it is ready.

Never expect to get paid for any news releases you submit (nor for interviews, for that matter). The only time when it is appropriate to ask for payment is when you are commissioned by a newspaper to write an article or invited by a radio or television program to make an extended guest appearance.

Other points to follow in making a news release are as follows.

Structure of a news release:
- the words 'News Release' at top of page
- a headline related to the main point
- most important point in first paragraph
- short sentences
- attribute all opinions to someone in your organisation
- give a succinct statement about your organisation and its aims
- precise dates and times of events; precise quantities for numbers
- name, address and telephone of a contact person
- photograph of person(s) who feature in the story

- Print the words 'News release' and the date near the top of the first page.
- Give the news release a headline, preferably related to its main point.
- Sometimes politicians put 'embargoes' on their news releases. This means they are asking the media not to report the item until after a certain date or time so that, for example, a formal speech will not appear in the media before it is delivered by the politician to his selected audience. Few other people have requirements like this, so it is usually best to forget about embargoes and similar devices.
- Report the most important issue first. Don't waste the opening paragraph with waffle or background information.
- Don't express opinions without attributing them to someone in the organisation.
- Don't assume the reader knows anything about your organisation or its aims. Include a succinct statement about both as part of the release.
- Give precise dates and times of events and precise quantities for numbers. Avoid unspecific quantities such as 'some', 'most' and 'many'.
- Write short sentences with one to three sentences per paragraph. (For other aspects of newspaper style, see Chapter Eighteen.)
- Don't forget to include the name of a contact person, plus both work and home telephone numbers.
- If you have head-and-shoulders photographs of people named in the news release, include them, making sure the name of each person is clearly attached to the back of the photograph. Ideally, photographs should be glossy black and white and sized 20 by 25 centimetres.
- Keep a file of all media coverage that your news releases generate. It will be useful as a reference for future releases.

NEWSPAPER AND MAGAZINE AUDIENCES

All newspapers and magazines are published with certain audiences in mind. The morning and broadsheet (large) newspapers generally have a smaller but better educated and more upmarket audience. Tabloid (smaller)

TREASURER

PRESS RELEASE

NO. 16

NO EMBARGO

STATEMENT BY THE TREASURER
THE HON JOHN DAWKINS MP

ENTRY INTO FORCE OF THE COMPREHENSIVE TAXATION AGREEMENT WITH INDIA

The comprehensive taxation agreement between Australia and India entered into force on 30 December 1991 following the exchange of notes with India through the diplomatic channel indicating that the necessary procedures to give the agreement the force of law had been completed in each country.

Signature of the agreement took place in Canberra on 25 July 1991. Details of the agreement were made public on the signature date and legislation providing for the agreement to be given force of law in Australia - *the Income Tax (International Agreements) Act (No. 2) 1991* - received Royal Assent on 24 December 1991.

The agreement is a comprehensive one for the avoidance of double taxation in relation to all income flowing between Australia and India. The allocation of taxing rights between Australia and India under the agreement generally accords with that provided for in Australia's other modern comprehensive taxation agreements.

The agreement with India will have effect in Australia, for withholding tax purposes, in respect of income derived on or after 1 July 1992 and for other income tax purposes in relation to income or gains of any year of income beginning on or after 1 July 1992. It will first have effect in India for Indian taxes covered by the agreement in respect of income derived on or after 1 April 1992.

CANBERRA

12 February 1992

CONTACT OFFICER: Neil Sidebotham
TELEPHONE:(06) 2751649 (Work)
:(06) 2512620 (Home)

A news release should look professional and, above all, be succinct and accurate newspapers are more downmarket, with the exception of the *Australian Financial Review*. Among magazines, the *Women's Weekly* is targeted to women in all age groups while *Cleo* and *Cosmopolitan* are aimed more specifically at eighteen to thirty-five-year-old women. Other publications have much more specialised readerships than these. The different audiences of the media will often require a different approach. If you are being interviewed by a journalist, try to work out from the content of the publication concerned the nature of its audience and pitch your message to people of that kind.

TELEVISION AND RADIO

Your organisation should have one or two people who can act as speakers on its behalf. Don't worry whether they are conventionally good-looking nor well-spoken. What matters is their commitment to, and ability to articulate, the cause. Such people are called by radio and television producers 'good talent' and, once discovered, will be sought to speak for the cause in the future.

Your speakers should expect to be available at any time. An early morning radio program, such as ABC's *AM*, often calls people at 6.30 am for their reaction to an item in that morning's press. Television journalists are usually fairly arrogant in their use of other people's time and will demand you fit in with them, rather than vice versa.

If you are invited for a studio interview, establish quite clearly beforehand what aspects of the issue will be covered, what line the reporter or program is taking and who else will be appearing with you.

You can also expect a fair degree of distortion of your views, especially on television news bulletins. Cutting and intercutting and editing can make you appear to say things quite different from what you actually said or intended to say. Your best recourse is to keep your answers and comments as short and as factual as possible and to realise the risks of distortion you run.

The typical comment used on the television news these days runs from five to twenty seconds. All you get is one or two sentences. On current affairs programs, you should expect your interviews to last from ninety seconds to three minutes. This means that you must be well prepared and have pithy comments and answers ready in advance. Try to anticipate the questions you will be asked. It is acceptable, in fact, to ask the interviewer beforehand to say what questions will be asked. It is also common to have a brief question-and-answer rehearsal with the interviewer before the television cameras roll.

If you are invited for a studio interview, establish quite clearly beforehand what aspects of the issue will be covered, what line the reporter or program is taking and who else will be appearing with you.

Despite a great many myths to the contrary, there are no special tricks to television interviews, apart from making your answers concise and punchy. If you believe in what you are saying, this will come across clearly. In the same way, insincerity is completely transparent. Talk to the interviewer as if he or she were the only one there, and never look straight into the camera. The latter does require some special talent and is best left to the professionals.

When they are speaking seriously, or when they are a little nervous, some people inadvertently pull faces. Some of these can be quite distorted by the television camera. If you suspect this problem, you will profit by rehearsing your answers and discussion before a mirror or, better still, if you have access to one, on your own video recorder.

Avoid using notes or written material of any kind before the camera or microphone. Even though notes cannot be seen on radio, reading anything always gives you away because you lose the conversational tone that is essential to effective broadcasting.

If you believe in what you are saying, this will come across clearly on TV. In the same way, insincerity is completely transparent. Talk to the interviewer as if he or she were the only one there, and never look straight into the camera.

Any television group appearance for your cause must be well orchestrated. There are few things worse on television than a group of people talking over each other. It can lead to instant disaffection for your cause—in fact, if a current affairs producer wanted to make your organisation look like a rabble, an unprepared group appearance would be a good way to do it. To be successful, a group appearance should have been prepared in the following way.

- You have held discussions beforehand on the issues you want to raise.
- There is a consensus of opinion about the most important points.
- You have elected individuals to speak on particular points.
- The group recognises different abilities in its members: persuasive speakers, well-informed speakers, and so on.

RADIO TALK-BACK PROGRAMS

Some lobbying organisations in the past have thought that talk-back radio was a medium they could monopolise by encouraging large numbers of their members to flood the switchboards of the major stations. They thought they could influence the public by having their views broadcast as often as possible.

The influence of talk-back radio, however, is now similar to that of petitions. There is now so much of it covering such a range of issues that little of it appears influential. It has become very much a medium that preaches to the converted.

At election times, however, talk-back radio takes on a new dimension because the leading politicians all feel they have to appear on it. This is when relatively fresh and influential issues are raised. A lobbying organisation should monitor the radio at this time and, if an issue is raised that is of concern to the group, its members should ring in with their comments.

The influence of talk-back radio is now similar to that of petitions. There is now so much of it covering such a range of issues that little of it appears influential. It has become very much a medium that preaches to the converted.

The main advantage of talk-back radio is that it provides a good vehicle on which to practise. You remain anonymous but you are able to get invaluable experience—overcoming nervousness, learning a sense of timing and how to speak in a modulated voice, neither too fast nor too slow. Make sure you record and playback your efforts and learn by criticising your faults.

NEWS CONFERENCES

A news conference can be useful when you want some publicity to stimulate interest in your cause, to make an important announcement, to introduce a visiting celebrity to the media or to display something new.

Draw up a news release announcing the news conference. Record the subject of the conference, a few brief background details (containing some drama and colour if possible), the time, date and location of the conference, plus a name and telephone number to contact. Send this release to all on your media contact list.

It is best to hold news conferences in the morning, preferably about 11 am. This gives both the morning newspapers and the evening television news, which both have early evening deadlines, plenty of time to come and to prepare their material afterwards. At this time of day, you should serve coffee, tea and biscuits, but there is no need for alcohol. You can, if you have the money, take the more interested media people for lunch. Do

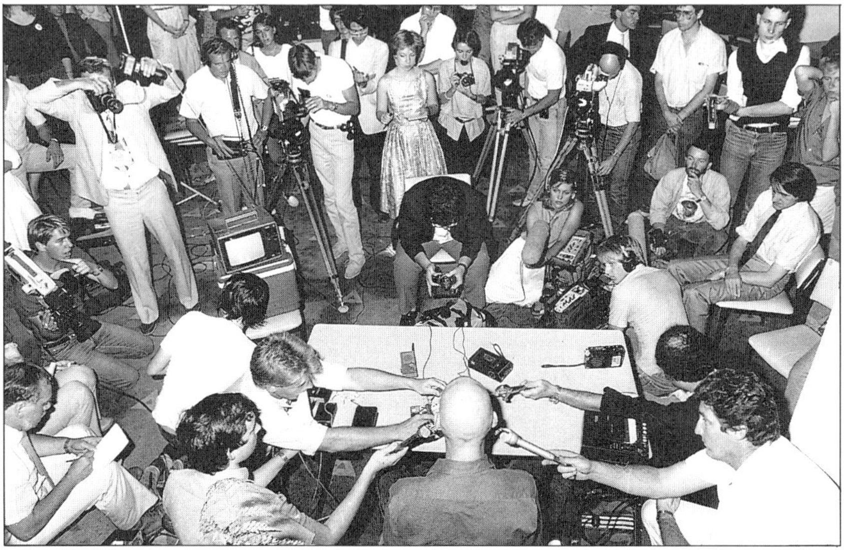

Rock singer Peter Garrett holds news conferences to publicise an environmental issue. Because he is a celebrity, the media are likely to give him coverage

not serve any food or drinks, though, until all the talk has finished.

Hold news conferences preferably about 11 am. This gives both the morning newspapers and evening television news, which both have early evening deadlines, plenty of time to come and to prepare their material afterwards.

A news conference should be held either in an uncluttered room, with plenty of space for television lights to be set up, or better still, at an outside location that has plenty of good 'visuals'—that is, scenes of colourful action.

The conference should consist of a prepared statement by one, two or three members of an organisation—no more. This should be followed by an open question time. The television reporters often want to record their own individual interviews with your people following the open question session, so give each the opportunity.

It is essential to have a typed set of copies of the opening statement. Give one to each journalist who attends. This need not be anything elaborate. Some public relations firms go to great lengths with expensive plastic covers, free pens and the like, which do little to enhance their prospects of being reported. A plain white, double spaced A4 typed sheet will do fine. A second handout, giving some background of your group, may also be useful.

You need one person to wait at the door or entrance to greet each journalist who arrives, to give each the handout and tell them where to sit or stand. You need someone else to act as chair, to introduce the person or people giving the prepared statement. In other words, you need a minimum of three people—one at the door, one as chair and one as speaker.

News conferences can sometimes be disappointing. They take a reasonable amount of effort to organise, but you might get little coverage for your trouble. News coverage will depend partly on how intrinsically interesting your announcement is and partly on what else happens that day. If something like the dismissal of the prime minister or a local disaster with a high death toll occurs, you will probably miss out, no matter how good you are. But if little else is making the news at that time, even boring and insignificant news conferences can get good coverage. Obvious times to avoid are those when you know the competition will be stiff, such as the middle of an election campaign or the day before the Melbourne Cup.

To conduct a news conference you need a minimum of three people—one at the door, one as chair and one as speaker.

Overall, any lobbying campaign that wants to make use of the media should prepare itself for both losses and victories. There will be times when very well-prepared news releases and conferences will hardly rate a mention. There will be other times when the media will turn against you, distorting your message or perhaps even denouncing you. The best way to respond is to do the same as those past masters of the media, the politicians. They simply keep coming back.

Hold news conferences either in an uncluttered room, with plenty of space for television lights to be set up or, better still, at an outside location that has plenty of good 'visuals'—that is, scenes of colourful action.

Apart from the communication skills offered throughout this book, the qualities you need most to succeed with the media are resilience and persistence. If you keep coming back, the chances are that the media will eventually take up your message and thereby provide you with some of the most powerful means of communication that are available to influence our society.

KEY POINTS: Chapter 38 How to use the media

- A large part of the knowledge and opinions most people have about current issues comes from the media, so it is worth putting effort into trying to attract media publicity.
- The most common way of getting news and views about your organisation into the media is through the news release, a short news story which is sent to the news editors of newspapers, radio and television stations.
- Now matter how good your story, it may not be published because other news of a higher priority occurs at the same time. Don't take failure personally—simply try again.
- Try to understand the audience that the publisher or broadcaster is trying to reach. Orient your story towards that audience.
- In a studio interview, establish beforehand what aspects of the issue will be covered and who else will be appearing with you.
- Keep answers in an interview short and factual to minimise distortion.
- If you believe in your cause, this will show in a television interview, but so will any insincerity.
- A group appearance on television is risky and needs to be carefully orchestrated beforehand.
- Radio talk-back programs do little to advance a cause that is not covered favourably elsewhere in the media.
- If you have a visiting speaker or can display something new, a news conference can generate good publicity.
- News conferences should be held in the morning and need at least three people—one at the door, one as chair and one as speaker.
- News conferences should be held either in an uncluttered room or, better, in a location that offers colourful visuals for television.

QUESTIONS FOR DISCUSSION

- When promoting a cause, is bad publicity better than no publicity? Discuss examples of the effects of bad publicity on issues you are familiar with.
- You have a very good story giving a new angle to an issue that everyone in your locality is talking about, yet when you send it to the capital city newspapers none of them use it. Discuss the reasons, and what you could do in response.
- You have an interesting story about a women's issue. Should you send it to every women's magazine? Discuss.
- You have an interesting story about a sporting issue. Should you send it to every sporting publication? Discuss.

EXERCISES

1. A public reserve in your locality is threatened by a new building development. Explain what steps you would take to publicise your opposition to: first, local newspapers and metropolitan dailies, and, second, radio and television. Compose a news release to present your side of the issue.

2. You are concerned about discrimination against a newly arrived ethnic group in your area. To date, the media has presented only one side of the story—that of the long-term residents. The situation reaches a crisis when a local resident seriously assaults a member of the ethnic group. As the president of a local service club, you decide to tell the real story to the media. Describe what steps you would take to call a news conference, whom you would invite and how you would present the case for the ethnic group.

3. Describe all the steps involved in conducting a media campaign to prevent the closure of the small arms factory discussed in Exercise 3 of the previous chapter.

4. Take a major public issue in which you have an interest or concern. As secretary of a community lobby group on the issue, work out a one-month media campaign to influence voters before the coming election. Schedule all dates of the actions you would take and compose all the news releases and public statements you would need.

REVISION LIST FOR PART XI

PUBLIC RELATIONS

- A wide range of organisations now engage in public relations including business, government, educational institutions, hospitals, community service organisations and religious bodies.
- They are trying to generate goodwill among several of their publics, including their customers, employees, the government, financial investors, their local communities, the media and the public at large.
- Whether they engage in public relations or not, most organisations have a public image that can serve them well or ill.
- The long-term aim of public relations is to communicate real information about clients' objectives, policies, standards, products and services.
- Public relations personnel are employed either in specialist departments within large organisations or in agencies who have a number of clients.
- Their role includes preventing conflict and misunderstanding, promoting respect and goodwill, improving industrial relations, projecting a corporate identity, researching public opinion, analysing and advising on future trends.
- Citizens in a democracy can lobby politicians to change the law and can lobby government departments and statutory authorities on a range of issues that affect their locality.
- Do not assume a politician has a great deal of knowledge of the subject about which you are lobbying. Politicians are ordinary people who get most of their information from the media, like everyone else.
- Your local member is obliged to give you a personal interview. Make an appointment through his or her electorate secretary.
- Politicians can be elected to Commonwealth, state or local governments. Try to decide which is the most relevant to your issue.

continued on next page

continued from previous page

- A delegation of two or three people is more effective than one, or more than three. Delegations have limited time and so should be well prepared.
- Try to persuade a politician on an issue in the same way you would an ordinary member of the public. But try, also, to see how the issue affects the politician's chances of being re-elected.
- Petitions today are largely ineffective means of lobbying politicians. Personal letters written by individuals can be far more effective.
- Demonstrations can be effective, but can also backfire if not enough people turn up. Save them for the last stage of a campaign, but use them only if you have nothing to lose.
- Lobbying involves risks in terms of finance and the law, so it is best to form a legal structure to handle both. The best type of legal structure for a lobbying group is either an incorporated association or a company limited by guarantee.
- A large part of the knowledge and opinions most people have about current issues comes from the media, so it is worth putting effort into trying to attract media publicity.
- The most common way of getting news and views about your organisation into the media is through the news release, a short news story sent to the news editors of newspapers, radio stations and television stations.
- No matter how good your story, it may not be published because other news of a higher priority occurs at the same time. Don't take failure personally—simply try again.
- Try to understand the audience that the publisher or broadcaster is trying to reach. Orient your story towards that audience.
- In a studio interview, establish beforehand what aspects of the issue will be covered and who else will be appearing with you. Keep answers in an interview short and factual to minimise distortion.
- If you believe in your cause, this will show in a television interview, but so will any insincerity.

continued on next page

continued from previous page

- A group appearance on television is risky and needs to be carefully orchestrated beforehand.
- Radio talk-back programs do little to advance a cause that is not covered favourably elsewhere in the media.
- If you have a visiting speaker or can display something new, a news conference can generate good publicity.
- News conferences should be held in the morning and need at least three people—one at the door, one as chair and one as speaker. They should preferably be held in a location that offers colourful visuals for television.

PART XI
KEY TEXTS AND FURTHER READING

Australian Media Directory, International Public Relations, annual editions.

B&T Year Book, Thomson Publications, Sydney, annual editions.

Binkowski, G. A., *How to Deal With the Government*, Information Australia, Melbourne, 1986.

Cutlip, S. M. and Center, A., *Effective Public Relations*, Prentice Hall, Sydney, 1985.

Hailstone, Robert, *The Australian Media Handbook*, Business Library, Melbourne, 1990.

Mathews, I., *How to Use the Media in Australia*, Margaret Gee, Melbourne, 1984.

Pesman, Sandra, *Writing for the Media: Public Relations and the Press*, Crain Books, Chicago, 1983.

Tymson, Candy, *How To Do Public Relations: A Do-It-Yourself Guide to Successful Publicity and Promotions*, Millennium Books, Sydney, 1988.

Tymson, Candy and Sherman, Bill, *The Australian Public Relations Manual*, Millennium Books, Sydney, 1990.

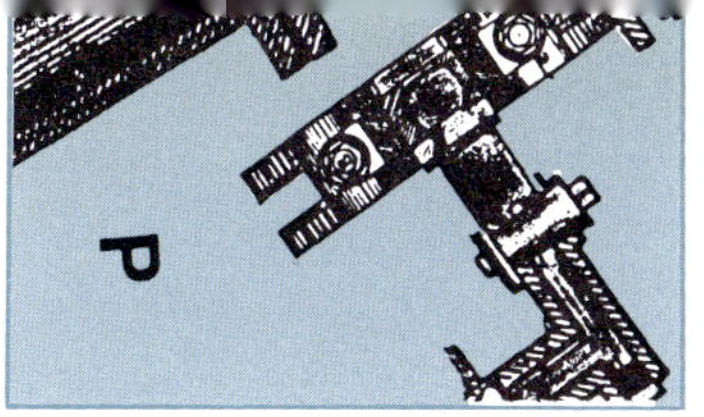

PART XII

MULTICULTURAL COMMUNICATION

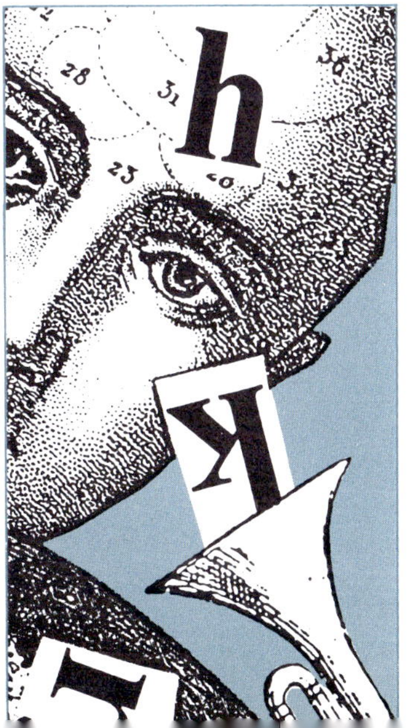

COMING TO TERMS WITH OTHER CULTURES

Dr Robert March tells how Australians need to lift their game in communicating with the Japanese and other people of Asia.

In this era of international business, companies are realising that success often depends on training their representatives to understand the cultural background of their foreign business associates.

The talents of Dr Robert March, lecturer/writer/seminar leader, whose specific area of expertise is on how to do business with the Japanese, are currently much in demand.

He is a visiting professor in Japanese business at the University of New South Wales and the author of several books including *Working For A Japanese Company: Insights Into The Multicultural Workplace*, *The Honourable Customer: Marketing and Selling to the Japanese* and *The Japanese Negotiator: Subtlety and Strategy Beyond Western Logic*.

His intimate knowledge of Japanese business practices comes as a result of intensive study in psychology, sociology and marketing, twenty years of international management consulting and living and working in Japan for fifteen years.

While he speaks and writes fluent Japanese, he is the first to agree that proficiency in a foreign language is only one part of coming to terms with people whose background is vastly different from your own.

He feels that the best negotiators are those people who are genuinely interested in learning about the values, beliefs and culturally defined mechanisms that influence the way people from other countries do business.

'In the 1970s and 1980s, a lot of the major Australian companies were employing people who didn't have the skills, affinity and background to really do a proper job of managing relations on a long-term basis with the Japanese,' he says. 'The people being sent over were often technicians and engineers (especially in the mining sector) who may have known a great deal about coal and iron ore, but were inexperienced in the basic protocol of business relations.'

While March now believes that Australian business practices are becoming more sophisticated and that negotiators are finally being selected on their 'people skills', he points to continuing deficiencies among Australians.

'Compared to the Japanese, Australians are short on international sense. They don't have the same comprehensive understanding of what's happening in the world,' he says.

He also warns about the dangers of stereotyped thinking.

'If you think that the Japanese are short, polite and introverted, you might behave in a way that would make many Japanese feel comfortable. However, there are also Japanese who are not at all shy and even quite extroverted. Since they won't be happy at being treated as shy introverts, you must modify your perceptions and adjust to the reality you're facing,' he states.

He points out that Australians are at a disadvantage when dealing with the Japanese because they certainly know more about our culture than we do about theirs, and are usually better informed about our way of life.

Surveys March has conducted with major Japanese companies that do business with Australians show that Japanese businessmen think many Australian negotiators are dogmatic, inflexible and become easily offended when problems of fact or interpretation are pointed out to them. They also feel Australians don't prepare very well for meetings and can be inclined to go back on their verbal promises.

With a view to enhancing relations between Westerners and the Japanese, March runs negotiation-training courses for educational institutions and companies in Japan, Australia, the United States and South-East Asia. While he believes they are beneficial, he says long-term contact with people from other cultures is the key to developing harmony with them.

'The role of training courses is useful but modest, since the capacity for people to learn by study or by talking to others is fairly limited. The only way to learn negotiation is to negotiate and the only way to learn properly about Japan is to live and work there, assimilating the culture from up close,' he declares.

He does acknowledge the importance of being aware of some fundamental differences in the way Westerners and the Japanese operate in the business arena.

While Westerners regard negotiation as a persuasive process, won by brilliant reasoning and bottom-line bargaining, the Japanese are different. The most important aspect to them is information gathering.

'They probe, question, check, re-state and verify all aspects of the deal before committing themselves, and such a drawn-out approach calls for considerable patience from the Westerner on the other side of the table. Westerners are more accustomed to working to the pressure of deadlines and frequently short-cut on information gathering,' he says.

Another problem characteristic of the Japanese is their tendency to understate and merely hint at things, expecting others to read their purposes and meanings. March states that this type of behaviour puts more emphasis upon trying to correctly interpret their non-verbal messages, which can be extremely difficult for an outsider.

He says the Japanese are very experienced at play-acting or putting a face over their true feelings and emotions. This is called *tatemae* in Japanese and means something like 'official policy' or 'dressed for public consumption'. Thus Japanese facial expressions can be misleading for foreigners.

A golden rule in Japanese business is that you have discussions and meetings face-to-face, as the Japanese like to develop a relationship of trust and goodwill with their business partners.

'Personal rapport is very necessary for the Japanese. They value people who will listen to them and take an interest in them as people, as well as being business negotiators. This family-type relationship is based on *amae* which concerns dependency on the goodwill of others,' says March.

Westerners concerned with doing a 'quick deal' and discussing money 'up-front' get nowhere in Japan, where there is less concern with time and a frequent disdain for what March calls the unvarnished 'merchant mind'.

The Japanese have developed more cohesive team work than their Western counterparts. The members of their negotiation teams have clearly defined roles to play in the various stages of information gathering.

'Most of the time the orientation of senior Japanese is to give experience to the younger people during negotiation and to let them make the mistakes in the low-risk phases of negotiation, which is a good method of training people, but alien to Western ways,' he says.

Westerners usually have more authority for on-the-spot decisions, while the Japanese may have to refer to superior team members. In some cases, the key decision-maker may not appear at the table until the closing stages of discussion. In this way, he is used as a 'secret weapon'. March calls this strategy 'concealing the top man'. On the other hand, when this senior man does appear, it is a clear sign that the Japanese are ready to do business with you.

Japanese culture approves the use of ambiguity, which extends even to the business setting. If the Japanese are unable to fulfil a request, they won't say 'no,' but will use indirect statements. Other Japanese are expected to understand, but this often confuses foreigners.

Great emphasis is placed on politeness and courtesy when the Japanese are doing business and they try to avoid confrontation at all costs. In fact, they will constantly apologise even for the most minor misunderstandings on their part, so that there can be no chance of misconstruing intended meanings.

'The Japanese do this to keep negotiations on an even keel, while Westerners tend to be more confrontational and adversarial when things go awry,' says March.

Over his many years of dealing with the Japanese, March has realised that Westerners are often unskilled in and unprepared for the subtleties of such an intricate culture. Consequently, in 1984 he developed some guidelines to facilitate effective negotiations among business parties which could be applied in a cross-cultural sense. He called his approach the Strategic Negotiation Process. Its main elements are:

1. Select negotiators who are first of all good managers, proven as both people and project managers.
2. Make a comprehensive opening statement in which negotiators present the context or background that has led them to adopt their current

stance on an issue. This statement should encompass what they see as the key issues at stake, the current trends in the environment or market place and what the predictions for the future are likely to be. March stresses that this opening statement is critical in minimising the possibility of later conflicts or petty squabbling.

3. The delay of bargaining is also advised, until as much as possible is known about the other side. This is similar to the Japanese information gathering orientation, and enables you to make offers or demands much later in a negotiation.
4. Conflict should be avoided wherever possible and resolved quickly should it eventuate.

Overall, negotiators should maintain a friendly and businesslike tone, whatever frictions occur along the way. 'This approach actually typifies a trend towards an international negotiation style that all international negotiators, Japanese as well as Western, gradually acquire with experience,' March says.

CHAPTER

39

UNDERSTANDING CULTURAL DIFFERENCES

After studying this chapter, you will:

- ☐ understand what it means to have a shared culture
- ☐ recognise that other people have different cultures
- ☐ understand the difference between a culture and a subculture
- ☐ know that a culture is not the same as a race or an ethnic group
- ☐ know what ethnocentrism means
- ☐ understand how communication can be distorted when interpreted by people from different cultural backgrounds
- ☐ understand how culture can be expressed through behaviour, manners, values, religion, status and body language
- ☐ recognise that people from other cultures may have different attitudes from us toward their use of time and space and their decision-making processes
- ☐ know where to begin when you want to understand another culture

More than ever before, it has become important for Australians to respond in positive ways to other cultures. For a start, it has become a matter of economic survival. Unless we can dramatically lift the levels of our exports to new markets, especially the growth areas in eastern and South-East Asia, the prospects for maintaining a stable economy and our present standard of living are grim. One of the essential criteria for expanding exports to these countries is to know what they want to buy from us, and this means gaining a much improved understanding of their culture. Second, although Australia has been a country of immigrants for all of the last two hundred years, the last two decades have seen an enormous increase in the number of countries from which immigrants have come. Today immigrants come from all of the continents and from almost every country on the globe.

Every day, all of us in the workforce and the education system find ourselves relating to people from widely varying cultural backgrounds. If these institutions are to work properly, and if the personal relationships within them are to remain as relatively harmonious as they have been until now, we all need to work hard at understanding each other's cultural differences.

Every day, all of us in the workforce and the education system find ourselves relating to people from widely varying cultural backgrounds. If these institutions are to work properly, and if the personal relationships within them are to remain as relatively harmonious as they have been until now, we all need to work hard at understanding each other's cultural differences.

UNDERSTANDING CULTURE

A culture is a shared system of behaviour, values, beliefs, attitudes, manners, symbols and assumptions. In some cases, a culture can have its own exclusive language, but in most cases this is not so. The English, the Irish and the Americans all speak English, but have clearly different cultures. The members of a culture can each have their own personal qualities and characters, which may differ widely, but when a large group has similar expectations about values, about how people think, behave and communicate, they can be said to share a culture.

The members of a culture can each have their own personal qualities and characters, which may differ widely, but when a large group has similar expectations about values, about how people think, behave and communicate, they can be said to share a culture.

Members of a particular culture often gravitate together and form a subculture, such as the Vietnamese in the Sydney suburb of Cabramatta

A culture is usually shared by a very large group of people within which there can be smaller groups who have their own identities. In these cases, the latter groups are generally called *subcultures*. Most people would agree that there is a dominant Australian culture, and that, within it, there are a large number of subcultures. Queensland sugar farmers would be one of these and another would be Tasmanian forest workers. Both share the overall Australian ethos but have maintained their own outlook, habits and personal relationships.

Cultures can vary enormously in the way that they relate to the culture of others. American culture, for example, tolerates and encourages diversity. Japanese culture is very homogeneous. Cultures can also change in important ways but retain their own uniqueness. Until the 1960s, Australian culture was wary and intolerant of non-European people. Today, despite problems that might occur between individuals, our culture as a whole is far more open and internationally oriented.

People who have lived all their lives within their own culture find it very difficult to imagine that others can be different.

A culture can sometimes be based on people of the same ethnic or racial background, but this is not necessary. People living in the United States have a myriad of ethnic backgrounds but an identifiable common culture. A culture usually arises when people have lived and mixed together for a sustained period of time. This, rather than the racial or ethnic background of their ancestors, appears to be the most important causal factor.

ETHNOCENTRISM

Ethnocentrism arises when people cannot appreciate the culture of others. Ethnocentrism can be both deliberate and innocent or unwitting. It is deliberate when it is overtly racist—when some people think that their culture is vastly superior to that of others. It is innocent largely through ignorance. People who have lived all their lives within their own culture find it very difficult to imagine that others can be different. Fortunately, the global reach of communications, especially in the form of cinema and television, means that most people in most countries are now aware that other people have different cultures and cultural values. There is far less ignorance of others today than there was fifty years ago.

Any form of communication with people of another culture runs the risk of being misunderstood, especially when it uses symbols that may have a positive meaning in one culture but a negative meaning in another.

Nonetheless, it will never be easy for people from one culture to fully appreciate that of another, even when they have the best will in the world. For instance, the more we recognise cultural diversity, the more we realise the inadequacy of an old Biblical saying which was once our byword for tolerance and consideration of others: 'Do unto others as you would want them to do unto you'. It is no longer good enough to treat other people the way *you* would want to be treated because your own demands are conditioned by your own culture. To be culturally aware is to treat people of other cultures the way *they* want to be treated.

THE VARIETIES OF CULTURAL DIFFERENCE

Any form of communication with people of another culture runs the risk of being misunderstood, especially when it uses symbols that may have a positive meaning in one culture but a negative meaning in another. For instance, an American cosmetics firm marketed its brand of men's cologne in North Africa using the advertisement that had already worked well for it in North America and Europe, a picture of a man and his dog in the great outdoors. The marketing campaign was a failure because the firm was unaware that in this Moslem country, a dog was a sign of either bad luck or a symbol of uncleanliness.

In another example, a manager of a company in Sydney that employed a group of Asian-born workers wanted to indicate that he was pleased with their work. At a staff meeting, he singled the group out for praise in front of the other workers, thinking this would make them proud of their achievement. He was puzzled when, instead of smiling, they looked at one another with much concern on their faces. The manager failed to realise that, in their culture, praise was only given privately and never in front of co-workers or customers.

To be culturally aware means to realise that other people differ from us in many ways: in their attitudes towards behaviour and manners, in their values and religion, in their concepts of status and social roles, in their decision-making practices, and in their attitudes towards time, personal space and body language.

BEHAVIOUR AND MANNERS

Almost all societies have rules of etiquette governing behaviour regarded as polite or considerate of others. They govern behaviour related to meeting and greeting others, eating, the use of names (when, for instance, it is appropriate to use someone's first name and when it is not), when and how people may touch each other, and the relations between the sexes. In some cases these rules are written down and can be learned; in other cases, they are informal and understood implicitly by members of a culture. In the latter case, outsiders often find it difficult to know how to behave and can only learn by watching and imitating the members of the other culture.

Etiquette varies greatly between cultures: what is polite in one country may be considered rude in another. To Japanese, slurping soup loudly is the proper way to act; in most Western restaurants this behaviour would attract frowns from other patrons. In Arab countries, a person visiting a family gives serious offence by bringing a present to the wife of the household, but is seen as generous by bringing gifts for the children. Among Australians, bringing a bottle of wine when you visit someone for dinner is a friendly gesture; if you did the same in Saudi Arabia, you could well end up in jail. In most countries of the world, the rituals and manners surrounding the eating of food are a cultural minefield. In all but a few, turning down an offer of food or drink gives an insult which will not be easily forgotten. When studying another culture, be sure you understand the etiquette that surrounds eating.

In some cases the rules of a culture's etiquette are written down and can be learned; in other cases, they are informal and understood implicitly by members of a culture. In the latter case, outsiders often find it difficult to know how to behave and can only learn by watching and imitating the members of the other culture.

The same is true for the relations between men and women. This is one area where what is acceptable in one culture is often regarded differently in another. For example, in Australia it is normal today for men and women to perform the same job and to work together in reasonably close confines. In a number of other cultures, however, this is unacceptable unless the men and women concerned are married to each other. There are a number of cases recorded where newly arrived immigrant women have been very disturbed to find, when they gained their first job, that they were required to work alongside other men. To avoid problems of this kind, Australian employers need to gain advice from compatriots about the cultural mores of new members of their workforce.

When dealing with other cultures, you cannot assume they will all be motivated by the prospect of individual gain. Nor can you assume that other cultures believe that those who work hard are better people than those who don't.

VALUES AND RELIGION

The 'Protestant ethic' that still determines the values of most English-speaking countries assumes that competitive behaviour is normal and that the acquisition of material gain by the individual is one of the major goals of life. However, the religious values of other countries regard our values with disdain. Buddhists and Hindus condemn materialism and place a much higher value on the spiritual life. Many Australian Aboriginal people believe it is unnatural for an individual to accumulate wealth and that the rewards of labour should be shared widely among relatives and friends.

So when dealing with other cultures, you cannot assume they will all be motivated by the prospect of individual gain. Nor can you assume that other cultures believe that those who work hard are better people than those who don't.

STATUS

The symbols that represent status are perhaps the most varied of all aspects of culture. You cannot assume that what is impressive in one culture will have the same impact in another. For instance, antiques in countries of European origin are highly prized and valued. But in many parts of China, if you give someone a gift of an antique clock you are assumed to be wishing them bad luck.

In most Western countries, the person who drives a prestige car like a Mercedes Benz or Porsche is attempting to demonstrate a certain kind of status; in many countries of Asia, people who have high status look down upon those who drive their own cars, no matter what the make, because it shows they cannot afford a driver.

DECISION-MAKING PRACTICES

In North America and Australia, people who are given the job of negotiating with others to make an agreement are given power to make their own decisions within a certain range of limits. We consider it inefficient for someone to go to a meeting without having this authority, and become impatient in a negotiation if, at a crucial point, the other side says they have to consult someone else. However, in other cultures, such as Japanese and Chinese, decision-making is a shared responsibility that an individual cannot usurp. Japanese negotiating teams, for example, take decisions only after all members of the team have arrived at a consensus.

In some cultures, such as Japanese and Chinese, decision-making is a shared responsibility that an individual cannot usurp.

A number of other cultures also place great store in dwelling on detail. In the West, this is usually taken as stalling or time-wasting. But many countries with a Spanish cultural heritage, such as Latin America or the Philippines, regard quick decisions as both anti-social and authoritarian. The trustworthy negotiator is one who is happy to go through a decision in the finest detail.

ATTITUDES TOWARDS TIME

Any Australian who has had business dealings with Americans will know that the two countries, though similar in many ways, have a different attitude towards time. To Americans, time is money and wasted time is income lost. Australians, on the other hand, are much more leisurely and regard time as something to be enjoyed rather than counted.

When doing business, there are many cultures whose members feel slighted if a deal is done quickly. If a deal is important, it should take an appropriate amount of time. What many Westerners sometimes interpret as indecision, prevarication or even haggling is often a desire to extend discussion to the amount of time regarded as appropriate. We often need to learn patience in order to deal with others.

There are many cultures whose members feel slighted if a deal is done quickly. If a deal is important, it should take an appropriate amount of time. What many Westerners sometimes interpret as indecision, prevarication or even haggling is often a desire to extend discussion to the amount of time regarded as appropriate.

With the internationalisation of business, many countries have adopted the Western attitude that punctuality is a great virtue and that it is inconsiderate of others to be late. However, in attitudes towards leisure, quite different practices can prevail. In Sydney, for example, if friends ask you for dinner at 7 pm, they would normally be annoyed if you actually arrived at this time, for they would still be getting things ready. The polite time to arrive is normally half an hour later, at 7.30 pm. This is something that most dinner guests will take as understood, but for formal occasions when printed invitations are issued, some actually will spell it out in the following terms: '7 pm for 7.30 pm'.

PERSONAL SPACE AND BODY LANGUAGE

We are often unaware of it, but like most others our society has certain expectations about the distance it is appropriate to keep between people in different circumstances. In general, when discussing business, people with an English cultural background tend to prefer to keep a greater distance between themselves and others than do people from Latin America, the Mediterranean or the Middle East. Our culture assumes that, by moving closer, someone is being aggressive, so we back away. We also use the gesture of leaning forward to someone across a table as an act of assertion, whereas to some other cultures it represents friendliness and agreement.

Many other signals that people give through their body language mean different things to people of different cultures. In general, people with an English-speaking background tend to verbalise, that is, to rely on the actual words they use to communicate. Other cultures, especially the Japanese, expect you to know that their words are only part of the message they want to get across and that, in some cases, their words may say one thing but their body language can modify the message greatly, even to the point of contradiction. When learning the languages of most other cultures, you need to ensure you also learn the meanings of their gestures.

Other cultures, especially the Japanese, expect you to know that their words are only part of the message they want to get across and that, in some cases, their words may say one thing but their body language can modify the message greatly.

LEARNING ABOUT A CULTURE

To communicate successfully with people from another culture, there is no substitute for hard work. If you plan to do regular business or to visit another country for a sustained period of time, you must learn the language. These days tourists can get by almost anywhere in the world with English, but you cannot develop business and personal relationships without learning at least some of their language. It is disrespectful, in most cases, not to. As we noted above, you cannot assume that another language is as word-oriented as ours. Gestures and body language can be a critical part of the communication process. Hence language learning tapes and phrase books are never enough—you need direct contact with someone from the culture itself.

Learning about another culture normally means reading widely. You will need some familiarity with its history, religion, politics and customs. For many newly developing countries, commercial activities have emerged only recently and are less than a generation old. This means there will often be a real cultural gap between older and younger members of the society. In these cases, you will need to find out who makes decisions and who determines the new rules and protocol.

Some of the developing countries have a newly acquired business subculture at odds with traditional values. But you cannot assume from this that the old culture has become irrelevant. In a changing world, many people—and this also applies to immigrants to another country—retain the most dearly held components of a traditional culture.

Every culture is continually evolving, so you can never assume anything is static. Some of the developing countries will have a newly acquired business subculture at odds with many of their traditional values. But you cannot assume from this that the old culture has become irrelevant. In a changing world, many people—and this also applies to immigrants to another country—retain the most dearly held components of a traditional culture but modify less important aspects to cope with the new conditions. Hence, understanding the past of a culture is often as important as understanding its present.

KEY POINTS: Chapter 39 Understanding cultural differences

- A culture is a shared system of behaviour, values, beliefs, attitudes, manners, symbols and assumptions.
- A culture is shared by a very large group of people within which there can be smaller groups with their own identities which can be described as subcultures.
- Cultures can vary enormously in the way they relate to others. Some, like that of the United States, are open and welcome diversity; others, like the Japanese, are much more homogeneous.
- Ethnocentrism means not appreciating the culture of others. It can be based on a sense of superiority over others, in which case it is racist, or it can derive from sheer ignorance.
- Any form of communication with people of another culture runs the risk of being misunderstood, especially when it uses symbols that may have a positive meaning in one culture but a negative meaning in another.
- To be culturally aware means to realise that other people differ from us in many ways: in their attitudes towards behaviour and manners, in their values and religion, in their concepts of status and social roles, in their decision-making practices, and in their attitudes towards time, personal space and body language.
- Learning about another culture starts by learning some of the language, reading about its history, religion, politics and customs, and questioning people about the process of cultural change.

QUESTIONS FOR DISCUSSION

1. What makes people ethnocentric? Why is this outlook a problem?
2. Discuss some symbols or gestures which mean different things in different cultures.
3. Discuss some aspects of eating in which Australian customs differ noticeably from those of other cultures.
4. Discuss some aspects of the relations between adults and children in which Australian customs differ noticeably from those of other cultures.
5. Discuss some aspects of the relations between men and women in which Australian customs differ noticeably from those of other cultures.

EXERCISES

1. Define and explain the differences between a culture, a subculture, an ethnic group and people who speak the same language. Give examples, apart from those used in this chapter, to indicate how each group is separate and to show where they overlap.

2. You are applying for a scholarship to one or more of the following countries: Indonesia, Malaysia, China, Japan and Thailand. One of the terms for winning is that you show an understanding of the culture of the country concerned. Do the research and prepare a ten-point list which describes the most important aspects of that country's culture. Elaborate each point in the list with explanations.

CHAPTER

40

COMMUNICATING WITH OTHER CULTURES

After studying this chapter, you will be able to:

- decide whether to learn a language to communicate with people from another culture
- display the sensitivity needed to communicate successfully with other cultures
- recognise your own cultural assumptions and prejudices
- communicate successfully in writing with other cultures
- engage in successful verbal communication with other cultures

Coming from an English-speaking country gives Australians an advantage in communicating with people from other cultures. English is the most international of all languages. It is not only the first language in at least ten countries, but is the most common second language in the world. Australians can normally write business letters to people in other countries who speak other languages and still be confident that the receiver can either read it directly or soon find someone who can translate it. Moreover, when people from other language groups write to someone in an English-speaking country, they normally write in English themselves. More than 90 per cent of the world's international business letters are written in English.

Although speaking English is very convenient, it has brought its own problems with it. People from other cultures need to learn our language but we are not forced to learn theirs. As a result, they tend to know much more about us than we do about them.

While this may be very convenient for most Australians, it has brought its own problems. People from other cultures need to learn our language, but we are not forced to learn theirs. As a result, they tend to know much more about us than we do about them. In terms of both doing international business and in relating to migrants to our own country, we are therefore at a disadvantage. This chapter offers some help in overcoming this.

INTERCULTURAL COMMUNICATION

Obviously, the best way to address the issue of intercultural communication is to learn the language of the country with which you want to communicate. This, however, requires a great deal of time and energy. To become fluent in another European language usually takes at least 240 hours of study, while to reach fluency in Chinese, Japanese or Arabic takes at least double this time.

Nonetheless, many people find it enormously rewarding to make this effort. Mastering another language is something that generates a great deal of satisfaction. Those who can achieve it often find that the language stays with them and enriches them all their lives.

Mastering another language is something that generates a great deal of satisfaction. Those who can achieve it often find that the language stays with them and enriches them all their lives.

A less arduous approach, especially for those who find they have to visit another country for a sustained period at short notice, is to take a brief course in which the vocabulary learned is focused on a particular industry or occupation area. For example, since the growth in the number of Japanese tourists to Australia, some language schools and hospitality colleges have introduced courses in what they call 'hotel Japanese'. These courses, which are generally conducted only for about half a day a week over about three months, provide a basis in Japanese grammar plus a vocabulary oriented to the needs of the hospitality and tourism industries, such as checking people into and out of hotels, greeting and taking orders in restaurants, and the like. While in this period of time, students do not by any means master the language completely, they learn enough to break down the cultural barrier that would otherwise remain if they had no knowledge of Japanese at all.

However, what if your job entails dealing regularly with people from a variety of cultures and language groups? It clearly would become impossible to learn even a little of all their languages. The following guidelines should assist you to communicate with any other person, no matter what their cultural background.

- Avoid attributing national or cultural characteristics to individuals. Treat the people you meet as individuals with their own personal qualities and avoid some of the more familiar cultural stereotypes, such as the Scots are thrifty, the Italians are romantic or the Americans are brash. Individuals rarely fit these stereotypes (and, indeed, many of the common stereotypes are themselves wildly mistaken anyway).
- Become culturally sensitive. If you remain aware that people from other cultures are likely to have different attitudes to the issues we discussed in the previous chapter, especially on matters such as manners and values, you are less likely to make a blunder. Being culturally sensitive means being cautious when these issues arise and waiting to see how others react, rather than assuming they share the attitudes of our own culture.
- Make your own position clear. People from non-English-speaking cultures are actually more likely to be culturally sensitive than the other way around. When meeting an Australian, they are more likely to be cautious and reticent. Rather than both of you standing there being nice and sensitive but doing nothing, the best way to proceed is to try to make your own meaning and position clear. At the same time you should avoid making any assumptions about the other party. Sending clear messages means being consistent in both your verbal and non-verbal communications. As we noted in the previous chapter, English-speaking people tend to rely more on words and less on gestures than other cultures but this means we are less aware of the kinds of gestures we make and the signals they convey. In making your own position clear, try to be sure that your gestures do not communicate something that might contradict your words.
- Recognise your own cultural position. As well as being more aware of your gestures, you really need to take stock of not only your behaviour but your attitudes towards people from other cultures. If you have a disparaging attitude towards another country, you may well communicate this without realising it. For intercultural communication to be successful, you need to bring your own prejudices and assumptions to the forefront of your mentality and to examine them carefully. Having done this, you are in a much better position to respond to others as human beings first.
- Develop empathy. Try to see things from the other person's point of view. Obviously, this is easier said than done when the person has a different system of values and customs to your own. Nonetheless you should try by listening carefully to what the other person is trying to communicate, by trying to understand their feelings, and, above all, by being patient and not rushing to judgment.
- Communicate respect. Whatever you want to communicate, you should recognise that the first task is to develop a relationship with the other person. Communicating is never mere message-sending. If the other person detects you have little respect for them, then any other messages you want to get across are likely to be lost in a cloud of emotional response. Whatever their culture, all human beings like to maintain dignity when meeting with strangers. Remember this and try to say some

Avoid attributing national or cultural characteristics to individuals. Treat the people you meet as individuals with their own personal qualities and avoid some of the more familiar cultural stereotypes.

Recognise your own cultural position. As well as being more aware of your gestures, you really need to take stock of not only your behaviour but your attitudes towards people from other cultures.

words or make some gestures that show your respect. To do this successfully usually means you will need to learn something about the culture of the other person before you meet.
- Recognise your own mistakes. No matter how well prepared you might be, it is always difficult to conduct a new intercultural meeting without a hitch. So be particularly sensitive to your own propensity for making mistakes. If this happens, don't pretend it hasn't but face it openly, smile, explain and, if necessary, apologise. Remain flexible and prepared to change your mind when it is necessary.

WRITTEN COMMUNICATIONS

Whatever you want to communicate, you should recognise that the first task is to develop a relationship with the other person.

Communicating is never mere message-sending. If the other person detects you have little respect for them, then any other messages you want to get across are likely to be lost in a cloud of emotional response.

When you write business letters to people in other countries, there are some guidelines that will make the process of communicating in writing much easier for all concerned. If you are not fluent in the language of the person to whom you are writing, then write in your own language. If you know the other person does not speak English and would have difficulty finding a translator, then the onus is on you to have the letter translated before it is sent. When you both speak different languages, helpful guidelines include the following.

- Write simple and direct prose.
- Use short sentences and the active voice.
- Keep your paragraphs short and confine each to one point.
- Avoid abstract words and obscure phraseology.
- Avoid metaphors and similes.
- Avoid jargon, slang and acronyms.
- Never use clichés or figures of speech. Most translate very badly.
- Realise that people in other countries may not be familiar with our current political or topical issues. If you mention our prime minister or ministers of trade or immigration, give titles and their names.
- Use numerical data wherever possible. Numbers translate directly in almost every other culture.
- Make sure your full address is included in your letterhead and that telephone and fax numbers are presented for international use. When people overseas dial Australia, for instance, they have to drop the first '0' in the area code of a telephone number. Ensure that it is clear that you are actually writing from Australia. In this country we might have no trouble recognising NSW or SA but, unless your letterhead actually ends with the word 'Australia', an overseas recipient could easily be mystified about your location.

VERBAL COMMUNICATION

Verbal communications have some advantages and disadvantages over written communication. On the one hand, receiving a written message is usually easier than a spoken message in another language because you can translate it at your leisure. On the other hand, writing in another language is always more difficult than speaking, because the latter gives you the chance to see immediately whether you are understood and, if not, to change tack or try again. In general, it is usually necessary to handle international business on a personal basis, through the spoken word, at some stage in a transaction. In most overseas countries, unless you establish personal rapport, you are unlikely to be successful in any business pursuit. You can speak to other people directly and get immediate feedback, which is almost always needed if either of you are communicating in languages that are not your own. Guidelines for intercultural verbal communication include the following.

In most overseas countries, unless you establish personal rapport, you are unlikely to be successful in any business pursuit.

- Remain sensitive to the other person's approach and style. If he or she appears direct and up front, then so can you. If the other party is reticent and cautious, adapt your behaviour to the situation.
- Pay attention and listen patiently. English speakers often interrupt each other before one has finished a sentence, because the other can readily anticipate what is coming. This, however, can be a disastrous habit in other languages. Wait until the other person has finished a whole statement, and then, if you are unsure what was said, ask for it to be repeated.
- Be aware of gestures. As we noted above and in the previous chapter, before you start you should understand the importance of gestures and body language in the culture you are dealing with. Pay particular attention to arm movements and facial expressions. Also ensure that your own gestures are not inadvertently saying something different to what you intended.
- Regard the other person as an individual human being first, and a member of another culture second. Don't impose ethnic stereotypes and try to avoid preconceived ideas. However, you should still expect and look for the other person to have different values, customs and beliefs.
- When the conversation is almost complete, ensure that you both agree on what has been said. Go over important points once more and reconfirm any decisions the two of you have made. In some cases, you will want to follow up a conversation with a letter of thanks in which you also go over the main points made.

English speakers often interrupt each other before one has finished a sentence, because the other can readily anticipate what is coming. This, however, can be a disastrous habit in other languages.

KEY POINTS: Chapter 40 Communicating with other cultures

- English has the advantage of being the most common international language, but it means that Australians tend not to learn much about either the language or the culture of other people.
- The best way to undertake intercultural communication is to learn the language of another country.
- Short language courses with vocabulary related to a particular industry can be useful for some international business.
- Treat the people you meet as individuals and not as representatives of some imagined cultural stereotype.
- Make your own position clear and avoid misinterpretations through words and gestures that might inadvertently contradict each other.
- Try to see things from the other person's point of view and through the eyes of their culture.
- Whatever their culture, all human beings like to maintain dignity when meeting strangers. Ensure you communicate respect.
- In written communications with people from other cultures, use simple, direct prose, short sentences, short paragraphs and avoid abstractions, jargon, clichés and flowery language.
- In verbal communications with people from other cultures, never interrupt. Wait until the other person has finished, and then go over the main points to be sure you both agree.

QUESTIONS FOR DISCUSSION

1. What are the advantages and disadvantages of having English as your first language?
2. What does it mean to be culturally sensitive?
3. Why is it important to communicate respect?

EXERCISES

1. You are the principal of a technical college in your region. You have to make a five-minute speech of welcome to a group of students from a number of different Asian countries who have just arrived in Australia to learn English. You have organised translators so that each student can hear your speech in his or her native language. Write the speech.

2. You have been appointed host to a group of Chinese students who are to visit your city on a student exchange program. They all speak English well but know little about Australia or its culture. Write a set of guidelines for them about what to expect from Australians and how they should respond.

REVISION LIST FOR PART XII

MULTICULTURAL COMMUNICATION

- A culture is a shared system of behaviour, values, beliefs, attitudes, manners, symbols and assumptions.
- A culture is shared by a very large group of people within which there can be smaller groups with their own identities which can be described as subcultures.
- Cultures can vary enormously in the way they relate to others. Some, like that of the United States, are open and welcome diversity; others, like the Japanese, are much more homogeneous.
- Ethnocentrism means not appreciating the culture of others. It can be based on a sense of superiority over others, in which case it is racist, or it can derive from sheer ignorance.
- Any form of communication with people of another culture runs the risk of being misunderstood, especially when it uses symbols that may have a positive meaning in one culture but a negative meaning in another.
- To be culturally aware means to realise that other people differ from us in many ways: in their attitudes towards behaviour and manners, in their values and religion, in their concepts of status and social roles, in their decision-making practices and in their attitudes towards time, personal space and body language.
- Learning about another culture starts by learning some of the language, reading about its history, religion, politics and customs, and questioning people about the process of cultural change.
- English has the advantage of being the most common international language, but it means that Australians tend not to learn much about either the language or the culture of other people.
- Treat the people you meet as individuals, not as representatives of some imagined cultural stereotype.
- Make your own position clear and avoid misinterpretations through words and gestures that might inadvertently contradict each other.

continued on next page

continued from previous page

- Try to see things from the other person's point of view and through the eyes of their culture.
- Whatever their culture, all human beings like to maintain dignity when meeting strangers. Ensure you communicate respect.
- In written communications with other cultures, use simple, direct prose, short sentences, short paragraphs and avoid abstractions, jargon, clichés and flowery language.
- In verbal communications with other cultures, never interrupt. Wait until the other person has finished, and then go over the main points to be sure you both agree.

PART XII
KEY TEXTS AND FURTHER READING

Bolton, Robert, *People Skills: How to Assert Yourself, Listen to Others, and Resolve Conflicts*, Simon & Schuster Australia, Sydney, 1987.

Hodge, A., *Communicating Across Cultures: An ABC of Cultural Awareness*, Janus, Sydney, 1987.

Neophytou, Charles, *The Japanese are Coming*, Travcorp Learning Systems, Sydney, 1988.

Sarantokas, S., *Living Together in Australia*, Longman Cheshire, Melbourne, 1984.

Tourism Training Australia, *The Art of Handling International Visitors*, TTA, Sydney, 1989.

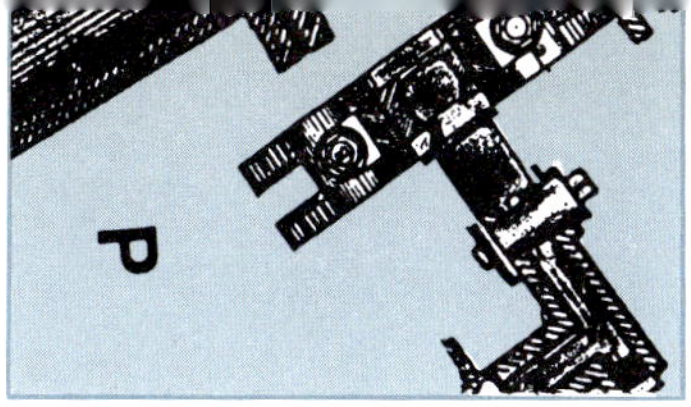

SPECIALIST TECHNIQUES SECTION

I

WRITING

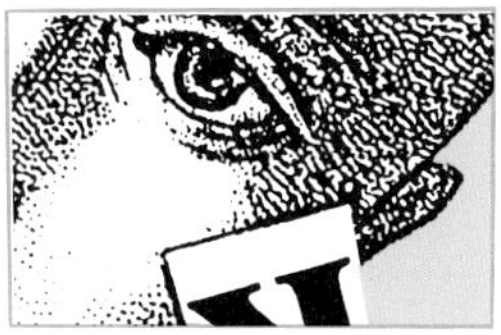

CHAPTER

41

GRAMMAR AND TECHNIQUE

After studying this chapter, you will be able to:

- write English prose that is internally consistent
- maintain parallel construction in your prose
- avoid the use of unnecessary words and phrases
- avoid misplacing pronouns, subjects and modifiers
- report quotations and indirect speech correctly
- use publishers' style for numbers, dates and times
- avoid sexist terminology

The English language can be described by a set of rules called grammar. For many years, children laboured through their schooldays learning these rules. They had to learn, for instance, to describe verbs as transitive or intransitive, to distinguish past perfect tense from pluperfect and to tell a present participle from a past participle. These days, children are spared these unproductive chores. Teachers now realise that the important thing is not to be able to describe the grammar but rather to *use* English correctly.

Correct usage of English is not something that can be laid down in a hard and fast way like the rules of mathematics or the laws of physics. English is an evolving language and the way people use it changes slowly over time. There are no authorities sitting like judges allowing or disallowing changes to the language. The rules of 'correct' English are made by the great majority of educated people in their daily practice of speaking and writing the language. People introduce new words, new phrases and forms of expression and if these are taken up in common usage, they thereby become accepted as correct.

This does not mean that anything goes. Large numbers of people will take up expressions only if they suit them, that is, if they help them to say what they want to say and help them to understand others. To be publicly acceptable, an expression needs to be precise, clear and to have a certain elegance about it. To achieve this it first needs to be internally consistent. If there is one rule about grammar that deserves to be preserved before all others, it is that of consistency. To give a simple example, it is never acceptable nor correct usage to have a plural subject in a sentence and a singular verb. 'The cars was in the parking station' is a sentence with a plural subject 'the cars' but a singular verb 'was'. To be consistent, the verb must be the plural 'were'. Other types of inconsistent language use are considered later in this chapter. Here we simply want to emphasise that consistency is the first rule people apply to language. To be grammatically correct, your sentences should be internally consistent in all aspects.

The second rule is that of precision and clarity. The meaning of a phrase or sentence should not be ambiguous, and it should say exactly what the writer intended. Consider: 'This year's report by the club president, the shortest we have had for many years, made no mention of the huge loss.' An ambiguous statement like this is a poor use of the language. It is an example of a modifying clause placed in the wrong position. There are many other examples of this kind described in the rest of this chapter. Overall, even though there is no set of hard and fast rules governing English expression, it is important to realise that there are still rules of a kind to be observed. Good writers always work within this framework of correct usage.

THE VIRTUE OF CONSISTENCY

Let us look at some of the most common forms of inconsistent usage. As we noted above, the subject and verb in a sentence should be consistent. In most cases there is no problem about using a singular subject with a singular verb or a plural subject with a plural verb.

A box of roses was delivered. (Not *were* because the subject *box* is singular.)

In other cases, the issue is less clear. Some subjects have a plural form but normally take a singular verb. These include: data, agenda and news.

The data shows a positive correlation. (Not *show*.)

Some subjects are always in the plural: *trousers, pants, scissors, shears, tongs, proceeds.*

The scissors were sharp. (Not *was*.)

However: 'The pair of scissors was sharp' is correct because the subject is now the word *pair*, which is singular.

When using the words *each, every, any, either, neither, anybody, everybody, nobody, anyone* and *none* you should always adopt the singular form.

Every boy and girl was present for the concert. (Not *were*.)
Each of them was responsible. (Not *were*.)
None of those in the room cares about her. (Not *care*.)

If in doubt about using any of these words, try to translate it into a form that exposes it as singular: Every single boy and girl ... , Each one of them ... , No one of those ...

Collective nouns often pose problems. Collective nouns usually refer to groups of people or things and should be treated as singular, that is, as one group of people or things. Typical collective nouns are: *audience, crowd, mob, herd, team, class.* They normally take a singular verb.

The crowd was restless. (Not *were*.)
The class showed its respect for the teacher. (Not *their*.)

An organisation or a company is a collective noun and should take a singular verb.

The report said BHP was planning to expand. (Not *were*.)
Woolworths is offering this special sale. (Not *are*.)

This is a rule that is frequently broken, however. There is one case where it is consistently ignored. Cricket journalists will often write:

Australia has gone into bat.

But they persist in referring to the English cricket team in the plural:

England were all out for 121.

The team is a collective noun and thus a singular subject. For the sake of consistency, any team or firm or organisation should have a singular verb.

The only exception permitted is where it is clear that individuals within a group are being discussed. Consider the sentence:

The team were told to improve their tackling.

Here it is understood that *the team* refers to the *team members* and so the subject takes a plural form.

There are some other problem areas with collective nouns. The phrase *the media* refers to the outlets for television, press and radio within a society. Depending on context, the media can refer to several media outlets, in which case it is a plural subject; or it can be a collective noun by referring to the totality of media outlets, in which case it takes a singular form. With words like this, you use the singular or plural form that is appropriate to the particular meaning you want.

Another source of inconsistent expression is the use of one group of pronouns *I, he, she, we, they, it* and another group *me, him, her, us, them.* Words in the first group are used as the subjects in a sentence: I ran away. Members of the second group are used as the objects in a sentence: The dog bit *him*. There are many times, however, when common usage breaks this rule.

Who broke the window? It was him. No, it was me.

The last two sentences are technically incorrect. The word 'him' is normally used for an object but in the second sentence here it is really being used as a subject. The sentence is understood to be saying: 'It was he who broke it.' In the same way, the last sentence is understood as: 'It was I who broke it.' Today, most people would regard the answers: 'It was he. No, it was I.' as fairly pretentious answers. In cases like this, common usage is strong enough to override consistency and so 'It was him. No, it was me.' are acceptable expressions.

In other similar cases, however, the issue is not so clear-cut. The following sentence:

He is bigger than me.

is incorrect. What the sentence is understood to be saying is:

He is bigger than I (am).

So the correct sentence should read:

He is bigger than I.

In speech, this last sentence would probably sound pretentious, but in writing we should try harder to be consistent. So, when you are writing and faced with examples like these, try to extend the sentence to mentally include the understood verb, which will tell you whether you need a pronoun that is a subject or an object.

As we said at the start of this chapter, the first rule of grammar to follow is to be consistent. Where common usage breaks this rule, especially in the use of collective nouns, writers should not follow meekly behind but should try to set a good example by upholding this virtue.

EXERCISES (A)

Write the correct versions of the following sentences.

1. A large crowd of soldiers made their way toward us.
2. Every member of the family, including distant cousins, aunts and uncles, were present at the dinner.
3. IBM have released details of the new computer.
4. The pair of shears were sharp and the sheep between his legs was bleeding.
5. After everybody had had their say, the detective decided that none of them were guilty.
6. No news is good news but bad news travel fast.
7. The media is a destructive influence on society and have no social responsibility.
8. I knew it was not him because he has always been she who helped out.
9. Let he and I get in first.
10. Us girls must stick together.
11. They gave we boys the time of our lives.
12. It was him who decided the first would be me.

PARALLEL CONSTRUCTION

As well as in grammar, consistency is also a virtue in sentence construction. In particular, when using one sentence to express two ideas, both ideas should have the same type of construction. Consider:

> Management is concerned about the high cost of labour and also worrying is the level of absenteeism.

The two things that are bothering management, the high cost of labour and the level of absenteeism, are similar in nature and should have been similar in construction. Either:

> Management is concerned about the high cost of labour and the level of absenteeism.

or:

> Management is concerned about the high cost of labour and worried about the level of absenteeism.

The following sentence:

> Please employ someone who can supervise the tradesmen and to keep the books.

should have been written as either:

> Please employ someone who can supervise the tradesmen and keep the books.

or:

> Please employ someone to supervise the tradesmen and to keep the books.

EXERCISES (B)

Rewrite the following sentences with parallel construction.

1. He was not only charged with stealing but also for possession of a deadly weapon.
2. She was dismissed from the job because she was often late and for taking extended lunch hours.
3. The problems of the unemployed are being studied through a detailed questionnaire and by examining all available statistics.
4. The new factory has easy parking, it is attractively landscaped but is already needing a new coat of paint.
5. Finding a job, treatment as adults and to receive good money are the main goals young people seek from employment.

TAUTOLOGIES AND REDUNDANCIES

Writing should avoid repetition, that is, in any one expression you should make your point only once. You should not keep on repeating yourself.

Consider the following sentence:

One after the other, the committee left the meeting in quick succession.

The phrase 'one after the other' means 'in quick succession', so the latter is redundant. A phrase like this can also be called a tautology.

The company's future prospects look bright.

Because the word 'prospects' contains the notion of being in the future, the word 'future' is redundant. It is the company's prospects that are bright.

EXERCISES (C)

Rewrite the following sentences removing redundancies or tautologies.

1. The discussion that subsequently followed was fruitful.
2. They mutually agreed to divide the spoils.
3. You don't have to study past history to know that nationalism is a cohesive force that bonds people together.
4. The essential book that is necessary for the course is widely available in libraries everywhere.
5. Writing is hard and difficult but don't give up or throw in the towel without a contested fight.

UNNECESSARY WORDS AND PHRASES

When people are speaking, they sometimes need a little time to think of the most appropriate next word. They also find sometimes that they start a sentence but can't finish it in a smooth or direct way. Public speakers who are faced with these problems all the time have developed a range of meaningless phrases that mark a little time while they bring up the right word or phrase from the depths of their minds.

I believe that, in this regard, the new tax policy will be a miserable failure.

The phrase 'I believe that' is meaningless. The statement by the speaker that the tax policy will fail is also a statement about his belief on the matter.

The same is true of other meaningless phrases such as 'I think that' or 'In my opinion'. When writing, save these phrases and only use them on rare occasions when you want to lend the weight of your reputation to a conclusion you believe is important.

The other phrase 'in this regard' is also meaningless, as is its mate 'with reference to'. Of course what you say has regard to or makes reference to the rest of your comments. It could not be otherwise. Some writers use the phrase 'as to' in place of 'in regard to'. Others use 'in the case of' and 'as far as ... is concerned' instead of 'with reference to'. In both cases the effect is the same—ungainly. Other unnecessary phrases and words are 'the fact that', 'the ... factor', and 'in terms of'.

These kinds of phrases indicate unplanned and sloppy writing and should not appear on the typed or printed page.

EXERCISES (D)

Rewrite the following sentences more concisely.

1. In the case of the Holden, the fitting of a single tow bar is quite satisfactory as far as pulling a caravan is concerned.
2. I don't think you can say that, in regard to his family, he has had a happy life.
3. With reference to the sale of tickets, there will be no refunds as far as the management is concerned.
4. In terms of parking, the shopping centre was a disaster.
5. As to his election chances, the fact that he has been divorced three times poses problems..

MISPLACED PRONOUNS

Pronouns can sometimes be misplaced so that a sentence becomes ambiguous or misleading. (Pronouns are: *I, me, you, he, she, him, her, it, we, us, they, them, which, who, whom, whose, that.)*

> I have placed the log on the chopping block and when I nod my head I want you to hit it.

Ambiguities like this arise because the pronoun 'it' which is the object of the instruction, has been placed too far away from the thing it refers to, 'the log'. A clearer version would be:

> When I nod my head I want you to hit the log I have placed on the chopping block.

EXERCISES (E)

Clarify the following sentences.

1. There is a huge pothole in the road which damages many drivers' cars.
2. Don't give grandfather any nuts. He may damage his teeth or swallow them whole.
3. After I drive the car away from the front of the house, I want you to photograph it.

MISRELATED AND MISPLACED SUBJECTS

Some sentences are written with hidden or unidentified subjects and this leads to an illogical construction.

Having switched off the power, the bulb can be safely replaced.

This should be corrected to either:

Having switched off the power, you can safely replace the bulb.

or:

Once the power is switched off, the bulb can be safely replaced.

EXERCISES (F)

Rewrite the following sentences to more clearly identify the subject.

1. Using the most advanced technology, two hundred cars come off the assembly line every day.
2. Lacking a jack, the flat tyre could not be replaced.
3. Withstanding hard knocks, I can strongly recommend this new plastic.
4. Looking through a powerful telescope, Halley's Comet came into view.
5. By choosing an innovative design, the product can be attractive and competitive.

MISPLACED MODIFIERS

Phrases and clauses that modify a subject or an object can be misplaced to alter the intended meaning of a sentence.

A briefcase was lost by a student with a broken handle and worn-out trim.

The description should modify the briefcase, not the student. To do this it must swap places.

A briefcase with a broken handle and worn-out trim was lost by a student.

EXERCISES (G)

Clarify the following sentences by relocating the modifiers.

1. The librarian will replace books for students that are lost from the library.
2. You will have problems if you continue to read notices placed on the board without careful attention.
3. The new dictating machines can pick up anything as described in this report.

QUOTATIONS AND INDIRECT SPEECH

When you want to repeat the exact words that somebody used, you should put those words within quotation marks without making any changes at all to the original.

'Friends, Romans, countrymen. Lend me your ears,' Mark Antony told the crowd.

Often, though, writers prefer to summarise someone else's words in order to be more economical.

Mark Antony asked the crowd to listen to him.

In the latter case, it is normal to put all the words in the past tense and to make appropriate changes to the subjects and objects of the expression. So:

'The evil that men do lives after them. The good is oft interred with their bones,' Antony continued.

becomes:

> Antony added that the evil men did lived after they were dead while their good deeds were usually buried with them.

And:

> 'I will return,' General Macarthur said.

becomes:

> General Macarthur said he would return.

If you make a consistent rule to translate all indirect quotations into past tense and to modify the subjects and objects appropriately, you will have no problems when paraphrasing other people's words. One more example:

> 'I am telling you to leave.'
> She told him to leave.

EXERCISES (H)

Translate the following original statements into indirect speech.

1. He told them, 'It is raining and we are all going to get wet.'
2. 'I am going to cross the continent,' Burke declared, 'and nothing can stop me.'
3. 'We hope everything turns out all right for you,' his parents said.
4. 'There is no truth in any of these charges,' the prisoner said. 'I am innocent.'
5. 'These new drugs will be no more expensive than existing varieties,' Dr King said.

NUMBERS, DATES AND TIMES

There are two main versions of how to write numbers, dates and times. One is preferred by book publishers, the other by daily newspapers. There is little to choose between these styles, and the only important decision is to make up your mind to stick to either one or the other in order to be consistent.

NUMBERS

Both book and newspaper publishers spell out numbers up to ten and use numerals after that. There are two exceptions:

1. When a number starts a sentence, they revert to spelling it out. 'Forty horses rounded the corner.' However, if the number is a long one don't spell it out at the start of a sentence but instead write: 'A total of 4013 inches of rain fell ...'
2. When a number less than ten contains a decimal point. Both publishers and newspapers have abandoned the use of fractions and convert them to decimal places; hence, four and a half becomes 4.5.

DATES

Book publishers write dates as: 19 September 1985, while newspaper publishers write them as: September 19 1985. Neither uses commas or any other punctuation marks with dates. They never use numbers to stand for months, nor include any letters next to the numbers (not 2nd nor 19th).

TIMES

Neither uses the word 'o'clock' and both insist on citing the time as 9.20 am or 10.45 pm, again without any punctuation (and never in the form 'half past ten' or 'a quarter to eight'). The only exceptions are '12 noon' and '12 midnight' which avoid any confusion at these times. Because airlines and hotels now operate on the twenty-four-hour clock and because this system causes fewer misunderstandings than the traditional twelve-hour clock, we will eventually all follow suit, but at present the twenty-four-hour system is a bit unconventional for everyday usage.

ABBREVIATIONS

The best rule to follow with abbreviations is: where an abbreviation has entered everyday language then use it, otherwise spell out the word fully.

There are many abbreviations that we take for granted today: exams, maths, car, bus, plane, photo, bike, TV, phone, and many more. If you think a majority of educated people use an abbreviation, it is probably OK to follow suit.

However, it is best to avoid those kind of abbreviations that have become initials, such as: e.g., to stand for 'for example'; i.e., to stand for 'that is'; or any mathematical symbols such as the 'equals' or the 'therefore' signs. These forms are more economical but they can be confusing to some readers, so it is best to avoid them. The only exception to this rule is the dollar sign, which is almost never misunderstood by anyone. In general, the best rule to use when contemplating an abbreviation or a symbol is, if in doubt, leave it out.

NON-SEXIST LANGUAGE

Writers should avoid sexist language that depicts women in a trivial or stereotyped way. There are two reasons for this.

One is a matter of social relations. From the experience of history we know how powerful a political weapon language can be. Most people today find it offensive to hear demeaning language directed at people on the basis of their ethnic background or religion. Relations between the sexes are in the same position and should be accorded the same status.

The second reason is a matter of accuracy. For example, to call all members of the police force 'policemen' when there are now a large number of women in the force is to describe police incorrectly. A more accurate, non-sexist term would be 'police officer'. Or take another example: 'The man on the land has been hit hard by falling commodity prices.' Both women and men live on the land and are affected by the price of commodities.

Sometimes sexist language is found in clichés with unfortunate results, as in the following newspaper report: 'A 35-year-old woman was taken by a shark while spearfishing off Port Lincoln today. Witnesses to the horror said the man-eater was a huge white pointer ...'

The words 'man', 'men', 'he', 'his' and 'him' are often used to describe people of either sex. When reference is to either or both sexes, but not specifically to the male sex, the words 'man' and 'men' can be avoided. Possible alternatives are 'person', 'people', 'human beings', 'men and women'. Avoiding 'he', 'his' and 'him' can be more difficult, since the repeated use of 'he or she' and 'his or hers' can be clumsy. But 'they', 'their' and 'them' can often be used instead.

For 'the motorist ... he', use 'motorists ... they'.

For 'the Australian ... he', use 'Australians ... they'.

Other words of the masculine gender should be avoided where they do not apply specifically to men.

For 'the man in the street', use 'the average person', or 'ordinary people'.

For 'mankind', use 'humanity', 'humankind', 'human beings'.

For 'manpower', use 'workforce', 'labour force'.

Occupational stereotyping is probably the most common form of sexist language because many jobs have traditionally been all-male preserves. Now that this has changed in a wide variety of occupations, our language should reflect the reality.

For 'foreman', use 'supervisor'.

For 'railwaymen', use 'railworkers'.

For 'policeman', use 'police officer' (not 'police woman').

For 'businessmen', use 'managers', 'employers', 'entrepreneurs'.

For 'salesmen', use 'sales representatives'.

For 'firemen', use 'firefighters', 'fire officers'.

For 'craftsman', use 'artisan' or 'craft worker'.

There is, however, one version of the way to overcome sexist terms which should itself be avoided, as it is unnecessarily awkward. This is the habit of simply replacing 'man' at the end of a job description with 'person'.

For 'chairman', avoid 'chairperson' and use 'chair' or 'convenor'.

For 'alderman', avoid 'alderperson' and use 'councillor'.

For 'spokesman', avoid 'spokesperson' and use 'speaker', 'representative' or 'media officer'.

For 'sportsman' and 'sportsmanlike', use 'sport' and 'sporting'.

Also to be avoided are terms that define occupations by gender.

For 'headmaster' and 'headmistress', use 'principal'.

For 'male nurse', use 'nurse'.

For 'authoress', use 'author'.

For 'actress', use 'actor'.

For 'air hostess', use 'flight attendant' or 'steward'.

In avoiding sexist terminology, there is no need to distort the language by sending up the process itself ('policeperson', 'alderperson'). With a little thought, appropriate substitutions can easily be found.

CHAPTER 42

PUNCTUATION

After studying this chapter, you will be able to:

- use punctuation to enhance the clarity of your writing
- use punctuation to make your writing more readable
- avoid common punctuation mistakes
- understand the conventions of punctuation used by publishers and professional writers

Writers should be careful to get their punctuation right. This is not because there is an abstract set of rules to which we must all conform simply to be 'correct'. Punctuation is one of the most important ways in which we help the reader understand what we want to say. When someone is speaking, there is no need for punctuation because rises and falls in the voice, changes of tone, pauses, emphases and inflections all help add meaning to the words used. The writer finds it more difficult to colour words this way, so punctuation has emerged as an important aid to conveying meaning. Punctuation also helps to clarify expressions and to indicate the logical relationships between groups of expressions.

To stress the importance of punctuation is not to say that the more of it you use the better. Punctuation should not be used as an ornament to words and sentences. It should be used sparingly. In modern writing, the tendency is to use less of it rather than more. In general, the rule 'If in doubt, leave it out' should govern its use.

FULL STOP

The full stop ends a sentence and marks the finish of a complete and self-contained thought. When read aloud, it indicates the point at which the voice should be lowered. Do not, however, use a full stop at the end of a heading or subheading, even though some of these may be the length of a short sentence. The heading itself tells the reader where it ends. The full stop is needed only within a continuous text.

It used to be a convention to place full stops at the end of abbreviations (such as etc or Pty Ltd), after contractions of words (such as Dr or Mr) or against initials (such as NSW). There is no good reason to do this, however. Abbreviations, contractions and the like can stand on their own. They do not need the full stop as a signal to tell the reader what is happening. Used this way, the full stop is a waste of time and effort. As consistency is a virtue, the best policy is to leave out the full stop in all these cases. So do not write:

Mr. John Brown M.H.R. for N.S.W., 10 a.m., David Jones Aust. Pty. Ltd.

but do write:

Mr John Brown MHR for NSW, 10 am, David Jones Aust Pty Ltd

The latter versions look better in print and take much less time and effort to produce.

Following this rule, you should not write Mr J. Brown but rather Mr J Brown. The latter may look a little unconventional today in a business letter but it is bound to become the norm soon, especially since most computer-printed names and addresses have now abandoned the full stop after the personal initial.

COMMA

The comma is assumed by many people to be the easiest form of punctuation to use and the least important. Both these views are wrong. More mistakes are made in the use of the comma and its misuse causes more problems for readers than any other punctuation mark. The most common mistake is to use too many commas. Writers often insert a comma into the text when they are unsure whether it is needed or not. A passage with too many commas, however, is worse than one with too few, because the text becomes disjointed, difficult to read and appears unsure of itself.

If in doubt, the best policy to adopt with commas is to leave them out. Part of the problem is that some people think a comma should be inserted at every place where, if the text was being read aloud, the reader would naturally pause. This is not so. The composition of words within a sentence usually bears its own natural pauses without the need for punctuation of any kind. To test this, read the previous sentence aloud and see if you tend to pause after the word 'pauses'.

There are at least six proper uses for commas.

1. Use commas to insert an aside, a qualification or an additional description into a sentence that would have been complete without it. For example:

   He bought the car, even though he couldn't afford it, because he had to get to work.

   It continually broke down, however, so he was no better off.

   He went shopping, yet again, and found a better model.

   John Brown, the well-known lawyer, was found on the premises.

   However, some writers habitually use commas when they insert a qualifying phrase beginning with 'which' or 'who'. Sometimes they are right to do so, but very often they are not. The following sentence is an example of overuse of commas:

   The teacher, who was appointed to the new school, found the environment stimulating.

   It reads better as:

   The teacher who was appointed to the new school found the environment stimulating.

   Similarly, in the following sentence the commas are more ornamental than useful:

   The package, which came three weeks late, was, nonetheless, very welcome.

A better version eliminates all these commas:

The package which came three weeks late was nonetheless very welcome.

2. Use commas to prevent a connection being made between words that would otherwise be confusing or misleading. For example:

Ever since he has tried harder and lasted longer.

reads differently to:

Ever since, he has tried harder and lasted longer.

And:

Please don't eat John.

reads differently to:

Please don't eat, John.

While:

The elementary principles of speech which everyone knows are difficult to describe.

is ambiguous. Commas remove the ambiguity.

The elementary principles of speech, which everyone knows, are difficult to describe.

3. Use commas to set off an interjection that adds emphasis or drama to a sentence. For example:

Yes, he certainly enjoyed the country.

So, we come to the concluding remarks.

Now, all this should make us stop and think.

However, she had omitted an important point.

4. Use a comma when you feel you want to slow the rhythm of a sentence to encourage the reader to notice that different points are being made. For example, the following sentence is perfectly acceptable without a comma.

They bought the new computer and then started to shop for the software.

But if the overall context in which you are writing is critical of people who arrange their purchasing in this order, you may find a comma adds the touch you want.

They bought the new computer, and then started to shop for the software.

In this example the comma throws the emphasis on the word 'then' and puts the two separate acts of purchasing into a new perspective.

This same use of the comma is usual after an introductory phrase or a long sentence-like start when the writer wants to throw emphasis onto these first segments. For example:

Weeping openly, the parents spoke to reporters.

If you want to be noticed, this is the colour to wear this season.

In a little more than three months, he destroyed the work of generations.

5. Use commas to separate several adjectives, descriptive terms or the items in a series or list. For example:

   Athletes from Third World countries were strongly represented, especially from Indonesia, Pakistan, Kenya and Zaire.

   It was a long, dark, cold hallway.

   The soldiers were badly armed, poorly fed, inadequately trained and hopelessly led.

   However, a short series of adjectives can usually dispense with commas.

   an old white building

   a playful young animal

   a strong military presence

6. Use commas to introduce a short quotation or the actual words of a speaker.

   The prime minister said, 'This issue has gone far enough.'

   'There is nothing to be done,' the policeman announced, 'so you can all go home.'

EXERCISES (A)

Put commas into appropriate places in the following sentences.

1. Although he was exhausted and wrung out sleep would not come.
2. He learned that despite everything she had still won.
3. There was little point obviously in fighting against such odds.
4. 'I will tell you a story' he said 'and then you can go.'
5. She added 'There are some times darling when you get too concerned too involved.'
6. These new vacuum cleaners whose reliability is well-known have been reduced in price.
7. I walked over to the small brown dog patted its scarred battered head and left as quickly as I could.

SEMICOLON

The semicolon is difficult to use and is best avoided. It is a fairly archaic form of punctuation, anyway, and is rarely used by professional writers. It is usually described as the punctuation to use when you want to inject a stronger pause than provided by a comma but not as strong as a full stop. As we said before, though, pauses are best handled by the natural flow of words themselves. You should rely on punctuation as little as possible to gain this effect.

The most legitimate use of the semicolon is in a long list where you want to join some items more closely than others and to distance other items. If you have a list that already is internally punctuated by commas, the semicolon will be useful to make broader divisions.

> He owned office buildings in Sydney, Melbourne and Brisbane; a hotel chain extending to Sydney, Auckland, Wellington and Suva; as well as retail shops in all major capital cities in Australia.

Similarly, if you want to run a continuous list over several lines but to maintain it all in one sentence, a semicolon will come in handy.

> The judge ordered the jury to consider four main aspects of the accused's testimony:
> 1. he denied having the conversation that was attributed to him;
> 2. there were no independent witnesses to the discussion;

3. he had nothing to gain from the suggestion;
4. to act this way would have been out of character.

It is legitimate to use a semicolon within a more normal sentence if you are joining long relatively independent sentences and don't want to use the conjunction 'and'.

The building retained few of its original features; its doors and casements had long been vandalised.

However, there is little to be gained from this and a full stop would probably have been more effective. Unless you are very experienced and well in control of your style, the use of semicolons within sentences like this will usually look showy and pretentious. Rather than run this risk, you are best to avoid them.

EXERCISES (B)

Re-punctuate the following sentences to include semicolons in each, where appropriate.

1. Popular music arose among the lower orders. Classical music was that of the court and the upper classes.
2. As well as providing entertainment, country music acted as a commentary on the news, as a vehicle for work songs, to set the atmosphere for political gatherings and as the background to many of the rituals that celebrated the lives of rural people.
3. The fantasies produced by some advertising to women are irresponsible, dream worlds which are impossible to attain.

COLON

Like the semicolon, the colon is not used often in modern writing. It should be avoided even more strongly within sentences. It is confined to a few technical uses. These are:

1. To introduce a list or series, such as the one you are reading now, or:

   There are three secrets of success in this business: blood, sweat and tears.

   Those named in the report include: three Supreme Court judges, two prominent State politicians and the Chief of Police.

2. To introduce a quotation, that is, the actual words of a speaker, especially when they are dramatic:

He stood up in the dock and declared: 'I never saw him before today.'

Normally, a direct quotation is introduced by a comma, as we noted earlier, so use the colon for this purpose sparingly and carefully.

3. To separate an example from the sentence that introduces it. Most of this chapter uses the colon for this purpose. Here is another example:

   Use the RX-20 spanner when the workload is particularly heavy. For instance:
   - to turn wheel nuts;
   - to remove spark plugs;
   - to turn the nuts holding the differential and gearbox plugs.

EXERCISES (C)

Place a colon where appropriate in the following sentences.

1. He had one ideal to serve mankind.
2. He used two illustrations for his example a red cross and a red crescent.
3. The list of books included *Jane Eyre, Wuthering Heights, Middlemarch, Silas Marner.*

QUESTION MARK

Use a question mark to end a sentence that is a direct question, such as:

Where are you going?

What does this tell us?

But in other cases that are less direct it is better to avoid the question mark. There are two of these other cases. The first is where a question is part of a larger sentence that is not a question. For example:

I asked him whether he wanted to go to the show.

Why someone with such a distinguished career would take a bribe was a question that puzzled everyone.

The second is the question for which no answer is expected and which is more an order or a command than a request. For example:

Would you shut up.

Do you mind not smoking in here.

EXCLAMATION MARK

Exclamation marks are difficult to use well, easy to overdo and are in most cases unnecessary. If you want to express a strong emotion such as surprise, disgust or indignation, your words should do it for you and there should be no need for an exclamation mark. Certainly, if the words don't already convey the emotion you want, the addition of this piece of punctuation will not do it for you. If you use it frequently, it will come to lose its impact.

So avoid the exclamation when you can and use it on rare occasions only, as in the following cases.

1. After you have made a short exclamation:

    Get out! Gotcha! You dirty rat! How sweet it is!

    Each of these phrases could have been written without exclamation marks. If so, they would have appeared a little less emphatic.

2. When you want to be sarcastic or comment on the irony of a situation:

    How generous you are!

    when someone has been particularly ungenerous. Or:

    Taxpayers' money was indeed saved!

a comment on the irony of Taxation Department staff cutbacks which were designed, according to the government, 'to save taxpayers' money' but which resulted in less tax being collected.

APOSTROPHE

Apostrophes are used for two purposes: to indicate that letters within a word have been omitted; and to show ownership. Like other forms of punctuation, the modern tendency is to reduce use of the apostrophe where possible.

When writing, it is usually better to spell out a word fully rather than give an abbreviated version that omits some letters. However there are times when abbreviations are useful or unavoidable, such as when you have to accurately report how someone spoke. In such cases the apostrophe stands for the omitted letters:

who's for 'who is'
there's for 'there is'
I'm for 'I am'
You're for 'you are'
he's and *she's* for 'he is' and 'she is'
I've, you've and *they've* for 'I have', 'you have' and 'they have'

It is still useful to use an apostrophe to show ownership because it avoids ambiguity and misunderstanding. In English, both plural endings and ownership are indicated by the letter *s*. By using an apostrophe when you want to show ownership exists you tell the reader that the *s* in this case does not indicate a plural. Where there is only one owner the apostrophe is placed in front of the *s*:

the girl's toys—the toys owned by the girl
the company's property—the property owned by the company

Where there are two or more owners, and you therefore place *s* at the end of the word to indicate plural, the apostrophe comes after the *s*:

the girls' toys—the toys owned by the girls
the companies' property—the property owned by the companies

If the plural word does not end with an *s* place the apostrophe before the *s*, as if it were singular:

the man's clothes—singular; the men's clothes—plural
the children's books

Avoid using a double *s* to show possession. Treat any word ending with *s* as a plural, even though it might be singular. For example, instead of:

Bob Jones's dog

write

Bob Jones' dog

The only place where it is normal to drop the apostrophe when indicating possession is the word *its*. For example:

Every dog has its day.

Sometimes you will see writers using an apostrophe to indicate a plural in a few special cases, such as:

In the 1980's.

He signs his cheques with X's.

It is easy to confuse 6's and 9's.

There is no benefit to be gained from this habit so it may be dropped. Better versions are:

Growing up in the 1960s.

Mind your Ps and Qs.

He couldn't pronounce 3s or 7s.

When using numbers in cases like the above, your meaning can sometimes be confusing. If you write 5s, some readers might mistake your meaning 'fives' for 'five shillings'. If there is even a slight chance of confusion when using numbers then spell them out. For example:

the sixties, the nineteen-eighties, sixes and sevens.

EXERCISES (D)

Rewrite the following sentences, using apostrophes where appropriate.

1. Womens shoes are incredibly expensive.
2. The Girl Guides hall was renovated.
3. Its late so lets go home.
4. He shouldnt have bothered so dont come complaining to me if you arent satisfied.
5. The Roaring 20s are over-rated.

INVERTED COMMAS

Inverted commas are sometimes called quotation marks because their main purpose is to mark direct quotations, or the actual words of a speaker.

She said, 'Do you know where he is?'

'I never want to see that place again,' he cried.

'There is one thing,' he said, 'that you have not considered.'

Do not use inverted commas, however, when you are reporting what someone said in your own words, rather than the exact words used by the speaker. In the following example, inverted commas are not needed.

He told us that he would be there just after eight o'clock.

When using other punctuation with inverted commas, there are two rules to follow.

1. If the punctuation was part of the original material you are quoting, put the punctuation within the inverted commas.

She asked him, 'Do you want to go now?'

2. If the punctuation derives from the sentence you have written, it goes outside the inverted commas.

The boy thought, 'I wish I was stronger', but he was too lazy to exercise.

Inverted commas are normally used to indicate a direct quotation has been taken from a book or article.

Few historians take this issue seriously any more. Edward Thomas has written in his most recent book: 'The idea was overturned by the investigations of the 1930s and has not been revived since.'

However, when taking a longer direct quotation from another author, especially if several sentences are involved, the normal practice is to place the passage in a paragraph of its own, drop the inverted commas and indent the whole passage, sometimes using smaller print, to indicate that it is a direct quotation.

The bible of amateur astronomy is Burnham's *Celestial Handbook*. The introduction contains all the basic information needed to get a grip on the subject, and his enthusiasm is contagious. You don't have to have Burnham's, but then of course you don't have to have electricity in your house either.

In some publications, quotation marks are printed as double inverted commas—"Help!"—and in others as single inverted commas—'Go away.' It does not matter much which version you use as long as you are consistent and don't switch from one style to the other within the one document. Book publishers these days tend to use single inverted commas. We prefer this style because on normal typewriter and word processor keyboards you can type the single inverted comma key directly, but to use the double inverted comma sign you have to press the shift key then the double inverted comma key. It is not an important issue and you should choose the style you prefer and adopt it as a permanent habit.

If you have a quotation within a quotation, it is normal to switch from single to double inverted commas, or vice versa. For example:

'What you call your "special reasons" seem very ordinary to me,' she said.
He said, 'Don't give me your "I don't understand" routine again.'

There is a fair degree of confusion and inconsistency in the use of inverted commas around the titles of things, especially works of art. Sometimes the names of newspapers, books, films and television shows will be given quotation marks—'Sydney Morning Herald', 'A Town Like Alice', 'Life on Earth'. In other places, you will see these titles without inverted commas but printed in italics. The best policy to follow is to be consistent and, for this reason, we prefer the style adopted by book publishers. This is to print all titles in italics, or with underlines: the *Age*, *Serpent's Tooth*, *Palace of Dreams*. The underline is accepted in the publishing industry as a signal to print the words in italics, so if you have a typewriter that cannot print italics, type the required words with an underline. When your writing is set in type, the appropriate words will be italicised. If your typewritten copy is to be the final version, the underline is the best way to indicate titles. The style of most book publishers is to use inverted commas to indicate titles only within other titles, for instance, when an article is contained within a book.

John Brown, 'Railways in early Victoria', in Henry Jones (ed.) *History of Australian Transport*, Bellbird Books, Melbourne, 1986.

For ordinary titles and names, however, there is no need for inverted commas. Capitals will suffice.

I still remember the first time I visited their property, Asprey Grove. They had a derelict Landau, a Surrey and several other horse carriages lying rotting in the front paddock.

Some writers use inverted commas to draw special attention to words, especially when using slang or words not yet accepted in normal English:

She thought there was something 'kinky' about him from the outset.

He did not want to 'bludge' on anyone.

However, using inverted commas this way indicates you are not willing to use the real strength of the word you choose, that is, you want to tone down the expression to indicate that it is a word used by others and not one you would choose yourself. If this is so, it would be better to choose another word with the more precise tone you want. In other words, inverted commas used like this are a sign of hesitancy or weakness and are best avoided.

A more appropriate use of inverted commas is when you want to define a word as a word:

There is no need to use the term 'charity' when it comes to helping members of the family.

Or when a writer wants to mark an expression as belonging to someone else not himself:

She still regarded him as her 'little boy' even though he had turned forty.

HYPHEN

The hyphen is a useful device that can often save you time and effort. If it is overdone, however, it can annoy the reader. Like all other devices of the language, it should be used with discretion.

It is particularly useful when you want to bring two or more single words together to form a descriptive term. You could write:

EXERCISES (E)

Add inverted commas and commas, where appropriate, to the following sentences.

1. Don't talk to me that way she said or you will regret it.
2. He replied that he would do whatever he liked.
3. The doctor said I want to see you again before the end of the month.
4. He told them he would look dumb in the costume.
5. She continued I heard him say Shut up and then I am sure I heard him hit her.

We are making a three stage journey

but your meaning is conveyed more immediately by:

We are making a three-stage journey

Similarly, instead of *bright eyed face* and *minerals based economy*, it is better to write *bright-eyed face* and *minerals-based economy*.

Some descriptive terms like these become so common that they form new single words: a *water-tight case* is now usually written as a *watertight case*; a *gun-shot wound* has become a *gunshot wound*. There are no rules to determine these cases. The only thing to do is follow common usage such as in newspapers or dictionaries (recently published dictionaries, that is).

In most other uses of hyphens there are also no guidelines except normal, educated usage in the community. In many cases, words beginning with 'ex', 'pre', 're' and 'co' have a hyphen between these prefixes and the main word that follows, as in

ex-convict, pre-wash, re-define, co-operative.

However, there are as many exceptions to this rule, such as

exempt, predict, rebound, cooperate.

And in other cases, a hyphen can be added to change the meaning of a word.

He will recount the story when he feels better.

He will re-count the votes when the officials return.

As we said above, the most common use of the hyphen is to join words to form a description that might otherwise be unclear or misleading. Only do this, however, when you have to. If possible, search for a better expression that does not need a hyphen. If you use hyphenated expressions too often, your writing will appear pretentious, as if you are trying too hard to invent new expressions yourself. Hyphens can be useful, but don't use them lazily to avoid thinking of the best way of making the point you want.

EXERCISES (F)

Use hyphens where appropriate in the following sentences.

1. Several flower covered boxes were lying outside.
2. He looked like the red haired, freckle faced boy in the description.
3. She tried to coopt him onto her female dominated committee.
4. You cannot pre date these events no matter how well you think you might re call them.

DASH

The dash has three main functions. The most common is to give special emphasis to a word or phrase at the end of a sentence.

Now she knew who the culprit was—her son.

Don't let this opportunity pass—buy it now.

It is also useful when you want to add an explanatory statement or an aside within a sentence. In these cases, dashes can be used instead of commas to separate more clearly the additional statement from the rest of the sentence.

He did not want to alarm her—he knew the stress she was already under from her parents' death—so he chose his words carefully.

The team had not reached a semi-final since 1942—and even then they lost badly—so their supporters had grown used to defeat.

The dash can also be used to signal an interruption to a statement or an abrupt change in thought.

I never meant to frighten—but what's the use of going back over everything?

I really shouldn't—oh, why not?

Like the hyphen, the dash is very easy to overdo and can become annoying to read. Too many dashes, especially to emphasise a word or phrase, make the reader feel you are trying too hard to be convincing. The more sparingly it is used, the more weight it adds where it is needed.

EXERCISES (G)

Put appropriate dashes in each of the following sentences.

1. 'I don't know why I bother talking to you oh I suppose I do really.'
2. At this stage the reader if he or she has persisted this far will be wondering what point is being made.
3. 'Come here take this.'
4. Even though he knew the whole family well not only the present members but parents and grandparents he never understood them.

BRACKETS

Curved brackets are used to make an explanatory statement or an aside within a sentence or within a paragraph. In this, they have the same function as the dash and it is usually a matter of personal preference which of these punctuations the writer prefers. Because they give a greater visual separation to the passage they enclose, brackets are best reserved for statements that are more strongly divorced from the meaning of the sentence surrounding them.

He was sentenced to life imprisonment (usually fourteen years in Victoria) but he escaped after serving only eight months.

There is considerable evidence that links smoking to heart disease (see, in particular, the American Surgeon-General's major survey of the literature published in 1971).

Square brackets are usually reserved for a direct quotation if you need to add an explanatory phrase of your own within the words of the person you are quoting.

He had written, 'I don't think there's a chance they [the Swiss Banks] will renege on the deal.'

EXERCISES (H)

Use brackets where appropriate in the following sentences.

1. Few people who write books earn a decent income let alone achieve any fame from them.
2. There were three Englishmen, two New Zealanders, two Australians Frank Field and Bert Cross and four Americans in the field.
3. 'Don't tell me they the Smiths are not coming after all.'
4. There are more details about the linotype machine discussed in Chapter Seven or Chapter Eight in the first edition.

ELLIPSIS

Like square brackets, the ellipsis is another device used to alter a direct quotation while still preserving its exact wording. In this case, the three dots signal that you have removed part of the original for the sake of brevity but that the rest has been preserved intact. The following are two direct quotations, one in full, the other shortened with an ellipsis.

'The strategy of pitching a newspaper deliberately downmarket, with revenues deriving mainly from sales, has no future.'

'The strategy of pitching a newspaper deliberately downmarket ... has no future.'

It is important when you are modifying a direct quotation in this way to do it in an ethical manner and to ensure that the original meaning has not been distorted by your abbreviation. You should not use ellipses to conceal or distort the author's original meaning. It would be unethical to modify the following statement in this way.

'Let me make it clear that there is no way I would employ him again.'

'Let me make it clear that ... I would employ him again.'

'The publicity said *Dark Journey* was a stunning film, but I found it boring and tedious'—review in *Daily Herald*.

'... a stunning film ...'—*Daily Herald*' (newspaper advertisement for *Dark Journey*)

Note that when inserting an ellipsis you don't include any other punctuation between the relevant words.

Ellipses should be used with discretion. Most readers would prefer to see the whole of a direct quotation rather than part of it. Only use ellipses to remove irrelevant or long and discursive passages that would be boring or distracting if left in.

EXERCISES (I)

Remove the qualifying phrase from the following sentences and replace each with an ellipsis.

1. He was in the game primarily to win and, although he had never been penalised for over-aggressive or violent behaviour, he was one of the fiercest competitors we have seen.
2. The hikers emerged from the desert with blistered feet, aching limbs and parched throats but feeling elated.
3. She told him, 'There is nothing you can do—not the slightest little thing—that will change my mind.'

CAPITALS

Capital letters should be used as infrequently as possible. They should be used on proper names, to start sentences and for very little else. The only titles that draw capitals should be those of highly placed public officials such as ministers of the government, the judiciary and vice-regal figures. The titles Mr, Mrs, Miss, Ms, Dr and Professor start with capital letters because they are used as part of proper names. Titles conferred by private and statutory organisations should be only given in lower case. It is Mr Brian Jones, chairman of the ABC, not Chairman; it is Professor Bill Smith, president of the Literary Trust, not President. The use of capitals is an attempt to make something look more important but these days their abuse can make people look foolish. A statement written as:

> The Members of the Board of the Company have just appointed a new Managing Director

looks pretentious and does more harm than good. Only the first letter of the above sentence should contain a capital.

Also, if you use capitals for anything but proper names and official titles, you are bound to use them inconsistently, giving capitals to some people and things you consider important but omitting them elsewhere in places others might regard just as important. The result is inconsistency throughout your presentation which will irritate some readers. The best rule to follow with capitals is the old standby: 'If in doubt, leave it out.'

EXERCISES (J)

Correct the use of capitals in the following sentences.

1. The Governor-General, Mr Bill Hayden, invited the Chairman of the Water Board, Dr Barry Holding, to an Official Dinner at Government House.

2. Richard Bolles has had his book, *What color is your parachute?* on the Best Seller Lists of the *New York Times* for the last twenty years.

3. In Australia's First Innings, the team was all out for 234 runs. When the English Side came in to bat, everyone thought it would win not just the Fourth Test but also the Ashes.

4. The new National Secretary of the Democratic party is a fifty-year-old former accountant, Mr David Parry. He said he was confident that the new management could restore the financial position of the Party.

CHAPTER

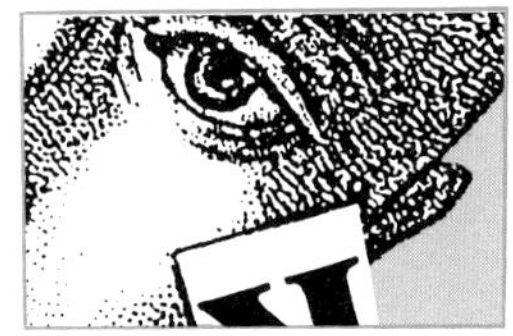

WRITING TECHNOLOGY

After studying this chapter, you will be able to:

- recognise the advantages and disadvantages of the different types of writing technology
- decide which type of technology suits your needs and budget
- see why keyboard skills and computer proficiency should become universal

Today a widely accepted standard of quality is expected for the presentation of documents in most contexts. Letters, memos, reports, articles and submissions should be presented in at least the quality that can be produced on a good electric typewriter. Handwritten notes, letters produced on old manual typewriters or reports in draft-mode dot matrix computer printout are unacceptable in many contexts for two reasons. First, they are often hard to read. Handwriting is notoriously hard to decipher and prone to misinterpretation. Some computer printout uses oddly shaped typefaces and the characters are often faint, which makes them difficult for anyone whose eyesight is not perfect. Second, you do not do yourself justice if you present your written work in a form that looks sloppy.

Of course, no amount of high quality, expensive printing can cover up the fact that something is badly written. But it nonetheless remains true that poor quality presentation can actually demean good quality writing. In recommending electric typewriter quality we are recommending only a minimum standard; if you have ready access to even better quality professional printing typefaces, by all means use them. The best kind of reproduction today is done on a laser printer linked to a good word processing package on a computer. This combination now has the capacity to reproduce work that is hard to distinguish from professional printing with the naked eye.

When you sit down to write something, the first thing to do is to decide what technology you will use. Given today's standards, this means thinking about both the technology that is best for you and the way you will get from this to an acceptable level of final production.

HANDWRITING

Handwriting probably remains the most common form of technology used for first drafts of written compositions. It is a very flexible medium. It is easy to correct by marking out or adding words and passages and for this reason alone is preferred by many people. Handwriting, however, is not an acceptable quality for most documents and this means a handwritten piece needs to be typed after it is drafted.

There are three disadvantages of handwriting. First, it is slow and, if the material is lengthy, it can be painful. Second, it involves the duplicated effort and additional time of typing the final version. Third, it is prone to error in the typing stage as words are misread or misunderstood.

One way to minimise the disadvantages is to handwrite the first draft, correct this in handwriting by adding and removing words and passages (either by writing on the original or by cutting and pasting in passages written on other sheets) and then typing up the final version on an electric typewriter. The original author, however, should ideally also be the typist, to use the opportunity provided by the typing stage to make last-minute corrections and improvements.

If the author cannot type, this whole process can be very laborious. The author is dependent on someone else to type the final version. This, however, is 'final' on only very rare occasions. The typist will usually make mistakes. The author has to read the typed version, correct the mistakes and send it to be typed all over again. This version then has to be corrected for mistakes once more. All this means that handwriting can be regarded as an efficient method of composition only if the author can type as well.

DICTATING

For those who cannot type, dictating is a better alternative than handwriting. Its main advantage is that it is fast. An experienced dictator can finish a one-page letter in the time it would take to handwrite the first paragraph. Dictating is also a fairly flexible medium. If you use a high-quality dictating machine—not a simple tape recorder but a machine specially designed for taking dictation—you can readily go back over your material, erasing some passages and correcting others.

Dictating has two main disadvantages. First, the dictator is still dependent on a typist to produce the final version which will itself need to be corrected for mistakes and misinterpretations. Second, dictating is a skill that needs some time and plenty of practice to develop proficiency. It is not easy to be able to speak in sentences that will read well on paper. There is also the difficulty of maintaining the sort of overall coherence you get from seeing your material as it is being written out. To overcome this last problem, many dictators adopt the sensible approach of handwriting a plan of what they want to say before they start speaking.

TYPEWRITERS

The writer who can type is always in a better position than the one who cannot. Most of the advantages of typing, especially speed and quality presentation, are gained mainly by the use of electric typewriters. Some electric typewriters are now relatively cheap and portable. Manual typewriters today are found only in secondhand shops and museums. Electrics, with either fabric or carbon ribbon, now produce the minimum standard of acceptable presentation quality.

Some electric typewriters are available with removable golfball or daisy-wheel-type printers. These allow you to change typeface for different documents or within the one document. This can be a handy feature, and these machines are thus more useful than those with fixed typefaces. Others offer proportional spacing and typefaces resembling those available from commercial printers. If your work needs to be of this quality, these typewriters may be worth their expense.

The best feature available to writers on electric typewriters is the correcting key. This allows the typist to go back over words and eliminate letters or words by typing them out, without having to rub out or use white correcting fluid. Correcting keys are now available on fairly inexpensive machines and any writer contemplating a typewriter would be foolish not to buy one with this feature.

Even with the most advanced typewriter technology, many writers still find difficulty composing directly onto a typewriter. It is never easy to go back to make major changes to the text. One way to reduce this difficulty is to adopt the old journalists' method of typing each paragraph of a story on a separate sheet of paper. This habit evolved in newspaper offices in the days before computerised typing because it was easier for editors and typesetters. It also helped in the business of composing a story. If some words or sentences looked unsatisfactory after they were written, then the paragraph could be thrown away and redone without affecting the rest of the text. In other words, to make a major change you only had to retype a paragraph not a whole page. Paragraphs can also be moved easily from one position to another when they are typed on separate sheets and this made composition easier as well. Instead of cutting up and pasting, you simply changed the order of your pieces of paper. Because journalists' paragraphs are very short (often only one sentence long) they were typed on small pieces of paper, usually half the old 'quarto' size, but most other writers who use the technique prefer full-sized sheets.

KEYBOARDS AND COMPUTERS

As we argued in Chapter Three, the Information Age is demanding that proficiency on the keyboard should be regarded as a universal skill, like driving a car or being able to swim. All children at school today should be taught the keyboard and any adult thinking seriously about his or her career prospects should make the acquisition of keyboard skills a high priority.

The biggest single reason to learn to use the keyboard is to become computer proficient. Small personal computers can be loaded with software packages that will handle not only word processing but filing, accounting and graphics. In other words, almost every form of communication that we once made on paper has now become computerised.

As we noted in our discussion of the electronic office, the great virtue of word processing is its flexibility and adaptability. You can correct simple typing mistakes, insert and delete words and passages, and move paragraphs and much longer parts of a text from one position to another. Successive drafts are all done on the one text—there is no need to retype the whole piece after you have made corrections or changes. The text is typed onto the computer's screen where all the corrections and changes are made. Once you are satisfied with the final version, you can print it out onto paper using a computer printer.

There are many computers and word processing systems on the market and it is not easy to choose between them. As well as word processing software you can also get computer dictionaries to check your spelling, an electronic thesaurus and functions to count how many words in a document. The top-of-the-market word processing software systems have all these features built in. They automatically handle just about every conceivable need in professional writing.

As well as word processors, our chapter on the electronic office listed a range of other software and hardware which can now be used with a personal computer. They include:

desktop publishing
database software
spreadsheet software

communications systems
CD-ROM

The combination of keyboards and computers offers a technological package that renders all the earlier forms of writing technology obsolete. The only decision to make is whether you can afford the money for a computer and a printer, and whether you can afford the time to learn to use the keyboard. If you are prepared to put in the money and the time, you will be a better writer than you would otherwise have been. Anyone who spends a reasonable amount of time on writing tasks should make the effort to become computer proficient.

CHAPTER

44

OVERCOMING WRITER'S BLOCK

After studying this chapter, you will be able to:

- recognise the reasons why many writers suffer an inability to start their work
- apply techniques that some successful writers have developed to overcome the problem

A recent survey of university academics found that no less than half of them had not produced any publications for five years, despite research and publication being specified as part of their job. In the great majority of cases they failed to deliver, the survey found, not due to a lack of interest in their subject matter, nor to the fact that they had not done the research that was required of them. They suffered from an inability to get started on the writing stage of their work. Many actually feared writing and put it off for so long that eventually their research topic had been taken up by someone else or had become out of date.

This inability to begin a writing task is often called 'writer's block'. It is not something confined to people who write infrequently. In fact, most discussion about the subject comes from professional writers. Some very famous writers, such as George Orwell and T. S. Eliot, have been almost chronic sufferers. Because of their obvious interest in the subject, most advice about how to overcome the problem has also come from professional writers. Useful as this material is, however, it is directed primarily at people who are frequent writers and who suffer a temporary lapse, whereas the real nature of the problem lies with that much larger group of people who never get to the ranks of the professionals. For these people, writer's block can be a real affliction that prevents them applying for any job where writing is involved and that can severely inhibit their careers all their lives.

To discuss writer's block we need to recognise there are two kinds: one that is long-term and affects people who write very little; the other that is short-term and affects people who write very often.

LONG-TERM WRITER'S BLOCK

The most important thing to understand about writing is that it does not spring from some 'talent' or 'genius' that lies deep within a lucky few of us, waiting to be unlocked. Like any other human skill, writing can be developed. And, like any other skill, if you practise often and work at it, you will develop the talents you need. Being a writer is very much like being an athlete. Unless you are fit you cannot perform. Developing writing skills is very much like exercising. You should begin by running a short distance or lifting light weights and, as your body adjusts, you can gradually increase your effort. No one has analysed what processes occur in the brain that make writing easy for some people and difficult for others. However, it must be something very much like other physical processes in the body. You have to exercise that part of the brain that handles writing and, the more exercise you do, the flows, currents and connections involved all work more quickly and smoothly. If you lay off exercising for several weeks, the body quickly deteriorates and you are soon unfit. The same seems to occur with writing—the longer you lay off, the harder it is to get started again.

If this analogy is correct, the way to handle long-term writer's block is to develop a writing plan in the same way you would an exercise regimen. Start with easy and light work, keep at it on a regular basis and work your way up. No one would dream of starting their first long-distance run with a marathon, and no one should think of starting off cold to write a major report or thesis.

If you feel completely out of practice, start writing letters to friends. Try to write something every day and look for slightly more difficult tasks each time. If you are involved with a long report or thesis, don't start with the introduction or Chapter One. (Introductions are actually best done last, when you know exactly what it is you are introducing.) Start with the very easiest jobs, perhaps letters to librarians requesting books or to someone else asking for information. Or you might start writing on some minor theme or side issue that you plan to bury deep within the report. You should even expect to discard your first few efforts once you have got going. They will not have been wasted if you have used them to build up your expertise so that you can get started properly on the main text.

Overall, long-term writer's block can be overcome by a persistent program designed to get your brain functioning within a writing mode. Like exercise, you should avoid overdoing it and, more importantly, you should avoid long layoffs that will take you back to the point where you started.

SHORT-TERM WRITER'S BLOCK

Some of the techniques used by well-known writers suffering writer's block can also be applied by most of us. The poet T. S. Eliot used to break his block by writing poems in French. This, he said, removed the pressure on him to perform in his mother tongue. In other words, he used French as a kind of warm-up exercise before getting down to the serious business of writing in English by which he would be judged publicly. Those of us who cannot write in another language can still use this as a model. When facing a block on a piece that will be made public, start with something that will not be published and which carries no pressure to perform. The American journalist Tom Wolfe blocked on his first article for *Esquire* magazine about customised cars, wrote a memo full of slang and jargon to his editor about the subject. The editor ran the memo as the article.

People who write often but who still suffer writer's block often do so after a brief layoff period. The layoff might only be a matter of days, but they need some stimulus to bring them back into their writing mode. The key to breaking the block is to write something easy, something that doesn't matter much. This will join the temporarily parted pathways along the synapses of the brain and kick-start the flows and currents of the writing process.

Ernest Hemingway is out of fashion these days. Although he won a Nobel Prize for his novels, the macho posturing and alcoholic decline of the last years before his suicide left him with few admirers. However, in the 1920s and 1930s he took the craft of writing very seriously and his essays still offer some of the most useful comments to be had on the subject. When you are engaged on a long piece of work, many people assume that it is best to keep writing until you have finished a whole section or a chapter. Hemingway's advice is much more telling: 'Stop writing when things are going well and you know what will happen next so that you will have sufficient momentum to continue the next day.'

The most effective way to avoid writer's block, however, is to prevent it from occurring. The best preventive strategy is to adopt the planning processes we have recommended in this book. By planning what you intend to write before you start to write, you overcome the great mental block that often occurs when you have a big project and don't know where to start. Studying the plan can sometimes indicate which sections would be the easiest and on which a start could most readily be made.

If you have not written for some time, examining and modifying the plan is a good writing exercise in itself, and the one most likely to help overcome both short-term and long-term writer's block. Working on the plan rather than the actual text is a useful way of developing the mental framework needed. In general, writers who plan their work to a high degree are the ones who have the least trouble in getting started, irrespective of how long their layoff period has been. In other words, those who plan most are the ones who suffer least from inhibitions such as writer's block.

CHAPTER

45

EDITING COPY

After studying this chapter, you will be able to:

- understand the techniques used by publishing houses to edit articles and books
- develop a work plan for editing a manuscript
- use editing conventions to mark copy to be corrected by a typesetter

Editing the text of your own writing or someone else's is an exacting task that should not be taken lightly. Editing should always be performed before the final version of a piece of writing is submitted to the printer, the typist or whatever other form of reproduction is appropriate.

THE SKILLS OF EDITING

All the major publishers of written work employ editors to go through the typescripts of writers to correct errors and ensure each work is readable. Book publishers and newspaper publishers have their own names for these typescripts. In book publishing, professional editors read, correct and rewrite the *manuscripts* submitted by authors to publishers. In newspaper and magazine publishing, subeditors do the same to the *copy* prepared by journalists. Editors and subeditors also mark up manuscripts and copy with symbols and instructions to printers about how to produce the finished job.

Unless we are employed in the publishing business, the editing that most of us do will be mostly our own work. The principles discussed below apply no less to our own than to the work of others. In fact, one of the rules of editing your own copy should be to try and distance yourself from it as much as possible and to look at it as an outside editor would. The best way to do this is to put as much time as practical between finishing the writing and beginning the editing. This way you will lose some of that closeness you have to your own writing which can prevent you being an objective critic of your own work. Even if you are really pressed on a dead-line, try and leave your writing at least overnight before coming back to edit it. The longer you leave your own work the more likely you will read it as another person would, and the better will be your editing.

Whether working on your own copy or someone else's, there are a range of specific responsibilities that editors are required to carry out. Anyone involved in an editing task should recognise them.

CONSISTENCY

The editor should ensure that a uniform 'style' is adopted throughout the work. The use of capitals, punctuation, quotation marks, italics and bold print, underlining, forms of abbreviation and spelling must be the same throughout. An inconsistency in the use of capitals, for example, would occur if the writer used capitals to describe one person's position ('Managing Director') but not to describe another's ('personnel manager'); or used commas between some numbers when designating thousands ('45,000 people') but not in others ('$250 000'); or if some subheadings were typed in capitals and underlined but other subheadings of the same order of importance were typed in lower case and/or were not underlined. The editor needs to decide on one consistent style and ensure it is main-tained throughout.

GRAMMAR AND USAGE

Here again, the underlying value is consistency. As we argued in Chapter Forty-One, the principal rule of grammar should be that of consistency. Singular nouns should relate to singular verbs and so on. The other points made in that chapter should also be firmly kept in mind when editing for correct grammar and usage.

ORGANISATION AND CONTINUITY

Editors should ensure the work is well organised and maintains continuity in both its ideas and its physical elements. A report should not have two Chapter Fives. The author should not make contradictory statements in different places. There should be no gaps in the argument. The author should not refer to a non-existent footnote or section.

WRITING STYLE

Even the most experienced writers sometimes write passages very badly. The editor needs to be able to recognise these when they occur and rewrite them in more acceptable English. This role, however, does not give the editor a licence to make major changes. The best editors, in fact, are those who rewrite the least. They do not impose their own concept of good writing onto someone else but rather correct the faults of others with a minimum of fuss, such as substituting one word for another, removing a redundant expression or breaking up one long, obscure sentence into three short, clear ones.

FACTUAL MISTAKES

It is difficult for the editor to check a work for factual content, as it is not the editor's job to go out and re-examine the evidence used by the author. However, editors can, if they are careful, catch misstatements, absurdities and obvious mistakes (such as a mistyped date of a well-known event) before the work reaches its final published stage. In newspaper and magazine offices, subeditors have a range of standard reference publications available on their desks such as *Who's Who*, the *Commonwealth Year Book*, the telephone book and the electoral roll, which they routinely use to check things such as the names, titles and addresses of people mentioned in stories. Other editors should emulate their practice and check all data of this kind.

WRITTEN CORRECTIONS AND ADDITIONS

These should be made neatly and legibly so that a typist or printer will have no difficulty in understanding them. The editor should thus always adopt a clear handwriting or printing style.

TYPESETTING

In most commercial operations, the editor has to mark up the copy for typesetting and must be familiar with the various marking conventions that convey the exact meaning intended. When a publication is computerised, the editor formats type with its typeface and font size directly on the computer screen. Increasingly, as word processing and desktop publishing grow in offices, there is a need for editors to adopt these same conventions for material that will be reproduced by in-house typists.

THE PRACTICE OF EDITING

Because there are so many different tasks in the work of editing, most professional editors break each down into one step. They then go through the manuscript several times, checking during each 'reading' on the one particular aspect. The following is a typical work plan used by an editor on a book manuscript.

WORK PLAN

NUMBERING

The editor checks all numerical sequences such as chapter numbers, section numbers, page numbers, numbers given to tables and diagrams and the numbering of simple lists.

HEADINGS AND SUBHEADINGS

The editor checks the sequence of all headings and subheadings to ensure that a consistent order of hierarchy has been adopted. All major headings should be typed or printed in the same style; all subheadings should also be typed and printed consistently and in a sequentially subordinate style to major headings. For example, if major headings are in capitals and underlined, subheadings may be in lower case and underlined, and in any sub-subheadings the underline may be omitted. The editor should ensure this format is maintained throughout.

STYLE CONSISTENCY

The editor goes through the manuscript to check consistency in capitals, spelling, punctuation, abbreviations, number style and so on. In some specialised works, such as a technical article or book, this step may be broken down into several—for instance, to check equations, to check alignment of tables, to check the spelling of technical terms. Pull out all recurring special material such as tables and references and ensure all have a consistent style. For publishing conventions in punctuation, numbers, capitals and other prose usage, see Chapters Forty-One and Forty-Two of this book.

SENSE AND GRAMMAR

It is difficult to separate these two and normally one 'read' to check both sense and grammar will suffice. For conventions in grammar, see Chapter Forty-One.

ORGANISATION AND CONTINUITY

However, 'sense' in the short term is a different matter from overall coherence, and so a separate 'read' is needed to ensure that the argument is consistent and follows logically and persuasively.

NAMES

Run a check to ensure all place names, personal names, institutions and publications are spelt consistently throughout the manuscript.

LANGUAGE

One point worth watching for is idiosyncrasies of a particular author. One author may begin too many sentences and paragraphs with 'However,'; another may be fond of 'not only but also'; another may be chronically unable to make a point directly without qualifying it: 'On the one hand ... On the other hand'. A good editor will pick up these tedious and sometimes embarrassing habits. If you are editing your own material, you have to be particularly aware to recognise your own foibles. Some word processor packages have checking systems to count the frequency with which a text uses its most common words and phrases. These are useful for detecting bad habits.

ADDING MATERIAL

Any text that is to go before an editor should be typed in one-and-a-half or double spacing. This makes it easier to read and easier to add changes. Any corrections or additions to the text are best made, where possible, on the spot and between the lines of text. If the material to be added is too long to fit between lines, it should be written in the side margin (which is another reason to have big margins top and bottom and both sides). If there is not enough space in the side margin, use the margin at the bottom of the page. Indicate clearly the extent of the new copy by drawing some kind of confining line. Also, indicate exactly where it is to go in the text, even if this means drawing a line from the additional material across the page to the point where it is to be inserted.

WRITING INSTRUMENTS

Consistency is a virtue not only in writing but in editing too. If you are working with a paper-based system rather than a computer, use a consistent pattern of writing instruments to make changes, to give style instructions and to write queries. The normal procedure of professional editors is to use a red pen to make changes, corrections and additions. To mark style instructions for the printer or typist, use a green pen. To query a point, either for checking at a later stage by the editor or to refer it back to the author, a pencil is always preferred. If the query comes to nothing, it can be rubbed out.

INSTRUCTIONS TO THE PRINTER

There is a formal set of conventions through which editors tell typesetters how they want the text to finally appear. This is a kind of shorthand that most people will find it convenient to follow. The full range of these instructions is too long to give here but is published in the Commonwealth government's book *Style Manual for Authors, Editors and Printers*, available from government bookshops. Unless otherwise indicated, copy will be typeset by printers as it appears in typewriter form. Typesetters will normally follow the capitals and lower case letters, the paragraph breaks, the indentations and most other styles typed in the text. The need for special instructions to the typesetter comes when the editor wants to change the typewritten version. The following are some of the more common instructions that editors give to typesetters.

1. Indicate capital letters by drawing three lines underneath the letter concerned: Australian council for education research.
2. Indicate lower case letters (when they are typed as capitals in the manuscript) by drawing a light diagonal line through them: AUSTRALIAN COUNCIL FOR EDUCATION RESEARCH. Note that in this case it was also helpful to indicate which letters should remain as capitals.
3. The following mark indicates the start of a new paragraph. ¶ Only use it in cases where there is not already a paragraph in the typescript.
4. Move copy from one position to another in the following way:
   ⟵ Australian Council for Education Research
5. Indicate that a line should run-on by:
   Australian Council for Education Research.
   This is one of the few research associations...
6. Indicate the need for space between lines by putting the following symbol between those lines: #
7. Close up spaces between lines by putting the following symbol in those spaces: ⁀
8. Underlining letters is a signal to a printer to use italic type for all those letters. It is not necessary to write 'ital' adjacent to the underlining, although some editors do this to be sure. To specify bold type, underline the letters or words and write 'bold' in a balloon next to each underline: chart (bold)
9. If a number should be spelled out, either write the word over the number or circle the number and write 'spell out' in the margin.
10. To indent a whole paragraph or section, indicate the section clearly by drawing a line around it. Then write 'indent 2 ems' or whatever indentation is required. An 'em' is a common measurement in typesetting and is the width of the letter 'm' in the typeface being used. In other words, the above instruction tells the typesetter to indent the passage by the width of two letters.
11. When letters or words need to have their order reversed, use the transpose sign. For example: the hosre kicked the gate front.
12. To delete a passage, cross it out and add a delete mark: For example: They have given up their interest. ~~It was too difficult at their age~~.
13. If you delete part of a text, then change your mind and want it left in, put dots around the words that are to remain and write 'stet' adjacent to them. For example: and, ~~therefore~~, can (stet)
14. To ensure that styles in chapter headings, section headings and subheadings are consistent, editors normally give instructions at the start of the text in the following way: Headlines labelled Ⓐ = caps, bold, underlined; headlines labelled Ⓑ = lower case, bold, underlined; headlines labelled Ⓒ = lower case, bold. They then go through the typescript and label all subsequent headings with the appropriate sign—Ⓐ, ⒷⒸ etc.

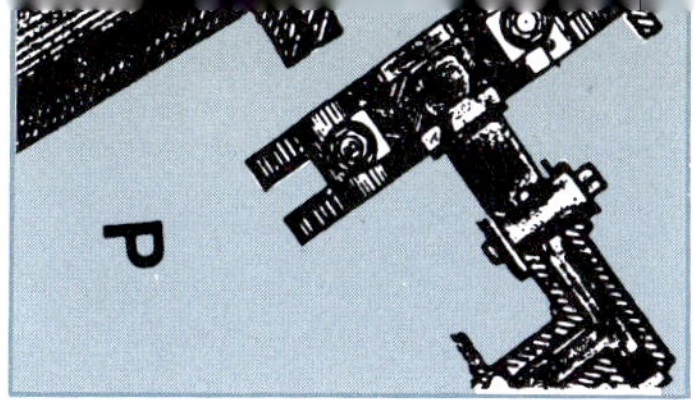

SPECIALIST TECHNIQUES SECTION

II

STATISTICS

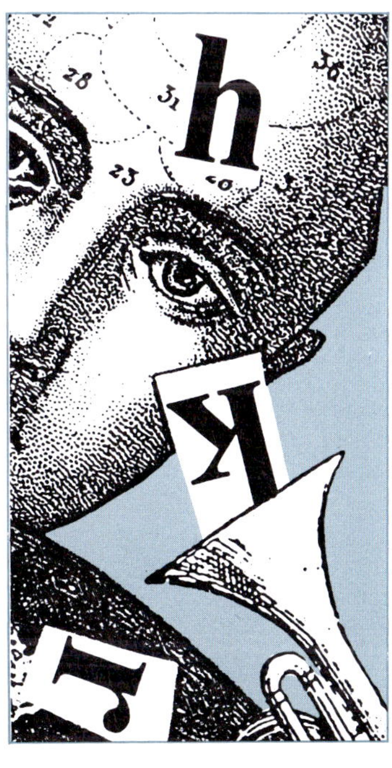

CHAPTER 46

USING STATISTICS

After studying this chapter, you will be able to:

- ☐ use numbers to make comparisons
- ☐ understand and use percentages
- ☐ use percentages to record change over time
- ☐ understand and use averages
- ☐ detect misuse of statistics

All types of communication are better if they use numbers whenever they discuss the quantity of anything. You can say the purchase price of a house was 'very expensive' but you do a better job of communicating if you add that it cost $300 000. This puts your meaning of 'very expensive' into an understandable context and rules out any other interpretations your istener might otherwise have, such as the idea that 'very expensive' might apply only to houses over $500 000. You can say a person 'is struggling to make ends meet' but you add much more to your meaning if you also say she exists on only $120 a week. Numerical data gives your audience confidence that you have done at least some investigation into the subject you are talking about. Anyone can say they think there is a great deal of crime around nowadays but the person who can actually report how many armed robberies or white-collar crimes have taken place within a city in the past year is taken much more seriously by most people. Ours is very much a numerate culture in which the quantification of issues, that is, the use of numbers and statistics, is often necessary to convince others of a point. Those who have difficulty in using numbers will always be less effective communicators than those who don't.

USING NUMBERS TO MAKE COMPARISONS

SIMPLE COMPARISONS

Very often, numbers on their own are not enough to provide meaningful information about an issue. If we take one of the topics mentioned above, the level of crime, this becomes clear. If someone says there were 250 armed hold-ups in Melbourne last year, this is better than saying there were 'a lot' of armed hold-ups, but we still need more information to know how seriously we should regard the problem. Is 250 an alarming figure for a city that size in that year? Is it worse than the numbers recorded in Sydney or Brisbane over the same period? Is it better or worse than the results of the previous year, or of the past five years? To make the figure really meaningful we need to compare it to those of other places and other times.

The most elementary form of comparison that could be made is by subtraction. If, in our armed hold-up example, Sydney recorded 270 robberies in the same year; if Brisbane recorded 240; and if there were 260 in Melbourne the previous year, we could do the following subtractions:

Sydney		Melbourne	
270	–	250	= 20
Melbourne		Brisbane	
250	–	240	= 10
1991		1992	
260	–	250	= 10

These figures show that Melbourne had 20 fewer armed hold-ups than Sydney but 10 more than Brisbane. Also, there were 10 fewer in the current year than in the previous year. In other words, Melbourne's total of 250 is not all that unusual for a city of its size and there is a slight downward trend in the incidence of this type of crime.

RATIOS

The examples given above tell us something about the relationships between the crime rates of the three cities. Sydney's is greater than Melbourne's. Brisbane's is less than Melbourne's. Very often, though, we want to express other relationships, such as by how much one thing is greater than or less than another. Take a different example. If the price of petrol in the city increases from 45 cents a litre to 54 cents a litre, we can express the size of the increase simply as 9 cents. If the price of a litre of petrol went up in country areas from 50 to 60 cents, then the increase was 10 cents. The country seems to have received the bigger increase. To work out who has been most affected by the increases we need to compare them to the original prices. One way to do this is to express each as a fraction of that original price. The new price in the city was an increase of 9 cents over 45. We calculate the fraction by dividing 45 by 9 which is 1/5. So the new city petrol price is 1/5 higher than the old price. To work out the country increase, we divide the old price of 50 cents by the 10 cents increase and find that the new price of 60 cents is 1/5 higher than the old. This means the proportion of the increase in both city and country is the same. Even though the country pays a higher additional amount, the relative difference between the two areas has been kept the same.

The comparisons here are made by expressing the extra cost as a ratio of the original price. We could have used a different ratio, that of the new price compared to the old price. This would be:

54 cents divided by 45 cents = 1 1/5 or 1.2
60 cents divided by 50 cents = 1 1/5 or 1.2

This tells us that the new prices are 1.2 times as high as the old ones. Or we could have divided the old by the new:

45 cents divided by 54 cents = 5/6 or 0.83
50 cents divided by 60 cents = 5/6 or 0.83

This tells us that the old prices were 5/6ths of the new. The ratio of 54 to 45 can be expressed in the following ways:

54:45 54-45 54/4 5 6/5 1.2

EXERCISES (A)

> What are the five ways of expressing the ratio of 45 to 54?

PERCENTAGES

Ratios are useful if you are making comparisons of a fairly simple kind, such as, in the example above, two prices for the one product. However, when it comes to comparing several things to each other, the limitations of ratios fairly quickly become apparent: for instance, if we are looking at government spending and we want to see what share education currently receives. In the 1985–86 Commonwealth budget education was allocated $4944 million. This is a difficult figure for most people to comprehend but it becomes more understandable if we compare it to the total Commonwealth budget that year of $69 067 million. As a ratio, education gets 4944 over 69 067, or about 1/14 of Commonwealth spending. If we want to compare this to the amount spent on assistance to industry of $1256 million, we could convert the figure to a ratio which comes out at about 1/56 of the budget. These two fractions have different denominators (14ths and 56ths) which makes comparisons awkward. If we wanted to compare these figures to other ratios of budget expenditure we get different denominators again (defence received about 1/9 and social security 2/7 of the budget) which makes clear understanding very difficult.

The way out of this problem is to convert all the ratios to fractions of the same common denominator which, by common agreement, has become 100. Instead of ninths, sevenths and fourteenths, we can now compare all the budget figures as their rate per 100, or their rate 'per cent'. The fraction 1/9 becomes 11/100, which we write as 11 per cent. The ratio 2/7 becomes 28/100 or 28 per cent. When we compare 11 per cent to 28 per cent we gain a much clearer idea of how the two amounts relate to each other.

Percentages are always percentages of something. That something is the sum total of what we are discussing (in the above case it is the total of the budget). This sum total is often called the base. A percentage without a base is a meaningless statistic. Advertisements that claim that a product sells 20 per cent more than its nearest rival, or travels 45 per cent faster than anyone else, are meaningless unless the claims are related to a base—20 per cent of what? 45 per cent of what?

EXERCISES (B)

1. What percentage of the budget total of $69 067 million did education receive with $4944 million? (Calculate by dividing 4944 by 69 067, then multiplying the answer by 100.)

2. The total number of people working in Australia is 7 million. If there are 700 000 people unemployed, what percentage of the workforce is out of work?

3. Spending on all forms of advertising in Australia in 1991 amounted to $4703 million. Spending on press advertising was $2319 million; on television $1614 million; on radio $420 million; on outdoor advertising $266 million; and on cinema $83 million. Calculate the percentage shares of each medium of advertising.

COMPARISONS OVER TIME

Another type of comparison that people frequently need to make is a comparison over time. In the simple comparisons of crime rates made earlier, we saw that armed hold-ups in Melbourne had declined from 260 in 1991 to 250 in 1992. This decline of 10 represents a ratio of decrease of 10/260 or 1/26 or 3.8 per cent. We can say there was a 3.8 per cent decline in the level of armed hold-ups in Melbourne between 1991 and 1992. Normally, social statistics like crime rates are more meaningful over a longer period like five years. So we could present them in the following way.

Table 46.1 *Crime rates in Melbourne 1988-92*

Year	*No. of hold-ups*	*Per cent change*
1988	190	
1989	200	+ 5%
1990	240	+ 20%
1991	260	+ 8%
1992	250	− 4%

From this table, it is apparent that the big change occurred in 1990 when there was a 20 per cent increase. Between 1988 and 1992 there was an increase of 60 hold-ups or a rate of increase of 31.5 per cent. In other words, the downturn between 1991 and 1992 is misleading because longer trends indicate a fairly substantial rate of growth.

EXERCISES (C)

Calculate the percentage rate of change in the price of petrol for each of the following years and for the whole period 1990 to 1995.

Year	*Cents per litre*
1990	60
1991	62
1992	64
1993	68
1994	65
1995	63

MISUSING PERCENTAGES

Although percentages usually work to clarify figures, they also present opportunities for obscuring them. You should avoid these forms of misuse yourself and be able to detect them in the work of others.

VAGUE CATEGORIES

Unless you know the extent of the category to which a percentage is related, you cannot be sure what it means. Take the following claim as an example.

> Sixty per cent of people in the dental profession use Brand X toothbrush.

At first glance this appears to be saying that 60 per cent of dentists use this brand. However, 'people in the dental profession' is a wider group. It could include dentists, dental nurses, receptionists in dentists' surgeries or even people who make toothbrushes and toothpaste—we cannot be sure. Since we do not know who is included in this vague category, we do not know the size of the base that is being compared, and so the percentage is meaningless.

MISLEADING COMPARISONS

One of the most common reasons given when companies increase prices is that their labour costs have gone up. A 3 per cent increase awarded under the national wage case will be used to justify a 3 per cent increase in prices. However, the assumption underlying this comparison is that labour costs are the entire costs of the organisation. This is rarely the case. Wages are usually only a proportion of costs that also include materials, transportation, power and so on. In a firm where wages represent half its total annual costs, a 3 per cent wages increase is really only a 1.5 per cent increase in total expenses.

Another common form of misleading comparisons occurs when different bases are involved. For example, to say that John increased his examination marks by 10 per cent while Harry dropped his by 10 per cent does not tell us much about who is the better student. It can be misleading, especially if John's result was an increase from 50 to 55 while Harry's was a decline from 100 to 90.

It is common for companies involved in takeovers to talk about their rapid rate of growth compared to those they want to take over. But if the base from which they have grown is low, their rate of growth may not be very impressive. A company with a $1 million profit one year may increase it to $2 million the next and so record a 100 per cent profit increase. But this may be far less impressive than a company that lifts its earnings from $12 million to $15 million. In absolute terms the second company has increased its profits by three times as much as the first, but in percentage terms on its previous year's profit, the increase is only 25 per cent.

FLATTERING MEASURES

Percentages are sometimes preferred by people wanting to make their case look better than it really is. For example, an employment agency that was not doing very well could nonetheless truthfully claim that '90 per cent of our clients found jobs last month' if it had only ten clients over this period and it placed nine of them. Similarly, a claim that 80 per cent of people in a 'taste test' preferred drink A to drink B may not be as impressive a statistic had we been told that only five people took the test. If percentages are to be meaningful statistical measures, it is always important to know the total numbers involved and the extent of the categories used.

EXERCISES (D)

Explain what is wrong with the following statements.

1. It is much safer to travel by plane than by train. Last year 450 people in the world were killed in passenger train accidents but only 145 died in planes.

2. Council rates last year increased by 4 per cent. So the landlord said rents should increase by 4 per cent.

3. The unemployment rate for adults is 6 per cent and the unemployment rate for teenagers is 20 per cent. Therefore, there are more youths unemployed than adults.

USE AND ABUSE OF AVERAGES

The normal meaning of 'average' is a figure produced by adding up the sum of a number of items and then dividing it by the number of items. For example, to work out a cricketer's average score over five innings, you would first list all his scores.

Innings 1	35
Innings 2	28
Innings 3	78
Innings 4	60
Innings 5	55

Then you add up the total runs scored: 256 runs.
Then you divide the total by the number of innings:
256 divided by 5
To get the answer that his average score was 51.2 runs.

This way of calculating an average produces what statisticians call the arithmetic mean, or more commonly the mean. In many cases it produces the 'typical' result we can expect from the thing we are studying. In the case of the cricketer's scores above, he never actually scored 51.2 runs but this is a figure that we can expect he will, under normal conditions, approximate.

Another way to measure the average is to work out the median. This is the mid-point of any distribution of figures. To work it out you arrange all the items in a line from smallest to largest and then find the middle one. In the cricket scores above, the line would be:

28 35 55 60 78

and the median would be 55. In this case the average calculated as the mean and the average calculated as the median are very close, but this is not always the case. Take the following set of cricket scores.

5 8 11 12 67

Here the mean is 20.6 and the median is 11. In this case the 11 is a better guide to the normal innings you could expect from this player because the mean has been distorted by his one good score. Similarly, in a class of schoolgirls, the mean time it takes each to swim 100 metres would be distorted greatly if one of them were an Olympic swimmer. The typical time would be better represented by the median.

Another way to measure an average is to calculate the mode. This is simply the number in a distribution that occurs most often. If we take, as an example, the seven most recent placings gained by a racehorse, it might look like the following.

1st 6th 4th 4th 2nd 21st 11th

The mode is the 4th placing because this occurs most frequently. In some cases, especially where there are a few results that are not typical and that would distort the picture if calculated by mean or median, the mode can be the best guide.

Like percentages, averages can be used to mislead and confuse. This is particularly true of social and economic statistics. For example, the average weekly adult male wage in Australia in February 1986 was $460.10, including both ordinary time and overtime. This is almost $24 000 a year and, in general, it is the figure most often cited by the news media as the typical wage of the Australian worker. However, it is a very misleading figure because it leaves out earnings by women and teenagers. The average weekly earnings of a woman in full-time employment was $360 and for the average woman worker (both full-time and part-time) it was $276.40. It turns out that about 75 per cent of employees earned less than the average male in a full-time job and that the average of all persons for all jobs at the time was only $364.10 or $18 933 a year. In other words, the typical worker is by no means as well off as the normally cited 'average' indicates.

Another example that indicates how averages can mislead is that of climate. A city with a temperature range of from 40°C in high summer to –5°C in midwinter is a far cry from one with a range of between 28° and 16°, yet both could have an annual average of 20°. To avoid being misled by averages we need to know the amount of variation in the data being averaged.

EXERCISES (E)

1. Calculate the mean and the median of the racehorse's performances given above.

2. Using the following cricket scores:

   39 44 34 48 31 39 46 48 34 36 41

   work out the mean, median and mode.

3. A mathematics class produced the following results in an examination:

   96 80 100 100 95 82 0 0

   The teacher said the average mark was 69. What is wrong with the teacher's reasoning?

4. Find some examples of misleading uses of averages in newspaper advertisements. Explain why they are misleading.

CHAPTER

47

UNDERSTANDING TABLES

After studying this chapter, you will be able to:

- read statistical tables on social issues
- understand social trends revealed by statistics
- use tables of statistics in documents of your own

STATISTICS AND THE HUMANITIES

There is an unfortunate division within our society between the humanities and the sciences. Many people who study or who work within the physical sciences and some of the social sciences, such as economics, believe they are the only ones in touch with reality because they deal exclusively in 'hard data', that is, in evidence that can be measured or quantified. The things that interest people in the humanities, such as social values and the quality of life, have long been regarded as less able to be discussed in numerical terms. In recent years, however, there has been a great increase in statistical information in many of those areas that concern people in the humanities. We now have good 'hard data' about areas such as family life, health, education, working life, housing, social welfare, crime and justice. The Australian Bureau of Statistics' series of publications called *Social Indicators* has opened up a wide range of statistical information in all these areas. Today there is no good reason why those studying or working in these fields should not make the best possible use of this data.

One of the problems, though, is that people who did not do well in mathematics at high school automatically shy away from numerical data whenever they see it. This is a great pity because you do not need a formal education in mathematics to be able to read, understand and use the more readily available kinds of social statistics. Tables and graphs of statistics are simply ways of showing social relationships or of making the kinds of comparisons we discussed in the previous chapter. Part of the problem lies not within readers of tables and graphs but in the way some writers use them. In many cases, articles and books that use statistics go overboard and present page after page of them. The sheer hard work involved in wading through them all is a daunting prospect for many readers. Tables and graphs should be presented in a way that makes understanding easier rather than more difficult.

While we wait for writers like these to mend their ways and to be more selective about their use of statistics, it is still a good idea to make the effort to read tables and graphs yourself and to use them in your own work. The next chapter discusses the use of graphs, while the rest of this one focuses on how to understand tables.

HOW TO READ A STATISTICAL TABLE

Let us take a real issue and see what the statistics can tell us about it. One of the most controversial issues of recent times has been the impact of the introduction of the Family Court on the divorce rate. The Family Court began operations in 1975 under a new set of principles: before 1975, if one partner in a marriage wanted a divorce, he or she had to sue the other partner and find some fault in him or her, such as adultery or cruelty of some kind. The person wanting a divorce had to hire a lawyer and go through a lengthy court hearing which was open to the public and which could be reported in the press.

After 1975, a 'no fault' divorce could be gained through the new Family Court on the simple grounds that a couple had been separated for a period of twelve months. Unless there was a dispute over property or over the custody of children, there was no need to employ lawyers or to go through a major court hearing. This 'easy' kind of divorce was a relatively inexpensive affair and there was no public airing of the couple's personal affairs. The number of divorces rose sharply after 1975. From an annual total of about 15 000 per year before the new Court was set up, the total number of divorces rose to over 60 000 in 1976. Some people have argued that divorce has now become 'too easy' and that families that might have stayed together are being broken up, to the disadvantage of the children within these families. On this line of thinking, the big rise in single-parent families can partly be blamed on the new divorce laws. Can the statistics enlighten us on these issues? We will start by looking at one of the tables from *Social Indicators No. 5*, which makes a comparison between the number of divorces per year for each year from 1967 to 1990, and the length of time the couples concerned had been married.

TABLE 47.1 *Divorces: duration of marriage*

	Duration of marriage (years)					
Year	*below 5*	*5–9*	*10–14*	*15–19*	*20 or above*	*Median duration of marriage*
			— per cent —			years
1967	7.1	25.4	20.2	17.4	29.9	n.a.
1970	10.0	29.4	19.4	14.0	27.1	12.5
1972	10.0	30.8	19.2	14.2	25.8	12.1
1974	9.5	31.7	20.2	13.5	25.2	11.8
1976	15.5	30.2	18.1	12.5	23.7	11.0
1978	19.3	28.6	18.5	12.2	21.4	10.5
1980	20.7	28.4	19.3	11.8	19.8	10.2
1982	20.3	28.0	20.0	13.0	18.8	10.4
1986	21.7	26.2	17.8	14.3	19.9	10.6
1990	20.9	28.5	17.3	13.1	20.2	10.1

Source: Australian Bureau of Statistics, *Social Indicators No. 5*

Take some time to look at Table 47.1. Read all the table's headings. The headings tell you what is being explained. Now try to understand what the table is telling you when you read *across* its columns, or from one side to the other. For each year the divorcing couples are divided up according to how long they had been married. We are shown what share (per cent) each group with the same duration of marriage had of the total of divorces that year. In 1967, some 7.1 per cent of couples who got divorced had been married less than 5 years. The same year, 25.4 per cent of those divorced had been married for between 5 and 9 years; 20.2 per cent had been married for between 10 and 14 years; 17.4 per cent had been married for between 15 and 19 years and 29.9 per cent had been married for more than 20 years. These percentages add up to 100 per cent. The last column gives us the median or average length of time couples had been married before they divorced. We can read the same figures for different years from 1967 to 1990.

The point we are interested in is what happened after 1975. What were the trends before that date, and what were they afterwards? To see these trends we now look down the columns. Straight away we can see that there has been a fairly big change in the share of divorces among the group who have been married less than 5 years. Only 7.1 per cent of this group divorced in 1967, but by 1990 the group accounted for 20.9 per cent of all divorces. No other group has had such a dramatic change. The share of divorces has remained much the same for these other groups between 1967 and 1990, except for the group married between 15 and 19 years who have had a fairly modest decline from 17.4 per cent of the total down to 13.1 per cent of their total.

So, one conclusion we can draw from the trends revealed by this table is that the introduction of the Family Court was followed by a increase in the share of divorces among the newly married. Note that the table is presenting percentage shares. The total number of divorces increased (as we said earlier, it went up from around 15 000 per year before 1975 to over 60 000 in 1976) so the number of divorces also increased for each of the groups in the table. But we can still say there was a relative shift in the divorce rate to the newly married.

TABLE 47.2 *Divorces: number of children involved*

	Number of children						
Year	*0*	*1*	*2*	*3*	*4 or more*	*Percentage of divorces involving children*	*Total number of children*
	per cent						'000
1967	33.5	25.4	22.7	11.1	7.2	66.5	13.2
1970	33.7	24.3	23.2	11.5	7.3	66.3	16.9
1972	33.2	23.6	23.4	12.0	7.7	66.8	22.2
1974	31.7	23.4	25.1	12.4	7.5	68.3	25.5
1976	37.3	23.3	22.8	10.7	5.8	62.7	73.6
1978	36.9	22.5	24.7	10.7	5.3	63.1	51.6
1980	39.4	21.4	25.2	9.9	4.0	60.6	46.8
1982	38.4	21.6	26.2	10.3	3.5	61.6	53.0
1986	40.3	21.2	25.8	9.5	3.2	59.7	45.2
1990	44.4	20.5	23.8	8.6	2.8	55.6	44.9

Source: Australian Bureau of Statistics, *Social Indicators No. 5*

Now let us look at another table about divorce. Table 47.2 shows us the number of children of divorcing couples. After reading the headings, we should look across each line of the table. For 1967 we see what proportion of divorcing couples had no children, what proportion had 1 child, had 2 children and so on. We can see the same for each of the following years up to 1990. When we look down the columns, we can see the trends involved. Again, the first column appears to be the most revealing. There was a sudden jump in the proportion of childless couples who divorced after 1975. This jump was not as dramatic as the trend revealed in the previous table, but it is still quite noticeable. If you study the other family size groups, you will see that, instead of increasing, their proportion of divorces actually declined between 1974 and 1976.

Now, if we put the conclusions from the two tables together, we find that there have been at least two clear changes in divorce trends since the Family Court was introduced. The share of divorces among newly married and among childless couples has increased. So we can conclude from all this that, although there has been an increase in the total number of children affected by divorce since the Family Court began, its main impact has really been on newlywed couples without children. We could draw other conclusions from this, if we wanted to, but the tables do seem to answer one of the concerns we wanted to discuss. This is that 'easy' divorce does not impact on children as much as we might have at first thought.

TABLE 47.3 *Exnuptial confinements and confinements within the first eight months of marriage (per cent)*

	Exnuptial confinements as percentage of total for age group, mother aged					*Confinements within the first eight months of marriage as percentage of total for age group, mother aged*				
Year	*Under 20*	*20-24*	*25-29*	*30-34*	*Total (a)*	*Under 20*	*20-24*	*25-29*	*30-34*	*Total (b)*
1971	32.8	8.7	4.3	4.9	9.3	40.9	9.3	1.6	1.0	8.6
1972	34.8	8.8	4.4	5.0	9.7	39.1	8.5	1.5	1.1	8.1
1973	36.3	8.6	4.5	5.3	9.8	35.4	7.6	1.4	1.2	7.3
1974	36.6	8.6	4.3	5.2	9.6	32.2	6.6	1.4	1.2	6.4
1975	39.0	9.4	4.7	5.7	10.2	27.7	5.6	1.4	1.2	5.5
1976	40.4	9.7	4.9	5.6	10.1	25.1	5.3	1.6	1.5	5.0
1977	43.6	10.4	4.9	5.1	10.3	22.9	5.3	2.0	1.9	4.9
1978	47.6	11.9	4.9	5.1	11.1	22.5	5.8	2.0	1.9	4.9

(a) Exnuptial confinements as percentage of total confinements.
(b) Confinements within the first eight months of marriage as percentage of total confinements.
Source: Australian Bureau of Statistics, *Social Indicators No. 3*

Let us take another, slightly more complicated set of statistics in Table 47.3. This is from *Social Indicators No. 3* and is a table of trends in the 1970s in exnuptial confinements (births to unmarried mothers) compared to confinements within the first 8 months of marriage (in other words, the bride was pregnant when she married). Look across the tables to see what groups are being compared. We find we are comparing unmarried mothers within several age groupings, to pregnant brides in the same age groupings. This is also a table of percentages, that is, we are looking at the shares held by these two groups of women, at their various ages, compared to total births to all women in the same age groupings. Next look down the columns to see the trends. The results are fairly clear. For two of the age groups of unmarried mothers (those under 20 years and those aged 20–24), there has been a substantial increase in their share of births compared to other women their age. However, for pregnant brides there is an opposite trend. Their share of births within the same two age groups (under 20 and 20–24) has declined fairly dramatically. From these comparisons we can draw one clear conclusion: in the 1970s, young women who became pregnant outside marriage had a growing tendency not to marry the father but to have their babies while remaining single.

There are many other kinds of statistical tables besides the trend types (or time series) discussed here. However, the broad method we have followed in studying these tables may be applied to any type. First, read and understand the headings. Second, read across the lines of the tables to understand the groupings or categories that the table is about. Third, read down the columns to pick up any trends, comparisons or relationships that appear to stand out as significant.

Let us take a table that does not show trends but rather focuses on the causes of a problem at one point in time. Table 47.4 looks at the reasons why people were absent from work or study in 1989–90. The table tells us that more students were absent that year because they had the common cold than for any other reason. Female students gave this as a reason for 25 per cent of the times they were absent while male students gave it as a reason for 23.8 per cent of absences. The main difference between the sexes is their tendency to be absent because of injury. Look at the figures opposite the condition 'injury' and you will see that male students gave this as a reason for 17.6 per cent of their absences, while female students gave it as a reason for only 11.4 per cent of absences. Similarly, male workers were absent because of injuries in 20.1 per cent of cases, compared to female workers in only 10.3 per cent of cases.

TABLE 47.4 *Students and employed people aged 15 years and over who had one or more days away from study or work in the two weeks prior to interview due to illness or injury: selected reason(s) for absence, 1989-90*

Reason(s) for action	*Males*	*Females*	*Persons*
	STUDENTS		
Illness conditions —		— per cent —	
Common cold	23.8	25.0	24.4
Injuries	17.6	11.4	14.2
Headache due to unspecified or trivial cause	13.5	13.2	13.3
Influenza	11.5	13.0	12.3
Asthma	15.7	9.4	12.3
Cough or sore throat	6.7	7.6	7.2
Dental problems	7.1	6.0	6.5
Virus	6.0	7.0	6.5
Abdominal pain	4.0	4.4	4.2
Diarrhoea, enteritis	4.4	3.6	4.0
		— '000 —	
Total students absent	**212.2**	**247.9**	**460.1**
	EMPLOYED PEOPLE		
Illness conditions —		— per cent —	
Influenza	18.8	17.2	18.1
Injuries	20.1	10.3	15.6
Headache due to unspecified or trivial cause	11.5	15.8	13.5
Common cold	13.1	12.6	12.9
Dental problems	5.5	8.1	6.7
Back trouble (unspecified)	7.5	4.4	6.1
Eczema, dermatitis	5.4	6.7	6.0
Virus	4.3	6.8	5.4
Hypertension	5.3	4.2	4.8
Asthma	3.9	4.8	4.3
		— '000 —	
Total employed people absent	**385.7**	**323.5**	**709.2**

Source: Australian Bureau of Statistics, *Social Indicators No. 5*

EXERCISES

1. Look at Table 47.5. What does it tell us about the age at which married women have children? What does it tell us about the ages at which unmarried women have children?

2. Look at Table 47.6 which shows the educational background of people in various occupations. What proportion of the category 'Managers and administrators' held a degree? What proportion of managers and administrators did not attend the highest level of secondary school available? What proportion of people in the category 'Professionals' held a degree? What proportion of professionals did not attend the highest level of secondary school available? What conclusions can you draw from the differences in these figures?

TABLE 47.5 *Median age of mothers at birth of exnuptial and nuptial child by birth order*

		Nuptial births birth order				
Year	*Exnuptial births*	*1*	*2*	*3*	*4*	*All births*
1981	22.7	25.6	27.4	29.3	31.3	27.0
1983	22.9	26.1	27.7	29.5	31.4	27.2
1986	23.4	26.8	28.2	29.9	31.6	27.7
1989	24.1	27.4	28.9	30.6	32.0	28.1

Source: Australian Bureau of Statistics, *Social Indicators No. 5*

PRESENTING TABLES IN A DOCUMENT

When publishing tables in reports and documents of your own, a few simple rules will assist both you and the reader.

First, give each table its own number, as we have done in this chapter. If there are no chapter divisions in your document, simply label each Table 1, Table 2, Table 3, etc. Where tables are located within chapters or major sections of a report, prefix each number with the chapter or section number, as we have done here: Table 47.1, Table 47.2, Table 47.3, etc.

Second, give each table a descriptive heading that can be clearly understood by anyone, whether they have read the text or not. Most headings take up one line but it does not matter much if you need two or more lines to make its description clear.

Third, make sure each column is labelled clearly with its own name. If you are using numbers or percentages or some other ratio, make sure it is clear and easily noticed by the reader.

TABLE 47.6 *Employed persons aged 15–69 years: educational attainment by occupation, 1991*

	Occupation								
Educational attainment	*Managers and administrators*	*Professionals*	*Para-Professionals*	*Tradespersons*	*Clerks*	*Salespersons and personal service workers*	*Plant and machine operators and drivers*	*Labourers and related workers*	*Total*
			— per cent —						
With post-school qualifications —									
Degree	11.8	58.2	8.0	1.4	5.9	3.9	1.3	1.7	11.4
Trade qualification or apprenticeship	15.6	3.8	13.5	56.9	3.2	6.4	18.0	11.5	16.2
Certificate or diploma	21.0	26.6	54.6	6.5	31.1	22.0	9.8	10.3	21.0
Total (a)	*49.0*	*88.7*	*76.7*	*65.0*	*40.8*	*32.8*	*29.9*	*24.0*	*49.0*
Without post-school qualifications —									
Attended highest level of secondary school available	13.7	6.8	10.4	7.3	22.1	22.8	10.2	14.4	14.3
Did not attend highest level of secondary school available	36.8	4.2	12.7	27.5	36.6	36.9	59.4	56.5	34.5
Total (b)	*51.0*	*11.3*	*23.1*	*34.9*	*59.0*	*60.0*	*70.1*	*71.5*	*49.1*
Still at school	*0.1	*0.1	*0.2	*0.1	0.2	7.2	*0.1	4.5	1.8
Total (c)	**100.0**	**100.0**	**100.0**	**100.0**	**100.0**	**100.0**	**100.0**	**100.0**	**100.0**
			— '000 —						
Total (c)	**834.9**	**983.5**	**452.6**	**1156.8**	**1348.3**	**1119.6**	**571.5**	**1184.6**	**7651.8**

(a) Includes persons with other post-school qualifications. (b) Includes persons who never attended school and those for whom attendance at a secondary school could not be determined.
(c) Includes persons with other post-school qualifications, persons who never attended school and those for whom secondary school qualifications could not be determined.

Source: Australian Bureau of Statistics, *Social Indicators No. 5*

Fourth, tables are easier to read if they are typed or printed vertically on the page (as has mostly been done here). Some larger tables, however, will need to be laid out horizontally so that the reader has to turn the page around. Avoid this unless it is absolutely necessary. If your table is so large that you decide you need fold-out pages, it is usually worth rethinking the quantity of data you want to convey. Very large tables like this not only become unwieldy to handle but are difficult to read. Try cutting out some of the less-essential columns to get the table down to a workable size.

Fifth, always include a line or lines to indicate the source of your figures. This gives readers confidence in your table and will allow some to go to the original to follow up any points that interest them.

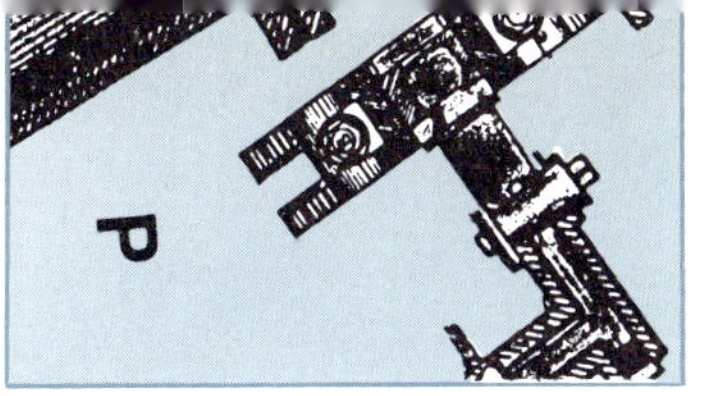

SPECIALIST TECHNIQUES SECTION

III

ILLUSTRATIONS

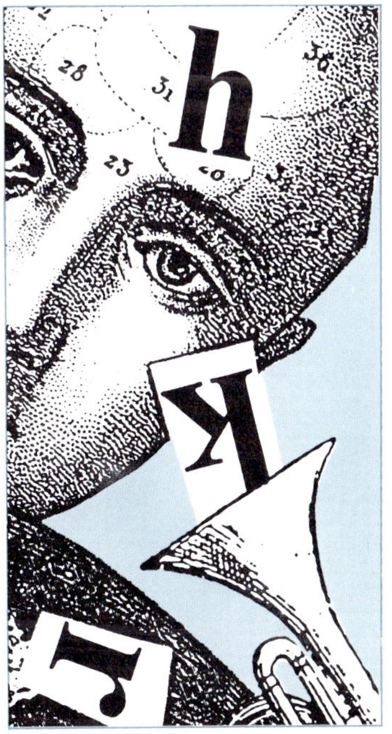

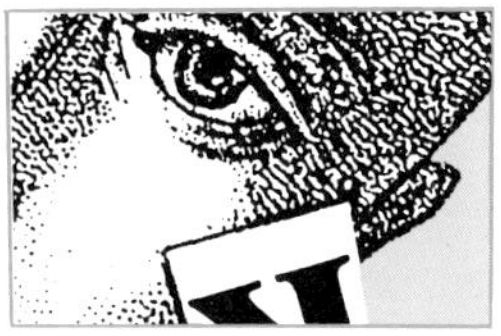

CHAPTER 48

ILLUSTRATING WITH GRAPHS

After studying this chapter, you will be able to:

- read and use a pie chart
- decide when to use a line graph to illustrate trends
- read and use a bar chart
- decide when to use a picture graph to illustrate data
- avoid being misled by graphs

Graphs are types of illustration that show the rows of columns in a numerical table in ways that make them more immediately understandable. They give us an overview of relationships between sets of figures and they quickly indicate trends, predictions and comparisons. They do not provide any information that cannot be found in a table but they are a good way to emphasise that information. Very often we see things in graph form that are not apparent from the figures alone.

A graph should not be included in a publication unless it is referred to in the text. Moreover, the reader should come to a written description of the data in the text before the graph is presented. It is not essential that the graph appears immediately after it is discussed—sometimes there is not enough room at the bottom of the page to do this. Nonetheless it should come as close as possible after the text reference, desirably on a facing page or immediately over the page. A graph should also be able to stand alone: that is, someone who has not read the text should be able to look at the graph and understand what it means. A descriptive heading should be placed above it. A reference to where the figures it describes came from (its source) should be placed below it. There are several kinds of graph, and each has its own uses and advantages.

PIE CHARTS

Sometimes called 'circle graphs', pie charts illustrate a fairly simple set of relationships. They show how a whole is divided up into its parts and what share or percentage each part has. One common use is to indicate how the expenditure of money is divided up, that is, who gets what share of the total. For instance, if we wanted to show how the total expenditure on advertising in Australia was divided, we could present the figures as a table in the following form.

Table 48.1 *Advertising expenditure in Australia, 1991*

	$ million	*Per cent*
Press	2319	49
Television	1614	34
Radio	420	9
Outdoor	266	6
Cinema	83	2
Total	4703	100

However, it would be much easier to see the relationships if we used a pie chart, as in Figure 48.1. This is a three dimensional chart which was generated by a computer spreadsheet program, Microsoft Excel, but it would be just as informative if drawn with pen, compass and ruler in two dimensions. Pie charts like this are very easy to read, especially if the name of the division and its percentage share is printed either in or next to its segment. This way we get a clear visual impression and at the same time we have the numerical data on hand for reference.

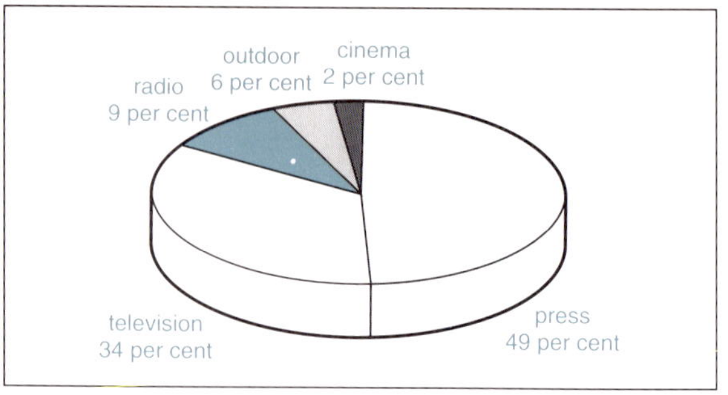

Fig. 48.1 Pie chart: Advertising expenditure in Australia, 1991

Pie charts are normally used to show static relationships, or how the whole is divided at one point in time. They are not well suited to indicating trends over time but, in some cases, they can be used for this purpose. Figures 48.2a and 48.2b show the changing educational levels of people in the workforce in Australia between 1987 and 1991. The growth has been among people who hold degrees, certificates or diplomas; the decline has been among those with trade qualifications or who did not gain any qualifications after they left school. Where the changes in relationships are reasonably clear, as they are in this figure, pie charts will do. But where change is more gradual, they leave something to be desired because the changes are not clearly discernible from chart to chart. If you wanted to show trends in educational qualifications in the workforce between 1987 and 1991, you could draw up to five pie charts, but this would not be a very helpful exercise.

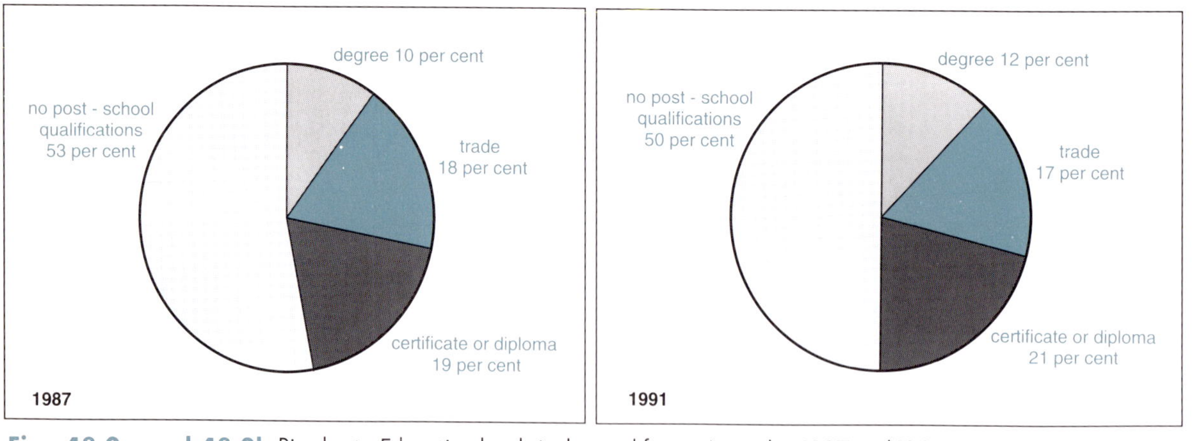

Figs 48.2a and 48.2b Pie charts: Education levels in the workforce, Australia, 1987 and 1991

EXERCISES (A)

From the figures in Table 48.2, draw two pie charts to represent (1) the leading causes of death among males aged 15–24 years in 1980, and (2) the leading causes of death among males aged 15–24 years in 1990. The source of the figures is the publication *Social Indicators No. 5*, Catalogue No 4101.0, published by the Australian Bureau of Statistics.

Table 48.2 *Leading causes of death among 15–25-year-old males, Australia, 1980 and 1990*

Cause of death	*1980 per cent*	*1990 per cent*
Motor vehicle accidents	62	44
Suicide	13	28
Accidents (non-motor vehicle)	19	22
Cancer	6	6

LINE GRAPHS

Line graphs are a better way to illustrate changes over time. They show the relationship between two sets of data. One of these is usually some quantity and the other is a range of points over a period of time. In Figure 48.3 the vertical line (sometimes called the Y axis) records the size of the Australian population, while the horizontal line (the X axis) records the years from 1901 to 1990. Even though the years named on the X axis are recorded as ten-year gaps, the line graph plots the population total for each individual year between those gaps. This graph records the line of

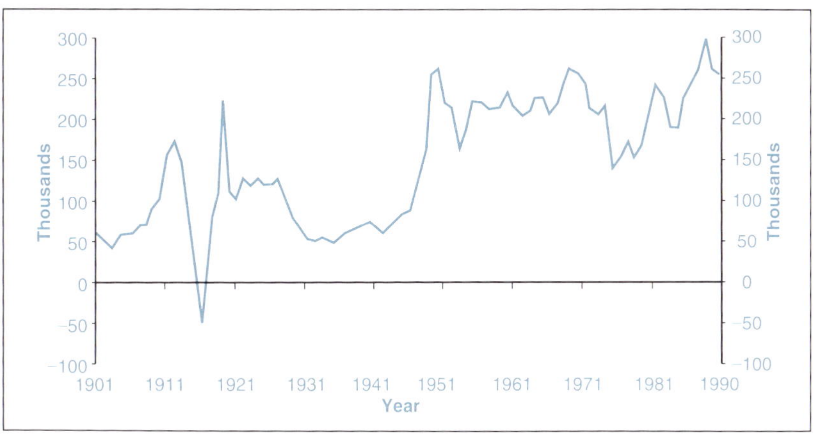

Fig. 48. 3 Line graph: Population growth, 1901 to 1990

one trend only, but it is more usual for line graphs to record two or more trends at once, so that they may be compared. Figure 48.4 records trends in the number of births per year compared to the number of immigrants per year in Australia from 1901 to 1990.

Not all line graphs are based on time series. Sometimes the horizontal line will record a set of figures different to years or months. Figure 48.5 shows the causes of death among males and females in 1990. The horizontal line records the various age groups. The graphs show clearly, for instance, that the most dangerous age for accidents among both sexes is the 15 to 24 years bracket. More often though a graph of this kind, which takes a snapshot of a social phenomenon and compares several types of people's experience of it, is presented as a bar chart, described in the next section.

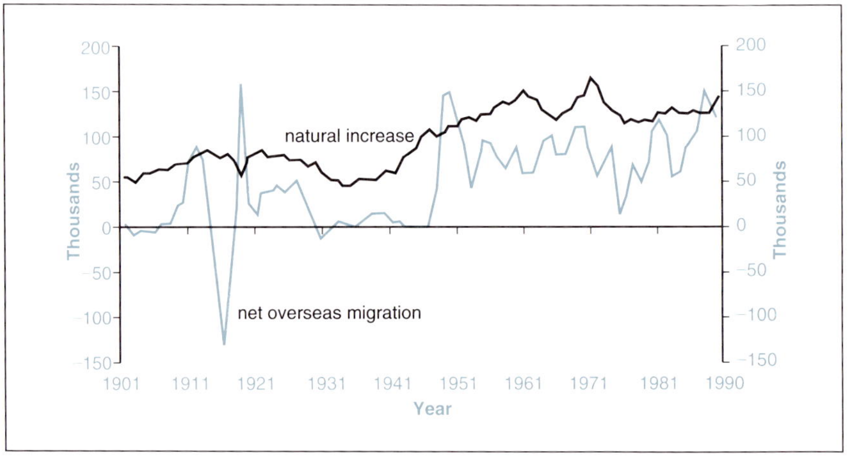

Fig. 48.4 Line graph: Number of births compared to immigration rate, 1901 to 1990

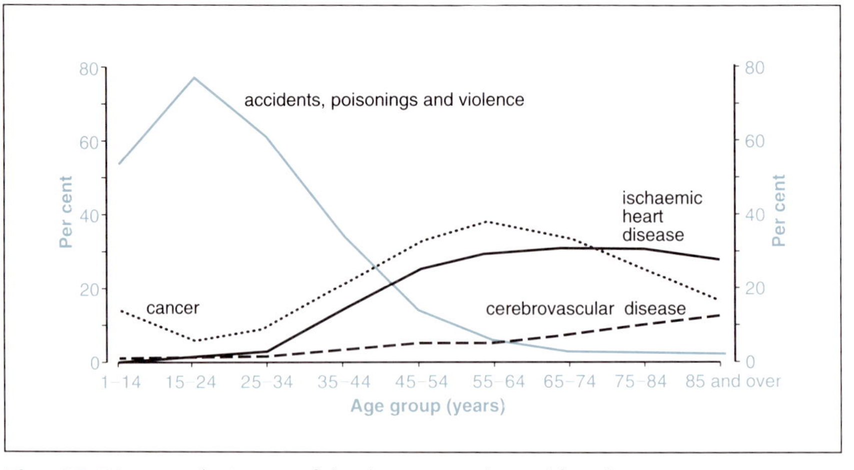

Fig. 48.5 Line graph: Causes of death among males and females, 1990

EXERCISES (B)

Draw one line graph showing (1) the number of male students remaining at school until Year 12 in Australia from 1985 to 1991, and (2) the number of female students remaining at school until Year 12 from 1985 until 1991. Use the figures in Table 48.3 as the basis of the graph. They come from the Australian Bureau of Statistics publication, *Social Indicators No. 5*, Catalogue No. 4101.0.

What conclusions can you draw from a comparison of the two line graphs?

Table 48.3 *Year 12 retention rates, Australia, 1985–1991*

Year	*Males per cent*	*Females per cent*
1985	43.5	49.5
1986	45.6	52.1
1987	49.4	57.0
1988	53.4	61.8
1989	55.5	65.2
1990	58.3	69.9
1991	66.1	76.7

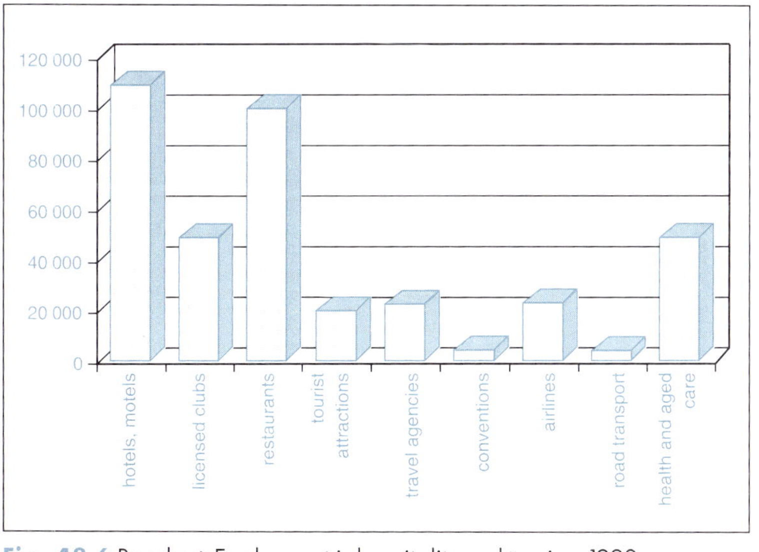

Fig. 48.6 Bar chart: Employment in hospitality and tourism, 1992

BAR CHARTS

Bar charts are normally used to take a snapshot of a group of things at one point in time, to divide them into groups and show the quantity of each group. Whereas a pie chart compares each division to the sum total of all the divisions, a bar chart has a much wider range of uses. Figure 48.6 is a bar chart which shows the number of people employed in various sectors of the hospitality and tourism industry in Australia. Figure 48.7 is another bar chart showing what proportion of people in each age group and in each sex was a cigarette smoker in 1989–90. The graph shows more teenage girls are smokers than teenage boys but at all other age groups, more men smoke than women.

Bar charts can also be useful for reporting reasons why certain things occur. Figure 48.8 shows various reasons why unemployed people in three different groups could not find jobs. This is a useful way to highlight the more important kinds of reasons. A complicated reporting job is made clear through visual presentation. In this chart, the two main reasons for unemployment are lack of job vacancies overall and lack of vacancies in the unemployed person's line of work. But one other reason stands out which, if published in a table, might have been overlooked. This is the difficulty that the long-term unemployed face because employers consider them too old, a reason which turns out to be the biggest single problem facing any of the three groups.

Bar charts are not always drawn vertically. In some cases they are published horizontally. This is particularly useful if you have a reason to make comparisons using a left horizontal axis and a right horizontal axis, as in Figure 48.9. This technique is most common when used, as it is here, to compare statistics for males and females.

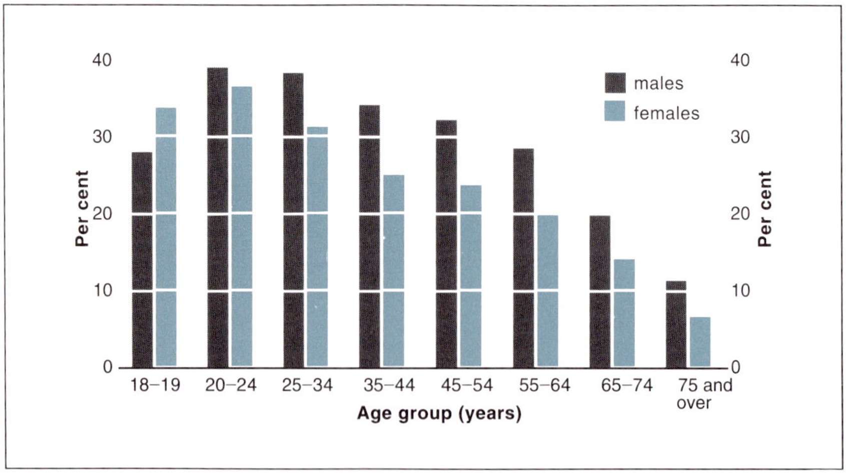

Fig. 48.7 Bar chart: Proportion of males and females in each age group who smoke cigarettes, 1990

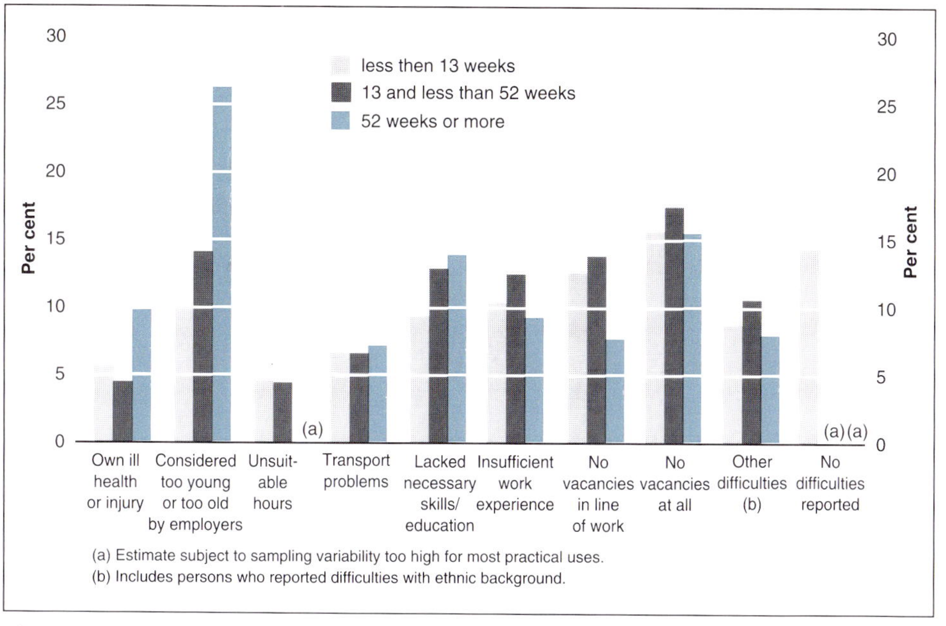

Fig. 48.8 Bar chart: Reasons unemployed people could not find jobs, 1988

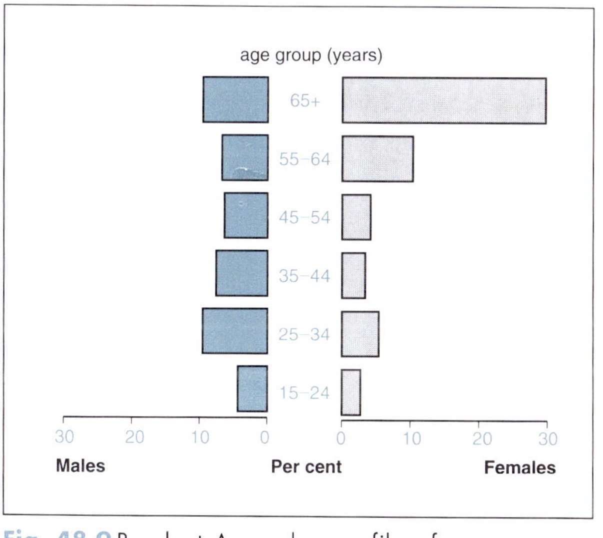

Fig. 48.9 Bar chart: Age and sex profiles of one person households, 1986

EXERCISE (C)

Draw one bar chart from the data given in Table 48.3 for Year 12 retention rates to illustrate the changes for both males and females.

PICTURE GRAPHS

To make a point more forcefully, some people who prepare graphs go further than lines and bars and use cartoon drawings of their subject to indicate size. This is called a picture graph or 'pictogram'. The cartoons can be purchased on plastic film and you can either add several of the same size to get the required proportions, or you can use bigger and smaller cartoons to indicate quantity, as in Figure 48.10. Computers can also generate graphs of this kind. The technique is acceptable when the quantities involved are simple and straightforward and where you want to add some light relief to pages of columns and bars, such as in an annual report. The measures, however, are necessarily fairly crude and, where more precise records are needed, lines and bars are better forms of presentation.

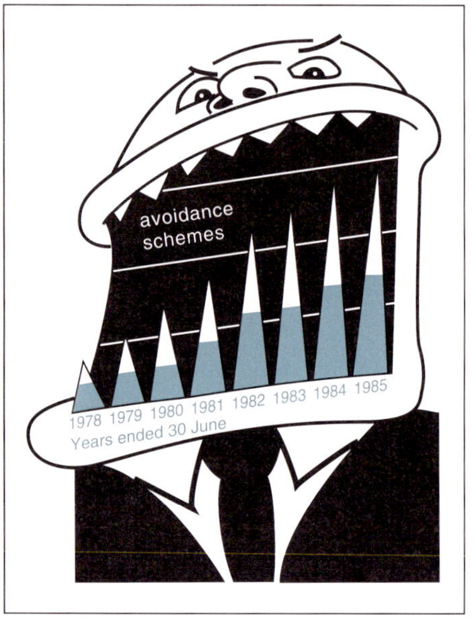

Fig. 48.10 Picture graph: Illustrations become the graphic indicators with striking results. Unpaid tax exceeds budget cuts, 1978 to 1985

EXERCISE (D)

Draw one picture graph to illustrate the changes in Table 48.3 Year 12 retention rates for males.

MISUSING GRAPHS

Numerical measurements and statistics are fairly objective ways of describing things. However, despite their derivation in numbers and statistics, graphs are far less objective. There is no fixed or certain way to draw any graph, so they are open to manipulation. The easiest way to manipulate numbers in graphs is through the scale you chose for the vertical line or Y axis. Depending on the scale of numbers you choose for this line, a graph representing the same set of results can appear fairly flat (hence giving the impression that the phenomenon in question shows little change) or quite steep (indicating a high degree of change).

Take the line graphs in Figure 48.11 and 48.12 as examples. Figure 48.11 shows the relationship of women's income as a percentage of men's income between the years 1950 and 1975. The graph indicates there was a slight upward movement in the late 1960s but, overall, there has been no fundamental change. Figure 48.12 portrays exactly the same figures but they have been drawn to a different scale (that is, there is more space between the numbers on the vertical line or Y axis). It is also cropped at the bottom (see the small break mark near the bottom of the Y axis) to compress the total space that would otherwise have been allocated to the whole figure. There is nothing inaccurate or dishonest about the second line graph, but it still gives a distinctly different impression to the first. It portrays the modest rise in women's income in the late 1960s as a much more dramatic or radical change than does the first.

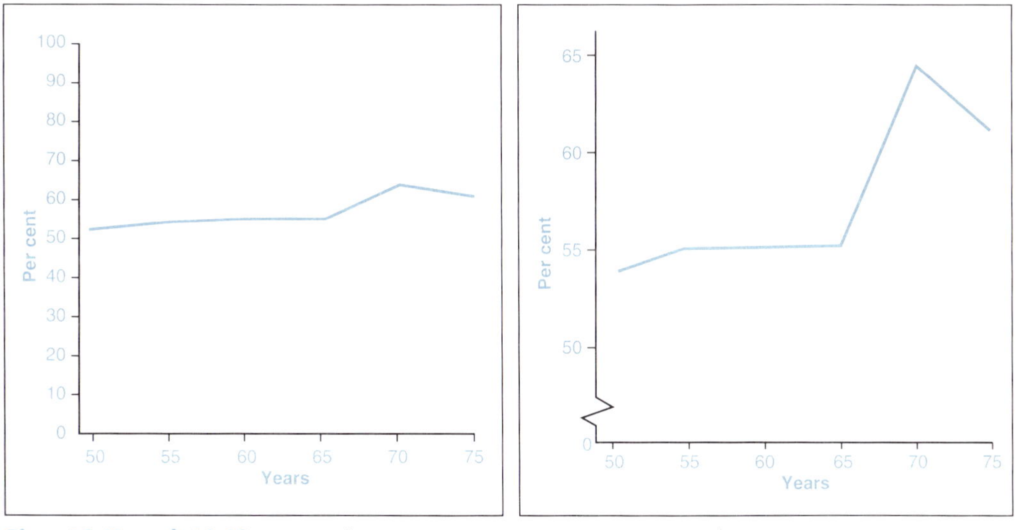

Figs 48.11 and 48.12 Line graphs: Women's income as a percentage of men's income, 1950 to 1975. By varying the Y axis the relationship looks different

Another pair of examples are given in Figures 48.13 and 48.14. The first comes from a newspaper report of how unemployment levels had allegedly fallen during the early 1980s. The scale chosen makes the decline look steep and dramatic, that is, it gives the impression that unemployment was much lower at April 1981 than a year earlier, and that the government of the day was getting on top of the problem. Note the break mark at the bottom of the Y axis. Many readers who are unfamiliar with this issue and who did not read the graph too carefully would have assumed that unemployment had almost been eliminated. In contrast, Figure 48.14, a graph published by the Australian Bureau of Statistics, shows its own measurement of unemployment from 1977 to February 1981. This second graph is not measuring exactly the same thing—its figures are percentage rates of unemployment, whereas the first graph's figures are for total number of people unemployed. Nonetheless, the Bureau's graph indicates that there had been little change of significance over the whole period and that any impressions created about a dramatic decline in unemployment would be a misinterpretation.

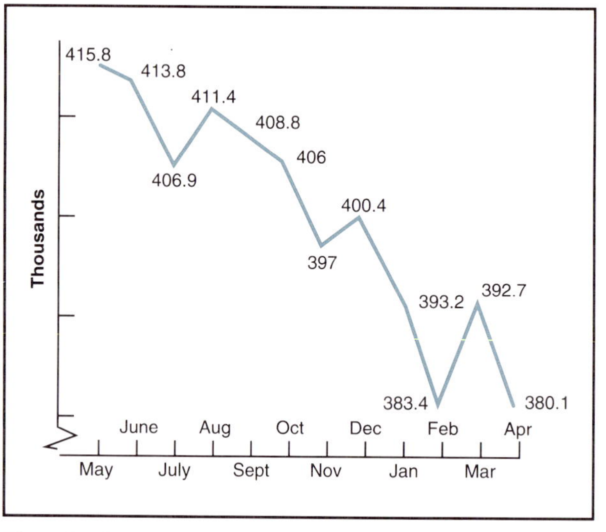

Fig 48.13 Line graph: Unemployed people looking for work, 1981. Compare this with Figure 48.14

EXERCISES (E)

Redraw your earlier line graphs of (1) male and (2) female Year 12 retention rates to give a different impression to the one you originally conveyed.

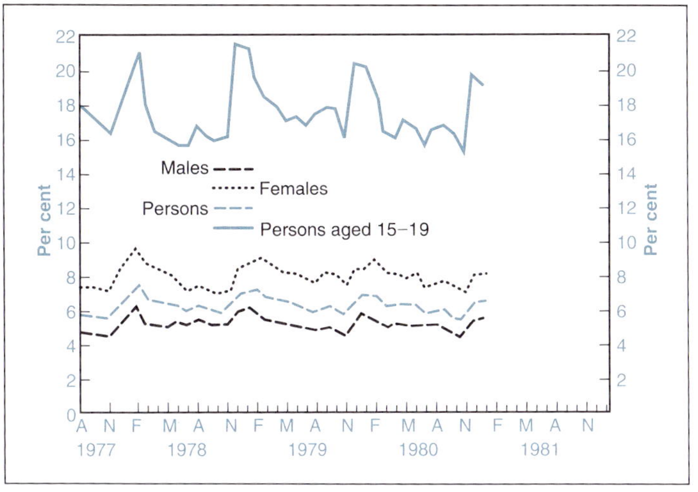

Fig. 48.14 Line graph: Unemployment rates, 1977 to 1981. Compare this with Figure 48.13

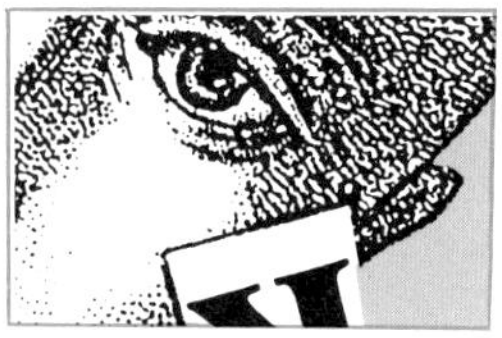

CHAPTER

49

PHOTOGRAPHS AND DRAWINGS

After studying this chapter, you will be able to:

- decide when to use photographs in a document
- write appropriate captions for photographs
- decide when to use technical illustrations
- understand the different uses of photographs and drawings

Articles, essays and reports always benefit from the addition of photographs or drawings. Readers who would otherwise be limited to a mind's eye impression of the subject matter can be given a much more vivid and concrete version through these kinds of illustrations. Dimensions, perspectives and relationships that are difficult to articulate in words can be conveyed quickly in illustrative form. Photographs and drawings also make complex subjects easier for writers to describe and for readers to understand. Photographs and drawings are often attractive additions to a text. The role of adornment, it should be emphasised, should not be regarded as something frivolous. An attractively illustrated text will draw readers and hold their attention much better than rows of grey columns of type.

Most newspapers and magazines have a policy of trying to accompany every story and article with either a photograph or drawing. They do not always maintain a 100 per cent success rate, but the general intention of the policy is maintained wherever possible. Writers of other material, especially reports and essays, are well advised to adopt a similar approach. While researching their subject they should always keep an eye out for suitable illustrations. The final version will be both more informative and more interesting for it.

USING PHOTOGRAPHS IN A TEXT

Although it remains true that pictures tell a thousand words, photographs still need words to describe them. It is sometimes unclear what a photograph is portraying and a description is needed to make it intelligible at all. More commonly, key elements of the photograph are not contained within it. The two most common elements that need to be added are time and place—when the photograph was taken and where—without which a great many misinterpretations are likely to be made. Many photographs taken of public figures would appear embarrassing or even incriminating if they were given the wrong context of time and place.

So, whenever a photograph is used within a text it should be accompanied by a descriptive caption. As far as possible, the caption should be self-explanatory and self-contained. It will obviously be related to material in the body of the document, but should be intelligible on its own to someone who is browsing through and not reading all the text. Sometimes this will mean writing longish captions, but it is always worth the trouble. The only acceptable exception to this rule is when the photograph is a head-and-shoulders portrait of a person. Here, the name and perhaps title of the person will be sufficient to identify him or her.

The worst kind of caption is one that says only 'Photo One' or 'Photo Two' and that thereby depends on the reader picking up its description through the body of the text. This misunderstands the way that readers approach photographs—they usually look at them before going to the main text—and it inhibits both browsing and reviewing. If the reader has moved on but wants to go back to examine the photograph again, this means not only finding the right page but combing through the text for the appropriate passage. By including a caption that provides a self-contained description of the picture, you show a proper appreciation of the reader's needs.

Why captions are essential to allow readers to see the relevance of photographs.

Fig. 49.1 The actions of the people in the photograph above do not make any sense until the caption tells us that the man in the centre is an acting teacher instructing a class. This is Richard Hayes-Marshall at the Actors Centre, Sydney, photographed for *SydneySider* magazine, October 1990

Fig. 49.2 In this photograph the subject matter could be related to geography until the caption tells us that the large round object is actually a cake made as a globe of the world. This is one of the custom-made products of Sweet Art, a Sydney firm which specialises in novel and sometimes bizarre cake designs. Photograph is from *SydneySider* magazine, December 1989

In a report, essay or article, a photograph should be placed as close as possible to the part of the text to which it refers. This does not mean that a photograph should always come after its relevant passage. Sometimes the layout makes it more convenient to place the photograph before the text and, if this happens, it is perfectly acceptable. If possible, place photographs on right-hand pages where they make more of an impact.

When selecting photographs for inclusion in a publication or in a report or an essay, a good rule to follow is to be generous. That is, give the photograph a generous amount of space and make the objects or characters within it a generous size. It can be counterproductive to try and squeeze a photograph into a confined space or to fit several into an area suitable only for one. If the figures being portrayed are thereby reduced to a size where they are difficult to discern, the whole point of using the photograph may be lost. Making characters and objects as large as possible usually means trimming the edges of the photograph or even cutting out other people or other details. This again is quite acceptable and, in fact, is the norm in newspaper and magazine publishing.

The above principles also apply to drawings when they are used in the same way as photographs. When you are using a drawing to illustrate a scene or people, it should be accompanied by the same kind of self-contained caption and placed as close as possible to the appropriate passage in the text. However, when drawings are used for technical purposes, to explain how something works, a different set of principles apply. The next section takes up this issue.

TECHNICAL ILLUSTRATIONS

For the production of manuals that explain how a piece of equipment or machinery works, technical drawings are the best option. They are better than photographs because they can show each part clearly and precisely. They can also be used to show several views of one object and to strip away part of the surface of an object to show what lies underneath.

Technical drawings also allow each part to be labelled so that references to parts in the text can be precise. Labelling can be done in one of two ways: first, by use of reference numbers or letters with a legend explaining the meaning of each reference (as in Figure 49.3); or, second, by including names directly on the illustration (as in Figure 49.4). The direct method should be preserved for fairly simple descriptions. The more complicated the procedure being described, the more need there is to use reference numbers or letters and a legend.

The ultimate aim in technical drawings is to make them so clear that descriptions in word form are unnecessary. One of the best models for this is the children's construction set Lego, which explains how to make items with increasing degrees of complexity without using words at all (see Figure 49.5). This approach was virtually forced on Lego because it could not assume any degree of literacy among its young customers. A number of manufacturers who sell to export markets have also adopted this approach. They are faced with selling to a range of different language communities and so, while they still produce multi-language brochures, their technical drawings work on the assumption that they should be self-explanatory without words from any language (see Figure 49.6). Again, this has forced a discipline on them that everyone producing manuals and brochures can use as models of effective communication.

Although photographs are more realistic, drawings are actually a 'friendlier' form of communication, probably because they involve more human interaction with the subject matter. This means that a report or article that is to be liberally illustrated should include both photographs and drawings. If it is possible, place a greater emphasis on drawings, and use more of them, if you want to make the best impression and get the best response from readers.

How to operate your Hoover cleaner

A – Hose entry
B – Power Socket (for Power Nozzle Model S 8140 – an extra cost option
C – On/Off switch (Foot operable)
D – Retractable Cord Reel release
E – Top Cover (Disposall bag compartment)
F – Air exhaust diffuser
G – Bag full indicator
H – Integral carrying handle
I – Retractable Cord Entry
J – Castor Wheel
K – Air Freshener Control

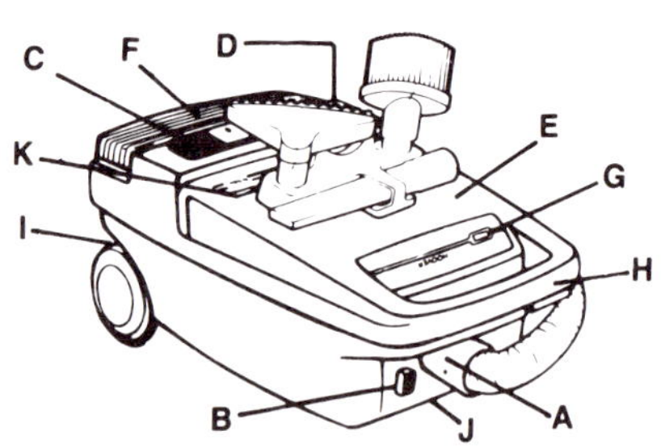

Fig. 49.3 Reference numbers with a legend describe the different parts of a Hoover vacuum cleaner

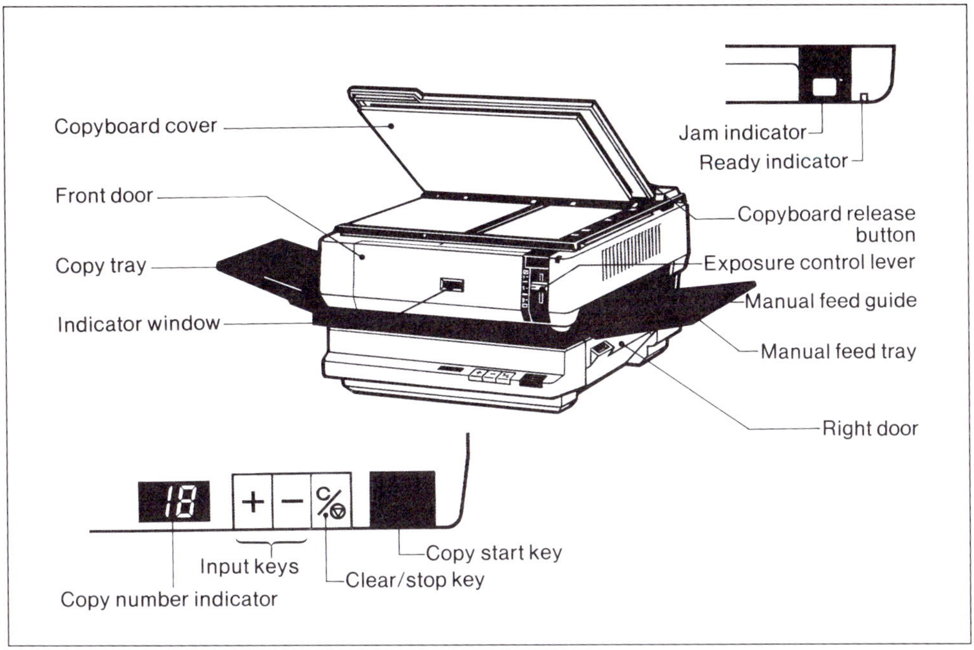

Fig. 49.4 Names of parts relate directly to illustrations of a Canon copier

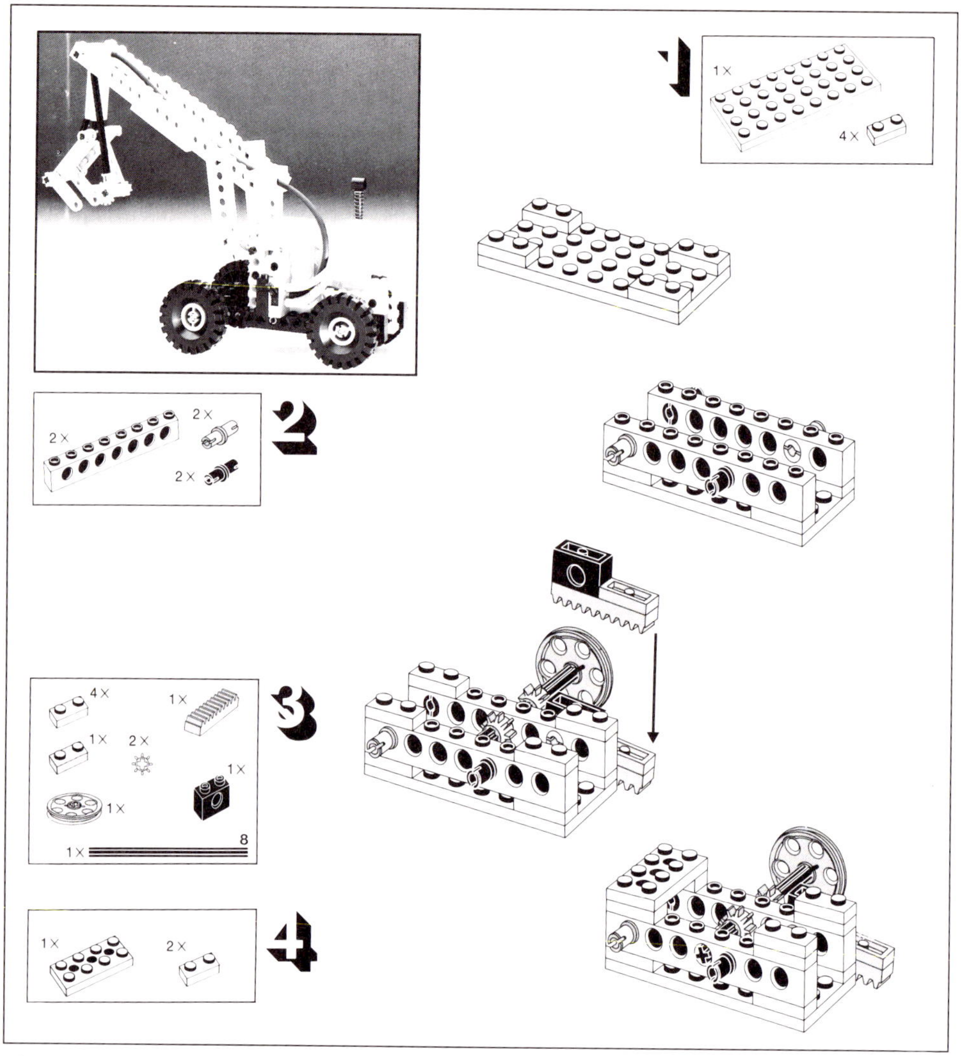

Fig. 49.5 Instruction book for LEGO construction set demonstrates how to use its parts without any recourse to words

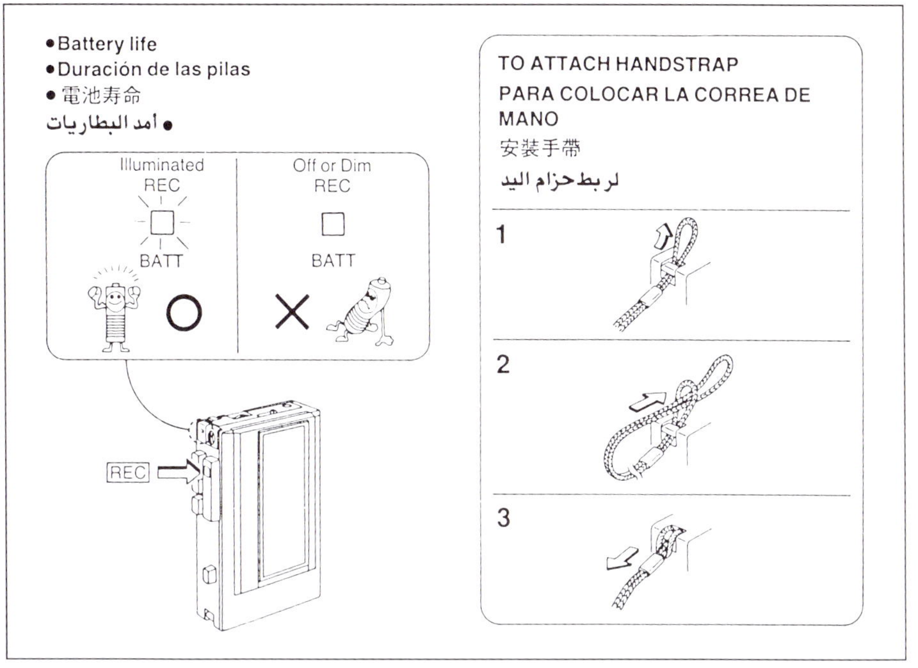

Fig. 49.6 Multi-language manual for National Walkman uses self-explanatory illustrations and symbols

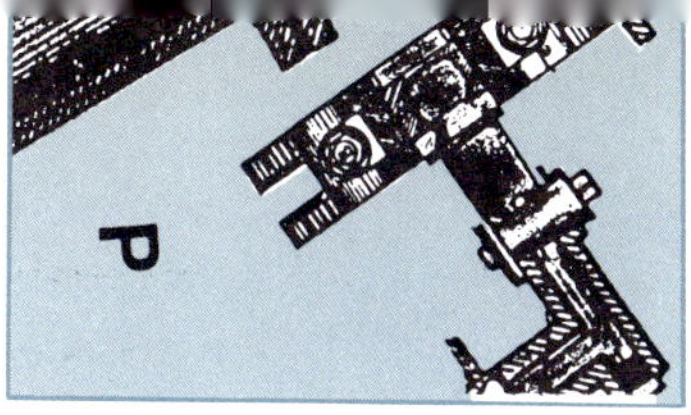

SPECIALIST TECHNIQUES SECTION

IV

REFERENCES

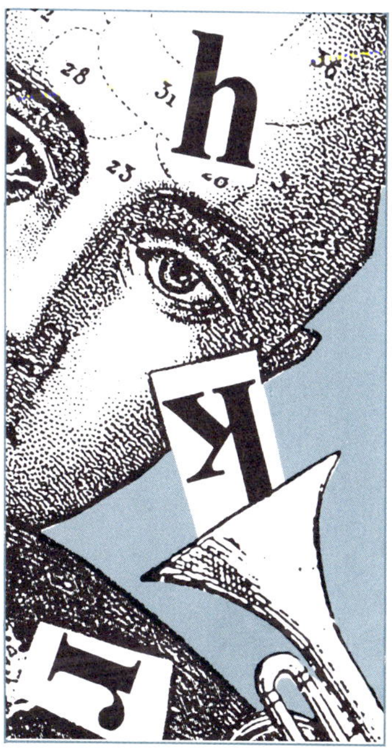

CHAPTER

50

ESTABLISHING A PERSONAL REFERENCE LIBRARY

After studying this chapter, you will be able to:

- plan a personal library to include the standard references most used by writers and speakers
- decide which versions of various kinds of references most suit your needs

Anyone who is part of the 40 per cent of the workforce now engaged in information-related occupations should have a set of reference works that are available when he or she needs them. Some of these references are expensive which inhibits people from buying their own. Unfortunately, if you have to rely on a library or even if you have a reference set which you share with your colleagues at work, there will always be times when you need something urgently but it is not available. If communication is an important part of your profession, it is difficult to avoid the need for your own personal reference library. This chapter is a guide to those works which we have found most useful in our own writing and lecturing careers. What we record here are some of the 'classics', works we think deserve a place on our readers' desks.

DICTIONARY

Everyone should have a good, printed dictionary. The computer versions are handy as spelling checkers but will never replace the best of the books. Although it does not get the most publicity, the book which many professional writers and others 'in the know', like compulsive Scrabble players, rate as the best is *Chambers English Dictionary*. You can buy the complete version for a reasonable price. The best value is probably the *Concise* edition which is almost as big as the original. The best Australian product is the *Macquarie Dictionary* which, if you can afford two, is a worthy addition.

THESAURUS

The *Macquarie Thesaurus*, published in Australia, is now superior to the original version by Roget. It comes in several editions, of which the best is the largest and most expensive. However, the concise edition of the Macquarie is still very good for those with limited desk space, and there is an even cheaper paperback *Penguin Macquarie Thesaurus* as well.

CORRECT PROSE

Stephen Murray-Smith's *Right Words: A Guide to English Usage in Australia*, Viking, Melbourne, 1987 (also available in cheaper paperback editions) is an essential reference. So is Nicholas Hudson's *Modern Australian Usage*, Oxford University Press, Melbourne, 1993. The two classic works on this subject are Sir Ernest Gowers, *The Complete Plain Words*, Penguin, 1948, and Eric Partridge, *Usage and Abusage*, Penguin, 1947. Both are still in print. All four books recommended here are fascinating insights into the language and may be read for pleasure as well as business.

PROSE STYLE

The best book on this subject is Robert Graves and Alan Hodge, *The Reader Over Your Shoulder*, published by Jonathan Cape in 1943 and reprinted by Random House, New York, in 1979. Good libraries have copies.

EDITING

The standard work which all publishers in Australia follow is the *Style Manual for Authors, Editors and Printers* published by the Australian Government Publishing Service, Canberra. The most recent edition is the 1988 one. This one is essential for any publishing job.

QUOTABLE QUOTES

Public speakers, in particular, always find it handy to spice their talks with quotations from well-known writers, especially if they can find something which is both witty and apt. There are now a large number of books of famous quotations on the market. It is better to buy one that is larger rather than smaller because the former has more quotations and thus give you a better range to select from. Some of these books are arranged alphabetically by writer's name and if you want to find all the witty sayings about, say, economists or marriage, then you have to use their index. A more convenient arrangement is by subject matter which give you the opportunity to browse more easily. Bloomsbury Publishing has two versions, one arranged by author, the other by subject. We prefer the latter. The best books of quotations, however, are those which focus on a particular subject area. If most of your work is in one field then you might find one of these more useful. A very good specialist book of quotations is *The Macmillan Book of Social Science Quotations* which covers anthropology, economics, history, politics, psychology and sociology. By far the very best of all the books of quotations is one which provides more than 3000 quotations by and about women, Anne Stibbs' *Like a Fish Needs a Bicycle*, Bloomsbury, 1992. This very political but entertaining resource would find a good place on either a male or female bookshelf.

THOUGHT AND THINKERS

Dictionaries give you meanings that are usually in a compact and literal form. Often, writers need more than this to make sense of a word or phrase. What, for instance, does 'hermeneutics' mean? Or 'performance art'? Or 'quantum mechanics'? To get a better idea of concepts of this kind, without reading a book on each subject, the most useful reference we know of is the *Fontana Dictionary of Modern Thought*, edited by Alan Bullock, Oliver Stallybrass and Stephen Trombley (1988 edition). If you need to know the key ideas of some modern thinkers—for instance, key ideas about the architecture of Walter Gropius, the notion of film-making of Jean-luc Godard, the management theories of Douglas McGregor or the positivist philosophy of Rudolf Carnap, then also extremely useful is the companion volume published in 1990, the *Fontana Dictionary of Modern Thinkers*.

MEETINGS

Citrine's book on the rules of meetings, *ABC of Chairmanship*, once enjoyed the same reputation as Hoyle's on the rules of card games. Today, however, rules 'according to Citrine' are increasingly regarded as unnecessarily cumbersome and restricting. A more modern, useful and sensible book is Sue Ward's *A-Z of Meetings*, Pluto Press, 1985. A more formal but nonetheless valuable Australian book is N. E. Renton's *Guide for Meetings*, Law Book Company, Sydney, 1990.

WHO'S WHO

For journalists and anyone else writing about public life, the only real contender is *Who's Who in Australia*, published by the Herald and Weekly Times. One of the great works of Australian publishing also relates to this field. This is the *Australian Dictionary of Biography*. It has published twelve volumes so far of biographies of people from 1788 to 1939. It is too expensive for most personal libraries but a delightful indulgence if you can afford it.

AUSTRALIA

Easily the best desk reference is the annual *Year Book Australia* published by the Australian Bureau of Statistics. Essential for anyone writing about contemporary issues. The Australian Bureau of Statistics bulletin, *Social Indicators*, which is published about every four years, is also one of the most valuable resources on a very wide range of issues.

ATLAS

By far the best value and the most relevant to our place in the Southern Hemisphere is the *Macquarie World Atlas*.

CD-ROM

If you have a personal computer, then one of the best favours you can do yourself these days is add a CD-ROM disc drive. Most suppliers will throw in several discs with the purchase and these can be some of the most valuable reference works you can have. CD-ROM titles are usually much less expensive than their printed versions and save enormous shelf space. You can have the whole 26 volumes of *Comptons Encyclopedia* on one compact disc, or the 21 volumes of the *Groliers Encyclopedia* on another disc. You can also get dictionaries for over twenty languages on one disc. CD-ROM publishing is the wave of the future and is one of the most efficient ways to build a personal library.

ACKNOWLEDGMENTS

The publishers and the authors wish to acknowledge the following sources for permission to reproduce illustrative material used in the preparation of this book.

Page 3: Graph, from *Sleepers Wake!,* Barry Jones, Oxford University Press, Melbourne, 1990
Page 27: Word processor, Macleay College, Sydney
Page 29: Database software, *dBase III Plus Fundamentals,* Alan & Linda Skinner, McGraw-Hill, Sydney, 1991
Page 84: Brochure, Bond University, Gold Coast
Page 98: Researching in library, Horizon/Penny Tweedie
Page 118: Michael Hudson, Rodney Hearne/Sydney Photos
Page 125: Mira Protruder, Macleay College, Sydney
Page 140: Interview, Norman Nicholls
Page 148: Negotiating, Horizon/Images Colour Library
Page 207: NSW parliamentary press briefing, Macleay College, Sydney
Page 248: Interviewing, Norman Nicholls
Page 299: Gantt chart, from *Microsoft Project for Windows Version 3,* Microsoft Press, Sydney, 1993
Page 300: PERT chart, from *Microsoft Project for Windows Version 3,* Microsoft Press, Sydney, 1993
Page 336: Bryce Courtenay, Heide Smith
Page 340: 'Geoffrey Robertson's Hypothetical', ABC Television Archives
Page 367: Audio-visual aids, International Photographic Library
Page 390: Karl Albrecht, the TQS Group
Page 404: Formal meeting, International Photographic Library
Page 408: Parliamentary debate, John Fairfax Goup
Page 438: Jan Murray, News Ltd
Page 449: Lobbyists, News Ltd
Page 455: Nuclear disarmament march, Brendan Read, *Sydney Morning Herald*
Page 466: News conference, Ross Willis, John Fairfax Group
Page 479: Subculture, Maria Sullivan
Page 569: Pie chart, *The Media,* Keith Windschuttle, 3rd edition, Penguin Books, Melbourne, in press
Page 570: Pie charts, *Social Indicators No. 5,* Australian Bureau of Statistics, cat. no. 4101.0
Page 571: Line graph, *Social Indicators No. 5,* Australian Bureau of Statistics, cat. no. 4101.0
Page 572: Line graph, *Social Indicators No. 5,* Australian Bureau of Statistics, cat. no. 4101.0
Page 572: Line graph, *Social Indicators No. 5,* Australian Bureau of Statistics, cat. no. 4101.0
Page 573: Bar chart, *Job Prospects and Career Paths in Hospitality and Tourism,* Alison Stott & Keith Windschuttle, Macleay Press, Sydney, 1992
Page 574: Bar chart, *Social Indicators No. 5,* Australian Bureau of Statistics, cat. no. 4101.0
Page 575: Bar chart, *Social Indicators No. 5,* Australian Bureau of Statistics, cat. no. 4101.0
Page 575: Bar chart, *Social Indicators No. 5,* Australian Bureau of Statistics, cat. no. 4101.0
Page 576: Picture graph, 'Australian Society', August 1986
Page 577: Line graphs, *Social Indicators No. 5,* Australian Bureau of Statistics, cat. no. 4101.0
Page 578: Line graph, *Sydney Morning Herald,* 8 May 1981
Page 579: Line graph, Australian Bureau of Statistics, cat. no. 6203.0
Page 584: Hoover vacuum cleaner, Hoover Australia
Page 586: Instruction book, © 1984 LEGO Group